Introduction to Clinical Psychology

Introduction to Clinical Psychology

Janet R. Matthews
Loyola University New Orleans

Barry S. Anton
University of Puget Sound

New York   Oxford
OXFORD UNIVERSITY PRESS
2008

Oxford University Press, Inc., publishes works that further Oxford University's
objective of excellence in research, scholarship, and education.

Oxford   New York
Auckland   Cape Town   Dar es Salaam   Hong Kong   Karachi
Kuala Lumpur   Madrid   Melbourne   Mexico City   Nairobi
New Delhi   Shanghai   Taipei   Toronto

With offices in
Argentina   Austria   Brazil   Chile   Czech Republic   France   Greece
Guatemala   Hungary   Italy   Japan   Poland   Portugal   Singapore
South Korea   Switzerland   Thailand   Turkey   Ukraine   Vietnam

Published by Oxford University Press, Inc.
198 Madison Avenue, New York, New York 10016
http://www.oup.com

Oxford is a registered trademark of Oxford University Press

Library of Congress Cataloging-in-Publication Data

Matthews, Janet R.
  Introduction to clinical psychology / Janet R. Matthews, Barry S. Anton.
    p. ; cm.
  Includes bibliographical references.
  ISBN 978-0-19-515767-3 (alk. paper)
  1. Clinical psychology. I. Anton, Barry S. II. Title.
  [DNLM: 1. Psychology, Clinical. WM 105 M439i 2007]
RC467.I5887 2007
616.89—dc22   2006053278

Printing number: 9 8 7 6 5 4 3 2 1

Printed in the United States of America
on acid-free paper

Contents in Brief

Contents

CHAPTER 15
Specialties in Clinical Psychology II

CHAPTER 16
The Dynamic Future of Clinical Psychology   438

Preface

To the Student

Clinical psychology is a specialty within the broad domain of psychology. This specialty includes both research and applied activities. We are both clinical psychologists although we reached that final professional destination in rather different ways, which we describe in chapter 1. An exciting and yet sometimes confusing aspect of clinical psychology is that it is such a broad specialty. During Dr. Matthews' doctoral oral exam, one of her professors asked her to describe the field of clinical psychology. When she was done, he asked her what she felt was left for the rest of psychology, since her description seemed to encompass all of psychology. This professor, by the way, was *not* a clinical psychologist! After using this book, you may come to understand why he made that comment.

As we wrote this book, we tried to capture that breadth while not being so general that you would find it difficult to decide if you might want to join us as a professional. All textbook authors want their readers to learn from their books as well as to pursue further studies on the subject matter. Our approach to this goal includes some special features we hope you will enjoy.

Questions to ask: We developed a series of questions to ask some clinical psychologists who are currently working in different settings. These questions include information about the courses they wish they had taken as undergraduates. This information may give you some ideas about possible elective courses you may wish to consider taking. We also asked them about their current activities as well as some personal information so that you might begin to see them as real people.

"Model" patients: We invented three patients to follow throughout your reading about interviewing, diagnosis, psychological assessment, and psychotherapy. Rather than merely read about these activities, you can see how they might be applied. These three people were designed to illustrate the many issues of diversity you see in clinical practice. They vary in terms of age, ethnicity, and clinical presentation. Of course, there are many other variables we might have used. We wanted to limit their characteristics, however, so that you would not find their cases overwhelming.

Ethical Conundrums: Each of the major chapters starts with an *ethical conundrum*. Each of these vignettes is designed to illustrate an ethical issue related to the topic of that chapter. We designed these vignettes to show you that real clinical situations do not necessarily fall within easy decision-making parameters regarding the appropriate action a clinician could take. At the end of the chapter we do not tell you what a clinical psychologist *would* do in each particular case but rather provide you with some of the things the psychologist might have considered when making a judgment about appropriate action.

Key Terms: Each chapter ends with a list of key terms. These terms are intended to provide you with a summary of what you may have learned in that chapter. Each of these terms is also defined in the Glossary.

References: References are provided at the end of the book by chapter, so that if you are interested in that particular subject you will find those references easy to locate.

Two subspecialty chapters: We set aside two chapters to consider specialties that have developed from clinical psychology. Although some clinical psychologists are *generalists*, others practice in more limited areas. In some cases, these psychologists have taken extra training, such as postdoctoral fellowships, to prepare for these careers, while others have taken specialty tracks within their doctoral programs and internships to do so.

Informal style: Our style of writing this book is somewhat less formal than is customary for books in psychology. We wanted our book to be analogous to one of our actual classes. Although you do not have the opportunity for dialogue with us as you would in a classroom setting, we wanted to set the tone from that perspective.

To the Instructor

This is the first edition of our book. We have tried to provide a balance between the research foundations for clinical psychology and the practical aspects that often appeal to undergraduate students. As a result, our text differs from other texts in a number of ways we hope represent significant improvements:

Reconsidered emphases: The history and research chapter is a bit longer than some may be accustomed to. We wanted to integrate these topics rather than subdivide and address them in separate chapters. There are also several chapters that are a bit shorter than other chapters. Chapter 2 on professional activities and managed care is written as a brief overview of two topics that are an integral part of active clinicians' lives but are not traditionally included in an undergraduate textbook. We therefore wrote a brief chapter covering these subjects. Our original manuscript did not include a chapter on personality theories. Based on comments from reviewers on the importance of having that material summarized in this book, we added chapter 4. This chapter is intended only as an overview, not as a replacement for a theories of personality course, and thus is somewhat brief. Chapter 13 provides a brief overview of the role of clinical psychologists in the broad realm of community work and public policy. This material is intended to alert the undergraduate student to these topics and provide a launching point for further research on their own, according to their particular wants.

A balance among theoretical orientations: One of the guiding principles in our writing was to have a balance among theoretical orientations. As we reviewed other books in this field, we noted that some seem to have a specific focus, such as empirically supported approaches to intervention. We believe that undergraduates benefit from reading about the entire domain of psychology and thus have tried to address options.

Diversity thoroughly incorporated: Another guiding principle was the impact of the changing demographics of this country on the practice of clinical psychology. Rather than have a single chapter devoted to diversity, we have attempted to include diversity issues throughout the text. This subject is part of some of our ethical conundrum issues as well as the text material. In chapter 9, we include a section on cultural considerations in psychotherapy. Because of the extensive literature on special issues of psychotherapy with women, we selected them as one of our special populations for consideration in chapter 11. When considering the future of clinical psychology in chapter 16 we not only discuss the changing demographics of the United States but also include a section on diversity.

Detailed coverage of psychological assessment: We wanted the material to address some topics in more detail than may be found in other texts. This was especially true in our coverage of psychological assessment. Although undergraduate students may take a course in tests and measurements, our text does not assume they have done so. Thus, we selected certain tests to represent various domains and covered them in greater depth. We also address the practical topic of malingering on psychological tests, why it may occur, and how it may be detected.

Inclusion of sex therapy: Based on prior student interest in the topic, we devoted a short section in our couples, family, and group psychotherapy chapter to sex therapy. We felt it was important for students to understand not only that this is a legitimate area of practice but also that most clinical psychologists who provide therapy for sexual dysfunctions have had specialty training in this area that is not typically part of general training in clinical psychology. We limited our coverage to sexual dysfunctions rather than also discussing the paraphilias.

Applied perspective on ethical issues of practice: We present ethical issues of practice from an applied rather than verbal rule perspective. We wanted our readers to understand that much of ethical practice is based on guidelines rather than standards as well as the type of decision-making that goes into ethical practice.

The text is accompanied by a **Test Bank.** The test bank is available for downloading at your convenience from www.oup.com/us/matthews. (The site is password-protected to ensure security; instructions for obtaining a password can be found at the site.) This Word document contains editable questions for every chapter of the text and was prepared by Amanda Schurle Bruce, The Pennsylvania State University, and Dana Figlock, The University of Iowa.

Acknowledgments

Many people have contributed to this final product. We thank the following colleagues who provided valuable feedback at the earliest stages of this project:

- Larry E. Beutler, Wm McInnes Distinguished Professor of Psychology; Director, National Center on the Psychology of Terrorism; Pacific Graduate School of Psychology
- James N. Butcher, University of Minnesota (Emeritus)
- Gerald P. Koocher, Simmons College
- David Lutz, Missouri State University
- Peter Vik, Idaho State University
- Ben Ogles, Ohio University
- Mikhail Lyubansky, University of Illinois, Urbana-Champaign
- Diane J. Willis, Professor Emeritus, Pediatrics, University of Oklahoma Health Sciences Center

As we developed the manuscript, several of our colleagues reviewed multiple drafts of chapters, providing extensive comments and much appreciated guidance:

- Amanda Schurle Bruce, The Pennsylvania State University
- Benjamin T. Mast, University of Louisville
- Jasper Smits, Southern Methodist University
- James Sullivan, Florida State University.

The test bank was also thoroughly reviewed—a valuable step too often skipped—for quality, consistency, and usability. We'd like to thank our colleagues who devoted their time to this review:

- Jerome Short, George Mason University
- William M. Grove, University of Minnesota—Twin Cities
- Randolph M. Lee, Trinity College
- Jefferson A Singer, Connecticut College
- Elissa Koplik, Bloomfield College
- W. Jake Jacobs, University of Arizona
- Brittany E. Canady, University of Houston

One of our reviewers, who chose to contact us directly and who provided ongoing responses to our questions, deserves special thanks—Dr. John C. Norcross from the University of Scranton.

At Oxford, we owe much to our original editor Joan Bossert and to our editor Shari D. Meffert for making this project come to fruition. We both received support from our universities for activities related to writing this book. Without the love and support of our families, this project would never have been completed. We therefore dedicate this book to our spouses, Dr. Lee H. Matthews and Maren Stavig, and to Amy and Eric.

We know that feedback is the best way to grow and improve, so we welcome all comments, criticisms, and suggestions. Please contact us at:

Janet R. Matthews
Loyola University New Orleans
matthews@loyola.edu

Barry S. Anton
University of Puget Sound
anton@ups.edu

Introduction to
Clinical Psychology

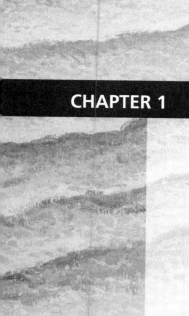

CHAPTER 1

Foundations of Clinical Psychology

Background

This chapter is the beginning of your journey into the field and the profession of clinical psychology. Before we start that journey, however, we want to tell you just a bit about ourselves. We each tend to start our classes this way, and we hope this book will be similar to the way we might tell you about these topics if you were in our classrooms. We will not go into extensive detail but rather will provide you with enough information so that we become real people to you.

I am Janet Matthews, and I have a Ph.D. in clinical psychology from the University of Mississippi. I completed my predoctoral internship in clinical psychology at the University of Oklahoma Health Sciences Center, funded by the Veterans Administration (VA), and my postdoctoral training was done at the University of Nebraska Medical Center with a specialty in neuropsychological assessment. I am a licensed clinical psychologist. I am board certified in clinical psychology by the American Board of Professional Psychology and in assessment psychology by the American Board of Assessment Psychology. I have been teaching undergraduate psychology for over thirty years. Currently, I am a full professor in the psychology department at Loyola University New Orleans.

Over the years, I have been faculty advisor to both the Psi Chi honor society and undergraduate Psychology Club on the campuses where I have taught. I am also active in professional psychological organizations. I have served on my state's psychology licensing board after being appointed by the governor. In addition to psychology, I spend my time with my husband and our cats and enjoy reading mysteries.

1

I am Barry Anton, and while I am a licensed clinical psychologist like Janet, my path to becoming a clinician was very different from hers. I should tell you that psychology runs in my family; my mother was one of the first women to receive a doctorate in psychology from Rutgers University in New Jersey.

After receiving my undergraduate degree at the University of Vermont, I decided to study brain–behavior relationships and received my Ph.D. in perceptual development at Colorado State University. After teaching and doing research for a few years, I pursued advanced clinical training at one of the teaching hospitals at Harvard Medical School (Massachusetts Mental Health Center—the original Boston Psychopathic Hospital), where I did my internship focusing on child clinical psychology. I then did a postdoctoral fellowship in child clinical psychology at Children's Hospital Medical Center and the Judge Baker Guidance Center in Boston.

Like Dr. Matthews, I have been teaching undergraduate psychology courses for a long time—over thirty years by the time you read this—and have been involved in all aspects of undergraduate education: teaching, research, administration, and service. I am board certified in clinical child and adolescent psychology by the American Board of Professional Psychology. For fun, I like to watch soccer, hike, and attend opera.

As you can see, we took very different paths to a similar end point. By the end of this book you will learn that there are not only many paths to becoming a clinical psychologist but also many different careers that exist under this general name. We believe it is important for you to determine not only if clinical psychology is a good personal career choice for you but also which path or paths are the best for you to follow toward that goal.

Our overall plan for this book is to give you a solid foundation about the activities of clinical psychologists. Related to each of those activities, we will present you with ethical dilemmas that may arise for the clinical psychologist who engages in them. One reason we are including this type of information is because we have found that students who read ethical codes tend to view them in absolute terms. Many of the clinical decisions that practitioners must make are not as clear-cut as the code might lead you to believe. It is also important to understand that parts of the code are really aspirational rather than mandatory. Our ethics code provides a solid grounding for our work rather than the answer to each of the dilemmas we face in our work. We are expected to use our skills to make the best possible decision for the specific situation at hand. When we are unsure about how to proceed, we seek collegial consultation. Even after years of practice and keeping up-to-date about ethical issues, we still face situations for which a second opinion is helpful. Because this book is about clinical psychology, we will generally refer to the Ethical Principles of Psychologists and Code of Conduct promulgated by the American Psychological Association (APA, 2002). This is not the only mental health profession that has an ethical code. We will occasionally make reference to the codes of other professions. Table 1.1 lists several related mental health associations and the web addresses where you can find their ethics materials. Because the APA accredits doctoral programs in clinical psychology in Canada, as well as the proximity of that country to the United States, we also have included the website for the ethics code of Canadian psychologists developed by the Canadian Psychological Association (CPA). We find that the world has become smaller in the sense that psychologists around the world are working together on many projects. As one way to help you see some of these issues in a broader way,

Table 1.1 also includes websites for the ethics codes of a number of other countries around the world. There is also some movement toward the development of an international set of ethical principles for psychologists. When Dr. Matthews attended the Third International Congress on Licensure, Certification, and Credentialing of Psychologists in Montreal, Canada, in April 2004, she had the opportunity to hear about the proposed framework for a Universal Declaration of Ethical Principles for Psychologists. At that time, an international working group was considering five such principles: respect for the dignity and rights of persons and people; caring for others and concerns for their welfare; competence; integrity; and professional, scientific, and social responsibility. Of course, even if this working group develops a set of principles, there is no guarantee it would be accepted by all jurisdictions. Most undergraduate textbooks do not discuss these international ethics issues. We have included this information because we believe the internationalization of clinical psychology will be an important part of the profession's future.

The APA Ethics Code has five general principles that are considered aspirational. These principles are beneficence and nonmaleficence, fidelity and responsibility, integrity, justice, and respect for people's rights and dignity. These general principles are followed by ten areas known as *standards*. The standards specify required behavior by psychologists. The term *standard* will be discussed later in the book. Although psychologists often talk about the fact that we need to be able to use our judgment depending on the situation and therefore need *guidelines,* or advice, about how to respond, we do have some concepts that are considered applicable in most situations and therefore the Ethics Code includes standards.

The CPA code is structured a bit differently. It starts with the four ethical principles of respect for the dignity of the person, responsible caring, integrity in relationships, and responsibility to society. These principles are followed by a *statement of values* that is used to define the principles. Psychologists are told that when there is a conflict in what behavior is suggested by the principles, the psychologists should weigh them in the order given in the list. Standards in the Canadian system illustrate the application of the principles and range from minimal expectations to more idealized ones. Psychologists who move from one place of residence to another thus must familiarize themselves with the relevant ethics code for the place where they are practicing.

The Code of Ethics of the National Association of Social Workers (NASW) also emphasizes a set of core values for the profession. The core values for social workers under this code are service, social justice, dignity and worth of the person, importance of human relationships, integrity, and competence. These values are thus used as a basis for the ethical principles in their code. We have given you information about these three ethics codes to illustrate the concept of professional ethics. Each code listed in Table 1.1 has some elements you may find of interest. Because times change, each code is updated on a regular basis.

To give you just a brief idea of the range of issues that may arise in the practice of clinical psychology, ten frequent ethical challenges faced by practitioners that have been identified by experts in this field (Smith, 2003) are understanding what constitutes a multiple relationship; protecting confidentiality; respecting people's autonomy; knowing your supervisory responsibilities; identifying your client and role; documenting, documenting, documenting; practicing only where you have expertise; knowing the

Table 1.1 Ethics Websites

American Association for Marriage and Family Therapy
    www.aamft.org/resources/LRMPlan/Ethics/ethicscode2001.htm

American Association of Pastoral Counselors
    www.aapc.com/ethics.htm

American College Personnel Association
    www.acpa.nche.edu/pubs/prncstan.htm

American Counseling Association
    www.counseling.org/resources/codeofethics.htm

American Group Therapy Association
    www.groupsinc.org/group/ethicalguide/html

American Psychiatric Association
    www.ama-assn.org/ama/publ/article/5009-4727.html

American Psychoanalytic Association
    www.apsa.org/ethics901/htm

American Psychological Association
    www.apa.org/ethics/code.html

American Society of Clinical Hypnosis
    www.asch.net/AboutASCH.htm

Association for Addiction Professionals
    www.naadac.org/ethics.htm

Association of Marital and Family Therapy
    www.amftrb.org/ethics.htm

Association of State and Provincial Psychology Boards (ASPPB)
    www.asppb.org/pubs/code

Australian Psychological Society
    www.psychology.org.au/aps/ethics/code of ethics.pdf

Canadian Psychological Association
    www.cpa.ca/ethics2000.html

Denmark (same for Finland, Norway, and Sweden)
    www.psy.it/normativa ue/scandinavian ethical principal.htm

International Society of Mental Health Online
    www.ismho.org/suggestions.html

National Association of Social Workers
    www.socialworkers.org/pubs/code/default/htm

National Council for Hypnotherapy
    www.hypnotherapy.org.uk/standards/ethics.htm

South Africa
    www.hpsca.co.za/legalmed/ethical.html#partnerships

Spain
    www.psy.it/normativa ue/spain/code of ethics.htm

difference between abandonment and termination; sticking to the evidence; and being accurate in billing. In coming chapters we will provide you with ethical dilemmas related to the topic of that chapter. At the end of the chapter we will give you information about issues the psychologist would need to consider when faced with these dilemmas. For more information about each of these codes, you may want to visit the websites listed in Table 1.1. You may also be interested in reading about the Hippocratic Oath, which was quite likely the first ethics code (von Staden, 1996).

Clinical psychology is both a science and a practice. The findings of science inform the activities of practice, and the activities of practice suggest hypotheses to be tested by science. Not all clinical psychologists are active researchers. We are all trained, however, to be knowledgeable about research. Using our psychological research training, we can read the studies conducted by our colleagues and evaluate their applicability to our practices. We can modify our clinical practices based on the data generated by our colleagues. In this way, we can continue to provide the most appropriate services to the consumers of our work. We will include information about empirical support for the clinical activities described in this book to illustrate ways the science of clinical psychology supports the practice of clinical psychology. These studies also illustrate the types of applied research done by clinical psychologists.

Throughout this book, we will discuss activities of clinical psychologists. There is no single job setting or activity that describes the role of a clinical psychologist. Among the places where clinical psychologists work are hospitals, community agencies, academic settings, and private practice offices. Some clinical psychologists have very general practices, while others are quite specialized. We will discuss some sample work settings in more detail later in the chapter. By the time you have finished reading this book, you will have a picture of the breadth of this profession.

Related Careers

As a starting point for this book, let's consider the range of professions that are similar to clinical psychology. Some of you may be considering a career as a clinical psychologist. Although we both strongly encourage you to learn more about this field, we also want you to be aware of some of the other professions that are similar to our field. You may find that a related field is really a better match for your interests than clinical psychology is.

Psychiatry

Psychiatrists are physicians who specialize in organic diseases of the mind. After graduating from medical school, these physicians do an internship and residency where they are trained to work with people whose behavior is sufficiently distressing to someone to have them be labeled as suffering from a mental disorder. Some psychiatrists specialize by the age of the patient (such as a geropsychiatrist, who works with the elderly), while others specialize in particular types of disorders (such as depression). Like their colleagues in other branches of medicine, some psychiatrists are generalists who see a wide range of patients; others are specialists. Psychiatrists may work in a variety of settings, including medical schools, state and private mental institutions, general hospital inpatient settings, or private practice. Psychiatrists also serve as medical directors of insurance companies, where they write the rules about access to care, determine patient benefits, and review appeals of denials of service. Many psychiatrists will work in some combination of these settings. When working in psychiatric hospitals, they may serve as administrators of specific units with an interdisciplinary staff, as hospital administrators, or as consultants to special programs.

Many students of psychology associate Sigmund Freud with the development of psychoanalysis, a form of psychotherapy. Freud was trained as a physician and thus would be considered a psychiatrist. Traditionally, psychiatrists have emphasized the use of medication, or other physical intervention like electroshock treatment, for the treatment of emotional problems. The use of psychotropic medication, as you may remember from earlier psychology courses, was once viewed as a major reason many people could be discharged from long-term care facilities. Prior to the availability of these medications in the 1950s, such individuals' behavior had been sufficiently extreme that they could not function outside a full-time care facility. Once a person was sent to such a facility, family members had to accept the idea that their loved one would remain there for life. These long-term care facilities were often located in geographically isolated areas of the state. The location made it difficult for family members to visit or be part of the treatment program. The calming effect of medication allowed many of these people to be placed in outpatient or partial care programs rather than living full-time in the hospital. When the use of medication allowed them to be discharged from the hospital, they could return to their home community and receive treatment there in community mental health centers. Ideally, family members could provide some emotional support for them during this transition period and participate in their treatment.

Over time, medications have been developed for less severe forms of emotional difficulty and are now routinely advertised on TV with the suggestion that the viewer check with his or her physician regarding the appropriateness of the specific product. The brand names of many of these medications now seem to be part of our common vocabulary and are among the most widely prescribed drugs in the world. Some psychologists have also been trained in the use of such medications with the hope that medication will become another of the tools with which they may practice their profession. We will discuss this development a bit more in chapters 3, 13, and 15.

Social Work

Social workers receive their postbaccalaureate training in **social work.** Most of the social workers with whom we have worked have a master of social work (M.S.W.) degree and are then certified on a state and/or national level after working under the supervision of a master's degree–level social worker for two years and providing three thousand hours of service. They also must pass a national written examination. The "diplomate in social work" is an even more advanced credential for social workers who have an additional three years of advanced clinical practice and have passed another national examination. Some social workers have continued their education and received a doctorate in social work (D.S.W.). Many of these professionals teach in graduate programs or serve as administrators.

Traditionally, social workers were the members of the mental health team who took the patient's history and made arrangements for community services once the patient was discharged from the hospital. They might also conduct follow-up home visits to check on the patient. These visits were intended to determine if the patient was functioning sufficiently well to remain in the community as well as whether or not additional services might be needed. In these earlier times, social workers did not serve as the patient's primary therapist in the hospital. Today, however, social workers are found in an expanding number of settings, including inpatient psychiatric services and private practice. When working in inpatient settings, they may be the patient's primary therapist or part of a therapeutic treatment team, depending on the structure of the program. In private practice, they may be in an individual or a group practice. A group practice might be one with several other social workers or with a range of healthcare professionals. When different types of healthcare providers work in the same setting together, it is called a multidisciplinary group practice. Social workers conduct both individual and group therapy as well as serve in administrative positions. According to information on the website of the National Association of Social Workers (www.nasw.org), "clinical social work interventions include, but are not limited to, assessment and diagnosis, crisis intervention, psychosocial and psychoeducational interventions, and brief and long-term psychotherapies." You can see from this brief description that social workers do many activities that are also done by clinical psychologists.

Some graduate programs in social work offer joint degree programs so that the student who attends school just a bit longer than the traditional three semesters of graduate social work study may receive two degrees rather than one. For example, one program near Dr. Matthews has the option, with the completion of one additional semester, for students to earn a master's degree in public health while also earning an M.S.W. degree. Students are able to do this because some of the coursework is designed to apply to both degree programs. Having these two related degrees gives these graduates greater employment flexibility. Other "joint" programs allow the student to earn both a social work degree and a law degree.

Expressive Therapies

Many specialized therapists may work in the same settings as clinical psychologists. Although we will not provide extensive detail about their training, we want you to know about some other possible mental health careers. Music therapists, dance/movement therapists, occupational therapists, recreational therapists, and art therapists frequently do group work in inpatient psychiatric settings. Although each of these professions is separate, a general term that is sometimes used to refer to them as a group is **expressive therapy.** As mental health professionals have come to have a greater appreciation of the calming effect of animals as part of the therapeutic process, we have seen an increase in such forms of therapy as equestrian therapy and the training of "therapeutic pets" who participate in traditional forms of "talking therapy." Among the animals used in therapy are cats, dogs, horses, and dolphins (www.therapyanimal.org). Many of these professionals also see patients on an individual basis to assist in their recovery.

In 1979, the National Coalition of Arts Therapies Associations (NCATA) was formed to provide a place for a number of different forms of expressive therapy to integrate their work. This organization includes six creative arts therapy associations with over eight thousand individual members. The professional groups in NCATA are art therapy, dance/movement therapy, drama therapy, music therapy, poetry therapy, and psycho-drama. If you would like more information about any of these careers, we suggest you visit their website (www.ncata.com). We will provide some basic information about music therapy and art therapy to illustrate these professions.

Music Therapy Although the use of creative approaches to dealing with human distress has a long history, the modern use of these approaches tends to be dated to the post–World War II period that also led to the growth of clinical psychology as a profession. Music therapists provided clinical services to help military veterans recover from the traumas of combat. In addition to their clinical work, these therapists also did extensive research in veterans' hospitals both during and after World War II. Research continues to be a significant part of the **music therapy** profession.

By the twenty-first century, the American Music Therapy Association represented over five thousand music therapists. Certified music therapists work in a range of set-tings that overlap clinical psychology, working not only with psychiatric patients and rehabilitation patients but also with people who are generally viewed as being healthy but have problems involving stress. Music therapists assist their patients in stress reduction. Stress reduction is important not only for patients with psychological problems but also for those in medical rehabilitation programs. Medical rehabilitation programs include ser-vices for patients recovering from strokes, spinal cord injuries, and heart attacks. Music therapists try to address patient problems both through their relationship with the patient and through the music they use with that particular patient or group. Music therapists use many different theoretical approaches. Some music therapists have developed specific methods to use with specialized forms of trauma. Rogers (1993), for example, suggests having different musical instruments represent different people in a child's life when working with sexually abused children. The child helps select the instruments as well as how they are played. Such factors as the size of the instruments, their relative placement, and which instruments are played with are then used to better understand the trauma from the child's perspective.

You do not need to be a professional musician to become a music therapist. You do need to have an appreciation of several forms of music plus some level of music ability. Within university structures, these programs are most likely to be located in the College of Music. Students enrolled in these programs complete music theory courses and applied music courses as well as **practica,** which are supervised experience in an applied set-ting. In order to become a certified music therapist (CMT), you must have a bachelor's degree in music therapy or its equivalent. There are nationally accredited programs in music therapy throughout the country. These programs include a nine-hundred-hour clini-cal internship as one of their graduation requirements. Music therapists with a master's degree in music therapy or a closely related field, one hundred contact hours in continu-ing education, and extensive clinical experience may apply for an advanced certification in music therapy. Currently, there are also some doctoral programs in music therapy as well as a national board certification process.

Art Therapy   **Art therapy** in the United States traces its history to European writing about the spontaneous art produced by patients in mental hospitals. Many abnormal psychology books include such paintings as illustrations. In China, calligraphy was viewed as a form of art therapy. Calligraphers studied handwriting rather than pictures. The modern profession of art therapy developed simultaneously in the United States and England in the 1940s and 1950s. The major forces leading to this profession were psychoanalysis and art education.

Art therapists use both talking about the art and the actual creation of art as part of their therapy. They may give the patient instruction in the use of various art media and select the specific media based on the patients' issues. With increased technology available, art therapists now also use videotaping and computer graphics to help their patient's express emotional issues (Wadeson, Durkin, & Perach, 1989). The first graduate degrees specifically in art therapy were awarded in the 1970s. In 2002, there were twenty-seven nationally accredited master's degree programs in art therapy.

Occupational and Recreational Therapy

The final two related professions we suggest you consider are occupational and recreational therapy. Both of these professions work with people across the lifespan as well as in both inpatient and outpatient settings. According to the American Occupational Therapy Association (AOTA), "occupational therapy is a health and rehabilitation profession that helps people regain, develop, and build skills that are important for independent functioning, health, well-being, security, and happiness" (http://www.aota.org). In some cases the work of the occupational therapist is aimed at preventing injury, and in other cases the focus is on preventing current problems from becoming worse. The occupational therapist helps the patient learn new ways to approach the job setting so that it does not become overwhelming. Consider, for example, the person whose job performance has been deteriorating following a change in equipment. Because of decreased productivity, the person has been told he may be laid off. The occupational therapist might work with this patient to break down the job role into segments and find better ways to complete the needed tasks. In some cases, the occupational therapist may also help the patient find or change employment either because the patient was not working or because return to the former occupation is not recommended. Suppose the patient has been in an automobile accident. Although she has been discharged from the hospital, she continues to have problems concentrating. Her job, prior to the accident, was as an air traffic controller. Obviously, concentration is an important part of her responsibility. Her neuropsychologist has determined that because of the location of her head trauma, she is likely to continue to have reduced ability to concentration. Thus, a return to her former occupation is not possible.

When working in the field of mental illness, the occupational therapist aims to help the patient function independently. The skills involved in these cases include time management, the ability to work productively with other people, and the ability to enjoy leisure time. These are the activities of daily living. Although traditionally, occupational therapists could be trained at either the bachelor's or master's degree level, that process is changing. Starting January 1, 2007, new occupational therapists must have education beyond the bachelor's degree. A list of accredited occupational therapy programs can be obtained from the AOTA on their website.

"The recreational therapist assists her/his patients' rehabilitation by offering recreational and other activities intended to promote recovery and wellness" (http://www.ceap.wcu.edu). The recreational therapist develops activities that can be used to teach positive interpersonal relations as well as to provide new forms of activity the patient can use outside the hospital or day treatment setting. For some patients, participation in recreational activities also allows them to feel sufficiently comfortable to talk to that therapist in a way the patient has not yet done in more traditional therapy settings. This information can then be given to the primary therapist for use in other interventions. Within the university setting, recreation therapy programs are most often found within recreation or leisure studies departments. In some schools, however, they are found in such departments as special education, nursing, and health and human performance. National standards for certification as a recreational therapist include making an acceptable score on a two-hundred-item national written examination offered by the Educational Testing Service (ETS).

Psychology Professionals

General Information

Even within the field of psychology, confusion sometimes arises about the differences between clinical psychologists and counseling psychologists. Both of us have colleagues who do the same type of work we do as clinical psychologists and yet their degrees are in counseling psychology. How do you decide which specialty is right for you if both do the same things? Let's start with the traditional distinction between these two specialties and then move to the current status. When we were training, we were told that clinical psychologists work with the more severe forms of psychopathology while counseling psychologists focus on less disturbed people. It was noted that clinical psychologists work with people whose diagnosis is one of the psychoses while counseling psychologists tend to work with anxiety disorders or career issues.

Today the distinction between these specialties seems to be a function of the particular graduate program and internship the psychologist attended rather than the specialty in the graduate program. Some **counseling psychology** programs still focus on the less severe forms of emotional distress. They may also provide training in career issues and other problems faced by people who are leading acceptable lives but feel they could be happier or more productive than they are. These are the programs that differ most from the clinical psychology programs. Other counseling psychology programs provide training opportunities on inpatient psychiatric units, work with the seriously mentally ill, and generally are quite similar to the clinical programs we will describe next. According to the definition of counseling psychology in the APA archives (http://www.apa.org/crsppp/counseling.html), "counseling psychology is a general practice health service provider specialty in psychology." This same phrase is used to begin the description of clinical psychology in the APA archives. Thus, we see that even within their professional organization, clinical and counseling psychologists have described their work in overlapping terminology.

Let's return to the question about finding the career that best fits your interests. We suggest that you may want to look at both clinical and counseling psychology graduate programs if you are considering a psychology–health service provider career and then make your selection based on the individual program rather than the specialty. Like clinical psychology programs, most counseling psychology programs award the Ph.D. degree. A few counseling psychology programs grant either the **doctor of psychology** (Psy.D.) or doctor of education (Ed.D.) degree.

Clinical Training Programs

Clinical psychology is the focus of this book, so we will spend a bit more time describing the training for this specialty than we did for the others. Students may also wish to read an additional description of this specialty on the APA website (http://www.apa.org/crsppp/clipsyc.html). The APA Council of Representatives accepted this definition of clinical psychology in August 1998. There are two major degrees that are found in clinical psychology programs. The older of the two degrees is the Ph.D., or **doctor of philosophy,** degree. This degree typically requires the student to complete both a master's thesis and doctoral dissertation as part of the academic program. These works are based on original research that is considered of publishable quality. This does not mean that every doctoral dissertation is published or must be published if you are going to graduate. The dissertation must be judged by the faculty committee overseeing the project to be of a quality that it "could" be published. For some students, the master's thesis is really the pilot study for the doctoral dissertation. Using this model also allows the future psychologist to begin to develop a personal research program that may be continued as a professional, especially if an academic career is selected.

The academic component of the training requires four to five years of study. Courses in both the scientific and applied aspects of psychology are included in this training. The foundation courses tend to cover such areas as the biological bases of behavior, social bases of behavior, cognitive-affective bases of behavior, individual differences, statistics, and ethical principles. Notice that these are broad areas of psychology rather than the very specific types of courses you probably have in your undergraduate program. This breadth allows some individualization for both students and programs while maintaining a common foundation among clinical psychologists. We will use one of these broad areas to illustrate some individual options. The biological bases of behavior domain includes courses in physiological psychology, biopsychology, psychopharmacology, and clinical neuropsychology. Depending on the particular program, the student might take one or more of these courses to satisfy the biological bases of behavior requirement.

The student also participates in an integrated series of practica. A practicum is a course for which the student receives academic credit but involves applied work rather than the traditional lecture or seminar. This applied work is done under the supervision of a professional and may occur in a range of possible settings. The supervisor is usually a psychologist, but in some cases supervision may also be provided by other licensed professionals, such as social workers or psychiatrists.

As students learn about psychological testing and various methods of intervention, they begin to use these tools with people who are seeking help. The further through the program, the less closely the student will be monitored by supervisors. Initially, the practicum may involve observing more advanced students engaged in clinical activities and/or participating in case conferences about the people seen in the department or university clinic. Next, the graduate student will begin to engage in these activities under close supervision. As students progress through this series of practica, they have increasing clinical responsibility and the supervision will not be as close. Regardless of the setting, the ultimate responsibility for the patient remains with the licensed professional, not the student.

In some programs, the early supervision is done "live" and later supervision is based on videotapes. Live supervision does not mean that the supervisor is in the same room with the student and the patient. Often this type of supervision is conducted in a room with a one-way window. The supervisor sits in a different room and observes. Other graduate students may also be in the observation room as part of their training process. The supervisor may provide instant feedback if needed through either an earpiece worn by the student or telephone communication. Of course, the patient is aware that this is a student therapist and that others may be observing. This same type of consent is given for videotaping a session. This tape is then discussed with the supervisor at a later time.

A series of examinations, called comprehensives, are typically administered near the end of the coursework portion of the graduate program to assess the student's overall knowledge of psychology. These exams often have both a written and an oral component. After passing these exams, the student is admitted to what is called "candidacy" for the doctorate.

Once the student has reached this stage of training, two things occur. One is the development of a proposal for the doctoral dissertation. The other is the application for the predoctoral internship. Although some doctoral programs have an approved predoctoral internship "on site," the most typical arrangement is for the student to move to a different location for that part of the applied training.

This move for the predoctoral internship is important for a number of reasons. First, if your internship is a long distance from your doctoral program you will need to consider how you plan to complete your dissertation. You will no longer have your major professor nearby for discussions. Although some "discussing" can occur through email, face-to-face meetings may be helpful at certain points in the process. You may need to budget for several trips from your new location to your university to discuss the project as well as for your final presentation and defense of your research. Second, moving can be both expensive and stressful. Your internship will start in the summer but you will not know where you are going to do it until February. Thus, accurate budgeting for the move may be difficult. As you learn personal coping strategies to teach patients, you also need to apply them to your own life. Third, you will have the opportunity to work with a new group of professionals as you fine-tune your clinical skills. This experience will broaden your knowledge base.

Unfortunately, not all students finish their doctoral dissertations by the time they have completed their internships. A variety of factors contribute to this situation. Perhaps expected subjects (now officially called participants) are not available. The student must look for new sources of subjects/participants before completing the project. In other cases, there are equipment problems or perhaps problems with the data analysis or final acceptance of the written product. A term that is sometimes used for students who have finished all of the work for their degree except the dissertation is ABD, which stands for "all but dissertation." The person is not allowed to use the title of "doctor" at this time because he or she has not finished all the work required for the degree. On the other hand, use of the term *ABD* allows others to realize the advanced level of this person's training.

Most doctoral programs have a time limit for completion of all degree requirements. This time limit usually starts when the student is accepted for candidacy. A problem faced by many students who are ABD is whether to take a job, since they have both skills and financial needs to consider, or to return to their university to complete their dissertation. Both of us know people who attended well-known doctoral programs, were solid clinicians, and have never received a doctoral degree in clinical psychology because their "clock ran out." What this means is that they took jobs after their internships and did not complete their dissertations. They reached the time limit specified by their program and thus would need to retake many courses plus complete their dissertations before receiving their degrees. To decrease the number of students for whom this occurs, some programs require that certain parts of the dissertation be completed before the student is allowed to start an internship.

Once the dissertation and internship have been completed, the doctoral degree is conferred. The person is still not ready to be called a psychologist or to practice independently. Requirements for licensure vary somewhat among jurisdictions (U.S. states or Canadian provinces), but a fairly typical sequence is for the person to be required to be supervised in a clinical setting for two thousand hours of work, which is completed after receiving your doctoral degree. There is also a standardized examination called the Examination for the Professional Practice of Psychology (EPPP), which is given nationally and must be passed before the candidate is eligible to undertake whatever specific requirements exist in that jurisdiction. These jurisdictional requirements may include a test on state law and ethics, explaining how to handle a case that is provided, and meeting with the state licensing board to discuss practice plans. These final requirements may be written, oral, or both. Once these requirements have been met, the person is finally permitted to use the title of "psychologist" and to engage in the practice of psychology without a supervisor.

Having the legal right to work independently does not mean that psychologists never seek assistance after receiving a license. For most of us, consultation with peers continues throughout our professional careers. Even if we can "legally" conduct all of our activities independently, there are times when it is helpful to get the advice of a colleague. This advice-seeking is done in general terms so that patient confidentiality is maintained.

Perhaps a brief example of this type of consultation will make the point clearer. One part of the 2002 APA Ethics Code is "Providing Therapy to Those Served by Others" (10.04; APA, 2002). Many people conceptualize this behavior as "patient-stealing." Recently one of us was consulted about a case in this area. The psychologist, who we will call Psychologist A, works in an agency setting. An outpatient was referred to Psychologist A for screening for one of the programs offered at that agency as well as for individual therapy. During the interview, the patient stated that she was "interviewing" several therapists in an attempt to find the best match. She gave Psychologist A the names of the other two professionals she either had seen or was scheduled to see. She stated she had already met with another psychologist, whom we will call Psychologist B, and was scheduled to see a social worker the next day. Psychologist A decided that the patient had not established a therapeutic relationship with anyone at this point and so did not seek a release of information to speak to Psychologist B. Subsequently, Psychologist B called and wanted to discuss this patient. Psychologist B noted that this was "patient-stealing" and was unethical and threatened to file a complaint with the state licensing board. Psychologist A sought consultation from a colleague about whether or not she could admit having seen this person, whether anything unethical had occurred given the patient's statement that she was in the process of trying to establish a therapeutic relationship, and how to document what had happened.

According to the APA Ethics Code, a major issue is to be sensitive to the therapeutic issues. This case becomes problematic because it does not involve an ongoing therapeutic relationship. Some professionals consider the point when the therapeutic relationship starts is when they first see the person; others would say that given the nature of the interview (interviewing therapists) this may not have actually started a therapeutic relationship. Thus, this is the type of case where the psychologist could elect to seek consultation. Patient confidentiality is not compromised because neither the name of the patient nor that of the other psychologist was used when seeking this consultation.

The pathway to the licensure process is quite similar in the other type of clinical training program. The degree in this case is the Psy.D. The major distinction between this program and the Ph.D. program is in the research–practice balance. Although both types of programs require training in the foundations of psychology mentioned in the description of Ph.D. programs, Psy.D. programs tend to start the practicum courses earlier and often have a broader definition of research. In some of these programs the final project may be a publishable quality case study, a survey, or an extensive literature review rather than an empirical research project. Students in Psy.D. programs receive a master's degree partway through the program just like their counterparts in the Ph.D. programs. The courses on research in the Psy.D. programs may place a stronger focus on being a good consumer of research rather than on being a producer of a body of knowledge. The length of time to complete the required coursework is similar to the Ph.D. program. Graduates of Psy.D. programs are less likely to be seeking traditional academic careers than are graduates of Ph.D. programs. This does not mean, however, that psychologists with a Psy.D. cannot or do not have full-time teaching careers. Graduates of Psy.D. programs often elect this training model because they are interested in applied careers in contrast to academic ones.

We are not providing great depth about the technical requirements for completing graduate school and for becoming licensed because those activities are a number of years in the future for you. There may be changes in the process by the time you are ready to enter the profession. We hope this chapter will give you enough information to be able to decide whether or not you want to learn more about this career for yourself. At least you will have an idea about the amount of both time and money you will need to plan to expend to reach your goal.

Education does not end for the clinical psychologist with the granting of a license to practice. As with many professions, the licensed psychologist may need to complete a specified number of hours of continuing education each year, or in each license renewal cycle, to maintain that license. Some jurisdictions specify topics, such as ethics, that must be included in the continuing education, while others leave the decision about the topics to the licensed psychologist. The continuing education must be relevant to the practice of psychology. In some jurisdictions only continuing education programs offered by sponsors approved by the licensing board are counted toward this requirement. The APA is one organization that evaluates continuing education sponsors, and its approved sponsors are found throughout the country. Some psychologists also choose to have their work evaluated by peers in order to become board certified in their specialty area. This process is similar to the board certification process common among physicians. Most of these credentialing boards require that the psychologist has been licensed for a period of years before applying for his evaluation process. Board certification typically involves submission of a work sample as well as an oral examination. These are activities for you to consider in your future.

Training Models

Clinical programs vary not only by the degree they offer but also by the model of training upon which they are based. In general terms, some programs place a stronger emphasis on the science side of psychology and others place a stronger emphasis on practice. Common terms used to describe these different training programs are clinical-scientist, scientist-practitioner, practitioner-scholar, and practitioner. The clinical-scientist programs emphasize training in empirically supported treatments. Their graduates are trained to use only those methods that have solid scientific bases. The scientist-practitioner programs strive for a balance between science and practice; these two areas are viewed as two elements that enhance each other rather than as two points on a continuum. Such programs train their graduates to be both researchers and practitioners and to model both of these skills as faculty members. These programs are based on the **Boulder model,** which we will describe next. The practitioner-scholar programs are based on the Vail Conference, which we will also describe shortly. Although these programs emphasize the mutuality of science and practice, their focus is on the practical application of scholarship. The practitioner programs emphasize the role of supervision and clinical judgment in clinical training. Each of these different approaches to training clinical psychologists tend to have their foundation in models developed at national conferences of psychologists.

In 1949, the Conference on Training in Clinical Psychology was held in Boulder, Colorado. This conference, usually called the Boulder Conference, established the scientist-practitioner model for training clinical psychologists. This model is also called the Boulder model. Seventy-two delegates were invited to spend two weeks in Boulder to design a model for clinical psychology training programs throughout the country. Like many of the major events in history, the need for this conference was based on what was happening outside the profession at that time. The United States was faced with many veterans returning from World War II. As a result of what these people faced during the war, many of them needed psychotherapy. There were not enough mental health professionals available to meet this national demand. Leaders at both the Veterans Administration and the United States Public Health Service contacted the APA. They had several requests. First, they wanted APA to name those universities that offered training at the doctoral level in clinical psychology. Second, they wanted APA to develop training standards so that additional programs could be developed. The underlying principle of these standards was that clinical psychologists needed to be trained as both scientists and as practitioners. This concept led to the inclusion of both lecture courses and applied courses in the training programs. These programs were designed so that students would spend four years at the university and then complete a twelve-month internship before being granted the doctorate. These delegates realized that their training model would need to be evaluated after being tested and so recommended that within the next five years a second national conference should be convened to consider what changes in the training program were needed.

The Institute on Education and Training for Psychological Contributions to Mental Health was held at Stanford University in 1955. This conference provided the follow-up recommended in Boulder. These delegates were not trying to start a training model but rather were trying to evaluate what was currently in place as recommended in Boulder. After spending four days on this task, the delegates determined that the previous delegates had developed a solid training model (Matarazzo, 1983). They made no recommendations for change at that time.

Ten years later, the Conference on the Professional Preparation of Clinical Psychologists met for six days in Chicago (Hoch, Ross, & Winder, 1966). This conference, often called the Chicago Conference, also endorsed the scientist-practitioner model initially proposed at the Boulder Conference. The delegates took a firm stand that training in clinical psychology should remain at the doctoral level. Some people had begun to question whether a practitioner really needed so many years in school to be effective. The delegates at this conference decided that this advanced level of education was necessary. It is interesting to note that this issue of how much education is needed to be an appropriate practitioner continues to this day. The impact of social needs of the time can be seen by the fact that the Chicago Conference also suggested that university training departments either establish psychological clinics or develop close relationships with existing clinics. These clinics were described as places where students could learn clinical skills, faculty members could conduct clinical research, and the social needs of the community could be addressed. A hint of changing times occurred at this conference when delegates debated the developing concept of a new training model, the Psy.D. Such a model was seen as an experiment that could be evaluated for future consideration.

The first Psy.D. program in clinical psychology started at the University of Illinois in 1968 and was discontinued in 1980. Three other Psy.D. programs began shortly after the University of Illinois program and continue to the present. They are located at Widener University (started at Hahnemann University's medical school in 1970 but moved to Widener in 1989), Baylor University (1971), and Rutgers University (1973). From this small start APA now accredits almost fifty Psy.D. programs. These programs train about half of the current graduates. Some of these programs are on traditional college campuses, while others are housed in freestanding professional schools. Freestanding professional schools are seldom located on a university campus. They were founded to teach only psychology. Because these schools are not part of a university, teach limited subjects, and yet are accredited institutions of higher education, they are called *freestanding professional schools*. In the twenty-first century, however, some of them have added related programs, such as advanced undergraduate training, and have changed their name to "university" but they continue to be quite different from traditional universities. Students need to consider these differences when searching for a graduate program that fits their learning style and interests.

The freestanding professional schools were designed specifically to train professional psychologists. One motivation behind the development of the freestanding schools was to have clinical courses taught by psychologists who were actually using these skills rather than by psychologists who only did research and supervision but did not actually see people professionally. In many of the early freestanding schools the majority of their teaching faculty was part-time. Only a few full-time faculty members worked in these schools. These full-time faculty members did the administrative duties as well as teaching courses. Over time, it was determined that the students needed more attention outside of class time than full-time private practitioners could provide. To provide this level of attention the concept of "core faculty" was developed. These core faculty members had full-time appointments at the professional school. They were, however, expected to maintain a private practice in order to keep their clinical skills current. Professional school core faculty members did not tend to have personal research labs like their counterparts in traditional research universities. One model used by these freestanding schools to facilitate this blend of academic and applied work is to have one day a week when the school schedules no classes. This form of class scheduling may be different from the students' undergraduate experiences. It is done so that all clinical faculty members have a designated time to see patients. They will not be available for students at this time.

The Boulder model of training in clinical psychology continued to be viewed as the traditional training model throughout the 1970s and 1980s. In 1990, a national conference was convened in Gainesville, Florida, to more fully articulate the model as well as show its applicability to other applied areas of psychology such as counseling, school, and applied developmental psychology (Belar & Perry, 1992). During this conference delegates met in specialty groups to articulate subsets of the model more completely. On the final day of the conference, these delegates voted word-by-word on a position paper articulating the scientist-practitioner model in more detail than previous conferences had done. Despite both the work involved and the level of agreement among these delegates, this report did not lead to any major national changes in training programs. This conference and its outcome illustrate an important point about the profession. Scholarly work does not necessarily lead to change; the suggested position must be accepted by the various factions within the discipline before change occurs.

The first major national conference to endorse Psy.D. programs as an alternative model for training clinical psychologists met in Vail, Colorado, for six days in 1973 (Korman, 1974). This conference, the National Conference on Levels and Patterns of Professional Training in Psychology, also departed from prior training models by suggesting that clinical psychology training programs did not need to be limited to university psychology departments. Appropriate settings for such training programs included medical schools, departments of education, and freestanding schools. Freestanding schools were a relatively new concept for psychologists in 1973, but by the twenty-first century we found that such schools were training many of our new professionals.

Development of Specialties

As clinical psychology continued to develop its identity, it also began to subdivide into specialties. One of those specialties is clinical child psychology. As more clinical psychologists developed practices that specialized in work with children, they felt the need to have a national conference to establish training standards in this area. This conference, The Conference on Training Clinical Child Psychologists, was held in Hilton Head, South Carolina, in 1985. Delegates at that conference decided it was not yet time to separate their specialty from the overall training of clinical psychology, but rather described the specific courses that should be offered to students wanting to pursue a specialty in clinical child psychology. These trainers viewed clinical child psychology as an area that could be pursued as a specialty track within a general clinical program rather than being a new major specialty. They also reaffirmed their support for the scientist-practitioner model first established in Boulder. Continued national interest in the importance of training clinical psychologists to work with children was seen when the National Institute of Mental Health (NIMH) sponsored a national conference on this topic several years later (Magreb & Wohlford, 1990). We will provide a further discussion of clinical child psychology as a specialty in chapter 15.

The professional school model first noted at the Vail Conference led to the development of many new training programs. To facilitate communication among these programs, the National Council of Schools of Professional Psychology (NCSPP) was established in 1977. This organization has hosted several national conferences to discuss the professional training model. Their first conference, known as the La Jolla Conference on Quality Control, was held in 1981 in La Jolla, California (Callan, Peterson, & Stricker, 1986). This was the first of several conferences designed to provide a forum for discussion of curriculum and quality control in professional schools. NCSPP includes both university-based and freestanding programs. What ties them together is the model of training used in their programs.

As the profession continued to evolve, the need for a national conference to discuss the role of the predoctoral internship arose. The first predoctoral internship conference was held in Princeton, New Jersey, in 1961. This conference was designed mainly to establish criteria by which the NIMH would decide which programs to fund (Belar, 1992). The first major conference to really consider the actual training that occurs during the internship was convened in Gainesville, Florida, in 1987 (Belar et al., 1989). Among the conclusions of this conference was to reaffirm the importance of the internship as part of the graduate educational process in clinical psychology. The conference continued to support the training model in which the degree is not conferred until after the completion of the internship. This model is in contrast to the physician training model, in which the internship occurs after graduation from medical school. Because the clinical psychology intern does not yet possess a doctorate, issues related to reimbursement and title have spurred a debate in recent years about possible changes in this part of the training model. Some psychologists advocate for conferring the doctorate prior to the internship; other psychologists maintain that the internship is part of the graduate program and that the graduate faculty needs to receive input from the internship trainers prior to certifying the student for graduation and readiness to enter the profession.

Over time, another issue arose related to training for professional practice. This is the issue of supply and demand. Were graduate programs in psychology producing so many psychologists that there were insufficient jobs for them? Were there enough places available for all students to find a predoctoral internship? The internship is a graduation requirement, and yet it is not offered within the confines of the university. Whose responsibility is it to find the internship for the student? Because the internship program may not be under the auspices of the university, the university does not have control over who is selected or how many students may participate in any given program. On the other hand, when the student enrolled in the university he or she had an expectation of being able to graduate as long as academic performance was acceptable. As a starting point to address some of these issues, a national conference on "Supply and Demand: Training and Employment Opportunities in Professional Psychology" met in Orlando, Florida, in 1997. This conference was cosponsored by APA and the Association of Psychology Pre- and Postdoctoral Internship Centers (APPIC). Although many points of view were expressed by delegates at this conference, no final changes in the training model were accepted by the conferees (Pederson et al., 1997). This topic continues to be an area of concern to both trainers and graduate students. When applying to graduate programs, students should ask about the program's success in placing their advanced students into predoctoral internships.

Recognizing the need to revisit many issues related to the relationship between training and readiness to practice professional psychology, 2000 APA President Pat DeLeon appointed APA President-Elect Norine Johnson as the chair of a thirty-member cross-constituency working group. This group was named the Commission on Education and Training Leading to Licensure in Psychology. This commission brought together the practice, training, and education communities to discuss barriers and possible solutions to entry into psychology practice. Among the driving forces behind the convening of this group were concerns expressed by new professionals about the availability of supervised postdoctoral training opportunities required for licensure, the timing of the granting of a license compared to other healthcare professionals, and issues of service reimbursement for nonlicensed professionals.

The commission recommended that licensure be granted after two years of "organized, sequential, supervised training" (Farberman, 2000, p. 44). The proposal further specified that one of those two years must be a predoctoral internship accredited by either the APA or the CPA or meet the definition of an internship developed by these groups. This recommendation was quite different from APA policy at that time, which specified two years of supervised experience, with one of those years being postdoctoral and no mention of an organized or sequential format for this training. The commission felt that a lack of specification of the nature of the training experience and its supervision was a weakness in its policy that needed to be corrected. Because the APA policy did not elaborate on the nature of postdoctoral supervision, candidates for licensure were often subjected to improvised experiences that were low-paying and uncoordinated. These "psychologists in training" were in a position of being inexpensive employees rather than being educated for the profession. A second reason the commission cited for needing a policy change was that the nature of predoctoral training had changed over the years but the training model had not. They noted that graduates at the start of the twenty-first century had many more hours of supervised practical experience than their predecessors had, often three or four times as many practicum hours. The commission did not specify a number of practicum hours that should be required for licensure. They felt that quality of practicum experience varied and therefore specifying number of hours would defeat the purpose of this experience. Although this commission represented many groups related to training, including graduate students, their recommendations were related not only to APA policy but also to licensing laws. At the time of this writing, these recommendations had impacted licensing laws in at least two states. In 2004, Washington became the first state where a person could obtain a license as a psychologist without completing a postdoctoral year of supervised experience. Utah followed in 2007. Even if other states agree to this change, psychologists licensed under this different format may be unable to get a license in other states that have not made this change. In 2005, the Association of State and Provincial Psychology Boards (ASPPB) surveyed their member boards to obtain reactions to this potential change in training requirements. Their delegates to the meetings of the commission were among the few to oppose this change.

In November 2002, another national conference was called by APPIC to consider "Future Directions in Education and Credentialing in Professional Psychology." Once again delegates from a wide range of backgrounds met to consider needed changes in both the education and credentialing of psychologists engaged in professional practice. The delegates were assigned to working groups that developed position papers on both the recommended form of education and the licensure process.

Applying to Graduate School

If you want to apply to graduate school in clinical psychology, there are certain steps to follow as well as a number of resources that will help you (Keith-Spiegel & Wiederman, 2000; Mayne, Norcross, & Sayette, 2000; Walfish & Hess, 2001). Some of these references provide information about many available websites in addition to specific information about the application and acceptance process. These books address such topics as contrasting Psy.D. and Ph.D. programs, dealing with both telephone and personal interviews, sample letters and personal statements, and how to handle various offers of acceptance and alternate positions. With the increased specialization of graduate programs in clinical psychology we now have a separate directory of graduate programs where you can focus your training on clinical work with children (Tarnowski & Simonian, 1999).

Ideally, you began the process of preparing for graduate school when you started your psychology major. Your transcript should include a balance of science and applied courses both within psychology and across subjects. For the more scientifically oriented programs, having conducted your own research as an undergraduate is important. Initially, you can gain research experience by assisting a faculty member in his or her research. Later, you are ready to do your own research. If you start your personal research project sufficiently early in your undergraduate training, you will be able to submit it for presentation at a psychology convention and possibly even submit it for publication. Summer research experiences are also available at many universities on a competitive basis. At these sites, you can learn research skills, possibly have access to a new research population, and generally broaden your background.

For more practice-oriented programs, it is important for you to have practical experience. While you are an undergraduate student, you can get practical experience through community volunteer programs or organized undergraduate internships. If your undergraduate department offers an internship or practicum course, it will allow you to obtain experience in an applied setting. This experience will not only make your application stronger but will also give you the opportunity to judge whether or not you really want to do this type of work. Reading about the work of a clinical psychologist in an abnormal psychology course, seeing TV and movie versions of the profession, or being the person to whom your friends turn for advice when they have problems is not necessarily the same as actually working in a clinical setting.

Your psychology advisor or campus career center may have resources to help you locate both research and applied internships. To supplement what they provide, you may also wish to use the Internet. For example, one of Dr. Matthews' students was interested in having practical experience with children. He was aware of a research and training program with children diagnosed with attention-deficit/hyperactivity disorder at SUNY–Buffalo. He went to their website (www.wings.buffalo.edu/psychology/adhd) and learned that this program offered both clinical and research summer internships. He also found links from this website to similar websites throughout the country. Thus, once you start this search process, you may find you will be able to obtain a wide range of options. It is important for you to start this search early. These programs are competitive and their spaces fill quickly. Some programs are also limited in terms of student classification (e.g., junior) or ethnic background. Some of our students have obtained one internship for the summer after their sophomore year and another one after their junior year. It is always good to have a faculty mentor or two become familiar with your work so they can write more personally about you when you apply for an internship or for graduate school. These summer internships are an additional source of training and do not eliminate the need for you to develop professional relationships with your undergraduate faculty.

When applying to graduate programs in clinical psychology, your undergraduate grades are an important factor, as are scores on entrance tests. Some students ask about the specific GPA they will need to have in order to be a strong applicant. The information you receive from graduate schools will probably include the average GPA for the students who were previously admitted to that program. There are also reference books that include this information. One of the books, called *Graduate Study in Psychology* and published by the American Psychological Association, is updated annually and includes information about admission requirements, cost, and housing for over five hundred programs located in the United States and Canada.

The most common entrance exam is the **Graduate Record Examination (GRE).** Information about the test center closest to you, the cost of the test, and application materials are usually available in psychology department offices and/or the campus career-counseling center or online (www.gre.org). If you do some practice testing in advance, or even take a test preparation course, you will have a better chance of your test score actually reflecting your abilities.

Start looking at material about graduate schools early in your undergraduate training. Some programs have special entrance requirements that are unique to those programs. For example, some programs list undergraduate courses that all successful applicants must have taken. Other programs may have specialized tests other than the GRE. You may want to study for these tests. There may also be limited sites and times when these tests are available.

Each application is likely to require the inclusion of a personal essay. You will not be able to write just one essay and include it as part of each of your applications. The questions asked will vary among schools. You will also need to focus on those aspects of your background and interests that are the best fit to that specific program when writing each essay. It is important to set aside sufficient time to write these essays. Do not plan to do them in a single weekend. After you have written a draft of one or two of your essays, ask your faculty advisor or someone in your campus writing center to critique them for you. Use the feedback you receive to improve your essays.

The deadline for having all of your materials arrive at the graduate program will vary with the program. In our experience, the earliest deadlines are in December of the year prior to starting graduate school and the later deadlines tend to be in February. You also need to allow your faculty references sufficient time to write their support letters. If you did a summer internship away from your university, you may want to request a letter from your supervisor there. Hopefully, you discussed this possibility before you completed the internship and determined whether or not this person was willing to do so. It will take time, however, for you to contact this supervisor and make the needed arrangements. When you approach faculty members to ask if they are willing to write recommendations for you, be specific about what you are asking. Start by asking if that person has the time to write letters for you and if that faculty member feels he or she can write a positive letter. Let the faculty member know approximately how many letters will be required as well as the due dates. When you take the forms to the faculty member, provide a cover sheet with a list of the programs, a short description of each program, and the due dates. Students who want a truly personal letter from their faculty members may also want to include information about the particular faculty member(s) at the school with whom they would most like to work and what research areas led to this interest. Also provide the faculty member with a transcript and a list of classes you have taken from that person, when you took the course, and the grade you received. Have a general sheet with your overall GPA, psychology GPA, GRE scores, and short summary of your career goals. If you have done undergraduate research or had applied experience, include brief information about that as well. It is important to complete all of the information required from you, the applicant, before leaving the material for your faculty reference. Most recommendation forms have a section that the applicant completes. This usually includes the applicant's identifying information as well as an indication of whether the applicant wishes to retain the right to see the letter or waives that right. Each application will be worded a bit differently, so be prepared to spend some time reading them. Not all faculty members will be willing to go to files to complete such information as your social security number, your phone number, and so on, so it is a courtesy to fill out as much of each form as possible. Because faculty members often have many students asking for multiple letters, they usually prefer to see a form as fully completed as possible. Remember too that these letters may be written over the winter holiday break when faculty members cannot reach you easily for needed information. Without that information, they may be unable to complete your letters and thus your file may be incomplete at the graduate school's deadline.

A frequent question our students ask us is how many schools should be on their application list. This question is not as simple as it sounds. One point to consider is the cost of applying. Most schools have an application fee. You will need to send transcripts of your undergraduate work as well as of your standardized test scores. Many clinical programs make an initial screening using these standardized scores and then invite the top people for an interview before making their final selection. It is typical for schools to invite many more applicants to be interviewed than they will be accepting. Each of the applicants invited to these interviews has the appropriate intellectual background for admission. Part of the reason for the interview is to see how well these applicants match the needs of the program. Matching the program needs involves more than just your academic interests and abilities. It includes such noncognitive attributes as motivation, teamwork, emotional maturity, and interpersonal skills. These characteristics may be evaluated not only in formal interview settings but also in social settings such as receptions or campus tours. It is important to remember that you are always being evaluated during your visit.

You will have the opportunity to meet with specific faculty members who are looking for graduate assistants and/or research fellows. Current graduate students may also be involved in formal interviews. In some cases, they may already be part of a faculty member's research team and will assist in the selection of additions to that team. It is this level of compatibility that may lead to being selected for a specific program. The interview will also give you the chance to see if you would really be comfortable in that particular program as well as in the community. During these interviews, you are also expected to ask questions. The graduate students you meet are a resource for you. Find out whether they are happy with the program, the program's general strengths and weaknesses, and what they plan to do after graduation. Ask faculty members about graduation rates and where former students are now employed. Thus, it is important for you to go to any interview you are offered. You will need to pay for your transportation and housing for these interviews. Occasionally, graduate programs will make arrangements for you to stay with a current student. If this option is offered, it is a good idea to take it. You will not only save money on the cost of a hotel room but will also have a chance to get to know one of the students well. Of course, you cannot count on these savings. All of these costs are part of your planning for the application process. Programs also differ in terms of the number of new students accepted each year. Some schools accept only five to ten new students while others may take thirty or forty. Information about the number of applicants and number of students accepted is often included in the material sent to you by the school. You will need to keep all of these factors in mind when you plan your application process.

We suggest to our students that they apply to at least fifteen to twenty schools if they can possibly afford to do so. How do you select the schools for your list? First, decide if there are any factors that would absolutely rule out a school for you. Some students have such strong feelings about certain geographical locations or community sizes that these factors would impact their ability to complete graduate school. Be honest with yourself about these factors before you spend time applying to programs you would not be willing to attend and complete if accepted. Remember you will be spending four to five years of your life in this community and many personal factors will enter into your decision. One of our former students, for example, commented that although she wanted to go away from home for graduate school, she realized that because of her father's poor health she was not willing to leave her home community. Such personal factors may impact not only the number of programs to which you apply, but also whether there are programs available in your interest area. The student who felt her father's health was her first priority had no clinical psychology programs in her home community. Although her career direction at that time was clinical psychology, she made the decision to explore related careers. Today she is a board-certified social worker who truly enjoys her profession. Another student, who did not have this degree of insight, accepted admission to a doctoral program in a rural community in a part of the country where he was not really comfortable. He dropped out of school within the first month of his graduate training because he was so uncomfortable with the community.

Look realistically at your academic record and test scores. Do not devote time applying to programs where you will not be competitive. Select a few "dream" schools that would be your first choice, and for which you qualify, but are highly competitive. Make the majority of applications to schools where you are a solid match in terms of your credentials and interests. Finally, select a few programs where your credentials exceed their average admission statistics and which you would attend if accepted. To make these decisions, you will need not only the general books about graduate programs but may also wish to do a literature search to get a better understanding of the faculty interests. Visit individual faculty member's websites. They may provide you with a quick summary of interests and activities. You can then apply to programs where your interests are a good match to those of at least one of the faculty members.

Should you apply to graduate school immediately after completing your bachelor's degree or should you take time away from studies? The answer to this question will vary among students. Part of the response relates to what you do in the intervening time. If you do work related to your area of graduate study, your graduate school application may be stronger after a year or two than when you complete your undergraduate degree. On the other hand, if you have had research and/or practical experience while completing your bachelor's degree and are reasonably comfortable that you know your career direction, applying to graduate school immediately after completion of your bachelor's degree may be advantageous. Your faculty references may be able to write a more personal letter than they will write after several years of not seeing you. If you are the type of student who finds you need time to adapt to the role of studying after school breaks, taking such an extended break may not be a good idea.

Another question we often hear is whether or not there are rankings of graduate programs. This question often comes from students who used ratings of colleges for their selection of their undergraduate program. Just as undergraduate programs are rated based on a number of factors, such as being a financial bargain or having a high percentage of national merit scholars, graduate programs are also rated on different factors. A general ranking of the *best* twenty-five clinical psychology training programs is published annually by *U.S. News & World Report* (http://www.usnews.com/edu/beyond/gradrank/gbpsysp1.htm). Little explanation is provided, however, about the criteria used for program selection. Thus, other resources may provide information that may prove more useful to individual students. For example, if your career goal is to teach in a doctoral program in clinical psychology once you have completed your own doctoral degree, you might want to consider the data provided by Ilardi and his colleagues (Ilardi, Rodriguez-Hanley, Roberts, & Seigel, 2000). They list those programs whose graduates most often obtain those academic positions.

As you can see, we recommend considerable study and research before you even start to complete graduate school application forms. Careful application for graduate study is a time-consuming process. This search should start no later than your junior year. We also suggest that if you know students who will graduate before you do, and who are applying to clinical programs, talk to them about their experiences. If your classmates are invited for interviews, talk to them as soon as possible after they return to learn about the interview process. There are also websites (e.g., www.interview.com) that provide useful information. Using multiple sources of information about interviewing allows you to prepare yourself better for your own interviews. Several of you may want to practice "mock" interviews with each other before having real ones. Ask your friends to tell you what they wish they had done differently during the application process; learn from their mistakes.

Work Settings

A new clinical psychologist might work in many different places. Some clinical psychologists choose to work in more than one setting. Both of the authors of your book work full-time in universities teaching undergraduate students. We also each see individuals through our part-time private practices. This combination of activities is not uncommon for academic clinical psychologists. Other clinical psychologists work in a range of hospital settings, including general medical hospitals, psychiatric hospitals, Veterans Affairs Medical Centers, and children's hospitals. Clinical psychologists who work in medical schools are housed in such diverse departments as psychiatry, pediatrics, and family practice.

Clinical psychologists also work full-time in private practice, some in individual offices and some in group practices. For example, Dr. Anton sees patients in a multidisciplinary practice with psychologists, psychiatrists, and social workers. Clinical psychologists in private practice may consult to a range of hospitals and nursing homes as well as with other professionals such as dentists and attorneys. Emerging trends for medical consultation include cardiology and surgery. Clinical psychologists may also serve as experts to the media on a range of topics and as expert witnesses in court.

Early textbooks about clinical psychology tended to include the typical workday of a clinical psychologist. Today there is probably no such thing as a "typical" day for a clinical psychologist. Not all of the work done by clinical psychologists today is on a face-to-face basis. As electronic telecommunications advances continue, further changes can be expected in clinical practice. We discuss some of these changes in chapters 9 and 16. Testing and assessment may be done on computer, and some therapeutic interventions occur over the Internet; issues of how to regulate these forms of practice are being discussed by licensing boards.

Sample Work Settings

Because most undergraduate students have been exposed more to the work psychologists do in psychiatric settings than to their work in other settings, we decided to present information about some nonpsychiatric settings to provide a more complete view of clinical psychology for your career options. We are only presenting a few examples for your consideration. There are many others.

Daw (2002) noted that psychologists are becoming key members of transplant teams. Her article describes the work of two psychologists who are actively involved with transplant surgery. One of them even accompanies the patients into surgery and holds the title of chief psychologist for a department of surgery. Although most of the psychologists who currently work with transplant teams do not actually observe during surgery, they use their psychological skills to assist both the transplant patient and family members in dealing with behavioral factors related to their health and coping with the stress of this type of surgery. The work of the psychologist in this setting is not limited to the time immediately surrounding surgery. Patients often must wait long periods of time before actually receiving the needed organ. Such waiting is stressful. Psychologists may provide assistance with this waiting process through individual and/or group therapy. Psychologists may also assist in screening donors for transplant. It is important for donors to be doing this without coercion. Consider the case of a person who is asked to donate an organ to a family member. Perhaps this person is the only viable donor and yet there are health risks in organ donation. Depending on the relationship between the donor and the recipient, this decision may be a very difficult one to make. There may be strong family pressure on this person to be a donor. The psychologist is in a position to talk to all family members in this situation. Psychologists may also be asked to assist in determining which patient should be placed where on the waiting list for a transplant. This decision is usually made by a team of healthcare professionals. These psychologists are literally participating in life-or-death decisions. Psychologists who work in this type of setting need to understand the effects of the various types of transplants on the person if they are to be effective in their role. Thus, they must do specialized reading so that they can prepare the patient for potential side effects of both the operation and medications.

Another surgical area in which psychologists are active members of the treatment team is obesity surgery. We frequently hear about the problems of obesity in the United States. A range of treatments for obesity has been developed. When obesity is severe, surgery may be recommended. We will use the work of one psychologist to illustrate the profession's role in this specialty area. Ayad (2004) is a clinical psychologist who has worked in bariatric surgery for many years. He conducts psychological evaluations on potential surgery candidates prior to the operation. Because so many of these surgery candidates have a history of having been mistreated by many people in their lives as a result of being morbidly obese, he recommends that they have some psychotherapy prior to actually undergoing surgery. He also conducts group therapy with postsurgery patients to help them deal with any postoperative personality changes as well as the needed period of special requirements related to food and liquid intake and activity level. Research on both the appropriate tools for psychological assessment and the most effective forms of psychological treatment is ongoing.

In chapters 14 and 15 we will discuss careers related to clinical psychology. If you are thinking of a career in clinical psychology some of these other careers may be of interest to you. We'll interview psychologists who are currently practicing in those interesting and unique areas. We hope that this additional information will also broaden your current view of clinical psychology.

As changes in laws occur, psychologists also find themselves in positions to use their skills in new ways. One example of this process occurred in Oregon when this state became the first to enact an aid-in-dying law. This law, called the Death With Dignity Act, allowed patients with medical conditions where a physician determined that they have six months or fewer to live to have a prescription for a lethal dose of medication. Two physicians must confirm the medical diagnosis before this lethal dose can be prescribed. In order to qualify for this assistance, however, the patient must be determined to be competent to make this decision by either a psychologist or psychiatrist licensed in Oregon. One of the few reasons for breaking patient confidentiality has long been when the psychologist views the patient as being dangerous to self. For many years, psychologists were legally and ethically required to support commitment procedures for suicidal patients. The Oregon law, however, placed these same psychologists in the position of being asked to confirm that the person should be allowed to have control over the dying process. The legislation does not use the word "suicide" even though many of this law's critics described it as such. It is not our purpose to raise moral issues here or to debate the question of whether "Death With Dignity" is equivalent to suicide.

Following passage of this legislation, a survey of Oregon psychologists reported that 53 percent of those responding indicated they would either refuse to do this type of evaluation or make a referral to a colleague to do it (Fenn & Ganzini, 1999). What about the 47 percent who said they would be willing to do this evaluation? What would be involved? As with any evaluation conducted by a clinical psychologist, it is important to obtain the patient's consent to consult with other treating professionals and review the patient's history. Significant others would need to be interviewed to obtain their description of the patient's past and current methods of dealing with major life events. Clinical interviewing and possibly psychological testing would also be used. According to the law, a final report must be sent to the Oregon Health Division (Farrenkopf & Bryan, 1999). This is an area of clinical practice that may be unique to Oregon, but it illustrates how ethics and personal values may interact with clinical psychologists' activities and how changes in a state's laws may impact a psychologist's practice. The survey data also illustrate the fact that not every clinical psychologist must do every activity allowed by law.

Some clinical psychologists have developed specialties that are now considered to be based in clinical psychology but are actually viewed as a specialized career. For example, some doctoral programs offer specialty tracks in areas such as clinical child psychology or clinical neuropsychology. Other related specialties are based on postdoctoral training. We have included two chapters, chapters 14 and 15, on careers to give you more information about some of these specialty careers. Rather than just describe these careers, we interviewed psychologists doing this type of work. Just as we described ourselves at the beginning of this chapter to make us more "real" to you, we are using these interviews to make some of these careers a bit more real.

Throughout this book, we will provide practical examples of the topics discussed. We will give you the histories of several patients and then add to that database as we discuss assessment and intervention strategies. These examples, however, will not address the full range of activities of clinical psychologists. Our sample patients are not real people. We have selected specific characteristics of patients we felt would illustrate points often seen in clinical practice. These characteristics are combined in one person. We have attempted to illustrate a range of ages and issues through only three patients. Thus, there are some limitations on what problems we can cover. They do, however, provide a start to your understanding of practice issues. We chose to have all three of our sample patients be seen outside a hospital setting. Today, psychiatric hospitals typically have rather short inpatient stays. Much of the traditional psychotherapy done by mental health professionals is done on an outpatient basis. Although physical questions are raised in some of these cases, our patient focus in this book is on more psychologically based problems.

A question that arises is what to call the recipient of the clinical psychologist's services. You may have read articles that use the term *client* and others that use the term *patient*. There are both theoretical and personal preferences for each of those terms. Often clinical psychologists who work in medical centers use "patient" because that is the accepted term in that setting. In outpatient settings, some practitioners prefer "client" in order to refrain from viewing the problem as medical in nature. Others, however, suggest that using "client" sounds more like a business rather than a helping relationship. One suggestion is to combine the terms and refer to the *client/patient*. We find that phrasing awkward. Throughout this book, we will use the term *patient* because this word implies a helping/healing relationship to us.

Key Terms

art therapy

Boulder model

clinical psychology

counseling
psychology

doctor of philosophy
(Ph.D.)

doctor of psychology
(Psy.D.)

expressive therapy

Graduate Record
Examination
(GRE)

music therapy

practica

social work

CHAPTER 2

Professional Activities and Introduction to Managed Care

Thus far, we have discussed the training and applied activities of clinical psychologists and have given you some information about related careers. In this chapter we discuss two topics of importance to clinical psychologists. One of these topics is participation in professional associations. The other topic is an introduction to the topic of managed care and how this healthcare phenomenon impacts the practice of clinical psychology.

Professional Associations

We decided to include this information in the book for several reasons. First, we are trying to give you an idea of what life would be like if you choose to enter this profession. Second, most of the associations we will describe have a student membership category. If you have an idea about how these groups fit into the total picture of the profession you may have a clearer idea about whether or not you want to spend some of your limited funds on membership. Student dues are typically much less than those of professional members. By starting your participation in professional associations early in your career path, you will have the opportunity to learn more about your chosen field through interaction with a larger number of psychologists than are found on your faculty.

You may also have the opportunity to become active in some of these associations, perhaps even take a leadership role. Such roles are available for students in many of these groups. The choice of associations described in this chapter has been influenced by our own memberships. We realize there are many other groups we will not mention that are also very popular among our colleagues.

Many clinical psychologists are active participants in a range of organizations related to their profession. The associations we describe in this chapter are not necessarily part of the life of *all* clinical psychologists. Associations are usually formally organized groups that include members who are interested in some or all of the activities of the group. Very large associations, such as the APA, are complex organizations with thousands of members and hundreds of employees. We will describe the APA in the next section to illustrate these large associations. Other associations, such as the Wyoming Psychological Association, have fewer than one hundred psychologist members and perhaps a part-time executive director. One reason for this small number of members is that although Wyoming is geographically a large state, it is not a populous state and thus has far fewer psychologists than are found in some of the geographically smaller states, such as Massachusetts. Some professional associations are highly specialized and thus of interest to only certain clinical psychologists. An example of a specialty association is the National Academy of Neuropsychologists. No matter the size of the association, each of these associations charges dues to sustain its operation and fulfill its mission. As you can guess, joining multiple associations can become quite expensive. Most psychologists make choices when they decide to join or not to join various associations; the same is true for students. By now you probably realize that clinical psychology is a very broad profession. Thus it is not surprising that the associations of interest to clinical psychologists also cover a wide range.

Why do clinical psychologists join these organizations? One reason is that these organizations provide an increased opportunity to meet others who have similar interests. This factor is often called "networking." A **network** is an informal link among psychologists with similar interests. The authors of your book met as a result of their activity within the APA. A colleague who knew both of us introduced us at a meeting we were both attending. He said he thought we had a lot in common. As we talked over breakfast at that meeting, we found that we agreed with him. We had similar interests and decided we could work well together. That initial meeting was followed by other professional meetings where we continued to talk. We then served together on a committee. Following that we agreed to collaborate on this book.

The development of email has allowed members of professional networks to communicate rapidly with each other on both a group and an individual basis. Most of the professional groups have listservs for their members. These listservs allow a psychologist with a question or an opinion to get responses from many colleagues in a short period of time. They also facilitate sending important professional information to a large group of interested people in a timely fashion. For example, if a clinical psychologist is looking for a referral source for a patient who is moving to another part of the country, posting this request on a listserv can provide multiple names quickly. Obviously you do not use the patient's name on the listserv because of the need for confidentiality. A request might be, "I need a referral for an adult female moving to Chicago. She works well in psychodynamic psychotherapy and is dealing with issues of death of a spouse." Where might this request be posted? Many listservs are for specific interest groups. This referral request might be published on the listserv for members of one of the practice divisions of APA, such as Division 12 (Society of Clinical Psychology), Division 29 (Psychotherapy), or

Division 42 (Independent Practice). Because of the interest in a particular approach to therapy, specifically psychodynamic psychotherapy, it might also be posted to Division 39 (Psychoanalysis) or to specialty organizations known to have practitioners who use this approach. Enough information was provided in the question that people who work with that age group from that particular theoretical frame of reference will be the ones who reply.

Another reason psychologists join these associations is because their professors and clinical supervisors are members of them and thus encourage their students to become involved early in their careers. Participation in these organizations becomes part of the student's view of the profession and continues once the student completes his or her studies and moves into the profession.

Many professional associations hold regularly scheduled meetings and/or conventions. These meetings provide a setting for expanding your network as well as learning early about contemporary issues that may appear in the professional journals at some future time. Because of the time it takes to write about professional issues, have the material peer reviewed, revise and edit it, and then wait for its actual publication, a considerable period of time may pass before it is widely accessible to the profession in published form. At conventions, this material may be presented in a symposium or poster session. The psychologist, as well as the student of psychology, then has the opportunity to discuss evolving ideas with their developer. Collaborative research projects may also develop from these meetings. As psychologists with similar interests meet to discuss their work they may also develop new projects they can do together. This type of collaboration also has the potential to increase sample size and generalizability of results. From a student perspective, these meetings may provide an idea for research projects such as your undergraduate thesis or an independent research project. They also provide a venue for students to present their work. Not only is such presentation good experience but it also gives students the same chance as professionals to discuss their work with others and perhaps get some ideas for the next study or the appropriate publication site for the data. Students who share rooms at these conventions find they can keep their expenses under control. The student registration fee, just like student dues, is typically much less than the fee charged to professionals.

Professional associations also provide a forum for group advocacy and action on issues impacting the discipline. We will discuss this activity more completely in the section of chapter 13 dealing with advocacy. Professional associations are also in a position to mobilize local psychologists when their services are needed. This factor is especially important for problems that arise unexpectedly, such as assisting with the psychological aftermath of natural disasters like floods or hurricanes. They may also organize local efforts to assist in community mental health days or develop programs to inform the general public about the roles psychology can play in their lives.

American Psychological Association (APA)

For many psychologists, the premier professional association is the APA. APA was founded in 1892 and incorporated in 1925 in the District of Columbia. The central office of the APA is located there, just a stone's throw from Union Station and the Capitol. Information about many of its activities, including those for students, can be found on its website (www.apa.org). According to 2003 membership data, the APA included 90,000 fellows, members, and associate members. A fellow is someone who has at least five years of work experience after receiving the doctoral degree and has made an unusual and outstanding contribution to the field of psychology. About 3 percent of APA members are fellows of a division. To qualify for member status in APA, the person generally must have a doctoral degree in psychology. Associate members have a master's degree in psychology or have completed at least two years of graduate study in psychology. After five years in this category of membership, they are allowed to vote in association elections. Others are in affiliate categories of membership. There were 4,000 international affiliates and 2,400 high school and community college teacher affiliates. A very large group of affiliates are the student affiliates. There were 53,600 student affiliates in 2003. These students are at both the undergraduate and graduate level. When we combine these affiliates with the members, we find an association with over 150,000 people.

The student affiliates of APA comprise the American Psychological Association of Graduate Students (APAGS). APAGS was organized in 1988 and approved by APA's Council of Representatives. Among its goals is to "promote the highest standards in the research, teaching and practice of psychology to further the education and development of all psychology students" (Williams, 2001a, p. 54). APAGS has its own full-time APA staff, governing body and committees, and a voting seat on the APA Council of Representatives. It also has a nonvoting seat on the APA Board of Directors. In 2003, APAGS began publication of a magazine, *gradPsych,* containing articles of interest to students and early career psychologists. Information about this magazine can be found on a special website (www.gradpsych.apags.org). Although the name implies this group is only for graduate students, undergraduate students may also affiliate with APAGS when they become student affiliates of APA by paying the annual APAGS dues. Undergraduate students comprise about 15 percent of the APAGS membership (Williams, 2001b). These dues support the APAGS office at APA as well as all of the APAGS programs. APAGS has its own website (www.apa.org/apags) with links to many resources of interest to students.

Because the APA is such a large organization, it has developed a rather complex working structure. Many of our students know we go to meetings at "APA." They do not, however, have a sense of how various parts of that structure fit into the general organization. We will describe briefly some of the parts of APA as a way to make that organization more real, much as we described our background in the first chapter of the book to make us more "real" to you.

Governance Because APA has a very diverse membership with intersecting and overlapping interests, it has developed a complex governance structure to represent the membership for the development of association policies and position statements. The Council of Representatives is APA's legislative body. Council members are elected by the membership of the fifty-three divisions and fifty-nine state associations, Canadian provinces, and associated territories that include Guam, the U.S. Virgin Islands, and Puerto Rico. This body meets twice a year. During these meetings, the members deliberate on and then vote to set APA policy and address budget issues. Council meetings are open to all members who are interested in attending. Since one of the two meetings of the council is in conjunction with the annual APA convention, students who attend the convention have the opportunity to observe how APA policy is created as well as to meet leaders in the field.

Structure The current structure of APA is not the same as it was in 1892 when the membership was quite small. There were twenty-six charter members when the initial organizational meeting was held at Clark University on July 8, 1892. By the time of the first annual meeting held at the University of Pennsylvania on December 27, 1892, five additional members had been added, bringing the total to thirty-one members. In its early years, the APA's growth was slow. It did not reach one thousand members until 1929. After that time, however, it grew rapidly so that changes in structure were needed to accommodate the needs of this more diverse group of psychologists. In 1945, APA made certain organizational structural changes, including the addition of special interest groups called "divisions." According to the APA bylaws, divisions represent major scientific and professional interests of the members. A member of APA can join as many divisions as he or she wishes or can elect to just have general membership in the association and not join any division. Each division has its own fees to support its activities. As of this writing, there are fifty-three divisions numbered 1–56. Two of the divisions (4 and 11) no longer exist, and their numbers were not reused. Number 4 was originally given to an external group, the Psychometric Society. This group was planning to become an APA division but later decided not to affiliate with APA. The Psychometric Society decided to remain an independent group. Number 11 was reserved for Abnormal Psychology and Psychotherapy. This division lasted only until 1946, when it decided to join Division 12 (Society of Clinical Psychology) rather than remain an independent division. Table 2.1 shows the current divisions and provides an overall picture of the diversity of interests represented by the divisions of APA. Students who want to learn more about the activities of any of these divisions can go to the APA website (www.apa.org) and then click on "divisions." This page provides more information about divisions as well as links to many of their individual websites. Many of the divisions publish newsletters on their websites. Reading these newsletters can give you a better understanding of the activities and interests of that division.

As technology has become more available and barriers to communication have dropped, psychologists from around the world have increased their interactions with each other. Thus, it is not surprising that professional associations might also interact more closely. Given the geographical proximity of Canada to the United States, it is not surprising that psychologists in one country have interests in the work of psychologists in the other country. Over the years, the APA has held some of its annual conventions in Canada. There is also a joint dues relationship between the APA and the CPA that allows members of one association to join the other one for only 50 percent of that association's regular dues. The most recent APA convention in Canada was the 2003 meeting in Toronto. Five previous APA conventions were held in Toronto with the first one occurring in 1931. APA has also held two of its conventions in Montreal.

APA has an extensive publications program. Members can subscribe to any of the thirty-seven professional journals at a reduced rate compared to the general public, institutions, or libraries. They can also buy books published by APA at a discount. Most students are familiar with the *Publication Manual* published by APA. Some of our colleagues refer to this book as APA's "most famous publication." This manual is often required as an undergraduate text for experimental methods courses. When undergraduate students prepare to apply for graduate school they may use another one of APA's popular publications, *Graduate Study in Psychology,* as a resource. APA also publishes many

Table 2.1 Divisions of the American Psychological Association

1. Society for General Psychology
2. Society for the Teaching of Psychology
3. Experimental Psychology
5. Evaluation, Measurement, and Statistics
6. Behavioral Neuroscience and Comparative Psychology
7. Developmental Psychology
8. Society for Personality and Social Psychology
9. Society for the Psychological Study of Social Issues (SPSSI)
10. Society for the Psychology of Aesthetics, Creativity, and the Arts
12. Society of Clinical Psychology
13. Society of Consulting Psychology
14. Society for Industrial and Organizational Psychology
15. Educational Psychology
16. School Psychology
17. Society of Counseling Psychology
18. Psychologists in Public Service
19. Society for Military Psychology
20. Adult Development and Aging
21. Applied Experimental and Engineering Psychology
22. Rehabilitation Psychology
23. Society for Consumer Psychology
24. Society for Theoretical and Philosophical Psychology
25. Division of Behavioral Analysis
26. Society for the History of Psychology
27. Society for Community Research and Action: Division of Community Psychology
28. Psychopharmacology and Substance Abuse
29. Psychotherapy
30. Society for Psychological Hypnosis
31. State, Provincial and Territorial Psychological Association Affairs
32. Humanistic Psychology
33. Mental Retardation and Developmental Disabilities
34. Population and Environmental Psychology
35. Society for the Psychology of Women
36. Psychology of Religion
37. Society for Child and Family Policy and Practice
38. Health Psychology
39. Psychoanalysis

(continued)

40. Clinical Neuropsychology
41. American Psychology-Law Society
42. Psychologists in Independent Practice
43. Family Psychology
44. Society for the Psychological Study of Lesbian, Gay, and Bisexual Issues
45. Society for the Psychological Study of Ethnic Minority Issues
46. Media Psychology
47. Exercise and Sport Psychology
48. Society for the Study of Peace, Conflict, and Violence: Peace Psychology
49. Group Psychology and Group Psychotherapy
50. Addictions
51. Society for the Psychological Study of Men and Masculinity
52. International Psychology
53. Society of Clinical Child and Adolescent Psychology
54. Society of Pediatric Psychology
55. American Society for the Advancement of Pharmacotherapy
56. Trauma Psychology

books and journals as well as videotapes. Many of these publications may be helpful to students. For example, students who are preparing a research project might benefit from APA's book about how to display your data (Nicol & Pexman, 2003). Magination Press, owned by APA, publishes books designed for children. Table 2.2 is an alphabetical list of the APA-published journals.

Because the APA is such a large association, it has a somewhat complex administrative structure. The APA Central Office handles the association's regular business under the direction of a chief executive officer (CEO) and a staff of more than five hundred employees in a building it owns in Washington, DC. This Central Office is subdivided into four major units, called directorates. Each directorate handles specific areas of the discipline: practice, science, education, and public interest. Of course, many activities overlap these artificial divisions and utilize staff members from each directorate to advance psychology.

The Practice Directorate is concerned with the practice of psychology and the availability of psychological services to the public. Many of the applied activities of clinical psychologists are related to the work of the Practice Directorate. There is also an incorporated companion organization, the APA Practice Organization (APAPO), that can engage in lobbying and other advocacy activities that are prohibited by federal law to APA because APA is a nonprofit entity. The APA Practice Organization began operation on January 1, 2001. Information about its activities can be found on its website (www.APApractice.org). Among the activities of these two practice-related groups are legislative **advocacy,** legal and regulatory strategies, marketplace activities, and public education. Within the legislative arena, they have worked on such topics as Medicare training funds for graduate students and mental health parity laws at both the state and

Table 2.2 APA Journals

American Psychologist
American Journal of Orthopsychiatry
Behavioral Neuroscience
Clinician's Research Digest
Consulting Psychology Journal: Practice and Research
Contemporary Psychology: APA Review of Books
Cultural Diversity and Ethnic Minority Psychology
Developmental Psychology
Emotion
European Psychologist
Experimental & Clinical Psychopharmacology
Group Dynamics: Theory, Research, and Practice
Health Psychology
International Journal of Stress Management
Journal of Abnormal Psychology
Journal of Applied Psychology
Journal of Comparative Psychology
Journal of Consulting & Clinical Psychology
Journal of Counseling Psychology
Journal of Educational Psychology
Journal of Experimental Psychology: Animal Behavior Processes
Journal of Experimental Psychology: Applied
Journal of Experimental Psychology: General
Journal of Experimental Psychology: Human Perception and Performance
Journal of Experimental Psychology: Learning, Memory, & Cognition
Journal of Family Psychology
Journal of Occupational Health Psychology
Journal of Personality and Social Psychology
Journal of Psychotherapy Integration
Neuropsychology
Prevention & Treatment
Professional Psychology: Research and Practice
Psychoanalytic Psychology
Psychological Abstracts
Psychological Assessment
Psychological Bulletin
Psychological Methods
Psychological Review
Psychological Services
Psychology and Aging
Psychology of Addictive Behaviors
Psychology of Men and Masculinity
Psychology, Public Policy, and Law
Psychotherapy: Theory/Research/Practice/Training
Rehabilitation Psychology
Review of General Psychology

federal level so that mental health coverage would be equal to physical health coverage. At the legal and regulatory level they have worked on such areas as the prescriptive authority for psychologists and disseminating professional guidelines in such areas as record-keeping and working with specialty populations. Marketplace activities include an Internet-based data collection system to gather information about practitioners' practice activities and educating the business community about the value of psychological services. Public education includes fostering media coverage of activities of psychologists. Thus, they are also part of the advocacy effort we will discuss in the next section of this chapter. We chose to talk about them here because of their special relationship with APA.

The Science Directorate was formed to coordinate member activities related to the needs of the scientific and academic members of APA. The Science Directorate has several committees that oversee policies on animal research and ethics and psychological tests and assessment. Of special interest to graduate students in clinical psychology is this directorate's awards program for the support of dissertation research. These awards can help students defray dissertation costs such as equipment or remuneration of subjects. The Science Directorate also maintains several programs of special interest to undergraduate students. During the summer, it sponsors the APA Summer Science Institute. This is a nine-day program designed to immerse undergraduate students in the science of psychology. Any undergraduate student may apply for this program. Although it is highly competitive, we strongly urge students to apply. Each year between four hundred and five hundred undergraduates apply for the thirty-two available positions. Does this level of competition mean that only students from the large research universities will be accepted? The answer is definitely "no." Several students from Dr. Matthews' department, for example, have been selected for this program. Her department offers only the undergraduate degree. At the time of this writing, the registration fee for this program was $200; some scholarships are available. Students also cover their own travel expenses, but APA pays for room and board as well as lab and lecture fees. Information about the application process as well as the dates and location of the next institute can be found on the Science Directorate website (www.apa.org/science/ssi.html). Another link on the Science Directorate website that may be of interest to undergraduate students is the list of internships and research opportunities. This list provides links to a range of sites to help undergraduates with the often difficult task of finding these summer experiences.

The Education Directorate is concerned with educational institutions and programs at all levels—high school, community college, undergraduate, graduate, internship and postdoctoral. It deals with both traditional and nontraditional educational settings and also evaluates continuing education programs often needed by licensed psychologists to maintain their licenses and continue lifelong learning. To assist educators at different levels the Education Directorate has developed a range of products. These products include a model high school psychology curriculum, standards for teaching psychology at the undergraduate level, and newsletters for educators that are published on a regular basis. The Education Directorate is also involved in accreditation activities. Remember that selection of an APA-accredited doctoral program in clinical psychology and an APA-accredited internship makes the process of obtaining a license to practice much smoother. The criteria APA uses to evaluate doctoral programs therefore impacts the courses offered in them. The directorate also works to impact public policy related to education.

The focus of the Public Interest Directorate is the application of psychological principles to human welfare. Among the many special interest groups in this directorate are
the Women's Program and the Office of Ethnic Minority Affairs. The staff and committees within the Public Interest Directorate address a range of topics, including children's
issues; urban and rural concerns; aging; disability; and lesbian, gay, and bisexual concerns.
Its Office on AIDS disseminates publications, sponsors training programs, and coordinates
dialogues among psychologists from a range of backgrounds with policymakers. This
office is active in obtaining grant money to fund a range of projects and conferences on the
topics listed here.

To give you a feel for the breadth of activities undertaken by APA, you should note
that periodic commissions, task forces, and work groups are constituted to address
contemporary issues. Examples of task forces that are of particular interest to the
Public Interest Directorate are the Task Force on Workplace Violence and the Ad Hoc
Committee on End-of-Life Issues. APA created a Working Group on Children's Mental
Health in 2001 in response to the U.S. Surgeon General's call for an action agenda on the
crisis in children's mental health. An example of a task force that reports to the Science
Directorate is the Working Group on Genetics Research Issues. The Practice Directorate
has an Advisory Committee on Colleague Assistance (for those psychologists who may
become disabled, impaired, stressed, or distressed) and a Task Force on Serious Mental
Illness/Severe Emotional Disturbance.

The Central Office also includes an Office of Legal Affairs with two full-time
attorneys, a Membership Affairs office, and a Financial Services division to handle
the association's finances. It is because of this range of activities that APA needs the
large staff we mentioned earlier. The full-time staff of APA has educational training
ranging from high school–educated people to doctoral-level licensed psychologists
and attorneys.

Boards and Committees A number of standing boards and committees also participate
in association work. The participants in these groups are members of the association who
are elected or appointed by the Council of Representatives. Task forces, work groups,
advisory committees, and ad hoc groups as well as other time-limited groups are often
created to address specific issues with members who have needed expertise appointed to
carry out those duties. To give you an idea of the range of these specialty groups, we have
provided Table 2.3, which lists some of them. You can obtain more information about
them from the APA website (www.apa.org).

In addition to these standing boards and committees, continuing committees were
developed to address specific topics of importance to the membership. Some examples
of these groups are the Committee on Disability Issues in Psychology; the Committee
on Ethnic Minority Affairs; the Committee on Gay, Lesbian, and Bisexual Concerns; the
Committee on International Relations in Psychology; the Committee on Psychological
Tests and Assessment; and the Committee on Rural Health. As you can see, the APA
addresses the needs of psychologists and the public from many different interest areas.

We have provided considerably more information about APA than you need to know
at this point in your career. We decided to include it as a reference for you rather than just
refer you to the APA website because it provides a good example of the range of activities of clinical psychologists.

Table 2.3 Standing Boards and Committees

Board for the Advancement of Psychology in the Public Interest
Board of Convention Affairs
Board of Educational Affairs
Board of Professional Affairs
Board of Scientific Affairs
Policy and Planning Board
Publications and Communications Board
Elections Committee
Ethics Committee
Finance Committee
Membership Committee

Specialty Associations of Psychologists

APA is a general member organization. Its interests and goals are broad. Other psychological associations are designed for specific subsets of the profession. For example, some professional associations developed to focus on the ethnic heritage of the psychologist and the needs of specific ethnic communities. Four such organizations are the Asian American Psychological Association (AAPA), the Association of Black Psychologists (ABPsi), the National Latina/o Psychological Association (NLPA), and the Society of Indian Psychologists (SIP). These groups also meet with the APA as the Council of National Psychological Associations for the Advancement of Ethnic Minority Interests to serve a networking function and share common concerns. We will provide some general information about each of these associations as well as their websites for students who want to learn more about them.

AAPA was founded in December 1972. Today it is the major national organization for psychologists dedicated to serving the Asian-American community (www.aapaonline.org). You do not need to be of Asian heritage to join AAPA. Its website provides information about its activities for students as well as for professionals. AAPA holds an annual convention at the time of the APA annual convention. Thus, you do not have additional travel expenses to attend two separate meetings if you want to participate in AAPA. AAPA is a nonprofit organization featuring a newsletter, monographs, student travel awards, and a division on women among its activities.

ABPsi was founded in San Francisco in 1968 by a group of black psychologists from around the country. In 2005, its website (www.abpsi.org) reported that its membership was over fourteen hundred. When ABPsi was founded, its stated purpose was to address the needs of black professionals and to have a positive impact on the mental health of the black community on a national basis. Among the categories of membership are *professional,* which requires either a master's or doctoral degree in psychology, and *adjunct,* which requires a bachelor's degree in psychology and/or one of the other behavioral sciences. Students who are currently enrolled in psychology programs qualify for either undergraduate or graduate student membership categories. This association works on significant social problems that impact the black community as well as other segments of the population whose needs are not being met. For example, with the assistance of a grant from the Centers for Disease Control and Prevention, ABPsi published a technical assistance newsletter about issues related to work with HIV/STD.

NLPA was originally named the National Hispanic Psychological Association. Its name was officially changed in 2002. This organization was established in 1979 by a small group of Latino psychologists at a conference at Lake Arrowhead. Unlike AAPA and ABPsi, the National Hispanic Psychological Association did not become a large national organization. At the time of the name change in 2002, the organization also began a major membership drive. In 2003, NLPA reported having 150 members. For information about NLPA, visit its website (www.nlpa.ws). NLPA offers three levels of membership: institution/organization, professional, and student. Starting in 2003, its newsletter published bilingual columns to model the value of bilingualism as well as increase accessibility to monolingual Spanish readers and encourage participation by mental health professionals in Spanish-speaking countries.

SIP states on its website (www.geocities.com/indianpsych) that its aims and purposes

> include but are not limited to the operation of a national body organized for nonprofit, charitable, and professional purposes; to provide an organization for American Indian and Native people who are vitally concerned with improving the mental well-being of their people; to create through an exchange of skill, expertise and experiences, opportunities for career development, positive inter- and intra-personal relationships, and general personal enhancement of American Indian and Native peoples; to encourage all American Indian and Native people to become involved in improving the quality of their lives.

SIP is the only freestanding professional association for psychologists and psychologists-in-training who are of American Indian or Alaska Native heritage. You do not have to be of this heritage, however, to affiliate with SIP. In addition to psychologists, SIP also welcomes people from other disciplines who are of Native American or Alaska Native heritage. The SIP website includes information for students, listserv material, information about how to join SIP, and links to related websites of interest. Several of these linked websites describe special university programs designed to facilitate the integration of Native American culture. SIP advocates for psychological research of service to its communities as well as the application of psychological knowledge and techniques to its issues. It also promotes needed policies at tribal, state, and federal levels. SIP works to ensure that the Indian/Native perspectives are honored at both the undergraduate and graduate training levels in psychology.

Other professional associations are formed on the basis of the specialty interests of their members. Some of the specialty organizations are interdisciplinary, while others are basically for psychologists. Many of these associations are of interest to clinical psychologists. There are too many of these associations for us to cover all of them here. Just as we will do with other topics in this book, such as theories of personality and psychological tests, we will present information about a select few of them. There are certainly many others we could have selected. We selected organizations with which we have some familiarity while trying to cover a range of interests to illustrate the field. We will present brief information about American Association for the Advancement of Behavior Therapy (AABT), American Association for Marriage and Family Therapy (AAMFT), American Group Psychotherapy

Association (AGPA), National Academy of Neuropsychology (NAN), Society of Behavioral Medicine (SBM), Society for Personality Assessment (SPA), and Society for Research in Child Development (SRCD) to illustrate these specialty associations. We also provide web-sites for those students who want further information about a specific organization.

AABT was founded in 1966 as an interdisciplinary association of mental health pro-fessionals who are interested in "behavior therapy, cognitive behavior therapy, behavioral assessment, and applied behavior analysis" (www.aabt.org). In addition to the national association there are also state and city chapter affiliate groups. Special interest groups within AABT reflect the members' interests. Among these groups are addictive behavior, disaster and trauma, and mental retardation. AABT holds an annual convention at which both research and clinical findings are presented. It also has a publication program.

AAMFT was founded in 1942. It has members, affiliates, and students in both the United States and Canada. Current information about membership requirements and conference dates can be found on its website (www.aamft.org). AAMFT was developed to provide a network for both the clinical and research interests of marriage and fam-ily therapists. Among the association's accomplishments are the development of training guidelines for marriage and family therapists and an ethics code for this specialty area of practice. AAMFT publishes both a journal and a newsletter to provide information about the marriage and family therapy. AAMFT has developed brochures for both professionals and the lay public to provide information about marriage and family therapy.

AGPA was founded in New York City, also in 1942. Its website (www.agpa.org) pro-vides both an address and toll-free phone number for those who want further information about the association. AGPA is an interdisciplinary association for mental health profes-sionals and students who are interested in the practice of group psychotherapy. In addition to the primary association, there are also affiliate societies located throughout the United States. AGPA's publications include a journal and a newsletter. Its annual convention includes continuing education programs for those in attendance. In chapter 12 we will discuss the issue of adequacy of training in group psychotherapy. One way psychologists can continue their education about this skill is through this professional organization. As a public service AGPA also publishes a consumer's guide for people who may have an interest in participating in group psychotherapy.

NAN was founded in 1975 and held its first convention with fewer than three hundred attendees in 1981. In chapter 14, we will provide a more extensive description of this specialty, which grew out of clinical psychology. By 2005, its membership had swelled to thirty-three hundred members located in twenty-four countries (http://nanonline.org). NAN members may be both clinicians and researchers or students in the field of neuro-psychology. Its annual convention provides a forum for the presentation of research. NAN also offers continuing education workshops for clinical neuropsychologists, students, and others interested in learning more about this specialty. Abstracts of the presentations from this convention are printed in NAN's journal, *Archives of Clinical Neuropsychology*. News relevant to the profession is presented in its newsletter. To address practice topics and advocacy issues, NAN established a Professional Affairs and Information Office. We will discuss this office a bit more in the section of this chapter on advocacy issues.

SBM was founded in 1978 as a multidisciplinary, nonprofit organization for health profes-sionals. In 2005, its membership included over three thousand individuals (www.sbm.org). A major focus of SBM is the integration of behavioral and biomedical research methods and data that relate to issues of health and illness. It also has a student membership category. Its annual convention provides a forum for the exchange of scientific and clinical information. SBM publishes a research journal and a newsletter as well as a directory of training opportunities. Students who are interested in this type of specialized training find this directory a good supplement to advice from faculty members.

SPA was initially incorporated as the Rorschach Institute, Inc., in 1938 but was renamed the Society for Personality Assessment in 1971 to reflect the fact that the group was interested in the full range of personality assessment issues rather than limiting its work to one measure. Their website (www.personality.org) provides information about the history of the organization, membership categories, and its annual meeting. SPA's literature notes that it is dedicated to work in three areas of personality assessment: advancing this professional activity, developing concepts and procedures for personality assessment, and the ethical and responsible use of personality assessment techniques. According to its 2003 membership directory, SPA members live throughout the United States and Canada as well as in twenty-eight countries around the world. Its members are also eligible for a reduced membership fee if they join the International Rorschach Society. Just as APA and CPA have the joint dues option because of the overlap of interest of their members, so do these two groups that are interested in personality assessment. SPA has two major publications: the *Journal of Personality Assessment* and a quarterly newsletter, *the SPA Exchange*. We talk more about personality assessment in chapter 7.

SRCD was founded in 1933 and in 2005 had about fifty-five hundred members in fifty countries (www.srcd.org). Its purpose is to provide an "informational network for scholars and professionals studying the development of children." SRCD's extensive publication program includes journals, monographs, and newsletters. To facilitate networking and interchange of ideas, SRCD holds conferences and conventions. It also has a committee structure to address such topics as public policy and the ethical conduct of research with children.

State, Provincial, and Territorial Associations

The specialty professional associations we have described thus far are organized on the basis of topic. Other organizations are based on geography. Many clinical psychologists view their state, provincial (in Canada), or territorial (e.g., Guam) psychological association as a primary source of professional support. Networking is frequently given as a reason for joining these associations. These organizations often provide continuing education programs as part of their annual meetings. Continuing professional education is one facet of remaining current with the profession. It may also be a requirement for renewing your license to practice. Having continuing education offered locally saves the psychologist money in terms of travel costs. These locally offered programs also tend to be developed to meet any unique requirements of that jurisdiction's licensing laws. These associations also monitor activities impacting the practice of psychology that may arise within the jurisdiction's governmental system.

Many of these associations hire professional lobbyists and directors of professional affairs to help them interact with legislators on issues of importance to practice. Because these organizations have major expenses, such as lobbyists, they often have higher dues than groups like the regional associations described next. Many psychologists feel that this is money well spent, since licensure laws, regulations, and advocacy are important professional issues that can greatly impact the practice of psychology. These organizations cannot serve their purposes, however, without a strong membership base. In tight economic times, it can be tempting to overlook the role they play in maintaining the psychologist's income and the psychologist may elect to resign because of the cost of their dues. Leaders of these organizations gather annually for a State Leadership Conference sponsored by the APA. During this conference they can share information across jurisdictional lines as well as visit Capitol Hill to talk with their congresspersons about psychological issues impacted by federal legislation. This legislation can affect the practice of psychology in many ways, including consumer access to mental health services. We will discuss the role of psychologists in advocacy activities later in this chapter.

Regional Psychological Associations

According to Hilgard (1987) the first regional association that specifically included psychology as a focus was the Southern Society of Philosophy and Psychology (SSPP). SSPP was founded in 1906. In these early years, psychology was often taught in the same academic department as philosophy, so it is not surprising that these two disciplines joined to form a regional professional association. As of this writing, SSPP remains an active organization. Psychologists, however, eventually decided they also wanted regional organizations specifically for psychology.

The United States is geographically subdivided into overlapping regions with each region having a psychological association. Historically, no one seems to know why these regions are overlapping, but some states are included in more than one of the associations. For example, the Southeastern Psychological Association (SEPA), founded in 1953, includes Alabama, Arkansas, Florida, Georgia, Kentucky, Louisiana, Mississippi, North Carolina, South Carolina, Tennessee, Virginia, District of Columbia, and Puerto Rico. The Southwestern Psychological Association (SWPA), also founded in 1953, includes Arizona, Arkansas, Kansas, Louisiana, Missouri, New Mexico, Oklahoma, Tennessee, and Texas. In this case, Arkansas, Louisiana, and Tennessee are included in both regions. The oldest of the regional psychological associations is the Eastern Psychological Association (EPA), which was founded in 1896. Psychologists may choose to join the association for the state in which they live as well as any of the other ones. You do not need to live within a region to be a member of the association.

The main focus of these regional associations is an annual convention for the presentation of scientific and professional materials. Because their range of activities is smaller than associations that are national in scope, they often have lower annual dues. For example, the dues for Western Psychological Association in 2003 was $50, while the dues for a state association, like the Washington State Psychological Association (where one of us lives), were $325 that same year. Also, annual conventions of regional psychological associations may be geographically closer than the APA convention and therefore less expensive for psychologists and psychology students in that area to attend. Attending meetings of these associations provides psychologists with an opportunity to network as well as to hear about and discuss a wide range of professional topics. Students are welcome at all of these conventions and may be able to have their registration fee waived in exchange for volunteering time to assist such activities as working at the registration desk at the convention. Many students report that this is a great way to meet professionals and to network. Often these conventions include special sessions sponsored by Psi Chi, the national honor society in psychology, as well as other activities specifically designed for students. For example, a common program at regional association conventions is the presentation of information by graduate schools in psychology. Students can not only obtain informational materials, but also may have the opportunity to talk to representatives of these programs. They may have the chance to meet current students who are making presentations, thus increasing their understanding of the appropriateness of various programs for their needs and determining if they would be a good match for specific programs. Information about each of these associations is available on its website. Table 2.4 provides the names of the regional associations and their websites. Information about the states included in that region, dues, membership categories, and date and location of annual conventions can be found on these websites.

International Psychological Associations

As we mentioned earlier, psychologists today are increasing their contact with colleagues in many countries. Within the APA, the Office of International Affairs coordinates the international activities of the association. This office also provides the staff support for the Committee on International Relations in Psychology as well as publishing a quarterly newsletter, *Psychology International*. Some of the professional associations to which American psychologists belong are international in scope and meet in countries throughout the world. Of course international travel can be expensive. Occasionally one or more of these international associations hold their meeting in the United States, sometimes in conjunction with the annual APA convention. Thus, even psychologists who do not feel they can attend international meetings may still choose to join one or more of these international groups. They may be able to attend the meetings when they are in this country and they also receive publications that give them a broader picture of international practice.

Many of these countries also have their own psychological associations. To give you an idea about psychology in some of these countries, you might want to access the websites

Table 2.4 Regional Psychological Association and Their Websites

Eastern Psychological Association (EPA)
 http://www.easternpsychological.org

Midwestern Psychological Association (MPA)
 http://condor.depaul.edu

New England Psychological Association (NEPA)
 http://www1.rider.edu

Rocky Mountain Psychological Association (RMPA)
 http://www.rockymountainpsych.org

Southeastern Psychological Association (SEPA)
 http://cas.ucf.edu

Southwestern Psychological Association (SWPA)
 http://www.swpsych.org

Western Psychological Association (WPA)
 http://www.westernpsych.org

of a few of them. It is important to remember when you access these sites that you may need to know the language of the country to read the information. For example, when we accessed the site from the Ukraine, we found that although some of the information was available in English most of it was not. We have provided a sample of these international websites in Table 2.5.

Table 2.5 Worldwide National Psychological Associations and Their Websites

Australia
http://www.aps.psychsociety.coom.au

Bangladesh
http://www.du.bangla.net/psycho

Belgium
http://www.ulb.ac.be/bps

Canada
http://www.cpa.ca

Chile
http://www.colegiopsicologos.cl

Croatia
http://www.psihologi.ja.hr

Czech Republic
http://www.ecn.cz/cmps

Denmark
http://www.dp.dk

Egypt
http://www.eapsegypt.hypermart.net

Finland
http://www.psykologienkustannus.fi/sps

France
http://perso.wanadoo.fr/sfpsy/

Germany
http://www.bdp-verband.org

Hong Kong
http://www.hkps.org.hk

Hungary
http://www/mpt.hu

Indonesia
http://www.himpsi.org

Ireland
http://www/psihq.ie

Israel
http://www/psychology.org.il

Italy
http://www.sips.it

(continued)

Table 2.5 Worldwide National Psychological Associations and Their Websites *(Continued)*

Japan
  http://www.nii.ac.jp/jpa/
Lithuania
  http://www.psd.fsf.vu.lt/lps/index.html
Mexico
  http://www.psicologia.org.mx
New Zealand
  http://www.psychology.org.nz
Norway
  http://www.psykol.no
Peoples Republic of China
  http://www.cpsbeijing.org
Poland
  http://www/ptp.psychologia.pl
Puerto Rico
  http://www/asppr.org
Republic of Panama
  http://app-panama.org/
Romania
  http://www.apsiro.home.ro
Singapore
  http://www.angelfire.com/sc2/sps
Slovenia
  http://www2.arnes.si/-dpsih/
South Africa
  http://www.psyssa.com
Spain
  http://www.cop.es
Sweden
  http://www.psykologforbundet.se
Switzerland
  http://www.unifr.ch/psycho/sgp-ssp/
The Netherlands
  http://www.psynip.nl
Turkey
  http://www.psykolog.org.tr
Ukraine
  http://www.ucap.kiev.ua
United Kingdom
  http://www.bps.org.uk
Uruguay
  http://www.psic-usuguay.org

Just to give you some general information we learned from a few of the websites that are in English, we will provide a tidbit to get you started in your search. From the Australian Psychological Society we learned that this group is the largest professional association in that country. This society of thirteen thousand members has its own code of ethics. Among the types of information on its website are financial information, membership snapshots, and marketing information. The British Psychological Society is even larger, with thirty-six thousand members. According to its home page, it has three major aims. These aims are to "encourage the development of psychology as a scientific discipline and an applied profession, to raise standards of training and practice in the application of psychology, and to raise public awareness of psychology and increase the influence of psychological practice in society." A complete history of this organization can be found on its website. Like many other societies, the Hong Kong Psychological Society also has its own code of professional conduct. You can get information about it on its website. This organization was founded in 1968 to encourage the growth of psychology in Hong Kong. Although there are specialty psychology organizations in that territory, the Hong Kong Psychological Society is the only one that represents all the different psychological specialties. These three organizations illustrate the English-language groups found in Table 2.5. As electronic communication continues to grow, other sites will be developed. The list we provide is based on material gathered by the APA Office of International Affairs in 2003. Many more countries had associations at that time, but we limited our material to those who provided websites.

Managed Care

The practice of clinical psychology in the twenty-first century has been influenced by the growth of managed care and its changes over the years. Throughout this book, we will refer to managed care, insurance reimbursement for psychologists' services, and the impact of this payment process on the possible direction of the profession in the future. In this section, we will provide you with some history of this concept as well as a general overview of how it works.

Clinical psychologists who are in independent practice may operate under a "fee-for-service" policy or accept reimbursement from insurance companies. The former means that patients pay for the services they are receiving. For many people in the United States, there is an expectation that any form of health care they receive, including mental health care, will be paid for by their insurance program. Over time, these programs have expanded to include a range of services either as options or as a regular part of the coverage. For example, dental insurance is a common option on group health insurance policies. Mental health coverage is becoming a fairly common part of a person's health care policy. Today, insurance is available for many kinds of health care, even for the health care of your pets!

The concept of insurance is not new (Starr, 1982). The basic concept of insurance is to manage risk. Many of you are familiar with the concept because you have automobile insurance or renter's insurance. Generally states require drivers to prove they have this type of insurance in order to obtain a driver's license or renew a driver's license. Some apartments require their tenants to provide proof of renter's insurance in order to live in their properties. By paying a periodic premium, the insurance company assumes a financial risk that individual drivers or tenants do not want to assume. Let's use car insurance as an example. Your insurance premium is based on a number of factors. Among those factors are your previous driving record, your age (people of certain ages are considered to be at greater risk to have an accident), where you live (some communities have a history of higher cost of accidents due to such factors as a high number of uninsured drivers), and the value of your car. If you have an accident, either your insurance company or the insurance company of the other driver will probably pay part or all of the cost of repair or replacement of your car as well as any associated medical costs. Different factors are used to determine renter's insurance premiums. They include the crime rate for the community, whether or not you have made previous claims, and the type of structure in which you live.

These same insurance concepts have been applied to health care, including mental health care. Various models have been used for this type of insurance coverage over the years. One model that has received considerable attention within the psychological community is known as the **health maintenance organization** (HMO). During the 1960s and 1970s, healthcare costs rose rapidly. In response to this economic issue, then President Richard Nixon signed the Health Maintenance Organization (HMO) Act in 1973. This act established funds to be awarded as grants to groups who would create a new form of healthcare delivery service. In this model, both the administrators and the healthcare providers are employees of the same organization. The focus of this approach to health care was on prevention of health problems. Providers were paid a salary and benefits by the organization, and their overhead costs, such as office space and malpractice insurance, were included in their employee contracts. Notice how this approach contrasts to that of psychologists who are in private practice. Private practice psychologists are essentially small business persons who have to cover all of their overhead costs. Depending on their location, they may even need to purchase a small business license from their local government. The original idea behind the HMO concept was that because these organizations were not paying externally for the services they provided, they would be less expensive than the previous fee-for-service approach (you pay for what you get). The focus on prevention was designed to lead to problems being addressed before they needed extensive and expensive treatment. In theory, both employers and individuals would save money.

The original HMOs were **closed panel,** indicating that the patient had little, if any, choice of service provider. You made an appointment at your healthcare facility and were assigned to a provider. When you joined an HMO as an insured, you might therefore have to leave a provider who had taken care of you for many years because that provider was not a member of your HMO. You also might see a different provider each time you made an appointment for service. This approach was supposed to be more efficient because you would have an appointment with the next available provider rather than needing to wait for one you saw the last time and who may have a full schedule. It was also intended to level the workload between the less popular and more popular providers. For mental health services, you might be assigned to a master's degree–level therapist rather than the higher cost doctoral level provider such as a clinical psychologist or a psychiatrist. All services had to be approved in advance by the HMO before they were provided. As you can see from this model, continuity of care was a problem. Although continuity of care is always a concern, it is especially so in areas of practice that are considered quite private or sensitive. For example, many women didn't like seeing different obstetrics-gynecology (ob-gyn) providers each time they needed care. Similarly, mental health patients had the same concern about continuity of care.

Over time, many of these HMOs evolved into a system of using a primary care provider (PCP) for physical health care so that the insured could at least see the same provider each time. When you joined the HMO, you were given a list of PCPs from whom to select one. This was most often a physician whose specialty was one of the general practice areas such as internal medicine or family practice. This PCP acted as a **gatekeeper** for the HMO. If you wanted to see a specialist for services you first needed to see your PCP. Only by referral from your PCP could you be reimbursed for specialty services. Often mental health services had even further restrictions, such as a referral from the PCP followed by a request for approval from an HMO administrator.

As this system continued to grow, complaints arose that HMOs were excluding newer and often more expensive treatments to contain costs as well as limiting access to needed services. In response to complaints about access to care, particularly by patients who had worked with mental health providers and by women who had regular ob-gyn physicians, the HMOs expanded their model. They contracted with additional providers in specialties where patients had concerns, thus increasing the number of available professionals. This change led to **open panels,** in which the providers were not necessarily employees of the HMO. A common practice of this open panel model was to enroll private practice providers in the community. These practitioners signed contracts with the HMOs to provide care for their patients. They were thus independent, but affiliated with the HMO. The move to open panels had specific significance for psychologists. Imagine being required to see a psychologist at the place where you also work if this person is the provider in your system. You might hesitate to do that because of the stigma that continues to surround mental health services. While it may be acceptable to see a colleague who is an ophthalmologist to have your vision evaluated, seeing a clinical psychologist "to have your psyche evaluated" may be viewed as embarrassing by many people. When even the open panel model was not found to be sufficient to address the mounting complaints, many HMOs began to offer a **point of service (POS)** option. This option allowed patients to continue to see a provider with whom they had a long-term, trusting relationship but at a somewhat higher cost than if they had selected one from the provider list of their HMO. The POS model provided for the insurance carrier to still pay part of the expenses but not as large a part as when you selected a provider from the approved contracted provider list.

During the 1990s HMO enrollments soared because their premiums were lower than those of traditional fee-for-service plans. HMOs also tried to find additional ways to divert financial risk and increase profitability. A form of reimbursement was created that can be explained by a schedule of reinforcement you may have learned about in one of your other psychology courses. The differential reinforcement of low rates of responding (DRL) seems applicable to what occurred at this time. DRL refers to those cases for which low rates of responding are rewarded. How does this apply to health care? HMOs began to "carve out" sectors of health care as separate from the overall policy. Specialists in these areas were offered a fixed amount of money each month to provide services to a specific population. Let's consider an example of how this approach worked. There are thirty students sitting in your class. Dr. Matthews and Dr. Anton agree to cover all of the mental health needs for this class for a fee of $300 each month. This model is known as a *capitated* (per head) model of reimbursement. Drs. Matthews and Anton will get that set amount of money each month no matter how much or how little service they provide. The advantage to the insurance company is that they know their cost in advance. It is now a fixed cost rather than being dependent on the number of people who seek such services. Thus, they know how much to charge their members for their insurance premium in order to generate the profits they desire. Providers who participated in these programs needed to know the *utilization rate* for their services by this population in order to decide whether or not they should participate. Returning to our example, let's say that previous research showed that 10 percent of a college student population will use mental health services in any given month. Further research indicates that college students average four sessions of this service. Based on the utilization rate, we would then predict that three of the students in this class of thirty will request our services that month. Each of these three students will be seen once a week for psychotherapy leading to twelve units of service during the reimbursement period. Divide the $300 by the twelve units of service provided, and you find that the average reimbursement to these clinical psychologists for their service is $25 per session.

Think about how this model can impact treatment. Ideally, it may encourage the provider to provide efficient, high-quality care to alleviate the referral problem as quickly as possible. This outcome is the best. There are, however, some reasons an ideal may not become a reality. After all, the psychologist will receive the same amount of money whether the treatment is a weekly group therapy session for all three students or individual psychotherapy four times a week for each of them. Is this decision about a psychotherapy format based on what is best for the patient or what is best for the provider? The motivation to actually *treat* patients may be reduced by this system of reinforcement. For example, after you interview the student you might recommend regular exercise to deal with stress rather than pursue the sources of stress in individual psychotherapy. In this case, you have reduced your number of sessions with the student and your reimbursement rate per session rises. The DRL model shifts the treatment cost and risks to the provider rather than the HMO. In essence, under the capitated model, the psychologist becomes an insurance company, fully responsible for the care of the covered lives that are included under the contract. Notice once again the use of business language under this model. For example, it uses the term *covered life* rather than *patient* or *client*.

Managed care organizations (MCOs) grew out of the HMO movement. MCOs were developed to manage how the insurance company carves out benefits. As they apply to mental health care, MCOs typically act as gatekeepers to the mental health benefits of an insurance program. In these organizations, the policyholder (covered life) typically needs authorization to see a mental health provider. Suppose you are severely depressed and concerned about your ability to care for yourself. You want to enter an inpatient mental health treatment program. The MCO would need to *precertify* your admission to the hospital as well as the length of time you would be allowed to remain there. How does this process work? You might start with an interview for admission at the approved hospital. The mental health professional who conducts that interview agrees that you are sufficiently depressed that you should spend some time in the hospital. The mental health intake worker then contacts the hospital business office. The business office of the hospital would contact the MCO to obtain their permission to admit you. Based on your diagnosis and the type of policy you have, a specified number of days in the hospital would be approved. This determination that the insurance company agrees to your admission as well as the number of days for which they will pay is what we mean by **precertification.** After you are admitted to the hospital, the inpatient staff reevaluates your status, and determines that additional days of hospitalization, beyond those originally approved by the MCO, are recommended. Once again the MCO would be contacted by the hospital business office to determine if it is willing to add days to your approved stay. If it does not agree with the hospital staff, you will need to pay for the additional days or leave the hospital before the professionals feel you should. You may also be able to transfer from this hospital to a public hospital if one is available and your income qualifies you for admission. Another possible outcome in this case is that the professional staff will appeal the decision and that appeal could be upheld. This process is sometimes called a "doc-to-doc" appeal. The attending physician on the hospital unit appeals to a physician employed by the managed care company to explain why the extra days are necessary. Finally, the hospital may agree to keep you for some additional time at a special rate.

Under this approach, hospitals bid for the HMO business, and the cost of the services they provide is a major determinant of whether or not that hospital gets business from the HMO. In other words, you cannot select the hospital where you want to be treated but have to go to one approved by the insurance company. You can see that patients and their families might object to this restriction of access. The MCOs also develop panels of providers. If a clinical psychologist is not a member of the panel of that HMO, they are not reimbursed for seeing one of its participants. The HMO and its MCO also set the reimbursement rates for these services. If psychologists want to get patients from this organization they have to apply to be a member of the panel and to accept the conditions set by them. Rates for services are quickly reduced under this system, and there seems to be little psychologists can do about it.

Impact on Psychologists

Psychologists are resourceful and creative professionals. They developed ways to deal with some of these problems. In the early 1990s, few psychologists who were in independent practice were part of a group. They were in individual practice and tried to become members of a number of those *panels* we described. Although there were often "office-sharing" arrangements through which they might share rent, overhead, and so on, they were each an independent provider. In response to the marketplace pressures, some psychologists began to work within multidisciplinary group practices. Other psychologists altered their practices to be more "managed care friendly," such as doing problem-focused short-term psychotherapy. Those psychologists who tended to do long-term psychotherapy tended to move to a fee-for-service practice. Some of them were well-established in their community and already had a sufficient referral base to be able to do that. Others had to change their reimbursement rates or expand into additional areas in order to practice their specialty.

Psychologists also have creatively adapted to the changing marketplace by developing practice niches. By this we mean that they find a need in their community for which they can provide services and center their work in that area. By using this strategy, they basically insulate themselves from managed care and the insurance reimbursement issue. For example, one psychologist reported that almost 98 percent of her practice was with patients suffering from **trichotillomania.** Her initial interest was in obsessive-compulsive behavior. As a graduate student she was working on a research project in this area and recruiting subjects. She included a line about hair-pulling in her subject recruitment pamphlet and was surprised with the number of responses she got for this specific problem. Following that experience, she sought further training about the treatment of this specific behavior, which led to her current "niche practice" (Holloway, 2003). Let's consider just one more niche practice to illustrate the range of possibilities. Sharkin and Knox (2004) noted that psychology has paid little attention to the impact of pet loss on their owners. In some communities, when a pet dies in the veterinarian's office, the veterinarian provides that person with grief counseling resources in the community. Psychologists have skills that could be useful not only in grief counseling with their current patients who may have lost a pet but also in other areas as well. They might develop community support groups for people who have experienced pet loss. Psychologists might work with both veterinarians and veterinary students about how to deal with their grieving clients. This skill would be especially helpful in cases of euthanasia. These veterinarians might then make referrals to support groups developed by the psychologist.

Not all psychologists realize the range of areas in which they might apply their skills. To assist them in this process, APA Division 42 (see Table 2.1) produces over forty niche guides to help psychologists develop these distinct practice areas. A key to approaching the development of such specialty practices is to evaluate your skills and how they can be applied to specific problems and/or populations. This does not mean just doing whatever seems to be popular at the moment. Following fads is not only not a good strategy for developing a practice but it may actually be unethical if you do not have the background to do what you propose to do.

Two national surveys examined the impact of managed care on the practice of psychology (Rupert & Baird, 2004). Data from these surveys suggest that managed care companies do not tend to reimburse for assessment services, except for neuropsychological assessment, to a high degree. Psychologists responding to these surveys indicated that psychological assessment was a much smaller part of their practice than psychotherapy. Although there is empirical support for the usefulness of psychological testing in both diagnosis and treatment planning (Kubiszyn at al., 2000), general clinical psychologists in the twenty-first century do not utilize it to the degree it was used in the past.

These surveys also reported many sources of stress resulting from dealing with managed care. Increased paperwork, decreased fees, and obtaining needed treatment authorization were among the causes of stress when working within the managed care structure that were much worse compared to fee-for-service patients. Although there are limitations on the generalizability of the data from these surveys, they do suggest that further research on the impact of managed care on the professional is important.

Other surveys have been more limited in scope but also provide relevant data for understanding the impact of managed care on practice. We will discuss a survey of New Jersey psychologists to illustrate one such survey (Rothbaum, Bernstein, Haller, Phelps, & Kohout, 1998). The New Jersey Psychological Association records indicated that somewhere between one-third and one-half of its members had called the association to complain about managed care companies. Although this survey is limited to practice in one state, this is a populous state. The 812 respondents to the survey represented almost 50 percent of those surveyed. This response rate is better than found in many surveys published in psychological journals. One interesting point in their data is that not all managed care companies were viewed equally. Psychologists need to review carefully the policies and procedures of any managed care company with whom they plan to sign a contract for service provision. Ethics and managed care was only addressed in one item in this survey, but the response to that item suggests that this topic needs to be included in future evaluations of the impact of managed care on the practice of psychology. Over 50 percent of the respondents who had managed care patients indicated that they felt pressure to compromise their ethics as a result of the company's policies. Although the data do not provide information about the specific ethical concerns, the fact that this high a percentage felt they were being pressured to be unethical raises a concern that needs to be explored further.

Concluding Comments

In this chapter, we have covered some topics that are not traditionally addressed in undergraduate clinical psychology textbooks. Why did we do this? Although it is important to know about the various academic areas that comprise clinical psychology, it is also important to have a broad picture of the profession if you are considering joining it. Professional activities play a larger role in the life of some clinical psychologists than others. Understanding the history of managed care can help new clinical psychologists make informed decisions about the type of practice that fits their needs.

Key Terms

advocacy	health maintenance organization (HMO)	managed care organization (MCO)	open panels
closed panel			point of service (POS)
gatekeeper		network	precertification
			trichotillomania

CHAPTER 3

History and Research

Some of you are probably wondering why you have to read a chapter about history and research in a clinical psychology textbook. You may even have taken a course in the history of psychology and another one in research methods and did not expect to find this information repeated here. We believe it is important to consider the roots of clinical psychology as a way to appreciate current issues and challenges faced by the profession. Of course, entire books describe important events in the history of psychology. We will not be providing you with that level of detail. We have selected specific events from that history that seem especially relevant to clinical psychology in the twenty-first century (see Table 3.1).

History of psychology textbooks and courses traditionally emphasize the experimental side of psychology's history rather than the clinical side (e.g., Boring, 1950). Hilgard (1987) did include a chapter on the history of clinical psychology in his history of psychology book, but the inclusion of material about clinical psychology is rare in history of psychology texts. It is our hope that in this chapter we will introduce you to some psychologists who may be new names to you but who have had an important impact on the field of psychology and to new concepts that are particularly relevant to clinical psychology. Experimental methods courses tend to focus on approaches that are used more often in animal research rather than on some of the unique methods that were developed for clinical research. Our focus when discussing research will be on those latter methods.

A common association with the practice of clinical psychology today is "psychotherapy." We will briefly consider this one activity to illustrate how several governmental

Table 3.1 Historical Highlights

1892 APA founded
1895 Breuer and Freud's *Studies in Hysteria* (importance of transference in psychotherapy)
1896 Witmer's clinic at University of Pennsylvania founded
1906 Simon and Binet scales published
1907 *Psychological Clinic* (first U.S. clinical journal)
1908 Vineland Training School (first clinical internship)
1920 Watson and Raynor classically condition fear
1921 Rorschach Inkblot Test published
1935 TAT published
1939 Wechsler Bellevue published
1942 Rogers' *Counseling and Psychotherapy* published
1943 MMPI published
1944 Connecticut passed first law regulating title of "psychologist"
1949 Halstead neuropsychological battery developed
      Boulder Conference established scientist-practitioner model
1950 APA published first internship standards
1952 DSM published by American Psychiatric Association
1953 APA published first edition of Ethical Standards
1958 Wolpe described systematic desensitization
      Ackerman's *Psychodynamics of Family Life* (presenting patient represents sick family)
1962 Ellis's *Rational-Emotive Therapy*
1963 Community Mental Health Center Act (designated mental health as national concern)
1968 First Psy.D. program (University of Illinois)
1973 Vail Conference (practitioner-scientist model)
1974 Exner scoring system for Rorschach published
1989 Psychologists authorized under Medicare
1990 California Supreme Court affirms psychologists' right to hospital practice without medical supervision
1993 First Department of Defense (DoD) graduates (prescribing psychologists)
1994 DSM-IV
1995 Empirically supported treatments list published
1996 Dorothy Cantor becomes first Psy.D. APA president
1999 NIMH first White House Conference on Mental Health
2000 Surgeon General's Conference on Children's Mental Health
2002 New Mexico becomes first state to grant psychologists prescriptive authority
2003 President George W. Bush's New Freedom Commission on Mental Health
2005 Louisiana psychologists granted prescriptive authority
2007 Evidence-based practice movement

agencies contributed to how clinical psychology as a profession changed over time. Clinical psychologists have not always conducted psychotherapy. At this point, some of you may be asking, "What did clinical psychologists do before they did psychotherapy?" It was not until the end of the 1930s that psychologists routinely engaged in the practice of psychotherapy (Louttit, 1939), and at that time they usually did so under a psychiatrist's supervision (Garfield, 1981). Office-based individual psychotherapy, as we know it today, was definitely not part of the professional practice of psychology at that time. What happened to change this situation?

World War II dramatically changed the way clinical psychology developed. As a result of this war, there was an extensive demand for mental health services for military personnel and veterans. Data from 1946 indicate that the neuropsychiatric patients (that's what patients with psychological problems were called then) in veterans' hospitals outnumbered the patients with other types of disorder by a rate of forty-four thousand to thirty thousand (Hilgard, 1987). Not only were these veterans suffering from war-related mental health needs, but they also needed vocational counseling (Humphreys, 1996). Because of this need for psychotherapy, the Veterans Administration (VA) established clinical psychology internships that were usually associated with psychiatric services, supported psychological research, and sponsored training conferences (Cranston, 1986; Herman, 1995; Miller, 1946). During their clinical training in the VA system, psychology interns were educated extensively in psychometrics, including the interpretation of personality, aptitude, and intelligence tests, as well as in diagnostic interviewing. In addition to the training programs, there was also a change in the status of the profession of clinical psychology within the VA system. Psychologists were given equal status with the psychiatrists as indicated by equality of both their rank within the government ranking system and their salary. This was also the first time nonmedical personnel were allowed to practice psychotherapy independently.

In addition, and perhaps more important for the way the profession of clinical psychology developed, the VA established the doctorate as the entry-level degree for clinical psychologists (Gilgen, 1982). This means that you are not considered to be a clinical psychologist until you have completed your doctoral degree. The doctoral degree remains the entry-level credential for clinical psychologists in the twenty-first century. Along with this educational requirement, clinical psychologists in the VA system were paid salaries commensurate with their doctoral level of training. Because of the relatively high pay scale for psychologists within the VA system, the compensation level for psychologists outside of the VA was raised in other settings to make them competitive. This competitive salary level increased the attractiveness of the field of clinical psychology to a wider range of individuals who were interested in healthcare professions and who previously went into other specialty areas (Humphreys, 1996).

Another governmental agency that is important in the history of clinical psychology is the National Institute of Mental Health (NIMH). Psychologists were involved from the beginning of this agency. The NIMH was authorized under the National Mental Health Act of 1946; its mission was both promoting mental health and addressing issues of mental illness. Within the original NIMH there were four major divisions: research grants and fellowships, training, community services, and intramural research. Thus, this agency provided training and research grants for students at the same time the VA was providing training sites. Between these two governmental agencies, clinical psychology was on its way as a profession.

Foundations

Clinical psychology is somewhat like a tree with many roots. Each of these roots has provided nourishment to the clinical tree. One of those roots is our grounding in *research*.

This book will not be repeating material about research methodology that is more likely included in your statistics and research methodology course. We will, however, make reference to research data and research methodology that supports concepts described in the book. Although clinical psychology tends to say it is based on scientific research, it is only in recent years that the gap between practice and research has begun to close. The terms *empirically based treatments* or *evidence-based practice* are currently used to refer to the research–practice connection. Early clinical psychologists used laboratory research, including animal studies, as the basis for developing clinical intervention procedures but not necessarily to evaluate those procedures. Perhaps as pressures for accountability have arisen from third-party payers as well as from the biologically based approaches of psychiatry, we have been forced as a profession to look more closely at the type of research we produce (Goldfried & Wolfe, 1996). Clinical psychologists still do basic research, but they also do research in the actual clinical setting to increase the potential generalizability of results.

Another root of our clinical tree is **assessment.** For clinical psychologists, this term is often used synonymously with psychological testing. If you talk with several clinical psychologists for whom psychological testing is a major part of their service provision, you are likely to hear the position that this activity is what truly makes our profession unique. Whether or not you agree with their position, psychological testing continues to be a fundamental part of the training requirements of doctoral programs in clinical psychology as well as a useful skill in many employment settings. In a survey of members of the Society of Clinical Psychology–APA Division 12 (Norcross, Karg, & Prochaska, 1997), 74 percent of the sample reported being engaged in psychological assessment. Norcross and his colleagues had reported similar numbers almost a decade earlier. A more recent survey, however, found a decrease in the percentage of this group of psychologists involved in psychological testing, with only 64 percent responding that they do so (J. C. Norcross, personal communication, November 21, 2003). Norcross and his colleagues also found, however, that among those psychologists who worked in hospitals, 80 percent of them were involved in diagnosis/assessment and spent about 18 percent of their time in this activity. Thus, the employment setting of a clinical psychologist may have considerable impact on the amount of time spent in assessment activities. Chapters 6, 7, and 8 of this book address various types of psychological testing done by clinical psychologists. Within the group of Division 12 members who continued to do psychological testing in 2003, Norcross and his colleagues found that there were differences when the type of testing was specified. For example, 61 percent reported doing intellectual/cognitive testing, 57 percent reported doing structured personality testing, and 39 percent reported doing projective personality testing. By contrast, 95 percent used a clinical interview as part of the assessment process. As we will discuss later in this book, the role of managed care and the activities for which it provides reimbursement to psychologists may have influenced these numbers.

A third root of our clinical tree is labeled **intervention.** This term is a bit broader than the more traditional term **psychotherapy.** Historically these two terms were considered to be interchangeable, but today there are many types of intervention used by clinical psychologists that are not considered forms of psychotherapy. We are using "intervention" to refer to the range of methods used by clinical psychologists to attempt to alter problematic behavior.

Historians of psychology enjoy tracing the heritage of contemporary psychologists to a handful of original trainers of psychologists like Wilhelm Wundt and Edward Titchener. That same interest is often reflected in history of psychology textbooks that are filled with the names of people from the past. Our students have complained about needing to read about, and remember, so many names. We decided in this book to use a somewhat different approach to the history of clinical psychology. We refer you to books in abnormal psychology (e.g., Barlow & Durand, 2002; Comer, 2001; Holmes, 2001; Seligman, Walker, & Rosenhan, 2001) for information about the history of the study of psychopathology and to books about psychological assessment (Anastasi & Urbina, 1997; Cohen & Swerdlik, 2002; Gregory, 2004) where you can learn about the history of that part of clinical psychology. For this book we selected the work of a few people to illustrate the work in research, assessment, and intervention in the history of clinical psychology. We selected a few of them for extra coverage about their lives in addition to their contributions to the field and practice of clinical psychology in an attempt to make them more "real" as individuals. We hope that by knowing them on a more personal level their work will make more sense to you. Let's consider the first root of our "tree"—research.

Research

Testing Research

An easy way to think about traditional activities of clinical psychologists is to subdivide them into assessment and intervention, as we did with two of the roots of our clinical tree. We will discuss some of the types of research that are used for each of these types of activity as background for studies given in later chapters of the book. Those students who want more detail about any of these methods should refer to one of the available books on research methodology in clinical psychology (e.g., Kazdin, 1998).

Research in the field of psychological testing takes many forms. Some studies compare the accuracy of test predictions with later behavior. Other studies consider how well a particular test supports independent findings in the same area. If test data are to be useful to the psychologist they must predict better than could be done using **base rates.** "Base rates" refers to the extent to which a particular variable, such as a personality trait, occurs in the population from which the patient comes. If you are testing people in a community where 50 percent of the people are clinically depressed, you will be accurate half the time if you just label the person depressed. Why bother to give the person a psychological test if your measure of depression is only accurate 50 percent of the time? You would need to develop a test that has a hit rate (accuracy) greater than 50 percent if it is going to be useful in this community. Thus, when developing or revising a psychological test, it is important to specify the group for whom it is intended. Comparison can then be made between the accuracy of the test in identifying the desired characteristics and its base rate in that population.

Research about psychological testing is also concerned about the impact of **false positives** and **false negatives** that may occur based on the test results. A false positive occurs when the outcome of your testing suggests the patient has a characteristic that he or she really does not have. A false negative occurs when the outcome of testing suggests the person does not have a characteristic that he or she actually has. Determining the relative importance of false positives and false negatives is partially a function of the reason you are doing testing. Which one is more important will vary from one patient to another rather than across tests. The question that needs to be answered is, "Which of these incorrect outcomes will do the least harm?" The answer to this question is the key to making your decision. For example, suppose you are developing a psychological test to measure concentration in people who are being screened for employment as air traffic controllers. A false negative on your test might mean that a person with good concentration does not get the job. In this case, there is a question of equity in employment. Based on the results of your testing, someone who might otherwise have been hired for this position did not get the job. A false positive could mean that a person with inadequate concentration ability is hired to coordinate the flight paths of numerous aircraft. The result of your assessment error could be a plane crash. Your false positive in this case has the potential to lead to a loss of life, while the false negative could lead to a qualified person being denied employment. In this case, therefore, the psychologist would be more willing to have a false negative than a false positive.

Another area of research related to psychological testing is **test bias.** For the lay person that phrase often suggests that the specific test is constructed so that certain groups of people will not do as well on it as people from other groups do. In the psychological assessment literature the term test bias means "a factor inherent within a test that systematically prevents accurate, impartial measurement" (Cohen & Swerdlik, 2002, p. 179). Basically, test bias is a complex statistical problem. This problem is different from **test fairness,** which refers to using tests in a way that gives preference to one group of people over another group of people. Test fairness is often debated as an ethical or legal topic rather than a psychological one.

Early research in clinical settings occurred in psychiatric institutions and facilities for developmentally delayed people, who were historically called mentally retarded. One of the earliest psychiatric institutions to include research as an identified function of the facility was the New York Pathological Institute. This facility, later named the New York Psychiatric Institute, established a research laboratory under the direction of a psychologist named Boris Sidis in 1896. In 1904, McLean Hospital in Waverly, Massachusetts, hired a psychologist named S. I. Franz for its new laboratory. McLean Hospital remains a training site for clinical psychologists in the twenty-first century and is a teaching hospital for Harvard University Medical School. A psychologist named A. R. T. Wylie was hired to conduct research on the treatment of developmentally delayed people at the Minnesota School for Idiots and Imbeciles in Fairbault, Minnesota, in 1896. Another early facility to add a psychological research component for the developmentally delayed was the New Jersey Training School for Feeble-Minded Girls and Boys in Vineland, New Jersey. They hired a psychologist named Henry R. Goddard as their laboratory director in 1899. The focus of the research of each of these psychologists was on the accurate assessment of the patients in the institution. These names are not the ones included in most history of psychology books. We mention them briefly to illustrate that it was not just one person but many who provided this foundation for the profession. All of these psychologists were working prior to the introduction of the individual intelligence tests, such as the Stanford-Binet and

Wechsler series of tests we take for granted today and which we will discuss later in this chapter as well as in chapter 6.

Psychotherapy Research

Early research about psychotherapy tended to focus more on the research methodology than on the potential practical applications of the results. Today, we find clinical research addressing psychotherapy from the perspective of the types of presenting problems that are seen in clinical practice, the process by which such change may occur, and ways to evaluate the outcome of psychotherapy (Goldfried & Wolfe, 1996). Let's briefly consider each of these types of research. Some psychotherapy researchers center their work on understanding psychopathology. From their data, practicing clinical psychologists hopefully will have a better understanding of the types of issues they may need to explore and work on with their patients. A second type of psychotherapy research addresses issues of the actual process of psychotherapy. The early research in this area led to the development of a number of different ways to analyze therapy sessions.

Based on these early studies, later researchers were able to focus on the specific parts of the therapeutic interaction that seemed to be the most important ones in terms of facilitating the therapeutic process. This type of research started in the 1950s and 1960s. At that time, the basic question was whether or not psychotherapy was useful. These early studies did not really consider the different approaches to psychotherapy that were available at the time but rather focused on the general activity called "psychotherapy." In the 1960s and 1970s, most psychotherapy research addressed questions about which approaches to psychotherapy worked best with which forms of psychopathology. Finally, in the 1980s much of the published psychotherapy research was similar to the large-scale medical clinical trials research previously associated with sponsorship by the pharmaceutical industry. These studies were designed to evaluate therapeutic outcome. Perhaps one impetus for this change in research focus was the availability of both industry and federal funding for this type of research. As a result of this shift in focus, there was less process research than was previously found in the psychological literature.

Dr. Martin E. P. Seligman of the University of Pennsylvania believed this shift in research focus away from process research led to certain forms of psychotherapy not being investigated to the extent that had previously been done. One result of this shift was that some types of psychotherapy were considered ineffective just because no recent studies supported their use. He suggested that much of the research in the 1980s was omitting consideration of what is actually "done" in psychotherapy. This real-life "field" research is called **effectiveness research** to distinguish it from **efficacy research.** As an illustration of the type of effectiveness research that might address his concerns, Seligman (1995) cited a large-scale study conducted by *Consumer Reports.* For some psychologists, a study conducted by a popular magazine is not considered real research. Seligman, however, was a consultant to *Consumer Reports* for this study and therefore had access to their data and found them useful. At the time the data were collected, *Consumer Reports* had about 180,000 readers. They conduct an annual readers' survey. One version of the 1994 survey was a hundred-item questionnaire covering a range of topics including mental health. Respondents were asked to complete the mental health portion of the survey if they had sought help for emotional problems from *any source* during the preceding three years. Approximately 32 percent of the survey respondents completed the mental health items. In other words, about one-third of these people acknowledged having had what they considered to be an emotional problem during the specified time period. Of this group, about 43 percent had talked only to friends, relatives, or clergy. Among those who visited a mental health professional, the most frequent professional reported was a psychologist (37 percent of the group). Despite the criticism by some psychologists about methodological flaws of this study, Seligman concluded that the data did provide empirical validation for the general effectiveness of psychotherapy. The respondents indicated greater satisfaction with treatment from a mental health professional such as a psychologist, psychiatrist, or social worker than from a marriage counselor or family physician. These individuals also reported that when their length of treatment or choice of therapist was limited by their insurance company they did not feel they had improved as much as those respondents who did not have these limitations on their choice of provider or the length of time they were allowed to continue in therapy. Because this is a survey, we do not have the ability to ask further questions about this topic to clarify possible reasons for this difference in perceived effectiveness. No specific type of psychotherapy was reported as being more effective than the others. Dr. Seligman did not suggest that a *Consumer Reports* model should be the only way to evaluate psychotherapy. Instead, he suggested that this type of approach should be added to the more traditional efficacy studies conducted by psychologists.

An efficacy study is the type of study most students read about in psychology classes. In this case, the patients are assigned randomly to the treatment group or the control group. In some efficacy studies there is more than one control group. One control group might be a "no treatment" control group. This group is included to address changes resulting from the passage of time. In other words, would the patient get better by just "waiting awhile"? Another control group receives a placebo intended to address such nonspecific psychotherapy factors as attention and patient expectation. Traditionally, efficacy studies have been used to evaluate forms of psychotherapy that are highly specific and well described so that each therapist can be said to be conducting treatment the same way. These treatment protocols are usually videotaped, and any variation from the prescribed approach is corrected. Most of these studies also use a specified number of sessions as well as have patients with operationally defined problems. Outcome evaluators do not know whether a specific patient is a treatment or control patient, although the therapist obviously knows who is receiving treatment. Thus, the evaluators of outcome for these studies are not the therapists. The *Consumer Reports* study is noteworthy not only because it returned to the topic of outcome from the patient's perspective but also because it brought the topic to a forum that was more readily accessible to the public. Remember that at the time of its survey, *Consumer Reports* had about 180,000 readers. We might hypothesize that these readers came from a range of educational backgrounds, vocational choices, and socioeconomic levels. By contrast, only psychologists and students of psychology tend to read psychology journals.

This shift in the type of research conducted about psychotherapy has been accompanied by a change in what is measured. A term associated with this type of research is whether or not the results are *clinically significant* (Kazdin, 1999). Most psychology research methods courses teach you about statistical significance. The term **clinical**

significance, however, adds an element to consider when evaluating the data from studies in the field of clinical psychology. After you have established a statistically significant effect you then need to determine whether or not that effect has any real-life impact on the person. The real-life impact is the clinically significant aspect of the evaluation. If we look at this very simply, clinical significance is a combination of statistical significance and results that would lead the patient to be included in the distribution of a normal population rather than a clinical population (Follette & Callaghan, 2001). Some researchers have taken the position that movement into the distribution of "normal" is not even needed for clinical significance. Kazdin (1999) suggested that even little or no change in the measured variable could have positive real-life implications for the person. In this case, the person might continue to be within the clinical population from a technical perspective but a positive outcome to the intervention has actually occurred. Consider, for example, the patient whose deteriorating memory cannot be treated. You might say that since there is no change in memory ability the treatment is not successful. If, however, the clinical psychologist has taught the person ways to cope with the decreased memory ability, you can make a case for an improved quality of life. It is this change in quality of life, as viewed by the patient, that is considered clinically significant. The concept of clinical significance appeared in the literature when clinical researchers in the 1980s and 1990s began developing measures of quality of life. Quality of life scales weren't new (Holmes & Rahe, 1967), but before the 1980s these scales were not linked to clinical issues. A major problem for these researchers is the fact that there does not seem to be consensus in the literature regarding a definition of "quality of life." Why can't psychologists just accept the comment, "I feel better" from the patient? As scientists, we are aware of the demand characteristics of therapy outcome research. If our patient continues to spend time and money on therapy, that patient may want to please us by indicating that life feels better even if there is no measurable change. This positive report may be the result of the patient wanting to make the psychologist happy because of the emotional attachment that has developed. This attachment is what Freud called **transference** and others have called the establishment of rapport. The patient may also have the feeling that if nothing positive is happening, he or she is really a fool for spending all that time and money on psychotherapy. It is easier to personally justify the expense if you think you are benefiting from the treatment.

When measures of treatment outcome focus on symptom relief, it is much easier to define the outcome. Let's consider a simple example. If the patient is concerned about being overweight, it is easy to select a target weight and then develop an intervention strategy to assist the patient in losing sufficient weight. Being overweight, however, may have a more far-reaching influence on the patient's life than the specified number of pounds. That extra weight may influence the person's social functioning and even job performance depending on the job requirements. As we noted in chapter 1 when discussing surgery for morbid obesity, these individuals also tend to experience considerable discrimination as a result of their weight. Thus, weight loss has the potential to impact a wide range of domains. To fully evaluate the effect of the clinical intervention requires this broader consideration of the data. Quality of life measures are often part of a larger assessment of the intervention; therefore, they need to be relatively brief. Like any measure that is part of an intervention evaluation, quality of life tests must be reliable, valid, and sensitive to the type of change that is being considered. For example, Mason (1998) developed the Quality of Life Inventory to assess how important each of sixteen areas of life is to the patient, as well as how satisfied the patient is with each of these sixteen areas. This inventory is used when evaluating patients for specialized surgery, such as the **bariatric surgery** we noted earlier. This is a growing area of clinical research.

Because of both ethical concerns and the considerable variability among patients, clinical researchers also publish other kinds of research. Case study research, for example, uses material about individual patients as a way to evaluate intervention methods. Some of these articles are really only single case descriptions and are thus not generalizable. By publishing a case study, clinicians give an overview of their experience and a suggestion to others about an intervention that seems to have been helpful. Sufficient detail is provided about both the reason the patient is in therapy and the intervention used so that other psychologists can then either try this form of intervention or adapt the described method for use in their individual practices. As the science of clinical psychology continued to develop, statistical designs were developed to evaluate single cases (or n = 1 designs). In these designs, the patient serves as his or her own control subject (Kazdin, 1998). One approach to the single subject design is known as an **A-B-A-B** design. Let's briefly consider how this research approach works.

The clinician/researcher gathers information about the patient before starting the planned intervention. This first information is "A" or the baseline that will be used for comparison later. In order to determine the stability of the behavior of interest, data may be gathered over a period of time before actually starting the intervention. The amount of time needed at point "A" will be influenced by the behavior of interest. Even in cases where the psychologist has strong concerns about the importance of starting the intervention, these data are needed to create a basis for comparison. It can be tempting to rush this part of the process as a result of concern for the patient, such as cases where the patient is experiencing some form of discrimination or personal distress as a result of the behavior. It is very important for the psychologist to have accurate baseline data, however, before proceeding. The clinician then introduces the planned treatment that is "B" in the design. The behavior that was measured at "A" is then measured again. In order to determine whether or not the intervention is having an impact on the behavior of interest, the clinician might then remove the treatment and see if the behavior reverts to its previous, baseline, level. Thus, the clinician goes from "A" to "B" to "A" and then back to "B" to reinstitute the treatment procedure. This design is found most often in the behavioral literature. A major reason for this is because of the need to operationally define the problem. That requirement fits with the behavioral orientation to treatment. An ethical concern with this type of research is that if you have helped the person change through your intervention and then remove that intervention you may harm the patient. The concept of *nonmalfeasance* (do no harm) applies here. Hippocrates included the concept of nonmalfeasance in his oath that physicians continue to take when they are first admitted to the practice of medicine. Nonmalfeasance is also a tenet of the APA Ethics Code (APA, 2002). Thus, this design is only used in cases where there is no major risk to the patient if you withdraw the treatment; it is also important to know whether or not what you are doing is actually what is controlling the behavior. A brief example of this design may make it clearer.

This example is adapted from one of our own cases. The patient was an adolescent male who was disruptive while attending a day program for children with developmental delays. The staff members of the program were unable to control him and were considering asking his family to remove him from the facility. After reading his case file and observing him, baseline measures were made of his disruptive behavior. An individual intervention program was designed for him. Because he had limited verbal ability, he was unable to select among possible reinforcers. Praise was tried but did not appear to have reinforcing value at that time. Since this secondary reinforcer was not successful, the use of a primary reinforcer seemed to be the next logical step in this case. He was given primary reinforcers in the form of food for certain appropriate behaviors. His disruptive behaviors decreased significantly. In order to determine whether it was the food or perhaps just the individual attention that was now controlling his behavior, the food was no longer provided. This is an example of the "B" condition in the design. At that point, there was an increase in the inappropriate behavior. This change suggests that the food was having an impact on the behavior. The food was then reinstated and later faded out for other environmental controls that were available. There are many examples of this A-B-A-B design in the psychological literature. This short description is merely intended to clarify the approach.

The A-B-A-B design is one of the more basic approaches to studying intervention outcome. Many real clinical cases, however, involve not just one problem behavior but rather many problem behaviors. In those cases, the clinical psychologist might consider using a multiple baseline design. When using a multiple baseline research protocol, the psychologist identifies more than one behavior of interest, but studies them in sequence rather than at the same time. Baselines are initially taken on each of the behaviors. Intervention is then attempted for one of those behaviors. The psychologist then measures each of the behaviors again. If you find that all of the behaviors you initially measured have changed rather than just the one you are currently treating it may be something other than your intervention that is leading to the measured change. Let's consider a simple example here. Suppose you have a patient who seeks your help for anxiety that often leads to feelings of nausea when attempting to sing and excessive perspiration when speaking in groups. This problem occurs at work when she presents material at staff meetings and at church where she sings in the choir. Your initial work with her centers on her singing in the choir. You use her anxiety at work as a control measure. The initial intervention program is related to anxiety while performing in the choir. After a specified amount of treatment has occurred, you measure her levels of anxiety in both the church and office settings. If your treatment has been highly targeted, you can expect to find that she is no longer experiencing feelings of nausea when she sings in church but continues to perspire excessively at work. The next step in this intervention program would be to apply your intervention to the work setting. You can also use a multiple baseline approach for multiple behaviors that occur in the same setting. In this case, you work on one behavior at a time while measuring each of the behaviors.

As you continue to study psychology, the term **meta-analysis** is sure to pop up. Meta-analysis is a statistical technique that has been used to combine data from many studies about clinical significance. Clinical researchers who want to do this type of research do not start with their own patients the way they did in the previous examples. Rather than starting with original data, these researchers go to the professional literature to find as many studies as possible that have addressed their issue of interest. By combining the data from many studies, the sample size is increased allowing for a range of statistical measures that might not have been possible with the smaller sample. Meta-analysis allows the researcher to determine the overall effectiveness of the intervention across many studies. This approach has been used to evaluate specific methods of intervention as well as assessment procedures. Such data are important for the profession but they may not be the final answer for an individual patient being seen by the clinical psychologist. To address the needs of the individual patient from a research perspective, clinical researchers have suggested that data need to be reported not only for group outcome but also for individual participants. This may be a different approach to research than you learned in your research methods course. Think about it, however, from a practical perspective. As a patient, do you really care about the outcome data from an entire group of people or are you really more interested in your own recovery? These are issues for the twenty-first century clinical researcher to continue to evaluate.

Some modern clinical researchers focus their work on what are called **empirically supported treatments** (**ESTs**) (Chambless & Hollon, 1998). Other studies use the term *empirically validated treatment (EVT)* or *evidence-based treatment (EBT)*. Early writing on this subject subdivided treatments into those that were considered well established and those that were probably efficacious (Chambless et al., 1998). The difference between these levels of research support included sample size of the studies involved when single-subject designs were used, the number of different researchers who produced the results, and whether or not the procedure was compared to another treatment condition or a control group. You are likely to find both of these terms in the clinical literature you read.

We will use EST or EBT rather than EVT in this book because we agree with Chambless and Hollon (1998) that EVT tends to imply that further research may not be needed. Using EST or EBT implies an ongoing evaluation for many researchers. This body of clinical research emphasizes those intervention methods that can be evaluated using controlled research conducted with a specified patient group. This approach is sometimes called efficacy research, as we mentioned earlier in this chapter relative to Seligman's view of the *Consumer Reports* study. To be considered an EST or EBT, some researchers believe that randomized clinical trials must be used. This approach to evaluating treatments is similar to the medical model of pharmaceutical research in which some patients are given a drug and others are given a placebo. As part of the control condition for these pharmaceutical studies, neither the experimenter nor the subject knows which subject gets what condition. This is called a **double-blind experiment.** In psychotherapy research, this means that patients who meet the diagnostic/behavioral criteria for inclusion in the study are randomly assigned either to the treatment being evaluated or to one of the comparison interventions. Other clinical researchers suggest that statistical controls are sufficient and that random assignment is not needed. Early studies from this perspective have centered on those interventions for which **treatment manuals** have been developed. A treatment manual is an integrated explanation of the phases of psychotherapy that can assist the clinical researcher as well as provide guidance to the clinical psychologist in practice. The manual must provide sufficient information to allow a trained clinical psychologist to apply the treatment in the same way that it was applied by the person who wrote the manual. These treatment manuals are not intended as a substitute for training. They are not used the way a person trying to learn to cook might use a cookbook. In the case of the beginning cook, the only assumption that is made is that the person is interested in learning to cook and can follow the printed directions. Treatment manuals, on the other hand, are designed for professionals who already have an understanding of the theory and practice of clinical psychology in the area for which the treatment is developed. The developers of these manuals assume that the clinician has already been supervised in providing such treatment by more senior members of the profession. We will refer to some of these studies later in the book.

Another term that is important in modern clinical research is **cost-effectiveness.** Just as we have seen the dramatic growth of generic drugs within the pharmaceutical industry to hold down costs, clinical psychologists have also felt the pressure of being cost-effective in their interventions. In most cases, patients would prefer the most cost-effective intervention as long as there is little or no difference in treatment outcome. A conflict may arise when the most effective treatment is also the most expensive one. How do you decide when it is acceptable to use the shorter or less expensive treatment rather than the longer or more costly one? Suppose your insurance company will pay for only twelve sessions with your psychologist. According to the psychological literature, there is a treatment that can lead to improvement in twelve sessions. There are other studies, however, that suggest if you see your psychologist for a year the potential for long-term recovery is greater. Do you invest your own money for those extra sessions, fight with your insurance carrier to try to get approval for the additional sessions, or try the shorter treatment protocol? If the shorter treatment protocol doesn't work, do you then try the longer one—when you may have used up your insurance benefit? Or, do you return at some future time when you have insurance coverage or if you once again experience problems? These are real-life questions that impact both the patient and the psychologist.

Issues of cost-effectiveness have led us to consider problems associated with the typical short-term intervention research found in the psychological literature. Some treatments may lead to continued improvement after the initial intervention while other treatments may have more limited effects. Thus, if we are to assess cost-effectiveness we need to do this over a period of time rather than just during the intervention process. Clinical literature and procedures do not specify a time period for collecting follow-up data. Ideally, the researcher would have multiple follow-up contacts. In this way, any changes during the post treatment period could be evaluated. To do this type of research requires a considerable time commitment from the researcher. Follow-up data collection may be difficult when you no longer have regular contact with the patient. In those cases where a former patient is not satisfied with the treatment outcome there is also a greater likelihood that the patient will not be inclined to provide the needed data. Thus, it is very important when evaluating these studies to consider what percentage of patients participated in the follow-up evaluation. If only satisfied patients participate, the data tell us very little that we need to know.

Psychological Assessment

Cognitive Measures

Clinical psychologists often subdivide the types of tests they administer into either cognitive or personality measures. We will continue that tradition and start with the cognitive measures. Standardized measurement of cognitive function in modern times owes much to the work of Frenchmen Theodore Simon (pronounced *sea moan*) and Alfred Binet (pronounced *bin A*). These men developed what many consider the first modern scale of cognitive abilities. The original purpose of their work was to assist the French public schools in determining which children would benefit from the regular school programs and which children might need some special educational programs. They published their first "intelligence" scale in 1905.

Their interest was not in the specific information the children had learned in school but rather their capacity to learn. This distinction is often referred to as the difference between **aptitude tests** and **achievement tests.** Aptitude tests try to predict what a person is capable of doing in the future, whereas achievement tests tend to measure what a person has learned to date.

Their original scale included both verbal items and sensory/perceptual items. The items were arranged from the least difficult to the most difficult. Binet and Simon's work on this scale provided us with many concepts about test development that we continue to use today. For example, they realized that if their scale was to be useful, then everyone who administered it should obtain the same results. They taught others to administer their scale and checked to see that similar scores were obtained no matter who administered the test. Today, when clinical psychology students learn to administer psychometric tests, they are taught the importance of standardized administration. At times, it may be tempting for psychologists to reword certain test items by using language they feel the patient might understand better than the standardized instructions. The standardized wording may also be different from the psychologist's typical speech patterns, leading again to the temptation to alter language from the printed instructions. One point we learned from these early test developers is that our results cannot be interpreted based on the normative sample if we do not administer our tests in a standardized manner. When clinical psychology students learn test administration today, they administer these tests many times, are observed doing so by an experienced psychometrician, and receive feedback about their performance so they learn how to effectively assess patients. It is easier to learn correct administration procedures when you start your training than it is to do it incorrectly and then need to extinguish one behavior (incorrect administration procedures) followed by learning a replacement behavior (correct administration procedures). Being a good clinical psychologist does not mean memorizing the directions for each test you plan to use in your practice. It does mean being sufficiently familiar with the test directions and test equipment so you use them effectively and consistently. This skill develops with practice. A clinical psychologist who has not used tests for an extended period of time in his or her practice may need to review the materials or even attend a training session or receive supervision before resuming this activity independently. Part of the process of learning test administration as well as keeping current doing it is derived from Binet's early concept of the importance of standardized test administration.

The Binet scales are sometimes described as being different from previous scales in four basic ways (Gregory, 2004). Because they were designed to assess general mental development, the result is classification rather than measurement. The Binet test was brief and practical and needed little equipment. It was developed as a measure of practical judgment because that was what they hypothesized was the essential feature of intelligence. The items in the scale were arranged in a level of increasing difficulty order rather than by content.

A premise of the Binet scales is that a child of a certain age should be able to answer correctly a certain number of items appropriate for that age. Binet conceptualized this as the child's "mental age," and then compared it to the child's chronological age. For example, if a seven-year-old child is asked the meaning of a list of words, Binet determined that the average seven-year old should get x number of words correct. If the child answered fewer than x words correctly, then that child had a deficit and Binet would recommend that he or she get extra help. If the child answered more items correctly than a typical child would answer, then the child would be considered advanced. Thus the concept of intelligence quotient, or IQ, was born. If a child's mental age (MA), based on test performance, was seven years old, and the child's chronological age (CA) was seven years old, then the formula MA/CA would yield a score of 1. By multiplying this result by 100, Binet derived a score that could be used to compare many children. You can see that a seven-year-old child who defined words at a nine-year-old level would then have an IQ of $9/7 \times 100$, or about 128. The IQ score allowed a quick comparison of children and helped identify who would receive extra services and who would not—exactly what the French government wanted to know.

Who Was Alfred Binet?

Because a person's background influences what that person becomes, we decided to provide personal information about some of the people we discuss in this chapter. Alfred Binet was born in Nice, France, in 1857 and died in Paris, France, in 1911. He was an only child. His father was a wealthy physician. His mother has been described as an artistic person (Francher, 1998). Alfred Binet's childhood has been described as financially privileged but not a happy one for him. As an adult, he reflected that he had been a shy child and attributed some of his shyness to a domineering father. Some of his father's expectations of him stayed with him throughout his life. For example, he remembered the time his father forced him to touch a cadaver. His parents separated when he was a young child and Alfred was raised by his mother. Alfred was a good student. He attended schools in both Nice and Paris. When it came time for him to select a career, he decided to become a lawyer. After completing his education, however, he found a law career was not stimulating for him. He then attended medical school. He became ill while in medical school. This illness may have been related to stress. He needed to spend six months in complete rest to recover from his illness. Toward the end of his convalescence he began to read about the young discipline of psychology. There was not much written about this new discipline in France but he sought the information that was available. He became excited about this new field and after he recovered he began some simple experiments in sensory psychology. After working in this experimental area, he sought practical training and obtained a job as an unpaid research assistant at Salpetriere Hospital in Paris working under Jean Martin Charcot, who was studying the use of hypnosis with patients diagnosed as "hysterical." Although most American psychologists associate Binet only with work in cognitive assessment, he had a rich background in many areas of psychology. We refer students who want to learn more about Alfred Binet to his biographies (Francher, 1998; Wolf, 1973). What

Alfred Binet with family *Archives of the History of American Psychology, The University of Akron.*

we covered about Binet illustrates how the time and place in which one lives, combined with one's family, can influence career directions.

Because the Binet-Simon scales were developed in France, they could not just be translated into English and then used clinically in the United States. Translation is the first step in the process of bringing a test from one country to another. Although several psychologists were interested in introducing Binet's test to the United States, Lewis Terman is the psychologist whose work seems to have had the most continued impact on cognitive assessment. After having the original scale translated into English, he needed to evaluate the appropriateness of the individual test items for the U.S. population on whom he planned to use it. He understood that what is common knowledge to children in France is not necessarily common knowledge to children in the United States. Those differences needed to be reflected in the test items. In other words, the test needed to be culturally relevant for this new population. It needed to be standardized for use in the United States. A new normative sample was needed to evaluate the changes Terman proposed from the original measure. Here we also find a key concept that has become increasingly important in psychological assessment as cultures become more mixed. In the twenty-first century we often hear about the idea of "cultural relevance." Early psychologists like Terman were already aware of the importance of culture even if they did not use the term. Thus,

Terman realized that the test needed to be assessed in the country where he wanted to use it and that modification of some items would likely be needed.

Today, psychologists must consider the appropriateness of many of our tests for specific subgroups within the United States. In early U.S. history, the term *melting pot* was used to indicate that people came to the United States from many places. Once they had relocated to the United States, however, these people tried to blend their culture into the current culture of the country rather than attempting to maintain the culture of their country of origin. The desire to assimilate was strong during much of the twentieth century. In the twenty-first century, there is a stronger tendency among immigrants to the United States to maintain the values and customs of their heritage. Clinical psychologists must now try to decide how much acculturation is needed for a particular test to be considered appropriate for use with specific segments of the population. To make this decision, clinical psychologists use a combination of interviewing skill and, when needed, inventories designed to measure a person's identification with a specific ethnic group (e.g., Cuellar, Arnold, & Maldonado, 1995; Vandiver, Cross, Worrell, & Fhagen-Smith, 2002).

It is important for psychologists who do testing to be aware of aspects of their patient's culture that may influence test performance. For example, many tests of cognitive ability require considerable verbal response. In some cases, extra points are awarded for more complete responses. Suppose your patient comes from a cultural group where brief verbal responses are considered the polite way to respond to authority figures. If the patient views the psychologist as an authority figure, it may be very difficult for the psychologist to obtain an accurate measure of the patient's cognitive abilities using traditional cognitive tests. In this case, the psychologist may need to use a nonverbal measure of cognitive ability. If such a test is not readily available for the person to take, the psychologist will need to note in the evaluation report that because of cultural issues the results may be an underestimate of the patient's abilities.

Another issue that may arise in assessment sessions is the patient who lives in the United States but for whom English is not the primary language. In many tests of cognitive ability, some test items are timed. The patient's response may be given extra points if it is given quickly. Other test items may not receive any credit if the response is not produced within a specified time period. Any factor that delays responding can impact the final score. Think about the child who sneezes when they are figuring out a problem and thus may take a second or so more than he or she would ordinarily need! That child's lowered score is not really a good measure of the child's "typical" performance; thus it is important for the psychologist to note this factor when interpreting the results. Also, if the patient is doing mental translation of the question before responding to the psychologist, this time lag may influence the outcome of the cognitive evaluation. Thus the obtained score may not be a true reflection of the patient's cognitive abilities. Can you use a trained interpreter in this case? Psychologists are divided on this issue. You would *not* use a member of the patient's family to translate during the assessment process. If there is no psychologist in the area who speaks the patient's language, the psychologist may elect to use a trained interpreter. The final report of the evaluation would need to make clear that because of the use of an interpreter, the test results might not be valid. The test was not administered according to the standard directions. Comparing the patient's responses to the normative sample is therefore suspect. Because the psychologist does not speak the patient's language, there may also be questions about whether or not the translator used the exact words or altered the language to make the item clearer to the patient. Decisions about whether or not to use an interpreter in psychological testing are made on a case-by-case basis by the psychologist, who uses his or her judgment to provide the best evaluation of the patient.

Lewis Terman, another early psychometrician mentioned previously, was working at Stanford University when he did his work on the Binet scales and so named this U.S. version of the test the Stanford-Binet Intelligence Test. This test was first published in 1916. Terman did more than make cultural and language changes in this test. He also understood that the measurement of cognitive ability, which we often call intelligence, is not limited to children. He added items to the test that were appropriate for adults. With these new items added to the test, it could be used across the lifespan rather than just with children. Another change from the original Binet-Simon scales was the inclusion of an IQ score for expressing the results rather than just a mental age. For many years, the Stanford-Binet was seen as the standard for intelligence testing in the United States. Over the years this test has continued to be revised to take into account cultural changes as well as changes due to the passage of time. The second edition was published in 1937, the third edition in 1960, and then it was renormed in 1972. The fourth edition of this test, published in 1986, was designed for people from age two through adulthood. The fifth edition of the Stanford-Binet was released in 2003.

Who Was Lewis Terman?

Lewis Terman was born in Johnson County, Indiana, in 1877, and died in Palo Alto, California, in 1956. Living to the age of seventy-nine was unusual for a man born in 1877. He noted in his autobiography (1961) that boys from families like his became either farmers or schoolteachers. He apparently decided that teaching was preferable to the physical demands of farming. In 1892, he left home to attend Central Normal College in Danville, Indiana. At that time, colleges for teacher training were called "normal schools." He spent five years at Central Normal College alternately taking classes and teaching at local schools. He earned both a bachelor of pedagogy (B.Pd.) and a B.A. (A.B.) degree during that time. Terman became a high school principal in Indiana following his graduation from Central Normal College and continued serving as a principal until 1901. At that time, he borrowed enough money to attend Indiana University, where he decided he wanted to become a psychology professor. When he decided to study psychology, he moved to Clark University because he felt Clark University was the center of psychology education in the United States at that time. While he was studying psychology at Clark University, he developed a strong interest in what was then called "mental testing" and was later called "intelligence testing." His doctoral dissertation was on a contrast between gifted and nongifted children and what tests might assist psychologists to make this distinction. Because Terman had a mild case of tuberculosis, he decided to move to California for his health following his graduation from Clark University. He was unable to find a psychology faculty position when he first moved to California and so he returned to his roots as a school principal when the opportunity arose in San Bernardino, California. The next year, he moved to the Los Angeles State Normal School, where he would spend four years as a professor of child study and pedagogy. Today, that normal school is called California State

Lewis M. Terman *Archives of the History of American Psychology, The University of Akron.*

University at Los Angeles. Finally in 1910, Terman was offered a faculty position in the School of Education at Stanford University. He would later spend twenty years as chair of the psychology department at Stanford University. His interests in cognitive testing and in the study of gifted people would become his life's work. If you want to read more about Lewis Terman, we suggest his autobiography (1961).

Who Was David Wechsler?

Another historically important name in the measurement of cognitive abilities who is often cited in the history of clinical psychology is David Wechsler. Wechsler wanted to develop an intelligence test specifically for adults rather than adding items to a test that was designed to measure children's cognitive abilities. Wechsler was employed at Bellevue Hospital in New York City when he developed this test. In 1939 he published the Wechsler-Bellevue Intelligence Scale. After that original test, he and his followers developed other tests based on the same model. Each test is appropriate for different age levels. Currently three different tests in the Wechsler series are available. The Wechsler Adult Intelligence Scale (WAIS) is used with people between sixteen and eighty-nine years of age. The WAIS is the modern version of the original Wechsler-Bellevue test. The third edition of this test, the WAIS-III, was published in 1997. In most cases, this instrument requires between sixty and ninety minutes to administer completely. It has also been

David Wechsler *Archives of the History of American Psychology, The University of Akron.*

translated into American Sign Language (ASL) to accommodate people who use ASL to communicate. Of course, the psychologist must be competent in this language to administer the ASL version of the test. The Wechsler Intelligence Scale for Children (WISC) is used with children and adolescents between six years of age and sixteen years, eleven months, of age. The third edition, the WISC-III, was published in 1991, and the current version, the WISC-IV, was published in the summer of 2003. In most cases, it takes an experienced psychometrician about fifty to seventy minutes to administer the WISC. The Wechsler Preschool and Primary Scale of Intelligence (WPPSI) is used with children between ages two years six months and seven years, three months. The third edition, WPPSI-III, was published in 2002. The typical administration time of the WPPSI varies depending on the age of the child and whether any of the optional subtests are administered. Younger children tend to complete the test in thirty to forty-five minutes while older children may require an hour or more for the core battery. A major reason for the shorter testing time with the younger children is that fewer items need to be given.

Some of you may be wondering why there is an overlap in the age ranges of the various Wechsler tests. Developmentally, there are important milestone periods that occur at different times in different children. Some children may be a bit slow for their age while other children are somewhat more advanced. The clinical psychologist uses his or her judgment regarding which of the Wechsler tests to administer based on the referral question, personal observation of the child, and the child's individual history to select the test that will give an optimal measure of cognitive functioning for that child. Many psychologists prefer the Wechsler tests rather than the Stanford-Binet because they view the Wechsler tests as being easier to administer (Cohen & Swerdlik, 2002). Psychologists often have options among available tests that are appropriate for their patients. Test selection tends to be based on personal preference and experience with the various tools.

Cognitive testing has not been without controversy. The concept of fairness of both cognitive and personality tests has been raised not only in the clinical literature (Brown, 1994; Lopez, 2000; Matarazzo, 1990) but also in the courts. Two early legal cases from California illustrate the issue of test fairness and how it relates to the activities of clinical psychologists. In 1970 in California, students were placed in special education classes based solely on their performance on intelligence tests. At that time, approximately 18 percent of the students in the California public schools had Spanish surnames. When the enrollment in special education classes was checked, it was found that 33 percent of the students in classes for the educable mentally retarded had Hispanic surnames. Further investigation showed that the intelligence tests were administered in English and that the tests used had been developed primarily on Caucasian children. Based on these findings changes were made in the education code of California so that future educational placements required a more comprehensive cognitive examination of the child than just an intelligence test (*Diana v. State Board of Education,* 1970). A second California case involved the placement of African-American children in these same special education classes (*Larry P. v. Riles,* 1979). As with the children with Hispanic surnames, there were a higher percentage of African-American children in special education than would be predicted from base rates. The court ruled that intelligence tests were not fair to African-American students. A major factor in this ruling was that when items from the tests that were being used were reworded to reflect their culture, the children in this test case performed within the normal range of intelligence. This case was appealed but the original ruling was upheld. In 1984 the courts ruled that intelligence tests could no longer be used in California to assess African-American children for potential placement in special education classes.

Not all courts have taken the same position regarding the use of standardized tests for class placement. In another legal case, at about the same time historically but in a different jurisdiction, a different ruling was obtained. The federal court in Illinois ruled in *PASE v. Hannon* (1980) that the schools could continue to use psychological tests for educational placement. The Illinois court decided that the tests being used in Illinois were appropriate for this process. Thus, it is important for the clinical psychologist who uses psychological tests to be aware of the laws related to the purpose of that testing and to be sure to use the most appropriate of the available tests for the group of people being assessed. The psychologist who moves from one part of the country to another must learn about any differences in the law that may exist, such as the difference between California and Illinois that we just noted. Test selection and use are ethical and legal issues for the clinical psychologist.

Many psychologists also struggle with the controversy over the origins of intelligence. You have probably heard the phrase "nature or nurture" in your psychology classes. Psychologists use these words to refer to the controversy over whether intelligence is innate or unlearned (*nature*) or derived from learning and experience (*nurture*). Today, the prevailing opinion among psychologists seems to be that both nature and nurture play a role in the development and expression of intelligence. In *The Bell Curve* (Herrnstein & Murray, 1994), the authors claimed that separated-twin studies represent the "purest" of the direct measures of heritability and that intelligence is strongly heritable. They also stated that social intervention can do very little to raise IQ. This claim is based on data from the National Longitudinal Survey of Youth (NLSY). This survey was an ongoing federal project that tested over ten thousand youths in the 1980s. Herrnstein and Murray argued that as American society expands, wealth and other social benefits are being distributed more prevalently on the basis of intelligence than on social experience. They also suggested that since intelligence is based more on heritability than on environment, social programs such as welfare and affirmative action should be abolished. According to them, genetic differences would contribute more to a person's future than would federal support from such programs as HeadStart. The implications of this book were far reaching. Data on intelligence test scores by ethnicity support the position that African Americans as a group score lower than Caucasians on the tests that were used to assess their ability. Herrnstein and Murray's book was used to support the position that African Americans are intellectually inferior to Caucasians. The firestorm that arose from this controversy continues to simmer, as does the debate over the relative contribution of nature and nurture in the development of intelligence. We discuss cognitive assessment in more detail in chapter 6.

Brain–Behavior Relationships

Franz Joseph Gall and Joseph Spurzheim (Temkin, 1947) considered assessment of human characteristics from a very different perspective. Believe it or not, they were interested in developing a better understanding of people based on the bumps and indentations on their heads! Gall, trained as a physician, tended to do much of the technical work on their theory, while Spurzheim was the publicist. They developed a "map" of the human skull. It was their theory that if you had an excess of certain characteristics, that part of your brain would grow, resulting in an external "bump." If you were deficient in certain characteristics, your brain would be concave in that region, resulting in a "dent." These bumps and dents could be measured and were the basis of their theory, which they called **phrenology.** Today, we realize that their theory cannot be supported, although the theoretical tenet that there is a relationship between certain areas of the brain and their functions was correct. In some books, phrenology is described in a rather joking or mocking way. We chose to include it because it provided important precedents for our study of assessment. First, Gall and Spurzheim attempted to test their theory by applying the concept to people whose major traits were demonstrated in other ways. For example, they hypothesized that a person who was found to be excessive in the area of "acquisitiveness" might become a criminal who stole property from others. Gall and Spurzheim measured the heads of known criminals to test this hypothesis. Second, they were willing to alter their map based on new data. Prior to their research, physicians believed that some brain fibers from one hemisphere crossed to the other hemisphere, but it was Gall's careful study that confirmed this concept, known as contralateral representation. Although these theorists were primarily interested in personality factors, their work really provides a foundation for our study of brain–behavior relationships that are part of training in neuropsychological assessment. We will discuss this type of assessment briefly here and then more fully in chapter 8.

Today psychologists do not look for bumps and dents in the head to assess people, but we have established that certain parts of the human brain have the major responsibility for certain types of behavior. If those parts of the brain are damaged those functions are impacted. Some of the factors are cognitive (language or perceptual), while other factors are emotional. Thus the work of Gall and Spurzheim, which was the basis for the notion of localization of function, constitutes an overlap between our history of cognitive assessment and personality assessment.

Neuropsychological Assessment

Neuropsychological assessment is a specialized form of testing. Although this form of assessment is not done routinely by clinical psychologists, many neuropsychologists were originally trained as clinical psychologists and then later specialized in brain–behavior assessment. Because of this overlap, we will provide some foundation for their work in our brief review of history. Ward Halstead's pioneering work illustrates part of the history of this approach to assessment. His work took cognitive assessment in a new direction. Prior to Halstead, the focus of test development was the measurement of educational abilities. Halstead was interested in a more biological approach to intelligence. He sought to develop measures that would reflect the state of functioning of the person's central nervous system. He developed a battery of tests that he then administered to people who were medically diagnosed as having recovered from recent head injury. The results of these assessments were evaluated by factor analysis to select the most useful tools. This process led to the identification of thirteen tests that identified four factors. He named these factors central integrative, abstracting, power factor, and modality directionality (Halstead, 1947). Halstead's research formed the basis for one of the more popular neuropsychological batteries currently in use, the Halstead-Reitan Neuropsychological Battery. This battery is described in chapter 8. A battery of tests is a group of tests that, when combined, give the psychologist a more complete picture of a person's cognitive functioning than any individual test provides.

Another historical figure whose work also forms part of the foundation for current neuropsychological practice is A. R. Luria (Christensen, 1975; Luria, 1980). Luria practiced in Russia, but his theories have had a major impact on current assessment practices in clinical neuropsychology around the world. Luria's approach is similar to what is done in many types of medical examination. A range of simple performances is evaluated in terms of being either normal or pathological. The examinations tended to be individualized with succeeding tasks being selected, in a hierarchical fashion, based on prior responses. This process of task selection allows the neuropsychologist to examine more extensively in domains where the person's performance is questionable and not spend extra time in those domains where abilities are clearly demonstrated to be within normal limits. We will discuss general concepts of neuropsychological assessment more completely in chapter 8.

Personality Assessment

Clinical psychologists tend to subdivide personality assessment into projective and objective forms. **Projective tests** are more open-ended in terms of both response and interpretation, while objective tests tend to limit the patient's response and are less subjective in terms of interpretation. There is some debate in the clinical literature about who was the first to use the term *projective testing,* but most authors credit L. K. Frank (1939) with popularizing the concept. Murray and his colleagues at Harvard had reportedly used the term *projection tests* to refer to not only their own test, the Thematic Apperception Test, but also to the Rorschach Inkblot Test. Some of their colleagues felt the term *projection* might be confused with Freud's use of that term defining a defense mechanism within psychoanalysis. Thus, *projective* seemed to be a more acceptable alternative.

Modern clinical psychologists trace the heritage of their projective personality testing to the work of Hermann Rorschach. Rorschach was a Swiss psychiatrist. The test that bears his name is often called the "inkblot" test in popular culture. His work standardized what many clinicians of his time were actually doing. He began work on his personality test in 1911 and published his famous book in 1921 (Rorschach, 1921). Various perceptual stimuli were being used at that time in attempts to assess personality. Some historians have suggested that Rorschach considered using cloud formations as stimuli, counting on the human tendency to "see" familiar objects in them as one method for understanding personality. Because clouds were not always available when a clinician wanted to evaluate a patient and they were not standardized, he turned to other media. Initially, he used geometric figures that were cut from paper of various colors. His reading led him to the idea of making inkblots. Rorschach learned that some people were using that approach and he decided it made sense for his work. He originally developed more than the ten blots we associate today with his approach. The publisher of his work was unwilling to include more than ten blots, so Rorschach decreased the number.

It is not unusual for one scholar to initiate an idea and another one to popularize it. That was certainly the case with the Rorschach. Rorschach's original book was not popular, even among scholars. It might never have become the widely used measure it is today if an American psychiatrist, David Levy, had not been studying in Switzerland in 1921. Levy brought Rorschach's book back to the United States and taught the test to a psychology trainee, Samuel Beck. Beck found the test interesting and applied his psychology training to its administration. As was noted with the Binet scales, standard administration procedures have been viewed as essential for psychological testing. Beck developed not only a standardized administration procedure for this new test but also a standardized scoring system (Beck, 1937). Another psychologist, Bruno Klopfer, also became interested in the Rorschach test and published a different scoring system the same year (Klopfer & Kelley, 1937). From that time to the present, the Rorschach has been a staple of clinical psychologists who do personality assessment. We will explain more about this test in chapter 7.

Not all early psychologists were interested in this projective approach to the measurement of personality. The modern use of objective measurement of personality stems from the work of Robert S. Woodworth with the U.S. military. Woodworth served as chairperson of the U.S. government's Committee on Emotional Fitness. The military needed to have large numbers of men evaluated for their fitness to serve during World War I. The time and expense of evaluating these men with projective tests of personality were prohibitive. Thus, a different approach was needed. Woodworth (1920) developed the Personal Data Sheet, the first of our modern objective tests of personality. It was called Personal

Data Sheet so that the candidates for military service would not realize its actual purpose. This test only required a "yes" or "no" response to a range of items that had been found to elicit different responses when previously given to patients who were diagnosed as "neurotic" and, as a comparison group, to individuals who did not have a psychiatric history. Later psychologists also used this method of test development. Woodworth's work on the standardization of the Personal Data Sheet was cut short because the war ended. The military no longer needed to do large-scale evaluations of inductees. Woodworth and his colleagues used what they had learned from their work on the Personal Data Sheet to develop a similar measure for the civilian population. Their new test was the Woodworth Psychoneurotic Inventory. Woodworth's second test became the first widely used self-report personality measure in the United States. According to the theory behind this test, the greater the number of symptoms endorsed by the patient, the greater the degree of neurosis. Chapter 7 provides more detailed information about personality assessment.

Who Was Robert S. Woodworth?

Robert Sessions Woodworth was born in Belchertown, Massachusetts, in 1869. His father was a minister and his mother was a teacher. He originally considered following in his father's footsteps as a minister but his undergraduate experience at Amherst College led him to a career in education. He taught high school math and science after graduating from

Robert S. Woodworth
Archives of the History of American Psychology, The University of Akron.

college. During his teaching career, he discovered William James' *Principles of Psychology* (1890) as well as some of the writings of G. Stanley Hall and decided that he would pursue a career in either philosophy or psychology. He enrolled at Harvard University, where he earned a second bachelor's degree as well as a master's degree. During this time, his interests turned more solidly to psychology. He moved to Columbia University to pursue his doctorate in psychology. After receiving his doctorate in 1899, Woodworth was appointed to the faculty at Columbia University. Other than a year he spent in England doing physiological research, he spent his entire academic career at Columbia. He retired from Columbia in 1939 at the age of seventy. He continued to teach part-time until he was eighty-nine and to write until he was ninety-one. Although we included him in this chapter because of his work in personality assessment, he was also known for his introductory psychology textbook that was published in 1921 and his experimental psychology textbook that was first published in 1938. He was a founding member of the Society for Research in Child Development in 1925. Like many of these early psychologists, he had a broad range of interests within the field. Among his professional accomplishments were election as president of the American Psychological Association in 1914 and receipt of the American Psychological Foundation's Gold Medal in 1956 for his outstanding contributions to psychology. He died in 1962.

Psychotherapy

In the early years of clinical psychology, intervention meant psychotherapy. *Psychotherapy* is a general term that refers to the interaction between one or more mental health professionals and one or more people who are either interested in making personal changes or whose behavior has sufficiently upset someone else that they are being forced to seek help. There is no single definition of psychotherapy that is accepted by all practitioners. Traditionally psychotherapy involved one therapist and one patient. Over time, the concept changed to include more than one of either the therapist or the patient. Psychotherapy is usually a highly verbal activity. With small children, the term may refer to what appears more like play than work on problems. Psychotherapy also implies that one of the participants, such as a clinical psychologist, has a degree of expertise about the issues that are of concern to the patient.

Freud's Impact

Modern psychotherapy traces its heritage to the individual psychotherapy of Sigmund Freud. Freud spent most of his career practicing in Vienna, Austria. There are numerous books written about the life and work of this pioneer (Freud, 1910, 1938, 1953–1964; Jones, 1953, 1955, 1957). A brief history notes that Sigmund Freud was born May 6, 1856, to Amalie and Jakob Freud. He was originally named Sigismund but shortened the name to Sigmund when he was an adolescent. Sigmund was raised in a home with half-siblings as well as full siblings because his mother was Jakob's third wife. Much of the history of Sigmund Freud has been tied to his concepts about sexuality and about women. For those students who want an in-depth understanding of this well-known figure from a less traditional perspective we suggest *Freud's Women* (Appignanesi & Forrester, 1992). This book provides both personal history and case analysis.

Freud's legacy to clinical psychology is immense. He described the use of verbal interaction to deal with a range of emotional problems. Today we call this activity psychotherapy. His methods also taught us the importance of the relationship between the therapist and the patient. Whether you call this relationship transference or **rapport,** training in clinical psychology includes learning how to develop an appropriate relationship between the therapist and the patient. Perhaps because the therapeutic relationship is so unique, modern ethical standards of many mental health professions include a prohibition against the patient and therapist developing a personal relationship either during therapy or for a specified period of time after the therapy has ended. In ethical terms, "dual" relationships between the patient and the therapist should be avoided. Freud also taught us that what we are told by the patient may not be accurate. This does not mean that the patient is actively lying to the therapist. There are a variety of reasons a patient's report may not be an accurate description of events. Perhaps what happened is emotionally very painful. In order to keep functioning, the patient's memory transforms some aspects of the situation into a more acceptable account of events. It is this latter description that the patient gives to the therapist. In other cases, the interpretation of events may be vastly different if several people who observed them are asked about the situation. As a therapist, you are getting your patient's view of what happened. We need to use our knowledge of theory/research as well as what we know about the person in order to make sense out of what we are told.

Freud gave us the concept that what happens in a person's early life is a major determinant of adult problems. Not all psychologists would place as much emphasis on early childhood as Freud did, but the idea that what has happened in the past influences current behavior is well accepted today. In chapters 9–12 we talk about specific techniques clinical psychologists use in psychotherapy. Some of these techniques are a direct result of Freud's work or a modification of those procedures to meet the needs of changing times. Other approaches to psychotherapy are more accurately described as having been developed to provide an alternative to Freud's methods.

In addition to the development of a major method of psychotherapy, Freud's approach to dealing with emotional problems also encouraged the use of projective tests of personality. Many early dissertations in clinical psychology were studies of the use of the Rorschach Inkblot Test or the Thematic Apperception Test (TAT). These projective tests, also noted in the section of this chapter on personality assessment, are described more completely in chapter 7.

Freud's approach to psychotherapy also included the use of hypnosis. The combination of hypnosis and psychoanalysis was called "hypnoanalysis." Hypnotherapy was quite popular during the rise of psychoanalysis in the early 1900s but then almost disappeared from the practice after that time. With the increased need for both psychiatrists and clinical psychologists following World War II, hypnotherapy once again became a popular form of intervention. Although no longer used in the Freudian approach of psychoanalysis, hypnotherapy was viewed as a way to address rapidly the emergency mental health needs of patients. Over time, hypnotherapy was used to treat a wide range of disorders, including habit problems such as overeating, anxiety-based disorders, and psychosomatic symptoms. In later years it would also be used in cases of pain relief and even in surgery for cases where more traditional forms of anesthesia were not feasible (Hilgard & Hilgard, 1983).

Freud also gave us examples of psychological autopsies. Although it is not one of his more frequently cited works, Freud wrote a book analyzing Leonardo da Vinci (Freud, 1914). He used available material about this historical figure to develop a personality description. The psychological autopsy is used today by forensic psychologists, especially in cases of questionable death. Psychologists use what is known about the deceased to make informed statements about what that person most likely thought or did at some time prior to death. Freud's work suggests a similar process can be used with historical figures.

Freud's concepts about psychotherapy were formally introduced in the United States in 1909 when he was an invited speaker at the twentieth anniversary celebration of the founding of Clark University in Worcester, Massachusetts. Clark University also conferred an honorary doctoral degree on Freud during this celebration. It would be the only honorary degree he received. Some of the early trainers of psychologists heard him speak during this event and thus began to teach his ideas to their students. Also the *American Journal of Psychology* published an article containing some of his comments allowing his ideas to reach a larger audience within the profession.

Several of Freud's colleagues also merit brief mention for their early work in psychotherapy, but we will refer interested students to other sources for more complete descriptions of their work. Alfred Adler, one of Freud's colleagues who would later move away from Freud's inner circle to develop his own theories, added the concept of the importance of patients' feelings of inferiority to the practice of psychotherapy. He suggested that people who feel inferior tend to "overcompensate" for these feelings when placed in certain situations. He also suggested that a person's place in the order of birth in the family had considerable influence on that person's personality development (Adler, 1927, 1935). Although many of Adler's concepts remain part of the practice of clinical psychology, his name is not as common as Freud's. Because his ideas seem to make sense to many people, the need to attribute them to a particular scholar has not seemed as important as concepts such as Freud's stages of psychosexual development or Jung's collective unconscious, described next.

When Freud came to Clark University, he was accompanied by a young colleague named Carl Jung. Jung's alterations of psychoanalysis would provide new dimensions to Freud's form of psychotherapy. Especially unique was his concept of the collective unconscious. Jung believed that we have latent memories we have inherited from our ancestors. He even went so far as to suggest that these memories went beyond human history and included our prehuman ancestry. Our other aspects of personality are built on these memories. How we learn from our experiences is influenced by these memories and therefore they are a key part of psychotherapy (Jung, 1959). We discuss some of Jung's other ideas in chapter 4.

Although Freud's psychoanalysis remains part of the practice of psychotherapy in the twenty-first century, some authors have suggested that its level of prestige began to decline starting in the 1960s when some prominent supporters of psychoanalysis started to question the research support for it (Shakow, 1969). At this same time there was a rise in the use of newly developed medication to treat emotional problems and a decline in the use of psychological forms of intervention.

Early U.S. Highlights

Historians place the first U.S. psychological clinic at the University of Pennsylvania. It was founded by Lightner Witmer in 1896. He is sometimes called the "father of clinical psychology." Witmer's first well-known case was a fourteen-year-old boy who suffered from chronic problems of bad spelling. This boy's teacher brought him to Witmer for help with this school-related problem. Witmer did extensive remedial work with this boy and later published a clinical report of his activities. Based on his description of the boy, today's clinical psychologists would probably give him a diagnosis of dyslexia. This initial case study was followed by more than twenty other case studies of children who Witmer evaluated. Witmer started his clinic as a place where teachers, parents, and community agencies could bring problem students. Much of the work done in this original clinic related to school problems rather than the type of childhood psychopathology often described in abnormal psychology books.

Witmer developed two tests for children, the Witmer Formboard and the Witmer Cylinders. He used these tests extensively in his clinic. These tests, however, were supplanted by the more popular Stanford-Binet scales. Although Witmer developed psychological tests, he also suggested that tests were overused by clinical psychologists. This position was not a common one for his time. When Witmer was practicing, testing was viewed as the activity that made clinical psychology a unique profession. Witmer also suggested changes in the graduate psychology curriculum of the time. Because of his interest in children's problems, Witmer believed the curriculum should include not only psychological theory but also the connection of this theory to education (Witmer, 1907).

Witmer conceived the role of clinical psychologists expanding beyond the consulting room (Humphreys, 1996). He argued that clinical psychologists should work within the schools and also engage in preventive social action to change harmful social conditions, such as slums (Reisman, 1991). In the twenty-first century much of the focus of prevention in contrast to intervention has been moved to the specialty of community psychology rather than mainstream clinical psychology. We talk more about prevention and social policy advocacy in chapter 13.

Who Was Lightner Witmer?

Lightner Witmer was born in Philadelphia, Pennsylvania, in 1867 and died in Devon, Pennsylvania, in 1956. His longevity was unusual for someone of his era. He was raised in an affluent family; his father was a successful wholesale pharmacist. Witmer entered the University of Pennsylvania in 1884 and four years later received a B.A. degree. He was described as an outstanding student. Following his graduation from college, he spent two years as a history teacher at a private secondary school in Philadelphia. During these two years, he also enrolled in psychology classes at his alma mater. In 1888, he became a full-time graduate student of psychology at Penn. Witmer became a student assistant to a new faculty member at the University of Pennsylvania. This new faculty member was James McKeen Cattell. Here we see an example of the role a mentor can have in career development. Cattell got his degree with Wilhelm Wundt in Leipzig. Wundt, one of the founders of modern psychology, was widely known for his work in psychophysics. When Cattell decided to leave the University of Pennsylvania for a position at Columbia University

Lightner Witmer *Archives of the History of American Psychology, The University of Akron.*

in New York, he made arrangements for his student. Cattell sent Witmer to Leipzig to study with Wundt with the understanding that after he received his Ph.D. he would return to the University of Pennsylvania to direct the psychology program. His doctorate was formally granted in 1883 but by then Witmer had already returned to the University of Pennsylvania, where he remained throughout his career with the exception of a leave of absence to serve in the U.S. Army during the Spanish American War. Witmer was known as a man of strong positions. For example, when a young faculty member was dismissed for having what the university considered to be radical political views, Witmer led the protest for his reinstatement. Although this protest was not successful, it did advance the concept of academic freedom. He retired from the University of Pennsylvania in 1937.

Early clinical psychologists were often associated with children's issues. It is not surprising that when the first U.S. juvenile court system was established in Illinois in 1899 psychologists were involved in testing and remediation. Work in the juvenile justice system led to the development of child guidance clinics. Many of these early clinics were associated with the juvenile justice system. Later they were affiliated with schools and social service agencies. Although most of these early clinics were directed by psychiatrists, the actual interventions with the children were done by psychologists and helped establish the role of psychologists as psychotherapists.

Early clinical psychologists were taught Freud's concepts about psychotherapy. As they applied his techniques, however, not all of these psychologists were pleased with the technique or the results. The training of clinical psychologists includes a strong understanding of both normal human development and personality theory. With this dual foundation, some American psychologists began to question the Freudian approach and began to develop other intervention methods. For those of you who wish to learn more about the range of methods of psychotherapy currently in use, we refer you to summary books on the subject (Prochaska & Norcross, 2002; Sharf, 2000). Here we highlight a few of the major approaches that provided the historical foundation for the development of various methods over time.

Rogers' Contributions

An American pioneer in the field of psychotherapy was Carl R. Rogers, who lived from 1902 to 1987. An instant reaction to his name by many students of psychology is "client-centered therapy." Rogers, a humanist, was an early proponent of calling the recipients of the services of clinical psychologists *clients* rather than *patients*. The focus of his techniques was on the person seeking help rather than the provider of the service (Rogers, 1942, 1951).

Being a well-trained psychologist, Rogers not only developed a theory to explain his work but also gathered data about the results of his methods and made changes in his methodology based on the data. Rogers was one of the early psychologists to record the actual conversations that occurred during a therapy session and then attempt to evaluate them to better understand the change process. When Rogers suggested that a microphone could be placed in the therapy setting, with the patient's consent, to record the therapy session, many of his peers believed the recording would be harmful to the therapeutic process. Rogers found that both the patient and the therapist quickly ignored the microphone. This methodology thus provided an exact transcript of therapy sessions. After the therapy sessions, Rogers and his colleagues did a content analysis of these transcripts so that the process of therapy could be considered from a quantitative perspective (Rogers & Dymond, 1954). Rogers also studied factors about the therapist that seemed to influence the process of change in psychotherapy. To do this type of research, Rogers developed rating scales to measure both therapist attitudes and patient attitudes. He did not limit his research about psychotherapy to just evaluating the recordings. His rating scales could be used with patients and the results of these ratings compared to the evaluations of the recorded session.

Based on his evaluation of the change process, Rogers suggested that there are three basic therapist characteristics that need to be present if psychotherapy is expected to succeed (Rogers, 1957). Over time, he used different terms for these factors. Regardless of the names used, these three basic concepts are important. These concepts are *congruence, empathy,* and *unconditional positive regard.*

Congruence refers to the therapist being honest about what he or she is experiencing in the therapeutic relationship. Rogers was not suggesting that therapists be rude or insulting to their patients. However, he suggested that if the psychologist feels angry about something the patient has said but says he or she is pleased with what the patient is saying that psychologist is giving the patient a confusing message. In other words, therapists need to be genuine in their reactions toward their patients. Most students of psychology who try using Rogers' method find that empathy is harder to use than it seems when they read about it. Rogers suggested that it is important for the therapist to be able to understand the patient from the point of view of the patient's internal frame of reference. This is what he meant by **empathy.** Some people have called this factor "seeing the world through the patient's eyes." Empathy also includes being able to communicate this level of understanding to your patient in more than words. **Unconditional positive regard** does not mean that the psychologist agrees with everything the patient says or does. It does not mean that the psychologist supports harmful behavior. This term refers to the ability to respect and accept the patient as a person regardless of specific factors that may be negative. This characteristic is often used today in books on parenting in which parents are encouraged to separate the behavior of their children from their love of their children. Parents are told to let their children know they love them for themselves and not for specific behaviors. For example, it is better for a parent to say, "I like it when you do your homework," rather than, "You're a good girl when you do your homework." This same approach is used in psychotherapy. The clinical psychologist accepts and values the patient as a person separate from the negative characteristics or behaviors the patient may express.

As times changed, so did Rogers' terminology. He moved from "client-centered" therapy to "person-centered" psychotherapy. When the group approach to psychotherapy for relatively healthy people who wanted to get more from their lives became popular, he also investigated these group therapy methods (Rogers, 1970). He applied his approach to many aspects of life, including educational issues and how to have a successful marriage (Rogers, 1972). Chapter 4 includes more details about Rogers' theory of personality.

Who Was Carl Rogers?

To help you get a better understanding of why Carl Rogers became the leader he was in the field of psychotherapy, we thought you might like to know a bit more about his life. When a person lived in history, where the person spent that life, plus the background from which he or she comes influences a person's development. Carl Rogers was born in Oak Park, Illinois, in 1902 and died following hip surgery in San Diego, California, in 1987. His family of origin is often described as highly religious, conservative Protestant, where great value was placed on hard work. When he was twelve years old, his family moved from a suburban area to a farm. This background led him to first consider a career in

Carl R. Rogers *Carl R. Rogers Collection, Humanistic Psychology Archives Mss 32, Department of Special Collections, Davidson Library, University of California, Santa Barbara.*

scientific agriculture and later the ministry. He received his undergraduate degree from the University of Wisconsin and then moved to New York City to attend Union Theological Seminary. This school taught religion from a more liberal perspective than his heritage. He also took classes at nearby Columbia University and would eventually leave the seminary to pursue graduate studies in psychology at Columbia. He received his master's degree from Columbia University in 1928 and his doctorate in 1931. His early practical training was basically Freudian, and he worked mainly with children.

His first job after receiving his doctorate was at the Rochester Child Guidance Center, where he met practitioners from diverse theoretical orientations. The center had staff conferences where they discussed practical aspects of psychotherapy with people of all ages. Rogers began to formulate his own approach to psychotherapy at this time. He became a psychology professor at Ohio State University in 1940, and two years later his *Counseling and Psychotherapy* (Rogers, 1942) was published. He expanded his ideas based on his work at the University of Chicago, where he worked as both a professor and counseling center psychologist in 1945. Each time he moved, Carl Rogers seems to have learned from his environment and modified his theory accordingly. From 1957 to 1963, he worked at the University of Wisconsin. During these years he did extensive research on psychotherapy with schizophrenic inpatients. His final move was to California in 1964, where he was associated with the Center for Studies of the Person. He was active at the center until his hip surgery. If you would like to learn more about his past, we suggest you read his autobiography (Rogers, 1967).

Behavioral Contributions

Behaviorally oriented clinical psychologists moved even further from the original Freudian approaches to psychotherapy than Rogers did. The early behavioral approaches to psychotherapy were based on the research literature in the psychology of learning (Pavlov, 1906; Skinner, 1938, 1953). The focus of their work was on overt, observable behavior. To illustrate this work, we decided to describe the classic study by Watson and Rayner (1920).

Watson and Rayner hypothesized that we learn associations between stimuli and responses through classical conditioning. They did a case study to illustrate that a simple fear can be taught to a child. Their subject, known in the literature as "little Albert," was not afraid of a white rat when they began their work with him. Over a series of trials, they paired the presentation of the white rat with a loud, unpleasant noise. Each time Albert reached for the rat, the noise was introduced. It took only five such pairings for Albert to start to show distress at the presentation of the rat without any sound at all. By the end of the study, Albert appeared to fear not only the rat but also other similar furry objects. You may remember from your learning course that this is called stimulus generalization. Watson suggested that one reason we often don't see the connection between our learning history and our fears is because of stimulus generalization. The fear on which we are now concentrating may not be the one originally conditioned. Several factors stopped Watson from conducting his originally planned reversal of this reaction in Albert. Albert left the hospital where the research was conducted shortly after the data were gathered. At this time, Watson was going through a rather messy divorce that ultimately led to a career change for him. These combined factors left it to one of Watson's former students, Mary

Cover Jones, and her case study of Peter a few years later (Jones, 1924), to demonstrate the removal of a fear. Peter was a three-year-old boy who was already afraid of such furry objects as a white rat and a rabbit. Her research involved presenting the feared animal in a cage gradually moved closer and closer to Peter while he was eating a favored food. After a few months of this "treatment" Peter no longer exhibited any fear of the animals. Of course, it was important for the fear not to be so intense that the child would transfer that fear to the food rather than have the desire for food overcome the fear. These studies were considered **analog studies**—they were conducted in a laboratory setting but considered to be analogous to the way such fears develop in real life. These case studies formed a foundation for later controlled studies of large numbers of subjects.

Over time, the term *behavior* was broadened from observable behavior to include thoughts or cognitions. Most of the behavioral approaches to psychotherapy are described as being short-term. Short-term can be somewhat deceptive depending on your frame of reference. Since earlier forms of psychotherapy tended to be applied in terms of "years," with four or five years not being uncommon, the behavioral approaches that were defined in terms of months were considered "short-term."

Psychotherapy Develops

Clinical psychologists who were commissioned into the U.S. Army during World War II had psychotherapy listed as a major part of their job description (Hutt & Milton, 1947). These early psychologists technically were under the supervision of a psychiatrist. Psychologists who were part of this early group of practitioners, however, reported that the need for psychotherapy was so great in the military that psychologists conducted psychotherapy with little or no actual psychiatric supervision (Garfield, 1998). This government program served as a model for later training programs that included the independent practice of psychotherapy by psychologists.

Not all psychotherapy is done with one patient at a time. Group psychotherapy became a major modality used by clinical psychologists in hospital settings and continues to be used by many mental health professionals today. Although some therapists used the group approach to psychotherapy with specific patients such as tuberculosis patients (Lubin, 1976), it was once again the needs of veterans following World War II that truly brought group psychotherapy to national prominence. Outpatient therapy groups also became popular with some of these people addressing specific problems, such as smoking cessation, while others dealt more generally with personal distress. Today the vast majority of theoretical approaches to psychotherapy are used on both an individual psychotherapy and group psychotherapy basis. Although many people have written about group psychotherapy, psychiatrist Irving Yalom (1975, 1995) is a major force in its popularization. We discuss his concepts in more detail in chapter 12. Specialized groups, known as families, are also seen together in psychotherapy. Nathan Ackerman (1958) was one of the early proponents of the idea that the presenting patient represents a sick family rather than a sick individual. The term *family* may refer to either the nuclear family or the extended family, depending on the particular psychologist's point of view or family structure.

Psychotherapy today is an activity practiced by many mental health professionals on an independent level. Historically, there was once an attempt to develop a new profession called psychotherapy. In 1963, a three-day conference in New York drew representatives of clinical psychology, psychiatry, psychoanalysis, and social work to consider developing a profession of psychotherapy (Garfield, 1998). Although this group discussed the training criteria for such a profession and produced an extensive report summarizing their ideas, the new profession never came to fruition. Today there are an even greater number of mental health professions engaged in psychotherapy than the ones who met in 1963. It seems unlikely that a separate profession of psychotherapy will become a reality. Just as there is no single profession of psychotherapy, there is no single method of doing psychotherapy. How many methods of psychotherapy exist today? We cannot answer this question for you. Garfield (1998) noted that a 1986 reference included over four hundred psychotherapeutic techniques. Of course, not all of these methods are taught in typical graduate programs. Nor can you expect to find all of them in research journals. Some methods are developed for work with special populations or unique cultures, while others are more general.

Intervention by clinical psychologists began to take a different direction starting in the 1990s. In 1986, the Council of Representatives of the APA endorsed a policy that the practice of psychology covers both physical and psychological interventions. This change in policy was described as putting into print what had been occurring in practice. We note some examples in the work settings presented in chapter 1. For many years, clinical psychologists had been working on physical medicine units as well as psychiatric units. The types of interventions they used varied with the patient population. For example, the psychologist in a department of pediatrics might be working with children and their parents to develop better compliance with a medical regimen such as medication and diet for diabetes. The psychologist working with patients on a chronic pain unit might be leading groups addressing ways to decrease attention to that pain plus lifestyle issues often faced by this population. The mission and bylaws of the APA were amended in 2002 to include "promoting health" among the objectives of the association. This change in the APA bylaws is an acknowledgment not only of the work of psychologists in medical settings but also of their growing interest in a wellness rather than solely an illness model.

Prescriptive Authority

This national policy of supporting the expanding role of psychologists as not only mental health providers but also as health professionals was reaffirmed by the APA Council of Representatives in 1995. This action also opened the door for advocates of prescriptive authority for psychologists. APA then developed model legislation that could be used by individual states seeking such changes to their laws as well as a recommended training program for those psychologists who wished to add this skill to their practice. Using their expertise in test development, APA worked with a test publisher to develop a standardized national **psychopharmacology** exam that could be used to measure the requisite academic content should prescriptive authority for psychologists be passed by legislative bodies.

After extensive advocacy by former APA president Patrick DeLeon (see chapter 13 for more information about him) and other dedicated psychologists, four military psychologists enrolled in a Psychopharmacology Demonstration Project developed by the U.S. Department of Defense in 1991. This program was originally funded by the U.S. Congress in 1988 with the actual program finally being developed in 1991 (Newman, Phelps, Sammons, Dunivin, & Cullen, 2000). By the time the project ended in 1997, ten psychologists had completed the program. Of those ten, four were in the Navy, three in the Army, and three in the Air Force. Although Congress ended the funding for the program, those psychologists who had already been trained were authorized to continue to prescribe in the military (Sammons & Brown, 1997). By 2002, seven of those ten psychologists remained in the military and continued to prescribe medication when needed as part of their psychology practice. They consider both biological and psychological components of their patients' problems and select the most effective interventions. Based on both government and external review, the program was found to be both feasible and cost-effective.

What about prescriptive authority for psychologists outside the military? In the American territory of Guam, the legislature passed a bill permitting psychologists to prescribe psychotropics under the supervision of a physician. Although the governor vetoed this bill, that veto was overridden. Psychologists in Guam received this right in January 1999 (Sammons, Gorny, Zinner, & Allen, 2000). Then, in February 2002, both the Senate and the House of Representatives of the New Mexico legislature passed a bill allowing psychologists prescriptive authority in consultation with a physician. After two years of physician supervision, if the supervising physician agrees, the psychologist's records will be given an independent peer review. If that peer review finds the psychologist's medication prescribing activity acceptable, the psychologist would be able to prescribe independently while maintaining a collaborative relationship with the physician. Thus, New Mexico became the first U.S. state to pass legislation granting psychologists prescriptive authority. The bill was then sent to the governor for signature. Governor Gary Johnson signed this bill into law in February 2002.

Two years later, Louisiana became the second state to pass such legislation. Governor Kathleen B. Blanco signed House Bill No. 1426 into law on May 6, 2004. This legislation used the term *medical psychologist* to refer to those psychologists who would be approved to prescribe medication. The "medical psychologist" title was inserted into current Louisiana laws as equivalent to the other prescribing professions: physician, surgeon, optometrist, and dentist. A medical psychologist was defined in this law as a licensed psychologist who had specialized training in psychopharmacology as well as passing a national proficiency examination specified by the psychology licensing board.

Although the APA endorsed the concept of prescriptive authority for psychologists, that position is not universally supported by American psychologists. An early article opposing prescriptive authority suggested that if psychologists have the right to prescribe psychotropic medication, the evolution of the profession would change considerably (DeNelsky, 1991). DeNelsky noted that without prescriptive authority, psychology was basically a behavioral field. If psychologists were given the ability to prescribe medication, the practice of psychology would become very much like a medical specialty rather than a behavioral specialty. An added concern was that in order for psychologists to be adequately trained to prescribe and continue to do their current forms of assessment and intervention, the length of training would need to be expanded significantly. This article also raised the issue of cost to the discipline if psychology actively pursued enabling legislation to be granted prescriptive authority. This cost would be both financial and personal. The author suggested that organized medicine would actively oppose such legislation. As the profession's relationship with organized medicine becomes strained, he noted that animosity might also impact physicians' reaction to psychology's requests for reimbursement for third-party payment, hospital privileges for psychologists, and other professional collaboration. Other psychologists questioned the statement that the majority of psychologists are supportive of psychologists seeking the right to prescribe (Moyer, 1995). Some of them raised questions about the entire identity of psychology as a profession if it moves to a pharmaceutical/medical model rather than its own philosophy of science. In a more recent article, George Albee (2005) argued against prescriptive authority because most mental disorders are not, in his view, diseases, but are caused by the damaging effects of poverty, inadequate parenting, poor schooling and limited access to mental health care. Like many professional debates, this one is likely to continue (Hayes, Walser, & Follette, 1995; Heiby, 1998). In an attempt to summarize the growing literature on this subject, Gutierrez and Silk (1998) integrated the psychological literature both for and against prescribing psychologists. They did not include the medical literature unless those articles were written by psychologists. They concluded that professional surveys have found the majority of psychologists support at least the option for psychologists to be able to prescribe. Their summary of previous articles suggested that the arguments against prescriptive privileges for psychologists fell within the categories of professional identity, motivation, practice issues, the interface of psychology with other professions, public interest issues, and training implications. Under public interest, they suggest that American society has become too reliant on using medication as a quick solution to personal problems. If those seeking help no longer have the option of a nonprescribing doctor for their emotional problems, they may become less willing to work on their problems. Despite the fact that two states now have legislation allowing properly trained psychologists to prescribe medication, this debate is likely to continue for a number of years.

In this chapter, we have covered many different topics. Because of the breadth of this subject, we were unable to provide as much depth on them as you may have liked. Some of these topics are also addressed in other ways in later chapters in this book.

Key Terms

A-B-A-B	cost-effectiveness	false negative	psychotherapy
achievement tests	double-blind experiment	false positive	rapport
analog study		intervention	test bias
aptitude tests	effectiveness research	meta-analysis	test fairness
assessment	efficacy research	neuropsychological assessment	transference
bariatric surgery	empathy	phrenology	treatment manual
base rates	empirically supported treatment (EST)	projective tests	unconditional positive regard
clinical significance		psychopharmacology	
congruence			

CHAPTER 4

Personality Theory

S ome of you may have taken a course in theories of personality and others may elect to take such a course before completing your undergraduate studies. A course in theories of personality is commonly offered in undergraduate psychology curricula. This course provides a foundation for the study of clinical psychology in graduate school. It is certainly beyond the scope of this book to provide an in-depth description of all the theories of personality that have been used by clinical psychologists. In this chapter, however, we will give you a general background about how psychologists have defined **personality** as well as a brief discussion of some personality theories to illustrate the field. This material will form part of the foundation for later chapters in this book about personality assessment and about psychotherapy. Students who wish to read more about personality theories than we present here are referred to one of the many available undergraduate textbooks (e.g., Allen, 2003; Engler, 2006; Frager & Fadiman, 2005; Hall, Lindzey, & Campbell, 1998; Schultz & Schultz, 2004).

Key Concepts

Let's start our discussion with what we mean by *personality*. There are numerous definitions of personality in the psychological literature. Some of these definitions arise from one of the many theories of personality that have been developed and others are more general. Because a psychologist's definition of personality is often linked with his or her theoretical orientation, it has been suggested that "no substantive definition of personality can be applied with any generality" (Hall, Lindzey, & Campbell, 1998, p. 9). An early attempt to categorize the existing definitions of personality divided them into either **biosocial** or *biophysical* definitions (Allport, 1937). The biosocial definitions of personality focus on the reaction of other people to the individual. These definitions are quite similar to the popular definitions of *personality* such as those you may have seen in magazines and newspapers at the supermarket. In other words, this definition refers to the public image of the person. We might also question whether these definitions imply that personality does not exist without the presence of others. The **biophysical theories** of personality focus on internal factors as being the most important ones for defining the term. In this case, personality exists without the presence of other people.

Using a biological approach to personality definition is not new. It may surprise you that in ancient Greece, Hippocrates, Galen, and other physician-philosophers presumed that personality differences were caused by biological factors. These early Greeks believed that bodily fluids, called **humors,** could cause both disease and disharmony when they were out of balance. Hippocrates' personality theory of the four humors was based on the classic four elements of nature: earth, wind, fire, and water. These four humors (blood, phlegm, black bile, and yellow bile) each correlated with the four elements and a particular temperament. For example, if you had too much phlegm relative to the other three humors you might be introverted, passive, and calm. Having too much blood led to being extroverted, easygoing, and sociable (Eysenck, 1970). It was therefore considered important to have a balance among these four elements if you wanted to have a healthy personality.

This idea of a relationship between physiology and personality persisted well into the twentieth century in both Europe and the United States. German psychiatrist Ernst Kretchmer assumed a correlation between body type and psychiatric illness. William Sheldon (1942) hypothesized that a person's physique was correlated with his or her personality. He coined the terms **endomorph, mesomorph,** and **ectomorph** to describe the basic body types of chubby, muscular, and thin. Based on his study of many Americans, especially college students, he correlated these body types with personality types called *temperaments.* For example, he found that mesomorphs would be adventurous, athletic, and competitive while the rounder endomorphs would be passive, lethargic, and sociable. Ectomorphs, on the other hand, would tend to be shy and studious. Although this may sound like a simple theory, he developed complex combinations of these body temperaments. He found that many people had mixed body types indicating that certain parts of their bodies were one type and other parts of the body were different. For example, a person might have rather muscular legs and yet have a thin upper body. His theory may no longer be popular, but think about the stereotypes we have that are related to these concepts.

Personality theories can also be subdivided into macro theories and micro theories (Engler, 2006). The macro theories are the ones that attempt to describe the entire person. They tend to be rather global in nature. These are the theories that are described in most traditional textbooks for undergraduate theories of personality courses. Micro theories of personality have a very narrow focus. They tend to be the result of research programs designed to study a specific aspect of personality such as outgoing or aggressive. These theories are more likely to appear in journal articles than in textbooks. We will include some of the specific definitions theorists have provided as we describe their theories.

In recent years, there has been a tendency to try to develop a taxonomy of personality traits. The attempt to develop such a modern taxonomy started with the work of Allport and his colleagues (Allport & Odbert, 1936), who used an unabridged dictionary to search for terms that seemed to describe personality traits. Over time, they were able to narrow their list to about forty-five hundred personality traits. Cattell (1943) applied factor analytic procedures to lists of personality traits and was able to reduce his list to thirty-five bipolar clusters of traits. The personality theories of Allport and Cattell are covered in detail in most of the textbooks we listed earlier. Their work formed a foundation for the development of a five-factor model (McCrae, 1992), which is currently receiving much attention in the personality research literature. Although McCrae and his colleagues agree that there may be more than five major personality traits, they take the position that an adequate description of personality requires at least these five factors. These factors are labeled extraversion (sometimes called surgency), agreeableness, conscientiousness, neuroticism, and openness to experience. According to this theory these five factors, also called basic tendencies, are biologically based. They have been found to be stable over time. These factors have been assessed in both Western and non-Western cultures. Some research has supported the concept that these factors are found across cultures although not necessarily in the same strength (McCrae & Costa, 1997). Questions remain, however, about the real differences between these groups and Western culture (Triandis & Suh, 2002), suggesting that considerable work will be needed before the cross-cultural validity of this theory is established. Career counselors use this personality model when helping people determine those occupations in which they may feel most gratified. The NEO Personality Inventory (Costa & McCrae, 1992), a test based on this model, is discussed in chapter 7 on personality assessment. This is just one example of the relationship between personality theory and clinical practice.

Psychologists study personality using one of two major approaches. The more common approach is the **nomothetic approach.** A common practice among clinical researchers is to study large groups of individuals with a goal of determining regularities in their behavior. Much of the published research on personality uses this approach. For example, one of Dr. Matthews' students conducted research for her senior thesis on the relationship between parental pressure, anxiety, and depression in ethnic minority college students. Issues of confidentiality were minimized because she was using group data. When a psychologist uses an in-depth case history to understand how various facets of a person's life have influenced that person's personality, the approach being used is the **idiographic approach.** Consider a clinical psychologist who is treating a thirty-year-old woman for obsessive-compulsive disorder. Although she had taken a patient history in their early work, she later decided to gather more in-depth material about her patient to better understand the woman's current symptoms and guide her treatment protocol accordingly. She got signed permission from her patient to conduct extensive interviews with the patient's parents, her older sister, and her husband. This psychologist is using the idiographic approach to personality evaluation. If she finds unique information that might enlighten colleagues who are treating similar patients she will be limited, however, in her ability to share it because of confidentiality. The group data generated in nomothetic evaluations do not generally pose this problem. Because issues of confidentiality may limit the details a psychologist includes in a case study, some personality researchers have turned to the evaluation of the life of historical figures when doing idiographic analyses. Often there is a vast amount of public information available about such prominent figures. This material can then be combined with information about the time when that person lived and psychological theory. The goal of such research is to better understand basic factors that influence the human experience.

Freud's Theory

Most psychologists today suggest that Freud's psychoanalytic theory was one of the earliest of the *modern* attempts to describe personality. His theory continued to evolve throughout his career and was still changing at the time of his death in 1939. Others have modified many of his ideas, resulting in a range of theories based on Freud's work. His theory is very complex. We refer you to the general theory texts for a more complete description of

Sigmund Freud
Bettman/Corbis © Austrian Archives/Corbis.

his theory. We illustrate his theory by briefly discussing Freud's ideas about the structure of the personality and the developmental stages through which it grows.

Personality Structure

According to Freud, the personality consists of three major systems he named the **id,** the **ego,** and the **superego.** The id can be considered the biological side of the personality, the ego represents the psychological side of the personality, and the superego represents the contribution of society to personality development (Allen, 2003). Although Freud was trained as a physician, he believed that the human personality was more than a biological process. These personality parts develop during childhood, and the way each part develops will have a major impact on adult personality patterns. These parts of the personality are not specific physical locations like our heart or our lungs. They are processes that organize our mental world. To do this, they must interact in a dynamic way. Freud wrote extensively about this interaction.

At birth all psychological energy is contained in the id. The other two personality components will develop from the id. The major goal of our id is to try to satisfy our primitive biological needs. How does it accomplish this goal? Freud suggested that the governing process of the id is the **pleasure principle.** When we have a need, the id's goal is to satisfy that need as quickly as possible. In other words, the main goal is to seek pleasure and to avoid pain. The id operates unconsciously through the use of inborn reflexes.

Because we live in a world with others, we must often modify our quest for need satisfaction. Immediate gratification is not always possible in the real world. The id therefore diverts some of its energy to the second structure of the personality, the ego. Freud said the ego had access to consciousness. Whereas the id operates based on the pleasure principle, the ego operates using the **reality principle.** The development of the ego allows us to delay gratification of our needs until we find an appropriate source of that gratification. For example, if you have a class with a professor who does not allow eating and drinking in the classroom, you may need to delay gratification of your need for food or beverage until after the class has ended for that day. If you try to eat that snack you have in your book bag, you may have negative consequences from the professor. Freud hypothesized that your ego allowed you to wait for this satisfaction. In other words, the ego is the part of our personality that allows our needs to be met without the potential of harmful consequences to us. The ego serves as our tie to the realities of the world in which we live.

Freud wrote less about the ego than the other two parts of the personality. It was only near the time of his death that he began to consider the ego more carefully. His daughter Anna Freud and others known as *ego psychologists* provided a more complete description of the ego's functions (e.g., Freud, 1936; Loevenger, 1976). This work illustrates a common pattern of theory development. One theorist starts the work and then others expand on the original material.

With further experience, we develop the third part of our personality structure, the superego. The superego is the part of our personality that has incorporated the norms and standards of our society. The superego functions using the *morality* principle. As the superego continues to develop, it also differentiates types of values. Thus, it has two major parts: the *conscience* and the *ego ideal.* The conscience is that part of our superego that punishes us when we have done something that is not consistent with our personal value system. Its role is to suppress many of the id's impulses and direct them in socially acceptable ways. At times, however, the person's goals may need to be modified by the ego because the superego operates only on moral grounds and reality also needs to be considered. The other major part of the superego is the **ego ideal.** This part is generally an internal picture of our idealized image of our parents. The ego ideal is the component of our personality that lets us feel proud of something we have done.

Stages of Psychosexual Development

Freud suggested that our personality develops sequentially in stages. He suggested that at each stage there is a different focus for our gratification. Because he viewed our needs as having a strong sexual component, he called these the stages of **psychosexual develop- ment.** These stages occur in the same order for each of us. We will briefly describe how these stages influence personality development.

At birth we are in the **oral stage** of psychosexual development. This stage lasts for about the first year of our life. Our psychological energy is totally located in our id dur- ing this stage. We tend to be highly narcissistic and do not consider reality when seeking gratification of our needs. Freud defined **libido** as the energy that drives the personal- ity. He believed that the focus of both our pleasure and potential for conflict was located in the region of our mouth at this stage of psychosexual development. Thus, an impor- tant activity related to personality development is the feeding process. Popular books for parents that focus on the importance of such factors as the method of feeding your new baby—breast-feeding versus bottle-feeding—for personality development may be using one of Freud's concepts. Regardless of the source of the nourishment, Freud suggests that if early feeding is unpleasant the person may become *fixated* at this developmental period.

Fixation means that although the person continues to grow physically and intellectu- ally, emotionally the person is stuck in this developmental period. Because satisfaction was frustrated, the person invests a certain amount of libidinal energy at this stage. This energy will therefore not be available for later developmental tasks. As an adult, this person will have certain distinct characteristics that tend to define his or her personality. These char- acteristics are most obvious to others when the person is faced with a stressful situation. Two common adult personality patterns related to fixation at the oral stage are the oral- receptive personality and the oral-aggressive personality. The oral-receptive personality type is fixated in the early months of life. This adult tends to be highly dependent on oth- ers. Dependency can be expressed in many different ways. The person also likes to "take in" many things. For some people, this need is translated to food and the person has prob- lems with obesity. Others tend to accept everything they are told and become extremely gullible adults. People who become fixated later in the oral stage, after the eruption of teeth, develop a different personality type. In this case they may be described as being oral- aggressive. As adults, they emphasize chewing and biting. For some people, this means that they are sarcastic, argumentative adults. They have transformed their aggressive needs to a verbal level. Others who are fixated at this period like to overindulge in the types of food they can chew. For example, these people would prefer to have a steak for din- ner rather than pasta. If they smoke, they will prefer a pipe to cigarettes because it fulfills their aggressive needs better. These interests provide the foundation for the development of many of their adult interests.

Freud's second stage is the **anal stage.** This stage begins after the first year of life and extends to about age three. The focus of both pleasure and potential for conflict is the anus. Toilet-training issues thus become extremely important for later personality development. Children who learn self-control easily at this period of development are likely to have appropriate levels of self-control as adults. When toilet-training is either too harsh or too permissive, however, the result may be the development of specific personality traits and values that impact the person's entire development. Once again, Freud emphasized a topic that continues to be popular in books for parents. Two possible adult personality types may develop from fixation at this period. They are called anal-retentive and anal-expulsive.

According to Freud, the issue for the child is power. During the anal stage, the parents want the child to use the toilet and the child must decide whether to do what the parents want or to just satisfy her or his own needs and go when and where the urge occurs. By defying their parents, the child is relieving anal tension but not learning to delay gratification to please others. Freud suggested that if the parents are very strict about toilet-training, the child may learn to withhold the expulsion of feces to the point of constipation. This type of child may become an anal-retentive personality type. The concept of withholding will be translated into other life areas for the adult. This person will save for the future in many areas of life, including money and need gratification, just as the child learned to save feces until just the right time. As an adult, this person is likely to be described as very neat and orderly in addition to being both stubborn and stingy.

What about the child whose parents were highly permissive during toilet-training or basically provided no training? This child may later develop an anal-expulsive type of personality. As adults, these individuals do not appreciate others telling them what to do. When restrictions are placed on them, they tend to do whatever they want to do just as they defecated wherever they chose as young children. Friends of these adults often describe them as being sloppy. According to Freud, many anal expulsives exhibit problems with emotional control as adults and therefore may have temper tantrums, behave aggressively toward people who offend them, and may even develop sadistic tendencies. Since toilet-training involves dealing with the rules of the real world, some of the child's psychological energy is diverted from the id to the newly developed ego. By the time the child has completed these first two stages of psychosexual development, around the age of three, the ego should be fairly well developed.

The third stage of psychosexual development is the **phallic stage.** This stage typically starts around the age of three and lasts until about age five or six. The focus of both pleasure and potential conflict is the genitals. Freud wrote extensively about the importance of the phallic stage in terms of adult personality development. He believed that children experienced their primary pleasure at this time through masturbation. Many adults have difficulty accepting Freud's concept about childhood sexuality, but it has had a major impact on the field of personality theory. It was not only the lay public who disagreed with Freud about childhood sexuality. Other personality theorists have taken very different positions about this developmental period.

According to Freud, male children experience erections at this age and find this experience pleasurable. Boys begin to show great interest in the genital area and also become aware that they have a penis and that girls do not have one. Because the penis becomes so important, boys also develop concerns that since girls do not have a penis perhaps something will happen to their penis as well. Freud called these fears *castration anxiety.* These fears become heightened as boys develop possessive love feelings for their mothers. They begin to view their fathers as rivals for their mother's love and affection. Freud called these feelings the **Oedipus complex.** This name comes from a play by the Greek dramatist Sophocles in which the hero, Oedipus, does not actually know his parents. Oedipus kills his father and later marries his mother. When he realizes both of these facts, he becomes so distressed that he gouges out his eyes.

Although the average person does not have such an extreme reaction to early feelings of sexual attraction, Freud felt that each male child goes through a tense and dramatic psychological struggle during the phallic stage. Over time, boys increase their desires for their mother as well as develop a combination of hatred and fear of their fathers. The father is not only a rival for their mother but is also much more powerful than they are. These boys come to fear that their fathers will punish them for their passionate desires for their mother and take away their prized organ, the penis. This fear increases their castration anxiety that began when they realized girls did not have penises. During this developmental period the boy learns to deal with his fears by repressing his sexual feelings toward his mother and increasing his identification with his father. By doing so, he can vicariously share his mother with his father and also decrease his fear that his father will castrate him. His feelings for his mother resolve into a tender affection. This resolution of the Oedipus complex also allows the boy to fully develop his superego. After all, he has appropriately quelled any desire he had for a sexual relationship with his mother. At this time, the boy adopts the value system he has learned from his parents as well as from society.

What happens to girls at this developmental period? Freud devoted less attention to female development than to male development. He ultimately concluded that girls generally resolve their conflicts from the phallic stage less completely than boys do. He believed that when girls realize they did not get a penis, they develop **penis envy.** A girl blames her mother for this lack of a penis because her mother gave birth to her. She also knows that her mother does not have a penis. Although her mother was her original love object based on her role as primary caregiver, her penis envy leads her to turn her love to her father. She desires to have a child with him so that she can have a penis. As a temporary measure, she will also masturbate with her clitoris, which she views as a stunted penis. Because the desire to have a child with her father cannot be fulfilled, Freud suggested that girls' superegos were not typically as adequate as those of boys. Over time, as the girl realizes that her attachment to her father is futile, she will begin to identify with her mother. Through this identification she can at least share her father with her mother. Although the girl gets some resolution of her conflict at this developmental period, Freud suggested that girls never fully resolve their Oedipal conflict until they have had a child of their own, especially a son. By giving birth to a son, this woman has now produced a person with a penis. She still does not have one of her own but has the satisfaction of having given birth to someone who does have one.

These first three stages of psychosexual development are collectively known as the **pregenital stages.** During these first three stages of development, the person's sexual gratification is basically from stimulation of one's own body. These stages are therefore considered basically narcissistic in nature. Freud wrote that what happens to the child during the pregenital stages of psychosexual development forms the most important component of adult personality development. By the end of the phallic stage, the basic ingredients of the adult personality are in place. The id, ego, and superego have been formed. Thus, about the time the child begins school in Western society, the basic personality of the individual has been established. From this description you can see the differential importance of family and society from a Freudian perspective on personality development. Before the child is separated from family influence for hours at a time in school the basic personality structure is in place.

Because so much happens to influence personality development in the first five to six years of a person's life, Freud believed it was necessary to have a time for the body and mind to develop and catch up with the internal, or psychological, development. He therefore suggested that a **latency stage** occurs from the end of the phallic stage at about the age of six to the onset of puberty. During this stage, the child learns the social and cognitive skills that will be needed for functioning in society. Sexual tension still exists in this developmental stage. During the latency stage of psychosexual development sexual tension is seen in such activity as the "dirty jokes" children tell.

The final stage of psychosexual development is the **genital stage.** This stage starts with the onset of puberty. Although there is conflict during the genital stage, Freud believed it was less severe than during the pregenital period. If the person has not become fixated at one of the earlier stages, a normal life may occur. A normal person adjusts to both love and work. To do this, the person must be secure in his or her identity as well as being responsible and motivated. Both boys and girls are aware of their sexual identities and needs. They begin to address these needs through the dating process and eventually marry and procreate. They also develop the ability to put the needs of others ahead of their own needs. This is quite different from the narcissism of the pregenital stages. They identify a form of work in which they are happy and can help others. This vocational planning guides their educational path. By the end of adolescence, the individual has moved from the infant who was narcissistic to a reality-oriented adult. This adult has transferred sexual tension and desire from a parent of the opposite sex to an opposite-sex peer.

Implications for Clinical Psychologists

Freud developed many techniques for therapists to use in order to help their patients understand the internal struggles that result from developmental issues. Regardless of the specific struggle, people are likely to seek therapy when their ego is weak and therefore they are unable to cope effectively with the demands of the reality of their lives. Freud said that mild emotional problems, historically called neuroses and now called anxiety disorders, involved the use of ineffective methods for coping with typical problems of living. More severe emotional problems, historically and currently called psychoses, involved ineffective methods of coping with people. Psychotic people are investing considerable psychic energy trying to control their instinctual impulses. Over time, they have begun to rely on various defense mechanisms to cope with life. As more and more energy is required to control these impulses, the person's level of functioning becomes less and less effective. Through therapy, unconscious material is brought to the surface and the ego is strengthened. This stronger ego will allow the person to better meet life's challenges and a more constructive form of growth can occur. They will also learn to develop an energy balance among their id, ego, and superego so that they are fulfilled in a socially acceptable way.

Thus, what is important for the therapist is not necessarily the specific reason the person stated for coming to see the psychologist, or what we call the presenting problem, but rather the imbalance of power among the personality structures. Some of you may be wondering if Freud's ideas are still considered important by clinical psychologists. Although not all clinical psychologists use his theory, it is definitely alive and functioning in the twenty-first century in both research and clinical practice (Westen, 1998).

Jung's Theory

Carl Jung (pronounced *Yung*), a Swiss psychiatrist who lived from 1875 to 1961, was a colleague of Freud who incorporated many of Freud's ideas into his theory of personality. Where Freud's theory is often called a psychoanalytic theory, Jung's tends to be called an

Carl G. Jung
Bettmann/Corbis © Austrian Archives/Corbis.

analytical theory. He also incorporated considerable information from both religion and mythology into his theory, making it somewhat unique among the major theories of personality. Some writers have referred to this theory as *mystic* because of his ideas about the connectedness between peoples' minds as well as between the minds of living people and those who are not currently living (Allen, 2003). We are including Jung's theory because it is quite different from other personality theories and because the twenty-first century's attention to diversity includes issues of religion. Jung's theory is one of the early personality theories to have this religious component.

Personality Structure

Jung described the personality structure as a complex system composed of a number of interacting systems. Among the important parts of the personality in Jung's system are the *ego,* the *personal unconscious,* and the *collective unconscious.*

The **ego** is the center of our consciousness but is not synonymous with consciousness (Jung, 1959). Within Jung's system, consciousness has several different components. The ego is the part of our personality that selects those perceptions from among many perceptions we have stored and then allows this material to enter our conscious mind. Thus, it has access not only to what is currently happening but also to our thoughts and memories. Our ego is responsible for our feeling of identity. Jung suggested that our ego develops around the age of four. Think about the similarities and differences between Jung's and Freud's concept of the ego.

The **personal unconscious** is composed of thoughts and feelings of which we are not currently aware. Some of these thoughts and feelings are just not important at the moment, while others have been actively repressed because of their potential to make us feel uncomfortable. These thoughts, however, can be brought to consciousness under the right circumstances. A clinical psychologist who is basing his or her work on Jung's theory would try to help the patient access material from the personal unconscious to facilitate the person's understanding of the current life situation. Each of us has different life experiences. Therefore, our personal unconsciousness is unique.

Because we have so many experiences in our lives, we need to have a system for organizing these experiences. They are grouped into associated concepts called *complexes.* As we have new experiences they can then be added to existing complexes and interpreted based on our previous experiences. Some of our complexes are conscious and others are not. Some of our complexes are so strong that they seem to dominate what others view as our *personality.* In a sense, a complex is almost like a personality all by itself because of its ability to take over our life. For example, Napoleon is often described as having had a power complex. This means that he was driven by internal forces to achieve power. According to Jung, Napoleon was dominated by this power complex and it forced him to engage in many aggressive behaviors to reach his goal of attaining power. Because of his power complex, he found it difficult to disengage from any situation in which his ability to achieve power might be questioned. For example, even when his combat experience might have suggested withdrawal from a particular battle, his need for power would dictate that he continue to fight.

The **collective unconscious** is found much deeper in the psyche than the ego and the personal unconscious. It is not unique. All humans have basically the same collective unconscious, although the specific ways they express it vary by culture and personal history. Some authors have suggested that the collective unconscious is the most controversial part of Jung's theory (Hall, Lindzey, & Campbell, 1998). The collective unconscious is composed of latent memory traces. These memories come from our ancestors. When Jung writes about ancestral memories, he refers not only to our specific ancestors but also to both human history and our prehuman ancestors. This part of Jung's theory suggests his agreement with the concept that humans evolved from other species. These memories are not representations like those in the personal unconscious. They are more like predispositions that lead to a selective interpretation of our world. The collective unconscious includes both instincts and archetypes. Jung found support for his idea of a collective unconscious in people's dreams, mythology, and data from cross-cultural studies.

Archetypes are an important facet of our collective unconscious. An archetype is a universal thought form. This universality is based on the common evolution of humanity as well as our common brain structure. An archetype is a predisposition to respond to the world in a certain way. Archetypes contain considerable emotion and are exclusively based on heredity. Let's consider a general example of this concept. Jung suggested that regardless of when or where you live, you inherited a tendency to handle extreme stress by turning to an all-powerful being. The name you give that being will vary, but the concept crosses history and culture. Suppose you call your all-powerful being God. Jung suggested that you do not need to try to prove the existence of God because God is an archetype. By accepting this archetype as unknowable, you are able to move toward a balanced psyche. Jung believed that people who do not acknowledge the presence of such an all-powerful being will have personal problems because they cannot deal with the parts of their world that are not rational. He firmly believed there are parts of our world that are not rational. It is tempting to suggest that archetypes are unique to Jung's theory because he wrote so extensively about them. Freud, however, suggested the concept of a *racial unconscious* that is quite similar to Jung's archetypes. He did not, however, expand on this idea to the degree that Jung did.

Not all of our archetypes are equally developed. Those that are better developed exert a stronger influence on our behavior than those that are less well developed. Archetypes can also combine and interact to allow us to use more than one concept to understand our world. Jung suggested that we have many different archetypes in our psyches. Some of these archetypes have become so well developed across people that Jung treated them almost as separate systems within the personality. In order to understand others, we must understand these well-developed archetypes.

One well-developed archetype is the **persona.** The persona is the mask or social facade we wear in society. It is our public personality. This archetype is universal because we all live in a world with other people. In some ways, it is similar to Freud's concept of superego. Our persona helps us keep our evil side under control as well as behave as society expects. A problem arises, however, when we become so identified with our social façade that we lose track of our true nature. This person has lost touch with the personal and collective unconscious. In this case, the person becomes only a reflection of society and his or her personality seems flat.

Another well-developed archetype is the **shadow.** This archetype represents our animal instincts. It is those shameful desires and motives that we do not want to admit we have. It is based on our evolution from lower life forms. Sometimes we try to deal with our shadow by projecting it onto others. For example, when we use negative terms to refer to people from a particular racial or religious group, we are actually failing to accept the fact that we possess those negative traits. Like other aspects of our personality, the shadow is not totally negative. It provides depth to our personality, and by acknowledging its existence we become more interesting and vital people. The shadow has some characteristics in common with Freud's concept of the id. The shadow is related to both the personal unconscious and the collective unconscious. From the personal unconscious, the shadow includes all of our experiences that we have rejected or repressed based on our morals. Our universal concepts of evil come from our collective unconscious. For example, regardless of the name given to it, Jung said that the devil concept is included in our collective unconscious.

A final archetype we will describe to illustrate this part of Jung's theory is **anima** and **animus.** This archetype is related to Jung's belief that we all have a bisexual nature. Jung noted that regardless of your biological sex, you secrete both male and female hormones. From a psychological perspective, he said we each have both feminine and masculine qualities. Jung's *anima* is the feminine archetype in men and the *animus* is the masculine archetype in women. As with all of Jung's archetypes, the anima and animus have the potential to be either constructive or destructive. The basis for these archetypes is in our sex chromosomes and sex glands. These archetypes have developed based on men and women living together. Jung said that this historical experience has led to a feminization of man and a masculinization of women. Some of Jung's descriptions of these archetypes sound like cultural stereotypes of men and women. The overall concept, however, is much broader than these descriptions. Our anima and animus assist us in understanding those of the other sex. This understanding facilitates the ability to marry, procreate, and raise a family. Problems arise when we depend totally on our archetype to the exclusion of the uniqueness of the individual to whom we are applying this knowledge. In such a case we may be disappointed by that person or develop misunderstandings in the relationship. It is this misuse of our archetypes that can form a basis for marital dysfunction.

Implications for Clinical Psychologists

Jungian therapists help their patients explore their inner lives based on Jung's theory of personality. Patients explore the parts of their unconscious that are either overdeveloped or underdeveloped. As a result of participating in therapy, these individuals are able to broaden their personality and improve their interpersonal interactions. Therapy from this perspective also includes developing a spiritual attitude toward a person's existence. This spiritual focus is more obvious in Jung's theory than in many others.

Jung (1954) said that psychotherapy includes the four key stages of confession, elucidation, education, and transformation. By confessing, the patient is acknowledging personal weaknesses to the psychologist. This starts the healing process. Elucidation permits the patient to reach an understanding of his or her ties to all of humanity and its ancestry. Education is when the patient is able to take this knowledge and incorporate it into new ways to fit more comfortably with the current life circumstances. Through continued work with the therapist, the patient is able to transform himself or herself in a way that is not merely adapting to the current society but rather moving toward fulfillment of the self. The patient will now be able to adapt to changing situations in life and understand when they can be controlled and when they cannot. This understanding will permit a healthier level of functioning. Thus, Jung used his personality theory to give us an outline for the therapeutic process. Although some authors suggest that Jung's theory has not had a major impact on Western psychology, we included it not only because it is quite different from other theories but also because of its potential for future research with the growing interest in cross-cultural factors. In some ways, Jung's writings are more compatible with Eastern cultures than with Western cultures.

Rogers' Theory

To provide a somewhat different view of personality, we will give you a brief overview of Rogers' theory. Carl R. Rogers, who lived from 1902 to 1987, identified with the humanistic movement within psychology. This approach grew in reaction to what some perceived as the rather pessimistic view of personality presented by Freud. The theories of Freud, Jung, and Rogers have also led to different forms of psychotherapy that continue

Carl R. Rogers
Carl R. Rogers Collection, Humanistic Psychology Archives Mss 32, Department of Special Collections, Davidson Library, University of California, Santa Barbara.

to be popular among clinical psychologists today. Consider the fact that between January 1, 1987, and September 6, 2004, 141 books, 174 book chapters, and 462 journal articles related to Rogers' work were published (Kirschenbaum & Jourdan, 2005). Most of these publications described new theories, research, or applications based on Rogers' work rather than merely citing him as a historical source. Rogers' death has certainly not led to his theory disappearing from the psychological literature.

Personality Structure

Rogers did not spend the amount of energy Freud or Jung did describing the structure of personality. He did not suggest any specific stages of personality development. He was more interested in the process of change and growth. He tried to identify the conditions that would either facilitate or hinder such growth. Within this process, he said that although genetics sets some foundation for our growth, the environment strongly influences the direction in which it occurs.

There are two constructs that are important foundation terms for Rogers' theory. They are the *organism* and the *self*. We will briefly discuss these terms before turning our attention to his concepts of personality development.

The organism is the center of everything that is available to awareness at any given time. It is the person as a whole. Rogers emphasized the uniqueness of individuals. Therefore, what is available to awareness is also unique. He called this unique characteristic the person's field of experience, or **phenomenal field.** Rogers' theory suggests that how we behave in any situation is dependent upon our phenomenal field rather than upon the stimulating conditions. In other words, how we react will be based on our internal definition of reality rather than on the external reality as viewed by others. Rogers believed that we use both conscious and unconscious information to decide how to react.

Over time, part of our phenomenal field becomes better organized. He called this organized part of the phenomenal field the *self* (Rogers, 1959). The self is a sense of who you are. The term *self* is used in many personality theories and has different definitions. It is important to remember that the self in Rogers' theory is an individual's self-view and not necessarily how others may see that person. It is "both a filter that selects the aspects of the outside world that the individual perceives and, simultaneously, an instrument that determines how the individual interprets and responds to that input" (Lakin, 1998). While the organism is what some call the *real self,* the self is that person's perception of himself or herself. When we have experiences that do not fit with our view of ourselves, we tend to distort them or deny their existence. Rogers said we do this because we have a need for congruence between the self and the organism. When there is congruence between the self and the organism, we tend to describe the person as being adjusted and mature. In cases where there is incongruence between the organism and the self, that person is likely to be described as being anxious or exhibiting behaviors that may be considered abnormal. Rogers did not describe the self as a concrete part of us. It is not an invisible person within us controlling our behavior. Instead, it is an organized set of perceptions that is available for our use when needed. Rogers also said we have an *ideal self.* This term describes the person we would like to be. Our feelings of worth, or the way we value ourselves, is related to our pursuit of our ideal self.

What kind of conditions lead to a sense of incongruence? This approach emphasizes external, interpersonal conditions that either facilitate or interfere with growth. A term often associated with Rogers is **unconditional positive regard.** Many people think of this term as it relates to psychotherapy. Rogers also used this term, however, in relationship to normal personality development. He believed that one of the unique characteristics of humans is that we have needs that can only be satisfied in positive relationships with other people. We need to feel that we make a difference in the lives of other people as well as to receive such positive responses from them as acceptance and warmth. In order for this to happen, we need to feel valued for the person we are and not some image the other person may have of us. Rogers was not suggesting that unconditional positive regard means that the other person approves each thing we do. We learn that others value *us* as a person separate from any of our specific actions. When we have this type of relationship with another person, we are comfortable and able to grow.

Accurate empathy is another interpersonal condition that contributes to the growth of a healthy personality. If we are going to have a sense of congruence between how we see ourselves and how others see us, important others in our environment must have the ability to understand not only our overt behavior but also our internal world. They are able to see the world the way we do. They do not have to agree with each of our ideas but they are capable of seeing situations through our eyes.

Congruence in our relations with others is the third major condition required for growth. We need to have genuine relationships with significant others. These important people in our lives must have a mutually comfortable relationship with us. In order to be mutually comfortable, we must each be able to be who we actually are at that time rather than who that person would like us to be.

A person who is able to grow in a healthy manner moves toward becoming a **fully functioning person.** This is someone who demonstrates five general characteristics (Rogers, 1961). First, he or she is open to experience. Unlike the incongruent person, the fully functioning person is able to acknowledge the range of his or her feelings. These feelings go from those society views as positive through those viewed as negative. He or she does not need to either deny or distort these feelings but rather experiences them as part of himself or herself. Second, a fully functioning person can be described as demonstrating existential living. He or she lives in the present situation and does not try to apply preconceived ideas about how a particular situation should flow but rather takes what comes. To do this, the person must be flexible. Third, this person demonstrates organismic trust. By this Rogers meant that fully functioning people do what *feels* right to them rather than what society would necessarily expect them to do. He did not mean that fully functioning people are always correct in the choices they make. He did, however, believe they make their own choices and have the ability to change those choices when the outcome is not sufficiently satisfying. Fourth, Rogers felt that fully functioning people are creative. He used the term *creative* very broadly to indicate that the person is open to new experiences and makes unique adjustments in order to benefit from these experiences. The fully functioning person trusts his or her own judgment and actively seeks ways to use it. Finally, they lead rich lives. Rogers did not imply that fully functioning people always have great wealth, although they may have it. Rather, he meant that their lives are exciting and meaningful.

Later in his career (Rogers, 1977), Rogers expanded his ideas about fully functioning people. We are using this information to illustrate one of the hallmarks of Rogers' personality theory—it was a theory that evolved throughout his life. He identified a small minority of people he called *emerging persons*. Although these people are small in number, they have a great influence on the society in which they live as well as on the future of humanity. Emerging persons are generally people who have moved in a very different direction from their roots. This category of people included corporate leaders who left their positions to lead a simple life and persons in minority positions in their culture who have taken an assertive position to create a more positive life.

He described emerging persons as having five common traits. First, they are open and honest. These are people who have resisted the structure of bureaucracy and focused on the needs of individual people. Second, they do not care about material things. Although they may have had great wealth in their past and lived an expensive lifestyle, they no longer do so. They prefer relating to others in more informal and equal ways. Third, they are caring people. Although they tend to distrust people in the helping professions, such as psychologists, they eagerly assist others on a volunteer basis. They refrain from telling these people how to live their lives but rather choose to just be there for them in a supportive and understanding way. Fourth, they tend to distrust science and technology. Their focus is on feelings rather than science as a basis for decision-making. Finally, they trust their own experience rather than external reality such as the law. When they believe a law is unjust, they will disobey it. They do not expect to be treated differently from others who disobey laws and therefore accept the consequences of this disobedience.

Implications for Clinical Psychologists

In addition to his theory of personality development, Rogers also developed a theory of psychotherapy. A major component of this theory is a focus on the relationship between the psychologist and the patient. Rogers suggested that without a positive relationship between the therapist and patient there will be no positive growth. The conditions required for this positive relationship are the ones he identified for congruence to occur outside the therapeutic setting. The therapist must be congruent, show empathic understanding of the patient, and demonstrate unconditional positive regard for the patient (Rogers & Stevens, 1967). The one clinical exception Rogers noted to these personal characteristics is when working with schizophrenic patients. He found that when dealing with grossly psychotic patients, the therapist may be more effective when showing some conditional positive regard. Although it is important for psychologists to value the person, they do not accept truly odd behavior. Because Rogers believed that we all have the personal ability to grow and change, he centered his attention on the facilitative conditions rather than on techniques. These conditions allow people to become what they actually are rather than what they have become because of the expectations of others. Under these conditions, patients will be able to express feelings they have about themselves and their lives. They can then integrate and reorganize their experiences more completely. In other words, they develop a congruence between the organism and the self. Through their relationship with the therapist, their self-concept will become increasingly congruent with their life experiences. Thus they can move toward their ideal self. Rogers did not want therapy to be just another situation in which the person develops in a way that is dictated by others, in this case the therapist.

Skinner's Theory

Most psychology students are familiar with the name B(urrhus) F(rederick) Skinner, who lived from 1904 until 1990. Considering Skinner's work as a personality theory, however, is perhaps a new view of his contributions. Although it is doubtful that Skinner would have considered himself a personality theorist, most general theories of personality texts have a chapter on Skinner's work, and therefore we decided to include him here to illustrate the behavioral approach to personality theory.

B. F. Skinner
Archives of the History of American Psychology, The University of Akron.

Personality Structure

Skinner approached the study of personality development from the perspective of trying to determine how we learn those behaviors that allow us to survive and grow in our world. From this perspective, personality can best be understood by studying the interactions of that person with the environment. During our lives, we learn to discriminate between those situations that tend to lead to pleasing outcomes for us and those situations that do not have pleasing outcomes.

This learning starts in infancy. According to Skinner, the person is under the stimulus control of his or her environment. Initially we are reinforced for those behaviors that allow us to take care of ourselves, such as dressing ourselves and using the bathroom at appropriate times. When we were first learning these behaviors, our parents and significant adults in our world probably rewarded us with praise or even something tangible immediately after successes or even approximations of success. As we continued to be successful, the reinforcement was probably delayed until we no longer needed that external reinforcement to engage in the desired behavior. Successful behavior was now its own reward. We even learned some of our behaviors by imitating what others did. Skinner believed that this type of learning occurs, however, only in cases in which the observed behavior has been reinforced many times (Skinner, 1990). Regardless of whether the behavior was directly reinforced or learned by imitation, over time we also learn to generalize our behavior to new situations.

One personality theory textbook described Skinner's theory of personality as an operant reinforcement theory (Hall, Lindzey, & Campbell, 1998). We will use their perspective here. Skinner noted that simple skills are learned first and then more complex skills are learned based on these simple ones. This learning is based on the reinforcement available in the environment. A reinforcer is anything that increases the likelihood that a response will reoccur in the future. Skinner does not mean, however, that we passively move through life waiting to see what will be reinforced. As we develop, we select environmental variables that are most likely to lead to need satisfaction. Thus, based on our past experience we make specific life choices.

Although Skinner's writings are often discussed as being significantly different from Freud's, Skinner also believed that Freud had made a major contribution to our understanding of personality development. Skinner suggested that we translate such concepts as ego defense mechanisms into behavioral terms so that we can study them scientifically. For Skinner, ego defense mechanisms were specific ways a person has learned to avoid or escape punishment. He did not automatically reject these concepts because they had not been studied from an operant perspective.

One of the key concepts in Skinner's theory for our consideration is **schedules of reinforcement,** or how often a reinforcer is applied to a behavior. Skinnerians use this term to explain the changes that take place in our personality over time as a function of reinforcers being applied to behaviors. This concept allows us to understand how some behaviors are acquired while others are extinguished. We will briefly review his ideas for you.

One possible schedule is *continuous reinforcement.* This means that each time we demonstrate a particular behavior we are reinforced. This type of schedule tends to produce a high rate of response. It is one thing, however, to demonstrate this schedule in the laboratory and quite another thing to do so in real life. There are few behaviors in our lives that will be reinforced each time we exhibit them. Consider the infant who is immediately picked up each time it cries. This infant is not likely to learn to function in a world where we do not get such immediate attention to our needs. Therefore, behavior like this is also likely to be lost, or extinguished, when this infant must deal with others.

The more typical schedules of reinforcement we find in our lives are *intermittent reinforcement.* This means that sometimes we are reinforced and sometimes we are not. Some intermittent schedules of reinforcement are based on time and are called *interval reinforcement,* while others are based on the absolute number of responses and are called *ratio reinforcement.* Behavior learned on intermittent reinforcement schedules is more resistant to extinction than behavior that is learned on a continuous schedule. Translated into personality terms, children who are raised on continuous reinforcement do not tend to be as hard-working or persistent as those who are raised on intermittent schedules of reinforcement because their behavior is much easier to extinguish when they are not reinforced.

Skinner was also interested in how we act on our environment to change it in order to increase the probability of reinforcement. He found that there are many different ways we do this (Skinner, 1953). Let's consider a few of them. We may use physical aids. In his later years, Skinner's vision was not as good as when he was younger. He therefore used a magnifying glass to assist him in his reading. He even designed a special frame for his magnifying glass so that it could be used most easily in the chair in his study where he often read. It is not unusual for college students to consume large amounts of coffee or other caffeine-laden beverages when studying late into the night as an aid to maintaining a state of wakefulness. Although questions could be asked about the health of this approach, it is an example of acting on your environment to increase the probability of reinforcement. In this case, the concept is that if you stay awake and study you will make a higher grade.

Another method we use to increase the probability of reinforcement is performing alternative responses to keep ourselves from engaging in a response that tends to lead to negative consequences. If you are having a conversation with a person who has very strong opinions on a topic and those opinions are quite different from yours, you may actively focus the conversation on other subjects to avoid the negative experience of a debate.

Finally, we may use self-punishment. Punishment, according to Skinner, is the application of an aversive stimulus when a behavior is emitted in order to reduce the likelihood of this behavior being expressed in the future. Punishment can be administered to us by others or we can punish ourselves. Consider the football player who spends an extra hour on the treadmill on Sunday because he missed a key tackle in Saturday's game and his team lost as a result of his missed play. If he chooses to do this himself, it may be self-punishment; if the coach requires it, it is punishment.

Implications for Clinical Psychologists

Skinner said that the acquisition of a repertoire of behaviors is the result of our reinforcement history. This repertoire may be labeled either normal or abnormal by our society. When the behavior pattern is viewed as abnormal, that person may be referred to a clinical psychologist. That psychologist might use *behavior modification* as a way to change the targeted behavior. Within behavior modification those techniques using operant conditioning-based procedures are most closely tied to Skinner's theory. We will use the token economy to illustrate this domain.

The **token economy** is an incentive system that has been used most often in psychiatric inpatient settings. Ayllon and Azrin's (1965) book describing this approach in an institutional setting provides a good example of the token economy. This book illustrates not only the application of the theory but also many of the implementation problems that may occur when designing and implementing such a system. Simply put, you need to have total control over the person's environment so that positive reinforcement for appropriate behavior comes consistently and only when the person is behaving as desired. Each behavior you desire to change is broken down into its components. The psychologist determines what approximations of the final behavior pattern are within the patient's current behavioral repertoire. When the patient exhibits these behaviors a staff member gives the patient a token. The tokens the patient gets may then be exchanged for specific rewards of interest to the patient. As with any normal behavior, over time you need to fade out (gradually stop using) the token so that the behavior itself becomes sufficient reward for the person. For example, suppose you want a patient to improve his attention to personal cleanliness. Each time this patient washes his hands after going to the bathroom, he receives a token. At the end of the day, if he has earned the required number of tokens, he can exchange them for the special candy he likes. This type of program requires careful analysis of each patient behavior plus consistent responding to appropriate behavior by the staff. Development and maintenance of this type of program is very time-consuming. Others have built on this initial description to increase the probability that the new, more appropriate behavior will generalize outside the initial setting (Kazdin, 1989). This generalization of appropriate behavior is what allows these former patients to live successfully in the world outside the hospital.

Cognitive-Behavioral Theories

Skinner and other behaviorists based their theories and therapies on observable behavior. Other theorists have suggested that although behavior is important for the understanding of personality you must also study the role of cognition. These theorists have come to be known as cognitive-behavioral theorists. Rather than focus on just one theorist this time, we will briefly describe the work of two of them to illustrate this approach and then cover the implications for clinical psychologists.

Albert Ellis and Personality Development

Albert Ellis, born in 1913, developed a *rational emotive* theory of personality. According to Ellis (1958), humans have four fundamental, interrelated processes. These processes are perception, movement, emotion, and thinking. Thinking in this model follows perception, movement, and emotion. We don't just think about things that happen to us; these other factors influence what we tend to consider thinking. Our thoughts and our emotions often overlap. Emotional problems are the result of the interdependence of these factors and not just one of them.

Albert Ellis
*Photo courtesy of
Albert Ellis Institute.*

Ellis developed an A-B-C theory of personality. This sequence is both interactional and bidirectional (Ellis, 1996). Previous theorists focused their attention on behaviors. For example, you might consider the frightened response of a child to the sight of a large dog. This emotional response is the *C,* or emotional consequence, in Ellis' system. From a behavioral perspective, you would consider the child's reinforcement history as a way to understand this behavior. You might learn, for example, that on several occasions this child was chased by his neighbor's German shepherd and once the dog actually ripped a piece of cloth from the child's shirt. This reinforcement history might then be used to explain why this child is now frightened at the sight of an Irish setter. This child has generalized his fear of the German shepherd to the Irish setter. Both are large dogs. Based on this reinforcement history and his responses, we might even predict that he will be afraid of other large dogs. Being chased by the dog is the *A,* or activating event, in Ellis' system. He contends you need more than *A* and *C* to understand the child's current response. You also need *B,* which represents the child's belief system. In this case, the child may believe that all large dogs are hostile and this is a terrible thing. It is this belief about the activating event that causes the child to run and scream. Ellis suggested that our belief system is the result of both heredity and environment. Unlike many of the behavioral theories, however, he suggests that the vast majority of our belief system is biologically based rather than environmentally based (Ellis, 1978). We inherit tendencies to react in certain ways but do have some free will to change our behavior patterns. We must alter our belief systems to do so.

Arnold Lazarus and Personality Development

Arnold Lazarus, born in 1932, is also a cognitive-behavioral theorist. He added to the work of his predecessors in both theory and application. Although he agreed that emotion, cognition, and behavior were all important for understanding personality, he felt other factors were also important. Lazarus suggests that our personality is composed of seven modalities. These modalities are behavior, affect, sensation, imagery, cognition, interpersonal processes, and drugs/biology. He developed an acronym using the first letter of each of these factors to summarize his theory—**BASIC ID** (Lazarus, 1973).

Behavior is Lazarus' term for what the person actually does in any given situation. This is the observable event of interest to such theorists as Skinner. *Affect* refers to emotion and in this case is used to describe the most prominent emotion in that particular circumstance. *Sensation* refers to sensory stimuli. It is important to know the specific sensory stimuli that are present in any given situation if you are going to

Arnold A. Lazarus
Photo courtesy of
Dr. Arnold A. Lazarus.

be able to understand a person's responses. *Imagery* may be either a memory or the deliberate imagining of a scene that the person finds positive. The difference between these two types of imagery is whether or not the scene actually occurred. Lazarus uses the term *cognition* very broadly. It includes intuition, beliefs, values, and attitudes. *Interpersonal* is Lazarus' term for our social relationships. This term includes not only daily social situations but also intimacy issues. His *drug/biology* factor originally indicated the neurological and biochemical factors that may influence behavior. Over time, this factor has come to include a range of facets of a person's physical well-being.

According to Lazarus, each of our responses can be understood if we know the influence of these seven factors. These factors will not all have the same influence on a person. Some people place more emphasis on imagery, while others may rely more heavily on sensation. Thus, the BASIC ID cannot be applied in a rote way to all people. You must also know something about that person's priorities. Our personality is a product of our genetics, our environment, and our learning. These three major factors interact to lead to the final product known as personality. Much of the basic personality comes from conditioning in our family life. This conditioning builds on our genetics. Although we have different levels of self-awareness of our BASIC ID, we can do structured self-assessments to evaluate the strength of each of these seven components. For that matter, Lazarus suggested that such a self-assessment performed on a weekly basis can make us feel better about ourselves (Lazarus, 2000). He suggested that this personal replenishment is especially important for psychotherapists. Lazarus did not feel that a psychotherapist needed to use his methods to benefit from such a personal self-care program. He suggested that this application of his concepts was useful regardless of the therapist's theoretical orientation.

Implications for Clinical Psychologists

Both Ellis and Lazarus have developed methods of psychotherapy based on their theories of personality. Ellis called his approach rational emotive behavior therapy and Lazarus called his approach multimodal therapy. Each of these approaches has continued to evolve (e.g., Ellis & Dryden, 1997; Lazarus, 1997). There are a number of other cognitive-behavioral forms of psychotherapy as well. These methods of psychotherapy are frequently cited in the psychological literature. They tend to be practical and directive, and many of them can be applied in group therapy as well as with individual patients. Because they tend to be more short-term and time-limited than some of the earlier approaches, they also fit with current demands of managed care companies (Sanchez & Turner, 2003). We discuss some other techniques developed by cognitive-behavioral therapists in chapter 9 on psychotherapy.

This chapter has provided a brief picture of the role of personality theory in the field of clinical psychology. It was not meant to be either comprehensive or exhaustive. As we noted earlier, there are many personality theories currently used by clinical psychologists as they develop intervention methods. The theories we included here illustrate a truly broad area of psychology.

Key Terms

anal stage of psychosexual development

anima/animus

archetypes

BASIC-ID

biophysical theories

collective unconscious

congruence

ectomorph

ego

ego ideal

endomorph

fixation

fully functioning person

genital stage of psychosexual development

humors

id

idiographic approach

latency stage of psychosexual development

libido

mesomorph

nomothetic approach

Oedipus complex

oral stage of psychosexual development

penis envy

persona

personal unconscious

personality

phallic stage of psychosexual development

phenomenal field

pleasure principle

pregenital stages of psychosexual development

psychosexual development

reality principle

schedule of reinforcement

shadow

superego

token economy

unconditional positive regard

CHAPTER 5

Diagnosis and Interviewing

In this chapter, we will introduce you to some of the clinical activities we first learned in graduate school. These activities form the foundation for our continued work with our patients. Before we define *diagnosis* and *interviewing* and discuss these activities, however, we would like you to read your first *ethical conundrum*. Throughout this book, we will present you with brief descriptions of situations that could easily happen in clinical practice. We ask you to think about the ethical issue as you read the chapter; then at the end of the chapter, we will provide further information about the points you might have considered. We are also going to introduce you to several fictitious patients. We will continue to refer to these patients throughout the book. Rather than merely describe the activities of clinical psychologists, we decided to relate these activities to individuals. Remember, not all of these people would necessarily be seen by the same clinical psychologist. As you have learned, psychologists may have different proficiencies and specialties. One of the ethical standards is that psychologists do not practice outside of their areas of expertise (APA, 2002). The patients we chose differ in terms of their age, background, and presenting complaint.

Patients

The following people are fictitious patients who might be seen by a clinical psychologist. In this chapter we are giving you information about them that might be obtained during an initial interview. In subsequent chapters, we will discuss the types of psychological testing

ETHICAL CONUNDRUM

You are a clinical psychologist in a solo private practice. You have been licensed for nine years. Initially you worked on an adolescent inpatient unit of a private psychiatric hospital but you have been in full-time independent practice for five years. You are having an initial interview with a seventeen-year-old female. She is a high school senior. Her parents are paying your fee. They have brought her to see you because they feel she has become distant, she won't talk to them, and her grades in school are dropping. They tell you she has had a 3.83 GPA throughout high school but that her grades during the most recent grading period were all Cs. They describe their previous relations with her as open. She had always talked freely with each of her parents individually as well as together. Now she does neither. At first, she does not want to talk to you. She tells you her parents are overreacting; there is nothing wrong. Later in the interview, however, she seems to develop a sense of trust in you. Her eye contact with you improves and she leans toward you as people often do when they want to say something that is both important and somewhat private. She confides in you that she is sexually active and that her menstrual period is now three weeks late. She does not want you to tell her parents. What do you do?

a clinical psychologist might choose to do with each of them as well as the possible outcome of that testing. We will also discuss them in the context of psychotherapy and why certain forms of psychotherapy might be best given their issues. We hope this approach to discussion of clinical activities will make them more real than merely describing psychological testing and psychotherapy.

Patty

Patty is an unmarried twenty-four-year-old first-year law student. When she called your office to make her appointment, she seemed to be crying. She told you that she had graduated from college with academic honors and majored in psychology. Her first semester grades in law school were marginal. She is now in her second semester and does not feel she is doing any better. Because law school classes only have exams at the end of a course, she does not have any objective measure of her current learning, but she sees no reason to believe her grades this semester will be different from those she earned last semester. She is worried she will have difficulty getting a clerkship this summer because her class standing is in the bottom 25 percent. She has begun to question whether she has the abilities to complete law school. Even if she does graduate, she wonders if she will have learned enough to pass the bar examination. She says she is depressed.

During the initial interview, you learn that Patty is the oldest of seven children from an intact biracial marriage. Her father is of Hispanic heritage and is a practicing physician. Patty's mother is African American and is trained as a nurse. She helps her husband in the office from time to time, but mainly stays home and takes care of her family. She worked in his office prior to their marriage and continued to do so until she became pregnant with their first child. Both parents are devout Roman Catholic and have raised their children in that faith.

Joyce

Joyce is a sixty-eight-year-old certified public accountant (CPA) with a large accounting firm. She has been with the firm for thirty years and is now part owner of the company. Joyce tells you that she has been a widow for three years, her husband of forty-five years having died suddenly of a heart attack. Joyce loves her work. Her presenting problem is that some days she has trouble concentrating and as a result of this problem just goes home early. She can do this because of her seniority and her efficiency level on other days when she is "on." Joyce made an appointment with you because she is afraid she is "getting senile." She does not want to retire but she also does not want to reach the point that someone will ask her to retire because she is unable to perform her work adequately. As one of the partners in this company, she also feels a financial obligation to the other partners to make sure her work is done efficiently.

During the initial interview, Joyce tells you that she has seen her family physician, and he reported that there are no obvious physical concerns. Joyce has gotten an annual physical from the same physician for twenty years. The most recent physical was two weeks before she came to see you. He notes in his report that Joyce regularly has had a "few drinks" every night since her husband died. Other than this change, Joyce is healthy and shows no major changes in her physical condition.

Trang

Trang is bouncy eight-year-old boy who was adopted at age two and one-half from Vietnam by his lesbian parents. He is currently in the third grade in a public school where he is having "mild discipline problems," according to his teacher. Trang's parents indicated that he adjusted well to living in the United States and that he acquired the English language quickly. He went to preschool beginning at age three and was described as "active" by his preschool teachers. In preschool he had friends whom he played well with at recess and worked cooperatively with in the classroom. At age five he entered kindergarten, where he continued to perform well and to get along well with his teachers and other children. His regular medical exam before entering kindergarten was unremarkable. He was noted to be of average size, with good listening skills and strong expressive language ability. His immunizations were current. At times he was noted by his teachers to be impulsive, but not overly so. He was never sent to the principal's office for disobedience or inappropriate behavior. First and second grade academic skills were readily acquired. In his school district, an effort was made to keep class sizes small through the second grade. Now that he is in third grade, he is in a bigger class and sits in the back of the classroom. Outside of school, he lives in a neighborhood with several kids his own age. He plays well outside and is often invited to birthday parties and other social events. He appears to be well liked, happy, and well adjusted. His teacher called his parents to note that he has become a little more of a management problem this year and that she has had to discipline him several times for getting out of his seat and blurting out answers. She said he responds well to her setting limits but worries that these behaviors are becoming more common.

Diagnosis

If you have already completed a course in abnormal psychology, much of the material in the first part of this chapter may be a review. If you have not had such a course, you may need to read this section several times because having a background about the diagnostic classification system will be important for later chapters of this book. A **diagnosis** is really a shorthand description of what you believe is the person's problem.

Much has been written about the diagnostic process. The pros and cons of using diagnostic labels are typically covered in psychology textbooks. We will briefly note some of them here to refresh your memory. (See also Table 5.1.) Diagnostic labels often provide a common language among mental health professionals. Although each of the professions has its own jargon, the use of a common classification system allows better communication among them. Diagnostic labels were designed to help professionals both understand behavior and predict behavior. Through this understanding, professionals expected to be able to select the best available treatment protocol for the patient. Although we have not really reached the point where a specific diagnostic label indicates a specific form of intervention, certain problems have been found to respond best to certain forms of intervention. Today professionals are practicing ethically when they select any one of a number of treatments, from among a range of possible forms of intervention, for most of the diagnostic classifications. Finally, the diagnostic classification process facilitates comparability of research samples in various locations so that our knowledge of psychopathology can increase. If research samples are sufficiently similar, and results of the treatment protocol are positive in each location, we are on more solid ground to generalize our results. This ability to generalize to various locations is the only way for progress to occur in the treatment of psychopathology. These reasons all appear to be positive. However, the reality of the diagnostic labeling process is that it has not always lived up to this potential.

Table 5.1 Diagnostic Labels	
Positive Reasons	Negative Reasons
Assist treatment selection	Behavioral inconsistency
Common language	Cultural biases
Facilitate research comparability	Societal stigma
Treatment selection	Uniqueness of people

Questions have been raised about cultural biases in the system. Of course that is a problem with a particular system, not necessarily the process of labeling. Another problem with the diagnostic classification system is that many of the behaviors associated with emotional problems are not consistent in all situations. The label implies that this "illness" is always present. We also know that behaviors change over time, but the diagnostic system does not take these changes into account. Once the label is placed, we tend to assume the behavior is present. Use of these labels also increases the probability that the uniqueness of this specific patient is lost. Although the labels may serve as a summary of behavior, it is important to realize that this person is unique. Over time, we have noted that some people will "live up to" the requirements of their label. If someone is told that he is "sick" he will not want to disappoint you. Thus, he may increase his inappropriate behavior rather than improve. Finally, in our society there is often a stigma attached to being labeled "mentally ill." Once that stigma is attached to the person, it is likely to remain regardless of behavior change or the fact that the "label" is no longer present.

Clinical researchers sometimes question the reliability and validity of the classification systems available. Briefly, reliability refers to the consistency of our labels and validity refers to whether the label is accurate for the problem. The reliability question is whether each clinician who uses the diagnostic labels uses them the same way. Validity, in this case, raises questions about whether there is a consistent group of symptoms that go with each of the labels. We will not debate these issues here. A reality of clinical practice is that a diagnosis is required for hospital charts when you work with inpatients and for insurance claims forms when such companies are providing any portion of treatment reimbursement. Thus clinical psychologists need to be familiar with the currently used classification system.

The most common system of diagnosis used by clinical psychologists in the United States is the *Diagnostic and Statistical Manual of Mental Disorders*, usually called the **DSM-IV,** published by the American Psychiatric Association (1994). This system is described in most abnormal psychology textbooks as well as in books specifically designed to teach mental health professionals how to apply the criteria required for each of the diagnoses (Morrison, 1995). As a brief review, we will provide a summary about the DSM system. The first DSM was published in 1952, and a second edition arrived in 1968. Psychiatrist Robert Spitzer is widely acknowledged as the person who transformed the DSM and developed criteria to help improve reliability. He began work on the DSM-III in 1974 (it was completed in 1980) when the manual was a spiral-bound notebook of just 150 pages. That edition provided brief descriptions of about one hundred mental disorders (Spiegel, 2005). The current version, DSM-IV-TR (text revision) has sold over 420,000 copies since its publication in 2000. For an overview of the development of this diagnostic system, see Spiegel (2005). The DSM-IV is a "multiaxial" system; that is, you consider the patient along five different dimensions, or axes. This does not mean that you will necessarily have something to report on each of the axes but only that you should "consider" each of these areas when assessing your patient. The first four axes in this system are:

Axis I Clinical Disorders and Related Conditions
Axis II Personality Disorders and Mental Retardation

Axis III General Medical Conditions (relevant to the mental disorder)

Axis IV Psychosocial and Environmental Problems: Life Events or Problems

Problems associated with Axis IV include:

Problems with primary support group: Death of a family member, family health problems, disruption of family by separation or divorce, remarriage, abuse or neglect, or birth of a sibling

Problems related to the social environment: Death or loss of a friend, living alone, adjustment to life cycle transitions such as retirement

Educational problems: Illiteracy, discord with teachers or classmates, academic problems

Occupational problems: Unemployment, threat of a job loss, stressful workplace, discord with boss or coworkers

Housing problems: Homelessness, unsafe neighborhood, discord with neighbors or landlord

Economic problems: Extreme poverty, insufficient welfare support

Problems with access to healthcare services: Inadequate healthcare services, transportation to healthcare facilities unavailable, inadequate health insurance

Problems with interaction with the legal system: Arrest, incarceration, litigation, victim of a crime

Other psychological and environmental problems: Exposure to disasters, war, unavailability of social service agencies

Axis V is the **Global Assessment of Function (GAF).** It is the overall level at which an individual functions, including social, occupational, academic, and other areas of personal performance; the GAF may be expressed as a numerical score. Axis V is for reporting the clinician's judgment of the individual's overall level of functioning. This information is useful in planning treatment, measuring its impact, and predicting outcome. Scores on the GAF range from 0 to 100 (Luborsky, 1962; Endicott, Spitzer, Fleiss, & Cohen, 1976). A score of 100 indicates that the person possesses superior functioning in a wide range of activities, doesn't let life's problems get out of hand, and/or is sought out by others because of his or her many positive qualities. This really means the person has no psychological symptoms. A score of 10 on the GAF would describe a person who was a persistent danger of severely hurting himself or herself or others, exhibited a persistent inability to maintain minimal personal hygiene, or was capable of a serious suicidal act with clear expectation of death. Between these extremes would be a score of 55, which would describe someone with moderate symptoms (e.g., flat affect and circumstantial speech, occasional panic attacks) or someone with moderate difficulties in social, occupational, or school function (e.g., few friends, conflicts with peers or coworkers). (See Table 5.2.)

Table 5.2 Global Assessment of Functioning (GAF) Scale

Consider psychological, social, and occupational functioning on a hypothetical continuum of mental health–illness. Do not include impairment in functioning due to physical (or environmental) limitations.

Code   (**Note:** Use intermediate codes when appropriate, e.g., 45, 68, 72.)

100 – 91   **Superior functioning in a wide range of activities, life's problems never seem to get out of hand, is sought out by others because of his or her many positive qualities. No symptoms.**

90 – 81   **Absent or minimal symptoms** (e.g., mild anxiety before an exam), **good functioning in all areas, interested and involved in a wide range of activities, socially effective, generally satisfied with life, no more than everyday problems or concerns** (e.g., an occasional argument with family members).

80 – 71   **If symptoms are present, they are transient and expectable reactions to psychosocial stressors** (e.g., difficulty concentrating after family argument); **no more than slight impairment in social, occupational, or school functioning** (e.g., temporarily falling behind in schoolwork).

70 – 61   **Some mild symptoms** (e.g., depressed mood and mild insomnia) **OR some difficulty in social, occupational, or school functioning** (e.g., occasional truancy, or theft within the household), **but generally functioning pretty well, has some meaningful interpersonal relationships.**

60 – 51   **Moderate symptoms** (e.g., flat affect and circumstantial speech, occasional panic attacks) **OR moderate difficulty in social, occupational, or school functioning** (e.g., few friends, conflicts with peers or co-workers).

50 – 41   **Serious symptoms** (e.g., suicidal ideation, severe obsessional rituals, frequent shoplifting) **OR any serious impairment in social, occupational, or school functioning** (e.g., no friends, unable to keep a job).

40 – 31   **Some impairment in reality testing or communication** (e.g., speech is at times illogical, obscure, or irrelevant) **OR major impairment in several areas, such as work or school, family relations, judgment, thinking, or mood** (e.g., depressed man avoids friends, neglects family, and is unable to work; child frequently beats up younger children, is defiant at home, and is failing at school).

30 – 21   **Behavior is considerably influenced by delusions or hallucinations OR serious impairment in communication or judgment** (e.g., sometimes incoherent, acts grossly inappropriately, suicidal preoccupation) **OR inability to function in almost all areas** (e.g., stays in bed all day; no job, home, or friends).

20 – 11   **Some danger of hurting self or others** (e.g., suicide attempts without clear expectation of death; frequently violent; manic excitement) **OR occasionally fails to maintain minimal personal hygiene** (e.g., smears feces) **OR gross impairment in communication** (e.g., largely incoherent or mute).

10 – 1   **Persistent danger of severely hurting self or others** (e.g., recurrent violence) **OR persistent inability to maintain minimal personal hygiene OR serious suicidal act with clear expectation of death.**

0   **Inadequate information.**

Source: Reprinted with permission from the Diagnostic and Statistical Manual of Mental Disorders, Fourth Edition, Text Revision *(copyright 2000). American Psychiatric Association.*

In addition to the axial diagnostic areas described here, *V codes* may be used in the diagnostic process. While not mental health diagnoses per se, these codes are frequently used to describe areas of concern. It should be noted that V codes are frequently not considered diagnoses that are reimbursable by insurance companies. Some V codes are shown in Table 5.3 to illustrate the area.

Table 5.3 V Codes

V15.81	Noncompliance With Treatment
V61.1	Partner Relational Problem
	Physical/Sexual Abuse of an Adult
V61.20	Parent-Child Relational Problem
V61.21	Child Neglect
	Physical/Sexual Abuse of a Child
V61.8	Sibling Relational Problem
V61.9	Relational Problem Related to a Mental Disorder or General Medical Condition
V62.2	Occupational Problem
V62.3	Academic Problem
V62.4	Acculturation Problem
V62.81	Relational Problems
V62.82	Bereavement
V62.89	Borderline Intellectual Functioning
	Phase of Life Problem
	Religious or Spiritual Problem
V65.2	Malingering
V71.01	Adult Antisocial Behavior
V71.02	Child or Adolescent Antisocial Behavior
V71.09	No Diagnosis on Axis II
	No Diagnosis or Condition on Axis I

Source: Reprinted with permission from the Diagnostic and Statistical Manual of Mental Disorders, Fourth Edition, Text Revision *(copyright 2000). American Psychiatric Association.*

If the patient is experiencing an emotional disorder, you will have a diagnosis on at least one of the first two axes. Your patient may have diagnoses on both of them or may have multiple diagnoses on one of the axes. On Axis III, you list only those medical conditions that are relevant to your diagnosis. The basis for this information is your patient's medical history. The clinical psychologist is not licensed to practice medicine and thus does *not* diagnose the medical conditions on Axis III. It is important, however, to be aware of these medical conditions as you plan your intervention because of the potential interaction of the medical condition and its treatment with your proposed treatment program. Depending on the medical condition, you may want to consult with one or more of the patient's physicians. If you want to either talk to the patient's physician or get copies of any of your patient's medical records, you will need to obtain a signed *release of information* form from your patient. Most patients are quite willing to provide this release so that their treatment program can be integrated with any medical regimen they may have. In some cases, you may need to recommend that your patient get a physical examination because the symptoms could indicate a medical condition as well as a psychological one. This referral for a physical does not mean that if a medical condition is found there is no further need for psychological services. Some medical conditions, as well as their treatment, are helped by psychological intervention in addition to the medical intervention. In other cases, such as learning that you have a medical problem that will lead to major life changes, dealing with the medical diagnosis may be helped by psychological intervention. Clinical psychologists need to know those clusters of symptoms that may indicate either physical or emotional problems. If the medical condition can be ruled out, you can then proceed to develop a treatment plan solely from a psychological perspective. On Axis IV you list only those circumstances that you believe may have an impact on the diagnoses you have listed on Axis I or Axis II. Remember, although you want to learn as much as possible that is relevant to helping the patient you are not developing a major biography. You need to be selective in terms of those factors that require investigation.

In some cases, especially during an initial interview, you may have insufficient information to evaluate the patient's current level of function. Under these circumstances, the GAF would be 0. You would then amend your diagnosis once you have sufficient information. Many psychologists make only a provisional diagnosis after the first meeting with a new patient. Although it may be quite obvious to the psychologist whether or not the patient is psychotic, for example, fine-tuning the diagnosis within that broad category may require more information than you usually get in one session. Thus a provisional diagnosis is made and amended later.

A psychologist might be asked to make a provisional diagnosis for many reasons. For example, a person who comes to a hospital emergency room for treatment may display behaviors that could indicate the need for psychiatric hospitalization. In this case, the emergency room personnel would contact the attending clinical psychologist or psychiatrist to determine whether or not an emergency commitment was warranted. Who is qualified to make emergency commitments varies from one state to another, but many states include clinical psychologists in their laws. Often this emergency commitment is for a brief period, such as forty-eight hours. During that time the person will be evaluated more completely. The role of the psychologist in the emergency room in this case is to form a provisional diagnosis rapidly. That diagnosis may be confirmed or amended following the more complete evaluation. In other cases, the patient is sufficiently distressed during the initial interview that the psychologist is unable to obtain enough information to form a diagnosis. It may be that this person needs sleep or medication prior to a complete diagnostic interview. Basically, a provisional diagnosis is made when the psychologist is unable to obtain sufficient information about the patient, for whatever reason, to apply the classification system.

The types of cases of disturbed behavior we have mentioned so far are the ones most often associated with clinical practice. With the increase in life expectancy, clinical psychologists are now more frequently asked to make a mental health diagnosis with older adults. One of the more common reasons for referral in this population is decline in cognitive abilities rather than grossly distorted behavior (Tuokko & Hadjistavropoulos, 1998). There are many potential causes of cognitive decline in the elderly. The research base for understanding these patients and providing an accurate diagnosis is relatively new (Gatz, 1995; LaRue, Dessonville, & Jarvik, 1985). Clinical psychologists who have been practicing for awhile may not have had this area included in their graduate training. Some experts suggest that at least 10 percent of people age sixty-five and older have diagnosable emotional and/or cognitive problems (Birren & Sloane, 1977). The clinical psychologist needs to be able not only to diagnose the problem but also to determine the types of treatment that are most appropriate.

In chapter 15 we discuss the growing specialty of clinical geropsychology and the guidelines available regarding qualifications for this area of practice.

Another system that may be used by psychologists to evaluate their patients, which is relatively new, is the **International Classification of Functionality (ICF)** developed by the World Health Organization (WHO) in 2001. The ICF is the result of a seven-year effort involving the active participation of about sixty-five countries. Rigorous scientific studies were undertaken to ensure that the ICF would be applicable across cultures, age groups, and genders to collect reliable and comparable data on health outcomes of individuals and populations. This system is an outgrowth of a WHO effort to associate the state of an individual not only to structures and functions of the human body but also to the individual's activities and participation in social life. Thus, the ICF is a substantial change in the way one evaluates a person in a mental health setting. In the ICF, there are no more references to a functional or structural problem, without it being related to a state considered "healthy." This document does not use terms such as *impairment, disability,* and *handicap,* which indicate that something is "missing" that prevents a full functioning of the body. Mental functions are defined as producing awareness of one's identity. The ICF takes into account the social aspects of disability and provides a mechanism to document the impact of the social and physical environment on a person's functioning. For example, consider a person with a serious disability who finds it difficult to work in a particular building because it does not provide ramps or elevators. The ICF identifies the needed focus of an intervention, that is, that the building should include those facilities, not that the person be forced out of the job because of an inability to work, as may be the case when the focus is on the "disease." ICF puts all disease and health conditions on an equal footing regardless of their cause. A person may not be able to attend work because of a cold or angina, but also because of depression. This neutral approach puts mental disorders on a par with physical illness. The ICF covers all aspects of human health, grouping them under the main "health domain" inclusive of sight, hearing, walking, learning, and remembering as well as those domains connected to the health domain, like mobility, learning, social life, and so on.

The ICF is not limited to people with disabilities. It relates to everyone and thus provides a context within which a person's mental state is understood (http://www.who.int/inf-pr-2001/en/pr2001–48.html). Because this system is still quite new, in contrast to the DSM system, we cannot predict whether or not it will become common for psychologists to use it. We note this system here so that if you see it in a journal article you will know what is meant. When we provide diagnoses of our patients throughout this book, we will use the more common DSM system.

Impact of Diagnosis

An issue to remember when thinking about diagnosis is the potential impact that diagnosis may have on the person. We may like to think that the twenty-first century has brought greater acceptance of emotional problems, but such acceptance appears to vary among people and circumstances. Think about Patty from the beginning of this chapter. Would the formal diagnosis of an emotional problem impact her legal career or perhaps a future in politics? We cannot tell her for certain that revealing such a diagnosis would not have a negative impact on her professional goals. Although it would be ideal to believe that such a history would have no impact on Patty's future, we know that such information has been used in a negative way in past political campaigns. Given the choice between a candidate who has a history of "emotional disturbance" and one who is described as "normal," who do you think will be the choice of the average voter?

We also know that information that should not be included in hiring decisions often impacts the final selection process. Although it may not be overtly stated that the reason a person was not selected for a position was a history of "mental illness," that information, if available to those doing the hiring, may subtly influence the process. For most employment settings, the final candidates for an opening are relatively equal in terms of the basic qualifications. Thus, it is the less obvious characteristics that may determine which candidate is hired. In some settings, for example, how well the person seems to "fit" with the others in the job setting may be the determining factor. If there is any concern that this person may not be emotionally stable, it can be quite easy to decide that one of the other candidates would make a more collegial impact. It is possible that potential employers overemphasize positive traits in some candidates who don't have a mental illness in order to avoid hiring someone with a mental illness.

During the 1960s, a popular topic of discussion was the "stigma of mental illness" (Szasz, 1960). No conclusion has ever been reached about whether or not the positive aspects of using a diagnostic classification outweigh the potential negative effects. It is possible that with the increased acceptance of various types of personal information being entered into databases, the addition of a DSM-IV code may seem less threatening than it was in the past. Only time will answer this question.

The impact of a diagnosis is not limited to the person's future. Consider a child who is given a mental health label. Teachers may react differently to that child because of their knowledge of that label. That diagnostic label may influence annual school reports and even class placement. If this happens, a child's entire educational future may be impacted. Think, for a moment, how you would react to a child you have just met if you are told this child is mentally retarded or has attention deficit disorder. Even with your background in psychology you will probably modify your behavior toward this child as well as your interpretation of the child's behavior because of that label. Suppose you had never studied psychology. You are a parent and you learn that one of your child's classmates has been in a psychiatric hospital. If you are typical of many parents, you will have concerns about your child's safety in the presence of this "different" child. You may not want your child to invite a child with such a history into your home for social activities, especially parties where you may not be able to have the ability to constantly watch this other child.

The potential impact of the label remains an issue for clinical psychologists to consider and discuss with their patients. For example, if a patient is having the psychologist reimbursed through health insurance, a diagnostic code number will be included in the form the psychologist completes for that company. It is not ethical to use a more "acceptable" diagnosis on your patient's records as a method of dealing with a potential societal reaction. You must use the diagnostic label that best describes your patient's problems. Discussing with your patient who may have access to those mental health records, however, and under what circumstances such access occurs, is very important.

Interviewing

Patient Interviews

We start this section of the chapter with a discussion of the clinical interviews each of our three fictitious patients had from the beginning of the chapter. We follow this patient information with more specific comments about interviewing skills.

Let's return to our patients from the beginning of the chapter. Patty has arrived in your office. The information from the interview starts as soon as you see her in the waiting area. What are your initial impressions? Think about what you notice the first time you meet people. How is Patty dressed? Does she make eye contact with you when you walk in? Is she smiling or frowning? Does she not demonstrate any affect at all? This is the type of information you want to remember and add to your observations from your upcoming interview. You observe that Patty is clean and neatly dressed. She appears to be of medium height, appropriate weight for her height, with a dark olive complexion and shoulder-length hair. Please remember you are not trying for exact measurements such as when you get on the scale at your physician's office. In this case, you are making a rough judgment about the appropriateness of certain observable characteristics such as body build and cleanliness. She makes eye contact with you and shakes your hand firmly when you offer it. You immediately feel comfortable with her. These reactions are part of the information you may want to include in the "behavioral observations" section of your report of this first session. Other information for this section of the report will arise as you continue to interview Patty. This opening section is basically what you have seen that may be relevant to the diagnosis and subsequent treatment planning.

Regardless of whether you are in a group practice, a solo practice, or a hospital- or clinic-based practice, an "office policy" statement is usually given to the patient. The contents of this form varies from practice to practice but always follows what is required in these forms by the state or province in which you practice. Because of concern about the potential for misunderstanding leading to lawsuits, many psychologists have increased the length of these policy statements in order to clarify a wider range of topics. In some states, your education and training, theoretical orientation, financial obligations and ways to arrange for payment, phone numbers to contact state licensing authorities if you have a complaint, and other issues must be included in the office policy statement. Patients are usually required to sign one copy of the form indicating that they understand and agree to the "rules" of the practice. This office policy statement is actually a contract between you and the patient and can be used in a court of law if there are disagreements between the patient and the provider.

As you and Patty arrive in your office from the waiting room, you make sure Patty is aware of the limits of confidentiality regarding what she is going to tell you. Many psychologists offer the patient the opportunity to discuss what is in the office policy statement at this time. You do this with Patty and she says it was clear. Your receptionist has also given Patty a form to sign regarding confidentiality; you ask her if she has any questions, and then she signs it. Even though the financial arrangements are made before your patient comes for the first session, you also ask her if she would like to go over this information. You can see from our discussion of the paperwork that not all of clinical practice involves purely psychological issues. Some students find it difficult to handle all of this business side of practice. Many graduate programs provide little or no training for the business side of practice. Part of what we have described is business and part is necessary for ethical reasons. All of it is necessary for the modern practice of clinical psychology.

You note from Patty's responses that her vocabulary is excellent, and this observation supports your perception that she has above average intelligence. Unless something arises during this interview to change your opinion about her cognitive abilities, you decide you will not need to do formal intelligence testing. You also make a decision about the style of questioning you will use with Patty and decide that you will go from general questions to more specific ones in this interview. This is a common style in initial interviews. You start with a very broad question and ask her to tell you why she is in your office. You follow that with a question about why she has chosen to come now rather than at some past time. During this initial session, you learn Patty has recently broken off a long-term relationship but that she is not certain the break-up was the best decision she could have made. Her former boyfriend sometimes calls her, but she has not seen him in several months. She gets upset when he calls her as well as when he does not. She tells you that she cries easily. You could have pursued more details about this relationship at this point in the interview but decide to save this line of questioning for either later in this initial interview or during a future session with Patty. You have already decided that Patty is a good match for your practice and thus expect to have future sessions with her.

At this point in the interview, you begin to have some concerns about the degree of her depression. In addition to questions about somatic concerns, changes in eating, sleeping, and use of substances, you ask probing questions to determine whether or not she is at risk for suicide. You determine that although she is depressed, she is not a suicide risk. You base this opinion on her responses to specific questions about suicide as well as her religious background, which is strong and forbids suicide. Many psychologists believe that it is important to ask the patient directly whether he or she has thought about suicide (which is not uncommon), has developed a plan (which is less common), or has actually made a suicide gesture or even an attempt at some previous time. The answers to these questions, combined with other factors, can give the clinician a good idea about the likelihood that a patient is a danger to himself or herself. Similarly, questions about assaultiveness can also give the clinician an indication about the level of danger the patient may impose to others. Remember that a psychologist may break confidentiality if the psychologist determines that a patient is a danger to himself or herself or someone else. Although Patty reports some difficulty sleeping, has experienced some appetite loss, and cries often, she is not abusing any substances and does not appear to be dangerous to herself or others. Even though you feel confident about your initial diagnosis, you will follow up later with psychological testing to provide additional information about her level of depression. Information about her degree of depression was more important at this time than the details of her relationship because of the lethality potential. You can pursue further details about her relationships in a later session with her.

In this first session, you decide to get some basic information about her family background and then pursue more information, as needed, in future sessions. Patty tells you that she was raised in a traditional Roman Catholic family. She describes herself as being fairly religious. She attends Mass most Sundays and attempts to live according to the dictates of her faith. Patty adds that she is probably the only twenty-four-year-old virgin in her law school class and that this is because of her religious beliefs. Her father is a second-generation American of Hispanic descent and her mother is African American. Patty is the oldest of seven children in the family; she has four sisters and two brothers. Her father is a family practice physician and her mother was the nurse in his office until Patty was born. Since that time, her mother has been a full-time home-maker who occasionally substitutes in her husband's office when his regular nurse is on vacation. Patty describes typical sibling rivalry but overall her statements suggest a solid family background. Religious values seem to be dominant in this family. These values seem to be stronger than cultural ones. The biracial nature of the marriage seems to have no impact on either Patty or her family. When she described her relationship with her parents, you got the impression that she is overly concerned about pleasing her father. You will want to pursue this in future sessions with her. Patty says that she has not told her parents about her appointment with you because her father does not believe psychologists are useful.

You ask Patty questions about her daily routine and study habits in an attempt to get a picture of her current life. This information gives you a framework for what will hap-pen in future sessions. You learn that her academic problems have led her to devote all of her time to what seems to be inefficient studying. Patty used to enjoy her daily jog but no longer gets any form of exercise. She is afraid to devote time to anything but her studies. The only time she sees other people is at school. Sometimes she has coffee at a campus coffeeshop with classmates between classes. Most of the conversation relates to classes, professors, and summer clerkships. Since she ended the relationship with her former boy-friend that she described to you, she has had no social life. Although Patty's family lives in a nearby community, she lives alone in an apartment not far from her law school. She decided a roommate would interfere with her need to study and living at home would require her to participate in too many family activities. She also did not want to take the time to commute from home to school. She tells you that she felt at her age she should be living independently. Her father is paying her law school tuition and her rent so she is not facing a student loan issue after graduation. Patty has a part-time job as a sales clerk in a jewelry store to earn spending money. She has kept her hours at the store to a minimum so that she has more time to study. She does not socialize with people from the store.

You need to know whether this lack of socialization has been typical of Patty or is something that started with her recent enrollment in law school. You thus ask her some questions about her social life when she was an undergraduate. You want to know whether she has always felt the need to devote so much time to studying. Did she need to spend all of her time studying in order to be an honor student in college? This information will help you determine what psychological tests may be needed. Patty tells you that when she was an undergraduate she was a member of a sorority and served as its secretary one year and as the vice president her senior year. She was also active in her Psi Chi chapter and served as its president her senior year. After college she spent two years working as a hospital administrator's executive assistant while she was considering career options. It was at that time that she met the former boyfriend. They began dating shortly after she started this position. They met at the hospital where he was doing his medical residency in family practice. Because of the time demands of his residency, she tended to work her schedule around his availability.

You know you will not be able to get all of the information you may want in this first session. You want to leave sufficient time for a summary and feedback before the session ends. Your overview of the session is that you spent the initial time generally trying to make Patty feel comfortable and giving her a broad idea of what would happen in therapy. The bulk of your time together was used for you to gather information about her background and lifestyle. At the end of this session, you summarized what you understood Patty to have said and gave her feedback about what you thought you might be able to do to help her.

In that final part of your first session with Patty, you tell her that you are proposing weekly psychotherapy sessions for six weeks. After that time, the two of you will discuss whether or not further work is desired. You explain that you will be asking for more information during future sessions, may ask her to take some psychological tests, and may also give her work to do between sessions. You explain that this work is really not that different from homework she does for school and will be just as important to complete. Patty expresses some concern about taking time away from studying to do your homework. You discuss the ways this work will lead to more efficient use of her study time.

Patty is concerned about having a potentially public record of her psychotherapy. She has therefore decided to pay for your services directly, rather than ask her insurance carrier to provide payment. She asks for further clarification of the confidentiality of what she says. She also asks you if she will need to admit to having a "mental disorder" when she applies to take her bar examination after law school. You discuss her concerns with her and schedule an appointment for the following week. After this initial interview, you form the following tentative diagnosis for Patty:

Axis I: 311 Depressive Disorder Not Otherwise Specified

Axis II: Deferred

Axis III: None

Axis IV: Educational Problems

Axis V: GAF = 60 (moderate symptoms)

There are also some diagnoses you will need to rule out with the additional information you get from further interviewing and testing. For Axis I, you need more information before you rule out 300.4 (Dysthymic Disorder) and 296.22 (Major Depressive Disorder, Single Episode, Moderate). For Axis II, you need more information before you can rule out 301.6 (Dependent Personality Disorder). As you decide what assessment tools you may want to use, as well as issues to pursue further in your next session with Patty, these diagnostic possibilities will guide you. We have provided the format of the diagnostic information a psychologist uses so that you would have an accurate picture of the process. Do not worry about the actual numbers from the DSM at this time in your education. If you choose to become a clinical psychologist, you will have references for that material.

The type of interview you have just conducted with Patty is often called an **intake** interview. This interview is designed to give you an overall understanding of the patient's problems as well as to determine whether or not you are an appropriate person to see her for intervention. Making this latter decision is based on your areas of expertise as well as your interpersonal reaction to the patient. If you determine that you are not an appropriate person to work with Patty, you need to explain why and also provide her with potential referral sources. It is important to attend to the issues of appropriateness of the patient for you in this session both for the sake of the patient and also for your schedule. The data tell us that about half of the patients who come for an initial appointment will not return for their next appointment (Morton, 1995). You do not want to fill your appointment schedule with patients who are unlikely to return. Although you hopefully have become a clinical psychologist because of your interest in people, you must also remember that this is your livelihood. You have both office expenses and personal expenses such as a mortgage and monthly bills.

With Joyce, you follow a similar pattern for the intake interview. Your observations of Joyce are that she is professionally dressed and gives no indication of either verbal or ambulatory difficulty. Eye contact is good. She appears confident when greeting you and tells you that her insurance company has told her you are on its list of approved providers of psychological services. She has completed the needed paperwork with your billing clerk so that your office can file for insurance reimbursement for your services. She will pay the required copayment at the end of each session. She understands both the office policies and the information about confidentiality.

Once Joyce reaches your office, some of her confidence seems to diminish. Joyce tells you that she has some days when her work level is solid and she is viewed as one of the best accountants in the firm. Because of her seniority and productivity level on "good" days, she is able to cover up her problems so that her colleagues are unaware of any difficulty. Thus far, no one has questioned her productivity or behavior. On bad days, she tends to leave work early, go home, and go to bed. Her sleep patterns have changed recently and she finds she often awakens in the early hours of the morning, lies in bed watching the numbers on the digital clock in her bedroom, and then feels tired for the remainder of the day. She demonstrates a number of symptoms of depression. You decide you would benefit from the type of information you can get from psychological testing to further explore her problems.

You learn that she has been a widow for three years after a solid marriage of forty-five years. Joyce has been employed by the same company for over thirty years and is now a partner in that company. Although the company does not have a mandatory retirement policy, she has begun to wonder if she will be able to continue working much longer. As she tells you this, she becomes sad and tears fall, but she does not fully cry. She has always loved her work. Since her husband's death, work has been her major activity. Joyce has two grown children, neither of whom lives in her community. Her son is a career diplomat and currently lives in Paris with his wife and daughter. She is proud of his accomplishments but notes that she has never felt they were emotionally close. Joyce's daughter is a computer scientist who is expecting her first child soon. Joyce had planned to take some vacation time to visit her daughter and help her in the first weeks after the delivery, but she no longer feels it would be safe for her to be around a newborn. She has told her daughter that she cannot get away from the office but that she will send money for a professional nanny to assist her daughter for a couple of weeks after the birth. So far, you do not have information about any local support system for Joyce. You therefore ask her some specific questions in an attempt to learn if there are any local sources of support as well as to further explore her closeness to each of her children. This information is important for treatment planning, especially if the neuropsychological testing you plan to recommend suggests early stages of a cognitive disorder like Alzheimer's disease. In addition to work, Joyce attends monthly meetings of the local business and professional women's association. For the past two years, she has served as a member of the board of directors of this group and helps plan its meeting agenda. She also attends annual meetings of the local chapter of her college alumni association. She denies that any of the members of these groups are close friends and says she sees them only at meetings. You make note that in future sessions you may need to ask more questions about Joyce's social life as she seemed to get somewhat uncomfortable at your suggestion that she may socialize outside these meetings.

In the summary portion of this session, you tell Joyce that you believe she will benefit from psychological services. You also tell her that you will need to have her do some psychological testing before you make a decision about the best direction to go in psychotherapy. Joyce seems comfortable with the concept of psychological testing. After this initial interview, you form the following working/tentative diagnostic impression:

Axis I: Deferred

Axis II: None

Axis III: Deferred

Axis IV: Occupational Problems

Axis V: GAF = 55

For Joyce, we don't have sufficient information after this first interview to make a diagnosis. On Axis I, we want to gather sufficient information to rule out both 290.0 (Dementia of the Alzheimer's Type) and Major Depressive Disorder (296.2). You would also want to refer her for a neuropsychological screening before making a decision about Axis III. You decided on neuropsychological screening rather than a full neuropsychological assessment because of the time and expense required of a full assessment. If the screening suggests one of the dementias, you may then need to recommend more extensive neuropsychological evaluation as well as further consultation with her primary care physician.

Your interview with Trang is very different from the previous two interviews. Children almost never refer themselves to a psychologist. Child and adolescent referrals almost always come from other people such as parents, teachers, pediatricians, and sometimes other relatives. For this reason, and because children are often poor historians, collateral contacts with "informants" are very important. Many child psychologists see the child's parents before they see the child. By doing this, the psychologist can obtain the circumstances surrounding the child's birth (Was the child premature? Did the mother have problems during the birth or shortly thereafter? Was the father involved in prenatal care? Were there unusual stressors during pregnancy, including the use of substances?). The psychologist can also obtain the developmental history from the parents or guardians, ascertaining when certain milestones occurred, such as when the child began talking, walking, and displaying other fine motor skills. Information about a child's medical history can also be obtained from the initial interview and a parent or guardian can sign a release of information form that will allow the psychologist to communicate with other healthcare providers, educators, and others who may be able to inform you about the case. In addition, the child's academic history can be obtained. Many child psychologists like to see a child's early report cards. Although the grades tell the psychologist something about the child, the psychologist is more interested in reviewing the narrative comments that the teacher(s) have made. Many times, this initial interview sets the stage for communication with other professionals who have information that can contribute to the therapist's understanding of the case.

You find out from the parent interview that Trang was adopted when he was two and one-half years old. The two women who adopted Trang traveled to Vietnam to retrieve him from an orphanage. They told you that he understood the Vietnamese language when they met him. This is what psychologists call receptive language. His expressive language, or his use of words to interact with others, was poor. You know from your training in developmental psychology that it is not unusual for receptive language to develop earlier than expressive language. Since he was living in an orphanage where he may have had minimal personal attention, this type of differential language development is more likely to have occurred. His parents share with you that Trang quickly learned English and that the developmental milestones occurred within normal limits. They report that he is a happy-go-lucky child, somewhat small for his age, who has good gross and fine motor skills. They tell you that they do not know what the pregnancy was like, but that he was born naturally and there were no physical concerns noted in the early medical record they were given. They also tell you that he had not been seriously ill, had never been hospitalized, and had no head injuries or other serious medical condition since they adopted him nearly six years ago. Both parents said that Trang had been in preschool from the age of three, attended a public kindergarten, and had an unremarkable first and second grade. Problems began in third grade when the teacher sent home a note saying that Trang was "aggressive" with other children, had some difficulty paying attention in class, and was disorganized. His teacher noted that he was sent to the office twice in the past month.

Your initial diagnostic impression of Trang, even though you haven't seen him yet, yields several intriguing possibilities. Trang could be developing an oppositional defiant disorder, attention deficit hyperactivity disorder, expressive language disorder, or some combination of these problems. You don't think there is any Axis II disorder (you rule out mental retardation following the interview based on his reported language skills and his parents' report of solid learning progress). Nor do you think there are any medical or physical factors influencing his behavior. You consider noting on Axis IV that there may be a parent–child conflict, as well as the possibility of school dysfunctions. Your GAF is 55, indicating moderate problems.

Your next step in this evaluation is to gather information from Trang's school. You plan to call his teacher, and perhaps the school counselor if there is one, as well as to contact Trang's pediatrician. You also remind yourself that this child comes from a different culture and has a different family constellation than most children, issues that you must remain aware of in your assessment.

Clinical interviews are done for a variety of reasons. The interviews we have described here were conducted to determine whether or not the person was an appropriate candidate for psychotherapy with a clinical psychologist. We chose this type of interview so that you would have background information about these people when we tell you about psychological testing and some of the intervention techniques later in the book. Clinical psychologists conduct interviews for many other reasons but the general interview skills used are similar. After you complete your interview, you will need to make formal notes for your files. There is no single format for these notes. Table 5.4 provides one sample of how a clinical psychologist might arrange the material from an initial interview of the type we have just described.

Table 5.4 Initial Interview Notes
A. General identifying information 　　1. Patient name 　　2. Place/date of interview 　　3. Date of birth B. Behavioral observations 　　1. Physical characteristics 　　2. Verbalizations 　　3. Mood C. Presenting problem 　　1. General description 　　2. Duration and strength D. History 　　1. Medical 　　2. Educational 　　3. Personal E. Tentative diagnosis F. Proposed treatment plan

Interview Skills

An interview is different from a conversation you have with a close friend. When you talk to a close friend, there is considerable give-and-take, even when one of you may be asking for advice. A clinical interview places emphasis on one of the participants (the patient) and is also much more goal-directed. When talking to a friend about your problems, you tend to just focus on your problem and how to solve it. In a clinical interview, you as the psychologist will be considering not only the patient's stated problem but also his or her strengths and whether there may be additional issues in the person's life that may be worth exploring. This interview does not just focus on negatives. Although the negatives are what brought the person to your office, you also want to know about the person's positive qualities. Your intervention strategies will build upon those strengths. In addition to the specific purpose of the interview, the psychologist is also trying to begin to establish a relationship, known as **rapport,** with the patient. In the personal conversation, you already have a relationship. When you talk to a friend, you probably don't spend time thinking about what skills that person has. You just want advice. Both for training psychologists in interview skills and for understanding how an interview actually works, psychologists have described and evaluated those characteristics that are important for good interviewers (Othmer & Othmer, 1994; Rogers, 1995; Shea, 1988).

A good interviewer brings multiple skills to the interview. One broad area of interest is communication skills. We are using this term to refer to both speaking and listening. Speaking is somewhat easier to define than listening. It is important to use language that your patient will understand. This is especially important when working with young children, people whom you suspect have lower or compromised (head injured, older, or possibly demented patients) intellectual skills, and people from cultures different from the culture with whom you most often work. Remember you are not talking to a professional colleague. On the other hand, it is also important to be realistic in your use of language. Do not try to use language you think sounds like your patient's language. This approach is not likely to lead to rapport; your patient will be able to tell that you are faking and will not appreciate it. During the interview, it is important to use your verbal abilities to paraphrase what the patient has said in such a way that your patient is encouraged to disagree with what you have said if you are not accurate. Although it feels good to be correct in your understanding of the patient, you do not want to have a false sense of being correct because that will interfere with therapy progress.

A term that is often used to describe the type of listening skills needed by clinical psychologists is **active listening.** Part of this type of listening is that you not only "hear" what the patient is telling you but also communicate that you are not judging the patient based on what you are hearing. You continue to value the patient regardless of what the patient tells you. The psychologist's interest in the patient can be communicated by a combination of eye contact, body language, and tone of voice in addition to specific comments expressed by the psychologist. Some of these nonverbal skills develop with supervised practice in interviewing. Listening skills can be divided into **primary listening skills** and **secondary listening skills** (Nystul, 1999). In this system, the primary skills are those skills that permit the psychologist to become more aware of the patient's true self. The secondary listening skills are also helpful to the therapy process but are not as directly related to understanding the patient. Primary listening skills are open-ended questions, paraphrasing, reflection of feeling, minimal encouragers, clarifying remarks, summarizing, and perception check.

Primary Listening Skills	Example
Open-ended questions	Tell me about your family.
Paraphrasing	So, you're feeling confused about . . .
Reflection of feeling	You say you're feeling anxious.
Minimal encouragers	I see—uh huh.
Clarifying remarks	Is that once or twice a week?
Summarizing	What I hear you saying is . . .
Perception check	So, you'd like to work on your feelings about work.

Secondary listening skills are normalizing, structuring, and probing.

Secondary Listening Skills	Example
Normalizing	You're not alone in that feeling.
Structuring	So, it looks like we'll learn relaxation first?
Probing	Tell me more about that.

Notice how this system seems to blend speaking and listening. It is probably more important for the psychologist to learn the skills needed for active listening than to rigidly subdivide categories of behavior. We are using this system to illustrate the concept and provide some samples of the desired behaviors. Let's consider each of these categories a bit more closely. In order to be clear about the information you would like to get from your patient, it is often tempting to ask very specific questions. This is probably not a good idea in most cases. Remember in our initial interview with Patty that we started with general questions. Many of these questions would be the kind that would allow Patty to choose the direction of her response. These are considered open-ended questions. We might have said, "Tell me about your family." This question would have allowed her to select how she defined "family" as well as whether she described them in terms of physical appearance, personality, occupation, or some other characteristics. Then if you want more information about part of the response you can follow the open-ended question with a more specific one. The key to open-ended questions is that they do not have one-word answers.

In order to **paraphrase** you must listen carefully to what your patient has been telling you. This skill is useful after a long response to one or more open-ended questions. When you paraphrase, you do not make your observations in absolute terms. You need to allow the patient the opening to indicate that your perception of what was said is not the same as his or hers. A handy way to start practicing this skill is to take a few key words from what you have heard, select synonyms for those words, and then develop a simple sentence using those words to summarize your understanding. Returning to Patty, you might say, "You feel confused about your feelings for [use the former boyfriend's name]."

Reflection of feeling is similar to paraphrasing but in this case you are moving a bit further from observable responses. You are taking information presented by your patient and then hypothesizing an underlying emotion based on a combination of the patient's words, the patient's nonverbal communication, and your knowledge of personality theory. With Joyce, you might say, "You feel ashamed about your lack of skill on some days." As with the paraphrasing, be certain to phrase your comment so that it allows your patient to correct your perception of this feeling.

Minimal encouragers are efforts made by the psychologist to keep the patient talking without actually interrupting what the patient is saying. Examples of ways to do this include the use of such sounds as "um" accompanied by a head nod and using an encouraging smile. This process encourages the patient to continue to speak but does not necessarily stop the flow of conversation or require the patient to reply directly to a question.

What about those times when you either don't hear what your patient has said or do not understand the remark? You do not want to let that pass because it may not be clear later to your patient if you ask about it. Thus, you may need to interrupt at some points during the interview to ask your patient to either repeat or clarify something. This is what is meant by a *clarifying remark.*

Summarizing refers to the concept we described earlier that you use near the end of your session. This term refers to the process of reviewing the major points of the session in preparation for making your treatment recommendations. Related to this is the concept of *perception check.* After you have reviewed the high points of the interview, you need to work with the patient to decide whether there is one particular problem on which he or she wishes to start or whether he or she would prefer to work on several related problems. This discussion is a smooth transition from your summary.

The first of the secondary listening skills is **normalizing.** Many patients who come to see clinical psychologists express concerns that their problems are so severe that nothing can be done for them. Others will be concerned that they have some extreme type of psychopathology when their reactions are more in the realm of moderate distress or even relatively normal reactions to some severe stressor. Normalizing refers to the process of helping your patient realize that the situation is not hopeless and that you believe you will be able to help the patient address the problem or problems.

Structuring is the term for your explanation of what to expect from therapy. What you say will vary depending on the format you plan to use with this patient. If you plan to use homework, you would tell the patient about it and how you plan to use this material in the next session. If this is the patient's first time in psychotherapy, you may also need to explain the active role patients are often expected to play in the process. Patients who are accustomed to seeing a physician who takes a dominant role, gives instructions, and then sends patient off to take pills may have difficulty with a collaborative treatment protocol.

Finally, *probing* is used when you need additional specific information to further understand something your patient has said to you. With Patty, you asked about suicide, a specific plan and possible method, and the role her religion may play in deterring this behavior because of your concerns about her level of depression. This was an example of probing. Manuals have been written to help psychologists develop a better understanding of the skills that may assist them in conducting good interviews (e.g., Evans, Hearn, Uhlemann, & Ivey, 1998). With this general background about interview skills, let's turn our attention to issues related to the setting in which the interview occurs.

The Setting

Psychologists conduct interviews in many different settings. We mentioned the role of the clinical psychologist in hospital emergency rooms earlier in the book. Many people think of the psychologist in terms of an outpatient office in a professional building. Regardless of the location of the interview, there are certain points to remember. First is the need for privacy. Even in the emergency room, the psychologist will try to minimize the presence of others when talking to the patient. Privacy is also an issue in the waiting room of the office. Psychologists do not keep sign-in sheets of the type seen in some types of businesses. Patients may check in with a receptionist or the psychologist may have some other method for the patient to indicate that he or she has arrived, such as a buzzer system, but names are not said aloud for reasons of confidentiality.

When clinical psychologists look for offices, one factor they must consider is soundproofing. You do not want to locate your office in a place where regular external noise will interfere with your clinical sessions. For example, having your office over a motor vehicle repair shop would not be a good idea. In addition to noise, there is also the issue of confidentiality. If you can hear external noise there is the possibility that what is being said in the office can be heard by those passing in the hallway or sitting in the waiting room. No office is likely to be perfectly soundproofed. It is important for the psychologist to take every possible precaution to ensure that external noise does not interfere with the session and that what is said in the office remains within the office. This is a matter of both ethics and facilitating the information flow.

Related to the noise issue is the question of interference with the session. Except in the case of an emergency, psychologists do not answer their telephone during a session. If there is a receptionist, that person takes all calls during a session. If the psychologist does not have a receptionist, then an answering machine is needed to handle calls that may occur during the session. There should be some system in place indicating that the psychologist is busy and that no one is to knock on the door.

There is somewhat less agreement among professionals about the furnishings of the office. Some professionals suggest that the office should be relatively neutral. From this perspective, personal items should be kept to a minimum. Others suggest that having family pictures makes the psychologist more "human" and facilitates the development of rapport. The office should provide a setting where the patient feels comfortable talking and yet realizes this is a professional setting, not a conversation with a friend. In other words, attention should be paid to the comfort level of the seats, cleanliness of the room, and appropriate levels of heat and air conditioning. Most psychologists have rules about whether or not to allow such behavior as smoking or drinking a cup of coffee during the session.

If the psychologist plans to tape record the session, the patient must be aware this is happening. Even if the recorder is not in plain sight, the patient needs to know the session is being recorded. Some psychologists like to tape record their sessions so that they can review the material later and devote themselves fully to the discussion without the need for note-taking. Many psychologists keep a note pad on their desk so they can make occasional notes of important phrases or issues to be pursued later. Most patients will give consent to recording once they are assured of the confidentiality of those recordings. If a patient is concerned about recording, or even note-taking, that concern will then need to be discussed with the patient. It has been our experience that most patients do not have objections to minor note-taking. We have also found that some patients try to read what we are writing. If you are noting phrases or subjects you want to learn more about, it is quite easy to just show that information to the patient who seems curious. By letting the patient know that there is nothing secretive about your notes but rather that you just wanted to remember some points for further discussion, you may actually improve rapport. Verbatim note-taking is generally not recommended because it interferes with the psychologist's ability to observe nonverbal patient behavior as well as his or her ability to mentally process needed directions for the conversation in this session.

Another issue psychologists need to consider is whether or not to keep a box of tissues on the desk. Some psychologists feel that having tissues visible encourages crying and may interfere with the session. Other psychologists take the position that encouraging emotional expression is part of the therapeutic process. Regardless of whether or not the tissue box is visible or in a drawer, psychologists have patients who cry and need tissues. They are essential office supplies for clinical psychologists.

Office size and furniture type varies among psychologists. Traditionally, we think of Freud and his patients lying on a couch. Today, many psychologists have offices without a couch. It is important to have comfortable chairs and sufficient space so that the patient feels at ease and willing to talk about personal problems. Specialized furniture may be needed for certain forms of intervention. For example, psychologists who frequently use relaxation training as part of their therapeutic process may find that having a padded reclining chair and a light switch equipped with dimming capability will facilitate the development of relaxation skills by their patients. Psychologists who work with children may want to have a section of their office devoted to toys and child-size furniture.

Occasionally, psychologists may feel that a meeting outside the office is warranted, but care should be given to maintain professional boundaries. For example, if the psychologist is treating a patient for fear of heights, the psychologist might feel it would be helpful to observe the patient on the observation deck of a high-rise building. A home visit may be useful when working with some children or families. In these circumstances the psychologist does not, however, stop and have a meal with the patient or give any impression that these "out-of-office" meetings are anything but professional. The psychologist must also consider whether there may be special confidentiality issues when planning any session outside the office. For example, you do not have a discussion about the patient's problems with height when riding the elevator to the observation deck of that high-rise building.

Interview Process

The specific format for interviews varies among clinical psychologists and among employment settings. Despite this variability, the general process can be summarized (Nietzel, Bernstein, & Milich, 1998). The first part of the interview process is when the psychologist sets the stage for what will occur during the majority of the time the psychologist spends in this session. Patients will not usually just come into your office and feel comfortable talking about very personal issues. They need to become comfortable with the clinical psychologist before revealing personal details. This process is known as establishing *rapport*. How you do this is individual to both the psychologist and the specific patient. If your office is located in a hard-to-find place, you may put the patient at ease by making a comment about how hard it is to find and that you are pleased he or she was able to locate you. Establishing rapport works quicker with some patients than with others, just as you feel more comfortable the first time you meet some people than others. You will continue to build rapport through the other phases of the interview process. The amount of time you take for this first part of the interview will vary with patients and circumstances.

The majority of the time you spend with your patient should comprise the second phase of the interview. This is the time when you gather information about the person. We talked about some of this process in the patient interviews earlier. Skilled clinicians use a range of techniques to gain information. Some of the questions you ask will be quite specific. They are designed to focus your patient on certain topics. For example, with Joyce you might have asked her what she does when she awakens during the night. Other questions are designed to allow your patient latitude in terms of what is discussed. With Patty, you might have asked her to tell you about her former boyfriend. You have provided a broad context but she may choose to discuss surface topics or emotional ones. At times during the interview, you will probably want to summarize, or paraphrase, what your patient has said to you. When doing this, it is important to make clear that it is "your" understanding of what has been said on this topic up to this point. By doing this, you have demonstrated not only that you are paying attention but also that you are willing to be corrected if you did not understand what your patient meant.

The final part of your interview is the closing or finalizing of this session. Just saying that time is up is not sufficient. You should allow sufficient time to recap what has happened, get feedback from your patient about accuracy, provide some information about what you would suggest should happen next, and come to some agreement with the patient about the next step. This may involve scheduling another appointment to obtain further information, scheduling psychological testing, suggesting a referral to another professional, or perhaps several related suggestions.

We have presented our description of the initial interview in stages. It is important to understand, however, that these divisions are somewhat artificial. You do not plan an interview so that you allow ten minutes for establishing rapport, thirty minutes for the body of the interview, and then ten minutes for the summary and ending period. When you are initially learning to do these interviews, it may seem most comfortable to you to do such specific planning in order to be sure you cover what you feel must be done in this session, but try to avoid that approach. Being that rigid tends to interfere with the establishment of rapport, leading the patient to feel uncomfortable with you and/or with the entire concept of therapy, and it is generally not a productive approach. It is important to stay within the general time frame of the session unless there is an unusual disclosure such as something that may warrant emergency commitment. Psychologists who allow their patients to continually use extra time are not setting appropriate boundaries or facilitating patient progress. With this background about clinical interviews, we now turn our attention to the mental status exam, crisis interview, and structured interview to illustrate other types of interviews conducted by clinical psychologists.

Mental Status Exam

One of the oldest types of interview is the mental status exam. This exam is most often used as part of an intake evaluation or initial screening process. Folstein, Folstein, and McHugh (1975) developed an instrument called the "Mini-Mental State" for the rapid evaluation of cognitive functioning that helps the clinician decide whether to undertake a more comprehensive neuropsychological evaluation. We return to this test in chapter 8 when we discuss neuropsychological assessment. Many psychologists, however, routinely use the mental status examination rather than a specific test as a way of formulating a diagnosis and helping in treatment planning. The mental status exam was originally developed by psychiatrists to be analogous to the physical examination done by other physicians. There is no single format or series of questions used in doing mental status exams. The names of the categories of behavior to be assessed vary somewhat from one text description to another (Groth-Marnat, 1997; Robinson & Chapman, 1997; Trzepacz & Baker, 1993).

Table 5.5 provides an example of behaviors that are usually covered in a mental status exam (Berg, Franzen, & Wedding, 1987).

Let's look at this process a bit more closely. Various terms are used for the broad areas of interest. One common category for the mental status exam is "appearance and behavior." Just as you did in the initial clinical interviews, the mental status exam includes notation about how the patient looked and acted. The patient's cleanliness, type of clothing, and unusual physical mannerisms may be indicative of certain disorders. Suppose you notice that your patient has a runny nose. What does that suggest to you? Three possibilities, and there are certainly others, are that your patient is sick, has been crying, or has been using drugs. The implications of this simple behavioral observation lead to diverse areas for further questioning.

Your evaluation of the patient's speech and use of language gives you an idea about communication problems, such as word fluency problems, as well as a rough indication of intellectual level based on vocabulary and sentence structure. Consider the patient's quality of speech. Based on patient comments, you note if the tone and rate of speech are appropriate. You make inferences about thought processes from the comments as well. Do you have any reason to suspect delusions or hallucinations from what the patient says?

Table 5.5 Mental Status Exam

Area Assessed	Behaviors	How Assessed
Orientation	Person, place, date, time	Ask the patient his or her name, where he or she is, the date, and the time
Attention	Distractibility	Does the patient follow the course of questioning? Serial subtractions
Language	Receptive (written and auditory comprehension)	Psychological testing Repetition, following commands
Language	Expressive (Symbolic) (Written) & spoken	Passage-writing, speaking
Memory	Short- and long-term verbal, visual, spatial, music, tactile, digit span	Repetition, paired associations, picture matching
Executive functions	Planning, monitoring	Vigilance tasks
Somatic concerns	Medical problems	Physical examination
Perception	Hallucinations or delusions	Verbal report, observation
Insight and judgment	Comprehension of situation	Verbal report, observation

Source: Adapted from Berg, R. A., Frann, M., & Wedding, D. Screening for Brain Impairement: A Manual for Mental Health Practice. *New York: Springer Publishing, 1987.*

In some cases, you may want to ask a simple question such as, "Do you ever see things that other people just don't seem to see?" In this case, you are exploring the possibility of visual hallucinations. If your patient's comments do not seem to flow logically from one topic to another, you may infer that the thinking processes do not connect appropriately either. In that case, you may need to probe rather carefully to rule out schizophrenic thinking. You might ask the patient, "Do strangers seem to pay a lot of attention to you?" In this case you are pursing the possibility of delusions.

Another area of concern is the patient's mood and affect. These terms refer to the patient's emotional state. Generally, we use the term **affect** to refer to what we observe in our patient that relates to emotional state and **mood** to refer to the internal emotional state. Your evaluation of the patient's mood and affect includes whether or not the affect fits the subject being discussed (are they congruent?), whether affect changes with changes in subject, and if there is a predominant mood (or perhaps no show of emotion, often called "flat affect"). You also note the intensity of the mood.

Another major goal of the mental status examination is to determine the patient's orientation. A common phrase in patient charts is the notation that the person is "oriented × 3 (oriented times three)," or perhaps less well oriented. The "3" in this notation refers to "time, place, and person." By time, you mean that the patient can accurately tell you the date and time of day. You are not as concerned that the patient is accurate to the precise second, without looking at a clock or watch, but that the patient is aware of the general time of day, month, and year. If it is currently 10 A.M., March 5, 2005, and your patient indicates that it is about 10:15, March 5, 2005, you would say this patient is oriented to time. The fifteen-minute discrepancy from the actual time is not important. On the other hand, if your patient indicates that it is midnight or that the year is 1975, your patient is definitely not oriented to time. This same general understanding is used to determine orientation to place. Does the patient know where this interview is happening? Occasionally, a patient will think you are asking the specific name of a building. Although it is often good to know the name of the hospital or office building, you are more concerned in this case that the patient is aware of the city and state in which the interview is happening than with a specific building name. The third part of your evaluation of orientation is person. Does your patient know who he or she is? You may have read in abnormal psychology books about patients who think they are historical figures or those who think they are children when in fact they are adults. You want to know if the patient knows his or her name and age in this case. Despite the colorful descriptions in books and the media, most patients are oriented × 3. Only the severely mentally disturbed or those with some form of brain trauma have difficulty with this part of the mental status examination. Typically you will need to ask only a couple of questions to determine orientation.

You also want a quick assessment of memory, both short-term and long-term. To accomplish this, you may ask the patient a couple of questions that tap both recent and remote memory and for which you can easily get the correct answer. For example, you might ask the patient, "What did you have for breakfast this morning?" Of course, you will need some external source to verify the patient response if you have any question about it. As a measure of both cognitive function and attention, you may ask the patient to subtract by a set number from a given starting point. A common approach is called serial 7s. In this case, you ask the patient to subtract by 7 from 100 until you say to stop. In other words, you expect the patient to answer 93, 86, 79, and so on. If the patient finds this a bit difficult, you might try serial 3s. This would be an important task with Joyce because of her concerns about her cognitive functioning. Although her performance here would not provide a final decision about Joyce, it would give you some very basic information.

Adult patients are often asked about their physical health and somatic (body) concerns. Some patients incur accidental head injury, infections, and viruses (e.g., HIV) that can affect their mental health. Psychologists ask patients if they have any physical conditions that they think influence their mental health. Likewise, many standardized mental status exams ask patients directly whether they use substances such as alcohol or street drugs. Occasionally, patients also have mental health side effects from medications that have been prescribed by other healthcare providers. Obtaining a release of information and speaking with the primary care physician, nurse practitioner, or physician's assistant can provide additional information that can help the psychologist make an accurate diagnosis. If it was not covered while probing cognitive and emotional issues, psychologists may ask specifically if the patient is feeling suicidal or assaultive. Getting these issues out on the table directly not only allows the patient to disclose important information but also emphasizes the point that the psychologist is exploring many different areas of functioning.

A final area of concern in mental status exams is "insight and judgment." Insight refers to the patient's awareness of both internal and external reality. Does your patient realize that certain behavior is problematic? Does the patient realize that his or her behavior impacts significant others as well as self? Judgment in this case refers to the ability to evaluate various sides of an issue. Does the patient seem to have reasonably sound judgment? A discussion of important life decisions the patient has made can illustrate past judgment. Since Patty and Joyce initiated contact, we may infer that they believe they have problems. If one of them had been referred to us by a third person and had come only to please that person but saw no problems, we might have to explore this area in greater depth. Since you haven't seen Trang yet, and know that because of his age his cognitive development is different from that of adults, you know that his level of insight and judgment is probably less well developed than that of most adults.

In many inpatient psychiatric hospitals, the initial information in the patient's chart is the admission note, perhaps a brief history, and the results of the mental status exam. Further psychological testing may be requested based on the results of this information. In outpatient settings, the mental status exam information will be included in the patient's chart and will influence the type of intervention that is recommended.

Crisis Interview

Another type of interview is the crisis interview. Some clinical psychologists, for example, spend part of their time "on call" for hospital emergency rooms. In this setting, if a patient arrives and the medical personnel feel there may be an overriding emotional problem, the psychologist is called in to make a rapid determination about whether or not this person needs an immediate psychiatric hospitalization. The psychologist in this case may be called not only during the day but also during the night and over weekends and holidays. Many hospitals require the on-call psychologist to remain within a specified distance of the hospital in case he or she is needed. A crisis interview may also be done over the phone. In addition to phone interviews done by psychologists, psychologists also may train and supervise paraprofessionals to work on suicide phone lines and other crisis telephone services.

What all of these interviews have in common is that information is gathered to allow the professional to make a referral for other services. Questions are usually targeted and address specific topics (e.g., Somers-Flanagan & Somers-Flanagan, 1995). Unlike the mental status examination where the professional may be planning to continue to see the patient, the crisis interview is more likely one where this is the only contact the clinical psychologist will have with this patient. Although the psychologist establishes rapport in order to quickly learn sufficient information to help the patient, this is not a therapeutic relationship.

Structured Interview

Not all clinical interviews are of the free-flowing variety we described with our patients. In some cases you may doubt the patient's ability to provide the needed information in a free-flowing conversation. Perhaps the patient has limited verbal skills or insight; perhaps the patient is resistant to providing information. A different way to approach the information-gathering process is to use what amounts to a structured script for your interview. A number of these "scripts" have been developed. Some are designed for use with specific populations, such as children, while others are designed to assess the possible presence of specific forms of psychopathology.

Structured interviews first appeared in the clinical literature in the late 1970s. An early example of this approach to interviewing is the Schedule for Affective Disorders and Schizophrenia, often called the SADS (Endicott & Spitzer, 1978). The SADS has two broad parts. One part was designed to consider current problems and the other part was designed to consider problems experienced in the past. A series of specific questions were asked and each response was rated on a Likert scale. This interview was designed to allow the clinical psychologist to determine whether or not the required symptoms for more than twenty diagnostic categories were present in the patient. Because of the popularity of the SADS, a separate version, the Kiddie-SADS (K-SADS), was developed for use with children and adolescents (Chambers et al., 1985).

Continuing the SADS tradition, the Structured Clinical Interview for DSM-III-R or SCID was developed for use with the DSM-III and then updated to be used with DSM-IV (Spitzer, Williams, Gibbon, & First, 1992). The SCID was designed for use by a trained clinical interviewer. One of the advantages of this particular structured interview is that once you have determined the patient is *not* going to meet the diagnostic criteria for a particular category, you can then omit further questions in this area and move to the next area. This process not only saves the interviewer time but also does not wear out the patient as quickly. There are multiple forms available for the SCID-IV depending on whether you are doing this interview in an inpatient setting, in an outpatient setting, or for research purposes with a nonpatient population. There is also a special series of items designed specifically to consider the symptoms of the personality disorders found on Axis II. These items are especially useful because individuals with Axis II disorders are less likely than those with Axis I disorders to exhibit openness about their problem or even view it as a problem since these are considered more lifelong behaviors.

One group of patients from whom it may be difficult to obtain sufficient information to make an accurate diagnosis is children. Although children may be accustomed to answering specific questions from adults, they may be shy with a stranger. They may also have difficulty providing the details the clinical psychologist needs to form an accurate diagnosis and treatment plan. The Diagnostic Interview Schedule for Children-Version IV (DISC-IV) can be used to help psychologists gain needed information from children (Shaffer, Fisher, Lucas, Dulcan, & Schwab-Stone, 2000). This interview has separate forms to be used with children, adolescents, and parents. Parents or a parent-substitute are routinely used as a source of information about children and adolescents. Their information provides both additions to what the patient provided and cross-validation of that material. As noted in chapter 1, the NIMH has a long history of interest in children's disorders. The development of the original DISC was partially supported by funds from NIMH. Not only is the DISC useful as a format for conducting structured interviews with children and adolescents, but the research on this tool has provided important information that can be used in any interview with this age group. Researchers have found, for example, that as the structured interview progresses, both children and parents will indicate the presence of fewer symptoms than they did in the beginning. This decrease in symptom endorsement is especially true of younger children and for mothers who are younger (Piacentini et al., 1999). Regardless of the type of interview conducted by the psychologist, it is important to note at what point in the interview with a child or adolescent the information was obtained and the age of the parent when making clinical judgments about its veracity. This is a basic example of science (research) informing practice. We will discuss other research issues in the final section of this chapter.

In some cases, a more nonverbal approach may be useful with children. This is especially true with younger children. One such approach is the Berkeley Puppet Interview

(Ablow et al., 1999). In this case, each of two hand puppets expresses an emotion and the child is asked to tell the psychologist which puppet's emotion is closest to the child's. This information can then be combined with observations and data from adults to obtain a more complete picture of the child.

Another example of a nonverbal approach to interviewing is the use of pictures (Valla, Bergeron, & Smolla, 2000). The Dominic-R centers on a child named Dominic. Dominic is shown in a range of situations, some alone and some with other children. Some of these situations are directly related to disorders of childhood, while others are normal childhood situations. The child is asked whether he or she has ever had a similar experience. Thus, the child does not need to be very verbal in order for the psychologist to obtain information.

As life expectancy increases, clinical psychologists have begun to need specialized interview materials for older adults. One example is the Clinical Assessment Scales for the Elderly (CASES) developed by Reynolds and Bigler (2001). The CASES was designed to assess the more prominent DSM-IV symptoms of older adults using a combination of a self-rating form and a form to be completed by someone who knows the older adult. It can be used with people between the ages of fifty-five and ninety.

Psychologists have also developed structured interviews to use with special populations or to assist in answering specific questions. One example is structured interviews designed for use in prison settings. There are times in those settings when the psychologist is asked to determine whether or not the prisoner is pretending to have emotional problems that he or she does not have. At other times in those settings, the issue is one of whether or not the prisoner is likely to engage in violent behavior.

Record-Keeping

There is no single record-keeping format used by all psychologists. Perhaps because of this variability in format, the APA developed a document entitled "Record Keeping Guidelines" (1993) to serve as a guide for psychologists. When APA uses the term **guidelines,** it is referring to something that is aspirational rather than mandatory. Behaviors that are mandatory are typically referred to as **standards.** The common understanding among healthcare providers is that deviations from standards can result in malpractice actions. A malpractice action means that someone files a lawsuit in civil or criminal court and/or files ethical charges with the state licensing board. In the case of guidelines for record-keeping, the document provides broad areas the psychologist needs to consider when developing a personal format. The purpose of clinical records is to document what the psychologist has done as well as to facilitate any future treatment that may be provided either by that psychologist or some other professional who later may be given access to those records. For the types of interviews we described in this chapter, some of the records will be included in patient charts in a hospital setting while others will be in an independent practitioner's office.

More recently (2003), the **Health Insurance Portability and Accountability Act (HIPAA)** mandates a different kind of record-keeping. Under the HIPAA Privacy Rule, which was promulgated by the U.S. Department of Health and Human Services, managed care companies and other covered entities are barred from requesting information beyond what is minimally necessary to accomplish payment or other administrative tasks. The HIPAA Privacy Rule applies to psychologists as well. Psychologists' employees, for example, should only be given enough information about patients to ensure that they can do their jobs. Some employees, such as a receptionist, might not need any clinical information. Under HIPAA's Privacy Rule, psychotherapy process notes can't be disclosed without patient authorization. In addition, managed care companies are barred from conditioning payment on the patient's authorization to release those notes to them. This egregious manipulation by managed care companies was common before HIPAA's protections.

Regardless whether a psychologist is using HIPAA guidelines or other record-keeping guidelines, a professional chart is started on the patient with his or her first session. That chart will contain a summary of the information from this initial meeting. For brief interviews, such as the crisis interview, we would expect considerably less material in the chart than from an intake interview. Any contact, however, is noted in a chart. For example, if the patient calls the psychologist and discusses issues over the phone the psychologist will make a brief note of that contact in the patient's chart. Of course if this is just a call to change an appointment, that information is not a clinical issue and need not be noted in the chart.

Various methods are used for keeping patient records. Three such methods are source-oriented, problem-oriented, and goal-oriented records (VandeCreek & Knapp, 1997). Let's consider the differences among these types of records and when you might want to use each type.

Source-oriented records might be used for inpatient programs in which a number of different professionals will be making notes about the person. There is one file for the patient but it is subdivided by discipline. There is a section for psychologists' remarks and another section for each of the other professionals who will be making notations. Notes are made chronologically within each of the professions' section but not in an overall sense in the chart. Thus, if you are interested in reading about this patient's history, you might read what the psychologist wrote and then move back chronologically to read what the psychiatrist reported. You would then repeat that process to learn what the nursing staff said and so on.

Another format is called the problem-oriented record. Typically, the record starts with a notation of the specific problems to be addressed. Each professional notation, whether by an individual psychologist or a professional team, would be based on the problem or problem number with the date of the notation. Suppose, for example, a patient had problems with (1) anger management, (2) time management, and (3) sleep. When a professional made a note in this patient's chart, the note would start with #2 if that information dealt with time management issues. If that same professional was also making comments about recent sleep issues, a new paragraph or section would start with #3. If further problems arise during the treatment of the patient, they can be added to the problem list. A problem is never erased, but a notation may be made that the problem has been handled. When describing activities later in therapy notes, reference would continue to be made to the ways these activities relate to the specific problems listed.

A similar type of record is the goal-oriented record. In this case, rather than noting a specific problem, the patient's treatment is viewed from the perspective of the outcome. After the intake interview, possibly supplemented by psychological testing, the psychologist and patient develop goals for the treatment process. Decisions about the treatment are all made from the perspective of these identified goals. For example, suppose your patient is a college student who has difficulty waking up for her early morning classes. She has routinely missed 50 percent of her first class meetings of the day. One goal might be to reduce missed classes to 10 percent of the time. Treatment leading to this goal might address such factors as placement of the alarm clock in the room, evening activities, and use of a "buddy system" for class attendance.

For some psychologists, the descriptions we have just provided seem a bit cumbersome. They would prefer a simpler format for making their records. Others prefer to make just a few summary notes following each session with the patient. Of course, there may be a prescribed format for record-keeping at the psychologist's place of employment. In that case, there is no choice about style. There may also be laws about the content that must be covered in the psychologist's notes. Psychologists must remain aware of any state or federal regulations that may impact the way they maintain their records. Keep in mind that what we have described is a suggestion. The psychologist might modify the suggested format. To facilitate the process of record-keeping, companies have developed computer programs using a range of formats.

When you read the clinical literature about record-keeping, you may find the contrasting terms **process notes** and **progress notes.** Some psychologists keep both types of notes, while others use only one of them. Progress notes describe what is happening in the treatment. These notes include information about changes that have occurred in the patient as well as a description of the interventions used by the psychologist. Process notes tend to be more impressionistic. These notes include the therapist's hypotheses that may be either supported or negated in later sessions as well as general impressions that are not necessarily grounded in data.

Regardless of the type of records you make, you must keep them in a secure place. This requirement is for both patient confidentiality and future availability. Because of confidentiality issues, the psychologist needs to be careful to remove patient records from his or her desk before another patient enters the office. Most records are kept in files with the patient name on the tab. Even the fact that this person is seeing you is confidential. You cannot risk the possibility that the next person in your office will see that name. Some authorities recommend that financial records be "backed up" and removed from the premises at regular intervals to protect these records from destruction by fire or theft. Tape backups have been supplanted in recent years by Internet-based backup systems. Regardless of what type of record-keeping system you use, you should be aware of the requirements that are mandated by your state licensing board, by ethical guidelines, and by any third-party payer contracts under which you accept reimbursement.

If you continue to work with patients after their initial interview, you need to make sure your intervention is consistent with the diagnosis and treatment plan found earlier in their record. Thus, whatever format you use for record-keeping, you need to have those records easily available to you and keep them current so you can modify the treatment plan based on new information.

There is some discussion within the profession about how long you need to keep your records following completion of a case. States differ in their requirements about how long professionals must keep records. Generally, the records of children must be kept longer than the records of adults. Most regulations related to children's records are worded in terms of a specified number of years *after* the child reaches the age of majority. Even with adults, courts have made distinctions about adult records depending on the type of pathology. Thus, for psychologists who have been in practice for a long time, storage of records becomes an issue. It is sometimes recommended that even if you plan to shred old records you keep a summary of the file for future use. When considering the need for keeping records, plans should also be made regarding patient records in case of the psychologist's death. Young practitioners may not think about this issue, but ethical practice mandates that it be considered regardless of the age of the psychologist. Within institutional settings, this is not a problem because the facility maintains the records. The psychologist in a group practice needs to have some understanding with the group about release of those records in case of the psychologist's death. What about the psychologist who is in an independent practice? What happens to patient records in case of death, or even retirement? Once again, the psychologist needs to make plans for someone to take over the records. Active patients need to be informed of this change of their records, and patients whose records are within the legal period of record availability need to know where they can get the information if needed. As you can see, the general topic of record-keeping is not a simple one.

Interview Research

As a closing topic in this chapter, we will make a few comments about interview research. As we mentioned in chapter 3, Rogers was one of the first modern psychologists to study the actual clinical interview. Since Rogers' time, much has been written about the clinical interview (Beutler, Machado, & Neufeldt, 1994; Beutler, 1996). Rogers' data on the importance of certain therapist characteristics, especially the ability to accurately reflect to your patient what you have heard, have been supported by more recent data on interviewing (Goldfried, Greenberg, & Marmar, 1990). The nonverbal behavior and noncontent behavior of the therapist in an interview have also been studied. Studies done in the 1960s found that the amount of time an interviewer spoke influenced the length of time the patient spoke. By increasing speaking time and then decreasing it during the same session, the interviewers found their patients followed their example of speaking time (Kanfer & McBrearty, 1962; Matarazzo, 1965). This phenomenon is known as **synchrony.** Synchrony was later found to vary depending factors such as the relationship between the patient and therapist (Pope, Nudler, Vonkorff, & McGhee, 1974). This line of research about nonverbal behavior was extended later to include studying the role of factors such as body language and voice tone on patient response (Siegman & Feldstein, 1987). For example, if the clinical psychologist used a somewhat negative tone when paraphrasing the patient's comments about a particular subject, this tended to close off further discussion of that topic, even if the psychologist's actual words encouraged further discussion.

When we described the mental status exam, you may have gotten the impression that this approach to evaluating the patient is so vague that it cannot, or has not, been evaluated. Researchers have applied statistical techniques to data from the mental status exam to develop better ways to do it (Spitzer, Fleiss, Endicott, & Cohen, 1967). Attempts have also been made to evaluate the reliability and validity of mental status exams (Spitzer, Fleiss, Burdock, & Hardesty, 1964). Remember that we noted that there is no single format for conducting mental status exams. Overall, because of the variability among approaches to mental status exams, the data do not support their reliability. Despite this lack of research support, however, they continue to be used on a regular basis and important patient decisions are made based on data from the mental status exam.

Another area of interview research involves the reliability and validity of the information obtained. Remember that reliability refers to the repeatability of the findings and validity refers to how well the measure actually evaluates what it is intended to evaluate. Studies investigating the reliability of interview data typically compare the diagnosis or patient description provided by several people who interview the same patient. When we consider the literature in this area, we find that structured interviews tend to have the highest levels of reliability (Segal, Hersen, & Van Hasselt, 1994); interviews with children or unstructured interviews do not do as well (Fallon & Schwab-Stone, 1994; Rogers, 1995). Validity of interview data is a more difficult question. As a result of physical and/or emotional problems, patients may provide the psychologist with inaccurate information. There are also patients who come to see a psychologist but are not there because they want help. They have made the appointment with the psychologist because having this appointment may be viewed as helpful with some problem. For example, a person who is under criminal charges for exhibitionism may find it helpful during the trial to "show remorse" by indicating he or she is currently in therapy with a clinical psychologist. If this person really does not want to stop this behavior, what is said in therapy will be only what the patient wants the psychologist to tell the judge. It may not be an accurate reflection of the patient's motivations. In this type of case, the psychologist can expect the patient to stop coming as soon as the trial has been completed unless continued therapy is part of the court mandate. Researchers have found that the validity of the interview increases when the patient feels more comfortable with the psychologist (e.g., Kane & Macauley, 1993). This finding further establishes the importance of establishing rapport with the patient. Regardless of the sense of rapport the clinical psychologist may feel with the patient, the potential for malingering must always be considered. In an attempt to address this question, specific tests to measure malingering have been developed (Hall & Pritchard, 1996). We discuss these tests further in chapter 8.

Advances in computer technology have provided researchers with the option of studying diagnostic accuracy without actually seeing the patient. Artificial intelligence computer programs have been used to simulate a clinical interview (Brammer, 2002). This approach allows a number of different people to consider the same information and form a diagnostic impression. Brammer asked both psychologists and graduate students to participate in his study. Each participant was given some basic patient information. After that, participants asked the computer questions and were given pregenerated answers related to psychosocial history and symptomatology. Each response was a paragraph. Of course, using a computer program does not allow the psychologist to make use of nonverbal clues that are available in a real clinical situation. By analyzing the types of questions asked Brammer learned that the more experienced subjects (the psychologists) asked the types of diagnostic questions leading to a correct diagnoses more frequently than did the less experienced subjects (the graduate students). The psychologists tended to avoid the types of questions that would not add to the needed database for an accurate diagnosis or perhaps be distracting in the diagnostic process. Further studies of this type can be expected to test these data.

ETHICAL CONUNDRUM POINTS TO PONDER

Let's return to that ethical issue from the beginning of the chapter. What are some of the issues you need to consider in this case? Who is the patient in this case, and does that have an impact on what you can do? First, you should have clarified with her the limits of confidentiality before she started to talk to you. In cases like this one, the clarification should have been done with both the parents and their daughter. Although this patient is seventeen years old and may look like an adult, she is legally a minor. In general terms, there are three instances when you might need to violate confidentiality, and you should explain them in the beginning (Pope & Vasquez, 1998). If a minor tells you that he or she is being abused, you must report that information to the police or child protection services in your state, depending on the law applicable in your jurisdiction. If the minor tells you about suicidal plans, you must tell the parents. If the minor tells you about plans to hurt someone else, you must warn the intended victim. In order to provide this clarification, you need to be familiar with the legislation and case law of your state relating to minors. How is a minor defined specifically in the area of mental health? This varies among jurisdictions as well as for different purposes. For example, in Louisiana, a minor is anyone under age eighteen, but there are special rules for people between ages sixteen and eighteen related to mental health issues. If you do not tell her parents about her missed period, you might talk to her about whether or not she sees an ob-gyn regularly. If she does, you could pursue with her the need to make an appointment and discuss her sexual activity with this physician as well as her delayed menstrual period. If your state requires you to tell her parents about this disclosure, you should not only inform her of this but also discuss with her how the two of you might talk about this with her parents. Perhaps you have thought of other issues. The point of these ethics vignettes is to have you think about cases that are not going to have easy answers and then provide you with some of the relevant issues to consider.

Key Terms

active listening	guidelines	intake	progress notes
affect	Health Insurance	mood	rapport
diagnosis	Portability and	normalizing	secondary listening
Diagnostic and	Accountability Act	paraphrasing	skills
Statistical Manual	(HIPAA)	primary listening	standards
of Mental Disorders	International	skills	structuring
(DSM-IV)	Classification	process notes	synchrony
Global Assessment	of Functionality		
of Function (GAF)	(ICF)		

CHAPTER 6

Intellectual Assessment

In this chapter we will discuss some of the tests used by clinical psychologists when they want to assess various aspects of a person's cognitive abilities. We will center our discussion on tests of intelligence and tests of achievement. Before we do that, however, we will discuss some of the theories of what is meant by **intelligence** and current research on this subject.

The idea of what constitutes intelligence is a thorny one. Some theorists believe that specialized areas of the brain serve particular functions. These "localizations" began with phrenologists Gall and Spurzheim in the 1800s and have supporters in the neuroimaging scientists in the twenty-first century. Although phrenologists had the right idea that some areas of the brain were responsible for specific behaviors, they had the wrong method. Gall and Spurzheim suggested that by feeling the bumps on a person's head, they could determine what major functions dominated that person's intellect. Additional scientific evidence to support the phrenologists' initial assumptions was provided by the French physician Paul Broca who, while examining patients with language deficits, found consistent lesions in the left temporal lobe.

Other theories of intelligence emphasize a hierarchal, or what others have called a dimensional, approach. Raymond Cattell (1971) proposed that intelligence is comprised of two factors: **fluid intelligence** and **crystallized intelligence.** Fluid intelligence includes speed, flexibility, and skill in acquiring new information, and understanding relationships and abstractions. Cattell suggested that this part of our intelligence is genetically based. It is basically nonverbal and allows us to adapt to the new situations we face throughout life. This is what some people call the ability to solve problems. Crystallized intelligence represents accumulated knowledge. This part of our intelligence is the focus of most intelligence tests used by psychologists. In contrast to fluid intelligence, crystallized intelligence is highly dependent on culture. Cattell's theory has been revised and elaborated upon using more recent statistical concepts. Fluid and crystallized intelligence are found at the top of the hierarchal model with numerous subcomponents such as specific sensory recognition and perceptual speed (Horn, 1994). Guilford (1967) also proposed a psychometric-based model of intelligence. In his theory, there are three dimensions of intelligence: operations, contents, and products. He used the term *operation* to refer to cognition, memory, divergent production, convergent production, and evaluation. The term *contents* refers to the types of information on which these operations are conducted. Within this system, they are figural, symbolic, semantic, and behavioral. The final segment of this system is *products*. Guilford identified six potential products: units, classes, systems, relations, transformations, and implications. Pictorially, this model is often shown as a cube to illustrate all possible combinations of these three factors. With five operations, four contents, and six products, this model proposes the existence of 120 separate intellectual abilities. Try to imagine developing a test to measure each of these 120 factors.

A third approach to understanding intelligence is found in the computational models that emphasize information processing. These theories consider how we mentally represent information and process it. There is a large literature in this area, especially those studies investigating the concept of **metacognition.** Some theorists have suggested that having the ability to use metacognitions is an essential part of intelligence (Wang, Haertel, & Walberg, 1990).

Some theorists have suggested that we should not even talk about intelligence in the singular but rather talk about intelligences. For example, Gardner (1983) proposed a theory of multiple intelligences. These intelligences were roughly based on the literature on brain–behavior relationships. His early writing proposed that the following seven types of intelligence were supported in the literature: linguistic, logical-mathematical, spatial, musical, bodily-kinesthetic, interpersonal, and intrapersonal. More recently, he added three more types of intelligence that were starting to have support in the literature: naturalistic, spiritual, and existential (1999).

A few theorists have approached the study of intelligence from a biological perspective. These studies have investigated various properties of the brain in an attempt to understand intelligence. Early investigators of the biological basis of intelligence studied brain wave correlates of intelligence (Ertl & Schafer, 1969). Technological developments have led to different approaches to the investigation of the biological bases of intelligence. For example, researchers analyzed positron emission tomography (PET) scans of people who were solving intellectual problems (Haier, 1993). They found that more intelligent people showed less brain activity when doing several different types of problems than less intelligent people did. Students who want to read more in this area might start with Sternberg and Kaufman's review article (1998).

Another perspective on intelligence is that it is inextricably bound to the culture in which a person develops. These contextualist theories focus on the relationship between intelligence and the external world (Suzuki & Valencia, 1997). And last, for our purposes, is the triarchic theory of intelligence by Robert Sternberg (1985). Sternberg emphasizes the point that successful intelligence is the ability to succeed in life according to your own definition of intelligence within your own environment. His theory places less emphasis on the speed and accuracy of performance than many of the other models do. Instead the emphasis is on

ETHICAL CONUNDRUM

You are a clinical psychologist who has been asked to evaluate a seven-year-old boy with possible need for special services in the school because of cognitive delay. He and his family have recently moved to your rural community from a village in northern India. He speaks very little English. You do not speak his language. The only person in your community who can act as a translator for your evaluation is his sixteen-year-old sister. What are some of the ethical issues for you to consider?

the person's ability to plan how to respond to various situations and then carry out that plan. Sternberg hypothesizes that intelligence is composed of three abilities: analytic, creative, and practical. As you can see, there are many different approaches to the study of intelligence.

We will review some of the more common ways of assessing the controversial concept known as "intelligence." Some of these tests have forms that can be used across the lifespan, while others are designed for specific age groups. We will note for each test the specific groups for which it is appropriate. The tests we have chosen to describe are only a small percentage of the tests available. Review sources are available for students who are interested in gaining knowledge about other psychological tests (e.g., Maddox, 2003; Plake, Impara, & Spies, 2003). Our selection of which tests to describe in this chapter was based on a combination of popularity among clinical psychologists and our personal familiarity with some of them. We do not mean to imply that other tests are less acceptable.

We noted in our description of the history of clinical psychology that intellectual assessment has played a major role in the development of the profession. The test development work of Binet in France and Witmer's clinic in Philadelphia are key parts of this domain. This chapter will build on that foundation. We will provide you with an ethical conundrum related to intellectual assessment shortly and then give you some points to ponder about it at the end of the chapter. Our ethical conundrum will be followed by a sample of current research in the field of clinical assessment. After describing our selection of cognitive tests, we will illustrate their use with our ongoing patients from chapter 5.

Research

Many of the standardized measures of intellectual ability are available in a condensed version as well as the original version. These condensed versions are called **short forms.** Managed care organizations often place strict limits on the amount of time that will be reimbursed for psychological testing. With this financial limitation, some psychologists who do intellectual assessment have sought to use short forms of the standardized measures rather than the longer original ones. This short form allows them to have a measure of cognitive ability and perhaps have time for other forms of assessment as well. Some of these short forms are described as serving a screening function rather than the complete diagnostic picture obtained from the complete version. Regardless of the reason for using a short form, it is important for clinicians to have information about its comparability to the longer form. Researchers have been challenged to develop short forms with validity similar to the full-length form. Not all psychologists have been pleased with the idea of short forms. Some psychologists have said they are acceptable for screening but note that the psychologist does not have the opportunity to adequately evaluate the patient's strengths and weaknesses when he or she uses a short form of the test. Periodically, psychologists review the literature on short forms of our tests (Levy, 1968; Silverstein, 1990). These reviews have also included suggestions about how to evaluate short forms. Short forms continue to be of interest to clinical psychologists (Smith, McCarthy, & Anderson, 2000). Smith and colleagues noted that psychologists continue to have mixed reactions to short forms of standardized tests. Little attention seems to have been paid to prior suggestions about ways to improve test development procedures. We presented this information to illustrate to you one of the professional controversies you may find as you read psychology journals. Throughout this book, we have tried to identify some of these "hot" topics to give you a start thinking about them.

Other researchers have focused on the use of specific parts of an intelligence test for understanding specific subsets of intellectual ability (Caruso & Cliff, 2000; Donders, 1997). This type of research is known as **component analysis.** Clinicians who want to either do this type of research or read it must have a solid foundation in statistics.

Another issue to consider in the field of psychological testing is the role of cultural diversity. This issue is broader than the ethical conundrum we presented earlier. Early intelligence test developers hoped to be able to devise measures of intellectual ability that were independent of one's cultural heritage. The term **culture-free** was seen in the literature related to those measures developed with special sensitivity to issues of cultural bias. Psychologists in the twenty-first century take the position that our culture influences all aspects of our development and therefore we cannot develop tests that are culture-free. Based on this evolving concept, the term *culture-free* tended to be replaced by the term **culture-fair.** Many culture-fair tests are nonverbal. One reason for developing nonverbal tests was based on the hypothesis that the use of language provided a major bias in testing. Specialists in assessment have questioned the appropriateness of replacing verbal tests with nonverbal tests. These specialists noted that we do not have data to support the concept that nonverbal tests assess the same cognitive abilities as verbal tests, nor do we have evidence that nonverbal tests are not just as culturally loaded as their verbal counterparts (Anastasi & Urbina, 1997). Awareness of the importance of culture in psychological testing has led to the publication of numerous materials to assist the psychologist when assessing members of diverse cultures (e.g., Dana, 1993, 1996). Developers of tests intended to be culture-fair have also tried to select test items that are common across a number of cultures. For this method of test development to be adequate, however, the measure would need to be validated in each of those cultures. This validation process takes time and significant funding and therefore is seldom executed to the degree desired by psychological assessment researchers. Others have suggested that the best approach is to develop different tests for each cultural group. Although that approach might have worked many years ago, it no longer seems feasible. The growing cultural diversity within the United States would require the development of many new tests. This would be a time-consuming and expensive process. Once these new tests were developed, their use would likely be specific only to those individuals who live in the United States and potentially not applicable to people in their country of origin. This is not a cost-effective endeavor for test publishers.

Reliability and Validity

Before we discuss the specific tests psychologists might use to measure cognitive ability, we want to review some of the basic characteristics of a good test. Two of the characteristics that are of importance are **reliability** and **validity.** We noted these terms in chapter 5 when we talked about diagnoses. We will now discuss them as they relate to psychological tests. Types of reliability and validity are listed in Table 6.1.

The *reliability* of a test refers to the consistency of the results of testing. In other words, does the person receive the same score each time that same person takes the test? Psychological tests, like many forms of measurement, do not have absolute reliability. Think about the implications of this test characteristic. If you are making important life decisions about a person based on the results of the testing, you want to have confidence that if the test had been given on a different day, in a different place, or by a different psychologist the results would have been the same, or very nearly the same. The following example illustrates this concept. Suppose you take your temperature and note that it is 98.6°F. You take your temperature again an hour later, and it is 98.4°F. You would probably not feel that your thermometer is broken and that you needed a new one if you obtained this slightly different result. Most of us would accept that this small difference might be a personal change or within an acceptable range of error for the thermometer. This same characteristic of slight variability relates to psychological tests. Test manuals provide information about the statistical evaluation of the reliability of the test, usually reported as a reliability coefficient. This statistic is the ratio of the true score variance of the test to the total variance of the test score. For a complete discussion of this topic, consult a general tests and measurements textbook (e.g., Cohen & Swerdlik, 2002; Gregory, 2004).

Psychologists use several different methods for evaluating the reliability of test scores. We will briefly explain test-retest, alternate form/parallel form, and split-half to illustrate reliability measures. One common approach is known as **test-retest reliability.** In this case, you correlate pairs of scores obtained by the same person on two different administrations of the same test. Of course, you use a large number of people's scores in this way before you have a good idea about the consistency of the scores. This approach to reliability is most useful for tests that are attempting to measure characteristics that are considered to be quite stable over time. For most psychological tests that are considered to be reliable, the test-retest reliability should be in the .80s or .90s range. Remember from your statistics class that a reliability coefficient of 1.00 means that the scores would be exactly the same each time.

When more than one form of a test is available, **alternate-form** or **parallel-form reliability** can be calculated. In this case, the alternate forms of the test were developed independently of each other but have similar content, normative properties, and level of difficulty. In this case, as with test-retest reliability, you need to administer the test twice to each person and then correlate the scores. It is expensive for test developers to make more than one form of a test because of the effort required to develop essentially two separate tests and to make them of equal difficulty. As a result of this increased cost, fewer and fewer tests are being developed with parallel forms.

There are situations in which it just may not be practical to test the same person twice. In this case, the test developed might use **split-half reliability.** You only need to administer the test once and then compare the person's score on equivalent halves of that test.

Many psychological tests are easier in the first half than the second half. Thus, to calculate split-half reliability, you would not want to just divide the questions in the middle. The most common approach to calculating a split-half reliability is to compare the odd-numbered items to the even-numbered ones. This evaluation of reliability is also used as an added evaluation when test-retest reliability has also been calculated.

Validity is the term psychologists use to indicate how well a test measures what it says it measures. After all, the purpose of doing a psychological assessment is to get a specific type of information. It is important for the psychologist to have confidence that this information is not only consistent but is actually a measure of the subject of interest. To determine validity, researchers must compare results of the test with other measures of that concept. To illustrate this process we will describe five types of validity: face validity, content validity, criterion-related validity, construct validity, and protocol validity.

Face validity is based on the surface content of the test. This concept appears to directly relate to the reason the test was made. Thus, questions like: "How happy are you?" and "Are you a jealous person?" simply ask what the test was designed to measure. Although the term *validity* is used here, this concept does not really guarantee that the test is valid in the way psychologists use this term. There are many reasons for this statement, but you can imagine that people may not always see themselves accurately or that they many want to manipulate the impression they are making and not tell the truth.

Content validity is a useful concept when a test is designed to measure a concept about which we have a great deal of information. This form of validity is a measure of how well the test samples the behavior associated with whatever concept is being measured. Content validity forms the basis for the selection of items when the test is first developed. Items are selected so that they are representative of the entire concept. It is much easier to determine the content validity of an achievement test, such as a basic math test, than it is to determine the content validity of a personality test designed to measure self-concept. Statistical measures designed to evaluate the various forms of validity we are describing here are discussed in detail in the psychological testing books we noted earlier in this section.

Criterion-related validity is an evaluation of how well a test score correlates with some other measure of the same concept. This other measure is called a *criterion*. A wide range of concepts have been used as criteria. This term has been used to include a psychiatric diagnosis based on interviewing, scores on another established test, and a rating by hospital staff on a standardized rating form. Under the broad heading of criterion-related validity are *concurrent validity* and *predictive validity*.

When the comparison test scores are obtained at about the same time as those on the test being evaluated, it is called **concurrent validity.** For example, suppose you are developing a test to assist in the diagnosis of depression. You might give your test to a sample of people who are also interviewed and diagnosed by a mental health professional. You would then compare the results of the two measures to determine how well your test differentiated those patients with and without depression. If you can get the same information another way, why would you bother to develop a test? The answer is quite simple. Your measure might provide the information more quickly than the other method or could be used later as a way to provide confirmation or support for the other method.

If you administer your test at one time period and obtain the comparison information at another time, it is called **predictive validity.** When you applied for admission to college,

Table 6.1 Reliability and Validity Types	
Reliability Types	**Validity Types**
Test-retest	Face
Alternate form/parallel form	Content
Split-half	Criterion-related
	Concurrent
	Predictive
	Construct
	Protocol

you probably needed to take a standardized test such as the Scholastic Aptitude Test (SAT) or the American College Test (ACT). The predictive validity of either of these tests could be measured by comparing your performance on them to your grade point average in your freshman year in college.

It is a bit harder to describe **construct validity** than the other three forms of validity. This is because a *construct* is a theoretical concept rather than something that is more easily quantified. Consider the construct *intelligence.* Later in the chapter, we will give you some definitions of this construct. Although *intelligence* is a concept most of us believe we understand, providing the type of definition needed for establishing construct validity is not easy. Psychological constructs have two common characteristics: Because there is no single referent for them, they cannot be operationally defined, and current theory provides interrelated suppositions about the construct (Gregory, 2004). Construct validity then refers to how well the test measures a theoretical concept. Generally it takes a long time and a complex procedure to establish the construct validity of a psychological test. Despite the difficulty in establishing construct validity, many specialists in the field today consider it the unifying concept within the overall area of validity of psychological tests.

Protocol validity is a term often associated with personality assessment, but we will introduce it here with the other forms of validity. This form of validity refers to issues related to the patient rather than the test itself. In this case, the issue is whether or not the patient is responding to the test items in a way that really represents that person. In some cases, the patient may be uncomfortable with the questions and therefore may choose not to respond correctly even if he or she knows the correct answer. In other cases, the patient may choose not to respond in a representative way because of factors about the testing situation such as characteristics of the examiner or the test setting.

Intelligence Tests

If you are going to study intelligence tests, you probably should think about what you are measuring. We all know what the term *intelligence* means, don't we? This may appear to be a simple question, but psychologists do not have a single definition of *intelligence* that is accepted by everyone. As a starting point for discussion of these types of tests, we selected two definitions of the term from the psychological literature. These definitions illustrate the concept sufficiently well for us to then discuss some of the actual measures we use. In his 1958 book, David Wechsler defined intelligence as "the aggregate or global capacity of the individual to act purposefully, to think rationally, and to deal effectively with his environment" (p. 7). Remember our discussion of him in chapter 3. Each tests and measurements textbook has at least one definition of intelligence. According to one of these books, intelligence includes "the abilities and capacities to acquire and apply knowledge, to reason logically, to plan effectively, to infer perceptively, to exhibit sound judgment and problem-solving ability, to grasp and visualize concepts, to be mentally alert and intuitive, to be able to find the right words and thoughts with facility, and to be able to cope, adjust, and make the most of new situations" (Cohen & Swerdlik, 2002, p. 224). A common aspect of these definitions is that psychologists use the term *intelligence* to refer to the ability to do certain things rather than knowing specific content information. Thus, it is not surprising to note that when Wechsler discussed what we are measuring with intelligence tests, he said it was "the capacity of an individual to understand the world about him and his resourcefulness to cope with its challenges" (Wechsler, 1975, p. 139).

These definitions of intelligence and intelligence testing are from the psychological literature. As we noted earlier, psychologists have also developed many theories to try to explain intelligence. Psychologists, however, are not alone in their attempts to understand the meaning of intelligence. When psychologist Robert Sternberg and his colleagues surveyed a sample of nonpsychologists regarding their understanding of intelligence, some of the common characteristics described were high reading comprehension, being open-minded, use of logical reasoning, and having common sense (Sternberg, Conway, Ketron, & Bernstein, 1981). Once again, the focus is on the ability to learn rather than on something specific the person has learned. Although the definitions used by psychologists and nonpsychologists use different words, the underlying idea is similar.

There are many different tests of intelligence available today. In this chapter we will describe a few of the intelligence tests used by clinical psychologists. We will limit our discussion to individually administered tests of intelligence because these are the ones most likely to be administered by a clinical psychologist. We do not mean to imply that group tests of intelligence are not good tests. To be practical in terms of space, we have chosen to be selective.

There are several terms from the assessment literature that are important to know as you read about psychologist testing. **Standard error of the measurement** refers to the variability of a person's score across multiple times the person takes what are found to be equivalent forms of a test. Occasionally this is also called *standard error of the score* to make it clear that it is not a change in the person but rather the fact that a person's performance on these tests should not be viewed as an absolute score but rather as part of a range of scores. Test manuals provide the psychologist with information about the standard error of the measurement for that tool. When summarizing a patient's test results, it is important to provide not only the person's score on the test but also the band of scores that is most likely to include the "true" score for that person. For example, if you were asked to look at Dr. Matthews and judge her height, you might say that she was 5'7" tall. You would likely be more accurate if you said that she was between 5'3" and 5'9" tall. This larger range of judgments increases the chances that you would be correct.

Another term appearing in the assessment literature is **accommodation.** In most cases in which this term is used, it refers to alteration of the testing procedure or apparatus because the patient has a specific form of disability. Before making an accommodation, the psychologist needs to consider how that modification affects the meaning of the patient's score. The report of that psychological evaluation needs to include information about the accommodation and how it may have impacted the assessment process. Issues of accommodation are quite common for psychologists who do school assessments. Because accommodations have become such a major issue since the passage of the Individuals with Disabilities Act, entire books address the topic (e.g., Burns, 1998). We will provide a couple of examples to illustrate the issue. Suppose you are asked to do an assessment of a person with visual difficulties. The type of accommodation you need to make will depend on the degree of visual impairment. There are times when you only know in advance that your patient is visually impaired but not the extent of their impairment. You will need to be prepared to alter your testing plans depending on the degree of visual difficulty you observe during the assessment process. Since many visually impaired persons need extra time for completing psychological tests, selection of tests that are timed may not be the best measure of the person's ability. You will also need to be highly aware of test fatigue. If the person has partial vision and is able to do the required tasks the effort to do this may be greater than for a fully sighted person. Although the psychologist should *always* be aware of the patient's physical changes during testing, this is an ongoing issue with patients who need accommodations. You may need to schedule testing breaks more often or plan fewer tests during one session than is usual in your practice. You may need to allow the patient to have time to handle your test equipment prior to the evaluation as well as to alter the lighting to allow the patient to provide as accurate a picture as possible of the domains being measured. You also need to be very familiar with the literature about specific parts of your test that may be impacted by the person's limitation. For example, subtest scores on the WISC may be influenced differentially in cases of blindness or severe visual impairment (Groenveld & Jan, 1992).

Another personal characteristic that may impact test performance is **test anxiety.** Test anxiety is a general term referring to a high level of concern about test performance. Most of the psychological literature uses this term to include not only the personal sense of fear but also its accompanying physiological and behavioral factors. Test anxiety often gets worse when narrow time limits are part of the testing procedure. Many of the most frequently used individual tests of intelligence have sections that are visibly timed. Highly anxious people have been found to do less well on timed subtests of the WAIS than low anxious people do (Siegman, 1956).

The Wechsler Tests

As we noted in chapter 3, David Wechsler developed a series of three tests of intelligence that are used with people from preschool through late adulthood. Each of the three **Wechsler tests** has its own test manual with specific administration instructions as well as technical information about that test. The tests in this series are grouped for interpretation into verbal and performance scales. Table 6.2 provides a comparison of the subtests included in the adult and children's version of the Wechsler tests. The version for preschool children is different because of the level of development. We will discuss that test separately.

Table 6.2 Wechsler Tests

	WAIS-III	WISC-IV	WPPSI-III
Verbal Tests			
Vocabulary	X	X	X
Similarities	X	X	X*
Arithmetic	X	X*	
Digit Span	X	X*	
Information	X	X	X
Comprehension	X	X	X*
Letter-Number Sequencing	X*	X	
Word Reasoning		X	X
Receptive Vocabulary			X
Picture Naming			X*
Performance Tests			
Picture Completion	X	X	X*
Digit Symbol	X		
Block Design	X	X	X
Matrix Reasoning	X	X	X
Picture Arrangement	X		
Symbol Search	X*	X*	X*
Object Assembly	X*	X	X
Coding		X	X
Picture Concepts		X	X
Cancellation		X	

*Supplementary or optional test.

The Wechsler Adult Intelligence Scale–Third Edition (WAIS-III) is the most commonly used test of intelligence when the patient is an adult (designed for people between the ages of sixteen and eighty-nine). According to the test manual, this test requires between sixty and ninety minutes to administer. The beginning professional or the psychologist testing a patient who requires breaks between subtests may need more time. We will briefly describe what is involved in each of the subtests of the WAIS-III to illustrate these types of tests. We selected this test for extensive coverage because of its popularity among practicing clinical psychologists. For the other Wechsler tests, we will not provide as much detail.

Including the supplemental test, there are seven verbal tests in the WAIS-III. The *Vocabulary* subtest requires the patient to define words from a list of increasingly difficult words. When you learn to administer this test, the first thing you will need to do is to make sure you are pronouncing each of the words correctly. You don't need to worry about knowing the definitions because they are provided in the test manual. Because the test was standardized on a large number of people, there is also information in the manual regarding some common responses that may be unclear. When a patient gives one of those "unclear" responses, you are required to ask for clarification. For example, you may say to the patient, "Tell me more," or use a similar prompt. *Similarities* is a subtest in which you present two words to the patient and then ask the patient to tell you how these two words are alike. This test allows you to get some impression about your patient's ability to form concepts and abstractions. For example, a person may be asked how a car and a train are the same. While it is true that both have wheels (and the person being assessed would get some credit for this response), a better response would be that they are both forms of transportation. *Arithmetic* looks like a test of basic math ability. Unlike many of the math tests you take in school, however, these problems are administered orally. The patient is not allowed to use paper and pencil to calculate the response. Although the psychologist can obtain a sense of the person's arithmetic skill, this test is also a measure of concentration, attention, and short-term auditory memory. *Digit Span* requires the patient to repeat aloud some numbers you have presented orally. As you progress through the subtest, the list of numbers gets longer. This task is performed in two different ways. Initially, you ask your patient to repeat the numbers in the same order you presented them. For example, if you said "5-3-9" the correct patient response would be "5-3-9." If the patient responded "3-5-9" the response would be wrong even though all of the numbers given are correct. The order is just as important as the specific numbers on this task. For the second part of this subtest, you ask the patient to repeat the numbers in a backward or reverse order. Using the same example numbers we gave for the other part of this subtest, if you said "5-3-9" the correct response would be "9-3-5." *Information* is a test of general knowledge. This subtest is designed to question the patient about topics that are likely to be familiar to anyone living in this country. The items included in this subtest are not believed to require any specific level of education. *Comprehension* is a subtest of the patient's common sense and ability to be practical in addressing daily living issues. This subtest contains several different kinds of questions. Some items require the patient to explain the meaning of a common proverb; others require explaining what to do in a certain type of situation. *Letter-Number Sequencing* is a new subtest with the third revision of the WAIS. For this subtest, you orally present letters and numbers in a mixed order. The task for your patient is to first repeat the numbers in ascending order rather than in the order you gave them. Your patient then must repeat the letters in alphabetical order. This subtest allows you to learn something about your patient's attention and concentration as well as verbal memory.

The WAIS-III has ten performance subtests, including three that are optional. *Picture Completion* is a task requiring your patient to identify what important part is missing in each of a series of pictures you present. Patients who have difficulty with this subtest often have concentration problems or difficulty attending to details. *Digit Symbol* is a code substitution test. At the top of the page, numbers are presented with a different basic symbol provided for each number. This information is followed by a page of numbers without the symbols being provided with them. The task for your patient is to write the symbol for each of the numbers. This is a timed task, so the patient must work rapidly but must also pay attention to the task to get the item correct. The numbers are repeated but not in any specific order. To be successful on this task, the patient needs to have the ability to remember what symbols go with each of the numbers or check the sample rapidly to complete the task. Clinically, you may also note "how" your patient approaches this task. Does the person keep checking back to the template for the symbol to use or has the person learned the correct symbol and thus can respond more rapidly? To be able to obtain this information, the psychologist needs to sit in a position that allows vision of the patient's eyes as well as the stimulus items. Combining information from the patient's approach to the different types of tasks involved in the WAIS-III allows the clinical psychologist to gain a more complete picture of the patient. *Block Design* is a matching-to-sample type of test. In this case, you present the patient with some red and white blocks. On some sides of these blocks they are all red, on some sides they are all white, and on some sides they are diagonally half red and half white. You present pictures of designs that can be replicated using the blocks. The patient must determine which side of each block is needed to make an exact copy of the picture. As you progress through this subtest, the designs become increasingly complex. This subtest is also timed. Although you try to use your stopwatch in a way that does not cause your patient undue anxiety, you do tell the patient that the task is being timed. Some patients get quite frustrated when you stop them to move on to the next item because time has expired. This information about patient behavior will be useful to you when you integrate the test data with your observations and develop an overall picture of the patient. Although the test score only reflects whether or not the patient was able to complete the design in the allotted time, your clinical observation about the person's reaction to "failure" can be quite informative. This observation can be useful in understanding other aspects of the patient's life. Such observations are sometimes called the "qualitative" aspect of the evaluation in contrast to the "quantitative" nature of the test score. *Matrix Reasoning* is also a new subtest of the WAIS-III (it was not part of the previous versions). This is a nonverbal task that provides information about your patient's perceptual organizing skills and abstract reasoning ability. The patient is presented with a geometric figure and then must select the correct shape from among five choices. *Picture Arrangement* is a task requiring the patient to arrange a series of pictures so that they tell a story. The psychologist lays out these pictures in a standard, but incorrect, order for the patient. For some of the trials, more than one order receives credit but not necessarily full credit. One order for the pictures is considered better than others and therefore receives more credit toward the overall score for ability. *Symbol Search* is also new with the WAIS-III. This subtest includes sixty items. Each item starts with a target group consisting of two symbols. This target group is followed by a group of symbols called the "search group." The task for the patient is to determine whether or not either of the original symbols is present in the search group of symbols. Finally, we have *Object Assembly*. If you played with jigsaw puzzles when you were a child this task will be familiar to you. As with Picture Arrangement, the psychologist lays out the parts of the puzzle in a standardized order on the table in front of the patient. You do *not* tell the patient what the picture looks like when the parts are correctly joined. Thus, it is different from those puzzles where you look at the box cover to give yourself an idea of the parts you want. There are several abilities needed to be successful on this task. Of course, you need to have some visual-motor coordination. In addition to that, you also need to be able to visualize a whole from looking at its parts. This subtest was required in previous versions of the WAIS but is now an optional test. Table 6.3 provides a summary of these subtests and their general purpose.

The Wechsler Intelligence Scale for Children–Fourth Edition (WISC-IV) was released in 2003. It was developed to update normative data so that it was closer to the current

Table 6.3 WAIS-III Subtests

Subtest	Index	Description
Vocabulary	Verbal comprehension	Word definitions
Similarities	Verbal comprehension	Abstract concept formation
Arithmetic	Working memory	Mental calculation, attention
Digit Span	Working memory	Short-term memory, attention
Information	Verbal comprehension	General knowledge
Comprehension	—	Social judgment, reasoning
Letter-Number Sequencing	Working memory	Mental control, concentration
Picture Completion	Perceptual organization	Visual recognition and perception
Digit Symbol	Processing speed	Visual-motor coordination
Block Design	Perceptual organization	Visual-motor organization
Matrix Reasoning	Perceptual organization	Visual-spatial organization
Picture Arrangement	—	Visual sequencing
Symbol Search	Processing speed	Visual scanning
Object Assembly	—	Psychomotor skill

U.S. census data. The issue of the changing demographics of the country and their impact on clinical practice will be a recurring theme in this book. Updating test norms and using current test materials is just one part of the process of ethical practice. From a practical perspective, this revision of the test also reduced the weight of the test kit to make it easier for clinicians to carry it to various sites where they may need to use it. Changes were made in the scoring of this version of the WISC based on research from both cognitive psychology and intellectual assessment. This test tries to do a better job of assessing fluid memory, working memory, and processing speed than the previous version did. The test developers also tried to make the test stimuli more colorful and engaging for the children who would take it. This test is used with children between the ages of six and seventeen. Keeping children engaged in the task is an important clinical skill in obtaining an accurate measure of their cognitive ability. Many of the children tested by clinical psychologists have a history of playing computer games and other colorful interactive activities. It may be difficult to engage them in the assessment process with traditional psychological tests that seem boring in contrast to their traditional activities. The theory is that the more attractive the test materials the greater chance of obtaining cooperation from the child and thus an accurate cognitive assessment.

The WISC-IV gives the psychologist a number of summary scores about the child. The traditional Full-Scale IQ score found in other measures of intelligence is retained. There are also four composite scores to assist the psychologist in making an evaluation of the child's pattern of cognitive abilities. These factors are Verbal Comprehension, Perceptual Reasoning, Working Memory, and Processing Speed. It is beyond the scope of this book to provide an in-depth discussion of each of the subtests of each test we name. This information tends to be included in undergraduate tests and measurement courses as well as graduate testing courses. We have limited our discussion to a naming of the subtests and then some explanation of the new ones added in the latest version because they illustrate changes in the field. The subtests retained from the previous version of the WISC are Similarities, Vocabulary, Comprehension, Picture Completion, Block Design, Object Assembly, Digit Span, Coding, and Symbol Search. Two other subtests from the WISC-IV, Arithmetic and Information, are now used as supplementary tests. Five new subtests were developed and standardized for the 2003 edition of the WISC. *Word Reasoning* allows the psychologist to evaluate the child's ability to reason using verbal material. The child is given a series of clues and asked to identify the underlying concept. *Matrix Reasoning* measures fluid reasoning ability. The addition of this subtest provides comparability to the WAIS-III and Wechsler Preschool and Primary Scale of Intelligence. On this subtest, the child is shown a partially completed grid. The task for the child is to select, from among the choices presented, the item that completes the grid. *Picture Concepts* is another measure of fluid reasoning. This subtest also assesses perceptual organization and categorization. The child is shown two or three rows of objects. The task for the child is to select objects that go together. The correct response is based on an underlying concept. *Letter-Number Sequencing* is a measure of working memory. This subtest is an adaptation of the supplementary WAIS-III subtest with the same name. The response is the same as we described for the WAIS. *Cancellation* is a measure of processing speed. Because the patients are children, the objects used in this test are animal forms. The objects that are interspersed, and not to be marked, are common items but not animals. The child's task is to cross out all of the animals on the pages. The score is the total number of animals selected over two trials, minus any errors that occurred when the child crossed out nonanimal objects. A qualitative measure on this task is to see whether the child's performance improves from the first trial to the second trial.

The Wechsler Preschool and Primary Scale of Intelligence–Third Edition (WPPSI, pronounced "whip see"), was published in 2002. This test is the third in the series and is used with children between the ages of two years six months and seven years three months. Although every effort has been made to keep these three measures as similar as possible so that performance over time can be evaluated, this revision places less emphasis on timed performance than either the previous edition of the WPPSI or the other two tests in this battery. Developmental psychologists suggest that cognitive processes change quite rapidly during these early years. Thus, this test is really divided into two distinct age groups: those children between the ages of two years six months and three years eleven months and those who are between four years and seven years three months. Testing time is shorter for the younger group who are less likely to sustain the needed attention over more than the suggested thirty to forty-five minutes.

For the younger group, the core subtests for the verbal component of the WPPSI are *Receptive Vocabulary* and *Information*. For the Receptive Vocabulary subtest, the psychologist shows the child a group of four pictures. The psychologist says a word and the child must point to the picture that represents that word. The Information subtest at the younger ages also uses pictures. Once again, the child is shown four pictures. The child responds to a question by pointing to the picture that represents the correct answer. This test is also used with older children. At the older levels, the responses are verbal and cover a broad range of general knowledge topics similar to those used on the WAIS. At this younger age, the two subtests comprising the performance component are *Block Design* and *Object Assembly*. The blocks used in the Block Design subtest are one- or two-color. Early items on this subtest use a constructed model that the child must copy.

As the child progresses through the subtest, pictures rather than actual models are used as stimuli. For the Object Assembly subtest, the psychologist places the pieces of a puzzle in front of the child in a standard way. The child has ninety seconds per puzzle to assemble these pieces into a meaningful whole. *Picture Naming* is a supplemental test available for the younger children and optional for the older ones. A stimulus book is used for this subtest. The child is shown pictures in the book and asked what they are.

For the children in the four years to seven years three months age group, the core verbal subtests are *Information, Vocabulary,* and *Word Reasoning.* We have already described the Information subtest. The Vocabulary subtest starts with pictures in a stimulus book. The child must name the pictures. As the child progresses through this subtest, the psychologist moves from pictures to reading words to the child and asking the child to define each of those words. The psychologist asks the child to identify the common concept in a series of increasingly specific clues for the Word Reasoning subtest.

The core subtests comprising the performance scores for the four years to seven years three months are *Block Design, Matrix Reasoning,* and *Picture Concepts.* We have already described the Block Design subtest. On the Matrix Reasoning subtest, the child is shown an incomplete matrix. Depending on the item, there are either four or five choices presented from which to select completions to the matrix. The Picture Concepts subtest involves presenting the child with two or three rows of pictures. The child must choose one picture from each row to form a group with a common characteristic.

The final subtest, Coding, is used as part of the full-scale IQ score but not as a component of the verbal or performance ones. *Coding* presents the child with a series of symbols paired with simple geometric shapes. The child uses this information as a key to draw these symbols in blank spaces for a page of these shapes.

For these older children, five supplemental tests can also be used: *Symbol Search, Comprehension, Picture Completion, Similarities,* and *Object Assembly.* We have already described the Object Assembly subtest. The child is given a "target symbol" on the Symbol Search subtest. The child is then presented with a group of symbols and asked whether or not the target symbol appears in that group. The Comprehension subtest is verbal. The child is asked a series of questions that relate to general principles and social situations. The psychologist shows the child a series of pictures on the Picture Completion subtest. The child is asked to either point to or name the important part that is missing in each of these pictures. The psychologist reads an incomplete sentence to the child on the Similarities subtest. This sentence contains two concepts that share a common characteristic. The task for the child is to complete this incomplete sentence in a way that reflects this shared characteristic.

With the recent move to spend less time doing psychological testing as well as having less time for it approved by third-party payers, we are starting to see an abbreviated form of the Wechsler tests used more often in clinical settings. Thus, we will present some brief information about the **Wechsler Abbreviated Scale of Intelligence (WASI)** that can be used with patients between the ages of six and eighty-nine (Wechsler, 1999). Unlike the other Wechsler tests, the WASI converts the raw scores to "t" scores rather than scaled scores to calculate an IQ. There are two formats for the WASI. One format uses four subtests—Vocabulary, Similarities, Block Design, and Matrix Reasoning. Using this format typically takes about thirty minutes of testing time and yields not only a full-scale IQ but also verbal and performance IQs. The other format uses only two subtests—Vocabulary and Matrix Reasoning. This format requires only about fifteen minutes of testing time. Because you have more limited information, you only get a full-scale IQ. The WASI is used in cases in which an estimate of the person's cognitive ability is sufficient to answer the referral questions as well as in cases in which the person has previously had a comprehensive evaluation and needs only a brief reassessment at that time. It may also be used in some cases as a form of screening to determine whether or not the entire test is going to be needed.

The Stanford-Binet

One of the major differences between the Wechsler tests and the **Stanford-Binet** used to be that the Wechsler tests were organized based on subtests within each of the three cognitive (IQ) areas—verbal, performance, and full scale—and the Stanford-Binet was organized by age level. Thus, if you were testing a person with the Stanford-Binet who had strengths in one area and not another you might repeat a particular type of test several times throughout the test administration. With the Wechsler tests, you administered a particular type of material, such as vocabulary, until the patient was no longer able to answer the questions and then moved on to another subject. The fourth edition of the Stanford-Binet, released in 1986, changed its format to one organized by type of test. This approach was continued in the most recent edition, Stanford-Binet Intelligence Scales (SB5), released in 2003. The normative sample of forty-eight hundred people for the fifth edition of this test was described as closely resembling the 2000 U.S. Census data in terms of gender, ethnicity, region of the country where they live, and educational level. The developers of the SB5 also evaluated test items on fairness relative to religious traditions using an expert panel. The panelists represented Christian, Jewish, Muslim, Hindu, and Buddhist backgrounds. Consideration of religious bias in this way is somewhat unique in test development at this time but can be expected to be used in other tests in the future.

This version of the test can be used with people between from the age of two upward. Thus, the psychologist using the SB5 only needs to buy one test kit rather than the three separate test kits of the Wechsler series. The developers of this test also relied on test theory and assessment research to design their revision. This test uses a five-factor model of cognitive ability as its base. These factors are fluid reasoning, knowledge, quantitative reasoning, visual-spatial reasoning, and working memory. These five factors are each viewed as having a verbal and a nonverbal domain. There is one subtest for each factor-domain combination, leading to the ten subtests of the SB5. Table 6.4 lists both the verbal and the nonverbal subtests of the SB5.

When a psychologist purchases a Stanford-Binet test kit, it includes a number of different items. The kit comes with a carrying case that holds the test equipment, examiner's manual, technical manual, and record books to write down the patient's responses and also to jot down any notes about the person's behavior in the margins for later reflection. There are three item books that contain the routing tests as well as the verbal and nonverbal items. Among the test equipment is a picture of a child to be used for the identification of body parts. Care was taken to make this picture both unisex and multiethnic. This is important to maximize the child's ability to identify with the picture. There is a plastic storage case that holds a form board and ten form board pieces, nine green blocks, twelve counting rods, thirty sorting chips, a spoon, a pencil, three plastic cups, and a number of

Table 6.4 Stanford Binet Subtests	
Verbal Subtests	Nonverbal Subtests
Verbal knowledge	Nonverbal fluid reasoning
Verbal fluid reasoning	Nonverbal knowledge
Verbal quantitative reasoning	Nonverbal quantitative reasoning
Verbal visual-spatial processing	Nonverbal visual-spatial processing
Verbal working memory	Nonverbal working memory

toys. As you can imagine, learning to administer this test will take some practice to make sure that reliability is assured.

Administration of the fifth edition of the Stanford-Binet begins with routing subtests from Item Book 1. There is one routing test for the verbal domain and one for the nonverbal domain. The starting point for the routing tests is based on a combination of the patient's age and estimated level of ability. The routing test for the verbal domain is *Verbal Knowledge* (basically a vocabulary test) and the routing test for the nonverbal domain is *Nonverbal Fluid Reasoning* (an object series and matrices). Item Book 2 contains material for the nonverbal domain. The remaining four subtests in the nonverbal domain, as well as their theoretical factor, listed in parentheses after the subtest name, are *Nonverbal Knowledge* (knowledge), *Nonverbal Quantitative Reasoning* (quantitative reasoning), *Nonverbal Visual-Spatial Processing* (visual-spatial processing), and *Nonverbal Working Memory* (working memory). Item Book 3 contains material for the verbal domain. The four remaining subtests are *Verbal Fluid Reasoning* (fluid reasoning), *Verbal Quantitative Reasoning* (quantitative reasoning), *Verbal Visual-Spatial Processing* (visual spatial processing), and *Verbal Working Memory* (working memory). Psychologists who work with children have shown some renewed interest in the Stanford-Binet because of this working memory factor. Because this factor includes both verbal and nonverbal tests, they hope it will provide information useful to understanding children with attention-deficit/hyperactivity disorder (ADHD).

The Stanford-Binet can be scored either by hand or using computer software, as can the Wechsler tests. The computer version provides not only conversion of the raw scores into standard scores and percentiles but also a graphical report and a brief narrative summary. Regardless of whether the psychologist uses computerized or hand scoring, the subtest scores can be used to compute four types of composite scores for the patient. The *Factor Index* score is a combination of two subtests. In this case, you combine the verbal and complementary nonverbal subtest scores. You can therefore obtain five such scores. Although we often think of cognitive abilities in terms of a single IQ score, having this more specific distribution of scores allows the clinical psychologist to have a better idea of the patient's strengths and weaknesses. There are two domain scales. The *Verbal IQ* combines the patient's performance on the five verbal subtests. Note this includes the routing subtest with the other four. The *Performance IQ* combines the patient's scores from the five nonverbal subtests. An *Abbreviated Battery IQ* can be determined based on the two routing subtests. This score might be useful to the psychologist who needs just a quick cognitive screen rather than more complete information about the patient's cognitive level. The traditional *Full-Scale IQ* is derived from a combination of the ten subtests.

According to the test publisher, it takes about five minutes per subtest to administer this version of the Stanford-Binet. Thus, the experienced psychologist can expect to need a bit less than an hour to administer the entire test. Of course, when you first start administering any test, you will probably take longer than the stated time. Some patients may need to take a short break between some of the subtests, but the Stanford-Binet is typically administered in one session. Despite the changes made to the fifth edition, the Wechsler tests remain more popular among psychologists than the Stanford-Binet. As with any major psychological test, there is a large research literature available. There are many sources for students who are interested in the Stanford-Binet's research literature (e.g., Caruso, 2001; Gridley & McIntosh, 1991; Kaplan & Alfonso, 1997).

Other Cognitive Measures

Differential Ability Scales (DAS)

The **Differential Ability Scales (DAS)** (Elliott, 1990, 1997) is an additional measure among the tests available for the individual cognitive assessment of children and adolescents. The DAS has three batteries that are appropriate for overlapping age ranges from two years six months to seventeen years eleven months. The lower preschool battery is used for children between two and one-half and three and one-half years of age; the upper preschool battery is used for ages three and one-half to six; and the school-age battery is appropriate for children between six and eighteen years of age. The subtests of this battery are grouped as core subtests, diagnostic subtests, and achievement subtests. The scores are based on a mean of 100 and a standard deviation of 10. A mean of 100 is common among cognitive tests, making it easy to compare results on various cognitive measures. On the other hand, a standard deviation of 10 is not as common as a standard deviation of 15 in these measures.

Because many of the test stimuli are both colorful and easily manipulated, they tend to hold the interest of children during the evaluation. Reliability and validity data are within acceptable ranges, although the normative sample sizes are not large. For example, one group of researchers (Dumont, Cruse, Price, & Whelley, 1996) compared DAS performance to performance on the WISC-III but used only fifty-three children. Such small samples have contributed to questions about its acceptability. Studies on the utility of the DAS with special populations are also appearing in the literature. For example, researchers have investigated its convergent validity with a group of Hispanic children (DiCerbo & Barona, 2000).

Peabody Picture Vocabulary Test

There are times when the clinical psychologist needs only a rough estimate of the patient's level of cognitive functioning. It would not be cost-effective to administer either one of the Wechsler tests or the Stanford-Binet because of time constraints, but the psychologist would like more information than the clinical interview provided. In this case, the psychologist might elect to use the **Peabody Picture Vocabulary Test (PPVT).** The PPVT originated in 1965 and is currently in its third edition (Dunn & Dunn, 1997). The first two editions of this test were most often used with children. The changes in this test over time illustrate many issues in test development. The first edition of the PPVT had only white children in the standardization sample. The second edition (PPVT-R) expanded the age range to forty in its standardization sample. The third edition includes norms for patients between the ages of two years six months and ninety. The pictures were updated not only to reflect the cultural changes in dress and style, but also to provide better gender and ethnic balance than the prior editions of the test. Independent consultants reviewed both the content and the artwork during this revision. These consultants represented the perspectives of women and people of diverse heritage—African Americans, Asian Americans, Native Americans, and Hispanic Americans. They also included persons with physical disabilities. Researchers have provided differential responses to the success of the test developers to provide a culturally fair measure. For example, one study found it culturally fair for African-American children (Washington & Craig, 1999) but another study (Campbell, Bell, & Keith, 2001) did not.

Depending on the patient's ability and cooperation with the task, test administration takes between ten and twenty minutes. The PPVT is a test of receptive vocabulary, so it is also useful when the patient is unable to read or has limited motor abilities. One of the scores obtained from the PPVT is the patient's standard score, which is based on a scale with a mean of 100 and a standard deviation of 15. As you can see, this is the same standard score system used for the Wechsler scales. Although this is only a screening measure, it does provide the clinician with information in a format that is familiar. This test is also portable. The test stimuli are contained in a flip-style book. Each page is divided into four segments. Each segment contains a picture and the numbers 1–4. The psychologist says a word and then asks which picture represents that word. The patient can either point to the picture or give the number representing the picture. The test manual provides different starting points in this book depending on the patient's age. This procedure also helps to keep testing time limited. Students wishing to read research on the PPVT might start with an evaluation of the construct validity of the PPVT-R (Miller & Lee, 1993) and the technical reference book for the PPVT-III (Williams & Wang, 1997).

Kaufman Brief Intelligence Test (K-BIT)

Alan and Nadeen Kaufman are a husband and wife psychologist team who were involved in the development of the WISC-R. During the 1980s and early 1990s, they developed a series of clinical instruments designed to be used in many of the situations where one of the Wechsler tests or the Stanford-Binet were used. They based their measures on test theory and evolving theories of intelligence and were interested in providing information that could be used in many different assessment situations. We are using the **Kaufman Brief Intelligence Scale (K-BIT)** to illustrate their work. The K-BIT (Kaufman & Kaufman, 1990) is intended for use at times when a brief measure of intelligence will meet the assessment needs. It was designed to measure both crystallized and fluid intelligence. This test can be administered to people between the ages of four and ninety. According to the test publisher, administration time is between fifteen and twenty minutes.

In contrast to the PPVT, the K-BIT has both a verbal and a nonverbal component. The verbal component of this test includes forty-five expressive vocabulary items (naming pictures) and thirty-seven definitions. According to the Kaufmans, this subtest is a measure of crystallized thinking. It is a measure of knowledge of words and their meanings. The nonverbal component of the K-BIT has forty-eight matrices. This component is a measure of fluid thinking, or the ability to understand relationships as a way to solve new problems. These matrices do not use words. They contain pictures as well as abstract designs. Some are 2×2 and others are 3×3 analogies. Thus, when language skills are somewhat limited this test can prove quite useful.

The K-BIT provides three standard scores: verbal, nonverbal, and composite. These scores were normed to have the same metric values as other intelligence tests such as those in the Wechsler series. Thus, they provide standard scores with a mean of 100 and a standard deviation of 15 for each of the three measures. This procedure was used so that scores on the K-BIT could be directly compared to scores from the longer tests. Despite this comparability of scores, it is important to remember that this test is a short form and thus is not a substitute for a traditional full-length measure of cognitive ability. The normative sample for this test was similar to the 1990 U.S. Census data in terms of sex, ethnicity, geographic region, and parental educational level. Both reliability and validity data are within acceptable range. The validity of the K-BIT has been evaluated with many specialized populations, including patients referred for neuropsychological evaluation (Naugle, Chelune, & Tucker, 1993), brain-injured children (Donders, 1995), and children with reading disabilities (Chin et al., 2001). There is a growing research literature for students who are interested in further investigation of this measure.

Bayley Scales of Infant Development

Suppose you are interested in the abilities of an infant. Because most general clinical psychologists do not do this type of assessment, these tests are often either omitted from undergraduate clinical psychology books or mentioned only briefly. Psychologists who are interested in very young children need such tools. We believe, however, that these are important measures in the profession and deserve more attention. Such testing is typically used when there are questions about possible developmental disability. Data from these tests are combined with information about the infant's birth history, health record, and measures of adaptive behavior. Infant tests used by psychologists are individually administered; it is obvious why we do not do group testing with this age group! Infants are tested while either lying down or on someone's lap. Although pioneers in this area believed performance on infant intelligence tests was a good predictor of performance on child and adult intelligence tests, this concept has not been supported by the data. Measures of infant intelligence evaluate very different skills than those we described for other cognitive tests. Predictive efficacy of infant tests is better at the extremes of performance than in the broad middle. Thus, the infant who scores in the highly gifted range or extremely slow range is more likely later to be at that level than the average infant who scores in the middle. The infants at those extremes are also the ones who are most likely to benefit from early intervention.

One of the more popular measures of infant ability is the **Bayley Scales of Infant and Toddler Development** (Bayley, 1969), revised in 1993 (BSID-II; Bayley, 1993), and revised again (BSID-III; Bayley, 2005). This test is used with children between the ages of one month and three years six months. The normative sample consisted of seventeen hundred children as a stratified sample representative of the 2000 U.S. Census.

The BSID-III includes the three areas assessed in the previous version—cognitive ability, motor skills, and language. A professional interacts with the child to administer these three parts of the test. Federal law about the areas that need to be assessed in preschool children has changed since the previous edition of the Bayley. Thus BSID-III added two new areas to meet federal guidelines. These areas are social-emotional behavior and adaptive behavior. A questionnaire is given to parents, or other caregivers, to assess these new areas. Let's consider just a few of the items to illustrate the developmental process. The cognitive scale includes tasks involving counting, matching colors, and pretend play. The motor scale is subdivided into gross motor skills and fine motor skills. Gross motor skills generally develop earlier than fine motor skills. Head control and sitting without support are among the early gross motor skills to be evaluated. As the child grows older, behaviors such as crawling, walking on flat ground, and going up and down stairs are added to the child's behavioral repertoire. Among the fine motor skills evaluated by the Bayley are visual tracking and various functional hand skills. Language skills are subdivided into expressive communication and receptive communication. In other words, you evaluate the child's ability to use language as well as to understand language. Early forms of expressive language include babbling and gesturing. Later expressive language skills are the ability to name objects and to make two-word utterances. The new adaptive behavior scale includes measures of self-care and home living topics. The social-emotional scale evaluates the child's progress toward mastery of the ability for social and emotional growth. This growth starts with an interest in the world around the infant. By the time the child is between six and nine months of age, he or she should be able to use emotions as part of interaction with others and to do so in a meaningful way. Toward the end of the evaluation period, the child should be able to demonstrate an understanding of the relationship between emotions and ideas.

The previous editions of the Bayley Scales have been described as being among the psychometrically strongest available for this population (Sattler, 2001). Infant tests of cognitive development like the BSID-III present a difficult problem to researchers interested in evaluating their reliability. Because there is only one form of the test, alternate form reliability is not an option. Developmental psychologists have long known that cognitive development during the early stages of life is both rapid and uneven. Thus, if you test an infant and then retest that infant six months or a year later, obtaining differential results does not necessarily mean a problem with the test. To address this issue, test-retest with the BSID-II was evaluated with an average of only four days between sessions. Although some questions could be raised about the infant "remembering" the tasks, at least these measures have demonstrated good test-retest reliability. In research settings, the BSID-II has been used to evaluate infants at risk for hypoxia (Raz, et al., 1998) and infants exposed to drugs (Alessandri, Bendersky, & Lewis, 1998), among other problems impacting early cognitive development. Niccols and Latchman (2002) questioned the stability of scores on this test with high-risk infants. At the time of this writing, the BSID-III was so new that research other than that done by its developers was not available.

Other Infant Scales

Although the BSID-II is often cited when considering measures of infant ability, there are many other measures also available. We will briefly note several others but not provide the level of detail we did for the BSID. The Neonatal Behavioral Assessment Scale (NBAS) was developed by pediatrician T. Berry Brazelton (Brazelton & Nugent, 1995). The NBAS is appropriate for a highly limited age range—infants up to the age of two months. It is most often administered during the first few weeks of life to evaluate early problems. It was developed as an aid to parents so that they could have a better understanding of their infants' problems leading to better parenting.

The Denver II is one of the most widely used pediatric screening tools in the United States (Frankenburg et al., 1990). It has also been translated into forty-four other languages. This test can be used with children between one month and six years of age. It includes 125 items grouped into four areas: personal-social, fine motor–adaptive, language, and gross motor behavior. It takes about twenty minutes or less to complete and includes direct observation of the child, parent report, and elicitation of behavior.

Several tests have been developed to apply specific developmental theories to the understanding of infant development. The Gesell Child Development Age Scale (GCDAS) applies Gesell's stage theory of child development to children between the ages of eighteen months and ten years (Cassel, 1995). The Ordinal Scales of Psychological Development (OSPD) applies Piaget's theory to the evaluation of children between ages two weeks and two years (Uzgiris & Hunt, 1989).

Nonverbal Measures

There are times when the use of verbal instruction for cognitive assessment is not appropriate. For example, patients who are hearing impaired or for whom there are verbal limitations, such as having English as their second language, are good candidates for this type of test. Thus, psychologists have developed cognitive measures that do not require either verbal instruction or verbal responding. One of the first well-known individual tests of this type is the **Leiter International Performance Scale.** This test was originally published in 1940. Subsequently it was revised and new norms were used for the 1990 version. Although the Leiter was originally developed for use with various ethnic groups in Hawaii, subsequent work included a broader range of individuals. The Leiter International Performance Scale–Revised (Leiter-R) is a nonverbal measure of intelligence and cognitive abilities appropriate for people between the ages of two years and twenty years (Roid & Miller, 1997). A feature used in this test and later adapted by other test developers is the almost total elimination of verbal instructions—although it is designed to measure a wide range of functions found in verbal scales. A criticism of previous "nonverbal" tests was that although the test did not require the patient to make a verbal response, the instructions were presented orally and therefore required the ability to process verbal information. This test, and others like it, is especially helpful for use with children who have speech, hearing, and motor impairments. The Leiter-R has been used with children diagnosed as autistic as well as with children with traumatic brain injury, speech impairment, and hearing problems and those who are from impoverished environments. It can also be used with patients for whom English is their second language and thus would be disadvantaged on some of the items of more traditional cognitive measures. On the Leiter-R, each of the tests begins with an easy task like those that will follow in that part of the test. This test is not timed. Reasoning, visualization, attention, and memory are the four measured domains. Although parts of this scale may be given independently, obtaining a measure of all four domains likely requires at least an hour and fifteen minutes. Research using the Leiter-R is somewhat limited, but it has been evaluated using medically fragile children (Hooper et al., 2000) and language-impaired children (Farrell & Phelps, 2000). Because of the ongoing need for nonverbal cognitive measures, other assessment tools are continuing to be published (McCallum, Bracken, & Wasserman, 2001).

Another nonverbal measure of cognitive ability is the Test of Nonverbal Intelligence-3 (TONI-3). The TONI-3 was designed for non-English speakers as well as for those who may be suffering from aphasia, those who are experiencing any of a range of neurological impairments, or those with hearing impairments who may have difficulty with more traditional measures of cognitive ability (Brown, Sherbenou, & Johnsen, 1998). This test can be used with people between the ages of six and eighty-nine. Unlike some of the other available tests in this area, there are two equivalent forms of the TONI-3 making retesting easier. The examiner pantomimes the instructions. The patient responds by pointing to one of six possible responses. Each form of the test includes fifty abstract/figural problem-solving items.

We presented this brief information about the Leiter and the TONI-3 to illustrate the area of nonverbal intelligence testing. Many other measures are available, but they do not tend to be as routinely taught to graduate students in clinical psychology as the traditional verbally based tests.

Social Competence

Another aspect of cognitive ability, especially important when questions of possible developmental delay are being considered, is social competence. A measure of social competence might be used to supplement the material from the cognitive measures. An illustration of this type of test is the **Vineland Adaptive Behavior Scales (VABS)** (Sparrow, Balla, & Cicchetti, 1984). The VABS was originally named the Vineland Social Maturity Scale (Doll, 1953) but the name was changed when it was revised. Most psychologists just call it "the Vineland." There are three forms of the VABS available. Two of these forms are interview forms and the third form is a classroom form. The two interview forms are designed to be used with children from birth to age eighteen as well as with developmentally delayed adults. One interview form is an expanded version of the other. Form selection is based on the amount of time available and the level of detail desired. There are 297 items on the shorter form and 577 on the expanded version. The expanded version includes all of the items on the first version plus additional ones. These forms are not designed for use with the child, like the BSID-II, but rather with someone who is very familiar with the child's abilities. The source of information is often a parent, but it is important for the psychologist to make certain the informant is neither overestimating nor underestimating the child's level of function. What the psychologist wants to know is what the child does on a regular basis, not what the informant believes the child is able to do or has done on only one or two occasions. The classroom form is used with children between the ages of three and thirteen and focuses on behavior considered important in the academic setting.

All three versions of the Vineland assess daily living, socialization, motor function, and communication skills. Each skill evaluated is broken down into small component parts. For example, how does the child use a knife at the table? Developmentally, children use knives for spreading before they are able to use them for cutting. A raw score is calculated for each of the broad areas and then converted to a standard score. As we see with so many psychological tests, the standard scores were developed with a mean of 100 and a standard deviation of 15. Thus, the psychologist can compare the patient's social maturity to overall cognitive ability. The relationship between these two scores is important in treatment planning. What is recommended for a child with an IQ of 65 and an adaptive level of 95 is quite different from a child of the same age with an IQ of 65 and an adaptive level of 60. We chose the VABS to illustrate the assessment of social competence because it is often cited as the most popularly used measure. There are a number of other measures available as well.

Achievement Tests

Achievement tests are designed to measure accomplishment rather than potential. These tests are associated with educational settings and making decisions about children's academic placement. On the other hand, clinical psychologists often have a need for basic information about academic skills when making decisions about children. To illustrate this area of assessment, let's consider the **Wide Range Achievement Test-3 (WRAT-III)** (Wilkinson, 1993). The WRAT-III provides scores for three areas of achievement: mathematics, spelling, and reading. The reading scale involves simple reading, not reading comprehension. The WRAT-III is the traditional measure of achievement used by psychologists and has been popular through its various editions. If the psychologist wants a more comprehensive measure of the child's academic skills, then the **Wechsler Individual Achievement Test (WIAT-II)** (Wechsler, 2001) is more likely to be selected. The WIAT-II measures eight areas: oral expression, listening comprehension, written expression, spelling, word reading, pseudoword decoding, reading comprehension, numerical operations, and math reasoning. When this test was revised, the applicable age range was expanded to include patients from age four through eighty-five. This test provides the psychologist with information about all areas specified in the Individuals with Disabilities Act. The psychologist can also select only those areas of skills of interest when a more limited evaluation is more appropriate.

Patient Test Data

You first met Patty, Joyce, and Trang in chapter 5. Based on their clinical interviews, we made some tentative or working diagnoses. Not every patient seen by a clinical psychologist will be given psychological tests. Even in cases in which psychological testing is recommended, not all types of tests are given to each patient. Although "full battery" testing, including cognitive and personality tests, was typical in the early days of the profession, that is not the case in the twenty-first century. There are many reasons for this change in testing philosophy. As you will read in chapters 14 and 15, when we provide interviews with psychologists in various specialties, managed care has placed tight limits on the services for which they will provide reimbursement. Psychological testing is one of the areas strongly impacted by this policy. Although the psychologist might "like" to have the data from a test, psychological testing may not be reimbursed by third-party payers and the cost must be borne by the patient. Psychological testing can be expensive and thus the patient may not want to pay for it without insurance coverage. Testing by psychologists today tends to address specific issues that cannot be addressed as well in other ways rather than covering the entire spectrum of possible tools.

In the following section we provide some cognitive test information about each patient for whom we chose to do this type of formal assessment. When formal cognitive testing was not recommended, we briefly explain why we decided not to do this.

We did not conduct a formal cognitive evaluation of Patty. Although we might decide later to do some cognitive screening, we already know that her undergraduate GPA was high and that she did well on her Law School Admission Test (LSAT). During the interview, her vocabulary and sentence structure were consistent with expectations for someone of her academic background. She did not seem to have any difficulty understanding any of the interview questions. Although she is seeking help for academic difficulties, the information from her interview seems to suggest an emotional rather than a cognitive reason for them.

With some older patients it may be helpful to do psychological testing to rule out organic brain pathology, which can result in mild cognitive impairments of various types. Some of the specific issues of concern for Joyce are cognitive. Although she seems to have no difficulty understanding questions during the initial interview and her vocabulary is consistent with her educational level, we will need to do some cognitive testing in this case. She is concerned about her ability to concentrate and pay attention. We need to consider whether her problem is emotionally based or perhaps due to some cognitive slippage. We therefore decided to do some testing. We also decided to use some of the cognitive measures with Trang. Next we provide a brief summary of the measures we used and the data we obtained.

Patient Test Information

Patty

We considered whether or not to do any cognitive testing with Patty. Remember, she is having academic difficulty and that might suggest some cognitive problems. However, based on her recent academic performance in college, her scores on the LSAT, and her verbalizations during the initial interview, we decided that cognitive testing was not needed at this time. Patty is a self-pay patient. That does not mean, however, that we treat her case any differently than we would if a third-party payer was responsible for her bills. We will do some personality testing and could always do other testing later if it seems warranted.

Joyce

Although Joyce is well educated and had good verbal skills during the interview, we decide to give her a WAIS-III. Information from this test may help us in our differential diagnosis. Our concern in this case is to distinguish between the early stages of one of the dementias, such as Alzheimer's, and depression. We also hope we will get some information to help us decide whether or not to refer Joyce for neuropsychological evaluation.

On the WAIS-III, Joyce earns a full-scale IQ score of 120. This level of cognitive functioning is consistent with her education and occupation. She does relatively well on the verbal subtests, but there are some noteworthy factors here. Her performance on Digit Span was below expectation based on her history. We also note that her performance was relatively the same on both forward and backward digits. On the Arithmetic items, she missed some of the easy items and yet was able to do many of the very difficult ones. On the Block Design subtest, she did relatively well for someone who may be in the early stages of one of the dementias but still below expectation based on her history.

Most of the Performance test items are timed. We noted that she had no difficulty completing items but did not get bonus points for speed on these items. There were also some items where she failed to get any points because she was too slow. She did them correctly but just not within the time limits. On items that were not timed, she did above expectation based on her performance on the timed items.

Based on her performance on the WAIS-III, we will do some neuropsychological screening before making a decision regarding referral for a full neuropsychological evaluation. From our knowledge of the clinical literature, we know that there is considerable overlap between patients with early signs of dementia and depressed patients on tasks such as general intelligence, reasoning, verbal fluency, and concentration. Patients with dementias do less well than depressed patients on verbal memory and temporal orientation. Personality testing will help but because of this overlap, we will also do some of the neuropsychological screening that is often done by clinical psychologists before making a decision regarding referral.

Trang

With Trang, we are using different measures. His parents were concerned about his mildly disruptive and aggressive behavior in school. They also had questions about his ability to concentrate. Remember that working with children is very time consuming, especially in the information-gathering stage. Collateral contacts with parents, teachers, pediatricians, caseworkers, and other important informants are a must for the psychologist to be effective. Several hypotheses come to mind as you review Trang's referral question and interview information. Is Trang possibly hyperactive? Is he an oppositional and defiant child who may develop a conduct disorder? Are there anxiety feelings from being adopted at age two and one-half that are surfacing at this time? How is the realization that his parents are lesbians affecting him? Is he being bullied at school because of his small physical size or for other reasons that have not yet become apparent?

As a clinical psychologist trained to work with children (we will discuss this specialty in more detail in chapter 15), you want to be sure of your diagnosis because the diagnosis will influence the treatment you recommend. One efficient way to gather information is to use questionnaires. Some of these questionnaires are covered in chapter 8 when we describe behavioral measures. We are discussing them in this chapter so that you can see how they relate to Trang's cognitive abilities. Luckily for the psychologist who assesses Trang, there is no limit on the psychometric testing that you can do to assess him. There are many appropriate tests for use with him and his parents are willing and able to pay for them. Because of the referral questions, you decide to administer the WISC-IV to assess cognitive ability and the WIAT-III, which will assess his achievement in school. Using these two instruments will also help you understand if Trang has a learning disability.

Many valid instruments are available that might assist you at this point. With Trang's parents' permission you send the Child Behavior Checklist (CBCL) to his teachers. You also ask Trang's parents to complete these measures. The CBCL will give you parent and teacher impressions of Trang's behavior on several dimensions before you continue with the formal assessment process. Although there are many personality tests specifically designed for children, you decide not to use any of them with Trang because your experience in this area suggests that the information you get from the CBLC will be sufficient to answer your questions. The CBCL is useful because research has shown that between 50 percent and 80 percent of ADHD-diagnosed children also meet diagnostic criteria for other psychological disorders (Jensen, Martin, & Cantwell, 1997). In addition, it is well known that children with ADHD frequently demonstrate academic underachievement (Hoza, Pelham, Waschbush, Kipp, & Owens, 2001). After talking with Trang's parents, collecting the rating scale data, visiting his school to observe Trang in both the classroom and outside at recess, and interviewing Trang, you conclude that ADHD is an accurate description of his behavior. You know that ADHD is the most commonly diagnosed disorder of childhood and surmise that ADHD is the most likely reason for Trang's disruptive behavior.

General Information About Psychological Tests

Within the APA, information about psychological tests is collected in the Science Directorate. Students who want to learn more about psychological tests might go to the APA website and then to the Science Directorate (www.apa.org/science/fac-findtests. html). One section in the Testing and Assessment part of the website is "Frequently Asked Questions/Finding Information About Psychological Tests." This site includes links to many other test sites as well as general information about tests.

Most university libraries have some or all of the major resources about psychological tests: *Tests in Print, Mental Measurements Yearbook, Tests,* and *Test Critiques. Tests in Print* provides basic information including test name, population for which it can be used, publication date, and publisher for a range of available English-language tests in psychology, education, and achievement (Murphy, Plake, Impara, & Spies, 2002). Once you identify the tests of interest to you, you may then want to refer to *Mental Measurements Yearbook* for more detailed information (e.g., Plake, Impara, & Spies, 2003). This reference lists only those tests that have been cited in the literature at least twenty times since the previous edition of the yearbook. Thus, it is a source of information about current, popular tests. Each test listed in this book also has at least one review by a qualified psychologist as well as information about factors such as reliability and validity of the test. Both *Tests in Print* and *Mental Measurements Yearbook* are published by the Buros Institute. Students who are interested in further information about these resources as well as links to related information should visit the institute's website (http://www. unl.edu/buros/.) *Tests* is a bibliography of tests in psychology, education, and business. Information in *Tests* includes the assessment instruments' major features, administration time and scoring method, cost, and publisher. *Test Critiques* is a companion to

ETHICAL CONUNDRUM POINTS TO PONDER

Now that you have read about cognitive testing, let's return to the ethical issue we raised at the beginning of this chapter. Start with some collegial consultation to make certain there are no psychologists in your area who may speak the needed language. Even if you practice in a rural area, there may be someone who does have the needed language ability. If that does not work out, consider whether you might be able to get sufficient information from a nonverbal measure so that you do not need a translator for the actual assessment process. The APA Ethics Code does not specifically rule out the use of an interpreter when doing psychological testing. Although you might be able to use the patient's sister to translate during the interview phase, you would probably be better off not using a family member during the testing process. According to the 2002 APA Ethics Code (APA, 2002), you will need to obtain your patient's informed consent to use an interpreter for psychological assessment purposes (Section 9.03, p. 1071). Because your patient is a child, and one who does not speak English very well, you have some issues about actually getting informed consent. Although parents give consent for a minor to receive psychological services, you are also obligated to explain what is happening in language that the patient can understand. In this case, to allow the sister to be the interpreter raises some concern. How much will you understand of what is specifically said to the patient, and is there subtle pressure since an interested person is making the request? Even if you do use the sister as an interpreter, you will need to take this combination of an interpreter and the relationship between the interpreter and the patient into account when interpreting your test results (Standard 9.06; APA, 2002, p. 1071). There are also issues of confidentiality in this case. You will need to talk to the sixteen-year-old about the confidential nature of both the responses and the test items. You must also consider whether any of the instruments typically used in the United States are actually appropriate for someone who has recently arrived in this country. Since most cognitive tests used in the United States were also standardized here, people living in India were not part of the standardization sample. Would the use of a nonverbal test solve this problem? There are also issues of the specific tests that the school system may require in order for the child to receive special services. You need to determine if any exceptions can be made for foreign-born children. If the psychologist decides there are just too many concerns to actually evaluate this child, does that mean the child will be denied needed services? Despite the fact that this case includes many ethical issues, it is not an unusual one. As a psychologist, you do not want to deny needed services to someone like the patient presented here.

Tests. Tests are selected for this volume based on surveys of the relevant professional organization.

There are also some general books designed to provide concise information about a range of tests. Corcoran and Fisher (1994) compiled a listing of available tests. They indexed these tests in two different ways: by population and by problem area. Their populations are children, adults, couples, and families. Maltby, Lewis, and Hill (2001) gathered reviews of 250 psychological tests covering a range of interests. Students who are looking for unique tests to use in their research may also want to consider the *Directory of Unpublished Experimental Measures* (Goldman & Mitchell, 1995).

Key Terms

accommodation

achievement tests

alternate-form (parallel form) reliability

Bayley Scales of Infant and Toddler Development

component analysis

concurrent validity

construct validity

content validity

criterion-related validity

crystallized intelligence

culture-fair

culture-free

Differential Ability Scales (DAS)

face validity

fluid intelligence

intelligence

Kaufman Brief Intelligence Scale (K-BIT)

Leiter International Performance Scale

metacognition

Peabody Picture Vocabulary Test (PPVT)

predictive validity

protocol validity

reliability

short form

split-half reliability

standard error of the measurement

Stanford-Binet

test anxiety

test-retest reliability

validity

Vineland Adaptive Behavior Scales (VBAS)

Wechsler Abbreviated Scale of Intelligence (WASI)

Wechsler tests

Wechsler Individual Achievement Test (WIAT-II)

Wide Range Achievement Test (WRAT)

CHAPTER 7

Personality Assessment

In this chapter we will discuss some of the tests used by clinical psychologists when they want to assess various aspects of a person's personality. Chapter 4 included some definitions of **personality** as well as an introduction to several personality theories. This chapter builds on that foundation by describing some of the personality tests used by clinical psychologists.

Regardless of the personality theory used, most psychologists agree that the term *personality* comes from the Latin word *persona*. This Latin word referred to a mask worn by the Roman actors in the Greek dramas enacted in Rome. Psychologists using the term today are interested not just in the mask but also in the underlying factors within the person. The "mask" may become obvious during the clinical interview, but the underlying factors are the ones for which the psychologist may elect to use personality tests to gain a better understanding. We are interested in what makes this person unique: What are the characteristics that truly describe this person? These are the factors that we try to measure with our personality tests.

There are also numerous popular definitions of personality. Most of these definitions seem to emphasize either social skills or the most notable characteristics of that person. Regardless of the definition used, most people believe they understand what is meant by the term *personality*. On the other hand, there is a mystique about its measurement, perhaps because it is not something tangible like your weight given in pounds. It is this mystique that leads some people to fear taking personality tests. They think the psychologist will learn their deep, dark secrets without them even realizing what they have told the psychologist.

ETHICAL CONUNDRUM

As a child clinical psychologist, you have recently completed a full psychological assessment of a nine-year-old boy. He was referred to you by the private school he attends. You are a consultant to this school. Although his parents agreed to have you do the evaluation, they also stated that the school was overreacting to his behavior and they did not feel he really needed to be evaluated. One recommendation you made based on your evaluation is that his parents send him to individual psychotherapy with a mental health professional who specializes in work with disturbed children. Further, you noted that based on his personality testing, you believe he has serious issues of impulse control that have the potential to lead to the development of an Axis II personality disorder if they are not addressed soon. His parents do not like your conclusions and demand to see his test responses that led you to form these conclusions.

Textbooks about psychological testing provide a starting point for considering what we mean by a **personality test.** One general textbook notes that personality tests are "instruments for the measurement of emotional, motivational, interpersonal, and attitudinal characteristics as distinguished from abilities" (Anastasi & Urbina, 1997, p. 348). This is a very broad definition of the domain. Another book places more emphasis on uniqueness when it defines a personality test as "a test that measures the traits, qualities, or behaviors that determine a person's individuality" (Gregory, 2004, p. 614). Psychologists using personality tests in practice tend to base their work on the theory that however you define personality, it is a relatively stable characteristic of the person. It is therefore something of interest to the psychologist as part of having a more complete understanding of the individual. This information may help the psychologist understand the patient's current distress as well as select the best method or methods for intervention.

Personality tests used by clinical psychologists tend to be subdivided into projective and objective types. Some of these tests are designed to measure a range of characteristics while others are more focused. We briefly discussed these two types of tests in chapter 3. In this chapter we will provide more detail about them as well as describe several examples of each type of test. Our selection of tests is based on a combination of test popularity among psychologists, our personal experience with them, and the contrast they provide. There are several hundred available tests from which we have chosen only a few to describe. We will also discuss some of the research literature in this area. As with the tests, the selected studies are only samples of the available literature.

Projective Tests

Projective personality tests are based on the **projective hypothesis.** This term refers to "the thesis that an individual supplies structure to unstructured stimuli in a manner consistent with the individual's own unique pattern of conscious and unconscious needs, fears, desires, impulses, conflicts, and ways of perceiving and responding" (Cohen & Swerdlik, 2002, p. 659). By placing structure on these unstructured stimuli, the patient is providing the psychologist with information about his or her psychological structure. This information is felt to be more personal than what may be obtained from the objective tests of personality. The final summary of personality resulting from projective tests tends to be a global picture of the patient rather than a focus on a particular trait, as may occur in some of the objective tests of personality. A range of stimuli has been used in these projective tests. We discussed Rorschach's selection of inkblots as stimuli in chapter 3. In this chapter, we will describe how clinical psychologists use those inkblots in their practices today.

One of the characteristics projective tests have in common is that they all present relatively unstructured stimuli to the patient. Regardless of the stimulus used, projective personality tests use indirect or disguised methods to measure personality. The clinician then infers information about the person from the responses given. When we discussed cognitive assessment, we noted the importance of standardized administration of the test. Students are taught to read the directions exactly as they are written in the test manual. When doing a projective test of personality, however, directions are kept to a minimum and may be slightly different from one session to another. These tests are intended to tap the person's latent characteristics—the hidden, unconscious part of the personality. The assumption in this case is that this material is buried sufficiently deeply in the person's unconscious that merely asking about it would not produce an accurate response. According to theory, the more vague the stimulus, the deeper into the unconscious the probe will be. Because of the nature of these tests, there is considerable subjectivity in their interpretation. Some theorists compare this process to movie projection. The subject matter of interest is analogous to the camera lens. The material the patient provides to the psychologist is the material we see on a movie screen (Rapaport, Gill, & Schafer, 1968).

Lindzey (1961) suggested that with the large number of projective personality tests available it is helpful to group them into categories based on the type of task involved. We are using his system to give you a conceptual framework for these tests. His system is comprised of five types of test. **Association techniques** are projective tests in which the patient is asked to tell the psychologist what a particular stimulus suggests to him or her. This stimulus might be verbal, such as a word association test; visual, such as the Rorschach; or even auditory. His second category of projective tests is **construction techniques.** In this case, the test stimuli provide a basis for the patient to produce material. For example, the Thematic Apperception Test (TAT) uses pictures about which the patient is asked to tell a story. **Completion techniques** require the patient to complete some process started by the test stimuli. For example, sentence completion tests provide the start of a number of sentences and the patient is asked to finish each of them in a personally meaningful way. **Choice** or **ordering techniques** ask the patient to arrange test stimuli in a meaningful way. For example, a series of pictures might be placed in an order to tell a story. These approaches are not used very often today, although examples can be found in the early literature in this field. Lindzey's fifth category, **expressive techniques**, does not really use stimuli to start the process. In this case the patient is asked to provide information in a sufficiently general way that a range of responses is possible. The psychologist then interprets these responses. For example, the patient might be asked to draw such things as a house, a tree, and a person.

Rorschach Inkblot Technique

This test is most commonly called just "the **Rorschach**" in the literature as well as by psychologists. Periodically psychologists conduct surveys to determine the frequency of use of the major psychological tests. In a survey of over one thousand members of the National Academy of Neuropsychology (NAN) and fifteen hundred members of the APA, more psychologists reported using the Rorschach than any other projective test of personality (Camara, Nathan, & Puente, 2000). It is often the major test described in tests and measurement books in sections about association techniques. We will therefore give you information about the test stimuli and administration procedure as well as research about this test.

The Rorschach can be used with patients ranging in age between five and adult. Unlike the complex test kits we described for the cognitive measures, the test stimuli for the Rorschach are limited. There are ten bilaterally symmetrical inkblots. Some of the blots are black and white while others have varying degrees of color. The amount of color increases as you move from blot 1 to blot 10. Each blot is printed on a separate 5½" × 8½" card. If you want to get an idea what these blots might be like, take a sheet of paper and splash a bit of paint on it. Then fold the paper from side to side with a crease down the middle. Quickly open the paper and allow the paint to dry. You have created an inkblot like those used for the Rorschach. Today, of course, these blots are created by machine because the blots are standardized. Each psychologist who administers the Rorschach uses the same ten blots in the same order. Because there is only one set of blots, the same test stimuli are used each time you test the patient. There are no alternate forms as there are for some tests. All ten blots are used with each patient.

There are no standard instructions used by all psychologists who administer the Rorschach. There are even variations in how the test is administered. We will describe a fairly typical procedure to give you an idea of how it is used. The amount of information recorded by the psychologist will also vary depending on his or her method of scoring and interpreting the data. For example, some psychologists record response time and others do not. Some psychologists record both the time between when the patient first looks at a blot and the initial response and total time the patient keeps each card. Other psychologists record only one of these times. Most psychologists who use the Rorschach develop their own method of abbreviating information because they want to get as much written down as possible. Over years of administering this test, they find their patients often use certain words. These are the words for which the psychologist probably has abbreviations or representative symbols. When psychology students first learn to administer the Rorschach, they may find they have some difficulty keeping up with verbal patients. With practice, this problem abates but can be an issue with a truly verbal patient or one who speaks quite rapidly. Psychologists do not tend to audiotape patients' Rorschach responses because of the need to refer to previous statements later in the testing process. Regardless of the method of noting the responses, psychologists sometimes need to ask the patient to repeat some of what was said. It is more important to get the information than it is to be concerned about having the patient repeat things. The psychologist may simply apologize for not having heard the entire response and then repeat what was heard. The patient is asked to give the missing information again. Although the psychologist does not want to interfere with the projective process, patients who speak very rapidly may need to be asked to speak a bit slower so the psychologist can write down their words. Most patients try to cooperate with these requests. When a patient is either unwilling or unable to comply, that provides the psychologist with additional information to be considered in the case formulation.

The equipment, in addition to the ten blots, consists of a location chart and either a recording sheet or a pad. The location sheet has pictures of each of the ten blots on it. Although some clinicians may use a stopwatch if they record time, most clinicians of our acquaintance use their wristwatches to record the time of interest.

Some clinicians present this test as one of imagination. Their introduction of the task is that they will be showing the patient a series of pictures and they want the patient to tell them what they imagine the picture to be. Others view this test as more reality oriented and say, "Tell me, please, what do you see? What might this be?" (Lerner, 1998, p. 74). Exner, developer of one of the more popular scoring systems, says that instructions should be even less than this (Exner & Erdberg, 2005). He recommends saying only, "What might this be?" when handing the first card to the patient. If the patient has never heard of the "inkblot test" then some explanation should be given about the test before actually starting the test administration but not after handing the patient Card 1. Even those patients who say they have heard of the test may ask why they are being asked to take it. The psychologist needs to be both honest and brief in responding to such questions. For example, the psychologist might remind the patient why the overall evaluation is being done and then add that this particular test provides some information about the person's personality.

The initial phase of Rorschach administration is called **free association**. Once the directions have been given, the patient is handed Card 1. The card is presented to the patient in a standard orientation. Some patients will ask if they may turn the card around. The psychologist usually gives a noncommittal response such as, "Do whatever you wish" or "That is entirely up to you." The psychologist records any cases when the patient uses a card orientation that is different from the standard one. Even if the patient returns to the standard orientation before giving a response, it is of interest to

Inkblot similar to those used in the Rorschach.

many psychologists that the patient turned the card around before giving a response, or perhaps failed to give a response. If the patient gives only one response to the first card and then hands it back to the psychologist, the psychologist will probably try to encourage additional responses by saying, "Some people see more than one thing in the blot. Do you see anything else?" This encouragement is provided for the first few blots. If the patient continues to provide only one response for each blot, this encouragement will be discontinued. Each response given by the patient is called a **percept.** The Free Association part of the testing process ends when the patient has been asked to provide responses to each of the ten blots. During Free Association, the psychologist has written the patient's statements on the response sheet or pad. As we noted earlier, every attempt is made to have a verbatim record of responses. If the patient has given fewer than fourteen responses by the time Card 10 has been returned to the psychologist, some experts (e.g., Exner, 1990) suggest the psychologist inform the patient that he or she has not provided enough information to allow an interpretation. The psychologist encourages the patient by noting that now the patient understands the task and so they will go through the cards again but this time the patient should try to give more answers. If the patient asks for a specific number, the psychologist says it is up to the patient but also lets the patient know how many had been given the first time. The patient is told it is OK to repeat some of the responses given the first time but that more responses are needed. If the patient really does not seem to be cooperating with the testing process, it is acceptable to tell the patient at this point that you need several new responses to each card. Not every patient has difficulty providing Rorschach responses; some patients have a different response style. Suppose the patient provides five responses to Card 1 and is still looking for others. It is considered acceptable to take the card away at that point and suggest the patient look at another one. Research has found that after about five responses to one card you do not get additional clinically useful information (Exner, 1990).

The second phase of the Rorschach administration is **inquiry.** Just as it was important to introduce the test in a way that facilitated patient responding, it is also important to introduce this second phase of testing in a clear way. The psychologist lets the patient know that it is important to see the things the patient saw in the same way they were seen. The psychologist will tell the patient that he or she wants to see them "like you do." The psychologist summarizes what will happen in this phase of testing by telling the patient that the task is to indicate specifically where each percept was seen on the blot plus what made that area look like that percept. The focus of the instructions is the need of the psychologist to see it the same way the patient saw it. The psychologist once again hands the first card to the patient. Using the notes made during Free Association, the psychologist repeats the first response the patient gave. It is not unusual for that initial response to be rather brief, such as "a cat." After repeating the response, the psychologist asks the patient to indicate on the blot where he or she saw whatever was said. For example, if the patient had initially said the blot looked like a cat the psychologist would ask, "Where on the blot did you see the cat?" The designated area would then be circled on the location sheet. The location sheet is a piece of paper with pictures of each of the ten blots on it. Each circled area is given a number corresponding to the response number in the patient's record so the psychologist can refer to this sheet when scoring the test later. It is important for the psychologist to be certain about the "exact" area used by the patient for later scoring purposes. Some responses will use the entire blot while others will use only small parts of it, or even a combination of the blot and its background.

The next part of the Inquiry is to determine what blot characteristics were used to lead to the response. The psychologist does not want to suggest characteristics that the patient may not have used. Thus, a general question such as, "What about the blot reminded you of a cat?" might be asked. The psychologist is interested to know whether it was just the shape, the color or shading, or other characteristics such as a perception of texture or depth. Once again, it is important for the psychologist to use the patient's exact words. For example, if the patient had said, "It looks like a cat playing with a mouse" during Free Association, the psychologist would now use all of those words in the Inquiry phase. In this case the psychologist is interested not only in the characteristics of the cat and the mouse but also in the implied movement of "playing." Some patients have more difficulty with this second phase of testing than they did with the first phase. They don't seem to be able to articulate the characteristics they used without more of a cue from the psychologist about what is desired here. Such patients may make comments like, "It just looks that way." The psychologist needs to collaborate with the patient without suggesting answers. At this point the psychologist starts by acknowledging that it may look like that to the patient but the psychologist is trying to see it exactly the same way the patient sees it. Thus, it would be helpful if the patient could explain some of the things that make it look like the given percept. This questioning procedure is repeated for each of the responses given by the patient. Thus, the amount of time required is related to both the number of responses and the length of reply given by the patient. The typical patient produces about twenty to twenty-five responses to the Rorschach blots. Thus, if you have a highly verbal patient this test has the potential to require an hour or more for complete administration.

Many different scoring systems have been developed for the Rorschach (e.g., Beck, 1944, 1945, 1952; Exner, 1974; Hertz, 1992; Klopfer & Kelley, 1942; Piotrowski, 1947). A detailed description of scoring is beyond the scope of this book. To give you a general sense of what happens, however, we will explain some of the typical processes. Common scoring categories in addition to the location are called determinants, form quality, content, and popular. **Determinants** are the qualities of the blot used by the patient in making the response. These categories are considered representative of the cognitive processing used by the patient in giving the response. Examples of determinants are form (the shape of the blot), color, shading, texture, and movement. Almost all responses to the Rorschach have some form to them. Thus, this category is used either alone or in combination with others for most responses. Movement may need a bit more explanation. It is not that most patients who give responses involving movement actually think the blot is moving. Some responses include the concept of movement, such as "a girl dancing." Characteristics of the picture make it appear that there is movement but the patient knows it is just a picture. This is no different from looking at a painting of a ballerina by Degas and saying that she is "dancing." For interpretation purposes, movement is usually subdivided into human movement, animal movement, and inanimate movement based on the subject of the response. **Form quality** refers to the degree to which the percept actually fits the space on the blot. In many cases the form of the response is obvious with no unusual features. Depending on the patient, however, some responses may be an unrealistic and distorted use of the space. Such responses are considered to have a minus form quality. Just because a response is uncommon does not make it minus form quality. There are cases where the patient gives a response that is uncommon but can easily be seen. This response is coded as unusual. Various scoring systems include lists of categories of responses for each of these form quality options. These categories are general and applied by the trained psychologist to the specific response. It would be impossible to list every possible patient response to each area of each of the blots. Thus, the manual might include the fact that for the specified area of the blot any four-legged animal is positive form quality while a human response is poor form quality for that area. **Content** refers to the general category of the response. Some examples of content are human, animal, anatomy, nature, and blood. The "girl dancing" would be "human" and the "cat playing with the mouse" would be "animal." An example of an "anatomy" response would be "a brain." "Nature" refers to broad responses such as an "ocean." It is not unusual for a response to have more than one content area. The content area considered most important to the percept is given first and receives greater priority in the interpretation. **Popular** means that the response is one that many people who have taken the test gave to that blot or part of a blot. A list of popular responses is provided as part of the scoring system for each system that uses this category.

Interpretation of the results of the Rorschach is based partially on the scoring system used and partially on the clinical psychologist's theoretical orientation. Variations in scoring the Rorschach are more likely to occur when different scoring systems are used than when comparing the results of psychologists who are using the same scoring system. This test requires considerable training and practice on the part of the psychologist before it can be used effectively. Just learning to administer this test takes practice. Becoming comfortable with personal abbreviations and getting the needed information without suggesting responses requires supervised practice. Even when these skills have been developed, the psychologist is not ready to include the Rorschach as part of a psychological battery. Learning how to interpret the test also requires considerable supervised practice. There is no set number of administrations required for the psychologist to learn this test. It is not a matter of saying, "I have now given twenty-five Rorschachs so I am qualified to give it." Ethical practitioners develop an internal sense of when they are ready to use a tool without consultation. They learn this skill as part of their training in a range of diagnostic procedures.

Clinical psychologists remain divided about the use of the Rorschach. Some take a very negative view of the scientific foundations and research literature on the Rorschach (e.g., Hunsley & Bailey, 1999; Wood, Nezworski, & Stejskal, 1996), while others take a very positive position (e.g., Meyer & Handler, 1997; Stricker & Gold, 1999). These discussions focus on the reliability and validity of the Rorschach and often generate rather heated debates in the journals. Some psychologists have suggested that the Rorschach should not continue to be used, while others respond that the problem is not with the test but rather with those who do not use it appropriately (e.g., Garb, 1999; Weiner, 2000). It is not unusual for articles on this subject to have strong rebuttals from psychologists who have very different points of view of the Rorschach (e.g., Lilienfeld, Fowler, & Lohr, 2003; Weiner, Spielberger, & Abeles, 2003).

Thematic Apperception Test

The **Thematic Apperception Test,** popularly known as the **TAT,** is the other projective test of personality we will cover in detail here. (When referring to this test, pronounce each letter separately [T-A-T] rather than having it rhyme with "hat.") Using Lindzey's

(1961) classification system we described earlier in this chapter, this is considered a construction technique. The term **apperception** refers to perceiving something in the present based on past perceptions. Christiana Morgan and Henry Murray developed the TAT at the Harvard Psychological Clinic (1935). Although only Murray's name is associated with the TAT today, the original articles about the TAT were published either by Morgan or by Morgan and Murray with her as senior author. The test stimuli, however, list the author as Murray and the staff from the Harvard clinic. After these original articles, little was found in the literature about Morgan until the publication of her biography (Douglas, 1993).

Although the TAT is considered applicable to both children and adults, an adaptation, the Children's Apperception Test (CAT), was developed in 1949 for use with patients between the ages of three and ten (Bellak, 1993). The CAT (pronounced *C-A-T*) follows the same process as the TAT but has animals rather than humans depicted on the cards. The animals are engaged in human-type activities much as children see in cartoons. With the increasing number of senior citizens, a special version for that population, the Senior Apperception Test (SAT), is also available, but many psychologists continue to use the TAT across the adult population (Bellak, 1993). In contrast to the highly unstructured Rorschach stimuli,

Card 12F of the TAT
Reprinted by permission of the publishers of Henry A. Murray, Thematic Appreciation Test, *Plate 12F, Cambridge, Mass.: Harvard University Press, Copyright © 1943 by the President and Fellows of Harvard College, © 1971 by Henry A. Murray.*

the stimuli for the TAT have some structure. Thus, theorists suggest it is tapping a slightly less deep level of the unconscious than the Rorschach does.

The TAT consists of thirty-one stimulus cards. One of these cards is blank; the other thirty are black-and-white scenes. Some of the scenes have a single person, some have groups of people, and others have no people. Some of the scenes look like photographs, while others contain impressionistic drawings. Some of these stimuli have been found to be especially useful with males, some with females, some with boys, some with girls, and some with a combination of those populations. Indication of this specialty use is noted on the back of the cards. The cards are not limited, however, to the groups for whom they have been found to have special attraction. This test was designed to reveal the patient's dominant drives, emotions, and traits as well as any conflicts that may exist for the person.

Like the Rorschach, there is no one set of instructions used by all clinical psychologists who administer the TAT. Unlike the Rorschach, it is not unusual for the psychologist to audiotape the patient's responses to the TAT. Since this is a storytelling task, it can be useful for the psychologist to listen to the story rather than feeling the pressure to write a verbatim transcript. By listening, the psychologist decides whether or not all needed elements of the story have been included and then ask for any missing elements before moving to the next card. The basic task is for the patient to tell a story based on the picture. The instructions to the patient might be, "I will be showing you a series of pictures. For each picture, tell me a story about what is happening. Include in your story what the characters are thinking and feeling, what led up to it, and what the outcome will be." Not all of the cards will be used with any given patient. There is no standard order for administering the cards. The psychologist selects those cards that seem most likely to be relevant to the particular patient. Many sources suggest that twenty of the thirty-one cards should be used, but it has been our experience that most psychologists use eight to ten of the cards. If the blank card is used, the patient is asked to describe a picture that might appear on the card and then tell a story about it the way they did for other cards. Thus, the blank card is not used as the first card presented to the patient. According to the theory behind the TAT, patients will base their stories on their own life experiences.

A number of different scoring systems have been developed for the TAT, but most clinical psychologists who use it do not use a formal scoring system. They tend instead to use a qualitative approach to this test. They look for overall themes across the stories produced. They also look for the needs that seem to be expressed repeatedly across the stories. Three terms from Murray's theory of personality associated with TAT interpretation are *need, press,* and *thema.* **Need** refers to the internal factors that motivate a person. **Press** is Murray's term for relevant environmental influences on behavior. **Thema** is Murray's term for the interaction of need and press. Special attention is given to the main character of each of the stories. This character, or "hero," is thought to represent the patient. As with any psychological test, interpretation of the test data will also include information noted by the psychologist during the testing about the patient's response style as well as any comments the patient made in addition to the stories.

A criticism raised about the TAT is that the people presented, whether they are clear or surreal, tend to have basic Caucasian features. Questions can be raised about the applicability of such figures to people from other ethnic groups. This is especially true if the clinical psychologist is planning to interpret the test based on the theory that the patient is projecting his or her needs and motives onto the main character of the story. Some attempt has been made to address this concern by developing alternative stimulus materials. Thompson (1949) developed a series of cards that are almost identical to the TAT cards except the characters have African-American features rather than Caucasian ones. Although these cards have been available for over fifty years, they have not received much attention from practitioners. One possible explanation for this lack of use is that the overall theme of the pictures is not seen as relevant to culturally diverse groups. Psychologists who want to use this approach to personality assessment may prefer to develop stimuli specifically designed for certain subgroups within the U.S. population.

An example of this subgroup approach is the **Tell-Me-A-Story-Test,** or **TEMAS** (Costantino, Malgady, & Rogler, 1988; Malgady, Costantino, & Rogler, 1984). One reason this test was developed was that prior research with the TAT and CAT with Hispanic and black children indicated they were less verbally fluent and more emotionally disturbed than other children (Ames & August, 1966). Research with the TEMAS compared to the TAT found both Hispanic and black children were more verbally fluent with the TEMAS than with the TAT (Costantino & Malgady, 1983; Costantino, Malgady, & Vasquez, 1981). The TEMAS is designed for use with urban Hispanic children between five and eighteen years of age in the United States. The culture-specific nature of the test stimuli was supported when attempts were made to cross-standardize the TEMAS with subjects in San Juan, Puerto Rico, and Buenes Aires, Argentina (Costantino, Malgady, Casullo, & Castillo, 1991). Although some of the TEMAS items were useful, they found that other items would need to be changed to be culture-specific with these different Hispanic subcultures. The test stimuli have a mixture of Caucasian, Hispanic, and African characteristics. This test has two forms, one for minority children and the other for non-minority children. Each form contains twenty-three chromatic cards, eleven of which are sex-specific. The test is scored for ten personality functions, ten cognitive functions, and seven affective functions. This type of test development requires considerable time and effort but is needed as the diversity of the U.S. population continues to increase. While Thompson's modification of the TAT and the TEMAS are not used as often as the TAT is, they illustrate psychology's concern with having tests that are appropriate for the increasingly diverse population of this country.

Completion Techniques

Among the more popular completion techniques are the various forms of sentence completion. We will use the Rotter Incomplete Sentences Blank (RISB) to illustrate these measures (Rotter, Lah, & Rafferty, 1992). The RISB has three separate forms depending on the patient's age—high school, college, and adult. Each of these forms has forty sentence stems with most of them being in the first person. The patient is asked to complete each of these forty sentences. Some psychologists score this using a qualitative approach. In other words, they read the responses and make hypotheses about the patient based on their collective meaning. The RISB also has an objective scoring system that can be used. In this system, each sentence is scored from 0 to 6 with "0" indicating good adjustment and "6" indicating very poor adjustment. The test manual provides examples of responses in each category. An overall adjustment score is then computed by adding weighted ratings.

Projective Drawing Tests

We will not provide the same level of detail for these tests that we gave for the Rorschach and TAT but instead will give a more general description of a group of procedures involving drawing. Psychological interpretation of drawings has been used for the evaluation of both personality and cognitive ability. Here we are only considering personality assessment. These measures are what Lindzey meant by *expressive techniques.* This approach to personality assessment has the advantage of not requiring much patient time or test equipment. The typical procedure requires only a piece of white paper and a pencil. The psychologist then develops hypotheses based on what the patient produces. These hypotheses are either supported or discarded based on other information. Some of these procedures focus on human figures while other procedures require the patient to make several different types of drawings. In addition to their diagnostic use, these drawing procedures can also be used to help establish patient rapport. This is especially true with children. When children first visit "the doctor" they may be expecting a shot or some other medical procedure and therefore be resistant to talking. Drawing is a common child activity and can be used to alleviate some of those fears. With adults, the most common reaction to these tasks is concern about artistic ability. Artistic ability is not required for these tasks; once this point is made most patients are cooperative. They are told to do the best they can.

These techniques became quite popular starting in the late 1940s with the introduction of the Draw-a-Person test (DAP) (Machover, 1949), House-Tree-Person (HTP) (Buck, 1948), and Family Drawing Test (Hulse, 1951). In most of these techniques, the patient is given a different sheet of paper for each drawing requested. Minimal directions are given to the patient. The specific items to be drawn vary from test to test. For example, the patient might simply be asked to draw a person. Once that task has been completed, the second request might be to draw a person of the opposite sex. Some psychologists then use these drawings in a further way by asking the patient to tell a story about the person, to give the positive and negative characteristics of the person, or other questions designed to explore personality. Buck (1981) developed a four-page form to be used for postdrawing questioning with the HTP. This form contained sixty questions addressing various elements of the drawings. Today, few clinical psychologists feel that the information gained warrants the time required for this process.

The Kinetic Family Drawing (KFD) (Burns & Kaufman, 1970) is derived from the Family Drawing Test and is more likely to be used today. In this case, the patient is asked to draw everyone in his or her family doing something. This test includes a picture of the patient as well as the other family members. Typical instructions for the KFD include the requirement that the people be engaged in some type of activity and that the drawings should not be either stick figures or cartoon figures. Psychologists who use the KFD test often report that they get considerable clinical information from their patients' comments while doing these drawings. In the case of the HTP, as the name suggests, the patient draws not only a person but also a house and a tree rather than just people as in the KFD. The way the patient draws each of these pictures is interpreted as indicating symbolism for the person.

This approach to personality assessment continues to be used by some psychologists. Although formal scoring systems have been developed for many of these tests, they are often not used. The more typical approach is a clinical judgment of the meaning of the drawings. Other psychologists question the psychometric support for these techniques

(Joiner & Schmidt, 1997; Tharinger & Stark, 1990) and question the appropriateness of using them.

Objective Tests

Within the field of personality assessment, the term **objective personality tests** refers to those personality tests in which the patient selects from among offered responses rather than generating unique responses. These choices may be in a true-false, multiple choice, or matching format. Whatever format is used, there is little, if any, interpretation by the psychologist regarding the meaning of the response. Scoring is standardized and may even be done by a computer program.

Some advantages of these types of tests are that they can be scored quickly to provide desired information about the patient, allow the psychologist to tap a wide range of topics with a few questions on each, and permit overseeing of the test-taking (although not of the interpretation) by an assistant, therefore allowing the psychologist to use this time for other activities. Some problems with this type of test include patients using a response set (e.g., all "true" answers in the true-false format), determining that the patient has the necessary abilities to read the items, and not having the clinical information about test-taking attitude found in projective testing. As we did with the projective tests of personality, we will describe several of the most commonly used tests and then give you the names of some of the others currently in use with references for further reading.

Minnesota Multiphasic Personality Inventory (MMPI-2)

The most frequently used objective test of personality is the **Minnesota Multiphasic Personality Inventory (MMPI-2).** The original MMPI, designed for use with patients ages fourteen and older, was developed by psychologist Starke Hathaway and psychiatrist/neurologist John McKinley (1943). It was restandardized and released as the MMPI-2 in 1989 (Butcher, Dahlstrom, Graham, Tellegen, & Kaemmer, 1989). The MMPI-2 is intended for use with adults only. A separate revision of the MMPI was done to develop a test for adolescents, the MMPI-A (Adolescent), and was released in 1992 (Butcher et al., 1992). Because psychological ethics require that we use the most recent version of out tests, we will focus on the MMPI-2 for our discussion. There are ten clinical scales (see Table 7.1); they are the same ones found in the original MMPI. MMPI scales are typically referred to by number rather than by their names.

Content component scales not included in the original were added to the MMPI-2. In addition to the clinical scales, the MMPI-2 has validity scales. These scales assist the psychologist in understanding the patient's attitude about taking the test.

The MMPI-2 is a 567-item true-false test. Of those items, 394 are identical to the original MMPI. The ten major clinical scales are listed in Table 7.1 with a brief description of their intent. The items on this test are quite simple. For example, you might be given the statement, "I see ghosts." You would then be asked to respond whether or not this was true about you. This approach is quite different from the projective tests we described earlier. It is also easier for the patient to lie. Because of this difference, the developers of MMPI included validity scales. These scales are designed to measure test-taking attitude.

Table 7.1 MMPI Clinical Scales

Scale Number	Scale Name and Abbreviation Used	General Meaning
1	Hypochondriasis (Hs)	Bodily complaints
2	Depression (D)	Presence and depth of symptoms
3	Hysteria (Hy)	Use physical/mental symptoms to avoid responsibility
4	Psychopathic Deviate (Pd)	Amoral and asocial symptoms
5	Masculinity-Femininity (Mf)	Traditional sex roles
6	Paranoia (Pa)	Feelings of suspicion, self-righteous
7	Psychasthenia (Pt)	Low self-confidence, subjective distress
8	Schizophrenia (Sc)	Alienation, immature, confused
9	Hypomania (Ma)	Heightened activity level
0	Social Introversion (Si)	Degree of introversion-extraversion

The original MMPI validity scales were Lie (L), Infrequency (F), Correction (K), and Cannot Say (?). Three additional validity scales were published with the MMPI-2. They are the Variable Response Inconsistency scale (VRIN), the True Response Inconsistency Scale (TRIN), and the F-Back scale (FB). A fourth new validity scale, F Psychopathology (FP) was added in 2001.

Why does the test need so many different checks of accuracy? There are many reasons a patient might be less than truthful on a personality test. We will give you a few examples but there are more you may see in practice. The patient might want to appear emotionally disturbed when that is not the case if having a diagnosis would allow the person to collect disability money or to mitigate a jail term. A patient who wants to stay in the hospital because home life is unhappy might also try to look more emotionally disturbed than is actually the case. On the other hand, if the patient wanted to be released from a psychiatric facility, it might be helpful to underreport emotional problems. Other patients may be confused and not able to respond appropriately to the test. The items included in each of these validity scales are found somewhat randomly throughout the test; they are not consecutive items. We briefly describe each of them but suggest that students who want more information refer to one of the available books describing the scales (e.g., Friedman, Lewak, Nichols, & Webb, 2001).

The L scale is a measure of underreporting symptoms. Some psychologists call this behavior **faking good.** All fifteen items on this scale are answered "false." When interpreting this scale, or any of the validity scales, the clinical psychologist also uses information about the person. Some patients who have a lack of insight into their problems, or are in denial about them, may also score in the elevated range on this scale. People who are very self-controlled as well as those in religious vocations may also produce elevations on this validity measure. Others who have been found to produce elevated scores on this measure are recent immigrants, especially those from Spanish-speaking countries. According to one MMPI expert, he adds 5 points to the traditional cutoff scores for these individuals (Ben-Porath, personal communication, November 8, 2003). The F scale is a measure of responding in an unusual way. The sixty items in this scale are considered a sensitive measure of the severity of the person's psychopathology. This scale is also elevated in people who are exaggerating their symptoms. The patient with an elevated score on the F scale is sometimes referred to as **faking bad.** The beliefs endorsed in this case are not endorsed by about 90 percent of the standardization sample. The K scale adds a correction factor to the clinical scales. This correction was added to deal with the number of false negatives that were occurring. People who score high on this validity scale tend to be defensive in their responding. This scale is used to iden-tify significant psychopathology. This factor is added to some of the clinical scales as a "correction" for those individuals, often inpatients, who may score within the normal range but are really disturbed. Cannot Say is the number of items to which the patient was unable or unwilling to answer either "true" or "false." Cannot Say, or the number of items omitted, is not really a scale, although it was sometimes called this related to the original MMPI. On the MMPI-2, it is not transformed to a standard score. The MMPI-2 is considered invalid if the patient has a Cannot Say score of 30 or higher. When the score is between 11 and 29, the psychologist should be careful in test interpretation because it may not be valid. Patients with elevations on this scale tend to be those who take a very cautious approach to the testing process, those who have difficulty making decisions, and those who really are not cooperating. It is up to the psychologist to determine what factor or factors contribute to this elevation.

As we told you, the MMPI-2 added validity scales to those from the original MMPI. Perhaps the need for additional validity scales is a combination of our developing knowl-edge of test-taking behavior and our concern about whether or not people are being coached in terms of their test responses. The 67-item VRIN scale measures inconsistency in responding. Within the MMPI are pairs of items that reflect the same sentiment but express it differently. Patients who do not respond the same way to each of these items get a point on VRIN. For example, suppose the patient says "true" to the statement, "I am often hungry" and later in the test replies "true" to the statement, "My appetite is very poor." These are conflicting sentiments and thus would be scored on VRIN as indicating a problem with the patient's responding to the test. TRIN is a 23-item all true response pairing. Marking all of these items "true" would be inconsistent. For example, the patient might mark true to both "I sleep well" and "I have trouble sleeping." It is used to clarify other validity scales. For example, when both F and TRIN are significantly elevated it suggests the patient is responding indiscriminately to the test. A moderate elevation of VRIN is used to interpret the clinical scales from the perspective that elevated scales may be magnified by the patient (faking bad). If the "T" score for either the VRIN or TRIN equals 80 or higher, the profile is considered invalid and is not interpreted. The 40-item F-Back scale was developed to add to the utility of the F scale. The items included in the F scale appear essentially in the first half of the test. Questions could be raised about response consistency later in the test-taking. Thus, the F-Back starts where F stops within the test. It can be useful to see how these two "F" scales compare. It is a measure of overreporting of symptoms. The FP measure of validity was added in 2001. These items are ones that are infrequently answered in the keyed direction even by severely disturbed people. It was designed to help psychologists differentiate between patients whose eleva-tions on the F scale were the result of true psychopathology and those patients whose elevations were the result of overreporting of symptoms. When the T score for these items is equal to 100, the profile should be considered invalid.

The MMPI-2 also has content scales. Each of these scales is based on a homogeneous collection of items that allow the patient to communicate concerns to the psychologist. They are more focused than the clinical scales. The scales that are most relevant to the reason for the assessment are the ones likely to be scored. Some examples of content scales are Anxiety, Low Self-Esteem, and Family Problems.

The Personality Psychopathology Five (PSY-5) was constructed from an analysis of the personality disorders on Axis II (Harkness, 1992). MMPI-2 scales were then developed to measure these constructs in order to allow psychologists to describe the patient in terms of major personality and psychopathology dimensions. These scales also provide a closer tie between personality theory and the test. We will provide a brief description of these scales; those students who want to learn more about them can go to the references (Harkness, McNulty, & Ben-Porath, 1995; Harkness, McNulty, Ben-Porath, & Graham, 2002; Rouse, Finger, & Butcher, 1999). The five areas are *aggressiveness (AGGR), psychoticism (PSYC), disconstraint (DISC), negative emotionality/neuroticism (NEGE),* and *introversion/low positive emotions (INTR).* The AGGR scale includes items mainly associated with antisocial and narcissistic personality disorders. The aggression in this case is directed toward other people and tends to be goal-directed. These individuals enjoy intimidating others and are prone to violence. The PSYC scale does not measure a full-blown psychotic episode but rather those characteristics associated with the schizoid, schizotypal, paranoid, and borderline personality disorders. These people often have unusual beliefs and sensory processes and may feel alienated from others. The items on the DISC scale include characteristics associated with the antisocial personality disorder. People who score high on this scale tend to have poor impulse control and are sensation-seeking. The NEGE scale measures characteristics associated with Cluster C personality disorders. These individuals tend to worry excessively, are self-critical, experience feelings of guilt quite easily, and often think about the worst possible outcome of events. They are also prone toward the anxiety disorders. The INTR scale measures characteristics most closely associated with the avoidant and schizoid personality disorders. These people have difficulty experiencing pleasure. They also tend toward the depressive disorders. Their therapists are likely to describe them as being socially awkward and insecure. These measures would be used in combination with the clinical and validity scales to get a more complete picture of the person.

More recently information has been published about the MMPI-2 restructured clinical scales (Tellegen et al., 2003). These scales are used to refine the psychologist's interpretation of some of the original scales by identifying their core components. Although a description of these scales is beyond the scope of this book, we mention them to illustrate the ongoing nature of scale development for this popular personality measure.

The MMPI scores are presented on a graph referred to as the patient's "profile." The following figure presents an example of an MMPI profile. Each of the scores on the clinical scales is converted to a T score. These T scores, based on the normative sample, have a mean of 50 and a standard deviation of 10. Using this profile, the psychologist interprets T scores over 65 as clinically important. By analyzing these scores in relationship to each other rather than individually, the psychologist gets a broader picture of the patient. If the profile is considered valid, based on the validity scales, then the highest of the clinical scales and the next highest or next two highest will be considered as a pair. Valid profiles usually include only two or three highly elevated scales. For example, suppose the patient

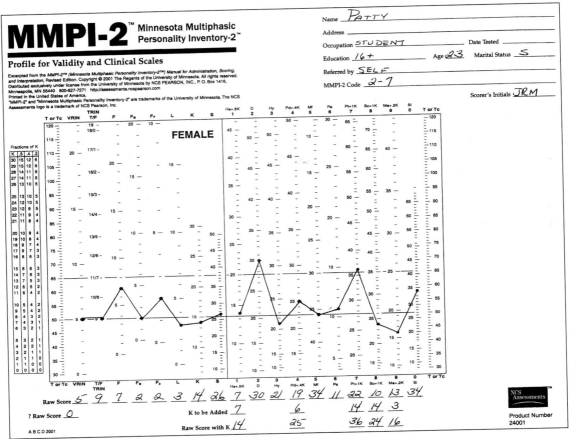

MMPI-2 Profile for sample patient Patty *Minnesota Multiphasic Personality Inventory-2 Basic Scales Profile. Form for use with the MMPI-2™ test as published by the Regents of the University of Minnesota. All rights reserved. "MMPI-2" and "Minnesota Multiphasic Personality-2" are trademarks owned by the Regents of the University of Minnesota. Used by permission of the University of Minnesota Press.*

has elevations on Scales 1 and 3. This pattern is known as the "Conversion V" because it is shaped like a "V" on the profile and is often found in a patient who is preoccupied with physical complaints. Although these patients still function, their level of functioning is considerably reduced.

The MMPI-Adolescent, or MMPI-A as it is usually known, is a 478-item test specifically designed for use with adolescents (Butcher et al., 1992). It is intended for use with adolescents between fourteen and eighteen years of age. We will not provide the details about this test we did for the MMPI-2. The MMPI-A has eight validity scales plus the same ten clinical scales we noted for the MMPI-2. The validity scales are somewhat different from those of the MMPI-2 and do not include the K correction factor. One of the content scales often of interest when assessing adolescents is the School Problems scale, which is unique to the MMPI-A.

As you can tell from reading about the MMPI, these tests take patients a considerable amount of time to complete. Thus, if the patient has problems with depression or concentration, it may be quite difficult to complete in one sitting. Even if the patient is capable of completing the test, remember you are administering the test because the patient is distressed. Thus, it is likely to be a difficult task. On the other hand, consider how much information is provided to the psychologist in a relatively short period of time by using the MMPI. It is not surprising that this test is so popular.

Millon Clinical Multiaxial Inventory

The **Millon Clinical Multiaxial Inventory-III,** known as the **MCMI-III** (Millon, 1997), is based on Dr. Theodore Millon's biopsychosocial theory of personality (Millon, Millon, & Davis, 1994). This theory suggests two major dimensions of personality—source of reinforcement and pattern of coping behavior. Millon's theory (1969) was used as background for the development of the Axis II personality disorders in the DSM system. This third revision of the test can be used with adults who are at least eighteen years old. It was revised to be consistent with the DSM-IV criteria for personality disorders on Axis II. The normative sample for the revision ranged in age from eighteen to eighty-eight, although 80 percent of the sample was between eighteen and forty-five. The normative sample included subjects from both the United States and Canada and represented inpatients, outpatients, and individuals in correctional institutions. A major limitation of the normative sample for this revision is the fact that 86 percent of these individuals were classified as white. After the 1994 publication of this revision, additional cross-validation studies were conducted. The data from these studies can be found in the second edition of the manual (Millon, 1997). The test creator also maintains a website where additional information about new studies can be found (www.millon.net).

The MCMI-III is a 175-item true-false test. This revision changed 45 of the 175 items from the previous version. Also, two scales were added to the third edition—Depressive PD and Post Traumatic Stress. Each item is a self-description to which the patient must respond. The score profile includes twenty-four clinical scales grouped into four major categories: Clinical Personality Patterns, Severe Personality Pathology, Clinical Syndromes, and Severe Symptoms. The Clinical Personality Patterns and the Severe Personality Pathology categories are designed to assess Axis II personality patterns from DSM-IV (see Table 7.2).

The Clinical Syndromes and Severe Symptoms are related to Axis I diagnoses (see Table 7.3). There are also Modifying Indices and a Validity Index. These scores assist the psychologist in evaluating facets of the patient's response style that may lead to questions about the interpretation as well as the general validity index.

This test was normed on a psychiatric population. Thus, you might wonder if it is appropriate to use it with nonpatient groups. Many psychologists suggest it should only be used in cases in which the person is being evaluated for treatment by a mental health professional (Strack & Craig, 2004). Millon has suggested that if the purpose of an evaluation is to determine if the person may fit the criteria of a diagnosable disorder then it is also appropriate. An example of this type of assessment is preemployment screening for someone who will be working in a nuclear power plant. Such a position is viewed as a high-risk position, and it is important to determine in advance if there are any indications of diagnosable psychopathology.

Table 7.2 MCMI-III Clinical Personality and Severe Personality

Clinical Personality Patterns	Severe Personality Pathology
Schizoid	Schizotypal
Avoidant	Borderline
Depressive	Paranoid
Dependent	
Histrionic	
Narcissistic	
Antisocial	
Aggressive (Sadistic)	
Compulsive	
Passive-Aggresive	
Self-Defeating	

Table 7.3 MCMI-III Clinical Syndromes and Severe Syndromes

Clinical Syndromes	Severe Syndromes
Anxiety	Thought disorder
Somatoform	Major depression
Bipolar: manic	Delusional disorder
Dysthymia	
Alcohol dependence	
Post-traumatic stress disorder	

Like the MMPI-2, there is an adolescent version of this test, the Millon Adolescent Clinical Inventory (MACI) (Millon, Millon, & Davis, 1993) for use with patients between the ages of thirteen and nineteen. The MACI has 160 items scored on thirty scales. These tests were designed specifically to assist in the DSM diagnosis of patients with the current versions corresponding to DSM-IV categories. Both the MCMI and MACI are intended solely for clinical populations and not for general personality research.

A major difference between the Millon tests and other objective personality tests is that the standard scores are not normalized scores. The Millon standard scores are called base rates (BR). The BR are tied to the occurrence of these problems in psychiatric populations. Some BR are adjusted depending on the particular population from which the patient comes to give a more accurate estimate of the accuracy of the diagnosis. The MCMI-III has also been used to evaluate intervention strategies (Retzlaff, 1995).

We do not think the MCMI will replace the MMPI in terms of frequency of use by psychologists, but some psychologists do seem to prefer it when interview data suggest an Axis II problem. To assist clinicians who want to become more familiar with the MCMI, a beginner's guide about its use is available (Jankowski, 2002). One reason for the need for such a book is that less attention tends to be given to this test than to the MMPI in graduate training in clinical psychology.

NEO Personality Inventory-Revised (NEO PI-R)

The **NEO Personality Inventory-Revised (NEO PI-R)** is based on the factor analytic adult personality research of Costa and McCrae (1992). This test is based on the five-factor model of personality, which includes neuroticism, extraversion, openness to experience, agreeableness, and conscientiousness. These factors are designed to address Axis II personality disorders. These descriptive factors provide an attempt to simplify the available data on personality by using a hierarchical model. Although a number of investigators have done work in this area, Costa and McCrae are most strongly identified with it in the clinical literature. Over a fifteen-year period of research, they developed the scales found in this test. The NEO-PI-R can be utilized with people seventeen years of age or older, requires a sixth grade reading level, and contains 240 items in each of the parallel versions. The patient rates each item on a 5-point Likert-type scale. This scale represents strongly disagree, disagree, neutral, agree, and strongly agree with each of the items.

The Neuroticism (N) scale includes anxiety, anger hostility, depression, self-consciousness, impulsiveness, and vulnerability. People who make high scores on this factor tend to be prone to psychological distress. The Extraversion (E) scale includes warmth, gregariousness, assertiveness, activity, excitement-seeking, and positive emotions. People who produce high scores on this scale tend to be people-oriented. They are described as optimistic and affectionate. Openness to Experience (O) includes fantasy, aesthetics, feelings, actions, ideas, and values. People who score high on this scale are portrayed as being imaginative and curious. They are sometimes also seen as having unconventional values. Agreeableness (A) includes trust, straightforwardness, altruism, compliance, modesty, and tender-mindedness. High scorers on A are often seen as being trusting and helpful people. Conscientiousness (C) includes competence, order, dutifulness, achievement striving, self-discipline, and deliberation. High C scores indicate a person who is considered reliable and hard-working. As you can see, the factor descriptions tend toward the positive characteristics. If you contrast the NEO with the MMPI-2, you will see they are measures of each end of the continuum of these factors. A major criticism of this test is the fact that it has only three items to serve as a validity check.

Some clinicians have suggested that the NEO-PI-R can also be used with adolescents. Attempts to validate the test with this age group have provided data suggesting that certain items are reliably difficult for these younger people to understand (McRae et al., 2002; McCrae & Costa, 2004). Preliminary attempts to provide a more readable version for adolescents have retained the factor structure of the previous version (McRae, Costa, & Martin, 2005).

Personality Inventory for Children-2 (PIC-2)

The **Personality Inventory for Children-2 (PIC-2)** can be used with children between the ages of five and nineteen (Lachar & Gruber, 2001). This test is administered to either the parent or a parental figure such as a guardian and provides that person's description of the child. To provide a more appropriate measure given the changing demographics of this country, there is also a validated Spanish-language version of this test.

The PIC-2 consists of 275 true-false items. According to the test publisher, a fourth grade reading level is needed to respond to these items. The responses are evaluated on three validity scales: inconsistency, dissimulation, and defensiveness. The Inconsistency scale includes 35 similar pairs to evaluate the consistency of the person's responding. The Dissimulation scale is also a 35-item scale. This scale is designed to assess whether there is a deliberate attempt to exaggerate the child's symptoms or possibly just respond randomly to the items. There are 24 items on the Defensiveness scale. This scale includes rather improbable virtues of the child and thus could be viewed as an attempt to make the child appear psychologically healthier than is actually the case. The PIC-2 yields nine adjustment scales. These same adjustment scales are also found on the child's version. They are cognitive impairment, impulsivity and distractibility, delinquency, family dysfunction, reality distortion, somatic concern, psychological discomfort, social withdrawal, and social skills deficits.

This test is often used in combination with a test completed by the child (Personality Inventory for Youth, PIY) and one completed by the teacher (Student Behavior Survey, SBS). The PIY requires a third grade reading level and can be used with children between the ages of nine and nineteen. Children who are poor readers but otherwise fall within the appropriate age range and level of understanding can take an audio version of this test. The SBS asks the teacher to evaluate the child in three broad areas: academic resources, adjustment problems, and disruptive behavior. It consists of 102 items. Within the Academic Resources domain, items address academic performance, academic habits, social skills, and parent participation. The Adjustment Problems items address health concerns, emotional distress, unusual behavior, social problems, verbal aggression, physical aggression, and behavior problems. The Disruptive Behavior items address attention-deficit/hyperactivity, oppositional defiant, and conduct problems.

Personality Assessment Research

A large research literature exists on each of the personality measures that were discussed in this chapter. Students interested in the types of studies that have been done on a particular test should do a literature search on the specific test. As a way to give some sense of the types of studies that are published in this area, we have selected a few to illustrate typical questions of interest.

One question of interest to psychologists who assess patients at ages of test overlap is whether to use the test designed for the younger or older person. For example, if the patient is eighteen years old, do you use the MMPI-2 or the MMPI-A? The MMPI-2 norms start at age eighteen and the MMPI-A norms are for ages fourteen to eighteen. Some psychologists make this decision based on their assessment of the maturity level of the patient after doing a clinical interview. From a research perspective, the question might be whether or not these two measures produce the same profile in the patient. In clinical practice, it is not practical to administer both tests. First, there is the time/cost factor. Second, consider the length of these tests. Imagine expecting a patient to take each of these tests as well as other tests that may be part of the psychologist's assessment procedure. Not many patients would cooperate with so many tests and the cost would escalate. In order to get the needed information, we need to look for some other samples. It is more likely that we can obtain at least some relevant information by administering both tests to students as part of their research participation credit within a university setting. In many universities, students become part of subject pools for credit in psychology courses. These students learn about research procedures by serving as participants for both faculty and student studies. Although the students are not expected to be identical to a patient population their scores would at least start to answer the research question we posed. One pair of researchers reported that in 46 percent of their subjects the profiles were inconsistent on these two tests (Osberg & Poland, 1992). Because they had used a counterbalanced design where half of the subjects had received the MMPI-A first and the other half had taken the MMPI-2 first, order effect is not an explanation of the results. For those students whose profiles were inconsistent between the two tests, the MMPI-A suggested there were no problems while the MMPI-2 profiles had clinically elevated scores. Thus, we might hypothesize that either the MMPI-A is missing significant psychological distress or the MMPI-2 is overly diagnosing such distress. To test which of these hypotheses might be more accurate, the researchers administered a different measure that has been found to be useful in screening for the presence of psychopathology. These researchers found that the MMPI-2 appeared to overdiagnose in this nonclinical sample of eighteen-year-olds.

What does this study mean for practicing psychologists? Should they stop using the MMPI-2 with eighteen-year-olds? The answer to this latter question is "no." The sample was not a clinical sample. It was also a reasonably small sample that was not necessarily representative of the population. On the other hand, these data do suggest that psychologists who elect to use the MMPI-2 with their eighteen-year-old patients should be cautious in their interpretation of any elevated scales.

One of the strong points about tests like the MMPI is the presence of the validity scales. Psychologists, however, are not the only people who realize tests have such scales. The legal profession takes an interest not only in the information psychologists can obtain from personality tests but also how they get that information. For example, one survey of both practicing attorneys and law students measured their attitudes regarding informing clients about such factors as validity scales on psychological tests and potentially how to respond to these tests (Wetter & Corrigan, 1995). Almost 50 percent of the attorneys and 33 percent of the law students indicated it was their responsibility as lawyers to give their clients this type of information. Previous studies had suggested that malingerers with validity scale information prior to assessment are less likely to be detected (Baer, Wetter, & Berry, 1995; Lamb, Berry, Wetter, & Baer, 1994).

These studies provided a background for a meta-analysis of the existing literature on underreporting of symptoms on the MMPI-2 (Baer & Miller, 2002). One problem found when doing this meta analysis was that many of the studies in the literature had used college students rather than real patients as subjects. These students were instructed to try to look a certain way on the test, but it was difficult to determine whether or not the students complied with these instructions. They did not have the incentive to comply that may be present in a real patient for whom the consequences of different types of profiles are quite meaningful. Overall, they reported that the L and K scales seem to do what they were designed to do when the patients/subjects has not been coached about test-taking.

Supplementary scales designed to detect malingerers need further evaluation, especially in patient populations in which coaching is suspected. The literature suggests that it is more difficult to detect underreporting of symptoms than overreporting of symptoms. Thus, if coaching is suspected, the psychologist needs to consider what type of profile leads to what patient benefits. It is also very important in cases where coaching may have occurred to consider other sources of information, such as behavioral observations and other sources of information available about the patient when evaluating the MMPI-2 data.

It can be tempting to look for meta analyses on psychological subjects and then assume that because they have the statistical ability to combine data they provide a better picture of the subject. Let's look at how this may be misleading when evaluating the Rorschach. One meta analysis of the literature comparing the efficacy of the Rorschach to the MMPI found the MMPI was more useful in understanding patients based on these studies (Garb, Florio, & Grove, 1998). By contrast, another meta analysis (Hiller et al., 1999) found that the criterion variables were the key to which of these personality measures is more valid. They found the MMPI produced larger validity coefficients when the criterion variables were psychiatric diagnoses or self-report measures but the Rorschach produced larger validity coefficients when the criterion variables were objective. Students who want to read further about the Rorschach research might start with special sections of *Psychological Assessment* devoted to this topic (Meyer, 1999, 2001). These articles provide a good framework for students to understand the professional controversies about this test.

Because of the extensive literature on the MMPI, it is often used as a comparison for evaluating other tests. There is a growing database comparing the personality measures of the MMPI and MCMI. Although many of these studies have restricted samples or limited populations, the available data suggest a significant positive relationship between the two (Schoenberg, Dorr, Morgan, & Burke, 2004). It is not unusual for psychologists to be required to testify in court about their psychological evaluations. This may occur even in cases in which the original referral did not involve forensic issues. Thus, psychologists must also know whether the tests they use will meet the requirements of the legal system. The MCMI has been evaluated for that purpose and has been accepted in court (Rogers, Salekin, & Sewell, 1999).

Although there is a smaller research literature on the TAT than the Rorschach and MMPI, there are studies available. One factor that seems to have contributed to this smaller research literature is the fact that few psychologists use a standardized scoring system for the TAT, thus making it more difficult to compare the work of various psychologists. Studies of the TAT in which trained examiners used the same procedure have reported acceptable to impressive interrater reliability (e.g., Sivek & Hosterey, 1992; Thomas & Dudek, 1985). Keiser and Prather (1990) summarized ten years of research on the TAT. Their work illustrates the conflicting data on its validity.

Although the research literature is smaller for some of the other personality measures we covered in this chapter, it also exists. Flanagan and di Guiseppe (1999) published a critical review of the TEMAS that provides an overview of the research on this specialized measure. Many of the early validity studies on the RISB, conducted in the 1950s and 1960s, used an expert judge as rater method to evaluate the measure. As newer statistical methods have been developed, they have begun to be applied to the RISB. For example, sociometric techniques have been applied to demonstrate the validity of the RISB (Lah, 1989). Because of the infrequent use of scoring systems for the figure drawing techniques, the research literature is also scarce for them. However, some experts in the field (e.g., Waehler, 1997) have suggested that these techniques provide a starting point to clarify differences between interview and drawing data.

The NEO PI-R has been used in a wide range of research projects. A rather unusual one considered the personality profiles of all U.S. presidents from George Washington through George H. W. Bush (Rubenzer, Faschingbauer, & Ones, 2000). How could they possibly give each of them a personality test? Of course, they couldn't do that. The researchers first identified experts in the biographies of each of these presidents. They then asked a biographer to complete the NEO PI-R as if that president were doing it. They had several biographers for each of the presidents. Based on the responses of these biographers, the researchers developed a typology of the presidents. They considered which characteristics seemed to be related to presidential success as defined by historians. The NEO PI-R has also been evaluated with "live" patients. For example, researchers (Ranseen, Campbell, & Baer, 1998) evaluated its effectiveness in evaluating adults with attention decifit disorder (ADD). Although their sample of twenty-five adults is sufficiently small that generalization is limited, this study illustrates the type of research that has occurred. They found that these adults scored significantly higher than a group of controls who did not have ADD on the Neuroticism domain and significantly lower than the controls on the Conscientiousness domain. These differences would be predicted from the diagnosis of ADD.

Patient Test Data

In chapter 5, you first met Patty, Joyce, and Trang. Based on their clinical interviews, we made some tentative or working diagnoses. Then in chapter 6, we provided you with data from cognitive testing on Joyce and Trang as well as a discussion about why we decided not to do any cognitive testing of Patty at this time. We will now discuss personality assessment of each of our patients.

Patty

Because of our concern about Patty's level of depression, we started with the Beck Depression Inventory (BDI-II). This test is described in more detail in chapter 8 because it is self-report measure of behavior. We also gave her the MMPI-2 as a way to better understand her overall personality profile and the Rorschach to examine any subtle signs that might be missed in more objective measures of personality. On the BDI-II, Patty endorsed items related to sadness, past failure, self-criticalness, crying, indecisiveness, changes in appetite and sleep, concentration difficulties, and fatigue. There were no indications of suicidal risk and this was consistent with her interview data. Her overall score on this test placed her in the moderate range of depression.

Patty produced a valid profile on the MMPI, indicating that she had cooperated with the testing process. Her outstanding emotional characteristics on this test were anxiety, depression, fearfulness, tension, nervousness, and guilt. Feelings of frustration and failure suggested self-blame. Her responses suggested that she tends to have overly high self-expectations that lead her to have a perception of personal failure or loss of self-confidence. She indicated a strong need for personal achievement and recognition. Her performance on this test was consistent with someone who has either an adjustment disorder with depressed mood, dysthymia, or major depression. Her pattern of responding to the MMPI-2 also suggest that she is a good candidate for psychotherapy and that she can be expected to remain in psychotherapy somewhat longer than the typical patient. Thus, you will need to watch for signs that she is becoming dependent on you as her therapist. People with her pattern of responding also may do well on short-term medication. You will therefore need to discuss this option with her.

You gave Patty the Rorschach and used the Exner scoring system to evaluate her responses. Patty produced enough responses on the Rorschach to provide a valid profile. Although she produced fewer responses than the average person, you are comfortable with her performance. Although there were depressive elements in the content of her responses to the blots, she did not have an elevation on the depressive index. Her responses also indicated a sense of uneasiness probably brought about by situational pressures. Her organizational efficiency in processing stimuli and integration was low, suggesting that she shows some neglect in processing information. She responded in a way that is consistent with someone who has high motivation and often invests more effort than she needs to use when facing life tasks. She also demonstrated some difficulty controlling her emotions and may have problems distancing herself from emotionally charged situations.

As you integrate the material from your interview with Patty and her test data, you decide to amend your original diagnosis (see chapter 5) of Depressive Disorder Not Otherwise Specified (311) to Adjustment Disorder with Mixed Anxiety and Depressed Mood (309.28). The stressors are the start of law school and her break-up with her boyfriend.

Joyce

Because we are considering a range of possible reasons for Joyce's symptoms, we decided to administer the BDI-II as an initial screen for depression, the MMPI-2 to give an overall profile of her personality, and the Rorschach to look for more subtle issues. We will also need to do some neuropsychological screening, to be described in the next chapter, to help us decide whether or not to refer her to a clinical neuropsychologist. Remember that one of her concerns was "senility."

Like Patty, Joyce's responses to the BDI-II placed her in the moderate range of depression. Most of the items she endorsed were in the somatic rather than cognitive area. As with any patient who scores in the moderate range of depression, we needed to evaluate her suicide potential. Based on both her interview data and her item endorsement on the BDI-II, we are not concerned about suicidality in this case.

On the MMPI-2, Joyce provided a valid profile. Her outstanding features were feelings of guilt and depression. Her pattern of responding also indicated someone who tends to be perfectionistic as well as both conscientious and methodical. These tendencies are consistent with both the interview data and people who are likely to select her occupation. On an interpersonal level, her responses suggest someone who avoids interpersonal involvement. This is not surprising given her status as a widow and is consistent with her self-description of social involvement. Her pattern of responding suggested that her thoughts are likely to be pessimistic and filled with worry. What is most surprising about her MMPI-2 performance is the elevation of her scores on both supplemental scales related to post-traumatic stress disorder (PTSD). There was nothing in the interview to suggest that she had recently experienced a traumatic event. She has been a widow for a sufficient period of time that the loss of her husband does not seem sufficient to explain her test results. Thus, the information from this test will need to be explored further in sessions with Joyce. You decide that because of this surprising information, administering a Rorschach is a good idea.

On the Rorschach, Joyce produced enough responses for scoring but not as many as might have been predicted given her educational level. This reduced number of responses is consistent with depression. Using the Exner system for evaluating Rorschach responses, you find that there were indications of loss of control and helplessness likely resulting from some type of situational pressure. She is likely to introspect, focusing on some negative emotional experience. Her responses suggest strong organizational efficiency and the ability to make decisions. This ability is not consistent with early stages of Alzheimer's disease or other forms of organicity. Her style of responding to the Rorschach indicated some overcontrol of her emotions and suggested that she does not like to deal with emotional stimulation. You will need to remember this when dealing with the potential causes of the PTSD symptom indicated on her MMPI-2.

Overall, her personality testing combined with the interview and cognitive assessment data suggests that she is not developing an organic disorder. You will still do the neuropsychological screening as a final check on this issue before discussing other options with Joyce. Her psychological testing thus far supports the idea that Joyce is a good candidate for psychotherapy and will probably benefit from short-term therapy. You must be sensitive, however, to the indicators of possible therapy termination if sensitive issues are not handled in a way that is comfortable for her. You continue to defer her diagnosis pending the neuropsychological screening and further interview material.

Trang

As we have noted, personality is a dynamic, developmental process that takes time to complete. For this reason, when you are evaluating a child's personality characteristics, you have to keep in mind that he or she is a work in progress. Nonetheless, as many developmentalists have found (Thomas & Chess, 1977; Thomas, Chess, & Birch, 1968) temperament and some personality characteristics appear to be innate and thus fairly unchangeable throughout life. Trang is eight years old, and as such is still in the formative stages of his personality development. Child clinical psychologists have to be aware of the scope of the referral question and the goals of the intervention. Trang was referred because he was mildly aggressive and disruptive in his classroom. Your task is to determine what the factors are that contribute to his behavior. You understand that Trang has a complex family history marked by adoption, relocation to a foreign country, and nontraditional parents who are both financially able to pay for his treatment and outside the mainstream of society.

When children are referred for assessment of disruptive disorders, one of the therapist's tasks is to determine whether the problems are likely to persist or are transient.

In addition, the therapist must determine whether the causes of the problems are within the child, the parents, or are exacerbated by the environment. If your goal is to address the behaviors that are disruptive in the classroom, your assessment would include compiling a complete developmental history, obtaining rating scales from the parents and teachers about the child's behavior, and understanding the context in which the behavior occurs. A marker for disruptive behavior is often familial stress, and an interview with Trang's parents can shed light on their family situation. A primary task for the therapist is to determine whether Trang's behavior can de diagnosed as oppositional-defiant disorder, attention-deficit/hyperactivity disorder, or perhaps conduct disorder. It is also possible that Trang has more than one disorder occurring at the same time, a condition that is known as **comorbidity.** Although some children are diagnosed with conduct disorder during early childhood, the more serious antisocial behaviors associated with conduct disorder do not usually appear until later in childhood, and frequently not until adolescence. Trang's history is not consistent with conduct disorder. After evaluating Trang, his parents, and his school setting, the clinician should have a good idea of the nature and severity of Trang's problems. It is not common for clinicians to administer personality instruments to children in cases where the referral question is similar to Trang's. Thus, you do not administer any personality tests to him.

ETHICAL CONUNDRUM POINTS TO PONDER

The first issue to consider is whether the psychologist followed ethical procedures in terms of explaining the assessment results. When a psychological evaluation is conducted, the psychologist not only writes a report but is also responsible for explaining those results to the patient. Because these results were definitely not what the parents had indicated they expected before the testing extra care was needed in providing feedback about this assessment. The parents do have the right to see the test data when they request it. The only rationale the psychologist in this case would have for not releasing the test data to these parents would be if the psychologist believed doing so would cause substantial harm to their child or that the parents would misuse the test data. Just noting that the parents were not pleased with the results does not constitute a reason for refusing to give them the information they have requested. Another point to consider in this case is exactly what constitutes the test data. In other words, what materials does the psychologist need to give to these parents? According to the APA Ethics Code, test data include the scores on all the tests, the child's responses to all questions, the psychologist's notes, and recordings made during the evaluation. Because of this requirement, psychologists need to take care in terms of what they write during an assessment. The psychologist does *not* release the test manual or test questions to the parents. These materials must be protected for reasons of test security unless the law requires otherwise.

Key Terms

apperception

association techniques

choice or ordering techniques

comorbidity

completion techniques

construction techniques

content

determinants

expressive techniques

faking good/faking bad

form quality

free association

inquiry

Millon Multiaxial Clinical Inventory (MCMI)

Minnesota Multiphasic Personality Inventory (MMPI)

need

NEO Personality Inventory-Revised (NEO PI-R)

objective personality tests

percept

personality

personality tests

Personality Inventory for Children (PIC-2)

popular

press

projective hypothesis

Rorschach

Thematic Apperception Test (TAT)

Tell-Me-A-Story-Test (TEMAS)

thema

CHAPTER 8

Neuropsychological Assessment and Behavioral Assessment

In this chapter we discuss two specialized forms of assessment. Although an entire chapter could have been devoted to each of these forms of assessment, we limited the material we chose to cover and combined them. A major reason for this shorter coverage is that these types of assessment are not as broadly taught to the general clinical psychology student as those measures we described in chapters 6 and 7. The general clinical psychologist may do some brief neuropsychological screening, but full neuropsychological evaluations are done by specialists in this field. We describe the related career of clinical neuropsychology in chapter 14. At that time, you will have an opportunity to read about this specialty in some detail. You will also have the opportunity to read the answers to questions we asked of two psychologists who practice as clinical neuropsychologists. Clinical neuropsychologists usually receive training in the basic intervention and assessment skills, just as clinical psychologists do, but they also receive extensive training in biological aspects of behavior, especially brain function. Their assessment training includes some of the diagnostic tools we describe in this chapter. Because many clinical neuropsychologists started their careers as clinical psychologists and because general clinical psychologists need to know when to refer patients to these clinical neuropsychologists, we are describing some of the major assessment tools used in clinical neuropsychology in this chapter. Although general clinical psychologists will not be using the major batteries we describe, they may receive reports based on them and therefore need to have at least a basic understanding of what is involved.

The other specialty orientation to assessment we describe in this chapter is the behavioral approach. Behaviorally oriented clinical psychologists have also added special-

ETHICAL CONUNDRUM

You are a clinical psychologist in a small group practice. There are two other psychologists, a psychiatrist, and a social worker in your office suite. Recently you scheduled a psychological evaluation of a thirty-six-year-old man who told you during your initial interview with him that he had been arrested for exhibitionism. His trial is scheduled next month but he wants to start therapy now so that he can start to work on his behavior problem. He informs you that his attorney has notified the district attorney's office about his scheduled appointment with you and his desire to begin therapy immediately. You discuss with him the special issues of confidentiality in this case as well as the psychological tests you think will help you gain a better understanding of his issues and therefore assist in the selection of appropriate forms of intervention. The prosecutor in his case called your office and said he wants to observe your testing session with this patient.

ized assessment tools to the profession. These tools may be used by any trained clinical psychologist but are most likely to be selected by a behaviorally oriented therapist. We have selected a sample of these tools for description to illustrate this approach to assessment.

Neuropsychological Assessment

General Information

According to Lezak (1995), the four major reasons for conducting a neuropsychological assessment are assistance with the diagnosis of a patient, understanding how neurological status is impacting current patient treatment and future planning, to develop and evaluate a treatment plan for the patient, and for research purposes. In many cases, the assessment is conducted for more than one of these basic reasons or information about one area arises even if the focus is on another domain. There has also been an increase in requests for neuropsychological evaluation for legal purposes. As our society becomes increasingly litigious, we find attorneys asking for this type of assessment more often. This is especially true in cases of personal injury or even when there is a suspected loss of function. In these cases, the neuropsychologist is asked to evaluate the amount of impairment, the potential for rehabilitation, and the amount of future care that is likely to be needed. Because these referrals may come from people who really don't have a solid understanding of the types of information that can be obtained from such an evaluation, the neuropsychologist may also need to spend time clarifying what can and cannot be learned from the evaluation.

Another growing area in which neuropsychological assessment is used is with athletes suspected to have sustained a concussion or mild head injury. Perhaps you have attended a football game, for example, and seen someone ask a player to say how many fingers the person is holding in front of his face. That is a crude measure of the player's cognitive functioning. To have a more accurate measure of functioning, some teams actually have a neuropsychologist ready to do an evaluation in the locker room while others may refer the player to their neuropsychologist after such an injury has occurred. Some of the areas of functioning that may be evaluated by the clinical neuropsychologist are the ability to handle abstract concepts, intellectual ability, language skills, various types of memory, and visual-spatial abilities. We will briefly discuss some examples of tools used by neuropsychologists to assess these functions.

Neuropsychological assessment of children is a separate specialty from general neuropsychological assessment. There is a growing need for the development of both psychometric tests and normative data on children (Baron, 2003). Such data are important in all areas of psychological assessment but are most lacking in the neuropsychological area. Although there are not currently separate standards for being considered a child neuropsychologist, ideally a psychologist who is practicing in this specialty has been trained not only in neuropsychology but also in "developmental theory, child psychopathology, and human development" (Franzen & Berg, 1989, p. 7). At the other end of the age spectrum, we are also seeing additional tests and normative data to assist in the assessment of people who are older than traditional test norms provide. These people are sometimes called the "older old" indicating their increased life expectancy. You can read more about clinical issues with this population in the section of chapter 15 on clinical geropsychology.

Within neuropsychological assessment, a distinction is often made between **fixed batteries** and **flexible batteries** (Williams, 2000). A fixed neuropsychological battery is one that includes a standardized group of tests administered in a standardized way to every patient who is undergoing a neuropsychological evaluation. This battery is designed to sample a range of types of functioning. Each of the areas of functioning measured by the fixed battery is considered to be important in understanding the overall functioning or dysfunctional behavior of the patient. In clinical practice, trained neuropsychologists who use fixed batteries find they may need to modify them with an individual patient to address specific deficits that become apparent during the evaluation process. They do, however, give the full range of tests to have an overall picture of the patient. A flexible battery means that the neuropsychologist selects the specific tests he or she believes will best answer the referral questions being asked. Tests are added to, or eliminated from, the planned assessment process based on hypotheses that arise during the evaluation itself. Once data from these tests are obtained, the neuropsychologist then needs to integrate the data from the various tests administered for the report. Since not all of these tests may have been normed on the same population, it can be difficult to integrate the findings. Certain criteria must be met if a neuropsychological test battery is to adequately serve the purpose for which it is going to be used (Reitan & Wolfson, 1993, pp. 51–54):

1. The battery must evaluate the full range of neuropsychological functions dependent upon the brain.
2. It must include tests that relate to the brain generally as well as tests that relate to specific areas of cerebral cortical function.

3. It must use "time-honored" methods of clinical neuropsychology.
4. It must use only tests that are carefully validated for their sensitivity to cerebral damage.
5. Included tests must provide an equivalent representation of both cerebral hemispheres so that a balanced interpretation of the degree of deficit may be determined.

Neuropsychologists have become increasingly interested in the role of culture and acculturation in the outcome of neuropsychological evaluations (Fletcher-Janzen, Strickland, & Reynolds, 2000). Researchers have reported that the level of acculturation may influence performance on some neuropsychological tests in Mexican-American (Arnold, Montgomery, Casteneda, & Longoria, 1994) and African-American (Kennepohl, Shore, Nabors, & Hanks, 2004) samples. Thus, it is possible that future use of the tests we describe in this chapter will need to be accompanied by a measure of acculturation if the test data are to be interpreted correctly.

An emerging area of evaluation in neuropsychological assessment is the use of telehealth technology. This term refers to the long-distance provision of services using technology such as the Internet and teleconferencing. This topic will arise in later chapters related to individual psychotherapy as well as future trends in the profession. Rural patients may find that they do not have easy access to trained neuropsychologists, and going to urban medical centers for evaluations can be expensive and difficult for some patients. Early data comparing evaluation of patients seen via teleconferencing from rural health centers by trained neuropsychologists at distant medical sites suggest no perceptible differences for general evaluations (Jacobsen, Sprenger, Andersson, & Krogstad, 2003; Schopp, Johnstone, & Merrell, 2000). Surveys of patient satisfaction with telehealth services for mental health issues suggest that the clinicians have more concerns than the patients do (Doze, Simpson, Hailey, & Jacobs, 1999). Perhaps the patients are more comfortable with the technology than the clinicians are, or these concerns may relate to the focus in psychological training on close observation of the patient. As technology advances, additional forms of assessment are likely to be evaluated.

Halstead-Reitan Neuropsychological Battery (HRNB)

A popular fixed battery used in neuropsychological assessment is the **Halstead-Reitan Neuropsychological Battery (HRNB)** (Reitan & Wolfson, 1993). This battery is based on the clinical work of Ward Halstead (1947). He used twenty-seven measures in his laboratory to study cerebral functioning. From these twenty-seven measures, Halstead eventually selected ten measures that he felt contributed to what he called an "impairment index." As with many forms of assessment, work by one psychologist would later be modified by another psychologist. Ralph Reitan (1955) discarded three of Halstead's original measures and developed further changes to the battery, leading to one of the major neuropsychological batteries in use today. The Halstead-Reitan Battery was designed for use with patients who are fifteen years of age and older. This battery has been modified over the years by its developer as well as by practitioners. As the name indicates, this is not a single test but rather consists of a large group of individual tests. The specific tests included in this battery that are used in an actual clinical setting vary by neuropsychologist.

Table 8.1 provides the names of the tests in this battery as well as a brief description of them. We describe in more detail some of the more frequently used tests included in this battery. These individual tests also may be used by general clinical psychologists as part of their patient screening prior to referral for a full neuropsychological evaluation.

In addition to the tests listed in Table 8.1, the clinical neuropsychologist using the HRNB test battery often administers an age-appropriate intelligence test as well as various personality measures. This is true of psychologists administering any of the neuropsychological test batteries. Administration of the HRNB requires a considerable amount of equipment. Thus, one of the criticisms of this battery is that it is not easily portable. It is difficult, for example, to take this material to the hospitalized patient. The HRNB is more commonly used in its entirety when the patient is able to come to the neuropsychologist's office. Some modifications of this battery have been made to make it a bit easier to use at least parts of it in other settings. For example, the original stimuli for the Categories Test were presented on 208 slides projected on a large specialized machine. A booklet form of this test was developed later and has become popular among neuropsychologists partially because it is easier to administer than the original version. To do well on the Categories Test, the patient must have the mental flexibility to form hypotheses and then to change these hypotheses when they are not supported by subsequent items. These 208 slides are grouped into seven sets of items. Each of these sets is organized based on a different principle. For example, the correct response in one set might be based on the number of objects in the picture. No clues are provided about the principle that is being used. The patient is told to select the right answer from among the pictures shown. Once the patient has responded, the neuropsychologist gives the patient the correct answer. The patient is encouraged to try to figure out the principle that is being used and apply that principle to the next item. The principle used to determine the correct response changes with each set so the patient must also be able to handle the frustration of this change. The patient is not given a warning that the set has changed. The only indication the patient has of this change of set is that perhaps he or she was giving a series of correct answers and then suddenly, using the same schema, he or she is told that the answer is not correct that time.

Table 8.1 Halstead-Reitan Tests

Test	Brief Description
Categories Test	Formation of categories of visual stimuli; abstracting ability
Tactual Performance Test	Fit various shaped blocks into formboard blindfolded
Seashore Rhythm Test	Discriminate between like and different musical beats
Speech Sounds Perception Test	Match audiotaped sounds to written list
Finger Tapping Test	Manual dexterity speed of index finger
Trail Making Test	Connect numbered and lettered circles
Strength of Grip Test	Comparison of left and right side grip strength
Sensory-Perceptual Exam	Unilateral and bilateral presentation of tactile, auditory, and visual stimuli
Tactile Perception Test	Left and right side perception and discrimination of tactile stimuli
Aphasia Screening Test	Language usage and recognition, figure reproduction, copy simple actions

The Tactual Performance Test requires bulky equipment that needs to be kept out of the patient's sight until it is time for this test. The patient is blindfolded before this test equipment is revealed. The patient is never allowed to see the equipment. Part of the task is to determine whether or not the patient can visualize the entire board after completing the task. Thus, it is important that the patient not see the equipment at any time. The adult version of the test uses a ten-hole formboard. Three trials are used with this formboard—preferred or dominant hand, the other hand, and both hands. After blindfolding the patient, the neuropsychologist tells the patient that there is a board on the table. The neuropsychologist then moves the patient's hand over the back of the board to feel the shapes of the various holes in the board. Many students note that this board is similar to toys they had as children. After feeling the board, the patient's hand is guided over the blocks that have been placed between the patient and the board. The patient is instructed that there is a block for each of the holes in the board. The task is to use the dominant hand only to place these blocks in the spaces. The neuropsychologist must keep a record of the amount of time it takes the patient to perform each trial of this test. After completion of the trial with the dominant hand, the process is repeated with the other hand and a third trial is completed using both hands. The board is removed from the area before removing the patient's blindfold. A blank piece of paper is placed on the table in front of the patient after the blindfold is removed. The patient is asked to draw an outline of the shape of the formboard including each of the shaped holes in their correct location on the board. As you can tell, this is a complex and time-consuming task to administer. Also, remember why neuropsychological testing might be done. A patient with neuropsychological dysfunction may find this task quite difficult, depending on the location of the difficulty. The clinical skills of the neuropsychologist may be needed to encourage the patient to attempt this task as well as to continue trying when the tasks become difficult.

Several of the HRNB tests require a tape recorder for stimulus presentation. The Seashore Rhythm Test is administered to assess auditory comprehension. This test includes thirty pairs of rhythmic patterns. The task for the patient is to indicate whether the pairs are the same or different. The patient is given an answer sheet for this test. The patient is instructed to write either an S (same) or a D (different) on the line after hearing a pair of rhythmic patterns from the tape. Sample items are used to make certain the patient understands the task. Once the regular stimulus items are started, however, the neuropsychologist does not stop the tape. Suppose the patient gets confused and loses his or her place on this task? The neuropsychologist just tells the patient to keep going. Another auditory test in this battery is the Speech Sounds Perception Test. This test includes six sets of ten items each. The patient hears a nonsense word presented on the tape. The task is to match this auditorially presented material with a written form of it on a sheet of paper given to the patient. All of the nonsense words used in this task were formed by adding a consonant before and after the two vowels "ee." Thus, one nonsense word might be "beeg" in written form. As with the Seashore Rhythm Test, sample items are provided before starting the actual stimulus items to determine that the patient understands the task.

Finger Tapping is a perceptual-motor task. It uses a small lever mounted on a board with a counter. The patient is instructed to place his or her hand flat on the board with the index finger on the lever. The task is to tap the lever, let it return to its original position, and then tap it again. This process is to be done as quickly as possible. The patient is given five ten-second trials with each hand starting with the dominant hand.

Grip Strength is measured by having the patient squeeze a dynamometer twice, first with one hand and then with the other hand. The patient is instructed to squeeze as hard as he or she can. The neuropsychologist demonstrates how to squeeze the instrument before starting the task and also makes any needed adjustment in its stirrup to fit the patient's hand. A mean strength is then calculated for each hand. As you can imagine, this test does not take very much time. Many patients feel comfortable doing this task because it does not really "seem" like a test. Thus, if the patient is becoming uncomfortable about his or her test performance this task may be helpful in terms of patient motivation.

The Sensory Perceptual Exam is a measure of tactile, auditory, and visual stimulation. Depending on the trial, stimuli are presented either bilaterally or unilaterally. Each of the three senses is evaluated separately. A standard format is used for both the location of the stimulation and the order of presentation. The patient is blindfolded for these tasks to eliminate the use of visual cues.

The Tactile Perception Test uses small common items such as a coin. The patient is blindfolded for this test. Part of the task involves placing various items in the palm of either the dominant or nondominant hand of the patient. The patient is then asked to identify these common objects by their feel and using only the hand in which the item has been placed. In other words, the patient must attempt to move the item, such as the coin, around in the hand being evaluated without using the other hand. When testing older patients, it is important to note whether or not the patient has any arthritic condition in the hands that may make this task difficult. In such a case, you would note in your evaluation of the patient's performance that this particular physical condition may have impacted the score on this test. This test also includes having the patient identify what number the neuropsychologist has written on the patient's fingertip using a small plastic stylus.

The Aphasia Screening Test is the major language test included in this battery. This test uses thirty-two of the original fifty-one items developed by Halstead and Wepman (1959). The original test was designed to assess all major areas associated with aphasia as well as other common language problems. The shortened version now used in the HRNB provides information that is used descriptively by the neuropsychologist in understanding potential areas of organic dysfunction. Among the items of this test are ones to measure language usage, language recognition, the ability to reproduce geometric figures, and the ability to pantomime simple actions presented by the neuropsychologist.

If the entire HRNB battery is administered, most neuropsychologists will need to spend a full day with the patient. For patients who must take frequent breaks, more than one day may be scheduled to complete the battery. This time is only the beginning of the psychologist's work. The scores on these tests need to be interpreted not only individually but also in relationship to each other by using knowledge of the underlying neurophysiology. Remember the type of specialized graduate training these psychologists received. They must have a solid understanding of how the various parts of the brain interact and what types of functions are likely to be impacted by problems in each brain area. Many types of interpretation can be made from this extensive battery. We are summarizing some of the most common forms of test interpretation.

The test data are interpreted based on a comparison of the patient's performance to the normative sample. This comparison is known as the level of performance. Each of the tests can then be evaluated in terms of the probability of the performance level indicating neurological deficits, and an Impairment Index is calculated. The neuropsychologist also considers the patient's **pattern of responding.** If some of the tests indicate deficits, do these tests measure skills controlled by similar parts of the brain? If so, there is further support for dysfunction in that area. There are several tests in which the patient is measured separately on the right and left sides of the body. It is important to know which is the dominant side when analyzing these data. Responses from a left-handed person would be expected to be stronger on the left side than on the right side. If performance on the dominant side is worse than on the nondominant side of the body, a different interpretation would be made. Finally, the neuropsychologist looks for **pathognomic signs.** This term is used to refer to specific deficits that are rarely seen in anyone who is not impaired. When these signs are present, they almost always indicate dysfunction.

Reitan (1986) has suggested that two major weaknesses of his battery are in its evaluation of memory and motor problems. Although it does include measures of these factors, when memory or motor function are a major part of the referral question it is probably best to include additional tests specifically designed to measure memory or motor functions. Over the years, many resources have been developed to provide data on specific patient populations (e.g., Batchelor, Sowles, Dean, & Fischer, 1991; Faibish, Auerbach, & Thornby, 1986; Heaton et al., 1995; Heaton, Nelson, Thompson, Burks, & Franklin, 1985). These norms have proved useful to neuropsychologists working with these specialty groups. As the need for neuropsychological evaluation of children increased, Reitan developed several downward extensions of his battery. His "intermediate" battery is designed for children between the ages of nine and fourteen and his "children's" battery is for those between the ages five and eight (Spreen & Strauss, 1998).

Luria-Nebraska Neuropsychological Battery (LNNB)

A second popular fixed battery is the **Luria-Nebraska Neuropsychological Battery (LNNB)** (Golden, Purisch, & Hammeke, 1980). This battery was developed to standardize the approach to patient assessment used by Russian neurologist Alexander Luria. In the revised version of the LNNB, two equivalent forms are available. Like the Halstead-Reitan, the Luria-Nebraska is intended for use with patients who are fifteen years of age or older, although some studies have reported data on twelve- and fourteen-year-olds. A separate version, the Luria-Nebraska Neuropsychological Battery–Children's Revision (LNNB-C), was developed for children between the ages of eight and twelve (Golden, 1987). This test is also sometimes used with adolescents who are thirteen and fourteen. The same eleven clinical scales found on the adult version are used in the children's version. There are also optional scales for spelling and motor writing. The typical amount of time needed for testing a child with organic deficits is about two and one-half hours. Golden notes that the LNNB-C requires that the child is reasonably cooperative and English-speaking. Screening batteries, requiring about twenty minutes to administer, are available for both children and adults. You will have a chance to "meet" Dr. Golden through our interview with him in chapter 14.

This 269-item battery is grouped into eleven subtests, as shown in Table 8.2. It is completely portable and thus can be administered at bedside if that is needed. In most cases, this battery can be administered in about two hours. There is also an equivalent Form II of this test that has ten additional items because of an added scale, Immediate Memory. Form II is computer scored, while Form I can be either hand scored or computer scored. The scoring of the LNNB is somewhat different from most psychological tests. Generally, high scores on psychological tests mean that you have done well on them. On each item of the LNNB, however, a score of "0" means normal performance, a score of "1" indicates a borderline level of performance, and a score of "2" means the level of performance was defective. Thus, the higher the score on the LNNB, the greater the deficit identified in that domain. The patient's T scores are adjusted based on the person's age and level of education in order to account for these factors in interpreting the performance level.

According to the manual for the revised edition of the Luria-Nebraska (Golden, Purisch, & Hammeke, 1985), the neuropsychologist using this battery should consider the data from four perspectives. First is the issue of whether or not there is significant brain injury. In some cases, because of the nature of the problem, this is not really a question. For many of the patients evaluated by neuropsychologists, however, the question is whether the problems leading to the evaluation may be caused by some neurological difficulty. In other words, previous evaluation information suggests that the problem may have an organic basis but may also be the result of other causes. The purpose of the neuropsychological evaluation is to provide further support for an organic basis for the problem or further support for the position that the problem is not organic in nature. Once you have established the presence of brain injury, the second step is to determine what behaviors are and are not within the patient's current level of abilities. A third point to consider is the probable cause of the difficulty. This information is derived from the

Table 8.2 Luria-Nebraska Neuropsychological Battery, Clinical Scales

Scale Name	Brief Description
Motor	Measures bilateral and bimanual skills
Rhythm	Attend to and discriminate among verbal and nonverbal stimuli
Tactile	Identify unseen objects, location and direction of tactile stimuli
Visual	Identify objects from pictures of differing clarity and complexity
Receptive Speech	Measures ability to discriminate sounds and understand grammatical structures
Expressive Speech	Ability to articulate sounds and construct sentences
Writing	Motor skills, copying, and spontaneous writing
Reading	Reading letters, words, sentences, paragraph
Arithmetic	Measures a range of basic math skills
Memory	Short-term memory for both verbal and nonverbal stimuli
Intellectual Processes	Concept formation, complex oral math, comprehension
Pathognomonic	Items from ten ability scales highly sensitive to brain dysfunction
Left Hemisphere	Items sensitive to left hemisphere sensorimotor strip
Right Hemisphere	Items sensitive to right hemisphere sensorimotor strip

behavioral manifestations seen during the evaluation. Finally, the neuropsychologist needs to integrate all of the information available to make hypotheses about the current level of brain functioning.

Two of the first studies to compare the Luria-Nebraska and Halstead-Reitan, using experienced neuropsychologists and the same patients, reported that the accuracy of the two batteries was comparable (Golden et al., 1981; Kane, Sweet, Golden, Parsons, & Moses, 1981). Subjects were drawn from brain-damaged, psychiatric, and normal controls. Although there was a tendency for the Luria-Nebraska to perform slightly better with the brain-injured and the Halstead-Reitan to do slightly better identifying psychiatric patients, the data do not support one battery being statistically superior to the other for their intended purposes.

Boston Process Approach

An example of the flexible battery approach to neuropsychological assessment is the **Boston Process Approach** (Goodglass, 1986; Kaplan, 1990). Neuropsychologists doing an evaluation from this perspective use the outcome from one test to determine the next test to be administered. The number of tests actually administered will vary across patients. The goal is to administer a sufficient number of tests to be able to evaluate both the strengths and weaknesses of the patient. For example, a common referral issue in neuropsychological assessment is to evaluate the patient's memory ability. The neuropsychologist using the Boston Process Approach would probably use several memory tests designed to evaluate specific facets of memory (e.g., verbal, visual-perceptual, tactile, short-term or working memory, and long-term). Suppose that during the process of this memory testing, the neuropsychologist noted some difficulty with motor function. In that case, tests of motor ability and control would be administered to evaluate what role these skills may have in the current state of this person's functioning. Throughout the evaluation the neuropsychologist is attending not only to the specific responses that are given to each specific test, but also to the strategies and processes used by the patient in responding to the tasks. Knowledge of the influence of the brain on these skills as well as the overlap of various skills may point to a cognitive area that needs assessment even if it does not seem obvious based on the referral question.

In some ways, the flexible battery assessment process is quite similar to the hypothesis testing used by experimental psychologists in the laboratory as they design one study based on ideas raised by another study. Many process-oriented neuropsychologists feel very strongly that the use of fixed batteries for assessment is not appropriate. One neuropsychologist noted, "The popularity of ready-made batteries attests to the need for psychological testing and to a general lack of knowledge about how to do it" (Lezak, 1995, p. 123). She obviously does not approve of the use of fixed batteries!

Screening Batteries

At times it is not feasible to do a complete neuropsychological assessment. As you have read, a full neuropsychological battery takes both extensive time and considerable professional expertise. Managed care companies typically will not pay for such extensive forms of evaluation. Thus, patients who desire this form of evaluation may find that they must pay for it independently rather than having their health insurance cover the cost.

In other cases, the patient may not be willing to undergo such a time-consuming evaluation. At other times, the referral issue is quite specific and may not require the amount of data generated from a full neuropsychological evaluation. In these cases, some more abbreviated form of evaluation may be sufficient to provide the needed information.

In some cases, the initial question may be to determine whether or not a full neuropsychological assessment is needed. In those cases, **screening batteries** can be used. General clinical psychologists use certain screening assessments, while others are used by clinical neuropsychologists. If a screening assessment provides sufficient support for conducting a full neuropsychological assessment, either a referral is made to a neuropsychologist or the neuropsychologist who did the screening will then add additional tests to gain a more complete picture of the patient's functioning.

Over time, attempts have been made to develop one test that could be used to differentiate between brain-damaged and non-brain-damaged patients. These attempts have not been successful. One reason for this failure is that brain damage is a very complex problem. Some tests are very helpful in determining whether or not the patient has problems in *one* aspect of functioning but will miss problems in other areas. An alternative is to develop screening batteries that can be used to evaluate all major areas of functioning. According to several experts on neuropsychological screening batteries across the lifespan (Berg, Franzen, & Wedding, 1987; Franzen & Berg, 1989), a good screening battery should measure several different abilities, including lateral dominance; motor functioning; auditory, tactile, and visual sensation; perceptual-spatial abilities; language skills; general information; and memory.

The term *screening battery* may give you the idea that it is completed very quickly. Many of the recommended screening batteries take several hours to complete. On the other hand, they are completed much more quickly than full neuropsychological batteries and often use tests that can be administered by the general clinical psychologist. Some of these screening batteries use only parts of specific tests rather than administering a full version of any of the tests. We will use one such battery to illustrate this concept. In this case, there is both an adult version and children's modification of the battery. Each version takes about an hour to administer. The adult version includes the Finger Tapping Test, Trail Making Test, and part of the Aphasia Screening Test from the Halstead-Reitan; the items comprising the Pathognomic Scale from the Luria-Nebraska; Digit Symbol from the WAIS; the Stroop Color and Word Test; and two subtests from the Wechsler Memory Scale (Wysocki & Sweet, 1985). Although most of the literature about psychological testing takes a negative view of using parts of tests, these batteries have been normed for the specific purpose of neuropsychological screening. In other words, this special combination of tests and test items has been evaluated for this specific purpose and found to be useful.

Bender Visual-Motor Gestalt Test

One test that has been popular for a long time as part of a neuropsychological screening process is the **Bender Visual-Motor Gestalt Test,** often just called the Bender (Bender, 1938). It is named for its originator, physician Lauretta Bender. This test was originally designed as a measure of visual-motor performance for use with adult patients and as part of a developmental screening exam with children six years of age or older. Studies have shown that this test is frequently taught in clinical and counseling psychology programs as well as being used by a large number of practitioners (Golden & Kuperman, 1980; Lees-Haley, Smith, Williams, & Dunn, 1996; Piotrowski & Keller, 1992). Among neuropsychologists, the Bender has been used to screen for visuospatial perception, constructional ability, drawing, upper extremity motor functioning, and verbal comprehension (Anderson, 1994). This test has also been used as a personality screening instrument (Aucone et al., 2001; Raphael & Golden, 2002). It is important to remember that the Bender is *not* used as the sole psychometric measure, even when doing a screening battery. Perhaps because it is so simple to administer, clinicians could easily rely on this test and draw inaccurate conclusions. When used as the sole measure, the Bender has been found to have a high rate of false negative findings. Research has suggested that Bender data are especially problematic when the differential diagnosis is between brain damage and a general psychiatric diagnosis.

The Bender test stimuli are nine index-sized cards. Each card contains a different geometric design (see the accompanying figure). The designs are drawn in black on white cards. They are based on the work of one of the early Gestalt psychologists, Max Wertheimer. The designs consist of dots, lines, angles, and curves. A number of different test procedures have been developed for use with these test stimuli. A common approach is to place several sheets of plain paper on the table within easy reach of the patient. The patient is provided with pencils with erasers. One reason for using pencils with erasers is that a common scoring item is the number of erasures the patient makes. The cards are handed to the patient one at a time. The patient is told to copy the design "the best you can." If the patient asks where to place the drawing or if more than one sheet of paper should be used, the psychologist gives a general response indicating that the patient can do whatever seems right. A recall or short-term memory assessment is often used after the completion of the original nine designs. The stimulus cards as well as the patient's reproductions are removed from view. Another sheet of paper is provided and the patient is told to draw as many of the designs as he or she can remember. The recall phase was not part of the original test procedure. Although there is no time limit for this test, the original copying phase typically takes between five and ten minutes. Unusually long or short administration times are considered of diagnostic significance.

When she originally developed her test, Bender did not have a formal scoring system. She meant for the clinician to use personal judgment to analyze the drawings. Over the years, a number of different scoring systems have been developed for use with the Bender (Hutt, 1985; Koppitz, 1975; Pascal & Suttell, 1951). Some of these systems are for specific populations, such as children, while others are more general. As you can probably tell, it is difficult to obtain strong validity studies on a test like this.

Some clinical neuropsychologists also use the Bender as a personality measure. Attempts to integrate the literature on this use of the Bender and to develop an empirically supported scoring system led to the development of the Advanced Psychodiagnostic Interpretation (API) scoring system (Reichenberg & Raphael, 1992). The API was developed using a factor analytic procedure and was later modified (Raphael & Golden, 1998), leading to 207 scorable items with high interrater reliability and seventeen personality factors. Because the most common use of the Bender is for neuropsychological evaluations, we are describing it here rather than in chapter 7 on personality measures.

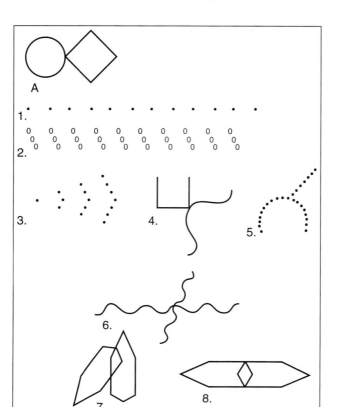

The Bender Drawings.

Cognistat

Neuropsychologists are often concerned about the patient's level of cognitive functioning. Over the years, a number of brief cognitive screening measures have been developed. To illustrate these measures, we will briefly describe the Cognistat (Kiernan, Mueller, & Langston, 1995). The Cognistat, known in its initial version as the Neurobehavioral Cognitive Status Exam (NCSE), measures a range of factors within a short period of time. Normal individuals can often complete this test in about five minutes, and even people who are cognitively impaired can usually complete all of the tasks within about twenty minutes.

The patient's *orientation* is measured in much the same way as we described for the mental status exam in chapter 5. *Attention* is measured by having the patient repeat digits. *Comprehension* is evaluated using orally presented commands, some of which require more than one step. *Repetition* is used to determine whether or not the patient can repeat phrases and sentences. *Naming* evaluates the patient's ability to name parts of objects or line drawings of objects. The *constructions* items require the patient to draw geometric figures from memory. These drawings are made immediately after the figure is removed from view. As you can see, this test is different from the Bender, which is a copying form of construction test. The Cognistat also includes items in which the patient needs to copy colored designs by using flat red and white pieces. A *memory* test requires the recall of four words without cueing and then with cueing as well as recognizing previously presented words when they are placed among a number of other words. This is a measure of verbal memory in contrast to the visual-spatial memory of the constructions task. Oral math problems are used to evaluate *calculation* skills. The *similarities* test requires the patient to state how two concepts are alike. For the *judgment* test, the patient is asked what he or she would do under described circumstances. The end product of this screening measure is not a single score but rather a profile of scores on the domains measured. These scores are plotted to reflect whether performance in each domain is average or falls within one of the impaired areas—mild, moderate, or severe. In addition to being used as an initial screening measure, the Cognistat is also used by neuropsychologists to follow the progression of change during either a disease process or as a result of treatment.

Dementia Rating Scale

As we mentioned previously, with the aging of our population, psychologists have needed to develop tests that are applicable to older patients. Earlier versions of many of our tests did not include these individuals in the standardization sample and thus they were not appropriate for use with these patients. Today, a frequent diagnostic issue with this patient group is whether or not dementia is present. The **Dementia Rating Scale (DRS-2),** now in its second edition (Jurica, Leitten, & Mattis, 2001), is used in cases in which the concern is the mental status of adults who have cognitive impairment. We chose it to illustrate a group of tests designed to meet this need.

The DRS-2 provides a general measure of cognitive ability in patients who are suspected of having some form of dementia. It can be used with people between the ages of 56 and 105. In addition to an overall level of cognitive functioning, the DRS-2 also yields five subscale scores: attention, initiation/perseveration, construction, conceptualization, and memory. The items are presented in a standard order starting with the most difficult items. If the patient is able to do the two most difficult items, generally the rules specify you to give credit for the easier ones. This procedure decreases testing time for patients who are relatively functional in that domain. The thirty-two stimulus cards are contained in a spiral bound booklet and depict items that are familiar to most people. For patients who are functioning well, this test takes about fifteen minutes to complete, while it may take twice that long for patients who are experiencing major cognitive dysfunction. The DRS-2 manual provides age- and education-corrected normative data, but that sample lacked information directly related to ethnicity and to people with fewer than eight years of education (Johnson-Greene, 2004). Therefore, DRS-2 scores for patients who are not Caucasian or who have fewer than eight years of education should be interpreted very carefully.

Mini-Mental State Examination (MMSE)

Suppose you do not already have information about cognitive impairment? Consider our patient, Joyce. Although she is concerned about being in the early stages of Alzheimer's disease, you do not have any solid information that her problem is not emotionally based. The **Mini-Mental State Examination (MMSE)** is a common screening test to assess cognitive functioning in adults (Folstein, Folstein, & McHugh, 2001).

This thirty-item screen for cognitive impairment takes between five and ten minutes to complete. It assesses orientation, registration, attention, calculation, serial subtractions, recall, short-term memory, naming, and language repetition. There are separate norms for patients who are illiterate, are over eighty years of age, and have less than a ninth grade education. If adults from these groups were merely included in a general sample, their results would likely have a negative impact on the range of scores indicative of dysfunction. Thus, clinical applicability of the measure would be decreased. Having separate norms for groups who are likely to do less well than the average adult but still not have major cognitive problems allows a more accurate clinical picture of an individual patient. Given the changing demographics we have discussed, the availability of a Spanish-language version (Taussig, Mack, & Henderson, 1996) adds to its utility. Students who want to read more about this popular measure might start with Tombaugh and McIntyre's (1992) review article.

California Verbal Learning Test (CVLT-2)

The **California Verbal Learning Test (CVLT-2),** now in its second edition, is used to measure immediate memory span, learning curve, and the effects of retroactive and proactive interference (Delis, Kramer, Kaplan, & Ober, 2000). It can be used with people between the ages of sixteen and sixty-nine. There is also a short form of the test, an alternative form for retesting purposes, and a children's version for use with people between the ages of five and seventeen. Although it usually takes only about thirty minutes to administer this test, there is also a delayed recall that must be done thirty minutes after completion of testing, so that needs to be taken into account when planning a testing session. Some people may have no problem remembering something they have just heard but have considerable difficulty remembering that same information a half-hour later because of the things they did during the passage of time. Thus, this test has very practical use in working with patients experiencing specific types of memory problems.

The CVLT-2 includes items intended to detect malingering as a way to decrease false results. Malingering has become such a major issue in neuropsychological assessment that special tests of malingering have been developed. We will discuss them a bit later in this chapter. Overall, this test is a list learning task used to assess multiple aspects of how verbal learning occurs.

Stroop Color-Word Test

Another screening test used by neuropsychologists is the Stroop Color-Word Test. Most patients take less than ten minutes to complete the task. Over the years, different formats of the procedure originally developed by Stroop (1935) have been used. Regardless of the format used, it is a quick test of organic impairment.

One common procedure (Golden, 1987) uses three sheets of 8½" × 11" paper. The first sheet has five columns of words. Each word is the name of a color (red, blue, and green). The task is for the patient to read the words down each column aloud. The patient is instructed to read as quickly as possible. The psychologist corrects any errors that occur. The score is the number of words read correctly in forty-five seconds. The second sheet of paper has columns of Xs. The Xs are printed in different colors (red, blue, and green). This time the task is to name the color. The patient reads down the columns and says the name of the color in which the Xs are printed. Thus the words the patient says are the same as on the first part of the test but the stimuli are different. Once again the score is the number of correct colors read in forty-five seconds. The third page uses the same words as found on the first page. The difference this time is that the words are printed in different colors from the name of the color. For example, the word *red* might be printed in green ink, or the word *green* might be printed in red ink. The task for the patient is to identify the colors and ignore the actual printed word. For example, in the case just described, the correct response to the first item would be "green" and to the second item would be "red." The score from each page is converted to a T score using tables provided in the test manual. Patients with concentration problems often find this test very unpleasant and difficult. In order to get their cooperation, it may be helpful to tell them in advance that this test may be difficult but has the potential to provide useful information. What you have measured in this case is the patient's ability to shift perceptual set based on the demand of each situation. You are also requiring the patient to suppress a typical response to stimuli in favor of an unusual response to those stimuli. Thus, it is a measure of selective attention and cognitive flexibility.

Trail Making Test

We briefly described this test as part of the Halstead-Reitan battery in Table 8.1. Because of the ease of administration, this test is also a commonly used test for neuropsychological screening, so we will describe it in a bit more detail here. This test is considered a measure of visual-conceptual ability and visual-motor tracking. It also has a large attentional component that makes it sensitive to the impact of many forms of brain damage.

There are two forms of the **Trail Making Test:** the Intermediate or Children's form and the Adult form. We will describe the adult form here. The Trail Making Test is administered in two parts, A and B. Each part is printed on a separate white page of paper. **Trails A** consists of twenty-five circles printed on the page in black ink. Each of these circles contains a number from 1 to 25. These numbers are not, however, found in their correct order. The patient is given a pencil and told to connect the circles in their correct order from 1 to 25 as quickly as possible. This is done by drawing a line from the circle containing the "1" to the circle with the "2" and so on. (Remember the connect-the-dots puzzles you might have done as child?) After the directions are given, the patient is provided with a short sample to make certain that the task is understood. This page contains only seven circles, numbered from 1 to 7. If the patient has difficulty with the sample, the psychologist explains the task again at this point. The psychologist records both the amount of time the patient needed to complete this process and the number of errors the patient made. The time is expressed in seconds. The psychologist must watch the patient carefully and point out any errors during the testing so the patient can immediately make corrections. Of course, this correction process adds to the total test time. Thus, the psychologist should not take an extended amount of time to explain the error. All that is needed, for example, is to say, "You skipped number 3. Or, remember, you go from 2 to 3 to 4."

Trails B is a bit different from Trails A and is more difficult. In this case, there are twenty-five circles numbered from 1 to 13 and letters from A to L. The task is to connect the circles sequentially alternating from number to letter to number. Thus, you would go from "1" to "A" to "2" to "B." Once again the score is the number of seconds required to complete the task and the examiner corrects mistakes as before.

Cutoff scores are provided to indicate whether or not the performance is suggestive of brain damage. Because many studies have reported that scores decrease with age, most of the scoring materials provide different cutoff scores for each age decade (e.g., 40–49, 60–69). According to Reitan and Wolfson, "It seems likely that the ability to deal with the numerical and language symbols (numbers and letters) is sustained by the left cerebral hemisphere, the visual scanning task necessary to perceive the spatial distribution of the stimulus is represented by the right cerebral hemisphere, and speed and efficiency of performance may be a general characteristic of adequate brain functions (p. 74)." The Trail Making Test has been found to be highly sensitive to brain damage (O'Donnell, 1983), closed head injury (desRosiers & Kavanaugh, 1987), and brain atrophy in HIV-positive patients (Di Sclafani et al., 1997), among other conditions.

Wechsler Memory Scale-III (WMS-III)

A common facet of brain insult is memory difficulty. With the increasing number of referrals of elderly persons for evaluation, further attention has been paid to the memory domain. Remember that one of the problems Joyce, our patient from chapter 5, brought to her psychologist was concern about memory and concentration. As you may have learned in other psychology classes, the term *memory* refers to a highly complex process. When faced with information, you must first be able to attend to that information. In other words, you must register it before anything else happens. Once you have determined that this information may be useful to you at some future time, you must then encode it and store it for future use. Psychologists often make a distinction between short-term memory and long-term memory. Storing memory on a short-term basis means that you do not plan to use it in the long run but need it briefly now. For example, you look up a phone number for a pizza delivery service. You only need it long enough to dial your phone. If, however, you want to retain this information for more than a few seconds, you will need to consolidate it into your long-term memory storage. The only information you will be able to retrieve later is found in this area. Although the ability to recall information may be assisted by various forms of cues, it must first have been stored in your long-term memory or it is lost.

Neuropsychologists have provided some evidence of a relationship between various forms of memory processing and specific anatomical areas of the brain. This is an area of research that needs further work so that we can continue to improve the clinical assessment process. We also know that memory can be influenced by your emotional state, the aging process, and various diseases such as Alzheimer's. It is beyond the scope of this book to describe all of the measures used by neuropsychologists to evaluate memory functions. We decided, however, to describe one of the more popular measures, the Wechsler Memory Scale-III (WMS-III), to illustrate these types of assessment tools. The original version of this scale was published in 1945 with the most recent revision being published in 1997 (Wechsler, 1945, 1997).

When administering a psychological test, an important aspect of test interpretation is to compare that person's performance to individuals from the standardization sample who are similar to the person in important demographic characteristics such as age and educational level. One of the changes in the norms for the WMS-III was the inclusion of people between the ages of seventy-four and eighty-nine to reflect the increased longevity of the U.S. population. The omission of this age group in the previous editions of the test was often cited as a major deficit.

The WMS-III includes seventeen subtests, of which seven are optional. The adjusted scores have a mean of 100 with a standard deviation of 15. Thus, it is easy to compare the person's memory score with an IQ score from an individual test of cognitive ability as one basis for understanding the level of functioning. It is essentially a measure of declarative episodic memory. As noted in the test manual, the test stimuli are new to the person and are specific to this testing situation. To perform well on this test, the patient must both learn and retrieve this new information quickly and accurately. Six of the ten required subtests measure immediate memory and the other four measure delayed recall. The delayed recall measures are taken thirty minutes after the immediate recall tests. Notice that this delay is the same one used with the CVLT. Thirty minutes is a common delay used in these types of tests. The patient is asked the same information as was used in the initial tests of this same information. These tests are listed in Table 8.3. Scores on these subtests yield eight primary indices of memory: auditory immediate, visual immediate, immediate memory, general memory, auditory memory, visual delayed, auditory recognition delayed, and working memory.

Information from the WMS-III is used in multiple ways by the neuropsychologist. Single subscale scores and single index scores provide information. In addition to these scores, the neuropsychologist will also look at the patterns of discrepancy that arise between scores. Damage to specific parts of the brain has been associated with specific types of memory deficit. For example, deficits in memory for nonverbal material may indicate right temporal lobe dysfunction. Deficits in memory for verbal material may indicate left temporal lobe damage. Individuals who have difficulty with tasks requiring memory for order of verbal or auditory material may have parietal lobe damage. The neuropsychologist would combine information from the WMS-III with biographical information as well as data from other tests that have been administered before suggesting such damage.

Table 8.3 Wechsler Memory Scale-III, Primary Subtests

Immediate Recall Subtests	Delayed Recall Subtests
Logical Memory I	Logical Memory II
Faces I	Faces II
Verbal Paired Associates I	Verbal Paired Associates II
Family Pictures I	Family Pictures II
Letter-Number Sequencing	
Spatial Span	

Rey Complex Figures Test

When the patient's memory problem is suspected to be a visual-spatial one, the neuro-psychologist might select a specialized test of this type of memory. One possibility is the **Rey Complex Figures Test** (Meyers & Meyers, 1995). This drawing test has four separate tasks. First, the patient is shown a card containing a complex figure based on the original one developed by Rey (1941). This complex figure was part of his published case study but was never commercially available. Thus, neuropsychologists who wanted to use this task tended to rely on photocopies of the figure from research journals. Such copies were not standardized and therefore scoring and interpretation of the data tended to be qualitative. In 1995, a computer-generated replica of the original stimulus figure became commercially available along with both scoring criteria and normative data.

The patient is given a blank sheet of paper and is told to copy the figure. After the patient indicates that he or she is finished copying the figure, it is removed from view and the patient's copy is taken from view as well. The neuropsychologist then talks to the patient for three minutes about any topic except the test. After three minutes have passed, the Immediate Recall portion of the test occurs. A new blank sheet of paper is provided to the patient and the patient is instructed to draw from memory the figure he or she just directly copied. The third part of the test is a Delayed Recall. Thirty minutes after the patient completes the original copy phase of the test, a new sheet of blank paper is provided and the patient is once again instructed to draw the figure from memory. The final phase of this test is a Recognition task. In this phase of testing, the patient is shown pictures of twenty-four geometric figures. Twelve of those twenty-four figures are elements of the original complex figure. The task for the patient is to indicate which of these items he or she recognizes from the original figure. The Rey Complex Figure Test can be administered to adults between the ages of eighteen and eighty-nine. The actual testing time for the test is between ten and fifteen minutes although you obviously need more time than this because of the delay. During that delay period, you may do some of your other testing or interviewing.

Interpretation of the scores on this test requires integration of scores from each part of the test. For example, interpretation of the score on Recall needs to take into account the score on the original Copy part of the test. The manual provides information on both quantitative and qualitative scoring.

Test Coaching

What do we mean by "test coaching," and why is it important to clinical psychologists? Test coaching can be defined as "any attempt to alter the results of psychological or neuro-psychological tests in such a way that distorts the true representation of the examinee's cognitive, emotional, or behavioral status, or hinders an accurate assessment of such attributes" (Victor & Abeles, 2004, p. 374). Test coaching is certainly not limited to neuropsychological assessment. For example, we read about a website on the Rorschach that provides information about the blots and how to respond to each of them if you are involved in a child custody evaluation. It also suggests that in this case, the best approach is to not take the test. This site provides instructions about what to say to the psychologist about your knowledge of the Rorschach so that the test cannot be used in your case (Victor & Abeles, 2004).

Because neuropsychological assessment has been associated with legal proceedings, we chose to address the issue of coaching here. A survey of members of both the National Academy of Neuropsychology and the Association of Trail Lawyers (Essig, Mittenberg, Petersen, Strauman, & Cooper, 2001) reported that 75 percent of attorneys not only prepared their clients for the tests for which they were being referred but also made suggestions to them about how to respond to those tests. Almost 50 percent of the neuropsychologists responding to this survey also noted that the attorneys who hired them requested that they focus on specific aspects of their findings rather than giving a total report. One published article told attorneys how to prepare their clients who are plaintiffs in mild brain injury cases (Taylor et al., 1992). These are just a few examples of the types of available coaching information.

Attorneys have described three levels of witness coaching (Abeles, 2001). One level involves overtly coaching the witness to provide false testimony. This form of coaching violates not only perjury statutes but also legal ethics. At a second level, the coaching is covert rather than overt and therefore seems to avoid the legal and ethical pitfalls of the first level. The third level is when the attorney does not knowingly do the coaching but it occurs as a result of regular interactions with the client. Consider how this information about test coaching relates to the ethical conundrum from the beginning of this chapter.

There are steps the neuropsychologist can take to at least reduce the impact of coaching on the outcome of neuropsychological assessment. First, the use of tests with built-in validity scales assists the neuropsychologist in determining whether or not the patient is being truthful. As we noted in chapter 7, however, much of the data we have on malingering comes from analogue studies and therefore further investigation is certainly needed here. It helps to use tests that "minimize the effects of witness coaching if at all possible" (Abeles, 2001, p. 5). Because it is harder to fake patterns of responding than specific scores on a measure, differences in these two areas are noteworthy (Victor & Abeles, 2004). Thus, it will continue to be important to develop more measures in which the pattern of responding is evaluated rather than just a single summary score. Neuropsychologists often use specific measures of malingering separate from their regular neuropsychological tests in an attempt to address not only malingering on the part of the patient but also the impact of patient coaching. We will discuss some of these measures next.

Malingering Tests

Malingering is defined as faking the results of a test. This behavior is associated with some type of personal gain for the individual. Why do you think you would need this type of test as part of a neuropsychological evaluation? In many cases in which malingering is a concern, there is a question of liability for the claimed deficit. Depending on the presumed deficit and the background of the patient, a considerable amount of money may be at stake.

In the early days of neuropsychological assessment, malingering was evaluated qualitatively. The neuropsychologist considered inconsistencies in the patient's performance and then determined whether or not there was sufficient reason to assume that these inconsistencies were the result of an active attempt to do poorly on the test. For example, if the symptoms reported by the patient did not make sense from a neurological perspective, the neuropsychologist might determine that the patient was malingering. Other qualitative signs used by neuropsychologists were instances when the patient provided responses that were close to the correct response but were not accurate. Such responses are sometimes called "near misses" in the psychological literature. These "near misses" sometimes occur on easy items such as, "What is 2 + 3?" and the patient replies "4." When more than one test was administered that measured similar functions but the patient's performance on each of these tests suggested a different outcome, this could also be viewed as supporting the possibility of malingering. Another qualitative measure of malingering was when the patient failed easy items of a particular type and yet passed more difficult ones. Psychological tests are generally developed so that the items are arranged in order of difficulty. Once the patient starts consistently missing items, many tests are terminated. You do not expect a patient to fail items early in such a series and yet pass the more difficult ones. Using such qualitative measures of malingering, however, is not necessarily reliable. For example, this irregular pattern of responding can also occur with patients who are anxious or depressed. They may not be concentrating on the easy items and therefore miss some of them. When they concentrate after making mistakes, they provide correct responses. Thus, a number of tests have been developed specifically to evaluate the probability that the patient is malingering.

Here we will describe the Test of Memory Malingering (TOMM) to illustrate these tools (1996). The TOMM is used when the psychologist believes the patient may be faking a memory problem. Memory difficulties are common complaints among patients who are evaluated by clinical neuropsychologists. This test can be used with patients who are sixteen years of age or older. The TOMM is a fifty-item recognition test. The testing procedure requires two learning trials and a recognition trial. Each of the learning trials involves showing the patient fifty line drawings of common objects. Each picture is shown for three seconds with one second between pictures. The learning trials use the same fifty pictures but in a different order on each trial. The patient is then shown panels containing two pictures. One of these pictures is from the learning trial and the other picture is new. The patient must indicate which is the familiar picture. You may recognize this procedure from your learning class as being a "forced choice" task. The patient is told after each item whether or not the response is correct. Normative data suggest that more than 95 percent of adults will obtain a score of 49 or 50 on this test (Tombaugh, 1997). A retention trial uses these same panels after a delay of about fifteen minutes. This retention trial is used to corroborate what was found on the initial test. According to the manual, a score lower than 45 on either the learning or retention trial should be viewed as important.

The TOMM is not designed, however, to provide a rigid answer to the question of whether or not the patient is malingering. Clinical judgment is still important for answering this question. The lower the score, of course, the stronger the probability that malingering has occurred. Neither the patient's age nor his or her educational background seem to impact scores on this test. It is also important to remember that even the person who does not score as a malingerer on the TOMM cannot be eliminated as a possible malingerer. It may be that a well-prepared malingerer will be able to determine that this test is too obvious or not relevant to the purported symptoms and therefore will perform well on it.

Patient Test Information

Joyce

As a clinical psychologist with some basic training in neuropsychological screening measures, you have decided to do some assessment of Joyce to determine whether or not to make a referral to a neuropsychologist for a full neuropsychological evaluation. Her performance on the WAIS-III did not support such a referral but some questions remain. You decide to administer the MMSE, Cognistat, CVLT, and Stroop. On the MMSE, her score of twenty-nine out of the thirty items was excellent. Her only error was on the last "serial-seven" item. This is an attention item and so is also consistent with your concerns about PTSD that were raised by her personality testing. On the Cognistat, she failed the screen item on Digit Repetition but completed all the individual serial items up to repeating six digits forward. Thus, she earned an excellent score on this Attention task. Although she made negative comments about her drawing skills, her Constructional Ability on a two-design immediate recall task was excellent, as was her block design. She correctly recalled all four words on the Memory task, and all of the other verbal and nonverbal subtests on the Cognistat were completed without error. Assessment of her new verbal learning and memory requiring learning two lists of sixteen items using the CVLT were generally within normal limits or higher based on her age and education. She showed no evidence of memory loss on this test. On the Stroop, her performances on the three tasks of Word naming, Color naming, and Word-Color naming were all above average for her age. Calculation of a separate Interference score between Color naming and Word-Color naming also indicated intact neuropsychological functioning.

The results of this neuropsychological screening, combined with her performance on the WAIS-III, were consistent with generally intact neuropsychological functioning. Although she showed some signs of very mild, transient deficits in attention these were consistent with the type of cognitive slowing associated with depression. You therefore decide you will not need to refer Joyce for a full neuropsychological evaluation. You also realize that you will need to look further for potential life stressors that may be causing her current distress.

Behavioral Assessment

General Information

For some psychologists, a key to treatment is the use of behavioral assessment prior to developing the intervention strategy (Peterson & Sobell, 1994). This type of assessment is not merely a single session with the patient for the purpose of treatment planning. Rather, it is an ongoing process. It is not unusual for the psychologist to administer the same measures to the patient before starting an intervention, during the intervention process, and at the completion of the intervention. Depending on the behavioral measure being used, they may even be administered each time the psychologist sees the patient. By using this approach, the psychologist is identifying specific behaviors that are targeted for change and then evaluating whether or not the intervention used is correlated with a behavioral change.

Many psychologists who use this approach trace its ancestry to Skinner's (1953) concept of conducting a **functional analysis of a subject's behavior.** Skinner described the importance of scientifically determining the antecedents and consequences of a behavior when trying to understand that behavior. If a psychologist is interested in developing an appropriate intervention, the first step is to carefully describe the behavior to be changed. Once you have determined the behavior you want to change, you then need to carefully explore what stimuli elicit that behavior from the patient and what are the consequences for the patient of engaging in that behavior. In the learning literature, these factors are called the *antecedent conditions* and the *consequent events.* Each of these factors is described in measurable terms. Thus, when the psychologist is trying to evaluate the success of the intervention there are objective factors that can be used. The psychologist cannot assume from his or her own history any of these factors. It is important to do this evaluation from the perspective of the patient's life. Using Skinner's theory as a basis for the clinical intervention the psychologist is operating from the perspective that the consequences of the behavior are what are maintaining the behavior.

When applying Skinner's theory to a clinical setting, some psychologists use an ABC model in which the "A" refers to the antecedent event, the "B" refers to the behavior, and the "C" refers to the consequences of the behavior (Haynes & O'Brien, 2000). Some current clinicians would call the *ABC model* an example of radical behaviorism. One problem with this model for some clinicians is that it does not seem to include internal mechanisms, such as thinking. They prefer an approach such as the **SORC model** to apply the Skinnerian approach to clinical cases (Kanfer & Phillips, 1970). In this model, "S" refers to the stimulus conditions that precede the behavior of interest to the psychologist. The "O" stands for "organismic." The organismic variables are those factors within the person that are relevant to the problematic behavior. Although Skinner focused on only observable behavior, later behavioral assessment models, such as the SORC model, include the facets of the person that may serve to modify the response to the stimulus. The "R" in this model refers to the patient's response to the "S" and "O" factors. It is this "R" that will be the focus of the psychologist's intervention. The "C" in this model refers to "consequences." What happens to the patient as a result of the identified behavior? Identifying the "C" is often the most difficult part of the interview process. Although on the surface the answer to "C" may appear quite obvious, the obvious consequence may not be the important one. For example, consider the four-year-old who repeatedly leaves her wagon in the driveway just before her mother comes home from work. When you interview her mother about how she responds to this identified problem behavior she says that she gives her daughter a verbal reprimand and negative consequences such as loss of computer game time. It may seem that there are only negative consequences for this child's behavior. After further investigation, however, the psychologist learns that the attention the child gets from her mother as a result of this behavior is an important consequence. The mother spends more time talking individually to her daughter when she misbehaves than when she behaves according to the family rules. Also, when she is not allowed to play computer games, she sits in the family room coloring while her parents are watching the evening news on TV. Thus, she is with both parents rather than alone in her room. Rather than being punished for her problem behavior, she is really being rewarded from her perspective.

Diagnostic categories in early editions of the DSM were hard to describe in behavioral terms. Thus, the early forms of behavioral assessment had little relationship to the diagnostic labels of the most common classification system. Changes in both the DSM and the role it plays in reimbursement in more modern times seem to have contributed to the development of behavioral assessment techniques that are specifically related to diagnostic categories (see Bellack & Hersen, 1998, for examples). Not only are the various categories described in more behavioral terms in DSM-IV than in previous editions of the classification system, but also the importance of the environmental factors that are stressful for the patient on Axis V are part of the behavioral "antecedents" of behavior.

Why does a psychologist decide to do a behavioral assessment? We will note four major reasons behaviorists have suggested (Compas & Gotlib, 2002). One goal emphasizes the "B" in the ABC model we described. The behavioral assessment goes beyond just naming the behavior involved. Conducting a behavioral assessment allows the psychologist to develop an operational definition of the behavior and also to place the behavior within a specific context for the person. Their second goal relates to the "A" in the ABC model. This operational definition provides information in quantifiable language. Such factors as the intensity of the behavior and its frequency would be included here. Their second purpose for the behavioral assessment is to investigate the relationship between the behavior of interest and the factors in the person's life that seem to control that behavior. In order to work with the patient, the psychologist will need to understand how proposed changes in the person's environment are likely to impact the problem behavior. Once this amount of information has been obtained, the psychologist is prepared for the third part of the behavioral assessment process—designing an individual treatment program based on the information obtained. The behavioral assessment process does not end with the development of the treatment program. The final step in this assessment process is to evaluate the effectiveness of that program. After applying the treatment program, the psychologist will measure changes in the behavior based on that original operational definition.

We will not spend time here discussing diagnostic interviewing because we covered much of the relevant material in chapter 5. It is important to note, however, that behavioral interviews tend to be highly focused on the factors needed for a functional analysis of the problematic behavior. The skills required are the same as those for any good interviewer. Those skills are applied in a specific way for the behavioral interview.

Behavioral Observation

Starting at the most basic level of behavioral assessment we have the **behavioral observation.** This level of assessment is most likely to occur following the initial interview. Thus, the psychologist already has some idea about the presenting complaint. The accuracy and depth of information provided in the behavioral interview will influence the behavioral observation. The better defined the behavior, the more quickly the method of behavioral observation can be determined.

Suppose your patient tells you that he "gets anxious" when he is in social situations in which he is expected to talk to people he does not know very well. What does he mean by "gets anxious"? You may have a subjective understanding of what that phrase means to you, but what are you going to observe in your patient? You may elect to do more questioning to get a sense of how his behavior changes in such settings. On the other hand, if you are using behavioral observation, you may also elect to observe your patient in conversation with people he knows well and people who are strangers. Ideally, you have trained observers who can observe your patient in a range of social settings. Realistically in clinical practice this will seldom be feasible. Many of the studies reported in the literature in this area are based on the work of trained graduate students who did this work as part of their course requirement. Dr. Matthews, for example, spent a full semester in graduate school doing a behavioral assessment of a developmentally delayed adolescent and then developing and conducting an individual intervention program with him. This project taught her how to conduct a functional analysis of behavior and provided a needed clinical service to the adolescent. This amount of time in most clinical settings, however, is not likely to be available. Thus, in these settings it may be difficult to do a behavioral assessment appropriately.

There are also several ethical issues to consider when doing observations outside the psychologist's office. Let's return to our patient who "gets anxious" when talking to people he does not know very well. If the psychologist observes him in a social setting, that setting will include people who have not given their consent to be observed as well as your patient. These people with whom your patient is talking have not agreed to be observed. The rights to privacy of these other people are being violated. In the case of Dr. Matthews' adolescent, he was in a day program in which enrollment included parental permission for students to observe the program. It was explained to parents that individual programs for one child might involve observing others. Classroom observations and home observations can be made under similar permissions, but that is not true of most social settings.

When making observations in naturalistic settings, the psychologist can use either continuous or sampling techniques. In other words, the psychologist may record behavior over a specified period of time or may choose to take samples of the person's behavior. Various aspects of the person's behavior may be included in these observations. For example, in some cases the important factor may be the frequency or rate of a particular behavior while in other cases the duration of the behavior may be more important. Of course, there are cases in which both of these factors are relevant. Other factors that may be measured include the intensity of the person's behavior and the specific location where it occurs. For example, suppose you are observing aggressive behavior in a child. Whether the child uses nasty words but a regular tone of voice or uses those same words while yelling may be an important factor.

To assist psychologists in doing observations in specific types of settings, rating forms have been developed for commonly requested behaviors. Let's return to aggressive behavior. The Behavioral Coding System (BCS) was developed to assess the behavior of aggressive, noncompliant, adolescent males in their homes (Patterson, 1977). This system includes twenty-eight categories of behavior. Given the number of behaviors included, and the need to record them systematically, it is used by trained observers who spend time in the patient's home. Behavioral researchers report that most families quickly ignore the observer's presence and demonstrate their typical interactions rather than being on good behavior because of the presence of a stranger. Research supports the premise that data collected by covert recording and overt recording of family interactions do not differ (Christensen, 1983). Using behavioral assessment measures combined with behavioral assessment can provide data that are helpful as a predictor of later problems with law enforcement (Patterson & Forgatch, 1995).

Some behavioral observations occur in a more controlled way. The **Family Problem-Solving Task (FPST)** was developed as part of a research project to assess family interaction patterns when one member of the family met the DSM criteria for a diagnosis of schizophrenia, schizoaffective disorder, or schizophreniform disorder (Bellack, Haas, & Tierney, 1996). The behavioral codes fall within the categories of problem-solving behavior, communication skills, expressed emotion behavior, and other behaviors. The FPST starts with a warm-up exercise followed by two problem discussion sessions. These sessions last ten minutes each and are coded on a range of specific behaviors. There are two participants, the diagnosed patient and a family member, in these discussions and the topics are selected from information previously obtained in the behavioral interview. Longitudinal evaluation of the FPST supports its utility in assessing the impact of family therapy with this population.

A number of behavioral observation measures have been designed for use with children. Because children are less likely than adults to be able to verbalize an in-depth description of their behavior and its antecedents, observation has the potential to add dramatically to the psychologist's ability to provide needed services. Observation of the child at play may be less threatening to the child than observation in other settings. Many tools have been developed to assist in this type of structured observation (Schaefer, Gitlin, & Sandgrund, 1991). Another case in which a structured observational system can be useful is when making a differential diagnosis between autism and mental retardation (Schopler, Reichler, & Renner, 1988). Observational information can be combined with information obtained from caregivers to assist in the diagnostic process.

When the behavior of interest involves avoidance, the psychologist may use a behavioral avoidance test as a form of controlled observation. Informal behavioral avoidance tests were used in early behavioral research, but later controlled performance tests were developed to address specific feared situations. For example, do you know someone who is afraid to go to the dentist? Psychologists have developed specific measures to use both in the dentist's office while the patient is waiting to be seen as well as when the patient is receiving dental treatment (Getka & Glass, 1992).

Self-Monitoring

Some behavioral assessment is actually done by the patient rather than by the psychologist or a trained observer. Depending on the nature of the behavior of interest and the functional level of the patient, there are cases in which the patient can be used as the behavioral recorder. This approach is often the best one to use for infrequent behaviors. Some behaviors may be problematic for the patient but do not occur in the psychologist's office. Because they are infrequent, it may also be difficult for the patient to describe the circumstances in which they occur in sufficient detail during an interview so the psychologist can do a functional analysis of the situation. Thus, if the patient monitors these behaviors some notation can be made of their circumstances and then discussed with the psychologist. **Self-monitoring** is also used in those behavioral treatment programs in which a focus is on internal behaviors, such as negative self-thoughts.

As with the clinical interview, self-monitoring may provide inaccurate data. If the patient is embarrassed about the behavior being monitored, that patient may be less willing to admit, even to the psychologist, the frequency of the problem. Some patients, for example, who monitor how often and what they eat may be embarrassed to report that they ate an entire quart of ice cream from the container after failing a test. Some patients may agree to do self-monitoring and then not comply while others adamantly refuse to do it. To maximize the effectiveness of self-monitoring, it is important for the psychologist to work with the patient to have as specific an understanding as possible of the behavior being monitored.

Suppose your patient complains of problems with anger management. You want your patient to keep a log of each time he gets angry and what the environmental trigger for the anger was. The two of you need to agree on a definition of anger. Does "anger" mean a specific type of language, physical contact, or internal reaction? Perhaps the definition varies for your patient depending on the situation or the people involved. You need to be clear about such terms even if they seem quite simple. A potentially positive impact of self-monitoring is that the patient becomes more aware of the behavior being monitored as well as the environmental factors that may be related to it. When you are implementing your intervention program you may need to spend less time demonstrating the relevance of some of your concepts if your patient has this background information from personal experience.

Depending on the patient, as well as the behavior being monitored, the psychologist may also make use of a monitoring aid. If you are interested in the frequency of a specific behavior, such as the use of profanity, you might have the patient purchase a small wrist counter. In this way, all the patient needs to do is push the counter with each occurrence of the behavior to be monitored. In other cases, having the patient carry a small spiral-bound notebook to record certain behaviors may suffice. For cases in which you want more description of a behavior and/or several different facets of the situation, helping the patient design a recording sheet works well. Let's consider a brief example. If you want the patient to briefly describe negative self-thoughts, environmental circumstances, and then try to give a more rational reaction to that situation, you might use a sheet with three columns for the data. The patient would then bring the "homework" to the therapy session for discussion. In this case, you have already identified that the patient has negative self-thoughts that are impacting his or her behavior. Rather than try to role-play life situations in the therapist's office and then report the thoughts followed by a more relational reaction, the patient supplies information from real-life situations. By recording the information at the time the negative self-thoughts occurred, the patient is more likely to have an accurate report of the situation. The patient is also given the opportunity to try to reply in a more realistic way without feeling the pressure of the psychologist in a one-on-one situation. This information becomes a point of discussion during the next therapy session.

Self-monitoring forms are also available for use with specified types of problems, for example, for recording panic attacks as well as specific symptoms of anxiety and depression (Street & Barlow, 1994). Computer technology has also helped with compliance with self-monitoring (Taylor, Agras, Losch, Plante, & Burnett, 1991). Some people prefer to record their data on small hand-held computers or personal digital assistants (PDAs). Others find the use of self-monitoring computer software helpful with compliance.

Psychologists have reported a number of factors that may impact the accuracy of report when self-monitoring. These factors should be taken into account when a psychologist is using this procedure. For example, when monitoring symptoms of anxiety, accuracy has been found to be higher when the targeted behavior is positively valenced than when it is negatively valenced (McGlynn & Rose, 1998). When the patient knows that some checking is being done on accuracy, accuracy is likely to be better than in those cases in which no attempt is made to check on it.

Self-Report Measures

As an aid to the interview process, behaviorally oriented psychologists have developed a number of self-report inventories and checklists addressing specific problem areas. They have also developed rating scales to provide data that may not be available through direct observation. Some rating scales address specific behaviors while others are a bit broader.

Beck Depression Inventory The **Beck Depression Inventory-II (BDI-II)** is a self-report twenty-one-item inventory of symptoms of depression (Beck, Steer, & Brown, 1996). This inventory can be used with patients thirteen years of age and older. It follows DSM-IV criteria by using a two-week time frame for the occurrence of the symptoms. Each of the twenty-one items presents a list of four statements arranged in increasing order of severity and related to a particular symptom of depression. Most patients need only five to ten minutes to complete the BDI-II and so it can be taken in the office while waiting for an appointment or just before leaving after a session. If the patient has reading problems or the psychologist has concerns about the patient understanding the items, it can be administered orally. Each of the twenty-one items is rated on a 4-point scale ranging from 0 to 3. If the patient has endorsed more than one response to an item, the higher alternative is scored. The score is merely the total number of the ratings. Thus, if a patient endorses the most extreme choice for each of the items, the score would be 63. This score is then interpreted in terms of general level of depression. A score from 0 to 13 indicates a minimal level of depression. Between 14 and 19 indicates a mild depression. Scores between 20 and 28 suggest that a moderate level of depression is present. Those patients who score 29 and higher are considered to have endorsed items indicating a severe level of depression. In this case, the psychologist would look carefully at the items endorsed and perhaps do additional questioning to determine whether or not the patient may need to be hospitalized.

This rating scale can be used as an initial measure of the degree of depression as well as the range of symptoms present and then repeated throughout the intervention process as a measure of efficacy of treatment. The BDI-II is not limited to use as part of a behavioral assessment; many psychologists use this test. We included it here to illustrate how this type of symptom-driven test can be used to measure behavioral change during intervention.

Achenbach System of Empirically Based Assessment Achenbach and his colleagues developed a rating system, the **Achenbach System of Empirically Based Assessment (ASEBA),** that is often used when the patient is a child or an adolescent (Achenbach, 1991; Achenbach, 2000; Wadsworth, Hudziak, Heath, & Achenbach, 2001). These behavior checklists were developed through a combination of research and clinical practice. They have separate forms for the child or adolescent, the parent or caregiver, and teachers and for use in direct classroom observation by the psychologist. Among the tests in this system is the Child Behavior Checklist that we noted was used with Trang in our description of his assessment in chapter 6. Items on this scale are rated as either "0," indicating that it is not true as far as the observer knows; "1," indicating that it is somewhat or sometimes true of the child; or "2," indicating very true or often true of the child.

The classroom version we sent to Trang's teacher gave us six factors that we used in establishing our diagnosis of ADHD (attention-deficit/hyperactivity disorder). These factors are withdrawn-inattentive, nervous-obsessive, depressed, hyperactive, attention-demanding, and aggressive. The form completed by his parents covered behavioral problems as well as social competencies rated in the broad areas of activities, social, and school. There is also a composite score indicating the overall level of the child's maladjustment.

Behavior Assessment System for Children We will discuss one other behavior rating system to illustrate the types of measures psychologists might use with children. The **Behavior Assessment System for Children (BASC)** can be used with children who are between the ages of four and eighteen years old (Reynolds & Kamphaus, 1992). Recent research has provided further support for the importance of having multiple views of a child's behavior rather than just one (Kamphaus, DiStefano, & Lease, 2003). The BASC is designed so that many or all of its five components can be used by the psychologist to facilitate the process of making a differential diagnosis. These components are the self-report form for the child to complete, a rating scale for the parents and another one designed for the teacher, a structured developmental history, and a form that can be used for direct classroom observations of the child's behavior.

The Self-Report of Personality (SRP) is completed by the child or adolescent. This form contains a series of statements requiring a true-false response. The results of this rating are grouped into three composite scores as well as an overall adjustment score. The three composite scores are School Maladjustment, Clinical Maladjustment, and Personal Maladjustment. The composite score is called the Emotional Symptoms Index. The child's responses are compared to national norms in general as well as those for the same sex as the child.

The Parent Rating Scales (PRS) uses a four-choice response format. This scale covers both adaptive and problems behaviors in both the community and the home setting. Like the SRP, the PRS ratings can be compared to a general national normative sample as well as to a sample who are of the same sex as the child.

The Teacher Rating Scales (TRS) can be completed by the teacher, teacher aide, or preschool caregiver. The TRS uses the same four-choice response format as the PRS. Both of these scales yield scores for Externalizing Problems, Internalizing Problems, School Problems, Adaptive Skills, and an overall Behavior Symptom Index. Each of these forms takes about ten to twenty minutes to complete.

The Structured Developmental History (SDH) can be used by the clinical psychologist as a structured interview in the office setting or sent home with the parent to be completed there and returned. This form includes a review of social, psychological, developmental, educational, and medical information about the child. Thus, it is important for the psychologist to have someone complete it who is familiar with all of these facets of the child's background. Some parents have difficulty remembering all of the information asked for in the SDH. This problem is especially true when there is more than one child in the family. It does not mean that these parents do not care about each child but rather that specific details, such as the age when the child said his or her first word or other developmental milestones, may not be readily remembered. Thus, if you as the psychologist plan to use it as a structured interview, it is helpful to let the parent(s) know in advance that you will be covering this type of information. You may suggest that some parents have found it helpful to bring their baby book to the interview.

The Student Observation System (SOS) is used in the classroom. The observer records both positive and negative behaviors using a time sampling procedure. It can also be used repetitively to evaluate the effectiveness of the intervention process. In contrast to the other measures within the BASC system, this one is less affected by bias because the clinician directly observes the child's behavior. The SOS includes four adaptive domains: response to teacher/lesson, peer interaction, work on school subjects, and transition movement. Let's consider an appropriate and an inappropriate behavior for each of these domains. An appropriate response to the teacher is raising your hand and waiting until the teacher acknowledges you before speaking. Talking back to the teacher is considered inappropriate. An appropriate peer interaction is talking quietly in a small group with other students. Kicking a classmate is inappropriate. Appropriate work on school subjects involves individual activity rather than activities with other students. This might mean working on an assignment on the classroom computer. Copying an answer from another student is inappropriate. Transition movements that are appropriate are nondisruptive ways to go from one place or activity to another. Walking around the classroom aimlessly is not appropriate. Before using the SOS, the psychologist will need to make special arrangements with the teacher and the school to observe in the classroom.

Psychophysiological Assessment

Some behaviorally oriented clinical psychologists supplement the more traditional forms of assessment with measures of the patient's physiological responding. The term **psychophysiology** refers to the fact that some of our physical changes are the result of our behavioral or emotional reactions. These measures focus on the sympathetic and parasympathetic portions of the autonomic nervous system. For example, researchers have identified physiological risk factors for schizophrenia (Hollister, Mednick, Brennan, & Cannon, 1994). The startle eye blink response has been part of the treatment of anxiety disorders in children (Waters, Lipp, & Cobham, 2000). In marital therapy settings, husbands who are dissatisfied with their marriage have higher levels of physiological arousal when interacting with their wives than do husbands who are satisfied with their marriages (Gottman & Levenson, 1992). These differences were found even when the dissatisfied husbands were verbally stating they were happy in their marriages. Assessment of these factors can be part of a behavioral evaluation. Although psychophysiological measures can provide a useful complement to more traditional forms of behavioral assessment, researchers have yet to establish the level of construct validity of their link to behavior that many people assume from their scientific aura (Tomarken, 1995).

A frequently cited form of psychophysiological assessment is biofeedback. This term refers to providing the patient with information about changes in such factors as heart rate or muscle tension as a result of having certain thoughts. Among the goals of biofeedback are to increase the person's awareness of internal processes and to establish control over them. Once a level of control occurs in the office setting, the psychologist then assists the patient to generalize that control to the real-life situations that have previously caused difficulty. Although the equipment originally used for this type of assessment was large and fairly expensive, technological advances have led to smaller, less expensive forms of equipment that can easily be used in either the psychologist's office or the patient's home. Baseline measures can be taken prior to the intervention and then as a measure of the efficacy of the treatment throughout the process. Physiological measures of penile erection have been used in the assessment and treatment of pedophilia (Freund & Blanchard, 1989; Freund & Wilson, 1991). In this case, continuous recordings are made of penile volume while the patient views a range of pictures or listens to taped messages. This assessment can be used initially to determine both specifics about sexual preference and degree of reactivity. During and at the completion of an intervention program, data from this initial assessment can be used for comparison purposes.

By now, you may be wondering how any clinical psychologist has room for all of the assessment tools we have described as well as how much time it would take to learn all of these measures. It is important to remember that not all measures are used by all psychologists. Also, some psychologists do very little assessment activity while others focus on it. Some psychologists refer their therapy patients to colleagues for assessment both because they feel it might impair their rapport with their patients by doing the testing and because they do not have the current skills to do what is needed.

ETHICAL CONUNDRUM POINTS TO PONDER

The first point to consider in this case is the impact of the observer on the assessment process. This is a hotly debated issue within psychology, especially neuropsychology. Neuropsychologists have suggested that the impact of an observer in the testing room is moderate to large (Gavett, Lynch, & McCaffrey, 2003). Thus, if the observer is present, you will need to take note of that factor in interpreting your data. Even indirect observation of the testing, such as a video camera, has been found to have a negative impact on patient performance and therefore threaten the validity of the tests. Of course, it also violates standard test administration procedures. You must try to explain these factors to the district attorney and attempt to dissuade such observation. If a judge orders the observation, you will need to take this into account when interpreting your data. It is best to request the least intrusive form of test observation, such as through a one-way window, rather than actual presence in the test room. Because your patient has brought his mental health into his defense, his confidentiality is already limited, so that factor is not the same as it might be on other cases. If the observation is to be recorded, you also have issues about test security to consider. You do not have control over who may see these tapes and how clearly they show the test stimuli. Thus, it is important to request that the judge limit the distribution of the recording as well as make special provisions for its storage or preferably disposal after the legal proceedings have concluded. Protection of the test materials is always important but is especially true when you plan to use a test of malingering, as you might choose to do in this case. Some of these measures are quite simple but also effective. You do not want people to view them who might misuse this information in future cases. If you believe you can obtain the information you need with paper-and-pencil measures, rather than measures that require viewing of test stimuli, you may wish to do so in this case. You do not, however, want to do a less complete evaluation as a result of the legal issues. Finally, if you feel you cannot comply with this legal requirement, you may need to transfer this patient and explain why you have done so.

Key Terms

Achenbach System of Empirically Based Assessment (ASEBA)

Beck Depression Inventory-II (BDI-II)

behavioral observation

Bender Visual-Motor Gestalt Test

Boston Process Approach

California Verbal Learning Test (CVLT-2)

Dementia Rating Scale (DRS-2)

Family Problem-Solving Task (FPST)

fixed batteries

flexible batteries

functional analysis of behavior

Halstead-Reitan Neuropsychological Battery (HRNB)

Luria-Nebraska Neuropsychological Battery (LNNB)

malingering

Mini-Mental State Examination (MMSE)

pathognomic signs

pattern of responding

psychophysiology

Rey Complex Figures Test

screening batteries

self-monitoring

SORC model

Trail Making Test

Wechsler Memory Scale-III (WMS-III)

CHAPTER 9

Introduction to Psychotherapy

One of the traditional methods of intervention used by clinical psychologists is **psychotherapy.** Psychotherapy traditionally has been viewed as a major activity for clinical psychologists. As we noted in chapter 3, efforts to establish a separate profession of psychotherapy were not successful. Therefore, today the activity we call psychotherapy is practiced by many professionals including clinical psychologists. In this chapter we provide a general overview of psychotherapy. Chapter 10 considers this subject from the perspective of schools of psychotherapy. Chapter 11 discusses individual psychotherapy. Chapter 12 provides information about psychotherapy involving more than one patient at the same time. After reading these four chapters, students who are interested in learning more about special approaches to psychotherapy are referred to other books (e.g., Ellis & Dryden, 1997; Horner, 1991; Rogers, 1951; Worell & Remer, 1992). In addition to books on specialized forms of psychotherapy, many books also provide a broad overview of the currently practiced methods of psychotherapy (e.g., Murdock, 2004). Students who pursue graduate training will have the opportunity to learn psychotherapy skills associated with specific schools of psychotherapy.

Many clinical psychologists today indicate that they use concepts from a range of approaches when actually practicing their profession. This combination of treatment approaches is called **eclectic** or **integrative psychotherapy.** Eclectic or integrative psychotherapy is the one most frequently reported by clinical psychologists, counseling psychologists, psychiatrists, social workers, and counselors when they are asked to describe their primary form of psychotherapy (Prochaska & Norcross, 1999). Rather than select specific theoretical approaches and presenting them in the traditional way, we will talk

ETHICAL CONUNDRUM

You are a clinical psychologist in solo practice in a community of thirty-five hundred people. You are the only clinical psychologist in your community. The nearest city is a three-hour drive. For the past six months, you have been seeing Mr. Roofer for individual psychotherapy. He owns the local home repair and roofing company. Following a major storm, you discover that the roof of your home has sustained significant damage and needs to be repaired. Mr. Roofer owns the only business in your community that provides roofing services. It is a small business employing only Mr. Roofer and his three sons. Can you ethically hire this firm to repair your roof? What are the issues you need to consider as you make your decision?

more broadly about individual psychotherapy. If you have taken a course in theories of personality, you have already been exposed to the background used to develop many methods of psychotherapy (e.g., Allen, 2003; Hall, Lindzey, & Campbell, 1998; Schultz & Schultz, 2005). If not, you will probably take such a course if you pursue graduate training in clinical psychology. You can then apply those theories to the general concepts we present here.

General Information

Definitions

Psychotherapy is a popular topic within psychology. One of the divisions of APA (Division 29) is the Division of Psychotherapy. Over the years, this division has been one of the larger of the APA divisions, indicating that many APA members have a strong interest in psychotherapy. Among the scholarly publications about psychotherapy are the Division 29 journal, *Psychotherapy: Theory/Research/Practice/Training,* which publishes articles on research, theory, training, and practice of psychotherapy, and the *Psychotherapy Bulletin,* which includes timely articles and news about psychotherapy. Many general clinical journals, such as the *Journal of Consulting and Clinical Psychology* and *Professional Psychology: Research and Practice,* also publish articles about psychotherapy. Psychotherapy remains a popular subject for students of clinical psychology.

There are many definitions of psychotherapy in the psychological literature. Perhaps one reason for the variety of definitions is the fact that there are so many forms or schools of psychotherapy. One author (Gold, 1996) suggested that over four hundred types of psychotherapy existed. Each of these types of psychotherapy included its own definition of the therapeutic process. Let's consider one definition of psychotherapy to illustrate what we mean. Psychotherapy is "the art and science of treating psychological, behavioral, and emotional problems by a trained and objective professional" (Cullari, 1998, p. 433).

Notice that this definition does not include any specific profession or indication of the number of participants involved in the process. As we mentioned in chapter 3, during the early 1960s there was some consideration of developing a separate profession of psychotherapy, but that did not happen; so the activity has remained one conducted by professionals from several different disciplines. Psychotherapy does not tend to be a legally controlled term limited to one or two professions. Thus people from a wide range of backgrounds may choose to identify themselves as psychotherapists. If you look in the yellow pages of the phone book of any large city, you are likely to find a section for people called "psychotherapists." Although some of these names will also be listed under other professions such as "psychologists" or "physicians & surgeons/psychiatry," they are also listed under "psychotherapist." One reason for this listing is that many people who are seeking the services of a mental health professional do not think of turning to the specific profession. Instead, they know they want psychotherapy and so that is the search term they will use. Depending on the phone directory, you may also find a range of services listed for, or populations served by, each of these "psychotherapists."

The word *psychotherapy* comes from the Greek and literally means the treatment of the psyche or mind. The reason for the psychologist to provide this service is to "help the patient/client with problems that may have aspects that are related to disorders of thinking, emotional suffering, or problems of behavior" (Sharf, 2000, p. 3).

Some people use the terms *psychotherapy* and **counseling** interchangeably (e.g., Young, 2001), while others suggest that these terms refer to different activities. Nystul (1999) suggests that "counseling tends to be developmental in nature whereas psychotherapy has a remediative emphasis" (p. 7). This distinction suggests that psychotherapy is an activity in which the goal is to change the patient in some way. This traditional distinction between counseling and psychotherapy implies that psychotherapy involves problems that are more serious, usually those that merit a formal DSM diagnosis, than those of people who are receiving counseling. Psychotherapy, as practiced in the early years of the profession, implied the commitment of an extensive amount of time. There are still people who engage in psychotherapy over a period of years. Others, however, for a variety of reasons, spend a more limited period of time in psychotherapy, leading to the appearance of the term **brief psychotherapy** in the literature. The terms *short-term psychotherapy* and *time-limited psychotherapy* are also used to refer to a limited form of intervention. Health insurance may include mental health coverage, but the number of sessions allowed is usually limited both within a given year and over the lifetime of the participant. Some of the currently used forms of time-limited psychotherapy have been developed and evaluated as a result of these fiscal policies. Thus, the person who wants to experience long-term psychotherapy will probably need to pay for this treatment outside the parameters of the insurance policy. This method of payment is often called "fee-for-service" in contrast to health insurance reimbursement. Regardless of the length of time involved or the type of psychotherapy used, most studies indicate that people who elect to engage in this process feel that it has been beneficial to them (Seligman, 1995; VandenBos, 1996).

When you hear the word *psychotherapy,* what is your mental image of the patient? For many people, both within psychology and outside the profession, the ideal patient is verbal and intelligent. After all, psychotherapy involves talking to a professional and delving into your deepest feelings. To do that, you need to have a good vocabulary plus the ability to understand yourself. A term that once was used to describe the "ideal" psychotherapy patient was **YAVIS** (Schofield, 1964). This acronym represented the characteristics of this ideal patient as young, attractive, verbal, intelligent, and successful. Notice that this definition goes beyond just being bright and verbal. The YAVIS is also young, attractive, and successful. You might actually begin to wonder why this person would even need psychotherapy. What about patients who do not fit this description? Obviously not all psychotherapy patients fit the YAVIS picture. Another acronym, albeit a derogatory term, has been coined to describe some of these other patients—**QUOID** (Sundberg, Taplin, & Tyler, 1983). This acronym stands for quiet, ugly, old, institutionalized, and different culturally.

Does a person who fits the definition of QUOID sound like a person with whom you would like to spend intense individual contact? Although this question may seem harsh, remember that psychotherapists are human. They do not lose all their biases with an advanced degree. Consider, for example, the people who are diagnosed as mentally retarded and developmentally disabled. A review of the literature on intervention with mentally retarded and developmentally disabled people notes that many psychologists avoid addressing the mental health needs of this population (Butz, Bowling, & Bliss, 2000). Perhaps because these patients don't fit the YAVIS model, some psychologists are unsure about how to work with them. In addition to the failure of these individuals to meet the definition of YAVIS, psychologists are less likely to have had practicum or even theoretical course material about this population than about many other patient groups. Training to work with these individuals is more likely to occur in departments of education or rehabilitation than in typical clinical training programs. It is difficult to determine if this lack of attention in training has led to lack of interest in conducting research in this area or if the absence of a research base has led to lack of training. Regardless of the reason, a search of the recent clinical literature indicates that unlike other areas of psychotherapy research, there are very few controlled studies with mentally retarded and developmentally delayed subjects. Most modern researchers suggest that modifications to the process of psychotherapy are needed when working with this population. However, this does not mean that psychotherapy is not appropriate. It should be recognized that a diagnosis of mental retardation does not exclude other forms of psychological maladjustment and that the use of psychotherapy may be helpful (Hurley, Pfadt, Tomasulo, & Gardner, 1996). Possible modifications when doing psychotherapy with this population are the type of language the therapist uses, being more open to questions about the therapist's personal life, and maintaining a more routine approach because violation of routine can be upsetting to them. Is this need for modification really anything more than being sensitive to the needs of your patient? As population demographics have changed, psychologists have become increasingly aware of the need to modify their approach to address cultural diversity, but we have not paid as much attention to the psychological needs of the mentally challenged. Our discussion of clinical geropsychology in chapter 15 includes information about the limitations of training for work with the older members of the population—another of the QUOID characteristics. Later in this chapter, we discuss ways to address issues of cultural diversity in psychotherapy. In chapter 11, we discuss the reasons for changing your therapeutic approach to meet the needs of individual patients. We illustrate this process by discussing special issues related to psychotherapy with children, women, adults with cognitive impairments, and suicidal patients.

General Concepts of Psychotherapy

Models Based on Purpose

A popular way of presenting the various forms of psychotherapy is to group them by the theory upon which each is based. Using this approach, you might find a book or chapter on humanistic psychotherapy or even within that broad category such subgroups as person-centered, Gestalt, and reality therapy. An alternative way to view forms of psychotherapy is to consider the purpose of the process. Wolberg (1967) was an early proponent of this approach to conceptualizing psychotherapy. His conceptualization scheme is quite different from those found in the typical psychotherapy book. We decided to use this model, with brief descriptions of how it can be used, to broaden the way you think about psychotherapy. Wolberg's method groups the major forms of psychotherapy into three broad categories: *supportive, reeducative,* and *reconstructive.* Within each of these general categories, you might place a wide range of theoretical orientations.

Among Wolberg's three forms of psychotherapy, **supportive psychotherapy** has the most modest goals. In this case, the major goal of psychotherapy is to prevent the patient from getting worse. Although improvement in some areas of functioning is always desired, the major goal of intervention in this case is to prevent further deterioration. Supportive psychotherapy can be used with a range of problems. For example, this approach could be used with a person who has faced a crisis or some form of stress. This person may not want to make major personal changes but rather needs help coping with current life events. Suppose a woman has just learned that her husband is terminally ill and he has fewer than six months to live. They have been married for fifty-five years and continue to have a happy marriage. Psychotherapy could help her deal with her feelings related to her husband's illness and her pending loss. Supportive psychotherapy might also be used with her husband as he deals with issues of his own mortality and shortened lifespan. This psychotherapy might be done for each of them independently or perhaps jointly depending on the couple and the psychologist.

Supportive psychotherapy may also be used following natural disasters. Much of the work of Red Cross disaster relief within the mental health arena is supportive in nature. These individuals provide assistance following such natural disasters as floods, earthquakes, and major hurricanes. In another case, a psychologist might recommend supportive psychotherapy to assist a patient who has been dealing with symptoms of schizophrenia for many years. This patient lives independently, receives disability money from the state, and takes medication on a regular basis. However, daily living can become difficult for the patient and thus some form of regular contact with a psychologist may allow him to remain outside an institutional setting. Psychotherapy might focus on such immediate issues as how to deal with pranksters on Halloween, finding shelter during severe weather such as hurricanes or tornadoes (depending on where the person lives), and more basic issues such as forms of recreation that are available within the person's financial limitations and abilities. Regardless of the specific details of any patient's problems, the goals of supportive psychotherapy are likely to involve such points as how to strengthen the patient's existing psychological defenses, assisting the patient to maintain control within his or her life situation, and ways to restore a sense of equilibrium if recent problems have occurred. Unlike more traditional views of psychotherapy, supportive approaches are not intended to lead to fundamental changes in the patient's personality structure. Also, they are not expected to lead to major changes in the way the person leads his or her life.

Wolberg's second form of psychotherapy is **reeducative psychotherapy.** In this case, the emphasis is on basically observable behavior. The patient's conscious processes will be of interest to the psychologist. If personality testing is used, objective rather than projective testing would likely be the choice. Topics of interest in psychotherapy will be the overt sources of conflict or difficulty in the patient's life as well as the patient's methods of handling these stressors. Although a patient history will be taken, the emphasis will be on the present rather than the past. Information about the past will be used to understand current distress but will not be used in an interpretive way.

Let's look at an example of how this might work. The patient is a twenty-six-year-old single male. A goal of his therapy is to increase his social life. After taking the patient's history, the psychologist decides that this patient needs to learn better interpersonal skills. Through the use of role-playing and homework assignments, the patient gradually learns better communication skills and increases his self-confidence. He is successful in obtaining dates and handles rejection without becoming depressed. He has learned the difference between those individuals with whom he may develop a social relationship and those who are not interested. In the past, he became depressed and withdrawn when he asked someone out and they declined. He is now comfortable with the concept that not everyone he asks for date will be interested. He has also developed conversational and interpersonal skills that have led him to have a second date with several people. No attempt is made in this case to look for developmental problems that may have contributed to his previous dating difficulties. His distress is viewed solely from the perspective of overt and conscious processes. Although new skills are learned, and behavior is practiced outside the therapy setting, there is also no attempt to make major changes in his worldview. His therapy is likely to be short-term. The specific length of time will be jointly decided based on his success in social skills development.

Wolberg's third form of psychotherapy is **reconstructive psychotherapy.** In these forms of psychotherapy a major goal of the process is for the patient to develop insight into the unconscious conflicts that are hypothesized as underlying the present feelings of distress. For this form of psychotherapy to be considered both complete and successful, the patient will achieve major alterations of his or her basic character or personality. Psychologists who focus on this type of psychotherapy tend to view reeducative therapy as being superficial. The focus in reconstructive therapy is not on the symptoms but rather on the underlying cause of those symptoms. The theory in this case is that if the patient understands the underlying cause of distress, then the symptoms will no longer be necessary. These symptoms will therefore cease to exist without being directly addressed in therapy. As the patient grows, the personality will change and new adaptive potential will allow the patient to handle further stress. If psychological testing is done, it is likely to include projective tests of personality to assist the psychologist in understanding hidden dynamics of this patient. Therapy in this case is likely to be viewed as long-term because the goals are extensive.

Let's return to our patient who had reeducative therapy. Suppose this patient had reconstructive therapy. Rather than focusing on the social skills training, the patient and therapist would have explored his internal dynamics and the personal history that had led to the current difficulties. The dating problems would be viewed as symbolic of more deep-seated issues for him. Perhaps he had problems talking to girls because he had never really dealt with the feelings he had about his mother. The psychologist would do an extensive exploration of his early childhood. Through the process of psychotherapy, this patient realized that he had always felt unworthy of love. His mother had, in his view, ignored him when he was a child and always spent time with his brother, who was two years younger than he was. When they were adolescents, his younger brother became a football star and was very popular in school. His younger brother had his growth spurt earlier than your patient and thus was often mistaken as the older of the two. Because of his smaller stature and lack of physical prowess, your patient's extracurricular activities were more intellectual in nature. He participated in the chess club and the math club, although he never had leadership positions. These factors had combined to lead your patient to feel inadequate. Once he developed insight into the fact that his social skills were related to his relationship to his mother and his brother, he was able to begin dating and see himself in a different way. As you can probably guess, this form of psychotherapy typically requires the greatest amount of time. Typically, reconstructive therapy is discussed in terms of years of therapy rather than months.

Goals of Psychotherapy

It is important to remember that the goal of psychotherapy may not be the same for all people involved in the process. When people involved in psychotherapy have divergent goals, these differences have the potential to interfere with the clinical process. It is important to be aware of the therapeutic goals not only of the identified patient but also of significant others in the patient's world.

Suppose, for example, a female patient makes an appointment with a clinical psychologist for help with weight control. She has correctly determined that she is over the appropriate weight range for her age and height. The psychologist, in this case, decides that reconstructive psychotherapy is the best approach to use. This psychologist views the patient's lack of control of caloric intake as symptomatic of issues not resolved at the oral stage of psychosexual development. Thus, a focus of the therapy sessions will be discussion of her early childhood recollections related to feeding and other uses of her mouth. Various techniques may be used to help her recall these early experiences. Your patient's husband, who travels a lot in his job, is happy his wife is overweight because he tends to be jealous of any other men with whom she interacts. He believes that as long as she is heavy she has a reduced probability of cheating on him or leaving him for someone else. Although he verbalizes his support for her psychotherapy, he does not really mean what he is saying. If these therapeutic goals (his and his wife's) remain divergent, the outcome of the therapeutic process is not likely to be successful. As she begins to lose weight, her husband is likely to find ways to sabotage the process. For example, he buys her boxes of her favorite candy to "show her how much he loves her." The psychologist may not pay attention to the weight loss because of the psychologist's interest in the underlying processes and not the overt behaviors. The patient then becomes frustrated with psychotherapy and no longer comes for treatment. In this case, a discussion among the relevant people about goals and concerns could have led to a different outcome. The patient might have remained in psychotherapy and gained a better understanding of the reasons she was overweight. She might also have improved her communication with her husband. It is possible that they might even have chosen to engage in couples therapy to consider some of the issues that contributed to their mixed communications and his trust issues. As a result of improved communication, he might not feel so concerned that she will cheat on him when he must take business trips. We will discuss couples therapy further in chapter 12.

Commonalities Across Psychotherapy Types

A number of characteristics tend to be found in the majority of forms of psychotherapy. These are descriptive factors rather than factors associated with one of the traditional classification systems found in the literature (e.g., Lambert & Bergin, 1994). We will leave the classification systems for graduate education or further independent reading by those students who are interested in this topic.

Table 9.1 lists six factors that are often associated with psychotherapy. We briefly discuss each of these six factors. When discussing individual psychotherapy, we usually find that there are two people engaged in a face-to-face interaction. One of these people is a professional and the other is the individual who is seeking help. This interaction deals with highly personal information. Some of this information may not have been stated aloud before it is said in the therapy setting.

This interaction is conducted in a professional way. Mental health professionals have a code of ethics that impacts how they conduct psychotherapy. State licensing boards may also have rules about how this process may be conducted. The rules and ethics codes are not identical for all professions that conduct psychotherapy. Certain general ideas, however, tend to be shared by all of them. For example, these rules often include limitations on socializing with patients and/or their families outside the therapy setting. The therapist usually does not discuss his or her own personal problems or life story with the patient or discuss what the patient has divulged with anyone else without the patient's permission. Regardless of how comfortable the therapist becomes with the patient, the purpose of these meetings is to help the patient, not to meet personal needs of the therapist.

Table 9.1 Common Psychotherapy Factors

Face-to-face
Professional attitude
Verbal activity
Professional setting
Ongoing process
Has a fee

Being professional also involves the therapist being available when the patient needs attention. When the therapist is not available, such as when attending a professional meeting or going on vacation, appropriate substitute coverage is arranged before leaving town. Patients are notified about this process well in advance. The rules about availability do not, however, mean that the therapist does not have the responsibility to exercise some judgment. Suppose, for example, the therapist is seeing a female patient who exhibits characteristics of a borderline personality disorder. She tends to call the therapist between sessions and indicate that she needs him. They have discussed during their sessions the need for limitations on such calls. She has been told that if she feels she might hurt herself she is to go to the nearest hospital emergency room. Despite these discussions, she continues to call the therapist in the evenings and on weekends. When his answering service pages him, he is given a phone number where he can reach her. If the therapist continues to respond to these "emergency" calls it may not be therapeutic for the patient. On the other hand, suppose she really is in danger? The therapist must make some decision about whether or not it is appropriate to respond to her calls. In this case, it may even be necessary to leave special instructions with the answering service about how to respond to calls from this specific patient. Although it is generally suggested that psychologists do not meet with their patients outside the regularly scheduled sessions, professional judgment must be used. If you know you have a severely depressed and potentially suicidal patient, special provisions may be needed for extra time or phone sessions that you would not use with the borderline patient we mentioned.

Professional behavior also includes paying close attention during the session (e.g., not take phone calls or fall asleep). Although this comment may seem rather obvious to you, it is not always easy to pay attention when you have other things on your mind and are seeing one person after another over a period of several hours. There are also some patients who may have speaking voices that tend to lead to lack of attention, such as speaking with a soft, rhythmic voice. Professionals learn to adjust themselves to these conditions and pay attention to what is happening in the office. Just as the psychologist expects the patient to be on time for appointments, the psychologist is also expected to be on time. This expectation holds not only for the first appointment of the day but also for ending sessions on time so that the next person can start on time. Of course, there are occasionally true emergencies that may require a bit of extra time. Except in most unusual practices, however, these occasions should be rare. If such an occasion occurs, the psychologist needs to make some judgment of the amount of time that is going to be needed to respond. Once that has happened, the psychologist can either make a brief call to the receptionist to let the next person know about the delay or, if needed, actually reschedule someone rather than have the person wait for an indefinite period of time.

Individual therapy, other than with small children, is basically a verbal interaction. The balance of who does how much talking varies among approaches, but psychotherapy remains a verbal process. Basically, psychotherapy is a specialized conversation. With small children the activity may look more like play than anything else, but that play actually has a specific purpose and the psychologist must pay attention just as much to the action in the play as to the words in the more traditional form of psychotherapy.

Psychotherapy is usually conducted in a professional setting. Although there are no specific requirements about furniture or type of office, there is an assumption that this interaction is different from one with a personal friend. Privacy of the activity is maintained as part of that setting. The office or setting where the psychologist actually conducts psychotherapy needs to be one where the conversation cannot be overheard by others. To maintain patient privacy, some psychologists try to arrange waiting areas so that individuals are not observed by others during that time period between arriving for their appointment and actually being seen. In many cases this is not possible and patients sit in a common waiting area. They do not, however, place their name on a sign-in sheet that can be seen by the next patient, nor is their name announced when it is time to go into the psychologist's office. Someone will need to get the patient rather than just calling out a name. This approach is used to maximize privacy. In some cases, a home or school visit may be warranted but in the majority of cases, psychotherapy is conducted in a professional office. Some specialized forms of psychotherapy do not fit this tradition. For example, some therapists report success using various forms of exercise as part of their therapy process. Such therapists could conduct part of their therapy while horseback riding. It is important when doing this outdoor form of therapy to maintain confidentiality, and thus the setting needs to be able to be controlled.

The term *psychotherapy* generally implies that this interaction will occur over a period of time rather than in one session. Unlike personal conversations about issues, psychotherapy tends to be a prolonged process. It takes time to learn the relevant factors and then address them. The specific length of time will vary with the nature of the problem and the theoretical orientation of the therapist. Some psychologists think in terms of months while others think in terms of years when discussing the likely length of psychotherapy with potential patients.

Session duration is also a factor in terms of the amount of time devoted to each meeting with the patient. Individual therapy sessions often last either forty-five or fifty minutes. A common phrase in the psychotherapy literature is the "fifty-minute hour." As managed care has become a more frequent part of the process, we also see thirty-minute sessions for certain types of problems.

Another common factor across forms of psychotherapy is the frequency of the sessions. Historically, patients participated in psychotherapy on a daily basis. Today, psychotherapy is often conducted using a once-a-week format. Insurance companies often have limits on the frequency of psychotherapy as well as on the number of sessions per year that are covered by the policy. Within the course of psychotherapy, the frequency of sessions may change. For example, if the patient is experiencing severe distress several sessions may be scheduled within one week. In some cases, toward the end of treatment, therapy sessions may be spread further apart before finally terminating the relationship. Using this process allows the patient to separate gradually from the support of psychotherapy. For example, the patient may move from weekly sessions to every other week or even monthly. In some cases, patients may also schedule follow-up or booster sessions to address potential relapse. Even if these sessions are not scheduled, patients are usually encouraged to make appointments in the future if they feel the need for a couple of additional sessions.

Therapists discuss the process of ending therapy with their patients. This process is usually called *termination*. When the therapist feels the patient has reached the desired goals of therapy, he or she will share this information with the patient. Usually one or two sessions are used to go over what has happened during the course of psychotherapy as well as the option of returning to psychotherapy should the patient feel the need to do so. Many therapists will also advise the patient that it is not uncommon to want to return for just a couple of sessions when something major happens in their lives. Just as patients beginning therapy may need to be assured that they are not unique in their level of distress, they also need to know at the termination of therapy that feeling the need to return to the therapist does not mean they will necessarily be facing another long period of therapy. Using the medical analogy of a booster shot following initial immunization for a disease often makes this process clearer to the patient.

Psychotherapy usually involves fees. Unlike talking to a friend or member of the clergy, patients who seek psychotherapy expect to pay for this service. In some cases, an insurance company may pay all or part of the cost. In other cases, the patient will pay for this service. In some cases, the psychologist will agree to provide psychotherapy to all people insured by a particular company at a set fee. When patients pay the psychologist directly for psychotherapy, they can expect the fee to be related to the location as well as the experience level of the psychologist. Information about fees for psychotherapy can be obtained over the phone before actually making an appointment and is always addressed at the time of the first session as well. There tend to be "community standards" for the typical cost or range of costs for psychotherapy. Psychologists with high overhead costs based on the location of their office will charge more than those located in less expensive areas. Most psychologists do agree to see a few people at less than their typical fee, or even at no cost (**pro bono**) as a service to the community.

Patient Rights

Although the focus of this chapter is on the process of psychotherapy from the perspective of the psychologist, we want to acknowledge that the patient does have certain rights. It is important for the psychologist to remember these rights. The American Psychological Association's 1996 president, Dorothy Cantor, had a patient's bill of rights approved by numerous mental health professions and patient groups as a major initiative of her presidency (Mental Health Bill of Rights Project, 1997). Table 9.2 summarizes some of these rights. We will briefly discuss each of them here. These rights can be applied to either inpatient or outpatient psychotherapy. We have limited our discussion to rights related to the relationship between the patient and the psychologist. The term *patient's rights* is also

Table 9.2 Psychotherapy Patients' Rights

Confidentiality
Respectful treatment
Respect for boundaries
Respect for individual differences
Knowledge of the psychologist's professional expertise
Choice
Informed consent to psychotherapy

Source: Adapted from Cantor, D. W. Patient's rights in psychotherapy. In G. P. Koocher, J. C. Norcross, & S. S. Hill, eds., Psychologists' Desk Reference *(2nd ed.), 181–183. New York: Oxford, 2005.*

applied to the relationship between the patient and the insurance company. We are not addressing these rights in this book but refer interested readers to Cantor's (2005) material about them.

Seven Basic Rights

Confidentiality is a key for successful psychotherapy. If your patient believes you will discuss his or her problems with other people, that patient is less likely to be open with you about all facets of the situation. Therapists need to discuss limits of confidentiality before actually starting to work with the patient. State law dictates some of these limits to confidentiality, and others come from professional ethics. It is probably best to actually have a form explaining these limits that your patient signs before starting psychotherapy. Some issues of confidentiality may not have occurred to your patient. For example, if an insurance company is paying for this service, that company probably includes the right to patient information as part of the policy. Most people do not seem surprised when their insurance provider wants records of their physical treatment, such as the results of knee surgery. On the other hand, these same individuals often become upset when they learn that the form filed with their insurance company included a DSM-IV diagnosis and that treatment goals and progress reports were filed with the company by their psychologist. This information needs to be clear to the patient in the beginning. Confidentiality extends beyond verbal transmission of information. It also extends to electronic storage and transmission of patient information. When computers are used, these files need to be password protected. Anyone who has access to these files, such as a receptionist in the office who first greets the patient, must abide by the same rules of confidentiality that the psychologist does.

It may surprise some of you that this list includes *respectful treatment.* Although you might assume that being professional would include respectful treatment, that may not always be the case. When we discussed commonalities among forms of psychotherapy, we mentioned professional behavior. Such behavior includes not only being responsive to the patient, meeting his or her needs in a timely fashion, but also being mindful of the patient's dignity.

Boundaries is a term you will often hear in your clinical training. Some of these boundaries are specifically noted in most codes of ethics. These boundaries include not having a sexual relationship with your patient and not accepting as a patient someone with whom you have previously had a sexual relationship. In general, boundaries for therapists refer to not having any relationship with the patient that is not part of the therapy process. It is important for clinical psychologists to develop an inner sense of when such a boundary may be in jeopardy and to seek peer consultation when that internal mechanism alerts them.

Respect for individual differences goes beyond the general concept of providing psychotherapy for people regardless of their personal characteristics such as race, religion, or sexual orientation. It also means that the psychologist will respect the patient's right to have opinions and values that are different from those of the psychologist. Psychotherapy is not intended as a way to convince the patient to think the same way you do. This right also means that the psychologist is competent to deal with the special needs of this person. Guidelines have been developed by the American Psychological Association to assist therapists in understanding the background they may need to work effectively with special populations.

Knowledge of the psychologist's expertise goes beyond the typical state law requiring the psychologist to display a professional license and the address of the state agency that granted it. Patients have the right to ask their psychologist about the treatment options that are available for their particular problem as well as the experience the psychologist may have in providing each of these options.

Choice is a term that is often associated with healthcare legislation. In that context, you may hear about *freedom of choice* bills in the legislature. What this term means in relationship to psychotherapy is that the patient has the right to choose a therapist rather than merely having one assigned by someone else. This right relates to the profession of the psychotherapist as well as the particular person.

Informed consent to therapy goes beyond the issue of confidentiality. When a psychologist gives the patient a form explaining confidentiality and its limits, that psychologist needs to be certain the patient understands what he or she is signing. In other words, the language should be written in a way that most of the people that psychologist sees will have no problem understanding it. When it appears a patient may not understand the provisions of this form, it is important for the psychologist to take time to explain them in different terms. Informed consent also means that the psychologist takes the time to explain what is involved in the proposed treatment, for example, whether the psychologist expects the patient to complete tasks between sessions or to commit to a specific number of sessions.

Many of the patient rights we have discussed seem to imply that the patient is capable of making independent decisions. What about patients who are sufficiently disturbed that they need to be in the hospital? These patients may also receive psychotherapy. If these individuals have been found to be incompetent, either a family member or the court will be asked to make decisions about their treatment. A number of court cases relate to concern about the rights of inpatients. The U.S. Congress has also taken an interest in this topic. We will describe two examples that relate to patient rights to psychotherapy.

Limited funds for state psychiatric hospitals can lead to overcrowded conditions in them. When staff members are responsible for a growing number of patients, these facilities may move from being treatment settings to providing only secure housing. A patient who has voluntarily entered such a hospital can elect to leave if treatment is not provided. The patient who has been committed, however, does not have this option. A landmark legal decision that included the mandate that such treatment facilities must develop treatment goals for patients and make positive efforts to reach those goals is one basis for the inclusion of psychotherapy for inpatients in mandated inpatient programs (*Wyatt v. Stickney,* 1972). Despite numerous court rulings about the care of psychiatric inpatients, patient advocates were still concerned that when treatment decisions were left to professionals the decision might not be the best one for the individual patient. Congress passed the Protection and Advocacy for Mentally Ill Individuals Act in 1986 to establish advocacy agencies charged with investigating issues of patient neglect and to provide these individuals with legal advice (Woodside & Legg, 1990).

Therapist Characteristics

No single trait or group of traits has been identified as necessary and sufficient for defining a good or successful psychotherapist. It is important for the psychotherapist to be aware of his or her strengths and weaknesses. In this section, we are combining the suggestions of many theorists about important characteristics to consider if you want to be a good psychotherapist.

Rogers' Model

Carl Rogers (1957) suggested that the presence of *congruence, empathy,* and *unconditional positive regard* in the therapist were needed to provide an environment in which patient change could be facilitated. When we discussed Rogers' theory of personality in chapter 4, we noted how these characteristics impact personality development. In this chapter, we expand on them as they apply to psychotherapy.

A general synonym for **congruence** is genuineness. The psychologist is expected to do more than serve in the role of a helper for the patient. Rather, the psychologist is expected to want to help that person. Part of what the psychologist is doing is serving as a role model for the patient. If the patient is going to be able to have authentic relationships with other people, that patient needs to start by having that type of relationship with the psychologist. If the patient has not achieved this type of interaction prior to beginning psychotherapy, then the patient may not know how to do it. At first this may sound basic. How does it translate into actual characteristics of the psychologist? The psychologist must be aware of his or her own relevant characteristics. Included here are the psychologist's motivations for being in this profession. The psychologist then communicates this information to the patient both verbally and through actions. The therapist has achieved a level of self-confidence that can be communicated to the patient as facilitative to the growth process and indicating an honest communication from the therapist. Included in this characteristic is the ability to take risks and share insights with the patient. If the therapist has told the patient, "I will be available to you whenever you are in crisis," for example, that therapist must be prepared to respond quickly to emergency phone calls that may occur between sessions. A psychologist who is not comfortable with that level of availability should share those reservations with the patient according to this approach. As we noted earlier, there are some patients for whom such availability is not therapeutic.

Rogers suggested that when a psychologist reflects **empathy,** the patient is empowered to handle his or her problems. "Empathy is achieved when one individual perceives the internal experience of another as if he were that person" (Murdock, p. 126). Others have built on this concept and added to our understanding of it. Egan (1998), for example, broadened the concept to include both primary and advanced levels of empathy. Primary empathy occurs on the surface level. At this level, the psychologist understands and feels what the patient is saying and doing. At the advanced level, the psychologist communicates an understanding of covert and unconscious levels of the patient's personality. To be able to have these levels of understanding with the patient, the psychologist must have strong self-knowledge. First, the psychologist is aware of personal values and how these values impact his or her life. Second, the psychologist is aware of how these personal values influence interpersonal situations. In addition to this self-awareness, the psychologist is also able to communicate this information to the patient. Communication occurs on both an overt and covert level. Some psychologists have suggested that although certain parts of this characteristic can be taught, the basic personality structure of the psychologist must be one that allows this characteristic to flourish.

Unconditional positive regard does not mean that the psychologist agrees to support and value every one of the patient's behaviors. It does mean that the psychologist believes in the worth of each person. If the psychologist successfully communicates this position to the patient, the patient can then begin to move toward taking responsibility for his or her own life. Some of the therapist characteristics that have been found to be related to the ability to provide positive regard are having self-respect, having a sense of self-worth and potential, having the ability to communicate these beliefs to your patient, and having the ability to move away from personal needs to control others to allow the patient to develop a sense of self-control.

Although these three characteristics are the ones traditionally associated with being a good psychotherapist, other characteristics have also been suggested. Another useful characteristic is the ability to help the patient acknowledge unpleasant things. If all that the patient needed was to hear positive, supportive comments then turning to a close friend might be sufficient to address most problems that bring patients to psychologists' offices. When psychologists feel their patients are not facing unpleasant realities in their lives, it is the psychologist's role to point out this avoidance to the patient. The patient may react negatively to the psychologist for doing this, but the purpose of psychotherapy is not to make the psychologist feel liked. If the psychologist has established sufficient rapport with the patient, any initial negative response to the therapist in this case will be overcome and therapy will continue in the needed direction. Of course, if adequate rapport has not been established, the patient may not return for the next session. Hopefully, the psychologist will have a sufficiently good understanding of the patient's reactions to be able to work with the resistant patient.

Young's Effective Psychotherapist

Young (2001) suggested five key elements of an effective psychotherapist based on an analysis of the work of fourteen different writers in the field. These elements are a positive view of other people, good self-esteem, good self-care skills, creative and intellectual competence, and courage (see Table 9.3). These characteristics are not totally different from those originally suggested by Rogers. We will try to contrast some of Young's terms with those used by Rogers and his followers.

A positive view of other people is quite similar to Rogers' use of positive regard. The therapist is nonjudgmental about such patient characteristics as lifestyle and values.

Table 9.3 Young's Effective Therapist Characteristics
Positive view of other people
Good self-esteem
Good self-care skills
Creative and intellectually competent
Courage

Source: Adapted from Young, M. E. Learning the Art of Healing: Building Blocks and Techniques. *Upper Saddle River, NJ: Merrill Prentice-Hall, 2001.*

A therapist who has a positive view of other people operates from the position that people do want to change and have the capacity to do so. After all, what is the point of the patient spending time and money for psychotherapy if that patient has no intention of making any life changes?

In order to help other people, it is also important that the therapist is psychologically healthy. A person who selects this career to be in a position to learn other people's secrets or have power over them does not make a good therapist. Depending on how such a person uses this information, it might even be unethical. People who choose this career because they think it will allow them to cure their own psychological problems rather than just going to a psychologist also do not make good therapists. Having good self-esteem allows the therapist to be self-critical and to consider his or her own limitations. Good self-esteem is related to Rogers' concept of empathy as developed by Egan (1998) when he wrote of the importance of self-awareness.

We periodically have students ask us why they need to learn so many theories and research methods if what they really want to do is psychotherapy, not research. Part of the answer to that question is that in order to be a good psychotherapist, you need to be able to follow the professional literature and evaluate information about various forms of psychotherapy. This information is then used to guide the practice of psychotherapy. Later in this chapter we talk about some of the research methods that are used in psychotherapy research and discuss some studies to illustrate how these data provide information that is important to good practice. The combination of skills and techniques used with a particular patient will be related to both the therapist's knowledge base and patient characteristics. To do this well requires both intellectual ability and flexibility on the part of the therapist. Thus another characteristic of good therapists is flexibility. Your intellectual ability is measured by entrance tests for graduate school, but your flexibility is not as easy to determine. This characteristic is more likely to be discussed with you by a practicum supervisor based on clinical observation than by a classroom professor.

Young uses the term *courage* to include both the ability to listen to great distress presented by the patient and to accept the fact that at times a psychotherapist is going to need to depend on his or her own judgment about how to proceed. The psychotherapist will not always have the "safety net" of a specific scientific study that perfectly matches the patient. Although psychologists tend to state, "Past behavior is the best predictor of future behavior," there is also considerable uncertainty when trying to predict your patient's behavior. The psychologist who is not comfortable with uncertainty is probably not a good candidate for conducting psychotherapy. Another aspect of courage is composure. When a patient is uncomfortable raising a particular topic, one common strategy is to mention just a small part of it. If the psychologist reacts with any indication of discomfort, the patient may assume this reaction is confirmation of severe psychopathology and not disclose further information. There are also circumstances in which the patient may react to the psychologist with very strong emotions such as anger or sexual feelings. The good therapist remains composed in these situations and helps the patient deal with them. Consider, for example, the situation in which the patient discloses to the therapist that she has had a romantic dream about him. The therapist is aware of the ethical implications of dual relationships and may feel uncomfortable. He may begin to question his prior behavior toward this patient. Such efforts, while certainly important, have the potential to interfere with the therapeutic relationship. In this case, the therapist needs to discuss with the patient possible reasons for that dream. These reasons are based on what the psychologist has already learned about the patient as well as their theoretical orientation. Regardless of the specifics of the discussion, it is important not to merely dismiss the topic as absurd. It is also important to let the patient know that his or her dream is not going to happen in reality. Of course, it is important to explain the ethics of the situation in a way that does not make the patient feel unwanted but clearly explains the boundaries between therapist and patient.

Cultural Considerations

As we noted in chapter 3 and will also discuss in chapter 16, the U.S. population is becoming much more diverse than when many of our approaches to psychotherapy were originally developed. The terms *race, ethnicity,* and *culture* now appear in the psychotherapy literature to begin to address concerns about psychotherapists' understanding of cultural diversity and its impact on their practice. Although the terms *race, ethnicity,* and *culture* are often used as synonyms in the psychological literature, they really have different meanings (La Roche & Maxie, 2003). Each of these meanings is an important consideration for psychotherapy in the twenty-first century. The term **race** refers to selected physical characteristics. These characteristics tend to be permanent ones such as skin color or the shape of one's eyes. Using these characteristics to define race leads to the inclusion of many ethnic groups and cultures within one "title." **Ethnicity** refers to a group of shared characteristics such as country of origin of one's family, language, and customs.

It is important for the psychologist to determine the degree of identification patients have to their ethnic heritage when formulating therapy treatment plans. During the initial interview, for example, the psychologist might ask about the neighborhood where the person lives. Some neighborhoods are essentially ethnic enclaves. Electing to live in such a neighborhood is one measure of the person's identification with ethnic heritage. Even patients who do not live in neighborhoods supportive of their heritage may have strong ethnic identification. It is important for psychologists to continue to consider these factors when doing psychotherapy.

Culture is a broad term representing a way of life that is transmitted from one generation to another within an identified segment of the population. Although many psychologists have acquired an academic appreciation of these factors, they may still find it difficult to use this knowledge effectively in their therapy practice. Given the wide range of factors included here, it seems almost inevitable that psychologists will be culturally different from their patients. Thus, psychologists must move beyond merely acknowledging that culture plays a role in the therapy process and must learn how to have open discussions with their patients about these factors.

It is also important for psychologists to remember that the race or ethnicity of a patient may not be obvious. This is especially true in multiracial patients whose physical characteristics may be different from those expected by the therapist. The best approach may be to ask the patient directly about his or her ethnicity (Cardemil & Battle, 2003). The influence of race and ethnicity may also be less obvious in cases in which the patient has family members from different cultural groups. The influence of their culture on the patient's issues needs to be explored.

Cultural Domains in Psychotherapy

The psychotherapist must consider many cultural domains when doing psychotherapy. We will discuss seven of them (Capuzzi & Gross, 2003): language, identity, generation, cultural custom styles, geographical location and neighborhoods, family constituency, and psychohistorical and religious traditions. Of course each of these domains will differ depending upon the background of the specific patient.

It is naïve to think that taking traditional language courses in college is sufficient preparation for conducting psychotherapy with patients for whom that is the preferred language. When seeing a patient whose primary language is something other than English, the psychologist needs to remember that the patient may use a blend of English and this language either in regular speech or in different settings. For example, the patient may need to use English in the employment setting but may use the primary language with relatives. Even in the work setting, if there are others who have the same primary language as your patient they may speak in that language among themselves and only use English when interacting with "outsiders." Regardless of where each language is used, it is likely that much of their emotional content was first learned in their primary language. The meaning of some of the words necessary to truly understand the patient may not occur easily through standard translation. Even when the patient is quite fluent in English, the description given in English may not carry an accurate picture of the patient's psychological state. There may also be subtle differences in the meaning of words even within groups that appear to an outsider to speak the same language. For example, the Office of Management and Budget of the U.S. government uses the term *Hispanic* to refer to people whose country of origin may be Mexico, Puerto Rico, Cuba, Spain, or any of a number of other countries. Having taken traditional Spanish courses is unlikely to prepare the psychologist for the linguistic subtleties characterizing the language of these diverse peoples.

Another issue is that of the existence of numerous dialects within any identified ethnic minority group. For example, among the recognized Native American tribes there are more than two hundred distinct tribal languages (Arciniega & Newlon, 2003). Although having the ability to use the language of the patient is important for all clinical psychologists, this ability is especially important for those psychologists who practice in parts of the country where there are large numbers of people for whom English may not be the primary or preferred language. A few examples will illustrate this point. More than a million people listed as Hispanic lived in Los Angeles and New York City in 2000. In East Los Angeles, this group comprised 95.8 percent of the population. Half of all Hispanic residents reporting in the 2000 U.S. Census lived in either California or Texas; the state with the largest percentage of its population having this heritage was New Mexico, with 42 percent of the total population classified as Hispanic (U.S. Bureau of the Census, 2001). Thus it is now very important for clinical psychologists practicing in those parts of the country to increase their understanding of the language and culture of this group.

Having an appreciation of your patient's cultural identity is important for the establishment of rapport. One aspect of this identity is the label the patient selects to represent his or her heritage. The simplest acknowledgment by the psychologist of this concept may be to ask the patient about the preferred identifier when obtaining general information rather than using governmental labels. For example, governmental surveys tend to use the term *African American* to refer to people with a black skin color. However, within this group individuals may prefer such self-referent labels as black or West Indian. Multicultural researchers have also provided information that will be useful to psychologists addressing this issue. According to these researchers, the identity process can be conceptualized as following a stage development process (Sue & Sue, 1999). Using this model can help the psychologist meet the patient's needs by fostering an appreciation of the development of identity.

Generation, in this context, refers to whether the patient was born in the United States or in some other country. Whether the patient is a first-generation American or a third-generation American may be a relevant factor in terms of acculturation. It is not unusual, for example, for a first-generation American to have stronger ties to his or her country of origin than do members of the family who were born and raised in the United States. Even as generations are born in the United States it does not mean they will abandon the cultural ways of their heritage. What often occurs in these later generations is that they blend traditions from the United States with those of their country of origin. Often this blend is unique to the individual patient or family and will need to be explored if psychotherapy is to be successful.

Without an understanding of the cultural custom styles of the patient, the clinical psychologist is likely to misinterpret many patient responses. We previously noted the verbal nature of psychotherapy. Communication styles vary considerably across cultures. Psychologists are taught the importance of making eye contact with others. In some cultures, however, not making eye contact with a person viewed as an authority figure is a sign of respect. Thus, one way to judge whether or not this patient respects the psychologist may be the presence or absence of eye contact. The role of the family, including the extended family, also varies across cultures. Attempting to convince the patient to become more self-centered may cause greater distress if he or she views responsibility to family as one's primary duty.

Another cultural factor of special importance to psychotherapy is the patient's concept of time. Most American psychologists are trained in a model that places considerable emphasis on time. Earlier in this chapter, we noted the importance of being on time for sessions and how to handle it if you have a patient in crisis and are not going to be able to complete a session within its scheduled period. When patients are late for psychotherapy sessions, it is not unusual for the psychologist to interpret this lateness as a form of resistance. Even if the psychologist does not favor a theoretical orientation that encourages interpretation, regular tardiness for sessions is not likely to go either unnoticed or uninterpreted by the psychologist. However, it may be that in the patient's culture social obligations take precedence over personal needs. Thus, missing an appointment with the psychologist or arriving late may be completely caused by this type of personal demand. If late arrivals become an issue, it is important for the psychologist to learn the reasons for them and how that reason may be related to the patient's culture before making a more "traditional" interpretation of this behavior. Psychologists conduct psychotherapy within a fairly rigid time schedule that may not work with certain patients. Much of the focus of the therapeutic work is on plans for the future and how to reach those goals. When determining these therapeutic goals, it is important to learn how the patient's culture may impact this process.

The neighborhood where the patient lives has been found to have an impact on patients. The literature suggests that patients who come from totally ethnic neighborhoods often have a different view of traditions and customs than do patients who live in more integrated neighborhoods. Thus, it is important for psychologists to have some understanding of the neighborhoods within their practice area. If the psychologist does not have that knowledge, a few simple questions need to be asked about the neighborhood where the patient currently lives as well as about the neighborhood where the person grew up.

The role of the family is important for many minority patients. Of course, family is an important factor for all patients, but it has been studied separately for certain ethnic groups. It is important to make sure that the psychologist and patient are using a similar definition of "family." The patient's definition of "family" may be different from the definition used by the psychologist. For example, in many Native American and Hispanic families that term refers not only to such extended family members as grandparents, aunts, and uncles but also to godparents and close friends. Within this network, it is considered important to create conditions in which each of these generations can be comfortable. There is a tradition of respect for the older generations that is often missing in the families with whom the clinical psychologist may have learned therapeutic techniques. The psychologist needs to understand the hierarchical nature of the family structure if individual psychotherapy is going to be successful.

When conducting psychotherapy with a patient from a cultural group other than one's own, it is important to understand that group's history. This includes the history of the group both before it came to the United States as well as after it arrived in this country. Key factors, such as child-rearing practices and their impact on personality development, may have been based on this history. The role of religion often has been found to be greater in the lives of ethnic minority patients than in the lives of other patients. As a result of the importance of religion, it is typical for many of these individuals to have sought advice from religious leaders before consulting a clinical psychologist. There is also a greater tendency to turn to religion for both comfort and socialization. Knowledge of the importance of religion as well as the resources available through the patient's religious community may be an important part of the therapeutic process.

Addressing Cultural Differences

Although all of these topics are important, psychologists must decide when to discuss cultural issues and how to do so. Of course, this process will vary depending on both the psychologist and the patient. This is not like a manual for constructing a toy. Psychologists need to use their training to adapt these ideas for the individual patient. They must consider many areas if they are to engage in appropriate psychotherapy. Table 9.4 provides a summary of ten suggested topics for psychologists who work with diverse populations to consider (La Roche & Maxie, 2003). We will briefly discuss each of them.

Table 9.4 Addressing Cultural Differences

1. Cultural differences are subjective, complex, and dynamic.
2. The most salient cultural differences should be addressed first.
3. Similarities should be addressed as a prelude to discussions of cultural differences.
4. The patient's levels of distress and presenting problem will often determine when and if cultural differences are discussed in psychotherapy.
5. Cultural differences should be addressed as assets that can help in the therapeutic process.
6. The patient's cultural history and racial identity development are important factors in assessing how best to conceptualize presenting problems and facilitate therapeutic goals.
7. The meanings and saliency of cultural differences are influenced by ongoing issues within the psychotherapeutic relationship.
8. The psychotherapeutic relationship is embedded within a broader cultural context that affects the therapeutic relationship.
9. The therapist's cultural competence will have an impact on the way differences are addressed.
10. Dialogues about cultural differences can have an effect on the patient's cultural context.

Source: Adapted from La Roche, M. J., and Maxie, A. Ten considerations in addressing cultural differences in psychotherapy. Professional Psychology: Research and Practice, 34(2003): 180–186.

Some people may wonder if the best approach to cultural issues would be to try to match therapists and patients based on culture. This solution is not practical. There are limitations on therapist availability to actually do this. Some research has suggested that differential levels of acculturation may interfere with the therapeutic process even in cases in which the patient and therapist are from the same culture (Berry & Kim, 1988). Because cultural differences are not only subjective and complex but also change over time and with context, it is important for psychologists to avoid making assumptions based on either academic knowledge or prior discussions with the patient. The interaction of factors such as sexual orientation and race may be more important for this particular patient, for example, than either of these factors considered separately. It will also be important to discuss how these factors may differentially influence the patient in various life situations such as work and family. When therapists note what appears to be a change in the patient's interactions with them, it is important to discuss how cultural differences between them may have changed because of some recent event in the patient's life.

La Roche and Maxie (2003), in summarizing the work of many people in this field, note that the psychologist needs to explore with the patient various cultural differences that exist between them and make some determination about which of these differences seem to be most important to the patient. It is these most important differences that need to be discussed initially if you expect to develop rapport with the patient and form a solid therapeutic alliance. Psychologists can facilitate the process of forming an alliance by discussing cultural similarities with their patients before starting the discussion of differences. These similarities may allow the patient to feel more comfortable with the psychologist and thus able to reveal issues of concern. Additionally, the psychologist needs to attend to cues from the patient during cross-cultural discussions. These cues should guide the psychologist toward the issues that are most important to the patient.

Although it is important to discuss cultural issues in psychotherapy, it is also important to be aware of the patient's emotional state. If your patient is in crisis or emotionally fragile, that is *not* the time to discuss cultural differences. The patient might feel the psychologist was just not in tune with his or her level of distress and may drop out of therapy. This patient might benefit from some discussion of similarities, but the focus should be on dealing with the major issues that brought the patient to the psychologist until the patient is functioning better. In this case, culture comes into play in the therapist's understanding of its role in the current distress.

Historically, people in the minority, as defined by the country in which they reside, have viewed the majority as seeing them as lesser beings. Positive characteristics tend to be described in terms of the majority culture. One result of this trend is for both patients and therapists to feel uncomfortable discussing cultural differences. Psychologists who openly note this tendency as well as the fact that this is a problem of the mainstream culture rather than something internal to the patient may find that the discussion proceeds better. Noting how the patient's differences from the mainstream culture are related to his or her strengths rather than as a deficit can set the tone for further positive exploration. As patients feel increasingly comfortable discussing cultural issues they also become more empowered to discuss the types of life changes they really want from therapy.

There is no single route toward gaining the level of cultural competence needed to follow the steps given here. Among the ways to become culturally competent are travel to various countries, participating in activities in ethnically diverse neighborhoods, reading about various groups, and seeking consultation and supervision from culturally diverse peers. Graduate training, as well as continuing professional education, also offers important information about relevant cultural factors.

Therapist Burnout

A common phrase related to emotionally draining professions is **burnout** (Skovholt, 2001). Psychologists who are employed in settings where they will be working with especially challenging patients in large numbers have been found to be especially vulnerable to burnout (Hellman & Morrison, 1987). A combination of the personality of people who choose this occupation and the needs of their patients has the potential to lead to overwork and feelings of stress. Added to this stress level is the increasing rate of litigation related to the therapeutic process and the accompanying increase in liability insurance rates. Although the therapist is not a "friend" of the patient, there is a relationship between them. As with any relationship that ends, there is a degree of pain on both sides. Psychotherapists with active practices must deal with issues of termination on a continuing basis. Although termination may be an indication of successful psychotherapy, it is also the end of a relationship and is a component of therapist stress. In order to be able to help other people deal with their problems, therapists must develop techniques that allow for the positive characteristics we have described but also allow therapists to "leave the problems after the session." This suggestion does not mean the therapist never thinks about a patient outside the therapy time or never allows the patient to call during a crisis. On the other hand, the therapist who internalizes all of the issues from the day is likely to become emotionally drained and no longer capable of a high level of functioning. It is important for the therapist to have a life separate from the demands of the profession. There are no specific recommendations about what activities may work best because they vary depending on the person. For example, Dr. Matthews likes to read mystery novels. Dr. Anton likes to work out. Some therapists find that playing tennis or some other physical activity on a regular basis is an important part of their own mental health.

It is also important for all therapists to be aware of signs of burnout. Kaslow (1986) provided a list of frequent signs of therapist burnout. This list is meant to be a guideline for practitioners. She noted that if two or more of them continue to appear with increasing frequency and duration it is time for the therapist to seek personal psychotherapy or make sufficient life changes to return to the needed psychological state to be an effective practitioner. Her signs include not wanting to go to work, developing frequent unexplainable illnesses, and constantly feeling overwhelmed by work. Having good self-care skills is important not only for the therapist but also for the probable outcome of the treatment. Research indicates that generally more well-adjusted psychotherapists are also the most effective ones (Lafferty, Beutler, & Crago, 1989).

Research

Psychotherapy research has many goals. In chapter 3, we provided some historical context for, and basic terminology used in, psychotherapy research. In this chapter, we build on that foundation. If we look at this subject broadly, a major goal is "to understand alternative forms of treatment, the mechanisms and processes through which these treatments operate, and the impact of treatment and moderating influences on maladaptive and adaptive functioning" (Kazdin, 1994). In order to reach this broad goal, psychologists have used true experiments, quasi-experiments, and naturalistic observation to evaluate psychotherapy.

Most of the psychotherapy research you will read uses a design that compares data from one or more types of psychotherapy compared to a control group. The simplest form of this design involves gathering data from each group before and after treatment, sometimes called a pretest-posttest control group design. In this case, you need a minimum of one form of psychotherapy and a control group. If the study is a true experiment, the patients will be assigned at random to either the real psychotherapy or the control group. Single-case research compares different interventions with the same patient over a period of time. Usually observations are made much more frequently than in the group comparison designs. Depending on the type of intervention, observation may even be made on a daily basis. This type of design usually starts with gathering baseline information about the behavior or behaviors of interest. These behaviors are then measured following administration of your treatment and then without the presence of the treatment or in a setting where treatment does not occur. Because these designs require the withdrawal and then reinstatement of treatment, they are more likely to be used in a research setting than in an actual clinical setting. Meta-analysis is also used in psychotherapy research. This statistical procedure allows the researcher to combine data from a number of different studies. By using meta-analysis, a researcher can evaluate more variables than can typically be included in an individual study. Meta-analyses also provide the foundation for hypothesis generation. Meta-analyses of psychotherapy began to appear in the psychological literature in the mid-1970s (Smith & Glass, 1977) and have continued to be popular since that time.

Psychotherapy research has a long history. Eysenck's (1952) evaluation of the data from more than seven thousand patients from twenty-four different research studies concluded that psychotherapy with *neurotics* was not more effective than no treatment at all. Many methodological questions were raised about Eysenck's data, including his definition of a control group, matching patients in the treatment and control conditions, and variable definitions of improvement across treating professionals. He conducted subsequent studies in an attempt to address some of these criticisms (Eysenck, 1965, 1966). His studies, regardless of the methodological questions, spurred the field to conduct more and better research at a time when this was not happening.

In chapter 3 we noted that a popular term in psychotherapy research is **empirically supported treatments.** Other terms that have been used in the psychological literature to refer to this body of research are *empirically validated treatments* and *empirically evaluated treatments.* A special section of the *Journal of Consulting and Clinical Psychology* was devoted to this topic (Kendall & Chambless, 1998). Special sections of major psychology journals occur when the topic is considered to be important and one of current interest to the profession. The term *empirically supported treatments* is used to indicate that the intervention method being discussed has been evaluated using acceptable methods of psychological science and has been found to be useful for the purpose for which it was developed.

Hopefully some readers are wondering what we mean by "useful." If you questioned that word as you read the previous material you are starting to think like a psychologist. Early intervention researchers tended to define *useful* in terms of being better than no treatment. Later researchers tended to define *useful* as not only being better than no treatment but also better than a placebo or perhaps an alternative treatment. According to Borkovec and Castonguay (1998), "If a therapy is superior to another treatment or matches the outcome of an already established treatment with adequate statistical power, then that therapy is said to have adequate empirical support" (p. 139). In order to get a broad understanding of an intervention, researchers test its efficacy in both the laboratory and the applied setting. The laboratory setting allows the researcher to have greater control of relevant variables and thus be able to make more specific comments about what does and does not work. Research conducted in applied settings, while usually not having as great a degree of control, allows greater ability to generalize to other settings. Methods of psychotherapy that are found useful in both settings are the preferred forms of intervention.

Psychotherapy Elements

Not all research about psychotherapy focuses on a specific method. Some studies address specific factors that are part of the therapeutic process. Based on concerns that the attention to empirically evaluated treatments was leading to insufficient attention to the role of the therapist in this process, the American Psychological Association's division of psychotherapy established a task force to "identify, operationalize, and disseminate information on empirically supported therapy relationships" (Norcross, 2001, pp. 347–348). This task force hoped to identify the specific elements of the therapy relationship that are most important for successful therapeutic outcomes. Once these characteristics were identified the task force hoped to be able to determine how to maximize their use based on specific characteristics of the patient. Table 9.5 lists the eleven elements of the therapeutic relationship evaluated by this task force.

After reviewing the available research literature, the task force concluded that there was evidence to support the effectiveness of the first four factors and the other seven had a promising level of support and were probably effective. Thus, these final seven areas need further study before being accepted as effective parts of the psychotherapy process. Because this material provides a broad picture of psychotherapy research, we will briefly discuss each of these elements here.

Therapeutic alliance "refers to the quality and strength of the collaborative relationship between client and therapist in therapy" (Horvath, 2001, p. 365). The data suggest that when this alliance develops over a period of time it is better than one that occurs in the first session. This early alliance may lead the patient to have unrealistic expectations about psychotherapy, and the disappointment when a quick change does not occur may lead to premature termination of psychotherapy. Patients who are seeking therapy because of relationship issues tend to find it especially difficult to form a therapeutic alliance with the therapist and may actually elicit negative responses that lead to premature therapy termination. Therapists who have good communication skills, are open with their patients, and are able to exhibit empathy build stronger therapeutic alliances than other therapists do.

Cohesion in group psychotherapy is defined as "the therapeutic relationship in group psychotherapy emerging from the aggregate of member-leader, member-member, and member-group relationships" (Burlingame, Fuhriman, & Johnson, 2001, p. 373). In other words, cohesion refers to the closeness the individual feels to both the therapist and the other members of the group. Good preparation for group therapy can increase the development of cohesion. We will talk more about this process in chapter 12.

We discussed *empathy* in chapter 4 as well as earlier in this chapter. This term is often associated with Carl Rogers' writing. When patients feel the therapist really understands

Table 9.5 General Elements of the Psychotherapy Relationship
The alliance
Cohesion in group psychotherapy
Empathy
Goal consensus and collaboration
Positive regard
Congruence or genuineness
Feedback
Repairing alliance ruptures
Self-disclosure
Countertransference management
Relational interpretations

them they are more likely to be satisfied with psychotherapy and therefore be compliant with the work of this process. For some people, experiencing empathy from their therapist allows them to move forward and participate in the therapy process because they feel worthy of the attention. Once the patient begins to work in psychotherapy he or she is able to explore himself or herself more completely and provide needed information for the therapist.

Goal consensus and *collaboration* refer to the ability of the therapist and patient to agree on the purpose of psychotherapy and then to work together toward that goal. You can see how this is related to the therapeutic alliance. It is easier to agree on the goals of psychotherapy when you have a strong bond with the therapist. When patients and therapists agree on goals and also work together to achieve those goals the outcome has been found to be more positive.

Positive regard is another therapist characteristic associated with Rogers' writing. Remember that his term refers to a nonpossessive type of warmth. Some of you may seem surprised to find this characteristic in the "probably effective" rather than "definitely effective" category. Thus far, the research on this subject has been moderately supportive (Farber & Lane, 2001). This is especially true when we consider it from the patient's point of view. Further research is needed on this subject before this therapist characteristic can be moved to the "definitely effective" level.

Congruence or *genuineness* is also one of Rogers' proposed necessary therapist characteristics. As therapists gain more experience they are generally able to be more genuine than when they first begin their training. This characteristic requires that the therapist is aware of those times when he or she is not being genuine. Beginning therapists may be so concerned about the techniques they are trying to use as well as their own fear that they will not do well with therapy that they do not have sufficient energy to also monitor their congruence. Even such simple factors as being in a good mood during the therapy session is related to increasing your congruence.

Feedback includes both a description and an evaluation of the patient's behavior and/or the effects of that behavior. Feedback in psychotherapy is a reciprocal activity. The therapist reacts to information from the patient. This reaction may be in the form of an interpretation, confrontation, or just noting something about the patient. If feedback is going to be effective there must be some reaction from the patient. Depending on the nature of the feedback, that reaction might be agreement, disagreement, or distortion. Perhaps because feedback takes so many different forms in psychotherapy, it has not been investigated to the degree that some of the other factors we listed have been. Feedback can be either positive or negative. When therapists give negative feedback, they have a better chance of having it accepted by the patient if they have already established a trusting relationship with the patient and precede the negative feedback with some positive feedback.

Therapy does not always proceed in a smooth, positive direction. There will be times when there is a strain in the relationship between the therapist and the patient. If this relationship is considered to be one of the important factors in a positive outcome for psychotherapy then a related factor is how to deal effectively with problems in that alliance. There is a small body of literature on *repairing alliance ruptures*. The available literature suggests that when therapists follow treatment manuals very closely they may miss problems in the therapeutic alliance, leading to its rupture. Therapists in this case need to adjust their behavior and pay closer attention to the therapeutic alliance rather than becoming defensive that their patient is becoming noncomplaint.

Self-disclosure refers to the therapist making statements to the patient that reveal something personal about the therapist. This is a highly controversial concept in psychotherapy training. Some psychologists are trained to reveal nothing personal to their patients; others are told it improves the therapeutic alliance. At this point, most of the research is analogue rather than in clinical settings so the generalization of results is limited. The available information suggests that the key is the reason for self-disclosure. Self-disclosure should only be done for the patient's benefit, not for the therapist's needs or in situations in which such disclosure could blur treatment boundaries.

Freud believed that countertransference, unresolved conflicts of the therapist being reflected in personal reactions toward the patient, was harmful to therapeutic outcome. He said it should be removed when it occurred. The therapist may need to seek personal supervision of this case if he or she decides to continue seeing the patient. Depending on the reasons for the countertransference the therapist may also need to seek personal psychotherapy to deal with these unresolved personal issues. *Countertransference management* is facilitated by empathy, self-insight, self-integration, anxiety management, and conceptualizing ability.

Helping the patient to become aware of information that is not currently part of his or her awareness is one aspect of psychotherapy. The quality of *relational interpretations* refers to how well the interpretation fits with the therapist's case formulation. The early work on this topic suggests that interpretations should be limited to those that address the major interpersonal themes of the patient.

General Issues

Introductory textbooks on psychotherapy often fail to be specific about the problems for which specific types of psychotherapy are intended or for which problems the research supports the use of those methods of psychotherapy. The descriptions are generic and students may complete these beginning studies with the idea that they must select a particular approach that will be useful for everyone they see as practitioners. Many practitioners have highly heterogeneous practices and may have patients who do not clearly fit the diagnostic criteria for a particular DSM-IV diagnosis. If psychotherapy outcome research is going to be effective, however, only those patients who fall within a clearly defined population should be included. By conducting research this way, the psychologist can then make statements about the usefulness of a particular treatment for a particular problem.

Many psychologists consider the National Institute of Mental Health (NIMH) Treatment of Depression Collaborative Research Program, which evaluated various methods for treating unipolar depression, as starting the modern era of this type of research (Elkin et al., 1989). This study compared the effectiveness of interpersonal psychotherapy, cognitive psychotherapy, the use of the drug imipramine with clinical management, and a placebo group that also received clinical management. One of the unique aspects of this study was that it was conducted in different parts of the country rather than at just one clinic. The design of this study also considered some of the previous criticisms of psychotherapy research. All of the psychotherapists were trained in a standard way and their adherence to that standard approach was monitored throughout the data-gathering process. The researchers also used multiple outcome measures during and at the completion of the treatment as well as at an eighteen-month posttreatment follow-up. The data from 560 patients were analyzed and then reanalyzed after subdividing the patients into two groups based on the severity of the initial depression. The initial data analysis indicated that patients in each of the three treatment conditions did better than the placebo group. When the patients were subdivided based on the severity of their initial depression, significant differences were found only for the severe depression group. This study provides a benchmark for future comparative psychotherapy research.

Just as the problem needs to be defined clearly, so does the intervention. Empirically supported treatment research often uses the term **treatment manual.** This term refers to "a cogent and extensive description of the treatment approach therapists are to follow" (Chambless & Hollon, 1998, p. 11). There are many different treatment manuals, and they do not follow a standard format. Early writers on this topic stated that treatment manuals must include a description of the basic principles upon which the treatment is based, concrete examples of each technique, and a method for evaluating whether the therapist is following the recommended procedures (Luborsky & Barber, 1993). Without the availability of a treatment manual it is difficult to determine if the procedure used in one research project is the same as that used in another research project. Thus less well-defined forms of psychotherapy are not as likely to be evaluated and appear in the research literature. Please remember this point as you read articles about psychotherapy in the psychology journals.

Not all clinical psychologists are comfortable with the treatment manual research. These psychologists have raised a range of concerns about the available studies. These concerns include whether therapists adhere to these procedures in clinical practice to the same degree they do in research settings, the potential for treatment manuals to lead to a rigid approach to psychotherapy, and the lack of attention to relationship factors in these manuals (Lambert et al., 2005).

It is also important that all therapists who are using any treatment are adequately trained in the procedure. If an intervention does not appear to be effective it may be because of inadequate training of the therapist rather than a poor treatment procedure. Some studies have been interpreted as suggesting that the experience level of the therapist has little to do with treatment outcome (Christensen & Jacobson, 1994). Many of these studies, however, measured experience level in terms of educational level or years in practice rather than amount of experience with the particular intervention being evaluated and thus may not be relevant (Chambless & Hollon, 1998). Overall, the data suggest that the relationship between the patient and therapist is the most important characteristic for predicting outcome success.

Other research about psychotherapy has emphasized the form of psychotherapy rather than the diagnostic category. These studies have sometimes reported conflicting results because of the definition of the specific form of psychotherapy as well as the outcome measures used. We will briefly summarize a few of these data to illustrate the findings. Meta-analytic studies have reported that short-term psychoanalytic therapy is preferable to no therapy (Crits-Christoph, 1992), and Weston (1998) reported considerable research support for many of the theoretical assumptions of psychoanalysis. A review of studies on experiential-humanistic psychotherapies reported that person-centered therapy resulted in significant change from pretherapy to posttherapy evaluation

(Greenberg, Elliott, & Lietaer, 1994). The importance of the therapist characteristics of congruence, warmth, and empathy for therapeutic outcome has been studied with varying conclusions (Beutler, Crago, & Arezmendi, 1986; Truax & Mitchell, 1971). There is a large research literature on rational emotive behavior therapy (REBT). Sharf (2000) noted that there are more than 250 studies on this form of psychotherapy. Lyons and Woods (1991) did a meta-analysis of 70 studies of REBT. They found strong support for this approach. Other REBT studies have centered on specific aspects of the theory. For example, data support the relationship between negative self-statements and dysfunction (Hutchinson, Patock-Peckham, Cheong, & Nagoshi, 1998).

ETHICAL CONUNDRUM POINTS TO PONDER

Establishing a business relationship with a patient is addressed in the APA Ethics Code in terms of multiple relationships, conflicts of interest, and exploitative relationships. In this case, the issue could easily have been handled if the psychologist lived in a larger community where there was a choice of roofers. The psychologist might consider contacting a roofing business in the city to determine whether or not it provides services in his community. If it does, it will be important for ongoing patient relations to explain why he chose to use this company rather than Mr. Roofer's. Another issue to consider here is whether hiring a roofing company would impair the patient or lead to any exploitation. As long as the psychologist pays the standard rate for this service and discusses the potential for conflict it may be that using Mr. Roofer's company will lead to less difficulty than using a more distant company. Because this psychologist is in solo practice, the use of consultation with a colleague is not as easily available but could still be tried. Regardless of the remoteness of the community, most psychologists do interact with peers through professional associations, workshops attended, and so on. Thus, the psychologist might consult with a colleague from another rural community about how that psychologist has handled similar situations to obtain a sense of local "standards of practice" as well as with a colleague from an urban area.

Key Terms

brief psychotherapy	empathy	QUOID	supportive psychotherapy
burnout	empirically supported treatments	race	therapeutic alliance
congruence		reconstructive psychotherapy	treatment manual
counseling			
culture	ethnicity	reeducative psychotherapy	unconditional positive regard
eclectic (integrative) psychotherapy	pro bono psychotherapy		YAVIS

CHAPTER 10

Schools of Psychotherapy

In chapter 9, we discussed general issues about psychotherapy. Many general clinical psychology textbooks have individual chapters on the major theoretical approaches to conducting psychotherapy. These theoretical approaches are sometimes called "schools" of psychotherapy. A broad classification system often used for such purposes is to describe the psychoanalytic and psychodynamic methods in one chapter, the humanistic and existential methods in a second chapter, and the behavioral and cognitive approaches in a third chapter. As we mentioned in chapter 9, most psychotherapists use elements of more than one theoretical approach, or school, in their actual clinical practice. The application of multiple theoretical approaches to providing therapy is often called an "eclectic" approach. On the other hand, basic knowledge about psychotherapy includes some understanding of these schools.

In this chapter we provide basic information about psychotherapy approaches grouped on the basis of the facets of the person's behavior that are emphasized (Seligman, 2001). We start with those schools of psychotherapy that emphasize the background of the person and the context of the behavior. Within this group, we discuss psychoanalysis and brief psychodynamic psychotherapy to illustrate these schools. Second, we discuss those psychotherapy schools that emphasize emotion and sensation. As examples of schools operating within this framework, we discuss person-centered psychotherapy and Gestalt psychotherapy. Third, we discuss methods of psychotherapy that emphasize the person's cognitions or thoughts. To illustrate these approaches, we discuss cognitive therapy and rational emotive therapy. Finally, we discuss those psychotherapy schools that

ETHICAL CONUNDRUM

You are a clinical psychologist with an outpatient psychotherapy practice. One of your patients is a twenty-eight-year-old woman who presented with classic symptoms of depression. You have decided to work with her from a cognitive-behavioral perspective and have been teaching her to debate irrational cognitions. As you work with her, you realize that your Jewish background is quite different from her background as a devout Roman Catholic. She is highly dependent on the word of her conservative priest, and her concern about using birth control is adding to her depressive symptoms. She often quotes church doctrine when discussing what you consider "irrational beliefs." Should you transfer her to another psychologist? What changes could you make in your approach to be able to work more effectively with her?

place emphasis on behavior or actions. Illustrative therapies in this case are behavior therapy and reality therapy. Before beginning our review of these schools, however, we present you with an ethical conundrum for you to consider as you read further about psychotherapy.

Schools Emphasizing Background and Context

Clinical psychologists would probably agree that the patient's past has an influence on the present concern. They do not tend to agree, however, on the extent of that influence and therefore on the amount of time that needs to be devoted to understanding and working through past events as a focus of current treatment. This section of the chapter discusses some of the schools of psychotherapy that emphasize the use of material from the patient's past and the context of that past in reducing current distress. These schools of psychotherapy that utilize historical information generally fall under the headings of psychoanalytic and psychodynamic approaches. We will use Freudian psychoanalysis to illustrate the foundation work in this area and brief psychodynamic psychotherapy as a twentieth-century approach with a similar historical focus.

Many patients expect the psychologist to ask about their past. After all, that is what they have seen in the movies! They may also interpret these questions as an indication that the psychologist wants to really get to know them. Questions about the past, except for those areas that are the most painful, may also be easier for the patient to discuss in early sessions than questions about their present difficulties. Thus, psychologists who use these forms of psychotherapy will tend to take extensive patient histories. They may devote several sessions to such information-gathering as well as ask the patient to bring historical mementos to future sessions. These mementos are then used to delve further into the events that made them important to the patient.

Freud's Psychoanalysis

In chapter 4, you read about Freud's ideas on the structure of the personality and the stages of psychosexual development. We now turn our attention to applying those concepts to psychotherapy. **Psychoanalysis** is usually described as a long-term psychotherapy. Because of the intensity of the process, modern psychoanalysis often uses a format of fifty-minute sessions, conducted between two and five times each week, for a period of three to five years. The process of psychotherapy involves the patient doing most of the talking while the psychologist processes the information and makes timely interpretations. The overall goal of this process is to obtain a good balance among the major elements of the psyche—the id, ego, and superego. Table 10.1 presents some typical objectives of psychoanalytic psychotherapy.

Practitioners of psychoanalysis use a range of techniques to achieve their goals. We will describe a few of them here to illustrate the process. Hypnosis is often associated with Freud's work. Although he did use hypnosis early in his career, he abandoned this technique over time because he found the results to be disappointing. The use of hypnosis allowed the ego defense mechanisms to continue their process of repression once the patient awakened from the trance. Thus, the therapist had greater insight about the core issues but the patient did not. Freud therefore sought other techniques that would allow him access to the patients' unconscious and would also allow the patients to become more aware of their unconscious material.

A core method used in psychoanalysis to understand the patient's unconscious is **free association.** Basically, this term means that the patients say whatever they are thinking without processing or cleansing it first. Although this sounds rather easy, it is a difficult task to learn. From the time most of us began to talk, we were taught to think about what we were going to say before the words came out of our mouths. We learned not to be rude or use certain words because they are considered inappropriate. In addition to the content of our speech, we were also instructed to speak in grammatically complete sentences. Psychoanalysts report that patients may need weeks, or in some cases months, before they are really able to free associate. On the other hand, free association is considered essential to the success of psychoanalysis (Freud, 1964).

Psychoanalysts recommend that the patient lie on a couch rather than sit in a chair for free association. The analyst remains out of the patient's direct line of vision, usually

Table 10.1 Goals of Psychoanalysis

Development of insight into the origin of one's difficulties
Improvement of the ego's control of irrational impulses and instincts
The release of psychic energy, or catharsis
Development of more mature, adaptable, and effective ego defense mechanisms
Development of perspectives based on clear assessment of reality
Development of healthy and rewarding relationships
Reduction of the rigidity, punitiveness, and perfectionism of the superego

by sitting just behind him or her. This is done to facilitate the free flow of unconscious material. The analyst listens carefully to what is said and hypothesizes about what is omitted. Disruptions in the flow of speech as well as sudden shifts of topic may indicate an important subject. These changes in the process are interpreted based on the analyst's knowledge of both personality theory and this particular patient's history. Free association may also lead to the appearance of a **parapraxis.** This term is sometimes referred to as a "Freudian slip." In this case, the patient uses one word while actually meaning to use a word with a very different meaning. The analyst would interpret this verbal error as having strong unconscious meaning for the patient. For example, suppose the patient meant to say that she hated to see her sister leave home to attend a distant college but she actually said she was happy to see her sister go to school so far from home. In this case, the analyst would interpret issues of sibling rivalry that had previously been denied.

Another type of interpretation of patient expression is **dream analysis.** According to Freud, when we are asleep our ego defenses are not as strong as when we are awake. Therefore our unconscious processes have a greater ability to express themselves, at least symbolically, in dream content. Psychoanalysts often ask their patients to keep a log or diary of their dreams. This log is brought to therapy sessions and discussed with the analyst. This log may even include waking dreams known as daydreams or fantasies. Freud talked about two types of dream content—*manifest content* and *latent content.* The **manifest content** of a dream is what the patient actually reports. The **latent content** of a dream is what the dream actually represents—the unconscious motives of the person. Psychoanalysts note that the real meaning of dreams is so personally distressing that people would awaken feeling anxious or depressed if it were not well disguised. It requires the skill of the analyst to understand the symbolism of the latent content and to know when the patient is ready to hear the interpretation. To better understand the latent content of the patient's dream, the analyst may combine dream material with a free association process. In this case, the patient is asked to free associate to various aspects of the dream. The patient is also asked to talk about the emotions that arise during this process. The analyst then combines this information with other patient information to form interpretations about the latent content of the dream and help the patient gain further insight about repressed material. Freud provided many examples of dream symbolism and its meaning to his patients in his extensive writings (Freud, 1953).

Another form of interpretation that is a key to psychoanalysis is the evaluation of the patient's relationship to the therapist. Of special importance is **transference.** This term refers to situations in which the patient reacts to the therapist as if the therapist were an important person from the patient's life. Freud's interest in this process began when he noted that some of his patients reacted to him much more strongly than was called for given their relationship. He interpreted that behavior as indicating that the patient was actually reliving an important emotional situation from the past and *transferring* the emotion felt toward that person to Freud. Transference is an unconscious process that does not include logic or time in history. Use of the couch so that the therapist remains a shadowy figure facilitates the development of transference.

Transference involves both positive and negative emotions. A common positive emotional expression of transference is when the patient believes he or she is in love with the therapist. In this case, the analyst might hypothesize that the patient did not resolve the Oedipal conflict successfully and is actually expressing those incestuous wishes from childhood. Positive transference may also explain those cases when the patient seems to show rather rapid improvement in the early stages of psychotherapy. This improvement, however, tends to be superficial rather than an indication of real improvement. Anger is a common form of negative transference. This anger may be expressed toward the therapist in the form of questioning the therapist's ability to actually help the patient. The analyst helps the patient work though the transference relationship as a method for gaining insight into unresolved personal conflicts.

Freud realized that therapists are human and may have inappropriate emotional reactions to their patients. He called this reaction **countertransference.** This countertransference is the result of feelings the therapist had toward significant others in his or her early life. The analyst needs to be aware of any such emotional reactions that develop so that they do not interfere with the therapeutic process. If the therapist cannot control these reactions toward a specific patient, then that therapist must transfer the patient to another therapist. One reason the training of psychoanalysts includes personal analysis is to help them understand their own childhood experiences and decrease the probability that countertransference will occur when they are doing therapy with others.

Analysts use these and many other techniques to help their patients improve. The key to this process is the use of interpretations. Interpretations must be timed correctly, at the correct depth, and be accurate if they are to help the patient understand the meaning of unconscious material. This is not a mechanical activity but rather one requiring considerable skill. If any of those three components are not present, the interpretation is unlikely to be successful.

Research evaluating the efficacy of psychoanalysis is limited. One reason often given for this paucity of data is that true psychoanalysts see a limited number of patients, making large-scale studies impossible. However, the Menninger Foundation collected data on forty-two analytic patients over a thirty-year period and reported moderately positive outcomes (Wallerstein, 1986). The nature of this form of psychotherapy makes comparisons with other, more time-limited, forms of therapy difficult.

Brief Psychodynamic Psychotherapy

Although some of Freud's colleagues developed brief forms of psychotherapy, the modern versions of this approach date to the 1960s. No single name is identified with this approach, as we find with many of the schools of psychotherapy (Demos & Prout, 1993). Among the practitioners who popularized these approaches are Davanloo (1979), Luborsky (1984), and Strupp (1992). Davanloo's approach, sometimes called intensive short-term dynamic psychotherapy, is one of the earliest and also perhaps closest to Freud's traditional methods. His approach has been used with people diagnosed with depression, anxiety disorders, and personality disorders who are treated in an outpatient setting. Davanloo uses the interpretation of transference relationships as well as the connection between these responses and other relationships in the patient's life. On the other hand, his approach is more active and confrontational than Freud's original psychoanalysis. Luborsky and his colleagues focus on what they call a core conflictual relationship theme (CCRT). This CCRT is viewed as an indication of the typical way the patient interacts with others. This interaction is not only the typical way the person interacts with others but is also viewed as the root of the person's problems. Interpretations are not used as frequently in this approach as they are in other forms of brief psychodynamic psychotherapy, and when they are used considerable attention is paid to the patient's readiness to hear them. This approach views symptoms as indicative of the patient's coping style rather than as indications of problems from the early developmental periods. Strupp's time-limited dynamic psychotherapy also focuses on interpersonal relations. In this approach, the therapist analyzes the interactions with the patient during the therapy session as a way to understand the patient's interpersonal style. This information is initially applied to current relationships. Once the patient understands the problems with current relationships, this same information is applied to earlier origins of the pattern of interacting. Strupp and his colleagues also place considerable emphasis on the level of rapport that is established with the patient. They report that when the therapist is warm and protective of the patient the therapy outcome is more positive.

Brief psychodynamic psychotherapy varies depending on the practitioner, but some commonalities are evident. In contrast to the typical three- to five-year process for traditional psychoanalysis, brief psychodynamic psychotherapy typically lasts for six months to a year. The therapist takes an active role in the therapeutic process, starting with setting achievable goals for therapy during the first few sessions. These goals usually involve interpersonal problems.

Not every outpatient is a good candidate for brief psychodynamic psychotherapy. Thus far, research supports its use with a range of patients, including those with a diagnosis of depression, personality disorder, and substance use disorder. The good patient also has a history of at least one meaningful relationship during childhood. On a personal level, the good candidate for this approach to psychotherapy should have introspective ability, at least some mature defenses, the ability to handle the eruption of strong emotions, as well as the ability to be introspective. The patient should also have an above average level of intelligence.

Much of the research on the efficacy of brief psychodynamic psychotherapy has been with adults rather than children, although the approach is used with patients across the lifespan. Meta-analyses of the data are often grouped into earlier studies and more recent ones. The earlier studies generally found that brief psychodynamic psychotherapy was more effective than a waiting-list control group but not quite as effective as some other forms of psychotherapy at the posttreatment evaluation period (e.g., Anderson & Lambert, 1995). Questions have been raised about the impact that the researcher's therapeutic preference has on the outcome of psychotherapy comparison studies. This **allegiance effect** has been reported to account for a large part of the difference reported among forms of psychotherapy (Prochaska & Norcross, 2007). Newer meta-analyses have been limited to studies that were not as likely to be impacted by the allegiance effect (Leichsenring, Rabung, & Leibing, 2004). These studies report equal effectiveness across forms of psychotherapy, with all of them being preferable to a waiting-list control group.

Schools Emphasizing Emotions and Sensations

People often seek psychotherapy because of their emotions. Most therapists would agree that emotions play a role in the reasons their patients come to them. Where therapists differ, however, is on how much attention they actually pay to those emotions as part of the therapeutic process. Some schools of psychotherapy view the identification of emotions and sensations as the core of their work. They assist the patient in identification of these feelings and how they influence the person's ability to function.

Not everyone is aware of the way their emotions impact others in their lives. Even when emotions are appropriate, their intensity may lead to problems. Some feelings, of course, are inappropriate. Whether or not an emotion is considered appropriate to the context in which it is displayed as well as the people involved. Emotions may also be either congruent or incongruent. When they are congruent, the emotion fits with the message that is being sent. Some people may indicate one emotion with their words and another with their tone of voice. Sometimes this is referred to as the difference between verbal and nonverbal behavior. Such messages tend to confuse the recipient of that emotion and can lead to problems. When people express emotions, they may facilitate relationships or derail them. Understanding the impact of emotional expression is the core of the following schools of psychotherapy.

Rogers' Person-Centered Psychotherapy

In chapter 4, you read about Rogers' view of personality structure and the implications of his theory for clinical psychologists. We will now discuss some of the psychotherapeutic techniques that grew out of that foundation. He originally named his approach *nondirective psychotherapy,* later changed the name to *client-centered psychotherapy,* and finally settled on **person-centered psychotherapy.** These changes in the name of this psychotherapy approach reflect the changes in Rogers' orientation throughout his career.

In person-centered psychotherapy, the goals of therapy are set by the patient rather than by the therapist. Rogers called them his clients, rather than his patients, to reflect his views that they were not ill. He placed less emphasis on techniques of psychotherapy than he did on the process of psychotherapy and the conditions that existed within the therapy setting. As he conducted research about psychotherapy, he adapted his methods.

Rogers did, however, suggest certain techniques to facilitate the therapeutic process. To facilitate the process of therapy, therapists make open-ended statements. These statements provide a broad topic to be discussed, but it is the patient who decides where to go within that broad domain. Consider the therapist who is seeing a woman because she has marital problems. The therapist would not start a session with a question like, "Did you fight with your husband this week?" A question like that could be answered with a brief "yes" or "no." The therapist interested in pursuing this area might ask, "Tell me about your interactions with your husband since our last session." This statement allows the patient to focus on both positive and negative interactions as well as to decide what types of interaction are important to her at this time.

Rogers recommended the use of noncommittal comments throughout the session. Examples of these statements are "hmmm" and "go on" at well-timed points during the session. These statements, when properly timed, encourage the patient to talk. They are viewed by the patient as an indication of the therapist's interest in what is being said. He also used **reflection** during therapy sessions. Reflection is an attempt by the therapist to acknowledge an important feeling expressed by the patient. For example, if a patient begins to cry while describing her relationship with her husband, the therapist might note, "Discussing your marriage upsets you." Doing this illustrates the characteristic of accurate empathy that we discussed in chapter 4 as part of Rogers' view of a fully functioning person.

Like Freudian therapists, Rogerians use **interpretation** as part of their work. Students are sometimes surprised to see the term *interpretation* applied to Rogers. They have heard that Rogers and his followers let the patient do all the talking. Rogers, however, found that interpretation did have a role in his approach to psychotherapy. The purpose of interpretation for these therapists is quite different from its purpose for psychodynamic therapists. For the Freudian therapist, interpretation is used to assist the patient in gaining an understanding of unconscious material that is impacting him or her. Rogerians use interpretation to help the patient recognize current emotions or motivation. In this case the therapist is expressing both empathy and genuineness. Rogerians also use **paraphrasing** in their work. Paraphrasing allows therapists to check the accuracy of their understanding of what the patient is saying. Patients use terms that may have different meanings. They may also use vague terms that allow many interpretations. When the therapist paraphrases the patient is given the opportunity to clarify the situation.

Although person-centered therapists may use various techniques to facilitate change in their patients, Rogers wrote that six basic conditions are both necessary and sufficient for personality change to occur (Rogers, 1957). First, the patient must be experiencing a state of psychological **incongruence.** This condition leads the patient to feel anxious or vulnerable. Using terms from his theory, incongruence means that there is a significant difference between the person's real self and the ideal self. In other words, there is a difference between the emotions the patient feels and the patient's self-view of what emotions should be felt in that situation. It is this incongruence that leads the patient to actually make the appointment with the psychologist. Second, the therapist must be *congruent.* This means that the therapist is able to accurately identify his or her feelings and then to behave in ways that agree with those feelings. The congruent individual is able to detect any changes in attitude toward the patient during a therapy session and match behaviors to those feelings.

Once the patient and therapist are actually in the office they must establish a close interpersonal relationship. Rogers called this relationship "being in psychological contact" with each other. He believed that it was not possible for personality change to occur if this type of relationship does not exist. Fourth, the therapist must experience **unconditional positive regard** for the patient. This does not mean that the therapist agrees with everything the patient says and does. It does, however, mean that the therapist truly cares for the patient regardless of what the patient says or does. There are no conditions placed on the therapist's caring. Fifth, the therapist is able to accurately experience the inner world of the patient. That ability allows the therapist not only to truly understand the patient but also to identify aspects of the patient's being of which that person is unaware. That information is used as part of the interpretation. Finally, the therapist must have the ability to communicate all of this understanding to the patient in a way that facilitates the patient's growth.

Person-centered psychotherapy is usually scheduled once a week. More frequent sessions, special sessions, and phone calls between sessions are discouraged because these extras could lead to dependence on the therapist and therefore not allow the patient to take responsibility for growth. When these conditions are present, the patient is likely to move through a sequence of seven stages (Meador & Rogers, 1984). During the first stage, the patient does not recognize his or her own feelings and is not ready to reveal personal feelings. When the patient moves into the second stage, the patient begins to recognize some problems but still externalizes rather than being in touch with personal experiences. During the third stage, the patient begins to describe past feelings as unacceptable and occasionally can see that these problems are internal rather than external. The fourth stage is characterized by a more accurate description of feelings and some sense that he or she is actually responsible for these feelings. The fifth stage brings acceptance of responsibility for personal distress and an awareness of the conflict that exists between thoughts and feelings. In the sixth stage, the person is willing to risk being genuine and trusting other people to be accepting of his or her true self. Finally, the patient is comfortable with the new person he or she has become.

Rogers and his colleagues were among the early therapists to conduct research about psychotherapy. These studies not only were pioneering efforts in the broad field of psychotherapy but also supported the effectiveness of the person-centered approach (Rogers & Dymond, 1954). Later meta-analyses supported the efficacy of person-centered psychotherapy over no treatment but did suggest that some other treatment methods may be more effective (Smith & Glass, 1977; Smith, Glass & Miller, 1980).

Gestalt Therapy

Gestalt is the German word for whole or pattern. Gestalt therapy, as developed by Frederick (Fritz) Perls and his colleagues, emphasizes the present in its attempt to treat the patient as an integrated whole (Perls, Hefferline, & Goodman, 1951; Perls, 1969). Perls believed that a major cause of psychopathology was a lack of awareness of one or more aspects of one's self. Within that context, the focus of therapy is to experience one's emotions and sensations. In contrast to forms of psychotherapy whose goal is to understand the cause of personal distress, Gestalt therapy emphasizes being in touch with your feelings and your environment as the way to decrease feelings of distress. Perls and his colleagues believed that as society became more complex, people lost contact with the true meaning of life. One goal of Gestalt therapy is to help restore a proper balance within the person. Gestalt therapists do not see their role as helping the patient solve problems. Instead, they use a range of techniques to help the patient feel more fulfilled and more whole. As patients progress through therapy, they become more comfortable experiencing their own sensations and emotions and using them in a complete way. Like person-centered therapists, Gestalt therapists note the importance of the therapeutic relationship if change is to occur.

Many patients who seek psychotherapy expect to spend considerable time talking about their past. Although Gestalt therapists do take a patient history, they place less emphasis on the past than on the present. The therapist provides his or her patients with some general guidelines, or rules, to assist them in addressing their current issues rather than those from the past. For example, patients are encouraged to speak in the present tense rather than the past tense. When the patient uses the past tense, the therapist will ask him or her to remain in the present. If the patient begins to describe an emotion rather than experience it, the therapist will redirect the patient by asking him or her to talk about the experience of that moment. Patients are encouraged to use the word "I" rather than "it" in conversations with the therapist. By centering on themselves rather than describing situations they are more able to remain in the present.

Dreams are an important component of Gestalt therapy. Unlike psychoanalysis, however, the Gestalt therapist does not interpret dreams. Perls recommended having the patient relive the dream in the present. The patient role-plays various parts of the dream in the present. By doing this, the patient is able to identify elements of the self that have become alienated. The patient takes responsibility for each of the segments of the dream. As patients come to view their dreams as part of themselves, they experience a sense of integration. They are able to understand that these emotions and sensations are really part of them. Prior to this activity, these same patients might have denied having such feelings. If that same information had been explained to them in the form of a therapist interpretation, the patient would be more likely to intellectualize it rather than experience it as part of the self.

Part of the development of a sense of being whole is more complete awareness of one's body. Even people who have reasonable contact with their emotions may have distanced themselves from their bodily sensations. Gestalt therapists remain alert to messages being sent by their patient's body. For example, if a patient starts to tap his fingers on the arm of the chair, the therapist might point out this behavior and then ask the patient to speak for his fingers. "What are your fingers trying to say?" Another way to help the patient understand the emotion tied to the finger-tapping is to ask the patient to exaggerate the behavior. In this case, the patient would be told to tap the fingers as fast and as hard as possible. Then the patient would be asked to talk about the feelings that are generated by exaggerating the finger-tapping.

Gestalt therapists make extensive use of role-play in their work. Although Perls was influenced by the psychodrama concept of Moreno that we will discuss more completely in chapter 12, he did not believe in using actors to represent various characters in the patient's life. He felt that adding outsiders could lead to fragmentation.

A common form of role-play is **topdog-underdog.** This activity is used to help the patient acknowledge conflicts arising from different parts of the personality. These parts of the personality have a conversation with each other and the patient plays both parts. The topdog is similar to Freud's concept of the superego. The topdog makes judgments based on the dictates of the person's parents and of society as a whole. The underdog is similar to Freud's concept of the id. The underdog's response to the demands of the topdog is to be meek and mild. On the other hand, the underdog makes no attempt to actually carry out the demands of the topdog. Although the topdog initially appears to be the stronger part of the personality, the underdog is really the part controlling what happens because it resists change despite feelings of guilt. By moving back and forth between these two roles in a dialogue, the patient is able to realize that both roles are facets of the personality and eventually to integrate these parts.

Some activities that Gestalt therapists utilize have been developed specifically for use in group therapy. One example of this type of activity is **making the rounds.** In this case, one member of the group becomes the focus of the activity. The identified group member interacts individually with each of the others in the group. The identified member might be instructed to tell each member something he or she wants from each of them or discuss some aspect of each person that reminds the identified patient of themselves. Making the rounds may also include having each of the members of the group give feedback to the identified patient. For example, each member might identify some strength they see in that person. Gestalt therapists describe making the rounds as an activity that can have a long-lasting impact on the patient.

Because most Gestalt therapists do not believe it is appropriate to do research on their treatment, the research base is somewhat limited. An early meta-analysis of the available studies supported the use of Gestalt therapy (Smith, Glass, & Miller, 1980). Although more recent studies have reported that Gestalt therapy is better than no treatment, they have not tended to find it preferable to other forms of psychotherapy for the populations investigated (Elliott, Watson, Goldman, & Greenberg, 2004). The use of Gestalt therapy to address issues of multiculturalism has received mixed reactions. Although Gestalt techniques may be quite useful in understanding self-perception in two different cultures in which the patient lives, this realization may lead to greater emotional distress about conditions that are beyond the patient's ability to change.

Schools Emphasizing Cognitions

Certainly psychologists are not mind readers. Schools of psychotherapy emphasizing thoughts do not imply that the psychologist has extraordinary powers. Most of us are aware of only a small percentage of our thoughts or cognitions. However, if someone asks us to focus on our thoughts about a particular topic we are usually able to do so. The average person can easily discuss the content of those thoughts with the psychologist. Cognitive therapists focus on the impact our thoughts have on our personality. From this perspective, inaccurate cognitive processes lead to personal distress and psychopathology. Therefore, if you alter the way you think, you will no longer feel that distress. Earlier schools of psychotherapy agree that cognitions are important but see them as less crucial than underlying unconscious affective processes. The cognitive schools view thoughts as primary. These cognitive schools of psychotherapy grew in the 1950s and 1960s.

Cognitions may be easier to analyze and change than emotions. You can write down your thoughts and then analyze the degree to which those thoughts are rational. You can learn skills, such as disputing irrational thoughts, that can increase your sense of empowerment. Focusing on cognitions, rather than attempting an extensive evaluation of the past, may require less time in therapy and therefore make the process acceptable to a wider range of people. Also, people who are not comfortable dealing on an emotional level may be more willing to participate in the therapeutic process if the process is described as focusing on thinking. The term *cognitive therapy* is used in several different ways in the professional literature. At times, it refers to those schools of psychotherapy that focus on the role of thoughts in both dysfunction and intervention procedures. It is also used specifically to refer to the method of psychotherapy developed by psychiatrist Aaron T. Beck. Beck's cognitive therapy is the first therapeutic approach we describe in this section. It is followed by Albert Ellis' rational emotive psychotherapy.

Beck's Cognitive Therapy

Within Beck's model, there are four levels of cognition: *automatic thoughts, intermediate beliefs, core beliefs,* and *schemas.* Because these terms are key to the process of psychotherapy, we will define them before describing the actual process of psychotherapy.

Automatic thoughts are the ones that provide our evaluation of everyday events. They occur rapidly and therefore do not tend to be in full sentence form. Because they do not seem to have a specific origin, they are called "automatic." Some automatic thoughts are functional while others are disturbing to the person. Regardless of which type of thought occurs, they do seem reasonable to the thinker. Because these thoughts occur so quickly the thinker is usually aware only of the emotion that follows them and not of the actual thought. *Intermediate beliefs* are the absolute rules and assumptions that underlie the automatic thoughts. *Core beliefs* is the term Beck uses to describe the most basic values a person has. These beliefs form the basis of the automatic thoughts and are the most difficult to change in psychotherapy. *Schemas* are the ways we organize the large amounts of information we constantly receive from our environment. Schemas allow us to make sense of our world. We each have unique schemas that allow us to understand our world, our future, and ourselves.

Cognitive therapy is usually a time-limited form of psychotherapy. Depending on the patient and the issues, cognitive therapy typically lasts from four to fourteen sessions (Beck, 1995). The overall goal of psychotherapy is to help the patient identify his or her cognitive errors and correct them. This requires the ability to recognize core beliefs as well as automatic thoughts and their associated emotions. These beliefs, thoughts, and emotions are then evaluated for validity and modified if needed. Therapy is a collaborative activity between the psychologist and the patient. The therapist brings the expertise about cognitions, determining goals for therapy, and how to reach the therapy goals. The patient brings the raw data that will be used in this process. Therefore it is important to establish good rapport so the patient trusts the psychologist. Although cognitive therapists accept the concept of transference as a possibility, they do not encourage it. If they note transference occurring, they treat it like any other cognition and work with the patient to analyze these thoughts. Typically the first few sessions are devoted to assessing the problem, establishing rapport, and outlining the procedures that will be used. This is followed by the use of various techniques to identify and alter inappropriate cognitions. The patient is often given assignments, called homework, to do between sessions. Finally, termination of psychotherapy is planned. Therapists and their patients discuss how the patients can use the information from therapy to help themselves in the future.

Much of the early work on cognitive therapy was with depressed patients. Beck found these patients typically had a similar cognitive triad—negative view of themselves, negative view of their world, and a negative view of the future (Kovacs & Beck, 1978). From this beginning, this cognitive triad of negative cognitions has been found useful in explaining information processing in general.

Cognitive therapists may use a range of techniques during the process of psychotherapy. Beck noted that the selection of technique is based on agreement between the therapist and patient about its use and that its purpose is to alter dysfunctional thinking (Alford & Beck, 1997). Cognitive therapists make extensive use of **Socratic questioning.** This term refers to the process of asking leading questions that guide the person to the conclusion you want him or her to make. Some samples of questions that are useful in dealing with automatic thoughts are given in Table 10.2.

Much work in cognitive therapy actually occurs between sessions. Patients are given homework assignments that are developed collaboratively during the session. The material from these assignments is discussed at the next session. One typical homework assignment

Table 10.2 Common Cognitive Therapy Questions
What is the evidence supporting my thought?
Is there an alternative explanation or explanations for this situation?
What is the worst thing that could happen?
What is the best thing that could happen?
What is the most realistic thing that could happen?
What is the effect of my believing my automatic thoughts?
What could happen if I change my thinking?
What should I do about my thoughts?
What would I tell a friend who was in my situation?

Source: Adapted from Beck, J. S., Cognitive Therapy: Basics and Beyond. *New York: Guilford, 1995.*

is to keep a dysfunctional thought record. This record can be kept on a commercially developed form obtained from the therapist or merely written on a piece of paper. The patient makes a series of columns on a sheet of paper as a guide to the needed information. When discussing automatic thoughts, it is helpful to have brief information about the date and time when the thought occurred. A brief notation of the situation is also made. Later, when going over the record during the therapy session, it may become clear that these thoughts occur more often in certain types of situations or at certain times of the day. Next, patients record their automatic thoughts and the strength of their belief in it. Belief strength is often assessed as a percent, with total belief being 100 percent. For example, the therapist might ask, "What emotion did you feel at that time, and how strong was it?" This information requires the patient to consider not only cognitions but also emotions. It needs to be done at that time rather than trying to remember a particular emotion later. The patient then tries to make a more adaptive response to the situation. Early in therapy, this column may be blank until the patient learns more adaptive ways of viewing distressing situations. The Socratic questioning method can lead the patient to make appropriate responses as long as the therapist is able to think logically from the patient's life data. In other words, if the therapist is going to lead the patient through this form of questioning, the therapist must select questions that are consistent with the patient's life situation. Finally, the patient is asked to write how the outcome is different when alternative responses are used.

Many patients who seek therapy are less active than prior to becoming emotionally distressed. Although this change is typical for depressed patients, it is also seen in other patients. Thus, some record of their activities may be useful in understanding what their life is actually like. In this case, an activity record is kept between therapy sessions. This can be done with a simple time grid for each day. Initially, the patient may just record activities and the length of time in which they occur. Once these baseline data are developed, this homework assignment might be expanded to include feelings of mastery and pleasure for each recorded activity (Beck, 1976). Beck recommends using a scale of 1 to 10 to record each of these characteristics. It is often illuminating for the patient to realize that some activities are done very well but with little pleasure. For example, few people really enjoy scrubbing the toilet in the bathroom. However, some people do a good job of bathroom-cleaning. In this case, the mastery might be rated quite high and the pleasure rated quite low. Such an activity helps patients to make a distinction between these two topics as well as to begin to experience some success, since mastery scores are often rated higher than pleasure scores by patients.

Suppose the patient is having difficulty identifying automatic thoughts. Although this concept may seem reasonably straightforward, some patients have difficulty just stating their automatic thoughts. Even when not under the time pressure of a therapy session, they may find it is easier to identify the emotions on their thought record than to identify their automatic thoughts when facing their clinical psychologist. In this case, the psychologist might use role-playing in the therapy setting. The patient imagines one of the situations described in the thought record and then, with the help of the therapist, visualizes that situation as vividly as possible. The therapist then uses questions to identify the thoughts once the patient actually feels as if the situation is actually happening in the office. Once the automatic thoughts have been identified, role-play can also be used to practice more adaptive responses to that situation.

Cognitive therapy comes from a research base. Perhaps because it was one of the early manualized forms of psychotherapy, was used as the treatment of choice for patients with depression, and yields good outcome measures, there is a rather large research literature on cognitive therapy. Generally these studies have reported positive outcomes for cognitive therapy with depressed patients (e.g., Dobson, 1989; Gloaguen, Cottraux, Cucherat, & Blackburn, 1998). A review of meta-analyses of treatment outcomes with a range of disorders reported large effect sizes for unipolar depression, generalized anxiety disorder, panic disorder with or without agoraphobia, social phobia, and childhood depressive and anxiety disorders (Beck, 2005). Cognitive therapy has also been reported to be effective in preventing further suicide attempts in an adult group of patients who had recently attempted suicide (Brown et al., 2005).

Ellis' Rational Emotive Psychotherapy

Rational emotive therapy (RET), also known as rational emotive behavior therapy (REBT), was developed by clinical psychologist Albert Ellis. This form of therapy involves a combination of cognitive, behavioral, and emotional changes combined with teaching the patient a life philosophy. Ellis (1991) noted that the philosophy of life component is what distinguishes his approach from other forms of cognitive therapy.

Like most forms of psychotherapy, RET includes the importance of the therapeutic relationship. Ellis suggests, however, that the best way to develop a good relationship with the patient is to solve the patient's immediate problem (Ellis & Dryden, 1997). Students who have seen films of Ellis conducting RET may find his style somewhat abrupt or assertive, but his patients tend to describe him with warmth and respect (Walen, DiGiusseppe, & Wessler, 1980).

Ellis developed a model of dysfunctional behavior that is sometimes called the A-B-C model. This model is explained to the patient in the therapy relationship. In summary form, he noted that it is not what happens to us that causes us to experience emotional problems but rather our interpretation of what happens that causes the problem. To make this system easy to understand, he used an alphabet model to label each stage of this process. He even included the intervention procedures in his alphabet description, thus adding "D" and "E" to the earlier three letters (Ellis, 1962, 2000).

The "A" in this sequence is the **activating event.** The activating event is what most people associate with their distress. They say that this particular event caused them to feel anxious, depressed, or some other negative emotion. In RET, there are two facets of the activating event. First there is the actual event and then there is what the patient perceived to have happened. It is important for the psychologist to ask sufficient questions to get a clear picture of what did happen. In some cases, this may even require obtaining outside information with the patient's permission depending on the nature of the event.

Although it is traditional to go directly through the alphabet when discussing topics that are alphabetized, most descriptions of RET cover "C" before discussing "B," and we will follow that tradition. In this system, "C" refers to the *consequences* of the event. These consequences are often the presenting problem that brought the patient to the psychologist's office. "I feel hurt by my husband" is a consequence. It is the reaction this patient has to something her husband said or did. It is important to distinguish between a belief and a consequence. A consequence is a feeling. Unlike a belief, that consequence cannot be disputed. The patient must be willing to have these consequences change but they will not be the focus of the therapy.

The "B" refers to *beliefs.* There are two types of beliefs. One type is rational and the other is irrational. Irrational beliefs are exaggerated and absolutistic. They do not facilitate constructive action because they view either success or failure in extreme terms. These are the beliefs that lead to upsetting feelings and may bring a person to decide it is time for psychotherapy. According to RET, we may not have a choice about activating events in our lives but we do have a choice about the beliefs we attach to them. Ellis and his colleagues identified twelve common irrational beliefs (Ellis & Grieger, 1977). Table 10.3 provides a summary of these irrational beliefs.

Table 10.3 Ellis' Common Irrational Beliefs

1. I must have sincere love and approval almost all the time from people who are important to me.
2. I must either be thoroughly competent and achieving or at least have real competence at something important or I am worthless.
3. People who do bad things to me, or just do bad things, are evil and I should blame them and they should be punished for their sins.
4. Life is awful and catastrophic when it does not go the way I want it to go.
5. My unhappiness is caused by external events that I cannot control. I cannot control my feelings or rid myself of negative emotions.
6. If I find something dangerous or fearsome, I must become terribly occupied with it and upset by it.
7. It is easier to avoid facing life's difficulties than to face them.
8. My past is all-important. If something once influenced my feelings, it must continue to do so.
9. Things should turn out better than they do and it is horrible if I can't quickly find good solutions to life's hassles.
10. I can find happiness if I am passive and noncommital.
11. I must find the single correct solution that always exists for life's problems, and if I can't find it I will be really upset.
12. I must give myself a global rating as a human being, and my sense of self-worth depends on how well I perform and how much others approve of me.

Source: Adapted from Ellis, A., and Greiger, R., eds. Handbook of Rational-Emotive Therapy: Vol. 1. *New York: Springer, 1977.*

In the RET model, "D" refers to *disputing*. After the patient learns the A-B-C model, then it is time to dispute the irrational beliefs. Disputing involves three different parts: detecting, discriminating, and debating. The psychologist starts by detecting the irrational beliefs in the client. Once that has occurred, the psychologist then helps the patient detect those irrational beliefs in his or her own perceptions. The same irrational belief may be detected underlying several activating events in this person's life. Next, the patient learns to discriminate between rational and irrational beliefs. Some key words that help the patient identify irrational beliefs are *must, should,* and *ought*. These terms tend to imply unrealistic demands patients are placing on themselves. Once these demands have been identified, it is time to dispute or debate those irrational beliefs. Psychologists use a range of methods to dispute the irrational beliefs, including the lecture, Socratic debate, humor, and self-disclosure. Ellis even developed some songs, such as *Love Me, Love Me, Only Me!* and *I Wish I Were Not Crazy,* which the psychologist can sing to patients about their irrational beliefs. These songs are set to such tunes as "Yankee Doodle Dandy" and "Dixie." Regardless of the method used, it is important to make sure the patient understands what has been explained. The psychologist does not accept a simple response of "I see" from the patient. The goal is not to have the patient merely accept the psychologist's position but rather to learn to think in a new way. When humor is used, it is important to make sure patients understand that the psychologist is not making fun of them but just making fun of their irrational beliefs. This distinction is extremely important for the maintenance of rapport between the therapist and the patient. Self-disclosure is used in some cases to indicate that the psychologist has used the A-B-C method to deal with his or her own irrational beliefs. This may give the patient greater confidence in the process.

Finally the patient is ready for "E," or *effect*. Patients who have successfully disputed their irrational beliefs are ready to develop an effective life philosophy. They develop rational thoughts to replace their irrational ones. The result of this change is engaging in more productive behaviors and experiencing less negative emotion such as depression or anxiety.

RET does not end when therapy is completed for that day. Ellis and his colleagues have developed numerous self-help books. These books are recommended to patients as a way to reinforce the points made during the session. Another technique often used outside the therapy session is to have the patient teach the principles of RET to friends. By trying to teach others how to use this method, the patient may also develop more effective ways to dispute his or her own irrational beliefs.

There is an extensive research base for RET. Many of these studies have been strongly supportive of RET (e.g., McGovern & Silverman, 1986). Some meta-analyses, however, have reported that although RET was found to be better than either a placebo or control group it was no different in efficacy from some other forms of intervention (e.g., Engles, Garnefski, & Diekstra, 1993).

Schools Emphasizing Behavior or Actions

Most psychologists accept the concept that thoughts and actions impact each other. Some schools of psychotherapy place significant focus on the behavior or action of the patient. This does not mean that they ignore other aspects of people's lives such as their history or cognitions. It merely is an indication of the emphasis of the therapeutic process.

In some respects, it is easier to deal with behavior than with the other concepts we have discussed. Consider the following two questions. What were you doing in the late afternoon last Saturday? What were you thinking and feeling in the late afternoon last Saturday? Most people find that answering the first of these questions is much easier than answering the second one unless something rather unusual was happening in the late afternoon last Saturday. People seldom come to a psychologist because they are concerned about their cognitions; they do come because of a concern about their behavior.

Because behavior is public, patients are more likely to be more comfortable talking about their behavior than they are talking about their emotions, which are private. Most of us have been socialized to keep our emotions private, so we are not accustomed to talking about them with anyone. Thus, patients may also be more accurate describing behavior than describing emotion because of their familiarity with discussing behaviors. It is also usually easier to measure behavior than it is to measure emotion. We can measure not only the behavior of interest but also any change in that behavior as a possible result of psychotherapy. We must infer changes in cognitions based on behavioral changes or accept the word of the patient about those changed cognitions.

Behavior Therapy

Behavior therapy is a general term that is used to describe the work of a number of different individuals. Regardless of the specific clinician, however, these approaches to psychotherapy are grounded in learning theory research. Some approaches emphasize classical conditioning, while others emphasize operant conditioning. Some behavior therapies even include cognitive components, but the emphasis is on behavior, and they are therefore considered behavioral rather than cognitive approaches.

Two early case studies are often discussed as forming the foundation for the rise of behavior therapy. The first of these studies was the conditioning of an eleven-month-old child named Albert to fear furry objects (Watson & Rayner, 1920). Watson and Rayner paired an initially neutral object, a white rat, with a sudden loud noise. Prior to the intervention, Albert demonstrated no fear of the rat but rather an initial interest in touching it. After multiple pairings of the white rat with the loud noise, Albert showed fear at the sight of the rat. This fear also generalized to other furry objects, such as a Santa Claus mask, that had not been feared previously. This study is often cited as evidence that *abnormal behavior* can be learned. This concept was in direct contrast to the focus on internal dynamics of the psychoanalytic and psychodynamic theories. A related early study demonstrated that fears can be removed (extinguished) by a similar conditioning process (Jones, 1924). In this case a two-year-old boy named Peter was already afraid of furry objects such as rabbits. The rabbit in a cage was gradually brought closer to Peter while Peter was eating favorite foods. Over time, this pairing led to the extinction of Peter's fear. Of course, it is important when using such a technique to make sure that the fear is not so strong that it will lead to the patient developing an aversion to food as well as to the previously feared object.

These two case studies illustrate one of the major features of behavior therapy—the emphasis on specific goals. In behavior therapy, the therapist and patient identify the reasons a problem behavior persists and then develop a method for removing that problem. Of course, many patients present with more than one problem. In most cases, the therapist and patient determine which problem needs to be addressed first and then move on to the next one. In some cases, however, problems may be treated simultaneously using either the same or a different behavioral technique. Some early behavior therapists worked only with observable, measurable behaviors such as those in the two case studies just cited. Contemporary behavior therapy, however, tends to include cognitive and emotional factors as well as observable behavior (Fishman & Franks, 1997).

The goal of behavior therapy is quite simple: You want to reduce or eliminate a maladaptive behavior and increase or teach an adaptive behavior to replace the maladaptive one. A number of techniques have been developed to assist the patient in reaching this goal.

One widely used and well-researched behavioral technique is **systematic desensitization** (Wolpe, 1958). The premise underlying this technique is that a person cannot be relaxed and anxious at the same time. The method teaches the patient to relax and then gradually introduces the anxiety-producing stimulus. Psychologists using this technique start with an extensive patient history. This history-taking may include a behavioral assessment plus several interviews in order to obtain a solid understanding of the problem and to determine whether or not systematic desensitization is an appropriate intervention technique. In cases in which systematic desensitization is determined to be appropriate, the psychologist will spend time explaining how the patient has learned to become anxious and what will happen during the treatment process. This treatment requires work on the part of the patient and therefore it is important to determine whether or not the patient is willing to commit to do that work. If the patient agrees, then two activities are needed. The patient must be taught a relaxation procedure and an anxiety hierarchy must be created. Because the steps of the anxiety hierarchy will be taken by mental imagery, it is also important to determine whether the patient has adequate visualization skills. This can be done by having the patient try to place himself or herself mentally in a pleasant scene and then describe that scene to the psychologist. The patient should appear somewhat relaxed since this scene is self-described as pleasant. As with dream analysis, the concept of anxiety hierarchies has led to publication of standard hierarchies. These are not actually recommended for use with an individual patient but may serve as a guide to the beginning therapist as well as be part of the learning tool for the patient. The actual hierarchy used with a specific patient needs to be individually designed for that patient's life situation.

A variety of relaxation methods have been used with systematic desensitization. It is important to teach the patient a relaxation method that he or she can practice and learn to use well. A common approach is based on the concept of progressive muscular relaxation (Jacobson, 1938). In this case, the patient is taught to tense and then relax each muscle group. This procedure is done until all major muscle groups in the body are relaxed. Part of this process is to teach the patient to note when muscles begin to tense rather than wait for muscle pain to indicate tension has occurred. Many patients do not even realize how tense they are until they have learned to relax their muscles. This relaxation process is learned like any other skill. It requires practice. Thus, although it is first taught in the therapist's office, the patient is asked to practice it daily between sessions. Psychologists who use this procedure on a regular basis may find it useful to have a reclining chair in their office. This type of chair provides support for more parts of the body than the typical office chair, thus facilitating the relaxation process. The number of sessions needed for the patient to learn this process will vary depending on the degree of tension, the amount of practice the patient actually does, and the skill of the therapist in teaching this behavior. Some therapists tape the relaxation instructions for their patients so that they do not have to remember which muscle group to tense after relaxing another one.

The patient and therapist work together to develop the anxiety hierarchy. A typical hierarchy includes about twenty to twenty-five items. Individual items are developed based on discussions of the situations in which the patient becomes anxious. Once a selection of these items has been formed, they are ordered based on the degree of anxiety experienced in each situation. They are listed from the least anxiety-producing situation to the most anxiety-producing situation. To make this list easier for the patient, some psychologists will suggest that they assign a number between 1 and 100 to each item. In this case, 1 is being calm and 100 is the most anxious the person has ever felt. It is important for the therapist to listen carefully to what the patient says about the personal experience of anxiety because hierarchy order may not seem logical to the psychologist but is actually correct for the patient. For example, a patient who is afraid of the dark might rate turning off the room light at night as producing more anxiety than lying in her bed in a dark room. The distance between items should be about equal numerically.

When the patient has learned to become relaxed and the anxiety hierarchy has been developed, it is time to combine these two aspects of the therapy. First, the patient is asked to relax. By now, this process should not require more than ten minutes or so. When the patient indicates a state of relaxation, the psychologist will assist with visualization of the least-anxiety producing item from the hierarchy. The psychologist will help the patient maintain visualization of this situation for about ten seconds unless the patient begins to lose the relaxation. In that case, the scene will immediately be removed from visualization and be replaced with a previously determined pleasant scene. After ten seconds or so of successful positive visualization, the scene is removed so that the patient can remain relaxed. This relaxation period occurs before revisualizing the anxiety-producing scene. This process of scene visualization and removal continues across therapy sessions until the patient is able to remain relaxed for all scenes. When the patient has more than one problem that fits this model, several hierarchies can be used. In those cases, part of each session may be devoted to each of the hierarchies. Although reaching the highest item and remaining relaxed ends the process, most psychologists also encourage their patients to experience these situations gradually in real life after they have reached the point of visual comfort with them before determining that therapy is completed.

Another behavior therapy technique is the **token economy.** This approach is used when the psychologist or others, like parents, have significant control over the reinforcements in the patient's life. Although it can be used on an individual basis it has been used more often in institutional settings, such as a unit in a hospital. One of the early descriptions of this behavioral technique was of a program designed to increase socially desirable behavior among hospitalized patients with a diagnosis of schizophrenia (Ayllon & Azrin, 1965).

In order to develop a token economy, the desired behavior must be operationalized. This behavior must be understood in the same way by each staff member as well as by the patients. Thus it requires both staff training and cooperation if the program is to be successful. The staff will need to keep detailed records of the occurrence of the behaviors of each patient in the program. There must also be a clearly understood token that is given after the desired behavior occurs. In some cases, this is a poker chip of a specific color; in other cases, a special mark on a chart. Finally, there must be backup reinforcers. The tokens are not sufficient for behavior to change. Patients must be able to exchange the tokens on a scheduled basis for backup reinforcers. Although some of the early token economy programs made all reinforcers in the institution part of the program, legal decisions now require certain things such as a bed, meals, and privacy to be part of what every patient receives. Therefore, if a token economy is going to be successful, there must be sufficient privileges of interest to the patient that can be earned with tokens. These reinforcers might include an extra dessert with dinner, extra TV time, or even selection of the TV program to be watched that evening on the hospital unit. Of course, the ultimate goal of these programs is to have the patients' behavior improve to a level where they no longer require hospitalization. The question then arises as to whether these behavior changes will generalize to other settings. Data have supported such generalization (e.g., Paul, Redfield, & Lentz, 1976).

Systematic desensitization and token economies are just two of many techniques that are used by behavior therapists. Individual research studies as well as meta-analyses have generally been supportive of behavioral techniques. For example, one meta-analysis of seventy-four studies reported that behavioral and cognitive-behavioral treatments were superior to person-centered therapy, psychodynamic therapy, and control groups (Grawe, Donati, & Bernauer, 1998). Similar data are reported by a number of other meta-analyses.

Reality Therapy

Psychiatrist William Glasser (1965) developed reality therapy. Although he is a psychiatrist, Glasser strongly objects to viewing mental illness from a biological perspective (Glasser, 2003). He feels that the trend toward medication for biological causes of psychological distress has led his profession to ignore the importance of the doctor-patient relationship and taking time to provide counseling. The original reality therapy was radically revised in 1996 to emphasize the importance of relationships (Wubbolding, 2000).

Reality therapists do not tend to use formal psychological assessment tools. For them, assessment is an ongoing process throughout therapy. They do this by asking patients what they need. These needs are met by closing the gap between what they perceive they are getting from their environment and what they would like to get. They also avoid using diagnostic labels whenever they can because they believe such labels are harmful to the patient rather than helpful. The focus of patient assessment is to understand what relationship or relationships are problematic for the patient.

The main goal of reality therapy is to help patients make better choices in life and therefore have greater control over their lives. Better choices are ones that help them but also do not harm others. Although the patient may want to focus on feelings, the reality therapist points out that feelings change only when he or she thinks and acts more effectively. When patients focus on the behavior of others, the reality therapist will point out that the only person's behavior they can control is their own. The patient and therapist work as a team to reach the goal. The psychologist helps patients to explore and evaluate their choices. This teamwork leads to a more friendly relationship between the psychologist and the patient than is found in most forms of therapy. This does not mean, however, that they form dual relationships or other unethical behavior. Reality therapy emphasizes the therapist characteristics suggested by Carl Rogers of empathy, genuineness, and positive regard to facilitate the therapeutic alliance.

Reality therapy uses a broad range of interventions to reach the desired goal. Reality therapists ask a large number of questions of their patients. One reason for these questions is to be highly specific about what the patient really wants. These questions are designed to get patients to take a careful look at their lives rather than having the therapist tell them what to change. They also enable the therapist to get a more internal view of the patient. Table 10.4 presents some typical questions that might be used by a reality therapist.

Reality therapists make considerable use of **bibliotherapy.** Glasser has written numerous books for patients rather than just for professionals. Reality therapists often recommend these books to their patients as a way to help them understand the therapeutic process.

In addition, reality therapists commonly use metaphors. Whenever possible, the therapist uses metaphors based on comments made by the patient. For example, consider the patient who says she really enjoys football and has season tickets for her local team. The therapist might talk to her about the fact that her attempts to reach her goals thus far have been like a quarterback who does not communicate well with his center and often misses the ball.

Glasser makes a distinction between positive addictions and negative addictions. He suggests that one method for overcoming such negative addictions as abusing substances is to develop positive addictions. Positive addictions help move you toward mental health but do not dominate your life. Some examples of positive addictions are journal-writing and regular exercise. Glasser lets his patients know that developing a positive addiction is not done quickly. He has found that most people require anywhere from six months to two years to actually do this. They must practice their positive addictions regularly before they reach the desired level. Practice requires between forty-five and sixty minutes each time the behavior is tried.

Reality therapists use paradoxical interventions that are similar to those suggested by existential therapist Viktor Frankl (1967). These interventions are most likely to be used

Table 10.4 Common Reality Therapy Questions

What do you want, or what do you really want?
What are you doing?
What is your plan?
What will happen if you continue what you are doing?
Is what you are now choosing to do (your actions and thoughts) getting you what you want?
What is going right in your life?

Source: Adapted from Glasser, W. Reality therapy. In J. K. Zoig, ed., The Evolution of Psychotherapy: The Second Conference, *270–278. New York: Brunner/Mazel, 1992; Howatt, W. A. The evolution of reality therapy to choice theory. International Journal of* Reality Therapy, 21*(2001): 7–11;* Wubbolding, R. E. Reality Therapy for the 21st Century. *Philadelphia: Brunner-Routledge, 2000.*

when the patient is resistant to actually following through on plans that he or she makes with the therapist. Paradoxical interventions involve telling the patient to do just the opposite of what is actually desired. Obviously, the psychologist must be careful when using this particular type of intervention. You do not want to suggest that your patient do something dangerous or harmful. Basically, paradoxical interventions are used when either following the requirement or not doing so will both lead to positive outcomes. They should not be used with patients who have paranoid tendencies because they tend to make that patient even more suspicious of the psychologist than he or she already was. Consider, however, a patient who tends to be perfectionistic. He is terrified of making mistakes in any part of his life. Recently, he has been reading about what wines should be ordered with what entrees at a restaurant. He becomes overwhelmed with long wine lists and fears he will not remember what wine he is supposed to order with that particular meal. A paradoxical intervention in this case would be to tell him to order the wine he feels is least appropriate for the entree his guest has ordered. If he resists the suggestion and orders a wine he has learned is appropriate, he no longer has the problem. On the other hand, if he orders a wine that totally overwhelms the food he has demonstrated that he does have control over his problem. In either case, the intervention has helped the patient.

Research has not been a major focus of Glasser and other reality therapists. They have been more involved in applying their ideas, especially in schools and human services settings, than in conducting outcome studies. Glasser and his colleagues noted, for example, that following the introduction of reality therapy at the Ventura School for Girls (a correctional facility), the rate of recidivism was considerably reduced. This is all the data of interest to them (Glasser, 1969). Some research about reality therapy is published in the *Journal of Reality Therapy* (now called the *International Journal of Reality Therapy*), but the numerous meta-analyses associated with some of the other forms of intervention described in this chapter do not exist. Case studies or descriptions of programs in schools are the most common type of article. One meta-analysis of twenty-one reality therapy studies found that there was a medium size effect but also noted that most of the studies were conducted in schools rather than in hospital or other clinical settings (Radtke, Sapp, & Farrell, 1997).

In this chapter, we presented material about various schools of psychotherapy. These are the traditional ways psychotherapy is first taught. Most practicing clinical psychologists, however, use techniques from more than one of these schools and become eclectic therapists. *Eclectic* does not mean that the therapist just randomly selects techniques to use with a specific patient. It means that the therapist uses those techniques that data support for the particular patient and problem. Because some people infer that *electic* means that the therapist doesn't understand any approach sufficiently well to practice from one school, the term **psychotherapy integration** has begun to appear in the literature (Prochaska & Norcross, 2007). This approach attempts to combine aspects of both the theory and techniques of psychotherapy to better meet patient needs. Today the term *integration movement* is also used for the broader concept. Some of the factors that have contributed to this integration movement are listed in Table 10.5. Over time, so many forms of psychotherapy have been developed that no one can study all of them. One way to handle this large number of approaches is to attempt to take the best aspects of many of

Table 10.5 Development of Therapy Integration

1. Proliferation of forms of psychotherapy
2. Patient needs are too diverse for any single approach
3. Demands for accountability
4. Psychotherapy outcome research
5. Increased use of short-term, problem-focused approaches
6. Organizations encouraging integration

Source: Adapted from Prochaska, J. O., and Norcross, J. C. Systems of Psychotherapy: A Transtheoretical Analysis (6th ed.). Belmont, CA: Thomson Brooks/Cole, 2007.

them and integrate that material. Despite the vast number of forms of psychotherapy that have been developed, no one approach has been demonstrated to be successful with all therapists and all patients. Realization of this fact has contributed to a greater number of therapists being willing to accept the concept that methods other than the one or two they prefer merit a place in the practice of psychotherapy. When a therapist realizes that his or her approach is just not working with a particular patient, that therapist may be more willing to consider the use of a different approach. As therapists see a wider range of patients, they are more likely to have such failure experiences. Issues of accountability in the field of psychotherapy occur for many reasons. Insurance carriers expect psychologists to provide justification for the payments the carrier is providing to them.

Increased attention to the empirical basis for psychotherapy has also led to more informed patients and legislators, who develop policies about psychotherapy reimbursement. Psychotherapy outcome research has continued to thrive. With increased available data, more meta-analyses have been conducted. These data are now available to inform good practice. Recent surveys of practicing psychotherapists suggest that the use of short-term, problem-focused approaches to psychotherapy is increasing. These psychotherapists are selecting those elements of various forms of psychotherapy that seem to work best with the patient with whom they are currently working. Professional associations are also contributing to the growth of integrative psychotherapies. These associations provide conferences devoted to research and practice from this perspective. They also publish journals that publish research from this perspective so that those who are involved have a forum for their work and those who are not using the integrative approach can read about it.

This trend toward integration is likely to be applied in the future to the multicultural approaches to psychotherapy that have arisen to address these needs of specialized groups. Most of the forms of psychotherapy that we have described in this chapter were developed to meet the needs of white, heterosexual patients who come from European heritage. As the U.S. population became more diverse, specialized forms of psychotherapy were developed for these groups (e.g., Comas-Diaz, 2005; Sue, 2003). The allegiance effect we mentioned when discussing brief psychodynamic psychotherapy has also been noted in literature reviews on the effectiveness of multicultural psychotherapies. To date, there are very few well-controlled studies about psychotherapy with culturally diverse patients. Thus we are not devoting a section of this chapter to these approaches but rather

ETHICAL CONUNDRUM POINTS TO PONDER

This psychologist has at least two broad areas to consider. One is competency to treat this patient and the other is the intervention method selected. One area noted under *boundaries of competence* in the *APA Ethical Standards and Code of Conduct* is religion. This does not mean that psychologists treat only those patients who are of their own faith. It does mean, however, that psychologists must note the role a person's religion may have in the treatment. In this case, we have a psychologist and a patient who are of different faiths, and the patient appears to be both conservative and highly influenced by her faith and her priest. The psychologist can do several things to increase understanding of her faith. Peer consultation with a colleague of her faith would be useful. This colleague might also recommend readings that could help the psychologist gain a better understanding of her ideology. The psychologist can also learn from this patient about her religion. Integrating her comments with the peer consultation and reading can give the psychologist a better understanding of how much of this patient's reaction is consistent with her faith and how much may be exaggeration because of her emotional state. It is possible that the plans for using cognitive behavioral interventions can still be used if this learning process is successful. If bibliotherapy has been used with her, the psychologist may want to have a short discussion, using the terms of the therapeutic method, about the role her religion may play in therapy. This discussion needs to be done carefully so that she does not feel her religion is being attacked or viewed as *irrational.* The psychologist may also consider whether some other forms of intervention may be a better fit for them if therapy is to continue. Since the process of debating irrational beliefs has already begun, and a therapeutic relationship may already have been established, transferring her to another psychologist may be harmful to her. If a different form of intervention is going to be used, the psychologist will need to discuss with her the reasons for changing at this point in the therapeutic process. If transfer to another psychologist is considered, this option and the reasons for it should be discussed and a transition process should be developed.

want readers to be sensitive to the research needs in this area. Several edited works provide foundation reading for those interested in pursuing this topic (e.g., Norcross, Beutler, & Levant, 2005; Norcross & Goldfried, 2005).

In the next two chapters, we will talk more about what actually happens in individual, couples, group, and family therapy.

Key Terms

activating event

allegiance effect

automatic thoughts

bibliotherapy

countertransference

dream analysis

free association

incongruence

interpretation

latent content

making the rounds

manifest content

paraphrasing

parapraxis

person-centered
  psychotherapy

psychoanalysis

psychotherapy
  integration

reflection

Socratic questioning

systematic
  desensitization

token economy

topdog-underdog

transference

unconditional
  positive regard

CHAPTER 11

Individual Psychotherapy

In this chapter, we discuss psychotherapy with individual patients. Individual psychotherapy is a common activity among clinical psychologists. It has been popularized in movies and on television. As we noted in previous chapters, members of many different professions practice individual psychotherapy. We will try to give you an overview of how this process works, describe the role expanding technology is playing in the practice of individual psychotherapy, and illustrate the use of psychotherapy with special populations.

Process of Psychotherapy

Psychotherapy moves through a series of stages. It starts with the initial visit by the patient. This first meeting is followed by an assessment of the patient's problems and the development of a treatment plan. Next is the ongoing activity of psychotherapy, in which it is important to maintain the flow and keep the patient involved. Finally is the termination phase. Psychotherapy ends when both the psychologist and the patient agree the time is right. This is not an abrupt ending; often several sessions are devoted to addressing separation issues. It is also important to realize that these stages of psychotherapy are not rigid. There is considerable overlap among them. Not all of the important information will be gathered during the initial interview. The psychologist continues to gather information through the therapy process. As new issues arise, there may be a need to return to the assessment phase. Let's consider this sequence of events more closely.

ETHICAL CONUNDRUM

You are a clinical psychologist in full-time private practice specializing in work with women. Mrs. Mom has an initial interview with you and you agree to accept her as a patient. After several individual psychotherapy sessions, she tells you that her husband's work schedule has changed for the next two months and he can no longer watch the children while she comes for her sessions. She believes therapy is helping her and wants to continue but is unable to come during any of your regular hours. A sitter is not an option in this case. She asks if you could conduct sessions by Internet until her husband's schedule changes. What are the ethical issues you need to consider?

Some psychologists view the psychotherapy process as starting with the *initial patient contact*. At this time, the patient may not really be aware of the exact nature of the problem. Many people do not know what to expect when they first enter the psychologist's office. This initial contact needs to be handled sensitively so that the patient is sufficiently comfortable to discuss personal problems. The limits of confidentiality need to be discussed before the patient begins to reveal information. During this session, the psychologist will also need to decide whether or not this patient-therapist match has the potential to work. Sometimes this session includes information about payment, availability of appointments, and overall technical parts of the relationship. In other cases, a business manager for the office handles these details before the patient actually sees the psychologist. By the end of this initial session, the psychologist needs to decide whether to schedule another appointment with this patient, determine if referral to another professional for services or consultation is needed, and in general terms provide the patient with information about the overall expected therapeutic process. The decision to continue meeting is not totally the psychologist's option. During this initial session, the patient is also deciding whether he or she is comfortable with the psychologist and what the psychologist proposes. If the psychologist and patient mutually agree, psychotherapy can proceed.

The initial contact is followed by a more detailed *assessment* of the patient in the next session or sessions. This assessment may involve some of the psychological tests we discussed in chapters 6, 7, and 8. Whether or not psychological tests are used will depend on a combination of the patient's problems and the therapist's orientation. Some health insurance policies that cover psychotherapy do not reimburse for psychological tests; those that do typically require prior permission from the insurance company. Some treatment facilities use specific psychological tests as part of their routine evaluation of patients who are treated there. The use of standard assessment batteries has decreased with the growth of managed care policies that frequently do not reimburse for psychological testing. In some cases, this assessment process will involve more detailed interviewing than was possible in the initial session. If the patient has a complex problem or has some difficulty expressing the problem, the assessment process may require several sessions. Some psychologists use psychological assessment at various points in the therapy process to evaluate their patients' progress.

If consultation with other professionals is part of the assessment process, the psychologist will need to wait for the outcome of that consultation before being able to establish a treatment plan. For example, suppose one of the patient's complaints is the frequent occurrence of headaches. It is important to rule out any medical cause of these headaches before assuming they are caused by psychological factors. Even in cases in which the psychologist has established a solid temporal relationship between stressful events and the onset of headaches it is important to have the patient evaluated by a medical professional to rule out such causes as tumors or other medical conditions that also cause headaches. Even when consultation is sought, the psychologist may continue to see the patient to obtain further information and begin therapy while awaiting the consultant's findings. The treatment plan can then be amended based on the consultant's findings.

When the psychologist has developed a reasonable understanding of what is involved in the patient's distress, he or she will develop **treatment goals.** These goals are the desired outcome of psychotherapy. Some psychologists use formal goals, while others discuss them in more general terms with the patient. As insurance companies continue to require greater documentation of service prior to reimbursing professionals, the more formalized process of having specific *treatment plans* has become more frequent.

Treatment Plan

If you think about the way individual psychotherapy is portrayed in film, you may believe that there is no overall plan for this activity. The patient sits down in the therapist's office and talks about problems and the wise therapist responds. In actual practice, however, psychotherapists develop **treatment plans.** A treatment plan is an overview of what the therapist hopes to accomplish with this patient. Because new issues may arise during the course of psychotherapy, this treatment plan is not static. It should be revised to reflect changes in the direction of psychotherapy. It is not unusual for the therapist to write a general plan and discuss it with the patient so the issues that will be the focus of psychotherapy are mutually agreed upon. The language used in the treatment plan will vary depending on the theoretical orientation of the therapist. For example, a behaviorally oriented therapist might include "completing the current semester with no grade lower than a C" in the treatment plan for a college student who is having academic difficulties but is intellectually capable of completing the work. A more dynamically oriented therapist might include "development of a better balance between the ego and superego" in the treatment plan of a patient who is seeking treatment for an overly rigid view of the world leading to social isolation. The written treatment plan helps both the patient and the therapist remain aware of the reasons for psychotherapy. Over time, the general purpose of therapy can become lost in individual events or crises. From a more practical perspective, the written treatment plan aids accountability with third-party payers.

How does the psychotherapist develop this treatment plan? Treatment plans vary depending on the theoretical model used by the therapist (e.g., medical model, insight-oriented, rational). We will use the medical model to illustrate this process. The first step is the patient history. We discussed the process of interviewing and assessment in earlier chapters. The psychologist integrates the information gathered from these activities into an understanding of the major issues the person faces. These issues form the basis for identifying specific problems. The problems will become the basis of psychotherapy.

Some treatment facilities have a specific format for writing a treatment plan; others leave the format to the psychologist. We will describe a six-step model to illustrate the development of a treatment plan (Jongsma, 2005) (see also Table 11.1).

During the initial interview as well as during assessment, patients discuss many different aspects of their lives. One role of the clinical psychologist is to sift through all of this information to find the actual problems that led this person to seek psychotherapy. We are not implying that patients try to trick you; most people who voluntarily seek individual psychotherapy help you sort through their issues for the core problems. Some issues may not be as urgent for the patient as others are. Thus part of *problem selection* is to set priorities among many problems facing the patient. For example, suppose you are seeing a fifty-five-year-old bank executive. During her interview, she talks about her company's retirement policy, her relationship with her daughter, her brief affair with a neighbor, her relationship with her husband, and her concern about the rising crime statistics in her neighborhood. These topics are interrelated but also quite broad. If you try to address all of them initially, you will have little focus to psychotherapy. On the other hand, if you select initial problems that are not high priority for her, she may not engage as well in the therapeutic alliance. Thus, as you developed this list you would also work with her about priorities. For example, you might think that since she is only fifty-five years old the retirement question is lower than the relationship issues she has raised.

You are now ready to work on *problem definition*. As you discuss this with her, you learn that the bank has developed a graduated retirement plan for senior executives who have been with the bank for at least twenty years. Since she started with the bank immediately after receiving her M.B.A. she qualifies for that program. On the other hand, she is not sure how this change will impact her identity. She wonders if some of her other problems are an outgrowth of her concern about the meaning of retirement. Further exploration of this topic should lead to a better definition of this problem.

Once you have a better understanding of the meaning of each of your patient's problems, you are ready for *goal development*. You want to have at least one goal for each of the problems you identify. Goals are broad statements. Let's return to our bank executive. One goal related to her concerns about retirement might be to have her determine what "retirement" means to her.

Patients reach treatment goals in small steps. These steps are called *objectives*. With our bank executive, one step might be for her to decide what psychological needs are

Table 11.1 Psychotherapy Treatment Plan Writing

Step 1: Problem selection
Step 2: Problem definition
Step 3: Goal development
Step 4: Objective construction
Step 5: Intervention creation
Step 6: Diagnosis determination

Source: Adapted from Jongsma, A. E. Psychotherapy treatment plan writing. In G. P. Koocher, J. C. Norcross, & S. S. Hill, eds., Psychologists' Desk Reference *(2nd ed.). New York: Oxford, 2005.*

currently being met by her job. Another step would be to consider other ways these same needs could be met.

Once the psychologist and patient have agreed on problems, goals, and objectives, it is actually time to begin the work of psychotherapy. The psychologist needs to decide which intervention processes will work best with this person and this specific problem. The psychologist's decision is based on a combination of prior training and experience, knowledge of the research literature on intervention with this type of problem, and patient characteristics. For example, if you are working with a patient who has a history of problems completing tasks, you probably do not want to start therapy with a focus on complicated homework assignments.

Before starting the actual process of psychotherapy, the psychologist also makes a *diagnosis*. Some psychologists do not approve of the current dominant classification system—DSM-IV. Diagnosis is a reality in today's health care. It is a necessity for third-party reimbursement. Even if your patient is on a fee-for-service basis, future requests for your records may be made. Diagnosis is considered a standard of good record-keeping.

Psychotherapy is really *implementing treatment.* After the psychologist has established treatment goals it is time to decide the best way to reach those goals. Some psychologists may decide to limit treatment to specific goals, while others will work more broadly at the personality change level. The psychologist will explain the proposed treatment to the patient and then they can mutually agree upon the process. This explanation includes at least a tentative timeline. The discussion will also include expectations for both therapist and patient contributions to the process. If the therapist is planning to ask the patient to do work between sessions, such as homework assignments or self-monitoring, this should be discussed before implementing the treatment plan. This is really part of the patient having informed consent for the treatment process.

Most people who enter psychotherapy expect this process will be time-limited. At some point, **termination** is considered. When the therapist determines that the patient is capable of handling his or her own life, discussions about ending psychotherapy become part of the discussion. How long termination takes will vary among both psychologists and patients. In some cases, termination means that a patient who was seen on a weekly basis changes to appointments every other week, then once a month, before finally leaving psychotherapy. Other patients may have a session or two in which they can discuss what has happened in therapy and how they feel about no longer seeing the psychologist. Ideally, the time for termination is a mutual decision of the psychologist and the patient. Some patients, however, may decide to terminate before the psychologist feels they are ready. In such cases, it is desirable whenever possible to discuss the reasons for termination and implications for the patient. Early therapy termination can be the result of changes in the patient's available time or finances. In this case, the psychologist will need to make decisions about whether there is any flexibility within his or her practice to accommodate these changes. If not, a referral to another professional may be needed. In cases in which the patient is moving, once again a referral can be arranged prior to the move. When early termination is the result of patient dissatisfaction with the psychologist, this point also needs to be discussed with the option of a referral or later return being offered. Early termination may also be the decision of the psychologist. In cases in which the psychologist determines that the patient is not likely to benefit from further work with this psychologist, the psychologist is ethically obligated to terminate treatment and make an appropriate referral. This referral is needed in cases in which progress is just not occurring as well as when the psychologist has developed problems that no longer allow effective treatment (APA, 2002). Psychologist problems might include personal psychopathology such as substance abuse/dependence or developing an inappropriate attachment to the patient.

Psychologists frequently offer the option of follow-up or "booster" sessions. In such cases, it is important to make it clear to the patient that taking advantage of this option does not mean that psychotherapy was not successful or that the patient is regressing to the point that many more months of treatment will be needed. These future sessions are intended to review the gains the patient has made as well as to address new problems that may have occurred since the end of therapy. In the case of new problems, it is likely that the psychologist can help the patient determine ways to address these problems using changes that were made in therapy rather than needing multiple sessions to develop totally new strategies. The typical time frame for such follow-up sessions is six months to a year after termination.

Termination is also a time for evaluation of the psychotherapy process. Ideally, the psychologist and patient do this as part of termination. Psychologists should also review their own records to evaluate their treatment program. This information then becomes part of the closing notes in the patient's file.

Special Populations

Although the general concepts about psychotherapy apply to a certain degree with everyone who is seen, there is a large literature about the practice of psychotherapy with special groups. We have selected several of these groups for further discussion. As with our selection of psychological tests in chapters 6, 7, and 8, we could have chosen different special populations to illustrate these issues. Our selection in this case was based on a combination of our personal interests, our desire to present a variety of populations, and the available literature. Two of the populations we selected are based on patient characteristics and the other two are related to the form of psychopathology involved. We use these four patient groups to illustrate the importance of customizing psychotherapy to the specific patient the psychologist sees.

Child Psychotherapy

The psychological functioning of children is related to the psychological functioning of their parents. Therefore, before starting psychotherapy with a child the psychologist needs to assess not only the child but also the parent and the parent-child interaction. Children are not just miniature adults. They are in the process of changing not only biologically but also cognitively and affectively. These latter changes may vary across situations in their lives. It is important for the psychologist not only to know about normal developmental changes in children but also to be aware of how these changes may influence the process of psychotherapy.

Psychotherapy with young children may look more like play than therapy and is sometimes called **play therapy.** It may involve many of the same toys and games the child also has at home or school. Some of the activities involve interaction with the psychologist, such as playing a board game. In other cases, the psychologist may talk to the child while the child is playing with a toy or engaging in an activity such as drawing. As you can see, this term covers a broad range of treatments. Early theorists such as Anna Freud and Jean Piaget wrote about the importance of play to help children deal with unpleasant experiences (Schaefer, 1979). Play therapy is a safe setting for resolving conflicts in the child's life. There are many publications about the meaning of play therapy as well as case studies illustrating the process (e.g., Landreadth, 1982), but little seems to have been published about controlled studies of this process. Child psychotherapy, like adult psychotherapy, has been influenced by managed care, leading to a greater focus on short-term approaches and empirically supported treatments. The role of cultural factors is influencing the development of child psychotherapy just as it is with adults.

Individual child psychotherapy typically involves the child meeting with the therapist once or twice each week for about forty-five minutes (Russ & Freedheim, 2001). During that time, the child structures the hour by choosing both the topics and the types of play. Children do not typically seek therapy; they are brought to the psychologist by their parents. They are referred to the psychologist by their parents, teachers, or pediatricians. Some children are aware of the problems that led to this referral, but others don't feel they have problems. These latter children may resent seeing the psychologist and initially be uncooperative. If the psychologist is going to overcome this resentment, he or she must be able to gain the child's confidence slowly.

There are special issues of confidentiality in child psychotherapy. Depending on the age of the child, the psychologist must clarify the limits of confidentiality with both the child and the parents at the beginning of the therapy process because children under the age of eighteen are not guaranteed confidentiality. Usually the issue of confidentiality becomes more important to the patient as the child approaches the teenage years and the therapist must be very careful about what may or may not be disclosed to parents or teachers. This topic is discussed carefully with both the child individually and in a meeting that includes the child and the parent or parents. Especially with adolescents, specific agreement about confidentiality on certain topics, unless the psychologist feels danger is involved, is important for the establishment of rapport as well as a successful psychotherapeutic outcome. Because school plays such a major role in the lives of children, teacher consultation is often a component of child psychotherapy. Thus, there would need to be an agreement about divulging to the teacher the fact that this child is receiving psychotherapy. Beyond that point, much of what is said in the sessions would remain confidential.

Child psychotherapists have attempted to understand how the change process occurs. Six proposed mechanisms of change are presented in Table 11.2. **Catharsis** and *labeling of feelings* refers to having the child release emotion and express important feelings during therapy. A major task of the psychologist is to help the child to understand that it is safe to express feelings to the psychologist. This is especially true of negative feelings that may have been labeled as inappropriate in other settings. In some cases of play therapy, feelings are attributed to a toy rather than the child. The therapist, when interpreting those feelings, also attributes them to the toy rather than to the child. For

Table 11.2 Child Psychotherapy Change Mechanisms

Catharsis and labeling of feelings
Corrective emotional experience
Insight and working through
Learning alternative problem-solving techniques
Development of internal structure
Nonspecific variables

Source: Adapted from Russ, S. W., and Freedheim, D. K. Psychotherapy with children. In C. E. Walker & M. C. Roberts, eds., Handbook of Clinical Child Psychology *(3rd ed.), 840–859. New York: Wiley, 2001.*

example, the therapist might note that a doll seems to be feeling sad today. The child may have noted that the doll was crying and the therapist then translated that feeling into a label—sad. Once the child has a word for the feelings he or she is experiencing, those feelings do not tend to seem so overwhelming.

The relationship between the psychologist and the child is especially important for developing a **corrective emotional experience.** This term refers to using the therapy situation to reenact emotional situations from the child's life but with different consequences to the child's responses. When a corrective emotional experience occurs multiple times, the child is able to be more comfortable with these emotions and then be able to look at them more closely. Let's look at an example of how this might occur. A six-year-old girl, speaking through a doll, uses multiple curse words toward the therapist. Based on her family experiences, she expects the psychologist to become angry with her and perhaps punish her the way her parents have done. That does not happen. Over time she has associated feelings of guilt and other negative emotions with the use of curse words. The psychologist notes that the doll seems to be angry and she wonders why the doll is angry. She has not told the girl that she is bad; she has not punished her in any way. This psychologist is accepting the girl's feelings of anger and is trying to help her understand the reason for these feelings. Over time, this girl can move away from her internalized feelings of guilt and begin to consider why she is so angry.

Part of child psychotherapy is the development of **insight.** This concept is the same as adult psychotherapy but is developed in a somewhat different way. Accepting verbal labels for emotions starts this process for children. The psychologist then uses these labels to help the child develop links between behavior and feelings. This is done through interpretation of various negative behaviors the child exhibits. Of course, the interpretation needs to be made when the child is ready to hear it and it must be accurate. If it comes too early or is not accurate, the interpretation may disrupt the process rather than facilitate it. Suppose you are working with a five-year-old child who has recently begun to have bouts of enuresis. This child has been toilet-trained since he was three. Your interpretation to him is that you notice that he seems to wet his pants when he thinks his mother does not want him. Your interpretation is related to the fact that his mother has recently told him she is going to have another child. Although the child is not ready to make that link, you can let him know you understand the feelings that have contributed to his enuresis. In addition to seeing the relationship between his feelings and his behavior, this child also benefits from a **working through** process. This child can emotionally reexperience learning about the forthcoming arrival of a sibling by acting out that experience with dolls. Really young children may never reach the cognitive level of insight because they have not developed to the point of being able to do so. They can, however, reexperience distressing events emotionally, for example, by having the mother doll tell the child doll about a new baby while the therapist talks about how that news must make the doll feel scared and wonder if he will get enough attention when the new baby comes. Playing can allow the child to express conflicts and then resolve them.

Psychotherapy often involves learning new ways to handle problems. This process of learning *alternative problem-solving strategies* and ways to cope is especially important in child psychotherapy. Because of their level of cognitive development, adults are more able than children to form their own new coping strategies with some assistance from the psychologist. Children, however, may not have reached that level of cognitive development. In those cases, the psychologist may need to be more directive and actually suggest alternative solutions to current life problems. Some of these suggestions will be made verbally, while others may be given through role playing or modeling new approaches (Singer, 1993).

Some children who enter psychotherapy have failed to develop the necessary personality structure and cognitive functioning to differentiate between fantasy and reality. They confuse their inner and outer worlds. Psychologists who work with these children serve as a stable force in their world. Empathy from the psychologist is one of the key factors in improvement. This ongoing relationship with a stable figure allows the gradual development of the child's cognitive functioning and the strengthening of the child's ego development.

Child psychotherapy specialists have recently begun to examine the importance of *nonspecific variables* in the outcome of their work (Russ & Freedheim, 2001). One such variable is the fact that the child no longer feels alone. Participation in psychotherapy gives the child some expectation that change can actually happen. The child is also aware that his or her family is involved in the psychotherapy, not just him or her. This awareness removes the feeling that the entire situation is a result of something wrong with the child.

Psychotherapy with Women

Some of you may be wondering why psychotherapy with women is any different from psychotherapy with men. With the growth of the women's movement in the early 1970s, some psychologists began to question whether there were gender biases in both the training for, and practice of, psychotherapy with women (Broverman et al., 1970). Gender bias contributes to misdiagnosis as well as ineffective psychotherapy. When a woman's behavior is viewed in the context of gender stereotypes, treatment is likely to focus on helping the woman live up to those stereotypes. This concern led to the growth of **feminist therapy.** Numerous books have been written about this approach to psychotherapy (e.g., Brown, 1994; Enns, 1997; Gilbert & Sher, 1999; Worrell & Remer, 2003). The field has become sufficiently organized that references are also available for work with special subsets of women, such as women of color (Comas-Diaz & Greene, 1994) and lesbian patients (Falco, 1991). There is no single person who is credited with starting feminist therapy. Most psychologists who indicate they practice feminist therapy combine these concepts with other theoretical approaches.

Feminist therapy emphasizes giving the patient more power in the therapeutic relationship by decreasing the power differential between therapist and patient. In many cases, the therapist will have more education than the patient does, regardless of gender. Even when the therapist is working with a well-educated patient, the therapist's specialized education related to emotional problems can facilitate a power differential. A goal of the feminist therapist is to promote an egalitarian relationship with the patient despite the factors that may work against it (Brown, 2000). The feminist therapist is more likely than many other therapists to reveal personal information to the patient. This openness further decreases the power differential. A basis of feminist therapy is to look externally, rather than internally, for significant causal factors of emotional disturbance. A major external focus of feminist therapy is the role of social, political, and economic stresses as a foundation for mental health problems among women. Some general goals of feminist therapy are summarized in Table 11.3. *Symptom removal* is a traditional goal of psychotherapy. In feminist therapy, *symptom* is defined carefully in terms of feminist theory. Symptom removal is only considered appropriate when is does not interfere with the overall goals of feminist theory. For example, consider a woman who is seeking treatment because of her anxiety over conditions in her work setting. The symptoms of her anxiety include feelings of nausea during meetings with her supervisor, who has not recommended her for promotion during the past three evaluation cycles. One treatment option in this case is to treat the symptom of nausea with medication. The feminist therapist would not take that approach. Instead, the feminist therapist would focus on assisting this woman to be more assertive about her qualifications.

Self-esteem refers to the way people feel about themselves. For many women, self-image is tied to public definitions of beauty and expected behavior. Feminist therapy attempts to help the patient move from dependence on external criteria of acceptability to internal criteria.

Interpersonal relationships exist with friends as well as family. A goal of feminist therapy is to improve the quality of these relationships, which means that they meet not only the needs of others but also one's own needs. Patients learn to be more direct and assertive with others. If those with whom the patient interacts do not also change, the relationship may be threatened. Because the quality of the relationship is the key, a

Table 11.3 Feminist Therapy Goals

Symptom removal
Improved self-esteem
Better interpersonal relationships
Body image and sensuality
Attention to diversity
Political awareness and social action

Source: Adapted from Sharf, R. S. Theories of Psychotherapy and Counseling: Concepts and Cases *(2nd ed.). Belmont, CA: Brooks/Cole, 2000.*

potential loss of any relationship is not as important as developing relationships in which the patient can be direct and assertive (Philpot, Brooks, Lusterman, & Nutt, 1997).

Eating disorders are diagnosed more often in women than in men. These disorders are linked to issues of body image. Women are socialized about the importance of physical attractiveness as defined by the media. A goal of feminist therapy is to help women accept their bodies as they exist rather than in comparison to an externally defined ideal. *Sensuality,* or sexual decisions, is closely related to body image. Sexual decisions are also made because of an individual's desires rather than because of coercive forces in that person's life.

Throughout this book, we have discussed the importance of cultural diversity. Feminist therapy was one of the early therapeutic approaches that emphasized valuing cultural diversity. Feminist values sometimes conflict with cultural norms. Feminist therapists value the cultural perspectives of their patients.

The goal of feminist therapy that is most unique is its focus on *political awareness* and *social action.* Part of feminist therapy is to encourage women to become aware of the diverse ways society influences them and then work to change these political systems. They are also encouraged to work for change on a more informal level by calling inequities to the attention of those in their regular life situation. A variety of techniques are used to help patients achieve these goals.

Regardless of the specific techniques, feminist therapists use empowerment, androgyny, and assertiveness training to help their patients reach their therapy goals (Gilbert & Sher, 1999). Empowerment focuses on the social factors that are part of the patient's problems. Through the use of various techniques, the therapist helps the patient become aware of those situations in which she has power in her life. Androgyny is part of the discussion of gender roles and gender stereotypes. Through both discussion and role-play, the woman can explore various masculine and feminine roles. Assertiveness training helps the women learn more active ways to handle her life. She learns to pursue her rights without violating the rights of other people. Assertiveness means being direct and honest without being aggressive.

Regardless of the techniques used, some general suggestions guide the therapy process (Brown & Mueller, 2005). Psychologists doing therapy with women are encouraged to keep up with the growing research on gender issues. This research base is a requirement for ethical clinical practice with women. In addition to the research literature, the psychologist also needs to read about women's psychological, sexual, and interpersonal development. Ethical psychotherapy with women means gathering information about women's diversity rather than viewing all women as being the same.

Some psychologists who work with women focus on particular groups of women and therefore can limit their area of expertise, while others have a more general practice. For example, some psychologists specialize in working with lesbian women and therefore must remain aware of the research and cultural issues of this specific group. If this psychologist also happens to be a woman, she needs to be careful not to make assumptions about her patient's experience as a woman. It is easy to assume that your gender-based experiences are going to be the same, but you may be incorrect. Test selection, when psychological assessment is part of the process, must include evaluation of the standardization samples to ensure that the major characteristics of your patient match that group. Psychologists doing psychotherapy with women are encouraged to pay close attention to the power dynamics in the therapeutic relationship because empowering the patient is a major goal. If the patient does not even feel empowered in her relationship with her psychologist, how can you expect her to feel empowered in other settings? Finally, both the social and political context in which the woman lives are included as part of the psychotherapy process. Thus, the psychologist needs to be aware not only of current laws and mores but also of any changes in law and social policy that specifically impact women.

Specialists in the field suggest that these goals and behaviors are important when conducting therapy with women regardless of whether or not gender is raised as an issue by the patient. Both male and female psychologists can do this type of therapy. The main issue about psychotherapy with women is to consider these topics from the onset of the therapeutic process.

Psychotherapy with Suicidal Patients

Students who are considering psychotherapy as a major part of their careers are likely to be faced with the special issues of working with patients who are at risk of committing suicide. It has been estimated that if you are a typical general practice psychologist, you may see five suicidal patients each month (Bongar & Sullivan, 2005). Psychologists therefore need to obtain the needed knowledge and training to work with these patients if they intend to have a psychotherapy practice.

The possibility that your patient may commit suicide has a number of ramifications for any psychologist. Of course, there is the potential for a malpractice inquiry and/or lawsuit. This outcome is not only stressful for the psychologist but also time-consuming and potentially expensive. The emotional toll on the psychologist also needs to be considered. The psychologist has developed a therapeutic relationship with this person. Like any relationship that is suddenly impacted by death, the psychologist will also feel the effects of a patient's suicide. The impact of patient suicide may influence the psychologist's ability to conduct therapy with other patients for a period of time. It can impair concentration as well as influence how the psychologist views statements and behaviors described by other patients. Data from surveys of psychotherapists suggest that dealing with suicidal patients is the most stressful of all clinical activities (Deutsch, 1984).

Clinical psychologists are typically taught about mandatory hospitalization of suicidal patients starting in graduate school. State laws require psychologists to seek involuntary hospitalization for suicidal patients who will not enter a hospital on a voluntary basis. On the other hand, the opinion of the psychologist may not meet the criteria for hospitalization of the managed care company that may be paying for this hospitalization (Hall, Platt, & Hall, 1999). This situation presents a problem for the psychologist. Most states have legal provisions for temporary hospitalization for observation and evaluation. This period is typically for somewhere between forty-eight hours and seventy-two hours. After that time, the staff in the hospital must convince the insurance company that the person needs further hospitalization if it is going to pay the hospital bills. The courts may also get involved if the patient is involuntarily committed for a longer period of time. We suggest that students who want an overview of issues related to working with suicidal patients should read Bongar's text (2002).

Now we will discuss some of the basic points psychologists consider when doing psychotherapy with patients they view as being at risk to attempt suicide. A core issue is making an accurate diagnosis of the patient. The majority of people who commit suicide were later judged to have been exhibiting the symptoms of a diagnosable mental illness at the time of their suicide. When conducting either an initial interview or doing psychotherapy with a patient who may be at risk for suicide, the psychologist must determine whether it is better to place the person in an inpatient facility for a short period of time or to treat this person in outpatient psychotherapy. Keeping the patient in an inpatient facility for an extended period of time, until the underlying problem has been handled, is not an option unless the patient has the financial ability to pay for the treatment. Insurance companies will not pay for such an extended hospitalization and most individuals cannot afford to pay for it themselves. There is also the issue of their employers. Most employers cannot hold a job indefinitely for a person. Thus, expecting a potentially suicidal patient to remain in the hospital for long periods of time is just not realistic.

A thorough risk assessment of suicidal patients is essential. This assessment requires the psychologist to ask numerous questions about suicidal thoughts and preparation. Has this patient made previous suicide attempts? Does the patient have a well-developed plan and access to the tools necessary to carry out that plan? Let's consider some examples of questions that might be asked. Today, it is quite easy to obtain a handgun. Suppose your patient says, "I would put a gun in my mouth and blow my brains out." An obvious question would be whether or not the patient already owns a gun. If the patient does not yet own a gun, does this patient have some idea of where to buy one and how to use it? Has the patient had any experience with firearms? Let's say the patient does own a gun and knows how to use it. The psychologist would consider the patient's daily routine and try to determine when and where the patient would be most likely to use it. That information would be used to develop supports in the patient's environment to deter such use.

Psychotherapy with patients who are at risk for suicide requires gaining permission to talk to the patient's support system more than most individuals' psychologists see. Although support from significant others can be helpful in many cases, it is essential in cases in which suicide seems probable. For example, consider a patient who does not want to be admitted to the hospital because of fear of job loss. The psychologist investigates and agrees that this perception is realistic. On the other hand, the person has strong suicidal ideation and has previously made three suicide attempts. The psychologist believes this person is "at risk." In addition, the psychologist believes losing his job will lower this patient's hope to the point that another suicide attempt is even more likely to occur. In this case, the psychologist might obtain written permission from this patient to talk to his wife about his condition. His wife would be asked to be sure her husband is not left alone at any time. The patient would also need to agree to this condition of remaining in outpatient psychotherapy. The patient would agree to call the psychologist if he decided he was going to commit suicide. The psychologist would also ensure that this man was aware of other community resources in case he was unable to reach the psychologist immediately. Although psychologists are required to be available through either an answering service or some form of backup coverage, suicidal patients may not wait for a return call. Thus, the psychologist in this case would also want to discuss suicide phone services as well as the nearest emergency room where the patient could go. All of this information, including risk assessment, is also documented in the patient's case records.

This documentation is necessary in case of later malpractice questions and as an ongoing best practice for all patients.

The psychologist must also be aware of any medical conditions that may be relevant to the suicidal ideation. In some cases, the patient may need to be referred to a medical specialist for evaluation of a medical condition that may be contributing to the suicidal ideation but has not yet been diagnosed. In other cases, the psychologist may need to refer the patient to a medical professional for medication to be used as an adjunct to psychotherapy unless the psychologist has prescriptive authority. In cases in which the patient is simultaneously under the care of a medical professional and the psychologist, it is imperative for the psychologist to get permission to speak to the medical professional. The physician needs to be aware of the suicide potential when considering medication for this person and the psychologist needs to know the potential side effects of any medication this patient may be taking.

Taking special precautions and continuously checking on them is certainly important when doing psychotherapy with suicidal patients. The psychologist must always remember that the therapeutic alliance may be the true key to success. During psychotherapy with these patients, the psychologist continuously reevaluates the relationship he or she has with the patient. The stronger the alliance, the better chance there will be of a positive outcome. If the psychologist feels uncertain about any of the facets of work with this patient, this is a case in which collegial consultation is essential.

Work with suicidal patients has been viewed not only from the individual patient perspective but also from an organizational perspective. We will briefly note one example of this broader perspective. Mental health services within the military have been conceptualized as somewhat unique. However, treatment of suicidal patients in that setting raises most of the same issues we have just noted. Therefore, programs developed by the military have the potential to assist other organizational settings in providing better services to their members. The Air Force Medical System designed a program, Managing Suicidal Behavior (MSB), to help its behavioral health practitioners provide better care to suicidal patients and to have more confidence in their ability to handle this problem when it arises. After they complete their evaluation of the effectiveness of the MSB, the Air Force hopes this program can be applied to such civilian organizational settings as universities, school districts, and other occupational-based communities (Oordt et al., 2005). This project illustrates not only the importance of working with suicidal patients but also one way various specialty settings can work together to improve patient care.

Psychotherapy with Cognitively Impaired Adults

There are many causes of cognitive impairment in adults. We chose this category for inclusion here because the goals of psychotherapy with these patients are somewhat different from those with many other patients. In these cases, the psychologist is working with the patient to assist in adaptation to changes in that person's life as well as personal changes. In chapter 15, we discuss the growing specialty of clinical geropsychology. Older adults are at greater risk than younger adults for such forms of cognitive impairment as dementia. Thus, clinical psychologists providing services to this population need to consider the modifications to psychotherapy that may be needed. Older adults, however, are not the only adult patients clinical psychologists treat who are cognitively impaired. Strokes and traumatic brain injury may also lead to such impairment. Thus, psychologists who work in nursing homes and other settings specializing in geriatric care as well as those who work in rehabilitation settings must be aware of needed modifications in their psychotherapeutic approaches. Clinical psychologists in general outpatient practices may also see these patients.

Cognitively impaired adults seldom seek psychotherapy on their own. These patients are more likely to be referred to the psychologist by medical personnel who are also treating them, by community agencies from whom they receive services, or from family members who are having trouble coping with their changed behavior. Thus, forming a therapeutic alliance with this patient is starting from a more distant point than with adults who are self-referred. The therapeutic alliance combined with the specific form of cognitive impairment will determine the modifications to psychotherapy that are needed. For example, these patients may not be able to work collaboratively with the psychologist to determine treatment goals. The psychologist must also be aware of any personal biases or assumptions that may interfere with developing the best treatment model. It is important not to place total focus on the person's impairment because this can lead to viewing the patient from a disability perspective. An alternative way to view these patients is from the perspective that they are a minority group (Kortte, Hill-Briggs, & Wegener, 2005). Psychologists who use this model are more likely to focus on the patient's strengths and how to maximize them in the patient's environment.

Psychologists who work with cognitively impaired adults are likely to find that they work closely with a number of other professionals who are part of this patient's treatment team. The treatment team approach is common in rehabilitation hospitals but it can also be part of the treatment plan for patients who are seeing psychologists in the community. These psychologists may develop consulting relationships with other specialties who also work with cognitively impaired adults—physical therapists, occupational/recreational therapists, speech-language therapists, and physicians. These psychologists also need to be aware of community resources such as support groups and vocational rehabilitation services for their patients. Of course, these psychologists should also be aware of the special legal rights of their patients as specified in the Americans with Disability Act (ADA) of 1990 (P.L. 101–336).

The psychotherapy modifications that are useful when working with cognitively impaired adults fall into the broad categories of communication, environment, and external aids (Kortte et al., 2005). Let's see how each of these categories alters psychotherapy. Psychologists spend many years in school. They usually have strong verbal skills and a good vocabulary. They are accustomed to speaking and writing in long, complex sentences. When working with cognitively impaired adults, however, they need to speak in fairly short sentences. Not only are these sentences short but their language needs to be kept simple.

The psychotherapy environment may require modification when working with cognitively impaired adults. Part of the assessment process will be to determine the time of day when the patient functions at his or her best level. Psychotherapy should be scheduled at this time of the day to optimize the outcome even if this means making some alternations in the psychologist's schedule. Because these patients often have difficulty attending for extended periods of time, shorter sessions should be scheduled, but they should also occur more often than is typical. Psychologists may also need to be more flexible about contact with the patient between sessions to assist the patient in using the information from sessions. It is important to keep distractions out of the psychotherapy office with any patient but is even more important with the cognitively impaired adult.

External aids can be used with any patient. They are especially important, however, when working with cognitively impaired patients. These aids help the patient follow what is happening. For example, the psychologist may develop an agenda for the therapy sessions and share that agenda with the patient. This may sound rather mechanical to some of you. However, it allows the patient to keep track of what is happening. It is also helpful to keep ongoing records of changes in the patient's behavior. These records may be rating scales or some other method depending on the nature of the problem and the psychologist's theoretical orientation. These patients often demonstrate subtle changes that are important. It may be difficult for the psychologist to realize they have happened without being able to follow data. Other external aids that may help the patient recover function are pictures or scrapbooks from the patient's past.

Technology

We discuss many technology topics in chapter 16 on the future of clinical psychology because this is a growing area. Technology, however, has some special uses related to psychotherapy. We will limit this discussion to current forms of technology that are especially important for psychotherapy practice and refer interested students to a special issue of *Psychotherapy: Theory, Research, Practice, Training* (Wolf, 2003) for more complete information.

The typical college student today is very comfortable with computers. Many senior clinical psychologists, however, were trained prior to this level of computer availability. These older psychologists have needed to learn about computers to practice in the twenty-first century. New terms have been added to the professional vocabulary to accommodate this new technology. In psychotherapy one of these terms is **e-therapy,** or Internet-based therapy (Castelnuovo, Gaggioli, Mantovani, & Riva, 2003).

Why would a psychologist want to do e-therapy rather than the more traditional form of psychotherapy? One reason is to be able to provide psychotherapy for patients who live in geographically remote places and tend to lack local resources. A second reason a psychologist might choose e-therapy is to provide service to a former patient who might benefit from this as part of the termination process or as a booster session with a former patient. Finally, some patients might choose to terminate therapy if e-therapy is not an alternative. These patients may enjoy the use of computers or have issues about being away from their home or office.

E-therapy allows the therapist to communicate in both real time and delayed time. One form of e-therapy is sometimes called **telepsychotherapy,** or psychotherapy provided via the Internet. When telepsychotherapy occurs in real time it is called synchronous. You may know this as instant messaging. The psychologist and patient communicate simultaneously in a way that is similar to what happens in the therapist's office. Each of them is sitting at the computer at the same time and they type in comments and receive immediate responses. A common form of delayed time psychotherapy, or asynchronous psychotherapy, is doing psychotherapy via e-mail. Of course, Internet-based psychotherapy limits the psychologist's ability to evaluate what is happening with the patient because there is no opportunity to evaluate nonverbal behavior or emotion. Although either person can indicate an emotion, this remains a verbal labeling of the emotion rather than observing its expression. Most psychologists view e-therapy as an adjunct to face-to-face psychotherapy rather than a substitute for it.

Computer technology can also be used in the psychologist's office to aid in the psychotherapy process. An example is virtual reality exposure therapy that is used to treat anxiety disorders. A head-mounted display covers the patient's eyes. The patient sees visual images through small TV monitors and receives auditory input through stereo earphones. The patient is then immersed in a computer-generated environment that relates to his or her particular area of anxiety. The program is customized to the patient's life circumstances. Both positive and negative responses of others can be provided to allow the patient to learn to handle these different situations. For example, suppose the patient has a fear of public speaking. Virtual reality exposure therapy can provide the patient with the experience of a positive audience response to a speech as well as a negative one. The patient can then practice various ways to handle the experience. In the past, such a patient might have initially been exposed to the situation using a hierarchy of mental imagery. In order to make the transition from imagination to reality, patients were asked to gradually expose themselves to the anxiety-provoking situations. Consider, for example, the patient who is afraid of flying. This patient might be asked to watch planes at an airport, then perhaps make arrangements to sit on a plane that is on the ground, and finally actually take a short plane trip. The psychologist needs to time this actual flight to a time when the patient can handle it. Virtual reality can place the patient in actual flight conditions while the psychologist is present in the room. If the patient proves not to be ready at that point, the psychologist can continue to work with the patient using this form of safe exposure prior to the actual flight.

Virtual reality technology is currently being evaluated for use with special populations such as the military. The U.S. Navy is studying its use with various types of PTSD. They are incorporating not only auditory and visual stimuli but also smell and other sensory factors in a therapy program for combat-related PTSD among naval personal. They are also studying its use for PTSD among noncombat naval personnel, such as medics. The positive results from early controlled research with this application of technology suggest it is likely to increase in use in the future (Krijn, Emmelkamp, Olafsson, & Biemond, 2004; Rothbaum, Hodges, Smith, & Lee, 2000)

Sample Patients

We will now return to the patients you originally met in chapter 5 to illustrate the process of individual psychotherapy. Of course, this is just a fictitious summary of a therapy session. In an actual therapy setting, there would be pauses, silences as emotionally charged topics were raised, and possibly some difficulty addressing these issues. We hope, however, that these summaries give you a picture of the types of information that arise in individual psychotherapy as well as how that information then guides further patient work.

Patty

In chapter 5, you first met Patty. We also gave you some personality test information about her in chapter 7. Although you may want to have some family sessions later with her, you decided to start with individual psychotherapy and told her at the end of the initial interview that you were proposing six weeks of treatment. Based on what she has told you thus far, it seems doubtful that she would be willing to have her father participate in her treatment, but perhaps her mother could be involved. You plan to use some behavioral homework assignments but also will use an interactive form of psychotherapy. In the first few sessions, you continue to get information about her family and life circumstances, but you also give her homework assignments. During your second session with her, for example, you learn that she cries easily and that this interferes with her concentration on her studies. You ask her to set aside a thirty-minute time period each afternoon at 5:30 for crying. She agrees to sit quietly in her apartment and cry at this time. She will limit her crying to this designated period. You initially planned to see Patty on a weekly basis for about six weeks and then to reassess your plans. At her third session with you, however, Patty asks if she can schedule another session that week. She reports that she has been crying more often and has had trouble sleeping. Earlier you had noted that you did not think she was suicidal but quickly go over this possibility again. Once again, you determine that although she has the typical signs of depression, her religious devotion is sufficiently strong that you do not think she is at risk for suicide. It is obvious, however, that she is in significant distress during this session. When you ask if anything new has happened since your last session, you learn that she had Sunday dinner with her family. Further discussion of this activity provides you with information that Sunday dinners used to be a regular activity, that she had not done this recently but her father insisted, and that he was angry about her first semester academic performance. He asked her if she had the ability to become a lawyer and even if she graduated if she really believed she could pass the bar exam and get a job. In your initial sessions, you noted the importance of pleasing her father and thus it is not surprising she has had a setback. You agree to schedule two sessions per week for the next two weeks and then decide what needs to happen after that.

You continue to see Patty throughout this academic year on a weekly basis. During the summer, because she has obtained a clerkship with the juvenile courts that has irregular hours, you see her every other week. This schedule seems to work and she continues to improve. You continue on this schedule throughout the second year of law school and into the beginning of the third year. You then move to once every three weeks and finally once a month as graduation approaches. Over that time, you continue to work with her about increasing her social activities. As she does this, she finds her studying is more efficient and her grades steadily improve. You also work with her on her relationship with her father as well as her view of her mother's role in her development. Because she remains steadfast about not wanting her family to know about her psychotherapy, family sessions are not scheduled.

Over her time in therapy, Patty learns a number of coping strategies she can use in her daily living, including relaxation skills and thought-stopping when she has negative thoughts about her abilities. She learned how to talk to her former boyfriend when he calls so that she no longer feels upset by his calls. He comes to visit at one point and she discusses this visit with you both before and after the visit. She has applied her new skills to this interaction and now decided that if he wishes to reestablish some contact with her she can handle that as an equal. She was able to see how she viewed him as a substitute for her father and allowed him to dictate to her how the relationship should progress. When his sexual demands were in conflict with her religious beliefs, she had been unable to handle the conflict. During therapy, she was able to evaluate the role of family and religion in relation to her self-image as a "modern" woman.

When therapy terminated, Patty noted that she still had issues with her family but that she no longer felt they needed to be handled. She had taken a position in another state and felt that living on her own would allow her to visit her family without being dominated by them. She wrote a letter to her psychologist six months after therapy termination to ask for a referral to a psychologist in her local community to help her address the stress of studying for the bar exam. She had not passed it the first time she tried but was sufficiently close to passing that she felt she would do so the next time. Follow-up notes from Patty arrived several times over the years following her therapy. She did pass the bar examination, she reconciled with her former boyfriend, married and later divorced him, and continued to work on the skills she learned in therapy.

One of the unique points about Patty's case is that psychologists often wonder what has happened to their former patients. This level of closure with Patty is not that common. Thus, it is important to determine how well you can handle not knowing the outcome of your work when choosing this profession.

Joyce

You first met Joyce in chapter 5. You also have read about her psychological evaluation. Based on both her psychological and neuropsychological testing, you have ruled out the organic problems of Alzheimer's disease and dementia that you were considering. Although Joyce showed signs of depression on her personality testing, she also showed many of the classic features of PTSD. This was not one of the original diagnoses you considered. The major life stressor she discussed previously was the death of her husband. Although it is possible that this event is the cause, you know you will need to do more questioning about that event. Based on further discussion of her life, you learn that she functioned well at work until quite recently. Despite the fact that PTSD symptoms can appear quite some time after the original event, you do not think the event in this case was in the distant past. You begin to review what the literature tells you about PTSD. You know that PTSD is less common in older adults than in younger ones and more common in women than in men. Therefore, it is quite possible that the issues suggested by her psychological test results are accurate.

You discuss the results of her psychological testing with Joyce and mention that her symptoms of anxiety, such as the ones she has been experiencing recently, may be alleviated on a temporary basis by medication. The records she supplied indicate she has a regular physician. You suggest that she see her physician about the possibility of short-term medication. You also offer to make a referral to a psychiatrist for medication if she would prefer that to going to her regular physician. You know that the use of medication is especially useful if you are correct that she is suffering from PTSD (Marshall & Pierce, 2000). Joyce seems quite relieved that she does not appear to be developing an organic disorder and asks for the psychiatric referral for medication. She would prefer that her regular physician not realize what is happening.

You are still left with questions about whether this reaction is a delayed response to her husband's death or something else. It seems likely that something has happened more recently that Joyce has not yet revealed to you. You spend several sessions with Joyce discussing her life and activities. You can find nothing in her relationships with her children or her colleagues at work that would qualify as a major stressor. At this point, you are beginning to wonder if you are the best therapist for Joyce. Perhaps she would be more comfortable with someone else. You share your concerns with Joyce indicating that although you are certainly willing to continue sessions with her you believe there are issues that are not being addressed. She says she is comfortable with you and would like to keep seeing you.

Although the medication she receives from her psychiatrist is helping, she views it as a temporary form of assistance. Joyce had previously said she did not feel especially close to any of the others in the business and professional women's club or her college alumni association. Despite these statements, you decide to explore those people a bit more to round out your understanding of her life. You ask Joyce if she ever socializes with any of these people outside of the meetings. Although Joyce replies in the negative, you notice a change in her tone of voice and she temporarily stops making eye contact with you. It is always important to be aware of subtle changes, especially nonverbal cues, in your patient during a session. When such changes occur, consider the topic under discussion and why it may have a special significance. You gently probe the subject of interactions Joyce has recently had with these people. Eventually, Joyce admits to having had "one date" with a seventy-year-old pharmacist from her college alumni association. You ask her to tell you about that date. Once again, Joyce looks uncomfortable. Eventually, however, she tells you that they had a lovely dinner at one of the better local restaurants prior to attending the symphony. After the symphony, he invited her to his home for a night-cap. She had known him for many years and so was comfortable accepting this invitation. She felt they had much in common not only in terms of the alumni association but also because he is a widower, having lost his wife about two years ago. As they sat on the sofa in his home, however, he began to make sexual advances. Joyce had not expected this and although she believes she was clear that she was not interested, she feels she must have done something to make him think she was. She describes a case of what we now call "date rape." From her perspective, however, it was her fault that this happened. She cries throughout the time she is describing these events.

You know that psychotherapy can help alleviate the symptoms of PTSD but also that in many cases the problem will never be completely reversed. You decide to use a behavioral extinction approach in addition to some supportive and educational work about date rape. You ask Joyce to describe the details of her rape as well as the thoughts and feelings she had at that time. You tape record everything she says. Initially you play this recording for her during therapy sessions to make sure she can handle hearing it over and over again. You then give her the tape and ask her to play it at home on a daily basis and think that it is currently happening. The purpose of this process is to extinguish her feelings. In addition, you give her literature about date rape so that she can learn more about this problem. During some of her therapy sessions, you also discuss ways she might handle dates in the future as well as role-play dating scenarios. After three months of this therapy, Joyce tells you that she is now ready to try to date again. She accepts a dinner invitation and is able to enjoy the evening. She has also found that she is no longer having the problems at work that initially brought her to therapy. Joyce discusses her progress with her psychiatrist, who suggests that she no longer needs medication. You and Joyce mutually agree to have her return for one final session in a month to "touch base" and also leave open the option to return in the future should she need to do so.

Trang

Trang is the third of our patients. Remember from chapters 5 and 6 that after interviewing his adoptive parents as well as gathering information from his teachers and pediatrician you determined that ADHD was the correct diagnosis. Now the issue is how to treat him. Similar to the requirements of a good assessment, effective treatment of ADHD requires awareness of comorbid conditions, availability of educational and psychological support services, and the consideration of medication management. In addition, conceptualizing ADHD as a chronic condition that will require ongoing monitoring is especially important. Coordination with Trang's pediatrician and his parents are essential for successful treatment.

Although there are many treatments for ADHD (Barkley, 1998), relatively few have been empirically supported. In treating Trang, you decide to use a multifaceted approach. You know you will also need to work with his parents to gain their support of the treatment protocol. Anastopoulos and Shaffer (2000) have pointed out that treatments for ADHD are not curative, but rather are aimed at reducing symptoms, improving emotional adjustment, and preventing the reoccurrence of pretreatment symptoms. Therefore, ongoing monitoring will help support both Trang and his parents. The usual treatment for ADHD includes pharmacology, counseling, parent training and support groups, and classroom management techniques. You therefore decide to get his parents' permission to consult with his pediatrician regarding medication for Trang. You will also work with his parents for several sessions (see chapter 12 for a description of these sessions) regarding their role in the treatment.

With Trang's parents' permission, you consult with his pediatrician regarding medication. Psychostimulant medications have been the most widely utilized intervention for ADHD. More than 70 percent of children diagnosed with ADHD who take psychostimulant medication exhibit behavioral, academic, and attentional improvements based on parent ratings, teacher ratings, direct observations, or a combination of these measures (Anastopoulos, DuPaul, & Barkley, 1992). The use of this type of medication has continued to receive support in the literature (MTA Cooperative Group, 1999).

You also work with Trang's teacher to develop a behavioral program for the classroom. Behavioral programs include instructing both parents and teachers about how to apply rewards for good behavior and how to use extinction for behaviors that are unwanted. For example, in applying rewards for appropriate behavior, you instruct Trang's teacher to praise Trang when he is paying attention, when he turns in his homework assignments, and when he is playing cooperatively with other children. In the same way, you help his parents understand that paying attention to those behaviors you want him to do at home, such as chores, focusing on his homework, or waiting his turn to speak are behaviors that they should attend to with positive verbal feedback. They should provide this feedback in their own words, such as saying, "Good job, Trang." You also tell his teacher and his parents to ignore behaviors that are inappropriate, such as when he approaches them and interrupts them when they are talking to others. You let them know that time-out is an effective intervention when children become distracted or engage in inappropriate behaviors. Parents and teachers also appreciate knowing that when using reward systems, not only are praise and attention effective, but also using visual charts with stars or points work well. Children like to see their progress visually, so posting a reward chart on the refrigerator or in a place where children can overtly monitor their progress in the classroom is often helpful. Trang's parents decide to use a chart on their refrigerator as part of their work with their son.

Trang's parents and his teacher are open and eager to help him. You therefore help them devise a more formal reward system for Trang. Many students have heard about "token economies" from their reading in other courses. You decide this approach would be a good one to use with Trang. You develop a system in which he can earn tokens for good behavior in the classroom. Thus, when he is paying attention, his teacher can reward him with a token. At home, you suggest his parents give him a nickel after each completed chore. As in many behavioral programs, the reinforcement schedule can be changed to reflect the needs of the child, the needs of the parents or teachers, and the effectiveness of the reward strategy. You work with both Trang's parents and his teacher to make these modifications.

As a child clinical psychologist, you know that comorbid conditions are not unusual in children with ADHD. You therefore decide to see Trang a few times to rule out other conditions. Depression, oppositional-defiant disorders, and learning problems are frequently found in children with ADHD. Before Trang arrives for his appointment, you decide to use play therapy (Axline, 1979; Kaduson & Schaefer, 1997), role-playing, and direct observation in your assessment of Trang. When Trang first comes into your office, you notice that he separates easily from his parents, has no stranger anxiety, and talks easily and clearly to you as you go to your office. As a therapist, you should remember that your evaluation and work with children really begins in the waiting room when you approach the child and introduce yourself. Many child psychologists ask the parents of their patients to tell their young children that they are going to see a "talking doctor." This information helps the child differentiate the psychologist from a medical doctor who may have given the child an injection or subjected him to some other unpleasant or painful experience. Even when children are primed in this way, it is not unusual for children to have some stranger or separation anxiety. How long they have that anxiety is an important marker. You are pleased that Trang demonstrates neither of these symptoms.

Psychologists who work with children frequently have toys, paper and crayons, and other age-appropriate objects in their offices. When Trang enters your office, you notice that he bolts for the toys and starts taking all of them off the shelves. This impulsive behavior supports your diagnosis of ADHD. Interestingly, Trang is also able to respond pretty well to the limits you set when you ask him to pick out one toy to play with at first. Trang chooses the paper and crayons and starts to draw. After a few minutes, you ask him to draw a picture of a person. This process is a frequently used projective test as well as a nice break for children. Trang draws a picture that resembles a boy, with lots of details and strong use of color. We will not go into detail about the interpretation of children's drawings. However, you know that an eight-year-old should be able to add details to pictures of people and that the portrait should be more than a stick figure. Trang's drawing meets this requirement. Trang is also able to engage you in conversation during the drawing task and you note that he has strong verbal skills that are highly correlated with intelligence. You then observe that Trang is able to engage in interactive play with you, by asking you to build with some blocks that he had previously taken out. You construct a small house with Trang. You then encourage Trang to tell you a story about the people who live in the house. You're pleased to hear that he is not conflicted about his lesbian parents in his story and he seems vibrant and interested in interacting with you. At the end of the session you tell Trang that you enjoyed your time with him and that you would like to see him again. He readily agrees. The following week, he returns, again separates easily, and engages in interactive play. This time the interactive play involves a board game. You conclude from these two sessions that Trang does not have a comorbid condition accompanying his ADHD. Because it appears that Trang has ADHD, and none of the accompanying comorbid disorders, you proceed to communicate your recommendations to his parents.

ETHICAL CONUNDRUM POINTS TO PONDER

The APA Ethics Code does not specifically address the use of the Internet for the provision of clinical services. Although it includes cautions related to the use of the Internet for providing public advice, it does not address your specific needs. You have already established a clinical relationship with this patient, so this is not an anonymous recipient of your services. You might consider going to the literature to get a better sense of the **standard of care** in this case since your professional ethics code is silent on the topic. Of course, you would also need to discuss with your patient the fact that information sent through the Internet has the potential to be accessed by others without either your knowledge or hers. Since both of you are in the same state, you do not need to be concerned that you are not licensed to practice where you patient is located. You should check to make certain that your licensing board has not developed any policies that prohibit such practice. If your patient's psychotherapy is being paid for by insurance, you will also need to determine if Internet-provided psychotherapy can be reimbursed. You might read the guidelines about online counseling developed by other mental health professions, such as the American Counseling Association, American Mental Health Counselors Association, and the National Board for Certified Counselors, each of whom have provided ethical guidelines for the provision of online counseling. These sources will help you provide the most secure service possible for your patient. Although this is a relatively new area of practice, it is one that could be used in this case if precautions are taken.

For students who are interested in a comprehensive review of treatments for ADHD and comorbid disorders, we suggest you start with Barkley (1998); Pelham, Wheeler, and Chronis (2000); and the consensus report from the National Institutes of Health (2000).

Assessment

Ideally, the psychologist is not only conducting psychotherapy with each of these patients but is also conducting assessments at various times throughout the intervention process. After several psychotherapy sessions, it is important to have some formal measure of the progress that is occurring. Patients are likely to want to please their therapist and report more change than may actually be occurring. The therapist needs to know whether the intervention chosen may need to be altered. In psychotherapy research and graduate student clinic settings, this assessment is likely to be more formal than what many practitioners use in their offices. Many practitioners use a short type of clinical interview to gauge progress rather than administering a series of psychological tests. This process of evaluation will occur repeatedly as the therapist determines when it is time to start termination of therapy process.

Key Terms

catharsis	feminist therapy	standard of care	treatment plans
corrective emotional experience	insight	telepsychotherapy	working through
	play therapy	termination	
e-therapy	self-esteem	treatment goals	

CHAPTER 12

Couples, Family, and Group Psychotherapy

In the previous chapter, we discussed individual psychotherapy. Not all psychotherapy done by clinical psychologists involves a single psychologist and a single patient. Although individual psychotherapy is used more often, there are cases when it is helpful to work with more than one patient at the same time. In this chapter, we will discuss couples therapy, family therapy, and group therapy. These are the general names for those situations in which the psychologist determines it is better to see more than the one person associated with traditional individual psychotherapy. We are using the term *couples* rather than *marital* because the basic concepts used are the same regardless of whether or not the participants are legally related or merely emotionally attached. Many family therapists are critical of the DSM-IV and its predecessors because the basis of that system is individual psychopathology and does not include the diagnosis of a dysfunctional family unit. Thus, working with dysfunctional families may cause problems with the typical insurance policies that are based on the DSM model of individual psychopathology.

Because of its differences from individual psychotherapy, family therapy needed to develop new theories as well as new techniques to meet its goals. In this chapter, we provide some general information about some of these theories as foundation material for the intervention process that is used. Over time, the definition of *family* has also changed. We discuss some of these changes in the section of the chapter dealing with family therapy. Group therapy is really a general term that could be viewed as including both couples and family therapy. The term **group therapy** is also applied when seeing more than one person at the same time and the patients are not related to each other. Most of our discussion of group therapy

ETHICAL CONUNDRUM

You are a clinical psychologist in private practice. You are currently seeing a family of six people (father, mother, three children, and grandmother) in psychotherapy. Their insurance company has been paying for the treatment you are providing because you are on the provider panel of the managed care company for the father's employer. After three months of treatment, the father loses his job because of company downsizing. At that time, his healthcare insurance was canceled because it was a company rate. He cannot afford the individual rate to keep the policy. He has not yet been able to find another job and the family cannot afford to pay for their psychotherapy. They are proud people and do not want to ask for free treatment. The grandmother is a talented amateur painter. They offer to give you one of her oil paintings in return for psychotherapy.

will be from this latter perspective. Special conflicts can develop in each of these forms of therapy. We will discuss some of these conflicts with our presentation of each approach.

Couples Therapy

Under what circumstances might a clinical psychologist recommend **couples therapy** rather than individual therapy? This is usually a situation in which the psychologist believes the problem is basically in the couple as a unit rather than as individuals. In some cases, one member of the couple may have made the psychotherapy appointment but after the initial interview the psychologist determines that the problem is really one of a relationship dysfunction rather than an individual dysfunction. Common problems leading to this conclusion include infidelity, sexual problems, disagreements about basic activities such as issues involved in raising children, power issues within the relationship, poor conflict management, specific complaints about the partner's behavior, violence in the relationship, and communication problems (Nystul, 1999; Wolcott & Glazer, 1989). Communication problems are often viewed as the core of many of the other issues.

An important concept to consider if you want to do couples therapy is, "What is the psychologist's role?" This question may seem simple to you but it is not. If a couple is experiencing relationship difficulties the psychologist can do two major things to help them. One is to help the couple have a more satisfying relationship. The other is to help the couple terminate the relationship if adequate changes cannot be made. Regardless of the psychologist's personal views about ending relationships, he or she must not impose those views on the couple. The role of the psychologist is to help the couple determine what outcome best meets each of their needs.

There may also be cases in which the members of the couple need individual therapy in addition to couples therapy. If the same therapist sees a person for both individual and couples therapy, rules about confidentiality need to be established clearly. Part of this issue of confidentiality involves the psychologist determining what information from the individual therapy is relevant to the couples therapy and what information should stay within the individual therapy setting. This combination of couples therapy and individual therapy raises issues about record-keeping as well. It is important to keep information about each person separate. If one patient's records are subpoenaed, you do not want information about someone else to be disclosed at the same time. Record-keeping is addressed in the APA Ethics Code, Standard 6. A combination of liability issues and multiple standards for record-keeping have made this a large topic beyond the scope of an undergraduate textbook. You can expect to have this topic addressed in multiple settings if you pursue a career in clinical psychology. Many references are also available for starting to learn about this issue (e.g., Moline, Williams, & Austin, 1998; Rivas-Vazquez, Blais, Rey, & Rivas-Vazquez, 2001). One resource that is particularly useful for clinical psychologists is the "Practice Update," which the APA Practice Organization publishes monthly. A review of record-keeping issues can be found in the July 19, 2005, issue (www.apa.org). To avoid this conflict, many psychologists refer each member of a couple to a different individual therapist for that part of the treatment. If such a referral is not possible, care must be taken to handle these conflicts in an ethical way.

When psychologists discuss couples counseling, or couples therapy, they frequently conceptualize it as marriage counseling. As you will see, marriage counseling is only one form of couples therapy. As we noted, couples present for therapy for a variety of reasons. These are cases in which couples present for help, not cases in which an individual who happens to be part of a couple seeks assistance. The patient experiencing domestic violence may have couples issues but receive individual psychotherapy because of the personal threat. In this section of the chapter we provide you with information about behavioral, psychodynamic, and humanistic approaches to working with couples. Because sex therapy has become a somewhat specialized practice, we discuss that topic separately.

Regardless of the reason the individuals specify when they come to see a psychologist, it is important to remember that there are probably multiple issues contributing to the marital discord. Each member of a couple brings a personal history into the relationship. That history includes cultural factors plus a view of relationships that has been shaped by the person's parents, peers, and the media. The goals of couples therapy are not static; they may change over the course of the treatment process. It is important for the therapist to be aware of the needs of the individuals and to discuss their treatment goals with them. In some cases, couples therapy will be designed to improve a couple's relationship by treating one of the partners. This approach is sometimes called **adjunctive marital therapy.** In other cases, therapy may involve helping the couple dissolve the relationship in a reasonable way that causes the least amount of psychological damage to them or, equally important, to their children or extended families and friends.

Over time, and among professionals, what comprises a "couple" may be defined differently. In contemporary terms, a couple may be straight, gay, or bisexual. Regardless of the definition of what constitutes a couple, therapy with more than one person involves ethical challenges and an understanding of the broader context in which the couple exists. Thus, knowledge about each individual's family, acculturation, employment history, and friendships can be very important factors in helping the couple. Taking a comprehensive history is just as important with couples as it is in individual psychotherapy. As in individual psychotherapy, the presenting issue may not be the most important concern for that couple. Thus, it is important for the therapist to remain open to other topics that arise during the course of treatment. These new topics may actually be the core issues for the couple.

Next, we briefly describe several different approaches to couples therapy to illustrate this specialty. We are using the traditional headings of behavioral, psychodynamic, and humanistic for these approaches.

Behavioral Approaches

Behavior therapists have adapted their stimulus-response approach to work with couples (e.g., Weiss & Halford, 1996). In a typical behavioral approach, the first phase is an assessment of the couple's relationship. Assessment provides two kinds of information: *content* and *process*. Content information refers to the reported concerns of the partners, such as a definition of their conflicts, thoughts about separation, and other topics they report about their relationship. Process information is defined as how couples interact and can only be obtained when the partners are together. Because the process in couples therapy can be intense, complex, and confusing, these couples sessions may be videotaped for future analysis by the therapist. Taping is a frequently used technique during therapist training. After an initial session with both partners, individual sessions are held. Content information is usually obtained from each partner individually or from self-report measures because it is more reliable to do it this way (Haynes, Jensen, Wise, & Sherman, 1981). For example, reports of physical abuse are significantly underreported in conjoint interviews (O'Leary, Vivian, & Malone, 1992). Although therapists may sense that some information is not being disclosed during a conjoint session, forcing one member of a couple to reveal information in that setting may lead to greater distress or a choice not to return for future sessions.

One of the pioneers in behavioral couples therapy was **Neil Jacobson** (Jacobson & Margolin, 1979). As his model evolved, he developed Integrative Couple Therapy (ICT) (Jacobson & Christensen, 1996). ICT is usually conducted in a conjoint format with a goal of altering interaction between partners. ICT has its foundation in behavioral therapy, and most of the approaches are based on two major components: *behavioral exchange* and *communication/problem-solving training (CPT)*. In ICT, emphasis is placed on determining what are the controlling variables in marital interactions. *Behavior exchange strategies* all involve attempts to increase the ratio of positive to negative behaviors exchanged by the couple at home. In CPT, couples are taught to be their own therapists through training in communication and conflict resolution skills. The theory of change is that if couples can be taught to solve their own problems, then they can function on their own when problems occur in the future after they have completed therapy.

Behavior therapists developed a range of assessment systems to better evaluate the couple's interactions. One such system, the Marital Interaction Coding System, is used to evaluate videotaped interactions by couples (Heyman, Eddy, Weiss, & Vivian, 1995). We cite this system as an example to illustrate this approach to working with couples. Of course, it is not the only available method. These researchers identified four factors for both men and women using their system: hostility, constructive problem discussion, humor, and responsibility discussion. After the therapist explores these factors with each individual of the couple, they can then be used when working with the couple as a unit.

Psychodynamic Couples Therapy

Not all couples therapy will be conducted from a behavioral perspective. Therapists who conceptualize human distress from a psychodynamic perspective may help couples gain an understanding of the use of such ego defense mechanisms as projection to place expectations on their partner. These defense mechanisms are the result of their own early childhood experiences. According to this approach to understanding couples, people often select mates who fit the dynamics of their own childhood. It is only after these projections are explored and clarified that the couple can develop a more positive communication style.

Ego analysts suggest that people develop dysfunctional relationships with their partners because they do not feel they deserve their own feelings (Wile, 1981). For example, consider the couple in which one partner used to stay home full-time and the other worked. Now they are both working and the partner who is new to the employment scene is investing long hours on the job in order to secure the position. The other partner may resent the decreased personal attention but not feel the right to have such negative feelings. After all, this job is important not only on a personal level to the partner but also to the couple's financial future. What is likely to happen, according to Wile, is that these feelings of resentment are going to be expressed in passive ways or occur in periodic explosions that do not seem to make sense. The ego analyst would help each partner deal with feelings of self-criticism. Therapy would also address the patient's ability to learn to accept not only his or her own feelings but also those of his or her partner. If each partner moves to a position of being on the other one's side, there will be no need for them to compromise. Any compromising that may be needed is likely to be spontaneous because of their expanded views.

Humanistic Couples Therapy

Relationship Enhancement (Guerney, 1984) is based on the client-centered approach to therapy developed by Carl Rogers that we discussed in chapter 10. It is a skills training approach to addressing couples' issues. Some of the skills included in this approach are being empathic, concentrating on your partner's internal world, and learning to listen intently. In addition to these personal skills, the partners are also taught basic problem-solving skills in much the same way that a behaviorally oriented therapist would do.

Emotionally Focused Couples Therapy (EFCT) centers on the quality of the attachment bond between the partners (Johnson & Greenberg, 1995). It is based on attachment theory (Bowlby, 1969). If the couple is securely attached to each other, they will not experience distress. Individuals who are not securely attached may, for example, fear they will be abandoned by their partner. This fear may then lead them to express unusual amounts of anger or to withdraw from their partner. To facilitate the establishment of a strong attachment bond between the partners, the therapist using this approach will encourage the individuals not only to experience their negative emotions but also to express these feelings to their partner. By expressing these emotions the individual gains self-insight as well as a greater understanding of the issues impacting the relationship.

We did not try to give you an in-depth description of how a clinical psychologist actually "does" couples therapy. Our intention was to provide brief information about several different approaches to illustrate the fact that clinical work with couples is done in many different ways. Students who want to learn more about the process of couples therapy should read general handbooks on the topic (e.g., Gurman & Jacobson, 2002).

Research on couples therapy has considered both improvement compared to no-treatment control groups and the magnitude of change that occurs (Alexander, Holtzworth-Monroe, & Jameson, 1994; Christensen & Heavey, 1999; Snyder, Wills, & Grady-Fletcher, 1991). Most of the studies indicate significant improvement initially after couples therapy compared to wait-list controls. These findings hold regardless of the theoretical orientation of the therapist. In terms of long-term improvement, several issues arise. There are limited available data on follow-up after the completion of treatment. There is also the question of whether a couple's decision to separate is considered a success or not a success. For example, a four-year follow-up of the seventy-nine couples in one study (Snyder, Wills, & Grady-Fletcher, 1991) reported that 38 percent of the couples who had received behavioral couples therapy were divorced by that time. Does the fact that they were divorced four years after completion of therapy mean therapy was successful or not? Your response to that question should not be based on your value system but on data about the individuals involved. Using group data does not allow us to consider the types of problems these couples may have had compared to those couples who were not divorced at the follow-up evaluation. Would such data really make a difference? There are also issues of the individual's views about marriage and divorce. Although criticisms were raised about the specific behavioral techniques used in this study, the issue of long-term effectiveness of couples therapy as well as the definition of success need to be addressed in future research.

Sex Therapy

A specialized issue for couples is sexuality. Thus, sex therapy developed as a special domain within couples therapy. Early sex therapists assumed that a person who was experiencing sexual difficulties was a deeply disturbed individual. The sexual difficulties were viewed as the outward manifestation of a deeply rooted problem. Today, however, sex therapy may be an adjunct to the types of couples therapy we described earlier or even the major focus of the work with the couple. Before starting sex therapy, the psychologist usually makes a referral for a physical examination to rule out a physical cause for the reported difficulty.

Modern sex therapy is often seen as starting with the work of **William Masters** and **Virginia Johnson** (1970). They developed a program of therapy conducted daily over a two-week period by a male and female therapist. This program was based on the work they had done as cotherapists. A major goal of this approach is to provide basic education about sexual functioning to the couple. Masters and Johnson found that many of their patients believed in myths about sexuality and had poor communication with each other. These problems led to performance anxiety during sexual activity. Based on these clinical findings, they developed their intervention program. Masters and Johnson's program was one of the main efforts leading to sexual problems becoming more accepted in the United States as legitimate reasons to seek treatment. Following their initial success, clinics based on the Masters and Johnson approach were established throughout the United States. As more therapists were trained in this method, they also conducted research to evaluate the procedures. Based on the data of researchers who were not part of the Masters and Johnson St. Louis clinic staff, some sex therapists modified the original format. For example, data suggested that using one therapist was just as effective as using two therapists (LoPiccolo, Heiman, Hogan, & Roberts, 1985) and that therapy sessions once each week were equally effective as the daily sessions recommended in the original approach (Heiman & LoPiccolo, 1983). These changes in format actually allowed many more people to be able to benefit from sex therapy. Some of these people did not have the resources to take the needed time away from work and to travel to St. Louis for treatment.

Sex therapy does not ignore the fact that sexual problems may be the result of relationship issues. The focus of sex therapy, however, is on that one aspect of the relationship. Not all clinical psychologists are trained to do sex therapy. If a clinical psychologist is seeing a couple who are experiencing specific sexual problems, that psychologist might refer the couple to someone who specializes in this approach and work with that other professional to coordinate treatment. It is important to determine the root of the sexual problem before deciding whether or not sex therapy is the best direction for a specific couple. For example, suppose the clinical psychologist is told that one member of the couple is experiencing decreased sexual desire. It is important to know whether this lack of desire problem is the result of some form of sexual trauma, such as rape or childhood sexual abuse, or from lack of knowledge about sexuality. The recommended course of treatment would be quite different in these two cases.

Sex therapists do *not* touch their patients, nor do they observe their patients' sexual activity. The approach developed by Masters and Johnson, and used by many professionals in this specialty, includes basic education about normal sexual functioning as well as a series of exercises practiced by the couple in the privacy of their home. The couple then discusses their successes and concerns with their therapist during the next session. For some couples, even this act of discussing their sex life may be quite difficult. It is important for the therapist to create an environment in which they can be comfortable with such discussions. The exercises used for sex therapy often start with sexual activity other than actual sexual intercourse and gradually build to that point over a period of time. Thus, if you plan to include sex therapy as part of your practice, you need to be comfortable discussing these issues as well as be knowledgeable about human anatomy and physiology related to sexuality.

Sex therapy is most often conducted with couples. In the early days, sexual surrogates were sometimes used when there was no regular sex partner or the partner was unwilling to participate. A sexual surrogate was a person trained to engage in specified sexual activity with the patient as the patient progressed through the therapy process. As a result of criticism of the use of sexual surrogates as being close to prostitution, combined with the increased incidence of such sexually transmitted diseases as HIV, surrogates are seldom reported as part of today's treatment approaches. There are also methods of sex therapy that can be used with an individual patient rather than a couple (Zilbergeld, 1992). These methods might work well for someone such as a male who is experiencing erectile dysfunction. There are numerous books for professionals and students who wish to learn more about sex therapy (e.g., Leiblum & Rosen, 2000; Wincze & Carey, 2001).

Family Therapy

Just as definitions of couples have changed with time, many definitions of *family* have also been suggested. As a start to this section, we will provide two of them to illustrate the range available. From a governmental perspective, a family is "two or more persons related by birth, marriage, or adoption and residing together in a household" (U.S. Bureau of Census, 1999, p. 6). Psychologists tend to consider roles of the individuals, and their definitions reflect this approach. For example, one psychological definition of family is "any group of persons united by the ties of marriage, blood, or adoption, or any sexually expressive relationship, in which (1) the adults cooperate financially for their mutual support, (2) the people are committed to one another in an intimate, interpersonal relationship, and (3) the members see their individual identities as importantly attached to the group with an identity of its own" (DeGenova & Rice, 2002, p. 2). As you can see, the definition of *family* changes with the times. Regardless of the definition of *family*, **family therapy** is a special form of therapy involving more than one member of this kinship group.

It is difficult to pinpoint a beginning date or founder of family therapy. Some historians of this specialty suggest it had its roots in Freud's practice. His family therapy, however, was quite different from what we see today. He tended to work with a parent who would describe a child's problem. He would then tell the parent how to work with the child. He did not tend to see either the child on an individual basis or the entire family unit. It is questionable whether modern family therapists would even consider Freud's approach part of their specialty. Before the modern concept of family therapy began, some families probably received services from clergy, family physicians, and attorneys. These professionals, however, were not operating from a theoretical foundation but rather from their professional backgrounds. These professionals usually had little formal training in psychological techniques, theory, or research and it is questionable whether or not they were helpful.

According to the American Association for Marriage and Family Therapy (AAMFT), marriage and family therapy is "brief; solution-focused; specific with attainable therapeutic goals; and designed with the 'end in mind'" (www.aamft.org). Interest in family therapy has even led to a broader topic called *family psychology* and a division of APA, Division 43, so that psychologists can have a forum to share knowledge about it. Family psychology can be defined as, "the scientific study of the family from a multifaceted perspective—its historical forms and variation, its structure and functioning across time, space, cultures, and generations, and its idiosyncratic and systems attributes" (Kaslow, 1987, p. 88). **Nathan Ackerman** wrote one of the classic early books discussing both the diagnosis and treatment of the family (Ackerman, 1958). Although Ackerman was trained as a child psychiatrist and psychoanalyst, his approach to family therapy involves the therapist actively confronting the family about its defenses. He then utilizes traditional forms of interpretation to help the family understand why it is having problems. For Ackerman, the therapist is a parental figure who is responsible for eliciting strong emotions within the therapeutic session. The basis of these emotions, from this perspective, is often found in issues of sexuality, aggression, or dependency. As you can see from our brief review, family therapy is a very broad term.

A term you may find in articles about family therapy is **family systems theorist.** Thus, before we provide some sample approaches used with families, we will discuss this more general concept. This term indicates that the therapist conceptualizes the family as a system. In other words, this therapist considers not only the fact that these people are interrelated but also how they function (Beckvar & Beckvar, 2003; Nichols & Schwartz, 2001). From this perspective, what one member of the family does impacts the actions of all of the other members of the family. The impact will then influence the functioning of the entire group, including the person who started the cycle of events. The focus of the work of a family systems therapist will be on these interrelationships rather than on any one individual within the unit. Although one member of the family may be the identified patient, that person's problems are not viewed as the reason for therapy. Rather, they are a symptom of the dysfunctional system known as the family. The real focus of therapy is the interlocking series of actions within the family. Therapy addresses the function of the system rather than an individual. Using this model, the therapist will attempt to understand the organizational structure of the family unit. This understanding includes the hierarchies that exist within the family as well as the types of boundaries that exist both between family members and between the family and the outside world. Family communication patterns must be understood as well as family rules. Although these rules are not always explicitly stated, they influence not only how the members interact with each other but also the overall level of functioning of the family unit. When you view the family as a system, you must remember that any changes that start to occur will impact the balance within the unit. Thus, family members may not be comfortable with changes. Part of the therapy process is helping family members to consider how proposed changes may influence not only individuals but also the overall family organizational structure.

For many families it is easier to focus on one member of the family, and that focus may allow the entire family to become engaged in the therapy process. Early theories in this specialty view families as resistant to change because they self-regulate. Thus, as one member of the family begins to change other family members try to reverse that change. More recent theorists have suggested that families are inherently flexible and capable of growth (Nichols, 2002). We will describe the approach of three family therapists—Virginia Satir, Murray Bowen, and Salvador Minuchin—to illustrate this specialty. There are certainly others we could have chosen, but these three provide a foundation upon which you may want to continue to build your knowledge about family therapy.

Virginia Satir

Virginia Satir was a pioneer in the development of what is known as **conjoint family therapy** (1983). In addition to her writing about the process of family therapy, she also traveled extensively around the United States conducting workshops to train mental health professionals to work with families. Her popularity extended beyond the professional community, and she even made a television appearance in 1979 on the *Phil Donahue Show*—a popular TV talk show of that era. She also created an educational organization called Avanta (www.avanta.net) to teach her therapeutic approach to working with families.

Satir's approach suggests that families go through three stages in the family therapy process (Satir & Baldwin, 1983). Satir did not suggest that families move rigidly from stage one through stage three and then are "cured." They may go through these stages multiple times before actually completing the process. The first stage is *contact*. A family must be in distress before they will seek therapy. Thus, the therapist needs to create an atmosphere in which the family feels there is hope for it. To do this, the family therapist actively shares with the family what he or she observes and may even have an explicit written contract to describe what will happen in future sessions. Notice that you must be able to conceptualize as you work with the family to provide such feedback. You do

not have the luxury of thinking about what happened in the session and then consider alternative explanations before discussing your ideas with the family. Interestingly, family therapists often find they are really tired after a therapy session because of the active nature of this process. Satir calls the second stage of therapy *chaos*. At this point in treatment, one member of the family takes the risk of revealing specific points of distress. The family therapist helps this individual family member remain focused on the present while providing support for both this family member and the others. The third stage of therapy she calls *integration*. At the point when the family begins to address the issues raised in the chaos stage, it has moved into this third stage of therapy. This does not mean that all of its issues have been handled, but the family has moved toward change on at least that one issue. It may then return to some level of pain or chaos as other issues emerge. The process then repeats for these other issues.

Satir viewed the family therapist as a teacher. For Satir, the specific area of expertise of this "teacher" is communication skills. Satir was a keen observer of nonverbal communication. For example, she observed the seating arrangement the family chose for the initial session as well as other nonverbal behaviors to better understand the role each member of the family occupied within the unit. Once she identified their communication patterns and family roles, she explained them to the family. This is another example of her collaborative approach to working with families.

In addition to observing the family in the office setting, Satir took an extensive family history. Part of that history she called the **family life chronology.** All members of the family participated in developing this chronology. The children were asked to describe their view of their parents and of family activities. The parents discussed their family of origin from the perspective of how they viewed themselves in relationship to their siblings. They also described how they had met each other and each of their expectations of their role as a parent. Think about the large amount of information you can get as the family discusses the family life chronology. Also consider how the therapist might have to act as a referee if one member of the family begins to question or disagree with the way another family member describes some of these subjects. Such discussions can provide useful information, but it is also important to intervene before they become too heated.

During family therapy sessions, one of her techniques was to have members reverse roles for fifteen minutes in order to better understand the other person's perspective. At different times or in different sessions, a daughter and her mother might change roles, a husband and wife, a brother and sister, and so on. Notice that neither age nor gender is a relevant factor for role reversal. Her sessions with families were very active. In addition to role reversal, she also used what she called *family sculpting.* In this technique, the therapist physically molds each family member into a position that represents that person's perception of family relationships. Satir believed that actually having this visual representation of family dynamics helped the family appreciate how they interact. For example, if one member of the family felt that she was seldom acknowledged by the others, that person might sit in the corner of the room, on the floor, facing the wall. If a family member seemed to dominate all family decisions, that member might stand on a chair to be "higher" than the others, who would all sit on the floor and look up to the person on the chair. She would then help the family members explore both their physiological and emotional reactions to the pose.

Satir also taught family members to communicate more directly what they felt. Helping the family members learn to speak this way led to greater feelings of empowerment as well as personal congruence. Part of speaking directly is to make greater use of the word "I" rather than the word "you" in your speech. For example, if a family member says, "I feel hurt," that statement takes responsibility for the feeling rather than saying, "You made me feel hurt." The statement, "You made me feel hurt," is debatable by the other person, while making "I" statements is not debatable and is empowering. Satir also helped patients attend to those times when their facial expression, body position, and voice did not match each other. Pointing out these incongruencies to patients helped them understand when they were sending confusing messages to other family members. The goal of these exercises was to teach family members to provide direct, clear communication that would not be misunderstood.

Satir's observation of family communication patterns led her to describe five major styles family members use to communicate with each other (Satir, 1972) (see also Table 12.1). Because communication is such a core part of family therapy, we will briefly describe each of these styles. One style she called the **placater.** This family member responds to others from a weak and tentative position. As you listen to family members in the therapy session, the placater can be identified as the person who tends to agree with whomever is speaking. Second is the **blamer.** This is the family member who does not take responsibility for anything. This person continues to find fault with various others within the family group. Third is the **superreasonable** member of the family. As you watch this person interact with the others, your impression may be that this is the calm one. The superreasonable person seems to be detached from the issues raging among the

Table 12.1 Satir's Family Communication Patterns	
Type	**Behavior**
Placater	Always agrees
Blamer	Takes no responsibility
Superreasonable	Detached and unemotional
Irrelevant	Distractor
Congruent	Open and honest

others. The supereasonable person usually shows little emotion during the discussion. The fourth style is **irrelevant.** The person who uses this style tends to make comments that have nothing to do with what is being discussed. By responding in this way to family discussions, this person tends to distract others from the actual topic being discussed. Finally, Satir noted that some family members are **congruent communicators.** These people are real and open. They are genuine communicators. A goal of Satir's family therapy is to increase the frequency of congruent communication.

Satir developed many techniques family therapists might use in their work. Some of them have been modified and used by others in the field. We have already described her technique of *family sculpting*. Related to family sculpting is the *family stress ballet*. In this case, rather than remaining in a posed position, family members move in different ways to illustrate their experiences within the family. This technique leads to a combination of dance and vocalizations. This approach may seem a bit more dramatic than what is often shown in movies when characters engage in family therapy, but Satir felt it facilitated the process of self-understanding as well as an appreciation of interpersonal dynamics.

Satir was known as a very physical person who often touched her patients. It was not unusual for her to hold the hand of each member of the family as a way to establish contact with that person in a special way. In the twenty-first century, professional ethical codes as well as fear of patient misunderstanding leading to lawsuits have significantly decreased the use of physical contact between therapists and patients. Although Virginia Satir died in 1988, her powerful approach to family therapy continues to be used today and has had a major impact on many other family therapy approaches.

Murray Bowen

Murray Bowen, a psychiatrist, was another early contributor to modern family therapy (1960, 1966). Bowen worked with children who were diagnosed as schizophrenic and being treated at the Menninger Clinic in Kansas. His approach to family therapy was to work with the parents so they could interact more appropriately with their family. A unique factor about the way he conceptualized the family issues was his focus on the emotional history of the family. He traced the emotional system of the family through not only the parents' family but also the grandparents' families to gain an understanding of the current family dynamics. Thus, his system is often described as an intergenerational approach. When Bowen worked with schizophrenic patients who needed to be hospitalized, he

Murray Bowen *Courtesy of the National Library of Medicine, Murray Bowen Papers.*

sometimes admitted the entire family to the hospital. In these cases, he conducted a form of group therapy with the entire family that has been called "family group therapy" (Kerr, 1981). It is unlikely that contemporary health insurance would cover this form of therapy and thus if it were chosen as the treatment of choice, only those families who could afford to pay for the hospital cost could take advantage of this aspect of Bowen's approach.

Bowen's system includes eight core concepts: *differentiation of self, triangulation, nuclear family emotional systems, family projection process, emotional cutoff, multi-generational transmission process, sibling position,* and *societal regression.* Table 12.2 provides a summary of these concepts. To illustrate his family therapy theory, we will provide a brief description of each of them. This theoretical basis is what differentiates the family therapy approach from those professions that had previously tried to help distressed families from a personal perspective.

Differentiation of self refers to a person's ability to understand which personal processes are intellectual and which ones are emotional. Think about the words "thought" and "feeling." Have you ever reacted to someone and then wondered why you responded the way you did? Bowen would suggest the first point to consider is whether you confused your thoughts and your feelings. People who are clearly differentiated can accurately communicate within the family environment and stand up for themselves; those people whose thoughts and feelings are not well separated are considered to be *fused.* Differentiation of self also applies to a person's relationship to the family of origin. Bowen believed that we are born with a need to balance feelings of togetherness and

Table 12.2 Bowen's Core Concepts

Concept	Description
Differentiation of self	Ability to separate thoughts and feelings, self and family
Triangulation	Use of third person to reduce interpersonal tension within family
Nuclear family emotional systems	People with similar emotional styles attract each other
Family projection process	Identify child as problem rather than parents
Emotional cutoff	Physical distancing from parents to minimize emotional interactions
Multigenerational transmission process	Similarity of emotional styles across family generations
Sibling position	Birth order impact on emotional development
Societal regression	Society from a family perspective

separateness from our families (Wetchler & Piercy, 1996). This is a difficult process, and most of us spend our entire lives learning to balance these two feelings of dependence and independence.

Triangulation refers to a method used by family members who experience interpersonal tension. Rather than deal with his or her relative about the negative emotion he or she is experiencing toward that family member, the person using triangulation brings another person into the interaction as a way to dilute the problem. This other person may be a member of the family, a friend, or even a therapist. Bowen suggested that when a family member is drawn into this type of conflict the selected family member is likely to be the least differentiated person available and thus more easily manipulated. This third person is viewed as reducing the level of tension between the original two. The larger the family, the more likely there will be multiple, interlocking triangles in existence before the family seeks professional assistance. During family therapy, members of a triangle are separated. Bowen felt one of the more successful ways to separate them was to work with the healthiest member of the family. This person, in Bowen's system, is the one considered most differentiated. This person could then be taught effective ways to intervene in various family relationships that are problematic.

Nuclear family emotional systems refers to Bowen's concept that people tend to seek partners whose level of differentiation is similar to their own. If these two people have low levels of differentiation, they are quite likely to become fused. When they have children, these children will continue this family pattern of low levels of differentiation. It is common to say that people seek life partners who are similar to them in some significant way. Historically, we have considered these similarities in terms of culture, religion, education, and other demographic factors. Bowen is using this same concept but applying it to internal family patterns.

Family projection process is Bowen's term for parents projecting their stress onto one of their children. This is likely to occur when the parents have relatively low levels of differentiation. This "problem child" may respond to the parents' projection in a variety of ways. For example, this child may be highly attached to the parents and therefore refuse to leave home to go to school. The level of stress within the family will impact how strongly the child reacts.

Emotional cutoff is seen in children who try to handle their overinvolvement in the family problems by separating themselves emotionally from that family. Children may try to run away from home as a solution to their problems. Older adolescents may choose a socially acceptable way to escape their parents by going away to college. Even if they attend a local college, these adolescents may elect to live in the dorm in order to separate themselves from the family issues. They keep their interactions with the family on a superficial level and try to make their interactions as brief as possible in order to remain emotionally separate from the family. If the child is unable to actually move out of the house and does not feel comfortable with the idea of running away, that child may choose to spend greater amounts of time in his or her room. Although this child may still be able to deal with routine family matters, when anything considered emotional arises, the child has developed a safe place for retreat. In families in which siblings share rooms, this method of escape may be unavailable.

Bowen's approach to understanding families uses a **multigenerational transmission process.** As with many approaches to family therapy, Bowen suggests that it is important not just to learn about the current family but also to gather information about previous generations. We mentioned before that this was one of his unique contributions to family therapy. He felt that people tend to look for spouses who have similar levels of differentiation to their own and to project their lack of differentiation onto their children. Thus, after a number of generations of this selection process, the family is likely to have increasingly fused couples. Learning about previous generations helps the family therapist to better understand family pathology. This part of Bowen's theory grew out of his work with schizophrenic children.

Early personality theorists, such as Alfred Adler, suggested that birth order was an important variable in personality development. Bowen agreed with this concept. **Sibling position,** according to Bowen, influenced how a person can be expected to behave as a parent. Unlike early personality theorists who placed great emphasis on the specific place in the family in terms of personality development, Bowen was more interested in the role the child played within the family of origin. An oldest child who was responsible for caring for his or her siblings was prepared for a later parenting role. A youngest child, however, who never had that level of responsibility did not have that preparation for becoming a parent. Thus, it might be predicted that this youngest child would have some degree of difficulty fulfilling a parental role as an adult.

Bowen's model of family therapy was not limited to a description of the family. He suggested that the development of the society in which the person lives also impacts family functioning. Just as families can be described as undifferentiated, so can societies. Some societies experience great stress. Societal stressors include natural conditions such as massive storm devastation or earthquakes as well as political conditions such as riots. He felt such stress could lead to **societal regression.** Under these conditions, the leaders of the society tend to make decisions based on emotion rather than distinguishing between their intellectual understanding of issues and their emotional reactions to them. Perhaps his system should be taught to politicians!

One of the tools Bowen recommended to assist therapists to better understand families is the **genogram.** A genogram is a diagram about the family. This diagram includes such information as marriage, birth, and death of family members as well as their ages and geographical locations. The genogram is not limited to the current family but includes the extended family as well. In this type of diagram, a male is represented by a square and a female is represented by a circle. The person's age is written within that shape. A couple is attached by a line and their children are attached to that line. Information from the genogram is used as part of the work with the family in therapy. An example of a family genogram can be seen in the accompanying figure (Petry & McGoldrick, 2005).

Overall, a major goal of this approach to family therapy is to help individual family members differentiate from their family of origin. One therapeutic approach to help reach this goal is to reduce the level of anxiety in both the individual family members and the family as a unit. Insight is used as part of understanding this process, but action in the form of a different pattern of family interaction is seen as the key to change. Individuals who do not live near their family of origin may be told to visit that family and observe family interactions as a start toward differentiation. Once a family member becomes differentiated, this does not mean that person separates from the family. Although the person remains in contact with the family of origin, the family no longer controls that person's behavior. Thus, the person no longer needs symptoms and is able to form appropriate relationships.

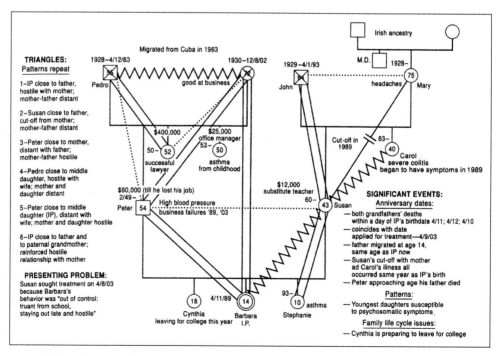

Sample family genogram *Reprinted from "Psychologists' Desk Reference, Second Edition," edited by Koocher, Norcross, and Hill III (2004), Fig. 1, Ortiz-Brown family genogram, p. 367. Reprinted by permission of Oxford University Press.*

Salvador Minuchin

Salvador Minuchin, a psychiatrist like Bowen, developed **structural family therapy** (1974, 1981). He has been described as both colorful and charismatic (Nichols, 2002). These personal characteristics have added to the popularity of his approach to working with families. Following his graduation from medical school, Minuchin worked in an inner-city setting at a school for troubled adolescents. The majority of these adolescents were from poor African-American families. This work led to the publication of one of his early books, *Families of the Slums* (Minuchin, Montalvo, Gurney, Rosman, & Schumer, 1967). Minuchin was particularly interested in psychological boundaries among family members. His work with families focused on changing the type and intensity of the relationships among family members.

Minuchin uses the term *family structure* to refer to rules developed within a family about who is supposed to interact with whom. Structures change over time as the family changes. Some structures last only a short time, while others are more long-term. Minuchin suggested that healthy families have a hierarchal structure. Parents have more power than the children have. Older children have more responsibility than younger ones do. Children learn the rules of their family in order to function in it. The family therapist needs to learn the family rules and structure before trying to help a dysfunctional family make changes. Although this may sound easy, it can be very difficult to learn the *actual* rules used by a family. The family therapist must attend to different versions of rules

Salvador Minuchin *Photo courtesy of the Minuchin Center for the Family.*

that are recounted by different family members as well as the nonverbal cues that what is described may not actually represent what occurs within that family.

Minuchin also analyzed families in terms of their subsystems. *Family subsystems* are alliances that develop within the family to address specific functions. Thus, family members may be in an alliance with family member X for one purpose and family member Y for another purpose. They may also form an alliance with the same family member but for a different purpose. Some alliances work well and others may not. For example, the father and mother may have a husband-wife subsystem to address marital issues. They may also form the parental subsystem to address child-rearing issues. Sibling subsystems teach the children not only how to relate to each other within the family but also how to build coalitions outside the family system and how to deal with their parents.

How these family subsystems interact with each other will also vary among families. Subsystems have rules that the family follows. These rules include who is permitted to participate and how the subsystems work with each other. Minuchin used the term **boundary permeability** to refer to the kind of contact members of the family may have with each other. Some families have highly rigid boundaries, or what are called nonpermeable boundaries. If the family is highly enmeshed, however, boundaries may be highly permeable. Consider the family in which a fourteen-year-old was sent home from school because he was caught smoking in the boys' restroom. If the family has highly rigid boundaries, the parents will handle this boy's discipline problem. They may determine a specific punishment, such as limited TV privileges for a specified amount of time or extra household chores. In an enmeshed family, however, the adolescent's behavior may be a topic for discussion over dinner that evening. Each parent will react differently. Perhaps the father will start to check his son's room for evidence of cigarettes, smell his clothing for evidence of further smoking, and so on. One of the siblings may begin to tease this adolescent about dying of lung cancer without any interference from the parents. Of course, this latter case would not be viewed as a healthy family.

Power within the family changes over time depending on the *alignments* and *coalitions*. For Minuchin *power* refers to the ability to make decisions within the family and then to carry out those decisions. By aligning with a powerful family member, you increase your power within the family. In Minuchin's system, an *alignment* is a joining of family members to advocate for, or oppose, an activity, while a *coalition* is a joining of family members against another member of the family. It is not always clear within a family who has power over what topic and so alignments and coalitions may shift. Generally, the more enmeshed the family the more vague the power structure. Families with either excessively rigid or excessively permeable boundaries have difficulty functioning effectively.

Structural family therapists form hypotheses about the structure of the family as the basis for understanding family dysfunction. They then work with the family to develop goals, such as changing coalitions and alliances, to allow better functioning. They focus on the present rather than the past of the family. In contrast to the genograms of Bowen, structural family therapists are more likely to do **family mapping.** Family mapping is a way to diagram the ways the family is currently interacting. These diagrams allow both the therapist and the family to consider which family subsystems are contributing most to the dysfunction as well as to plan ways to change the situation. Structural family therapists also use *enactment* within the family session. This role-playing process allows the family to actually see, rather than merely describe, its interactions. Enactment may also provide the therapist with a clearer picture of family dynamics and therefore increase the therapist's ability to develop interventions. As problems become clearer, the therapist may help the family *reframe* certain problems. A common family issue is to view problems as belonging to individuals rather than to the family as a whole. A family member may be viewed as "sick" and therefore the problem needs to be addressed at the individual level. If that "sick" person's behavior is reframed as being not an illness but rather that the person is "frightened," the family can then consider ways to change circumstances so that person can be more comfortable. This process moves the issue into the entire system rather than considering it an internal problem of one person.

Concluding Comments

As we saw with couples therapy, family therapy tends to include work on improving communication within the family group. Unlike individual psychotherapy or even couples therapy, however, it is rare for a family to seek family therapy. The more common scenario is for the first appointment to be made for one member of the family. This member is often called the *identified patient* within the family. Frequently, the identified patient is an adolescent. After the interview process, the psychologist may decide that the problem is not really an individual one but rather an issue within the family system itself. At that point, the psychologist suggests that some sessions for the entire family would be helpful.

Some students may be wondering why a psychologist would not recommend at least some form of family therapy with all patients. After all, when one member of the family unit is experiencing problems these problems are likely to impact the other members of the family. There are several reasons family therapy is not the universal answer for all patients. First, the family may be so dysfunctional that family therapy would have no chance of being successful. Individual therapy may be used to help members adjust to conditions that cannot be changed easily or perhaps to provide a foundation for later family therapy. Second, there are cases in which one or more members of the family refuse to participate in therapy. Unless family therapy is court-ordered, or the person refusing is a minor and the parents require that minor to attend, other forms of intervention will be needed. It may also be that if a family member is forced to attend family therapy that person may be so uncooperative or disruptive that therapy is sabotaged. Another issue is that the psychologist to whom the patient was referred is not trained in family therapy and may not consider family therapy as an option.

We all think we know what we mean by "family." This is not as clear as you might think. We started this section with some definitions of this term. Now that you have read about some of the forms of working with this hard-to-define group, let's see how we can summarize this information. The term *family therapy* is used to refer to intervention with a range of subsets of emotionally related people. In some cases, therapy may include parents and children. Other family therapy may expand on this base and include grandparents or even further removed relatives such as aunts and uncles. Thus, family therapy could be viewed as a specialized form of group therapy. There may actually be more people involved in a family therapy session than in the typical group session, depending on the size of the family. If a relative is considered to have an impact on the family dynamics of the family unit that family member is asked to participate in the family therapy process.

In some cases, people who act "as if" they are members of the family but actually are not members of the family may even be asked to participate. The key is the person's role rather than the legal relationship.

In addition to the general term *family therapy* there are also some other terms you may find as you do additional reading on this subject. A popular term in the psychological literature for the concept of seeing the whole family together is *conjoint family therapy*. Although this is the name Satir used for her method of working with families, it is also used more generally in the family therapy literature. A related form of family therapy is **concurrent family therapy,** in which the same therapist sees all members of the family but does so on an individual basis rather than in the same session. Finally, there is **collaborative family therapy,** in which each member of the family sees a different therapist but all members are in therapy at the same time. It is called "collaborative" because the therapists meet to discuss their individual patients and the family unit as a whole rather than the family unit meeting together.

Overall, family therapy in its various forms assumes that if you influence one part of the family system you will influence the other parts. Each form views dysfunction as relating to the unit as a whole rather than to individual members of the system. Despite this focus on the family unit rather than the individual, family therapists must also be aware of the developmental issues being faced by each member of that family system.

Family systems therapies have not gone without criticism. For example, these approaches have been charged with being culturally biased because most of the models used in the United States were developed on the basis of Caucasian, middle-class nuclear families (Imber-Black, 1990). As we noted earlier, Minuchin's approach, based on his early work with inner-city, poor, African-American families, is an exception to this criticism. This narrow cultural vantage point could lead family therapists to ignore other forms of adaptive family structure. For example, encouraging a Latino family to differentiate actually works against the tradition of **familismo** that is central to many Hispanic/Latino cultures (Sue & Sue, 2003). This term refers to the tendency to emphasize the needs of the family above those of the individual. These individuals find their identity through belonging to the family. For example, if a relative is ill, it is considered not only appropriate but also important to stay home from work or school to care for that person. Of course, such behavior may be viewed as illegal in the case of an older sibling staying home so that both parents can work if the ill person is a younger sibling. Most school systems do not accept familismo as an appropriate excuse for missing classes. Helping families integrate the demands of society with their cultural values can be difficult. On the other hand, if family therapists spend all of their time centered on the unique family traditions of a given group, they may ignore how these traditions may be contributing to the current distress in the family. A balance between cultural values and societal norms is likely to serve the family best.

We also note that until recently the focus of work on family therapy has been on heterosexual issues. There is an increasing interest in work with gay, lesbian, and bisexual families (e.g., Johnson & Colucci, 1999). This can be expected to be a growing area of need and is one reason we described Trang as one of our ongoing patients in this book. For example, between one and five million lesbians in the United States are either biological or adoptive mothers (DeGenova & Rice, 2002). Current data indicate that the majority of these children were conceived as a result of a heterosexual relationship. After leaving that relationship, the mother may form a relationship with another woman who may then serve the role of stepparent to the child or children. If this second woman also has children, the same issues that arise for children when their heterosexual parents divorce and remarry occur as these stepsiblings become acquainted. In other families, the child was conceived through artificial insemination or was adopted, as is the case with Trang. Studies of children who were raised in gay or lesbian families suggest that these children have no greater likelihood of developing psychological problems than children who are raised in heterosexual households. However, therapists need to be aware that there are situations in which child custody has been denied because it was judged that living in a same-sex parental family would adversely impact the child (Patterson & Redding, 1996). These issues may be important and yet unspoken parts of family distress. These concerns need to be addressed as part of the treatment process.

Family therapists are continuing to develop their specialty to address common life stressors that may impact family functioning. One illustration of this direction in the practice of family therapy is attention to the impact of suicide on the surviving family members. The annual thirty thousand suicides in the United States result in between five and six million bereaved individuals (Kaslow & Aronson, 2004). Family therapy can be an integral part of addressing this problem. After a thorough family assessment, the psychologist may recommend some combination of individual therapy, family therapy, medication, and support group. Family therapy with this special population should consider "psychological distress and painful affects, understanding denial as a protective coping strategy, appreciating concerns about family disintegration, helping families deal with stigmatization, and creating a suicide story" (Kaslow & Aronson, 2004, p. 240). The *suicide story* is a unique part of this therapeutic process. Each member of the family contributes to this shared family narrative. Family members discuss their understanding of why their loved one committed suicide and reconstruct both the psychological and behavioral indicators prior to the act. Cultural attitudes about suicide must be considered when helping the family come to terms with the suicide and develop a shared picture of what occurred. This area of contribution illustrates not only family therapy but also the active role psychologists take in considering where they may contribute to society's needs.

Group Therapy

Group psychotherapy involves multiple patients being seen in the same session. The couples and family therapies previously described in this chapter are specialized forms of group therapy. Other therapy groups are composed of individuals who are not related to each other in either a legal or an emotional way. These are the groups that are most likely to be described in books about group therapy. In this section, we will give you some history of group therapy, discuss the overall process of group therapy, assess some issues that must be considered when doing this type of therapy, and describe psychodrama as a unique form of group psychotherapy. Students who want to read more about this topic are referred to one of the many general textbooks about group psychotherapy (e.g., Ormont, 2003; Sadock & Kaplan, 1993; Yalom, 1995).

There are no specific numbers of either patients or therapists required for group therapy. Often therapy groups include between six and ten patients and one or two therapists.

When there is more than one therapist, they are called cotherapists. Play therapy groups for children typically include no more than four children. The family therapy groups we described earlier may be larger depending on the family constellation. As you can imagine, with so many unrelated people involved, group therapy can be very intense. It can be hard to keep track of what is going on in the therapy session. Because there are so many people involved, group therapy sessions may require more time than traditional individual psychotherapy sessions. Group therapy sessions typically last ninety minutes.

History

Although we described the history of clinical psychology in chapter 3, we will make a few additional historical comments specific to group psychotherapy here. Group therapy traces its origin to Joseph Henry Pratt's work with tuberculosis patients in Boston in the early 1900s (Hersen, Kazdin, & Bellack, 1983). Those group therapy sessions included having patients give testimonials and a public recording of their weight. This weight focus was because a major problem for people with tuberculosis is in maintaining their weight. Certain modern therapy groups, such as Alcoholics Anonymous (AA), are based on this early work. In AA groups, part of the session involves publicly noting the number of days you have been sober. There were other early influences on group therapy as well. Psychoanalysts in England at the Tavistock Clinic were among the early leaders of using a group approach to psychoanalysis (Ezriel, 1973).

Group approaches with psychiatric patients increased during World War II because of the increased need for mental health services and limited personnel available to provide these services. This situation has been both positive and negative for group therapy. Although this increased need for group therapy led to the development and ongoing evaluation of the group therapy process, it also led to a common misconception that group therapy was just a "cheap" form of individual therapy. Further study of group process led to a better understanding of those factors that may be unique to the group approach. Even with this information, it is not unusual for psychologists to need to "convince" some patients that group therapy is actually the treatment of choice for them.

During the 1970s, there was a proliferation of many types of group therapy. In an attempt to provide some order to this rapidly developing field within psychology, Lieberman (1977) suggested that the many approaches could be grouped into four major types: psychotherapy groups, peer self-help groups, human potential groups, and consciousness-raising groups. In this conceptual system, professionals lead psychotherapy groups. The purpose of psychotherapy groups is to improve the patient's mental health. Peer self-help groups are designed for people who share a similar life problem. These groups usually do not involve professional leadership but rather a mutual sharing of problems and peer support system. For example, some high schools have organized peer self-help groups to address problems of adolescence. Participants in human potential groups do not view themselves as having emotional problems. These groups have a leader whose role is different from that of the members. The aim of these groups is personal growth or self-actualization. The leader provides structure and assistance to help the individuals in these groups reach their goals. These groups may include a range of group exercises in addition to general discussion to achieve the desired goal. A major criterion for joining a consciousness-raising group is membership in the same large subgroup of the population (e.g., female). These groups focus on the meaning of being part of the specified group within the larger population. The 1970s were a rich time for theorizing about group processes. Frank (1979) added two other group types he felt were not covered in Lieberman's system: marriage and family groups and counterculture groups. We have already discussed the marriage and family groups that can be considered naturally occurring groups. Frank used the term *counterculture* to refer to groups composed of individuals who view themselves as living by a philosophy or code of conduct that is different from, and considered superior to, that of the society in which they live. Our focus in this chapter is on the psychotherapy groups.

Group Composition

Why would you want to use the time of two professionals as cotherapists rather than having just one therapist for a group? Over the years, many advantages of using cotherapists for group psychotherapy have appeared in the literature (Corey & Corey, 1997; Nystul, 1999). We will briefly note seven of these advantages here. First, the patients can benefit from the expertise of the two therapists. Second, using a male-female cotherapist team may give a more balanced approach to the therapy process. Although some readers may find this suggestion somewhat "sexist," the group therapy literature is filled with material about the benefits of this combination. Third, the two therapists benefit from postsession discussion of what happened. This discussion can provide additional insight about the group as a whole as well as about individual group members. Fourth, one therapist may be able to focus on an individual group member who needs the attention while the other therapist can attend to the group process. Fifth, using cotherapists in group therapy also decreases the probability of therapist burnout because of the peer support. This is especially important when working with really intense patients. Sixth, having cotherapists means that there will be knowledgeable coverage of the group in case one of the therapists becomes ill. Finally, both therapists are assured that they will be able both to consult with each other regarding patient progress and to provide support, insight, and planning opportunities.

How does the psychologist decide which patients go into which group? A number of factors will be considered in this case. The psychologist must first decide what type of group he or she is going to have. Some groups are described as **homogeneous** while other groups are **heterogeneous.** Group therapists often debate the meaning of these two terms for group composition. They ask, "Homogeneous or heterogeneous for what?" What characteristics are included in this delineation? Do you need to consider just the diagnostic label, or do you also mean such demographics as age, sex, educational level, and socioeconomic status? There is no single answer to this question that will satisfy all group therapists. Any combination of these factors might be used to construct a psychotherapy group. Yalom (1970) suggested that heterogeneous groups are better when the purpose is an intensive form of treatment. Although homogeneous groups tend to feel comfortable with each other more quickly, they may also remain on a more superficial level than heterogeneous groups.

Another way to distinguish therapy groups is to describe them as either **open** or **closed.** An open group is one that generally maintains its size by adding members when members of the group leave. Open groups don't have a fixed ending date. Some people leave group therapy because they no longer need it or can't afford the time or cost, while others may just drop out of treatment either permanently or for a "break." Open groups may continue indefinitely. The major limitation to continuing open therapy groups is the availability of new patients to fill the openings left by those who no longer participate. A closed group does not take new members once it has started. Closed groups today tend to be ones designed for a specific purpose and with a specific time commitment expected before the group will end. Good examples of a closed group are a parenting skills group and a smoking cessation group. For example, a person may agree to attend six weeks of a parent skills training group. Of course, he or she still has the right to quit before the end of that time period if he or she wishes. The expectation at the beginning of this group is that all parents who start the group will stay for the six sessions. Closed groups may also be used in settings where attrition is not an issue, such as long-term prison settings. Just as there is no specific format for determining group composition, there is no specific length of time for a group session to last. We noted earlier in this section that traditionally individual therapy lasts for fifty minutes and group therapy lasts for ninety minutes; however, a range of session lengths are used for both individual and group psychotherapy. Group therapists also use a range of theoretical orientations for their work.

How Group Psychotherapy May Help

Many theorists have tried to understand the specific ways group therapy helps patients. Psychiatrist Irving Yalom suggested a number of factors that may be relevant. His ideas are among the most common cited in the group psychotherapy literature and so we will discuss them here. Yalom (1970) suggested ten primary categories of what he terms **curative factors** that operate through group psychotherapy. Although variations of this list have emerged over the years, we are presenting his original list. These curative factors provide the foundation for much of the later work in this specialty.

Imparting of information refers to the didactic function of group psychotherapy. This information comes from both the therapist(s) and the other patients. Although Yalom noted that his experience was that information was not generally of direct use to patients, provision of such information demonstrated mutual caring. This mutual caring was helpful. Although the therapist may not provide didactic information in every group session, Yalom noted that he had never conducted a group session in which patients did not provide advice to other patients. Whether or not patients give or seek advice in the group is also a clue to their individual interpersonal behavior. This information is useful to the psychologist in helping the patients.

Instillation of hope is important for keeping a person in therapy. Yalom suggested that therapists should point out patient improvement to others in the group to highlight hope as a powerful factor in helping patients improve. Therapists do not do this every time something positive happens but rather on a periodic basis. Patients will also make spontaneous observations about others' improvement that serves the same purpose. Hope is a major positive variable in self-help groups, but it also operates powerfully in more traditional therapy groups.

Universality refers to the fact that many patients who seek therapy believe their problems are unique to them and no one could possibly suffer from the same problem. Their sense of being completely different, in a negative way, from everyone else tends to become exaggerated as they isolate themselves from others. The therapist doing individual psychotherapy can explain that despite the unique nature of the patient's life experiences his or her overall distress is not unique. Such comments are quite routine in individual psychotherapy. However, for many patients accepting this concept may be difficult. In group psychotherapy the patient hears directly about the problems faced by the other group members. Because this experience often happens early in the group therapy experience, the patient's relief at no longer feeling so alone can be a powerful tool to aid the psychologist in working with him or her. Common themes or topics are likely to occur. This experience can debunk the myth that his or her problems are unique and allow him or her to appreciate the fact that other patients have very similar issues. This realization can lead to mutual problem-solving within the group.

Altruism refers to the fact that patients help each other. Group members tend to point out each other's strengths and weaknesses. Feeling needed is a common human desire. This feeling may contribute to a sense of self-worth. When they first enter therapy, group members often feel useless. They may have low self-esteem. When the idea of group therapy is presented to them they may question what they could offer others as well as what other patients could possibly offer them. As they learn that they can help others, they begin to value themselves.

The corrective recapitulation of the primary family group refers to the fact that the therapy group can seem like a family. Having a male and female cotherapist simulates a family. It is easy to view them as traditional parents. This is not meant to imply that same-sex cotherapists are not used or that when they are used this factor does not work. Just having two authority figures in a setting with a number of people who are looking to them for advice simulates a family setting regardless of the sex of those authority figures. Many adult patients have a background that includes living in a dysfunctional family. Group therapy allows them to recreate, understand, and deal with group members in a way different from the dysfunctionality of their family experience. They see and experience a more positive way to interact.

Development of socializing techniques refers to the social learning that occurs in group therapy. In some therapy groups, this factor is facilitated through the use of role-play. Regardless of whether or not role-play is used, feedback from other group members is likely to be more honest than in general society. Patients who have poor interpersonal skills or some specific annoying behaviors may get feedback about them. These behaviors are often ones that lead others to just ignore or avoid the person rather than tell the person what is wrong. For example, consider a person who tends to use considerable profanity in her speech. Rather than tell her that her language is annoying, some people may just stay away from her. In a therapy group, others are likely to confront her about her language.

Imitative behavior refers to the tendency of patients to copy the behavior of their therapists. In group psychotherapy, patients have more models from whom to select aspects of behavior. Bandura's research on social learning has demonstrated that learning can occur through vicarious reinforcement. In group therapy, patients may learn adaptive behavior by watching other members of the group change their behavior without ever discussing their own problem in that area. For example, one patient might note that she sometimes has difficulty falling asleep at night when she has had a long day at work in her office and had not been able to get any exercise. She tells the group that now when she has this type of day she routinely takes a long, brisk walk around her neighborhood in the evening before bedtime. This combination of fresh air and exercise has led to fewer sleepless nights for her. Several sessions later, a patient who never mentioned having sleep problems thanks her for the suggestion and notes, "Those walks really work!"

Interpersonal learning "is a broad and complex curative factor representing the group therapy analogue of such individual therapy curative factors as insight, working through the transference, and the corrective emotional experience" (Yalom, 1970, p. 16). As patients continue to attend group sessions, they have the opportunity over a period of time to integrate small pieces of information from others. They can then develop a picture of how their behavior impacts others as well as how others influence them. This information provides a foundation for understanding their current level of distress.

Group cohesiveness refers to the "patient's relationship to his group therapist, to the other group members, and to the group as a whole" (Yalom, 1970, p. 37). Members of a therapy group tend to develop a sense of togetherness. Rather than disappoint the others in the group, a member may continue to attend rather than quit therapy. At other times, they may maintain improved behavior for the same reason. Some patients have the same reaction to their psychologist in individual psychotherapy. In group psychotherapy, however, the patient tends to develop this tie to a number of people rather than just one. There is still a bond with the psychologist but also one with the group as a whole and perhaps with some individual members of that group. Yalom suggested that the strength of feelings of group cohesiveness is a major predictor of therapy outcome. A feeling of group cohesiveness can be seen, for example, when a patient is unable to attend a group session, for a good reason, and calls in advance to let the therapist know why he will miss the session. That patient does not want others in the group to worry about his absence.

Catharsis refers to the patient's ability to express feelings in an open and honest way. The strong expression of emotion is not only therapeutic but also seems to increase group cohesiveness. Group sessions provide a safe place for the patient to express strong emotions that may not be acceptable in the outside society. Of course the therapist must be vigilant about the way this expressed emotion may impact others in the group and address any concerns about it within the session.

Although Yalom suggests that group therapy does not progress through stages, some others in the field have developed a stage model (e.g., Corey & Corey, 1997). This four-stage model suggests an initial stage, transition stage, working stage, and final stage. The initial stage involves preparation for the group and the early sessions when the patients are learning to be comfortable with each other and understand group process. Once patients begin to understand what is happening, they may become uncomfortable about discussing their problems with others as well as have concerns about being accepted by these new people. Support from the therapist allows the patients to move into the working stage of group process. In this stage, they explore their issues and translate their understanding into needed life changes. The final stage involves preparation for leaving the group. In closed groups this period will occur at the same time for all members, but in open-ended groups this stage will occur at different times for each member of the group.

Getting Ready for Group Therapy

Patients are not usually just placed in a therapy group. Some prior preparation is needed before attending the first session. In outpatient settings, the psychologist is likely to have at least one individual session with the patient before the first group session. After determining that group therapy is an appropriate intervention method for this person and that a group is available, the psychologist will need to discuss how groups work. The idea of socialization for group therapy is no different from providing some overview of what to expect in individual therapy, but some of the topics are different. Patients who have received pregroup preparation have been found to have more faith in group psychotherapy and also to engage in significantly more group interaction than those who do not have this pregroup experience. These differences exist not only initially but continue over time in the group (Yalom, Houts, Newell, & Rand, 1967).

Preparation of patients for group therapy includes some unique ethical issues. As you have learned, psychologists must maintain patient confidentiality except under special circumstances. These exceptions are explained to the patient prior to starting therapy in both the office policy statement and by the therapist. The other patients in the therapy group, however, do not have these professional constraints. Thus, patients in group therapy are asked to keep what is discussed in therapy confidential to members of the group. Patients must depend on each other to maintain confidentiality. There are no ethical or legal requirements that members of a group maintain confidentiality. Part of the trust developed within the group is that others will not discuss their issues outside the group setting. Until this trust develops, patients are likely to be careful about what they discuss in the group.

Many group therapists, especially those conducting outpatient groups, also ask their patients not to form social relationships outside the group setting. As with confidentiality, there is no enforcement mechanism related to socialization. Patients are seldom rejected from a group because of socialization patterns. When this request is made, the reason for it is explained. Patients who form social relationships outside the group develop material that is separate from the group's activities. They may not choose to share that material with the entire group, thus interfering with the flow of the group sessions. It may also add stress to these individuals because of their concern that others will learn of their violation of the rules or that they will divulge something they learned about the person in their social setting. Thus, participation in the group sessions may be impacted. This decreased participation hurts both the individual patient and the group as a whole.

The APA Ethics Code (2002) has a special section for group therapy—10.03. This standard notes that psychologists "describe at the outset the roles and responsibilities of all parties and the limits of confidentiality" (p. 1073). Of course, the other members of the group are not held to the same consequences as the psychologist for violation of confidentiality. When psychologists consider both their ethical code and relevant state laws they quickly note that these regulations tend to be written for professionals who are working with individual patients rather than for a group therapy format. Despite its limitations, these rules must be applied to group psychotherapy and thus impact some of the patient preparation we discussed.

Training for Group Therapy

How much training do clinical psychologists receive about group psychotherapy? Early studies indicated that group psychotherapy did not tend to be a required area of study in clinical psychology training programs (Butler & Fuhriman, 1986; Zohn & Carmody, 1978). It may have been an elective course but that meant that only a subset of the clinical students would take it. As the number of Psy.D. programs increased, some psychologists wondered if perhaps these practice-oriented programs might provide more training in group psychotherapy than was reported in the early surveys. A survey of APA-accredited clinical programs reported that all of the Psy.D. programs did offer a group psychotherapy course while only about a third of the Ph.D. programs offered such a course (Weinstein & Rossini, 1998). If you stop examining the data at this point, you might get an erroneous impression, however, about group psychotherapy training today. When the data are considered further we find that only 40 percent of the programs offering a course in group psychotherapy actually required that course of their students. We have no idea how often group psychotherapy courses were actually offered in those programs where it was not required or how many students elected to take this course.

   If clinical psychologists do not get group psychotherapy training in graduate school, where do they learn this skill? The next step in the training process is the predoctoral internship. Perhaps this is where the training occurs? Over 422 fully accredited predoctoral internships in clinical psychology were surveyed about the training they provided in group psychotherapy (Markus & King, 2003). About 62 percent of the facilities that responded to this survey indicated that they provided a didactic seminar about group psychotherapy. In addition to the time predoctoral interns spend seeing patients, they also receive didactics. These are typically time-limited seminars and individual lectures on relevant topics. However, the amount of time devoted to group psychotherapy according to this survey varied considerably—from 11/2 to 158 hours of training. Examination of topics covered in these seminars led these researchers to conclude that they were inadequate to provide a solid foundation for group psychotherapy practice.

   The majority of predoctoral interns do have the opportunity to lead a group, even without the didactic foundation. They may serve as a cotherapist with a psychologist or other mental health professional from whom they learn how groups function. Leading one or two groups, however, is not considered sufficient background to become a specialist in group psychotherapy. Where else might they receive this training? Perhaps this training occurs during formal postdoctoral programs. This topic has not yet been reported in the research literature, partially because many postdoctoral experiences are not within organized training programs. Instead, they are individually designed learning experiences. The available data raise concerns about preparation of clinical psychologists for the practice of group psychotherapy.

Psychodrama

We decided to conclude this chapter with a description of a rather unique form of group psychotherapy called **psychodrama.** Although this form of therapy is not widely practiced today, it is sometimes credited as one of the earliest forms of modern group psychotherapy (Nystul, 1999). Therefore, for historical purposes we wanted our readers to have a general knowledge of it. It is different from the types of group psychotherapy typically shown in films and thus may be new to you. Psychodrama is a combination of therapy and acting. It is a method of working with an individual patient in a group setting. Jacob L. Moreno developed psychodrama (1946, 1959). He recommended using an actual stage if possible. One of the goals of psychodrama is to assist the patient with self-expression. This self-expression is considered in the context of the patient's relationships with significant others in her or his life. It also allows the patient to test reality by enacting important situations with real people rather than just talking about them.

There are four major roles in psychodrama. The therapist serves as the *director* of the drama. In this role, the therapist leads the interactions. At times, the therapist may describe a scene that is going to be enacted before it occurs. The therapist is also expected to develop an accepting atmosphere in the setting. If someone verbally attacks the patient, the therapist intervenes to maintain a productive process. The patient who is the current focus of the session is the central character, or *protagonist,* in the drama. The protagonist describes a problem that will serve as the starting point of the drama. Other patients in the group, as well as staff members, serve in the role of *alter egos,* or auxiliaries. These auxiliaries represent significant others from the patient's life. Initially, the auxiliaries enact perceptions of these significant others. They are encouraged to put considerable emotion into their enactment to make it more real for the protagonist. According to Moreno, the auxiliaries may get insights into their own lives about issues that are similar to the role they are playing. The fourth role is the *audience.* The role of the audience is to provide acceptance of the patient as well as spontaneous participation in the drama. The director may also call on members of the audience to share experiences related to what they are observing.

The actual process of a psychodrama goes through three phases. It starts with a warm-up. During this phase, the participants prepare for the action to follow. They begin to develop a sense of trust and a willingness to enact new behaviors. New participants to psychodrama may need some explanation of the process during this phase.

The action phase of psychodrama involves the protagonist and auxiliaries acting out a situation and working through the issues involved in it. The director may assist the others in moving furniture and other props to help the protagonist set the scene for the drama. At times, the director may also ask others to change roles with the protagonist so that the protagonist has the opportunity to view his or her role from the perspective of another person. All participants in the drama are encouraged to act as if they are actually in the situation rather than merely talking about the situation. Many techniques have been used in the action phase of psychodrama. We will describe a few of them to illustrate this procedure. The *mirror technique* is one form of feedback that may be used. The purpose of this technique is to give the patient information about how others see him or her. This technique is monitored closely by the therapist so that the patient does not feel ridiculed. One of the auxiliaries plays the role of the protagonist while the protagonist observes this action. The auxiliary may use a combination of body postures, gestures, and verbalizations. Another technique used in psychodrama is the *double technique.* In this case, one of the auxiliaries takes the role of the protagonist. The auxiliary expresses what he or she believes are the patient's inner feelings and concepts. In some cases, multiple doubles may be used to address various aspects of the patient's personality. To facilitate this interaction, the double is asked to stand very close to the protagonist during this process. A third technique is *surplus reality.* This technique moves into fantasy rather than enacting a current situation. Surplus reality could involve an auxiliary portraying a monster or demon from the protagonist's dreams. The protagonist would have a dialogue with this fantasy creature. Surplus reality is also used to allow the protagonist to redo an experience from the past that was painful. Auxiliaries play characters from that situation and the protagonist has the opportunity for a corrective emotional experience.

The final part of the psychodrama is a sharing and discussion period. The auxiliaries and other group members share their observations with the protagonist. The therapist assists the protagonist in dealing with these observations and ensures that the feedback is helpful rather than critical. If only one session of psychodrama is planned for the patient, it is especially important that closure be complete. Regardless of whether or not there will be additional sessions, it is important for emotions to be decreased to a reasonable level before people leave the theater.

We noted that preparation of patients for group therapy includes some unique ethical issues. Certainly the use of psychodrama as a specialized form of group psychotherapy raises ethical concerns as well. For example, this approach to psychotherapy utilizes considerable emotional disclosure based, to a degree, on Freud's concept of catharsis. Although this approach may be working for the central individual in the drama, the leader needs to be aware of the fact that others may become overwhelmed or threatened by such a level of emotion (Glass, 1998). Another ethical issue related to psychodrama is how much training is necessary in order to use this technique. According to the APA Ethics Code, psychologists provide only those services for which they are competent and when they want to provide new services, they receive training in them. Since most doctoral programs do not have a course in psychodrama, how does a professional learn this technique? The standard in the field of psychodrama requires clinicians to "spend many hours as a client in the therapeutic process prior to using the technique with clients" (Klontz, 2004, p. 174). One reason a specific number of hours is not given is because of the differential time these clinicians may need to address their own unresolved issues. This process is considered especially important in psychodrama because these exercises may cause unexpected emotions to surface for the psychologist as well as the participants. As with any therapeutic technique, the psychologist must also be aware of populations for whom it is not appropriate. Some individuals for whom psychodrama may be contraindicated are those who are actively abusing substances, those with dissociative or psychotic disorders, and those who have difficulty regulating their affective state.

Although psychodrama is certainly not a routine technique used by clinical psychologists, it continues to be used. Psychodrama was a major force in group psychotherapy in the United States in the early years of the twentieth century but decreased in popularity here by the end of the century. As the twenty-first century began, it continued to be very popular, however, in many parts of Europe, South America, and the Far East (Kipper & Ritchie, 2003). Observers have suggested that perhaps its decline in popularity in the United States is correlated with the rise in emphasis about using empirically supported treatments. Much of the literature about psychodrama tends to be anecdotal or case studies rather than empirical research. As we noted previously, research on specific topics in psychology often starts with the developer of those subjects. In this case, Moreno was not a strong advocate of traditional psychological research. Thus, practitioners of psychodrama have tended to be clinicians and not academics. A meta-analysis of the available research on psychodrama published between 1965 and 1999 reported a moderate to large degree of patient improvement for all of the techniques evaluated (Kipper & Ritchie,

2003). Psychodrama worked equally well with college students and clinical samples. Although these results seem to suggest that psychodrama should once again be taught and included in clinical psychologists' repertoire, these authors found only twenty-five acceptable studies in that entire time period. These results do suggest that this is a topic worthy of further empirical study. There are about three hundred certified psychodrama practitioners in the United States and over six thousand in the world (Blatner, 1997). Students who are interested in learning more about psychodrama will find relatively few books available (e.g., Blatner, 2000; Sacks, Bilaniuk, & Gendron, 1995). We covered psychodrama in more detail than many clinical books do to illustrate the point that what is popular in one part of the world or at one time historically may be different from what is popular at other times or in other places.

Concluding Comments

Group psychotherapy continues to be a very popular therapeutic modality. Articles appear in the professional literature not only of clinical psychology but also of specialized groups or approaches for particular problems. Division 49 of the APA is the Division of Group Psychology and Group Psychotherapy illustrating the merging of theory and practice in this area. We have only scratched the surface of a very broad topic.

Sample Patient Data (Trang)

As we noted earlier in treating Trang's attention-deficit/hyperactivity disorder (ADHD), a multimodal approach is often best. To be effective, a child's developmental level and the individual strengths and the needs of the family and the child (Waschbusch, Kipp, & Pelham, 1998) must be taken into consideration. Family members may also need help managing their child's behavior as well as dealing with their own and other family members' feelings. Siblings may feel neglected or resent the time their parents spend with the ADHD child (Mash & Wolfe, 2005). Family counseling can be helpful in giving each family member a chance to share his or her feelings, expectations, and frustrations with a therapist. Support groups like Children and Adults with Attention-Deficit/Hyperactivity Disorder (CHADD) have local, regional, and national meetings to discuss the latest approaches to treating ADHD, as well as a forum for parents and family members to share their feelings. Online discussion groups and bulletin boards can be helpful to parents as well. Counseling the family can give family members more effective skills in relating to each other, developing behavior management skills, and dealing with feelings. Family counseling can also be a forum in which contracting and goal-setting with the ADHD child can be created. We decided that Trang's parents would benefit from a family session to discuss their feelings about the behavior management program we developed with them as well as to have a chance to express any frustrations they had been feeling. After one such session, we determined that they were doing well with the program. We therefore gave them the names of several local support groups for parents of ADHD children and let them know that they were welcome to return if they had any questions or problems with the program.

ETHICAL CONUNDRUM POINTS TO PONDER

This case involves what is often called "barter." The APA Ethics Code, Standard 6.05, indicates that psychologists may engage in barter only when it is not either clinically contraindicated or exploitative. In this standard, barter is defined as accepting goods, services, or some nonmonetary form of reimbursement for psychological services. This limitation in the family's finances could not have been expected when therapy started. Thus, it was not discussed in advance with the family. The psychologist might consider how it might be expected to impact the family if barter occurs or if it does not. If the psychologist strongly believes the family is benefiting from therapy and will not continue to benefit if they are not allowed to make this form of payment, then barter may be appropriate in this case. Once these issues have been evaluated, the psychologist might also benefit from consulting with a colleague before agreeing to it. This type of consultation would be done without violating patient confidentiality. If the colleague also agrees that barter is neither clinically contraindicated nor exploitative in this case, the psychologist can then agree to it. In terms of record-keeping, the psychologist will need to have the painting evaluated and record it in the office records at its fair market value.

Key Terms

Nathan Ackerman

adjunctive marital therapy

blamer

boundary permeability

Murray Bowen

closed therapy group

collaborative family therapy

concurrent family therapy

congruent communicators

conjoint family therapy

couples therapy

curative factors in group therapy

differentiation of self

emotional cutoff

family life chronology

family mapping

family projection process

family systems theorist

family therapy

familismo

genogram

group therapy

heterogeneous therapy group

homogeneous therapy group

irrelevant

Neil Jacobson

William Masters and Virginia Johnson

Salvador Minuchin

multigenerational transmission process

nuclear family emotional systems

open therapy group

placater

psychodrama

Virginia Satir

sibling position

societal regression

structural family therapy

superreasonable

triangulation

CHAPTER 13

Community Intervention and Public Policy

In the previous chapters, we discussed the traditional roles of clinical psychologists providing intervention with individuals, families, and groups. In this chapter, we talk about intervention on a broader level—the community. We will consider two ways psychologists work on the community level. The first of these approaches is to provide intervention programs in the community and the second is to develop public policy.

ETHICAL CONUNDRUM

As a psychologist, you have treated many patients for problems with attaining weight loss. Part of your practice involves evaluation of patients who are being considered for obesity surgery. You are asked to serve as a consultant, for a large fee, to a company that is planning a nationwide campaign for its new natural diet products. Although they will be using a professional advertising company for the actual wording of the ads, they want you to work with this company about the best ways to attract truly overweight people to their product. You ask the company for their research on product effectiveness to help you develop a marketing strategy. The company provides you with information that everything used in their diet products is natural with no chemical additives, but they have done no studies of product efficacy for weight loss.

Community Intervention

The development of a range of medications to treat emotional problems resulted in many people who previously were expected to spend their entire lives in institutions being released and returned to the community. Not all of the communities to which these former patients moved were prepared to provide the follow-up services they needed. As with any major societal change, communities needed time to determine ways to provide needed services to these new residents. Addressing the needs of former mental patients was not limited to individual communities. States also considered these issues on a broader level to integrate what was being done in individual communities.

Initiatives on a national level led to the passage of the Community Mental Health Centers Act by the U.S. Congress in 1963. This bill, often called the Kennedy bill because of President John F. Kennedy's strong support both for the bill and for initiatives designed to prevent mental disorders, provided funds to construct community mental health centers. The location of these centers was based on a combination of size of the population and distance from a center. It might seem to be logical to place more facilities in large urban areas than in smaller communities. These urban settings have larger populations. Developers of this legislation realized, however, that in more rural states some people might live too far from the nearest mental health center to be able to use its services if center placement was based solely on population. Therefore, a formula was developed to combine population and distance from the nearest facility to identify where centers should be located. This type of planning was an early indication of the special needs of rural healthcare in the United States.

Psychologists were members of the staff of these community mental health centers and were involved in all of their mandated programs. Each of these centers was mandated to provide what were considered five essential services: inpatient care, outpatient care, partial hospitalization, twenty-four-hour emergency services, and consultation and education. Each of these services had to be provided if the center was to qualify for federal funds. An early result of the construction of the mental health centers was an increased use of mental health services by all segments of the population (Veroff, Douvan, & Kulka, 1981). We do not know, however, if this increased use of mental health services was a result of the new community mental health centers or if it was because of changing popular views of psychotherapy. About the same time these facilities were constructed, there was an increase in positive media attention to diagnosis and treatment of mental disorders. One goal of these early community mental health centers was to promote community involvement with prevention efforts (Smith & Hobbs, 1966). Although these facilities were designed to provide treatment, prevention was also one of their mandates. Work on prevention included providing programs for various community groups and consulting with such community organizations as schools and businesses. Psychologists continue to view prevention as a key to their work in the community.

Money is needed to pay for staff and the development of services in these mental health centers. These funds were expected to come from state and local sources rather than from the federal government. Thus, the success of the community mental health center movement was ultimately dependent on the priority of mental health issues at the local and state level. Some of these centers did very well and continue to thrive in the twenty-first century, while others eventually were forced to close their doors.

When considering the need for community mental health services, it is helpful to know something about the potential number of people who might require such services. The number of people in the United States who experience emotional problems in any given year is hard to estimate but has been estimated to impact between 20 percent and 30 percent of adults and between 10 percent and 15 percent of children (Sundberg, Winebarger, & Taplin, 2002). Thus if some of these people can be helped through prevention programs before they develop problems it is not only a personal benefit but also a financial one. This philosophy is the basis of the prevention aspect of community mental health. Because prevention is so central to psychology's work in the community we will spend time examining this concept more closely.

Prevention

The concept of prevention started with work on physical illness. The Commission on Chronic Illness (1957) divided prevention into three subtypes—primary prevention, secondary prevention, and tertiary prevention (see Table 13.1). These terms were adapted for use by psychologists working in communities.

Primary prevention refers to attempting to change conditions that have the potential to lead to problems before those problems arise. The goal is to decrease the rate at which new cases of the identified disorder develop. Achieving this goal means reducing those conditions that are potentially harmful before they can cause problems. Suppose, for example, you have identified lack of problem-solving skills as a common problem among children diagnosed with conduct disorder. Primary prevention in this case might involve teaching preschool children basic problem-solving skills and then measuring the rate of conduct disorder in their cohort. Primary prevention often involves some form of social change. Some of the work we discuss in the section of this chapter on public policy involves primary prevention.

Secondary prevention focuses on people who are in the early stages of the disorder. This type of intervention is sometimes called early intervention. The major thrust is to correct problems before they become overwhelming. Most people do not seek the services of a psychologist at this stage of their disorder. They may believe their problem will go away without treatment or that it is not sufficiently troubling to justify the time and money to seek help for it.

Using the concept of secondary prevention, psychologists might recommend screening large numbers of people so that those who have early signs of the disorder can be

Table 13.1 Prevention Classifications

Physical Illness Model	Mental Disorder Model
Primary	Universal
Secondary	Selective
Tertiary	Indicated

Source: *Adapted from Commission on Chronic Illness.* Chronic Illness in the United States, Vol. 1. *Cambridge, MA: Harvard University Press, 1957; Mrazek, P., & Haggerty, R.* Reducing Risks for Mental Disorders: Frontiers for Preventive Intervention Research. *Washington, DC: National Academy Press, 1994.*

identified and treated at this stage. For example, you might work with elementary school teachers to identify children who are too withdrawn for their age. The teachers are using their knowledge of the range of age-appropriate social skills combined with cultural variables to identify children who fall outside these parameters. As a psychologist, you use your knowledge of children's emotional problems to theorize that this withdrawn behavior has the potential to lead to a diagnosis of social phobia as these children continue to develop. A special program would then be instituted to help these children gain self-confidence and interact more appropriately with others.

Unlike primary prevention, secondary prevention is not applied to all members of a group. Those who are identified as being at risk may be stigmatized within their group without actually having developed a diagnosable disorder. If the intervention is successful, we have no way to determine if they ever would have developed that disorder. Thus, secondary prevention does have a potential negative result. We may identify children as being at risk, and thus stigmatize them, when they did not belong in this group. Because of the risk of negative peer reaction as well as the impact on self-perception of being identified as being at risk for a mental disorder, it is important to continue to refine definitions of the at-risk group based on new data. The goal is to decrease the number of children who are identified as being at risk who would never have developed the problem.

Tertiary prevention is what we have generally described in this book. The purpose of this type of prevention is to decrease the duration of the disorder that already exists and to reduce its negative consequences to both the individual and those around that person. Part of tertiary prevention is to prevent future reoccurrence of the problem for this person. Some authors use the term *rehabilitation* synonymously with tertiary prevention, while others consider rehabilitation as part of the tertiary prevention process.

Although the terms *primary prevention, secondary prevention,* and *tertiary prevention* are quite common in the psychological literature, an alternative view of prevention subdivides it into *universal prevention, selective prevention,* and *indicated prevention* (Mrazek & Haggerty, 1994). Because this classification system seems to be gaining popularity, we decided to include it briefly as a contrast for you.

Universal prevention is similar to primary prevention. These programs are designed for all members of a particular group regardless of whether or not they seem to be at risk for a specific disorder. Universal programs are designed to decrease the *incidence,* or rate of new cases, of the disorder in the specified population. Most universal prevention programs involve nonintrusive interventions that are of value to the target group.

Selective prevention programs are designed for groups of people who appear to be at greater risk of developing the target problem than are members of the general population. Thus these programs target a larger group than secondary prevention targets. Groups are selected because they have some common characteristic. This characteristic may be personal, environmental, or a combination of the two. One example of a characteristic that has been used is poverty. Selective programs try to decrease or eliminate the impact of the risk factor, in this case poverty, while increasing the impact of protective factors. Protective factors may be personal characteristics or external resources that seem to insulate the persons so that disorders do not develop.

Indicated prevention programs are similar to the traditional role of clinical psychologists. These programs are designed to alleviate a current problem but also include a strong relapse prevention component. The programs include people who have some characteristics of a diagnosable disorder but have not yet developed the full syndrome. The targeted populations are those that are at greatest risk for either relapse or the development of additional emotional difficulty. Programs include elements of both secondary and tertiary prevention. Regardless of which conceptual framework you use, these systems imply significant understanding of both the causes and likely course of the mental disorder involved. As you know, this knowledge base is imperfect. Thus, these models are ideals rather than easily applied outlines.

Psychologists doing prevention work have identified a number of important concepts that need to be investigated. Research about each of these concepts is used to help design prevention programs in the community. Among those concepts are *risk, protection, resilience, strengths,* and *thriving* (Dalton, Elias, & Wandersman, 2001) (see Table 13.2). We will discuss these five concepts as illustrations of the community intervention approach to psychological practice.

Risk is a common term. In this context, "risk processes can be defined as those features of individuals and environments that reduce the biological, psychological, and/or social capacities of individuals to maintain their well-being and function adaptively in society" (Dalton et al., 2001, p. 270). Let's consider how risk might operate over a period of time to lead to difficulties for a number of people. It is important to note here that being at risk does not mean that the person will always develop a problem. It merely means that given the circumstances they are more likely than others to do so.

In our sample case, we have a family of four—mother, father, seven-year-old girl, and four-year-old girl. The mother has just given birth to her third child, a son, who is diagnosed as severely mentally retarded. As with many cases of severe mental retardation, her son also has physical complications. The addition of this child into the family constellation puts them *at risk* for problems. Because this infant needs constant attention, the others in the family are expected to help with his care, take additional responsibilities around the house, and give up former activities. The seven-year-old must now ride the school bus home each day because her mother cannot come to school to get her. This means that she can no longer participate in the afterschool activities she enjoys. The four-year-old has been attending a gymnastics program for preschool children and her coach says she has talent. She really enjoys gymnastics and has made friends with several of the other students. They do not live near her and so the only time she sees them is at the gym. Because of the cost of medications for their son, this family can no longer afford to pay

Table 13.2 Key Prevention Concepts
Risk
Protection
Resilience
Strengths
Thriving

Source: Adapted from Dalton, J. H., Elias, M. J., & Wandersman, A. Community Psychology: Linking Individuals and Communities. *Belmont, CA: Wadsworth, 2001.*

for gymnastics lessons. They also do not have the time to take her to these lessons. Thus she has lost an activity she enjoyed as well as the opportunity to see her friends. Both girls are beginning to resent their brother and are starting to act out at home. Their mother, who has always been very supportive and scheduled individual time with each of her daughters, is now tired most of the time and has become short-tempered with them. Her husband is spending extra time at work to earn additional money for the special services they know their son will need as he grows. This family has enough money that they do not qualify for public assistance but not enough money that they can afford live-in help. Both of these girls are at risk to develop diagnosable behavioral problems. This family is at risk to develop family problems, including increased risk for divorce. Unfortunately, there is no simple formula to tell us just how many risk factors are required before an individual or a family unit actually breaks down. Some authors have suggested that these multiple factors are additive, while others have suggested they are multiplicative (Haggerty, Sherrod, Garmezy, & Rutter, 1994). Researchers seem to agree, however, that multiple factors do increase the risk for problems.

Protection is really the opposite of risk. These are the personal and environmental factors that help the person cope with the risk factors and function successfully in the world. Psychologists try to determine the types of protective processes that most help people handle risk factors and then assist them to use these behaviors. For example, research suggests that when we are feeling especially stressed we tend to recall truly positive experiences. These positive memories provide a sense of protection and allow us to handle the current negative situation. Let's return to our at-risk family. Suppose some relatives live nearby. This family might work with these relatives to provide some respite from its stress. For example, the daughters might be able to spend some quality time and receive individual attention from these relatives. This attention could make the girls feel special and give them time away from the changed home environment. Depending on the relatives, they might be able to spend some time with the son so that the rest of the family could have some positive time together. Working further with this family, we learn that the mother's college roommate is now a pediatric nurse. This former roommate may know about respite services available through local agencies for which this family does qualify. These services could allow the rest of the family to have quality time together. Contacts might also be made with parents of some of the seven-year-old's classmates whose children participate in afterschool activities of interest to her. If some of them live near this family, they might be willing to drive her home with their own children so she can continue to participate. Even maintaining one or two of her former activities would be helpful. Once again, we are approaching the topic from the perspective of multiple factors. We have identified many different protective factors that could be activated to insulate this family from the risk factors that exist.

Resilience is a term that has become quite prominent in the psychological literature. It refers to a personal kind of protective process. Resilience is the factor that helps us handle really difficult situations and then continue our lives in a productive way. In other words, people who are high in resilience are less susceptible to stress than others. For example, psychologists have found that in families in which the parents are warm and yet set limits and are consistent in enforcing those limits the children are more resilient when faced with stressful events than children from families with different parenting styles (Cicchetti & Toth, 1998; Rodgers, 1993). Thus, fostering resilience in this case might involve teaching parenting skills. Over the years there has been some change in how psychologists use this term. When you read early articles, resilience seemed to be described as a trait. Because of concerns that this trait-based approach might lead to a focus on genetics rather than environment, more recent researchers have used resilience to refer to an interaction between the person and his or her environment. Although they do not discount potential genetic factors, these psychologists view changes in the environment as being more feasible than genetic changes as a way to improve resilience.

Hardiness is a term that is sometimes used as a synonym for resilience. Let's look briefly at an example of how this factor has been studied and then apply the data to the development of training programs to help people become more hardy. In 1981, Illinois Bell Telephone Company was forced to downsize. During that year it decreased its number of employees by about one-half. One result of this downsizing was that those employees who kept their jobs were required to change tasks and supervisors frequently. Most people find this type of change quite stressful. They must learn new jobs as well as how to deal with different supervisory styles. About two-thirds of the employees showed significant negative reactions and the other third did not. Psychologists studied these employees to try to understand what characteristics were different between those employees who had problems with the transition and those who did not. They used what they learned to develop a training program for the employees who were having problems (Maddi, 1987). This training program was later expanded for use with other companies as an early intervention to improve employee health as well as performance (Maddi, 2002). This project is one illustration of how psychologists might apply their research and intervention in a community setting. In this case the community is a large business rather than the more traditional use of the term.

Clinical psychologists work with individual patients to build upon their **strengths** as part of their intervention strategies. Clinical neuropsychologists often help patients use compensatory functions to take over functions that are no longer available as a result of some physical trauma. The focus on strengths rather than weaknesses in community settings is a bit newer. One example of this community use is a strength-based approach to prevention with adolescents who are considered at risk. First their strengths are identified. Psychologists then work with them on enhancing those strengths rather than focusing on their problem behavior. As they begin to realize their positive attributes, they then learn how to use these attributes to deal with their areas of difficulty (Brendtro, Brokenleg, & Van Brockern, 1990).

Thriving is another positive concept that goes beyond strength. It refers to individuals faced with negative situations who not only avoid problems but also actually continue to grow and develop. Part of this development seems to come from gaining personal insight as a result of their success in coping with these negative circumstances. Thriving seems to follow survival and recovery in the face of trauma. It could be defined as "a transformation of one's personal priorities, sense of self, and life roles (O'Leary, 1998). *Thriving* is a term that has been applied to entire countries that have survived and grown despite a long history of disaster when their neighboring countries have collapsed (Karakashian, 1998). Psychologists hope to learn from people in these countries and then apply that knowledge to other groups. This is similar to what we described with the Illinois Bell Telephone Company employees. Psychologists are trying to determine what characteristics differentiate citizens of the thriving country from those in the country that collapsed.

Challenges to Prevention

What we have described thus far sounds very positive. Then why have prevention programs not been more widely adopted? What challenges do they provide for psychology if we are to move forward with such program development? We will discuss some of the obstacles to the effective use of prevention and promotion techniques that have been identified (Dalton et al., 2001). As we summarize these factors, try to consider the way you would apply your understanding of research design to maximize your understanding in each case.

Clinical trials of medications use the same chemical substance in different settings. Trials of the types of prevention programs we have described place considerable dependence on the personal characteristics of both the developer of the program and the individuals who are charged with carrying out the program. These *operator-dependent* characteristics must be considered when planning programs and when applying them in diverse settings. Explaining the importance of varying certain conditions among demonstration programs to funding agencies can be difficult.

The developer and staff are not the only people involved in these programs. There are also the people who are the targets of the program. It can be difficult to identify all of the relevant personal characteristics for program development. Let's return to our contrast with clinical trials of medication. Although questions can be raised about diagnostic accuracy, careful attention to the criteria that are used can minimize this factor. When implementing community intervention programs, psychologists have a bit more difficulty balancing this *context-dependent* characteristic.

Overall program design may be based on a combination of theory and understanding of the population involved. On the other hand, it can be difficult to determine the specific factors of the program that are necessary for change to occur. The more vague the description of key parts of the intervention program, the more difficult it will be for people in new settings to understand their responsibilities.

Prevention researchers consider the difference between *core components* and *adaptive components* of their programs. The core components are those factors that are considered crucial for the effectiveness of the programs. Adaptive components are the parts of the program that can be changed to meet the needs of the people or location where the program is being implemented. As program developers work with various communities, they help them develop the best ways to adapt the program to meet their unique needs while maintaining the core components. The more difficult it is to specify the core components, the harder this task becomes.

The implementation of prevention programs may require major changes in the community involved. Most of us are not comfortable with great change unless we feel there are major issues that need to be addressed. In some communities, people realize that change is needed but think it is only needed in specified areas. If you want to make *organizationally unbounded* changes, this may take more time.

Let's consider an example of this situation. You are working in a company that wants to develop a prevention program about substance abuse among its employees. In that setting, many of the managers believe that drug abuse should be handled by the employee assistance office and not elsewhere. They are therefore likely to be resistant when the prevention plan includes employee training videos about the impact of substance abuse and the use of peer counselors to assist on site with colleagues who may be developing substance abuse problems. In this hypothetical setting, supervisors are now told that when they suspect an employee has a substance abuse problem they are not to take a harsh stance but rather try to convince that employee to use one of the forms of intervention that are now available. Those supervisors who do not believe in this approach will resist such changes until they are convinced they are the best way to handle the problem.

Psychologists in the community may also work with advocacy organizations. State and local statutes establish bodies to serve as watchdogs over human services agencies in the area. For example, many states have protection and advocacy agencies that oversee services for those considered disabled. Usually these agencies have the right to inspect clinical records from institutions where the disabled may be treated. This inspection is intended to ensure that they receive effective treatment. States also appoint individuals, usually called ombudspersons, to investigate patient complaints in human services facilities.

Public Policy

Psychologists in the twenty-first century are actively involved in both public policy development and lobbying about public policy issues. **Public policy** is "policy at the community or governmental levels that influences what resources are allocated where so that the quality of life is improved" (Cullari, p. 355). Lobbying involves a group of individuals with similar interests working together to promote a common political cause. Psychologists have founded political action committees, often called PACs, to raise money for their lobbying efforts. These PACs have provided campaign funds for candidates who support psychological issues. They have also raised money to hire professional lobbyists to work with psychologists as they try to influence relevant policy development. Professional lobbyists often work for a number of different clients but they do this work full-time. Because lobbying is their profession, they have a better understanding of how to influence legislators than the average psychologist does.

Lobbying can also cause some legislative problems. Psychology is not the only profession that hires lobbyists. In the mental health field, lobbying has a history of various factions taking positions that are quite different. That situation can lead to the group with the greatest available resources being successful or to the legislators deciding that no resources will be allocated until these competing groups are able to present a coherent picture of the situation. For example, a lobbyist for psychiatrists might advocate for additional government funding for clinical trials of certain medications, while a managed care company might lobby that same governmental agency to pass legislation that would limit the amount of prescribed medication for which they must reimburse their enrollees. Such diverse positions often lead to resistance to enact policy changes.

Advocacy

An attempt to change a legislator's position or to influence legislation is sometimes called **advocacy.** Over the past twenty years, there has been a growth in the role of psychologists as advocates for professional issues. There are many reasons for advocating, but the primary reason is to protect or enhance the ability of psychologists to practice.

In a broad sense, advocacy means to try to change someone's opinion or urge their support for something. In other words, advocacy means speaking for another person or group. Psychologists sometimes define advocacy as "promoting or advancing the science and profession of psychology by actively attempting to influence a specific group's (the public, the government, a special interest group, etc.) perception of psychology through the provision of information and education." In the case of legislative advocacy, we actively try to influence public officials and especially members of Congress to enact legislation that is beneficial not only to psychologists but also to the consumers of mental health services (personal communication, Stephen Pfeiffer, August 19, 2004).

Psychologists do mental health advocacy on an individual basis and also through organized groups. We will discuss some of these activities. Former patients and their families are also active in the mental health advocacy arena of the twenty-first century. Perhaps you have read about the advocacy work of Dorothea Dix in the 1800s. This schoolteacher was an early advocate for improving treatment facilities for the mentally ill. Although she was not a former mental patient or relative of one, she met mental patients through her teaching and became an advocate for their needs. She spoke to legislators on behalf of these patients. Former mental patient Clifford Beers wrote about his experiences as a way to raise national consciousness about the treatment of mental patients (Beers, 1908). This is also a form of advocacy.

Many of the early efforts at mental health advocacy were really consciousness-raising rather than the political version we associate with the term today. Psychologists may be asked to speak to groups of former patients or their families to help them understand their particular form of pathology. This is also a form of advocacy.

These early advocacy attempts eventually led to federal action. For example, in the late 1970s the Community Support Program was developed through the National Institute of Mental Health. Today this group is named the Center for Mental Health Services. This group is charged with involving more "consumers" of mental health services in national policymaking activities. In 1985, Congress held hearings about the conditions in various mental health treatment facilities. These hearings led to further advocacy by the federal government for the rights of mental patients.

Over the years, the field of advocacy has become more organized. Unlike the early work of individuals like Beers and Dix, today's advocacy tends to occur through groups. Planning is the first requirement of effective advocacy. An early step in this process is to develop clear goals. Once you have defined the goals of your advocacy, you need to identify other groups with whom you might form an alliance in order to have a larger base group for your work. You also need to identify the specific legislators or political leaders whose support is crucial for your project. An example would be finding out who chairs the committee within the state legislature that will need to approve any bills before they are seen by the whole body. Once you have identified the key people, you then need to learn how the process occurs and how to make your concerns known to those key people. This is the type of advocacy that is most likely to be coordinated by a lobbyist for a professional association.

Political Office

Psychologists also serve in governmental positions, both appointed and elected, as a way to apply their training to public policy issues. Let's consider some of the ways that psychological training makes these individuals special assets to governmental service as well as some of the issues these psychologists face.

Mediation is often required in the political arena. Psychologists are trained to listen to what their patients say on both a verbal and nonverbal level. When serving in public office, they may apply this skill to work with their colleagues. One psychologist who served in his state legislature noted that his peer interactions sometimes reminded him of his clinical work with dysfunctional families (Kennemer, 1995). Psychologists' training in statistics allows them to be useful when comparing data from different sources or determining what questions may need to be asked about specific projects. Psychologists are trained to take large amounts of material and summarize it for abstracts and other summary sources. This skill is quite useful in a legislative setting where there is often a large amount of material for each of the many votes that occur. Even though many legislators have staff members who are responsible for synthesizing information for them, legislators still have much material to digest.

One topic of relevance to clinical psychology is health care. It is important for psychology to have a voice present in the room when healthcare issues are discussed because the role psychology could play in many healthcare programs is not necessarily recognized by legislators. If one of those legislators is a psychologist, or has a psychologist on his or her staff who has provided needed information on the topic, psychology's relevance is more likely to be considered. Psychologists' training also makes them useful when the legislative body addresses issues related to mental health, education, corrections, and professional licensing laws.

Psychologists who choose to run for public office must remember that it is unlikely that they will be able to maintain a traditional clinical practice despite the fact that this job is considered part-time, at least in state legislatures, and requires reelection on a regular basis. So why would any psychologist choose to do this? One psychologist who served multiple terms in her state legislature noted that "psychologists have the skills and caring to make significant, positive, and needed legislative changes for the present of one's state, one's profession, and oneself" (Buffmire, 1995). We are not suggesting that the majority of clinical psychologists will run for elected office. On the other hand, students entering this field should know it is an option.

Many psychologists have served in state and national offices. We will not attempt to summarize the legislation sponsored by these psychologists but rather select a few cases to illustrate their contributions. Congressman Ted Strickland of Ohio, a psychologist member of the U.S. House of Representatives, sponsored the Mentally Ill Offender Treatment and Crime Prevention Act (Sullivan & Reedy, 2005). This law actually expanded on a law he had previously introduced that was passed in 2000. Dr. Strickland's professional career includes work in the federal prison system as a psychologist. Thus, he had firsthand knowledge about mentally ill individuals who were placed in those facilities. This legislation established demonstration projects of mental health courts. Outcome data from these projects can then be used for future social policy change. Part of the rationale for this legislation comes from the history of the treatment of the mentally ill that we have already discussed. The deinstitutionalization of the mentally ill led to many of these individuals returning to their communities without adequate support services. One outcome of this return to the community is that, as of this writing, some of the largest collections of diagnosed mentally ill people are found in penal institutions rather than mental hospitals. Among the penal institutions identified as having large numbers of mentally ill inmates are the Cook County jail in Chicago, Los Angeles County jail, and Rikers Island jail in New York (Sullivan & Reedy, 2005). A goal of Dr. Strickland's demonstration projects is to illustrate the utility of using more appropriate settings for the incarcerated mentally ill so they do not continue to have problems functioning in society.

As we noted in chapter 11, work with suicidal patients is an important part of clinical practice. Politicians are also concerned about suicide, especially youth suicide. Within the U.S. Congress this concern led to the passage of the Garrett Lee Smith Memorial Act in 2004. This act provided funds for suicide prevention programs targeting young people. Dr. Tom Osborne, a member of the U.S. Congress from Nebraska, sponsored a part of that act that funds competitive grants to college campuses for mental health and behavioral services to students. These student services are part of the suicide prevention movement. These are just two of many examples of applying the specialized education of psychology to the legislative process.

Other Governmental Options

Of course, not everyone is willing or able to serve in elected office. There are other ways for psychologists to impact public policy. One option is to work for someone who holds one of these elected offices. For example, clinical psychologist Patrick DeLeon serves as chief of staff for U.S. Senator Daniel Inouye of Hawaii. To give you an idea of what Dr. DeLeon does in this position, and whether or not this type of career might be of interest to you, we asked him to respond to a series of questions. We asked psychologists in various career areas to respond to these same questions; their answers appear in other chapters of this book.

PATRICK H. DELEON has a Ph.D. in clinical psychology from Purdue University. He also has a master's degree in public health from the University of Hawaii and a law degree from Catholic University. At the time of this interview, he worked as administrative assistant to U.S. Senator Daniel K. Inouye of Hawaii.

If you were talking to an undergraduate student who is considering a career in clinical psychology, what psychology courses would you recommend as good preparation? Dr. DeLeon recommended taking courses in psychological testing.

What courses in other disciplines would you recommend? He would recommend that students take courses in computers and in nursing in addition to their psychology courses.

What courses didn't you have that you wish you had taken? Once again, Dr. DeLeon noted coursework in computers. This focus illustrates the importance of computers in many careers in the twenty-first century.

When you think about the work you do, what do you find most rewarding? Dr. DeLeon told us he finds the creation of programs one of the most satisfying aspects of his job. Working within the federal government, he is in a position to recommend the creation of new programs to meet specific societal needs. These may be either the creation of

Patrick H. DeLeon
*Photo courtesy of
Patrick H. DeLeon.*

new programs being considered by the federal government or the continued funding of current programs. His position allows him to evaluate these programs and make recommendations to the senator.

What do you find most frustrating? Here he noted the difficulty of making change occur. He told us that change takes place very slowly. Once he and the staff in the senator's office have identified a need and developed a program they must then work their way through the mandated procedures before it is actually implemented.

Were there specific life experiences that influenced you to become a psychologist? Dr. DeLeon's response was general rather than centering on a specific incident. He told us that he liked working with people and thus clinical psychology seemed to be a good fit to this interest.

Why did you decide to work in your specialty? Dr. DeLeon told us that clinical psychology was the hardest program to get into. Because he likes challenges, he decided to apply for that specialty within psychology. He later obtained his public health and law degrees.

Did you have a mentor or role model who influenced you to become a psychologist? He said that Dr. Bob Birney, professor of psychology, was that person.

Please write one or two paragraphs about each of two days in your professional life that describe a sample of what you do. Dr. DeLeon told us that he listens to the problems brought to the senator's office by his constituents. He must then consider what types of programs work to address those problems. He must also consider why these particular programs work and which ones seem to be most effective. After reviewing that information, it is his job to look for ways to create and fund the programs that will meet the needs of these people. This information is then used within the governmental system to do so.

Looking toward the future of your specialty, what are your predictions for such factors as growth, new directions, and so on? Dr. DeLeon told us he believes there will be an expansion of practice, especially through the acquisition of prescription privileges for psychologists. He also sees practice expanding to meet the needs of the truly underserved. Finally, he sees a changing perspective of the court system as influencing future practice.

Looking over the time since you received your degree, how has your identity as a professional changed, and to what do you attribute these changes? Dr. DeLeon told us that there has been an expansion of his scope of influence because of the greater numbers of psychologists in practice as well as the changes in our society over that time period. He also noted that the changes in the communications field have influenced how he works.

If you could have dinner with any person, living or dead, who would you select and why? Dr. DeLeon would have dinner with his son and his daughter. The reason for this choice is that he finds them to be "enjoyable folk."

Although Dr. DeLeon has a very busy schedule, he does have time for hobbies. In his case, however, one of his hobbies is also part of his professional life. He names writing psychology articles and columns as a hobby. His other major hobby is golf.

Notice how the work Dr. DeLeon does exemplify many of the aspects of community psychology we discussed. He uses his knowledge of psychology to evaluate what the literature says about current needs and ways to address them. He combines this knowledge with his training in law and public health to work on the development of interdisciplinary community programs to try to meet these needs. It is important to note that he did not obtain all of these academic credentials at the same time. If you pursue a career in clinical psychology, you may find that your interests move in a direction that leads you to want additional formal education. In Dr. DeLeon's case that work led to two degrees after his Ph.D. in clinical psychology—law and public health.

Psychologists also have options for short-term experiences in governmental settings through various fellowship programs such as the congressional fellowship program sponsored by the American Psychological Association and health policy fellowships sponsored by the Robert Wood Johnson Foundation. Through these programs, psychologists spend a year in Washington, DC, working for a member of Congress, with a Congressional Committee to assist in public policy development, or in relevant governmental agencies. An example of the latter type of fellowship is one sponsored by the APA Practice Organization to learn about health policy development at the Substance Abuse and Mental Health Services Administration (SAMHSA) in Rockville, Maryland. Fellows in this setting analyze large amounts of data provided by outside contractors. They meet regularly with a range of professionals including those in mental health, economics, and public health as well as consumer advocacy. They also plan conferences to bring a range of professionals together to coordinate services. After these fellows complete their time at SAMHSA they are in a position to apply their newly acquired policy development skills to issues in their home states. This same transfer of learning occurs for fellows in other settings.

As the practice of psychology has moved into areas of health care other than mental health care, fellowships have also become available in primary health care (Dingfelder, 2004). Psychologists awarded these fellowships increase the visibility of the profession within the public policy process as they learn how it works. We note these experiences to let students know that even after you become a practicing psychologist there are opportunities to have specialized learning experiences.

Illustrative Activities

Psychologists also act on an individual level to impact relevant policy. In some cases this individual action is coordinated so that large numbers of psychologists act individually on the same topic. For example, the American Psychological Association works with individual psychologists, called grassroots coordinators, to advocate with their legislators for relevant bills. These grassroots coordinators then mobilize other psychologists in their community or state who also individually contact these legislators. Forsyth (2004) noted, for example, that over a three-year period more than two hundred psychologists contacted members of the U.S. Congress about funding for the Graduate Psychology Education Program (GPE). These contacts included traditional letters, e-mail, phone calls, and even personal visits. GPE is a federally funded program that provides grants to APA-accredited doctoral programs, internships, and postdoctoral fellowships in which students are trained to provide services to *underserved* populations. This is the term that is used to refer to those groups who have traditionally not received an adequate level of service. These populations include the elderly, children, seriously mentally ill persons, and trauma victims. Although these activities are coordinated by an organization, the focus is on the individual psychologist speaking as a constituent of the legislator rather than on behalf of the entire profession.

Over the years, many professional organizations like the APA have developed advocacy efforts. Because of tax laws, these efforts must be organized separately from the organization. The American Psychological Association Practice Organization (APAPO) does advocacy work for psychologists. According to their website (http://www.APApractice.org), one of the primary reasons for this organization is "to promote the professional interests of practicing psychologists in all settings through a wide range of advocacy activities, focusing on policy makers, consumers of services, and the healthcare marketplace."

The American Psychological Foundation (APF) is a nonprofit organization founded in 1953 by a group of former APA presidents and other distinguished psychologists. The mission of APF is to advance psychology through fostering the best students and recognizing outstanding research and careers within the profession. The research supported by APF addresses issues of our society such as understanding and eliminating prejudice and understanding and preventing violence. These activities are a form of advocacy for the profession.

The Association for the Advancement of Psychology (AAP) was founded in 1974 as an organization to advance the science and profession of psychology. According to their website (http://www.aapnet.org/mission.htm), "AAP promotes the interests of all psychologists in several ways including: (1) representation of psychologists before public and governmental bodies; (2) cooperation with other organizations and agencies in furtherance of the profession and science of psychology, and (3) support and operation of a political committee known as Psychologists for Legislative Action Now (AAP/PLAN)."

This bipartisan political committee has been described as the first such group designed solely to advocate for the interests of psychologists.

The National Academies of Practice (NAP) was founded in 1981 as an interdisciplinary organization devoted to promoting quality health care. In 2005, NAP included the professions of dentistry, medicine, nursing, optometry, osteopathic medicine, pharmacy, podiatry, psychology, social work, and veterinary medicine (www.nap.vcu.edu). These organizations are just a sample of those involved in advocacy for psychology.

Psychologists also influence public policy by testifying before relevant governmental bodies about psychological knowledge relevant to their work and providing briefings to congressional staff members. These staff members are the ones who will later read related proposed legislation and make recommendations to the congressperson about whether or not to support any given piece of legislation. For these sessions to be effective, psychologists need to be aware of the most relevant data and express it succinctly in language that fits the audience. They must remember that they are not making a convention presentation to a group of their peers but rather are speaking to educated audience members who may have little background in psychology beyond an introductory course when they were in college. These congressional staffers, however, are aware of proposed legislation. One goal of these briefings is to indicate ways psychological science and psychological practice can contribute to specific topics and programs.

Psychologists also use their research skills to assist them in their advocacy activities. In this case, it is called **policy research.** The purpose of policy research is to generate empirical data about social issues of interest to the profession. Later the data may be used not only with legislators but also by attorneys in related court cases. One outcome of policy research is the demonstration of the need for new social policies. Once that need has been demonstrated, psychologists often form an alliance with people on one side of a controversial issue. The data are combined with the other skills we noted to sway legislative action.

ETHICAL CONUNDRUM POINTS TO PONDER

You need to consider whether your work has the potential to cause harm. You might make the case that since the product is composed entirely of natural contents the people who use it will not be buying anything that is harmful. If this is correct, you have met the requirement of the APA Ethics Code that states that you take reasonable steps to minimize foreseeable harm because you have checked the ingredients of the product. Because your name will not appear in any of the literature about this product, you are not likely to be faced with any professional repercussions, such as an ethics complaint. Perhaps more relevant is whether or not the psychologist is making a deceptive statement. Although the advertising will not be attributed to this psychologist, the psychologist is using professional expertise about obesity to create the marketing campaign.

Key Terms

advocacy	protection	secondary prevention	tertiary prevention
indicated prevention	public policy		thriving
policy research	resilience	selective prevention	universal prevention
primary prevention	risk	strengths	

CHAPTER 14

Specialties in Clinical Psychology I

Neuropsychology, Health Psychology, Forensic Psychology, and Sport Psychology

In this chapter and the next one, we describe some of the careers and several niche opportunities available to clinical psychologists. As we said in the first two chapters of this book, clinical psychologists do many different things. Some clinical psychologists have diverse private practices in a multitude of settings, while others focus their work in a specific direction, providing services that depend on specialized training. When a new employment direction is created, it may even lead to the development of a new specialty area within psychology. We have selected some of those specialized areas for more extensive coverage.

First we will describe a specialty, including some of its research base and current areas of investigation. We will include special training the clinical psychologist may need in order to do this type of work. For areas that have evolved into well-defined specialties, we will also provide further readings for those students who may want to learn more about it. We will give you some general information about the type of work done by psychologists in this area. This information will be followed by interviews with some clinical psychologists who actually do this type of work. We hope these interviews will make this material more reality based than merely describing it. We also want you to see the range of work activities associated with these subsets of clinical psychologists. To do that, we decided to interview one or two people for each specialty described so that different perspectives are presented. Each of these psychologists responded to the same questions you read in chapter 13's interview with Dr. DeLeon. An additional resource for you is *Careers in Psychology: Opportunities in a Changing World* (Kuther & Morgan, 2003).

Clinical Neuropsychology

Clinical neuropsychologists are specialists in understanding the relationship between brain function and behavior. Clinical neuropsychologists often work closely with neurologists, neurosurgeons, physical therapists, occupational therapists, and rehabilitation psychologists in a multidisciplinary team. While many neuropsychologists work in private practice settings, a significant number work in medical schools, universities, and specialty clinics.

Let's briefly consider these other professions so that it becomes clearer why clinical neuropsychologists need the training that is recommended. Neurologists are physicians who specialize in the diagnosis and treatment of nervous system disorders. Their assessment and treatment approaches are often described as *invasive*. By this term, we mean they use such procedures as injecting chemicals into the nervous system in order to locate areas that are malfunctioning and prescribing medications and other interventions to address the problems they find. Neurosurgeons are physicians who operate on the brains and spinal cords of people who have tumors, epilepsy, or one of a long list of injuries or diseases of the nervous system. Physical therapists help patients preserve, develop, and restore optimum physical functioning. They also emphasize wellness, fitness, and quality of life as it relates to movement and health. Physical therapists also help eliminate pain, prevent injury, and assist the patient restore function after an injury. When normal behavior has been permanently damaged, the physical therapist helps the individual learn to adapt personal motor performance within the limits of personal loss. We briefly described occupational therapists in chapter 1. Occupational therapists teach skills of daily living. These skills include modification of eating utensils for people with brain injuries, ramps and the design of cabinets and furniture for better access and mobility, and other techniques for dealing with changed physical and mental abilities. The American Occupational Therapy Association is a vital organization that advocates for legislation to help people with physical and mental disabilities. Information about them can be found at www.aota.org. Rehabilitation psychologists also work to help restore optimum functioning of patients and are acutely aware of the psychological effects of injury and loss of functioning that can occur after an injury or illness. Division 22 of the American Psychological Association is dedicated to the work of these psychologists.

Clinical neuropsychologists infer organic involvement based on the patient's behavior on specific tasks. They may also work with other medical specialties to assist in the diagnosis and treatment of specific disorders. Many presenting symptoms could be the result of either emotional or neurological conditions. The role of the neuropsychologist in these cases is to help clarify the basis of the problem as well as to suggest methods of remediation.

In chapter 1, we gave you definitions of both clinical and counseling psychology from the APA archives. Those archives also include a definition of **clinical neuropsychology:** "Clinical neuropsychology is a specialty that applies principles of assessment and intervention based upon the scientific study of human behavior as it relates to normal and abnormal functioning of the central nervous system. The specialty is dedicated to enhancing the understanding of brain-behavior relationships and the application of such knowledge to human problems" (http://www.apa.org/crsppp/neuro.html). This archived definition states that the practice of clinical neuropsychology is based on the research literature in both physiological and cognitive psychology, the development of both quantitative and qualitative principles used in clinical practice, and the growing body of knowledge about the relationship between central nervous system lesions and their behavioral consequences. Clinical neuropsychology includes both assessment and intervention activities. Within these broad categories, the clinical neuropsychologist might be asked to either support or rule out a tentative psychiatric or medical diagnosis, make predictions about potential recovery of function, and assist with the rehabilitation process.

To fulfill these different roles appropriately, the clinical neuropsychologist must have the ability to carry out all of these activities—based on appropriate training—to evaluate the person completely. This means not only the biological bases of a disorder but the cognitive and emotional bases as well. The material you read about cognitive and personality assessment earlier in this book is also important to the clinical neuropsychologist. In addition, this specialist is able to include information about the influence of biological systems on the presenting problem. It is important to note that the clinical neuropsychologist approaches patient evaluation very much like the clinical psychologist does.

A neuropsychological evaluation of a patient can be viewed as consisting of current and background information, the neuropsychological evaluation itself, and the feedback provided to the patient and/or significant others as well as the referral source (Incagnoli, 1986, p. 3). Clinical psychologists get a patient history to better understand that person's current problems. Sometimes the patient is not a good historian as a result of his or her problem. In those cases, a relative or friend must give the pertinent history. Of course, the psychologist must obtain permission from the patient before talking to these other information sources. Depending on the problem involved, the neuropsychologist may benefit from information obtained from multiple sources rather than just one. This historical background on patients is especially important to the clinical neuropsychologist. We discussed many of the assessment procedures used by clinical neuropsychologists in chapter 8. The assessment data are interpreted in terms of this information. Consider a patient one of us evaluated. This man had suffered a head injury. Among other information, his current IQ test performance yielded a full-scale IQ in the high average range (IQ = 113). Without his history, you might conclude that he was experiencing no cognitive deficit based on this current test performance. However, his documented academic history and performance on nationally standardized admission tests for postbaccalaureate education suggested that his prior cognitive level was considerably higher. Other background information also supported the hypothesis that he had been functioning cognitively on a superior level for many years until the trauma occurred.

Neuropsychologists often conduct assessments as consultants to other professionals. They must then obtain a release of information from the patient to communicate their findings to that referral source. Because of the type of problems that neuropsychologists evaluate, it is quite common for feedback to be given not only to the identified patient but also to a significant other. The significant other is often going to be the primary caregiver for the individual and thus may be a good source of some of that background information as well. The causes of the types of deficits evaluated by clinical neuropsychologists vary and include accidents or trauma caused by some form of negligence. In these cases, the clinical neuropsychologist begins to overlap the forensic psychologist in that court testimony will likely occur. Clinical neuropsychologists frequently serve as expert witnesses in cases such as trauma following an automobile accident or resulting from toxic waste.

Currently, there are doctoral programs in which you can specialize in clinical neuropsychology rather than in clinical psychology. Many of the original clinical neuropsychologists were trained in clinical psychology doctoral programs and then, because of their interest in brain–behavior relationships, focused their practice on work with patients who had potential organic dysfunction. Although there are now specific guidelines for training and practice in clinical neuropsychology, there is no single way to reach that educational goal (Hess & Hart, 1990). Some psychologists take the position that it is best to first be trained as a solid clinical psychologist and then add the specialty course work in neuropsychology, while others believe the best training background is to specialize in clinical neuropsychology from the onset of graduate education. Regardless of which approach to becoming a clinical neuropsychologist is used, the student will need to learn basic neuroscience, neuroanatomy, neuropathology, and psychopharmacology in addition to the general clinical skills. To prepare for this type of graduate study, it helps if undergraduates complete advanced science and math courses in addition to the courses required for the psychology major. Because this is also a "clinical" field, students will need to have a background in both normal and abnormal development. An understanding of principles of psychological testing also helps. In addition to the doctoral programs in clinical neuropsychology, specialty predoctoral internships and postdoctoral fellowships in clinical neuropsychology build on this basic academic foundation. It is in these latter settings that the student fine-tunes the clinical skills related to the academic knowledge base of clinical neuropsychology.

Psychologists have been interested in the relationship between brain function and behavior for decades. Many neuropsychology textbooks suggest that the beginning of this specialty was Broca's famous 1860s case study of a patient whose speaking ability was lost following damage to the anterior temporal region of his left cerebral hemisphere (Broca, 1960). This research was followed by the work of others in both Europe and the United States who attempted to localize brain function. Roger Sperry and his colleagues devoted over twenty-five years to studying the impact of **commisurotomy** on both humans and animals (Sperry, 1982). Commisurotomy is a surgical procedure in which the two hemispheres of the brain are separated by cutting a thick bundle of fibers that form a bridge between the left and right hemispheres. This procedure has been used successfully to treat severe epilepsy that has not responded to other types of treatment, such as medication. Fascinating results were found about how the left and right hemispheres of the brain were different and led to some truly innovative methodology. Sperry was awarded the Nobel prize for his efforts. Interest in "split brain" research led to the development of behavioral measures that are used to assess brain function. Early research in neuropsychology centered on ways people with brain injuries were different from those without them. From this point, research moved to consideration of the specific areas of the brain involved with specific types of behavior. In the twenty-first century these are still areas of interest to clinical neuropsychologists but to a lesser extent than before. The technical innovation in imaging techniques, such as PET scans, has made localization of lesions a lower priority for neuropsychologists. Today, interest lies in developing accurate assessment tools leading to appropriate forms of remediation as well as doing the intervention. There remains a strong experimental foundation to the discipline of clinical neuropsychology in addition to its clinical focus.

In chapter 3, we noted the strong impact World War II had on the growth of clinical psychology. The same can be said of clinical neuropsychology. Many veterans suffered from head wounds. Some were closed-head injuries while others were the result of penetrating head wounds. Much of the early work in clinical neuropsychology was done in veterans' hospitals as part of the treatment program to assist these veterans. Having a large number of patients with a range of head injuries provided a good source of data for this growing field. On the other hand, this population was predominantly male. Very few female veterans were in these programs and so there were insufficient female subjects to be included in the basic research. Research on sex differences in neuropsychological factors does exist, but it is limited. Much of it was conducted in the 1970s and early 1980s. Three primary areas of investigation into gender differences were in neuroanatomy, spatial ability, and verbal ability (Browne, 1983).

After that point in time, the research on sex differences seems to have decreased. It is possible that as psychologists became sensitized to sexist issues within the profession researchers on sex differences may have felt their work was problematic. This decreased research on sex differences may also be a result of changing interest by those researchers. Whatever the reason, there seems to have been a decline of this type of research since the 1980s. Several authors have noted that the significance of the person's sex on neuropsychological factors has not been investigated to the same extent as other factors (Filskov & Catanese, 1986; Matthews, 1992). Whether or not there will be a resurgence of interest in this area of neuropsychological research in the twenty-first century remains to be seen. Other areas of neuropsychological research, such as inquiries into various pediatric and geriatric disorders, are flourishing.

One of the pioneers in neuropsychological assessment was Ward Halstead, whose work was described in chapter 8. His approach resulted in the neuropsychological test battery that was the major one used in the United States until an alternative approach was developed in the mid-1970s by Charles Golden and his associates (Golden, Hammeke, & Purisch, 1980). At this time, both batteries are still in clinical use. A solid understanding of this form of assessment is part of the training of clinical neuropsychologists. A number of textbooks cover the basic principles of neuropsychology as well as specialty topics in the discipline for students who wish to do further reading (e.g., Fletcher-Janzen, Strickland, & Reynolds, 2000; Kolb & Whishaw, 2003; McCaffrey, Duff, & Westervelt, 2000; Stirling, 2001; Wilson, 2003).

Research by clinical neuropsychologists covers the same breadth as what is reflected in their practice. In contrast to what some psychologists call "basic research," which means it is laboratory based, much of the research we see in clinical neuropsychology is applied. It is conducted in the practice setting of the psychologist. To illustrate this aspect of the specialty, we will briefly discuss a review study on pediatric sickle cell disease (SCD) (Kral, Brown, & Hynd, 2001). This research comes from the growing subspecialty of pediatric neuropsychology. Neuropsychologists in child, or more frequently called pediatric, neuropsychology often consult with, or are employed by, pediatric departments in hospitals and medical centers. In contrast to the work with general neurologists noted earlier, they work with pediatricians and other pediatric neurologists.

SCD is a chronic disease affecting about one in four hundred African-American newborns in the United States, with one in twelve African Americans carrying the recessive gene that causes the disease. It is important for neuropsychologists to understand the changes that may occur throughout the course of a disease that afflicts so many people. To develop this knowledge base, researchers not only must know how to administer and interpret the typical psychological tests but also must have an understanding of data from various neuroimaging procedures. Neuropsychologists researching SCD study not only magnetic resonance imaging (MRI) data but also data from less well-known procedures such as transcranial Doppler ultrasound (TCD). By combining these data with data from more traditional sources, they can provide assistance in terms of both preparation and intervention. Researchers have learned, for example, that a major source of both morbidity and mortality in children with SCD is neurological complications. The side effects of the neurocognitive impairment are seen in impaired social and academic functioning. Kral, Brown, and Hynd (2001) reviewed the existing literature on pediatric SCD to be able to make some general conclusions about what has been found as well as to suggest directions for future research on SCD. To do this type of research, you must be able to understand and evaluate a range of studies. Once you integrate the data from the empirically sound studies from the available literature you apply your knowledge of neuropsychology to suggest further research. For example, they found that very little had been published about preschool-aged children with SCD. These children need to be followed longitudinally to gain a more accurate picture of the progression of the disease. From a more traditionally psychological perspective, they also found that further work is needed to understand peer reaction to SCD children and to be able to develop effective intervention techniques to address peer skill issues. Many of the available studies used correlational data. These data need to be verified through the development of experimental studies.

Because of the strong research basis of this career, clinical neuropsychologists periodically review the literature to summarize the state of the discipline (Parsons & Prigatano, 1978; Prigatano, Parsons, & Bortz, 1995). Prigatano and his colleagues (1995) suggested ten concepts that should guide research in clinical neuropsychology. Because they seem to summarize the suggestions of many others in the field, we are providing them in Table 14.1 for you and suggest that any students considering a career in clinical neuropsychology read the original article.

Table 14.1 Clinical Neuropsychology Research Issues

1. Make studies pertinent to important clinical questions.
2. Recognize when present-day methodology cannot properly test an interesting idea.
3. Replication of findings may be more difficult than you think.
4. Apply, when possible, experimental and cognitive (neuro)psychology techniques to the study of clinical problems.
5. Application of electrophysiological, psychophysiological, and neuroimaging techniques to clinical neuropsychological research is highly desirable.
6. Negative treatment effects can be as clinically useful as positive findings.
7. Study brain–behavior relationships across the life span.
8. Consider the role of premorbid factors in understanding neuropsychological symptoms following brain insult.
9. Scientific investigations require controlled observations and careful consideration of threats to reliability and validity.
10. Nonneurological variables may influence research findings more than we anticipate.

Source: Adapted from Prigatano, G. P., Parsons, O. A., & Bortz, J. J. Methodological considerations in clinical neuropsychological research: 17 years later. Psychological Assessment, 7(1995): 396–403.

The activities of neuropsychologists will be illustrated through interview information from two professionals. Their comments represent only a small selection of the myriad activities and interesting careers of clinical neuropsychologists. As we developed the standard questions we wanted to ask in these interviews, we decided we wanted to know not only about their professional activities but also about their personal lives. We did this to illustrate that professionals actually have personal lives as well as to make these select individuals become more real for you.

ALISON N. CERNICH has a Ph.D. in clinical psychology from Fairleigh Dickinson University. Her specialty area within that clinical program was clinical neuropsychology. At the time of this interview, Dr. Cernich was completing her postdoctoral training as a research associate in the neuroscience research department of Medstar Research Institute in Washington, DC. She is currently a clinical neuropsychologist at the Baltimore VA Medical Center, where she trains students, see patients, conducts research, and directs a dementia clinic. The specific questions we asked Dr. Cernich are followed by her responses.

If you were talking to an undergraduate student who is considering specializing in neuropsychology, what courses in psychology would you recommend as good preparation? Dr. Cernich listed tests and measurements, clinical psychology, learning theory, physiological psychology, statistics and research design, abnormal psychology, developmental

Alison N. Cernich
*Ernie Brown, Baltimore VA
Medical Center.*

psychology, and a practicum if available. Although having a field experience in clinical neuropsychology would be best, just having the applied experience is the most important aspect of this course suggestion.

What courses in other departments would you recommend? She noted that a strong concentration in biology with a special concentration on cell function and human anatomy is very helpful. Dr. Cernich also recommended neurophysiology, calculus, and English composition. Her recommendations may sound like a pre-med curriculum to you, but you will see the connection later in the interview when she discusses her current activities within this specialty.

When you think about the work you do, what do you find most rewarding? We asked this question in our interviews to give you some sense of what it is about these careers that makes the psychologist want to continue to do whatever he or she is doing. Of course, everyone has days when work is just not enjoyable. Overall, however, if there is nothing positive about your work setting you are likely to burn out and want to change occupations.

Dr. Cernich said, "The thing I enjoy about my work and what I find most rewarding is the constant pursuit of knowledge. I am relatively certain this can be said about many disciplines. However, for me neuropsychology allows you to apply and pursue knowledge in various ways: There is the clinical application of your knowledge to a patient's presenting problem; the research application of your knowledge to the study of disease, a measure, or a treatment; and the continuing education and clinical research needed to be helpful in both of these arenas. A great part of my job is to help patients understand why they are experiencing certain symptoms, aid them in seeking treatment or compensating for deficits, and defining their behaviors in a way that is helpful to clinicians in other disciplines. Another fascinating part of my job is working with other disciplines and within my own to generate hypotheses about neurologic disease or how an assessment measure behaves in a population and to explore scientific questions in clinical research."

What do you find most frustrating about your work? "I am often frustrated when I feel that I have a firm grasp on a subject area in my specialty, and then I find one more article that points out how much more I have to learn, either from the point of view of another discipline (neurology, pharmacology, etc.) or from another school of thought within my own discipline. Additionally, because I am just beginning my postdoctoral training, I often become frustrated with how much there is to learn in the field and how little I feel I know."

Were there specific life experiences that influenced you to become a clinical psychologist and specialize in clinical neuropsychology? "I had done some work as an undergraduate in psychiatric hospitals and found them exciting and interesting, but felt that I would probably burn out in what I felt was a high-intensity and highly emotional setting. I then was assigned to an acute brain injury unit for an undergraduate practicum and found myself spending more and more time reading about neurologic disorders, their etiology, their symptoms, and their differing presentations. I also always had an interest in the biologic bases of behavior, so the intersection of neuropsychological assessment and brain insult was fascinating to me. When I was in graduate school, I discovered that research was not as dry or boring as it seemed in undergraduate school, especially when you had a hand in generating hypotheses and testing them. The fact that these two facets of a field could be combined to make a career solidified my decision to combine clinical and research practice in neuropsychology."

Mentors are often important both for entering a specialty and for advancement. Thus, we asked Dr. Cernich, *Did you have a mentor or role model who influenced you to become a psychologist? If so, tell us about that person.* "In high school I took an introduction to psychology course and was encouraged to pursue further study in the field by my instructor. When I reached the undergraduate level, I initially found it difficult to pursue my chosen profession because my undergraduate advisor was often unavailable or interested in a different application of psychology and tried to encourage me to pursue this instead. I finally identified a professor at the university who had a similar interest in clinical psychology and was willing to encourage me to pursue graduate study in clinical psychology and advise me on relevant courses and practical experience. I found that mentors do not often search for you; in fact you often have to pursue them and make yourself a desirable mentee."

Given this background about Dr. Cernich, you may wonder what she actually "does" during the day. We thus asked her, *Please write a couple of paragraphs about each of two days in your professional life that describe a sample of what you do.* Her response to this question illustrates the variety of activities she noted earlier was important for her happiness in a career.

"My postdoctoral fellowship divides my week into three components: research, clinical assessment, and continuing education. My research focus at National Rehabilitation Hospital is in the area of concussion, but I am also involved in projects concerning systemic illness (lupus, fibromyalgia), medication effectiveness and cognitive side effect profiles, effects of alcohol hangover, and civilian applications for military technology. A typical day finds me coordinating ongoing studies in our department, conducting statistical analyses and presenting results to my research team, searching for and reviewing current articles regarding our projects, developing new ideas for grant proposals, preparing documents for Institutional Review Board (IRB) review, and preparing presentations and manuscripts for presentation at conferences or publication in peer-reviewed journals. The clinical assessment component of my training involves inpatient and outpatient consultation-liaison service at a Veterans' Affairs Medical Center. I interview patients, administer full neuropsychological batteries, and provide feedback regarding the assessment to patients and their families. The continuing education facet of my training involves classes one to two times a week in the following areas at a local medical school: neuroanatomy (including brain dissection), pharmacology, diseases of the central nervous system, psychopharmacology, and some experience with neuroradiology."

Although Dr. Cernich is just starting her career, we asked her to predict the future of clinical neuropsychology. *Looking toward the future of clinical neuropsychology, what are your predictions for such factors as growth, new directions, and so on?* "The field of neuropsychology has become more competitive, and specialization in this area requires significant training even before the predoctoral and postdoctoral level. The field is experiencing considerable growth and will probably continue to do so. I think this is concomitant with the substantial increase in our knowledge of the brain at the cellular and molecular level and our ability to image brain function. I believe the research component of neuropsychology will continue to be the high growth area in the field, simply due to the numerous areas of study, the continued refinement of assessment and imaging techniques, and our need to understand the cognitive profiles of diseases that affect the central nervous system and the cognitive effects of medications in order to improve the patient's quality of life. Clinically, the field will continue to grow because of the need for evaluation of cognitive symptoms with an increasingly elderly population. However, my training was focused on giving brief and well-defined batteries that were targeted to the patient's symptoms, instead of long and comprehensive neuropsychological assessment batteries that evaluated all areas of function in great detail."

From the perspective on someone just entering this specialty, we asked Dr. Cernich, ***What changes would you like to see occur in clinical neuropsychology?*** "There are two changes that I would like to see, one professional and one more personal. The professional change I would envision is more attempts in construct validation for neuropsychological measures. It seems to be an area that has been pursued more ardently in personality assessment, possibly because some of those constructs are more abstract and amorphous, but it still feels needed within the field. The more personal change I would like to see is more support in psychology as a whole for professionals who are beginning families or caring for family members that are older or are ill. I often hear colleagues talk about 'getting behind' or 'losing time' when they are in these situations and feeling a pressure not to engage in caring for children or ailing loved ones. I find it incomprehensible sometimes that we work in a field above all promoting mental health and yet place so much pressure on our colleagues or trainees to not take time out to care for themselves or their families."

If you could have dinner with any person, living or dead, who would you select and why? Her response to this question reflects her interest in the diversity of activity that we saw with her professional activities.

"It's truly a toss-up and depends on what side of me I would like to tap into and what it would gratify. Professionally, if I could have dinner with Ward Halstead, I would pay for a dinner at a bistro, uncork a great French red, and listen to him wax philosophic about brain function and degrees of impairment. He was a fabulous writer and from all accounts an engaging speaker. Historically, I would love to have a hearty steak with Theodore Roosevelt simply because it is hard to think of a person more passionate, stubborn, and well-educated and because he seems to have been an enjoyable fellow. Artistically, kicking back a few beers with the Indigo Girls would be an enjoyable evening. Personally, I would love to have dinner with my deceased grandfather at the racetrack in New Orleans so he could tell me to 'bet the house' and so that we could talk about the latest books we've read."

As a final bit of personal information about her, we asked Dr. Cernich about her hobbies. She told us she enjoys running, hiking, backpacking, traveling (anywhere), attending theater productions, and reading. She noted that if you do not enjoy reading you should not plan to attend graduate school.

Our second interview is with a well-established senior neuropsycologist, **CHARLES J. GOLDEN.** Professor Golden has a Ph.D. in clinical psychology from the University of Hawaii. He completed his neuropsychology internship at the Hawaii State Hospital. At the time of this writing he was a professor of psychology and coordinator of the neuropsychology concentration in the doctoral programs (Ph.D. and Psy.D.) at Nova Southeastern University in Fort Lauderdale, Florida, as well as engaged in the practice of clinical neuropsychology. He has over three hundred publications in books, chapters, and articles, with the majority of them addressing the development and validation of neuropsychological and assessment procedures in general. Earlier in this chapter, as well as in chapter 8, we noted his work in the area of neuropsychological assessment. We asked him the same questions we asked Dr. Cernich.

If you were talking to an undergraduate student who is considering specializing in clinical neuropsychology, what psychology courses would you recommend? The undergraduate psychology courses he recommended as good preparation for a career in clinical neuropsychology were "all basic psychology courses for a broad background with an emphasis on physiological psychology, research methods, test and measurements, and statistics."

What courses from other disciplines would you recommend? "Ideally students would take human neuroanatomy including brain and central nervous system anatomy and chemistry at least up to organic chemistry and biochemistry."

What courses didn't you have that you wish you had taken? He noted that neuroanatomy was not offered to undergraduates at his university when he was an undergraduate.

When you think about the work you do, what do you find most rewarding? "I get my rewards in several ways: helping clients and families understand what is wrong with them and how they can work around the limits set by a brain injury, helping clients get appropriate justice within the legal system for injuries, preventing malingerers from misusing the system, and completing research which illuminates some aspect of brain–behavior relationships."

What do you find most frustrating? He noted "the inability to help a client or family when they refuse to listen and cooperate or when the 'help' system aligns itself against patient needs."

Were there specific life experiences that influenced you to become a psychologist? He said he selected psychology as a career mainly because he had an intense curiosity about why people are so different. He wanted to know why people behave the way they do.

Why did you decide to work in clinical neuropsychology? "I thought neuropsychology offered the ideal blend to study all the forces which shape people's behavior: organic contributions (both normal and those arising from injury), experiential influences, and social forces."

Did you have a mentor or role model who influenced you to become a psychologist? Although he did not have a single mentor to whom he credits his career direction, he noted that he was taught by many excellent professors who encouraged him to think outside current beliefs.

Please write one or two paragraphs about each of two days in your professional life that describe a sample of what you do. "My job is an academic/clinical job, which leads to many varied days. On a teaching day I might teach a course in assessment or advanced neuropsychology from 9 to 12 o'clock after arriving at work at 8 A.M. to prepare, answer phone calls, deal with leftover problems, and the like. At noon, I have supervision for practicum students in neuropsychology that can last until 2 P.M. After that I would typically work on a research or writing project, while seeing students who need support for their projects or patients. On nonteaching days, my time is spent between research and writing commitments, clinical cases which I may be seeing (primarily forensic cases), and university commitments like the Institutional Review Board (which reviews research for human safety) or the Department Administrative Committee or faculty meetings of various kinds. I will meet with clients, families, insurance company representatives, and lawyers. Occasionally, I will give a deposition in a case. I try to be generally available in my office, especially in the mornings, to meet with students who need to see me but who don't have a specific appointment. I will also prepare class materials and lectures. The actual balance of any given day will differ considerably depending on what is most 'crucial' at that time."

Looking toward the future of clinical neuropsychology, what are your predictions for such factors as growth, new directions, and so on? "The role of organic factors, both in normal development and as a result of injury or disease, is increasingly being recognized as a major contributor to behavior. As the human genome is deciphered, the extent of this role will be better understood and likely broadened. I see more involvement in psychopharmacology, helping to tailor drugs that have very specific effects on emotion and cognition. I see a better understanding of how toxins, injuries, mild traumas, medical illnesses, and the like impact brain function. I see a greater emphasis on personality issues in addition to the past emphasis on cognition."

What changes would you like to see occur in clinical neuropsychology? "I would like to see more focus on personality issues as a result of brain dysfunction. Increased involvement in the design and validation of innovative medical and psychological interventions for the treatment of the effects of brain injury is also needed. More interaction between the clinical scientists and the basic scientists to better integrate the disparate sources of data on human function is also important. More pie in the sky: Develop ways for experts to help in the forensic system (criminal and civil) which are based on finding the truth rather than advocacy for one side or the other, which can lead to bias and distortion."

Unlike Dr. Cernich, who is a recent graduate, Dr. Golden has spent some time in the profession. He is one of the authors of the Luria-Nebraska Neuropsychological Battery we described in chapter 8. *Looking over the time since you received your degree, how has your identity as a professional changed, and to what do you attribute these changes?* "I have increasingly broadened myself from being a neuropsychologist to an assessment psychologist, recognizing more strongly the need to consider the role not only of brain injury but also of personality, family, environment, and premorbid behavior in describing brain-injured individuals. This has been due primarily to experiences with clients which forced me in this direction."

If you could have dinner with any person, living or dead, who would you select and why? Dr. Golden selected A. R. Luria as the person with whom he would like to have dinner. He described Luria as "probably the most innovative thinker this field has ever seen. He was a genius who constantly expanded what he did and believed."

To give you some idea about Dr. Golden's life outside the profession, we asked him about his hobbies. He stated that his hobbies are his family (a wife and three daughters) and Broadway musical theater.

Integrating the Interviews

There was considerable overlap in the undergraduate preparation suggested by Drs. Cernich and Golden. Although they are at different points in their careers, they appear to have similar perceptions of their specialty. Both of them suggest that it is important to be a solid, well-trained, *psychologist* as a foundation for becoming a clinical neuropsychologist. Thus, undergraduate preparation needs to cover the range of courses offered by the department. Among the specific foundation courses in psychology they both recommend are a course in tests and measurement, physiological psychology, statistics, and research methods. They also agree on the importance of a course in human anatomy, often provided by biology departments. These courses give the undergraduate student a foundation for completing the graduate courses in general clinical psychology and the specialty training in neuropsychology. These courses also provide a foundation for the graduate student interested in clinical neuropsychology to both conduct original research and appreciate the existing literature in this specialty. It is also interesting to note that each of them mentioned the importance of personality evaluation as part of clinical neuropsychology. When you read basic texts in this field, it is easy to get the impression that it is totally centered on physiological factors and perhaps it has been that way. Each of these neuropsychologists noted that a change they would like to see in the future of clinical neuropsychology was an increase in attention to personality assessment. With active people like Drs. Cernich and Golden in the profession perhaps their wishes will come to fruition.

Clinical Health Psychology

According to the APA archives, "**Clinical health psychology** applies scientific knowledge of the interrelationships among behavioral, emotional, cognitive, social and biological components in health and disease to the promotion and maintenance of health; the prevention, treatment and rehabilitation of illness and disability; and the improvement of the health care system" (http://www.apa.org/crsppp/health.html). Clinical health psychologists work not only with the identified patient but also with their family members. The nature of this specialty requires that these psychologists do interdisciplinary work and have the skills to work in a range of healthcare settings. They apply their psychological training to understanding the bases of a range of health and disease entities. As psychologists have become more involved in healthcare policy, it is not surprising to find that clinical health psychologists have played an active role in this area. Thus, they are not only interested in the bases of disease but also the improvement of the healthcare delivery system as well as disease prevention strategies.

As we noted with clinical neuropsychology, there are doctoral programs in which you can get your degree in health psychology as well as clinical psychology programs with specialty tracks in health psychology. Many of the founders of the health psychology specialty were trained in clinical psychology. Their ties to clinical psychology are evident when you read the three special issues of the *Journal of Consulting and Clinical Psychology* that are devoted to "behavioral medicine and clinical health psychology." The first of these special issues appeared in 1982, the second in 1992, and the most recent in

2002. Not only do the articles in these special issues of this journal describe the developing specialty but they also have had a role in shaping it. Articles address individual issues of behavior and culture, intervention strategies, and relevant public policy. Several books also describe this specialty (e.g., Brannon & Feist, 2000; Johnson, Perry, & Rozensky, 2002; Rice, 1998). Health psychology has even grown to the point that some of its practitioners specialize in terms of the setting where they work. In 1990, the term *occupational health psychology* appeared in the literature (Raymond, Wood, & Patrick, 1990). The occupational setting is related to many health problems so it is not surprising that health psychologists would see the occupational setting as an important site for the application of their skills. This clinical specialty is sometimes viewed as a merging of clinical psychology with public health (Quick, 1999).

Traditional clinical psychology, centered on assessing and treating mental health issues, has tended to operate on a tertiary prevention level. In other words, clinical psychologists have centered their work on emotional problems that already existed in the individual. Among health psychologists, there is often a focus on primary prevention. In this case, efforts are made to promote health and reduce risk factors that have been found to increase the probability of developing various forms of illness. For example, consider a program designed to decrease risk factors for developing skin cancer. This program was a combination of providing facts about skin cancer with teaching behavioral change skills and helping people handle barriers to behavior change. Analysis of patient data supported the program's value in reducing behaviors associated with the increased risk of developing skin cancer (Rodrigue, 1996).

Psychologists provide a range of services in the healthcare delivery system. APA's Board of Professional Affairs (BPA) established a Work Group on Expanding the Role of Psychology in the Health Care Delivery System to investigate some of these changing roles. This group noted that these activities include assessment, intervention, and liaison roles (Brown et al., 2002). In the assessment domain, health psychologists might be asked to assess whether or not a given individual has the emotional characteristics needed to undergo the rigors of an organ transplant or to adhere to a needed medical treatment program. Specific psychological test batteries are now being evaluated to assist psychologists in making these assessments (e.g. Streisand et al., 1999).

Psychological assessment in the healthcare setting occurs at the *primary, secondary,* and *tertiary* prevention periods. Consider the research on breast cancer. At the primary level, assessment might involve evaluating candidates for genetic screening (Carter & Hailey, 1999), at the secondary level it might involve evaluation of the emotional reactions of women recently diagnosed with breast cancer (Tjemsland, Soreide, & Malt, 1996), and at the tertiary prevention level it might involve assessing memory functions of women who had received chemotherapy as breast cancer treatment (Wieneke & Dienst, 1995). Psychologists have also been active in developing forms of psychotherapy specifically designed to deal with issues faced by breast cancer patients. Support groups have become quite common for these women and psychologists often lead these groups. Numerous books are available for psychologists who want to learn more about the unique nature of these groups (e.g., Antoni, 2003; Baum & Andersen, 2001; Spira & Reed, 2003).

Intervention activities have also been used at all three levels of the disease process. Primary intervention would include the development of educational programs designed to teach healthy eating habits to adolescents in order to prevent obesity. At the secondary intervention level psychologists might provide smoking cessation programs for cancer survivors. An example of tertiary intervention is a treatment program designed to help patients cope with chronic pain.

There are also times when health psychologists provide information to other health-care professionals who will work directly with the patients (Frank, McDaniel, Bray, & Heldring, 2003). At the primary intervention level, liaison activities might involve teaching physicians about the role psychologists can play in their specialty patient care. An example of secondary intervention liaison activity is the provision of an in-service program for child life workers in a hospital who will help sick children make the transition from the hospital to their home. Finally, at the tertiary level, health psychologists may provide training for hospice workers who will be dealing with the daily emotional needs of terminally ill patients.

Researchers in clinical health psychology have noted that understanding the role of the environment in the disease process is an important direction for this field (Keefe, Buffington, Studts, & Rumble, 2002). In the early years of this specialty, the focus tended to be on the individual, as is typical in clinical psychology. As clinical health psychology moved into the twenty-first century, however, both researchers and practitioners realized the impact of the community as well as public policy on individual behavior. Social isolation has been identified as an important factor in both health and illness. To address this factor, the family and possibly even the wider community need to be active parts of the treatment process. When working on prevention programs, clinical health psychologists may consider the school and work environment, the role of advertising, and the impact of changes in the economy in the development of various disorders.

Technology is also an important component of clinical health psychology. Many of the patients seen by these practitioners have traditionally needed to travel to specialized sites to receive services. Telehealth applications in the form of automated phone and computerized systems have been developed to provide easier access to clinical health psychologists. Clinical researchers have empirically evaluated Internet interventions for a range of problems, including diabetes self-management (McKay, Glasgow, Feil, Boles, & Barrera, 2002), weight loss (Tate, Wing, & Winett, 2001), and pediatric encopresis (Ritterband et al., 2003).

Assessment services have also been provided using these distance methods. Let's briefly consider an example. One small sample study, using twenty-seven patients, evaluated the reliability of distance neuropsychological assessment of patients considered to be alcohol abusers (Kirkwood, Peck, & Bennie, 2000). Reliability was found to be high when face-to-face evaluation was compared to distance evaluation of these patients. Patient satisfaction with distance evaluation was also good. This latter factor is important when considering the development of telehealth procedures. If the patient does not feel satisfied with the process it may be that he or she will not complete the program. Thus, the cost would not be considered worth doing. Cost is a factor that must be considered when telehealth programs are developed. Some researchers have suggested that before such programs can really be considered to be cost-saving, the profession will need to see a significant increase in the number of patients served this way (Lamminen, Lamminen, Ruohonen, & Uusitalo, 2001). To achieve this increase in the number of patients served, there will need to be acceptance of these procedures by the third-party payers (insurance companies).

Other issues that need more complete study involve patient confidentiality and issues of jurisdictional control. For example, if the standard of care is not met for the provision of these services, who is responsible for disciplining the provider? Although no one has suggested that all future services will be provided in this way, there is the hope that it will assist in the treatment of people in remote areas. Another area that has been explored to determine its usefulness in the delivery of healthcare is virtual reality. For example, virtual reality has been used to provide patients with exposure to distressing circumstances while in a safe environment (e.g., Hoffman, Doctor, Patterson, Carrougher, & Furness, 2000). Another growing area of research is to determine which interventions work best with specific populations and why (Whitfield, Weidner, Clark, & Anderson, 2002). This type of research has become more important as the U.S. population has developed in a more demographically diverse way. We no longer assume that one treatment approach is the best one for all people.

How are psychologists trained to perform these new activities? There has been considerable professional discussion about training models in health psychology. Traditionally, the APA has taken the position that graduate education should focus on training general practice psychologists and specialty training should then occur on the level of the predoctoral internship and postdoctoral study. This position applies to each of the specialties we are discussing in this book. In 1983, a national conference was convened to discuss education and training models in health psychology. One of the recommendations of this group was that training in health psychology should occur at the postdoctoral level. This training would require two years following the completion of the doctorate (Sheridan et al., 1988). Despite this recommendation, health psychology has continued to grow as a specialty track within doctoral programs and predoctoral internships. Some of these programs focus on specific areas of practice, such as eating disorders or psycho-oncology, while others are more general in nature. More recently, training models and programs have been developed for primary care health psychology because primary care is the setting where many emotional problems first become evident under the modern managed health care system (McDaniel et al., 2002). Psychologists who work in this setting with physicians are able to provide an integrated system of care to their patients. Our two interviews with practicing health psychologists illustrate some of their varied activities.

RONALD H. ROZENSKY has a Ph.D. in clinical psychology from the University of Pittsburgh. He is a diplomate in both clinical and health psychology from the American Board of Professional Psychology (ABPP). At the time of this interview, he was chairperson of the Department of Clinical and Health Psychology at the University of Florida in Gainesville, Florida.

If you were talking to an undergraduate student who is considering specializing in health psychology, what psychology courses would you recommend as good preparation? Like many of the psychologists with whom we conducted interviews, Dr. Rozensky took the position that it is important to become a good "psychologist" before thinking about becoming a specialist. He thus suggested that undergraduate preparation should include good basic and advanced courses in learning, motivation, emotion, perception, personality

Ronald H. Rozensky
Photo courtesy of
Ronald H. Rozensky.

development, normal development, abnormal psychology, psychometrics, research design, and statistics. Then, he said, courses in biological bases of behavior, neuroanatomy, psychophysiology, public health, health promotion, and aging will help you see where health psychology is headed.

What courses in other disciplines would you recommend? In this case, Dr. Rozensky recommended two rather different directions in terms of course selection. When you read the interview with Dr. Haley in the next chapter in the clinical geropsychology section, you will find he has a similar recommendation. Dr. Rozensky suggested that courses in medical terminology, biology, chemistry, pharmacology, anatomy, and neuroanatomy are helpful. In addition to these science courses, he recommended taking a couple of courses in Shakespeare. These courses will help you think about the human condition in general, what motivates people, and why they become happy and sad.

What courses didn't you have that you wish you had? Dr. Rozensky responded that he did not have courses in public health, disability, medical disorders, and pharmacology. He noted that at the beginning of health psychology, students picked up biological bases of behavior and pharmacology as part of their clinical training. These courses are now often available more broadly, such as on the undergraduate level.

When you think about the work you do, what do you find most rewarding? For Dr. Rozensky, the answer to this question is seeing people learn to manage their illnesses or see their medical problems improve because of psychological interventions.

What do you find most frustrating? Like many psychologists of his time, Dr. Rozensky discussed some of the practical and business challenges that face the profession in the twenty-first century. He expressed frustration with the business side of practice, insurance, and physicians who have no knowledge of psychology or psychological issues. He added that these problems have a direct impact on medical illnesses and patients' lives both in terms of quality of life and longevity.

Were there specific life experiences that influenced you to become a psychologist, and why a health psychologist? "Yes, I had a suicidal roommate in college. I managed getting him into treatment with the student health services. They said I should think about becoming a psychologist. I started out as a chemistry major and wanted to teach high school chemistry. I took a psychology course as a required course when I was a sophomore. I was excited by the science of learning research and the eloquent studies we read. The rest is history!"

Did you have a mentor or role model who influenced you to become a psychologist? "When I was an undergraduate, the entire faculty at the University of Illinois, Champaign, were at the cutting edge of many areas of research, including abnormal psychology, child development, psychophysiology, community psychology, and learning and emotion. The excitement of the science and how it could be applied in the clinical situation was very motivating to me. I had three major mentors in graduate school—Drs. Alan Bellack, Lynn Rehm, and David Lazovik. Each of them came from the scientist-practitioner philosophy and continued to excite my interest in the scientific study of, and application of, psychological principles in clinical situations. Dr. Arnold Friedman at the Pittsburgh VA Hospital introduced me to clinical health psychology during a training rotation there. The work with medically ill patients was a very intriguing application of all the psychological principles I had learned up to that point. We were doing 'clinical psychology' in a medical setting. The term 'health psychology' was still on the horizon at that time."

Please write one or two paragraphs about each of two days in your professional life that describe a sample of what you do. "Right now, I am the chair of the department of clinical and health psychology at the University of Florida. Thus, administrative activities take the better part of my day, but I will not focus on my administrative duties. I can see a variety of patients with medical disorders who are having difficulty managing their reactions to their illnesses. I also see patients who present to their physicians with medical problems but the physicians find no medical diagnosis. Thus they are sent to me to work on various emotional and psychological issues that contribute to their physical problems and complaints. I also supervise students in their work with medical patients as well as their work in diagnostic assessment and psychotherapy with traditional patients with mental health problems [depression, anxiety, panic disorder, etc.]. We see patients who must learn how to adhere to their medical regimens in order to stay well. We see patients who present with a wide range of stress-related and psychological-related problems but focus on physiological symptoms and must learn to talk about their depression, anxiety, or life situation rather than about their medical concerns. I have a grant from the Substance Abuse and Mental Health Administration [SAMSHA] that funds the National Rural Behavioral Health Center. In that center, we train psychologists to work with underserved rural populations and we do research on access to health care, school violence prevention, and depression and anxiety in primary care settings. I edit a journal, *The Journal* *of Clinical Psychology in Medical Settings,* which has been published for ten years. Some time each day is spent reviewing manuscripts for publication in that journal."

Looking toward the future of clinical health psychology, what are your predictions for such factors as growth, new directions, and so on? "We will see more interface between psychology and public health as we, as a discipline, direct our empirically validated treatment protocols to larger populations. Psychologists will be spending more time in primary care settings working side by side with pediatricians, family practice physicians, and nurse practitioners as well as in ob-gyn practices. We will be working with patients with the entire spectrum of psychological disorders but in primary care settings we will see those patients sooner and this earlier diagnosis will help them address their psychological problems sooner and more effectively."

What changes would you like to see occur in your specialty? "In clinical health psychology we have already seen the identification of specialties such as rehabilitation psychology and pediatric psychology. These two specialties, along with clinical health psychology, all work with medically ill patients and do research within their areas of focus. I would see ongoing 'subspecialization' where health psychologists will work specifically with cardiac patients, cancer patients, etc. There will be a clinical health psychologist in every medical clinic and on every medical unit from the emergency room to the surgical suite to the intensive care unit doing direct patient care and research to improve quality of life and longevity."

Looking over the time since you received your degree, how has your identity as a professional changed, and to what do you attribute these changes? "I have maintained my roots as a scientist-practitioner, thus bringing the skeptical mind of a hypothesis tester to the clinic, classroom, and the research lab. If anything, I find this belief in the scientific basis of the practice of psychology has gotten stronger as I see how the field has become and how it continues to evolve. If you do not have that strong scientific basis, then you will not be the best psychologist you can be."

If you could have dinner with any person, living or dead, who would you choose and why? Dr. Rozensky chose to alter this question a bit. Rather than select *one* person, he would host a dinner party. "One person would not be enough to satisfy my curiosity," he told us. His guests would be William Shakespeare, Marie Curie, Henry David Thoreau, E. B. White, Rosa Parks, King David, Sigmund Freud, Carl Rogers, and B. F. Skinner. He said that these people give us a true picture of people and why we are who we are.

As a final bit of information to help us get a more complete picture of Dr. Rozensky, we asked him to list his hobbies. He said they are sailing, amateur astronomy, and reading Shakespeare.

JALIE A. TUCKER has a Ph.D. in clinical psychology from Vanderbilt University. At the time of this interview, she was a professor in the Department of Health Behavior, School of Public Health, University of Alabama at Birmingham. Her research interests in substance abuse led her to the conclusion that public health, health economic policy, and health policy issues were crucial to increasing access to, and utilization of, substance abuse services. To gain a more solid grounding in these areas, she returned to school and earned an M.P.H. (master of public health) degree in healthcare organization and policy. Among her many professional activities are service as the first elected president of the Division on Addictions (Division 50) of the APA, service on numerous APA governance

Jalie A. Tucker
*Photo courtesy of UAB Creative
and Marketing Group.*

groups, and being a regular recipient of research grants from the National Institute on Alcohol Abuse and Alcoholism. The specific questions we asked Dr. Tucker are followed by her responses.

If you were talking to an undergraduate student who is considering specializing in clinical psychology with specialization in addictive behaviors and healthcare systems, what psychology courses would you recommend as good preparation? Dr. Tucker recommended courses in the biological bases of behavior, abnormal psychology, learning and memory, sensation and perception, statistics, and social psychology.

What courses in other disciplines would you recommend? Dr. Tucker noted the importance of taking math through calculus. For this area, she felt it was also important to have multiple science courses selected from biology, chemistry, ecology, and physics. Students would also benefit from taking courses in such social sciences as sociology and anthropology. Because of the importance of developing good writing skills and analytic skills based on reading, she recommended English composition and literature courses. Finally, she noted that it is important for undergraduate students to take some courses just because they like them. She felt that a well-rounded liberal arts education is basic to being an effective psychologist.

What courses didn't you have that you wish you had? Dr. Tucker noted that she would like to have had courses in economics, especially microeconomics, and computer programming.

When you think of the work you do, what do you find the most rewarding? "The research process, especially the initial literature review and design phases followed by data analysis and manuscript preparation phases are really rewarding. Writing is a challenging but rewarding aspect of much of what I do."

What do you find most frustrating? "What I find most frustrating are most meetings, especially regularly scheduled meetings with no compelling agenda."

Were there specific life experiences that influenced you to become a psychologist? "Not really—I drifted into a psychology major from a chemistry major in my junior year when I transferred from Stetson to Duke University and found that I'd probably have to spend an extra year there finishing a chemistry major. I'd taken some psychology courses before and found it to be, by comparison, enjoyable and easy. I liked psychology, especially the more research-oriented areas, because it allowed me to use my basic science background in an area of human interest and application. This is why I was drawn to my specialty area of substance abuse, which cuts across disciplinary boundaries from the biological to the social sciences and requires some consideration of broader policy and economic forces. I've never been bored as a result."

Why did you decide to work in health psychology? Dr. Tucker had already answered this question as part of the preceding ones.

Did you have a mentor or role model who influenced you to become a psychologist? If so, please tell us about this person. "Robert C. Carson, Ph.D., my honors thesis advisor at Duke University, influenced my decision to go to graduate school at Vanderbilt University from among the places where I had been accepted. That was an excellent choice, and I owe him a debt of gratitude for steering me toward a science-oriented program in clinical psychology. But I otherwise was not encouraged to become a psychologist. My father had a dim view of the field from his experiences with I/O [industrial/organizational] psychologists in banking and pushed me to become a physician, but I knew that wasn't the life for me. I needed the intellectual engagement of the research process and found getting a Ph.D. much more compatible with that than a medical education."

Please write one or two paragraphs about each of two days in your professional life that describe a sample of what you do. "There are few constants in my schedule from day to day, and I value that highly. I am involved in many different endeavors that cycle over time (e.g., grants management, grant submissions, journal editorial activities, teaching class, and writing of many kinds). I serve on several boards and committees at the university and national levels that have a scholarly or policy focus. I've avoided administrative roles as much as possible, although I've done my share of that kind of service, including a stint as codirector of a doctoral program in clinical psychology."

Looking toward the future of your specialty, what are your predictions for such factors as growth, new directions, and so on? "The healthcare environment has changed fundamentally during the last twenty-five years, shifting from a provider-dominated enterprise with a fee-for-service arrangement to a corporate enterprise driven by marketplace economic forces. Much headway has been made in recent years in moving psychological services into the healthcare system, but the applied research base and doctoral education in psychology has lagged behind these developments badly. The line of critical conflict in psychology today, as I see it, is between education and practice."

What changes would you like to see occur in your specialty? "Yesterday's training models that emphasize assessment and therapy skills and comparative research evaluations of technically different psychotherapies that are otherwise delivered in the same dyadic format are not serving tomorrow's clinical psychologists well. They will be working as researchers and service providers in a healthcare environment that is fundamentally different from the one that birthed yesterday's training models, when the battle line was between psychiatry and psychology and resulted in psychologists moving out of supportive roles as assessor and into independent practice. Tomorrow's clinical psychologists will need to understand the healthcare system, and many will likely participate in the delivery of behavioral health care in ways other than direct service delivery (e.g., as supervisors of services provided by subdoctoral therapists, as coordinators of outcomes assessment, and as health services researchers). To do so effectively, they need to acquire knowledge about the healthcare system and newer research approaches. To that end, I recommend taking courses on health economics, health insurance and managed care, health outcomes assessment, and health promotion and disease prevention."

Looking over the time since you received your degree, how has your identity as a professional changed, and to what do you attribute these changes? "The changes I just described became apparent to me in the 1990s through developments in my research area and also from the vantage point of overseeing a doctoral program in clinical psychology. To get out ahead of these developments, I obtained a career development award (from the National Institute of Alcohol Abuse and Alcoholism) that allowed me to obtain a master's of public health degree in healthcare organization and policy. My advisor was a health economist and managed care expert who gave me considerable latitude in learning about mental health economics and related policy issues. It was a perspective- and life-changing experience that led to my present position in a department of health behavior in a school of public health. I highly value my psychology roots, with its rigorous behavioral science foundation and emphasis on measurement, but my evolution toward a broader public health perspective on the content areas of concern to psychology has been very useful, necessary, and satisfying to me."

If you could have dinner with any person, living or dead, who would you select and why? "I'd like to say a Buddhist mystic, but I probably wouldn't get it. So as a fallback, I'll say a rock star like Mick Jagger who has survived a life of temptation and drugs and lived to tell the tale. How some drug abusers and addicts pull back from the extremes and others don't is at the heart of the addictions puzzle."

As a final bit of information to help us get a more complete picture of Dr. Tucker, we asked her about her hobbies. She told us her hobbies are dance and gardening.

Integrating the Interviews

We were surprised to learn that both Drs. Rozensky and Tucker started college as chemistry majors. Perhaps that interest in science helped them select their direction within clinical psychology once they reached graduate school. Do not think, however, that you must start in chemistry to become a health psychologist! Within the broad field of clinical health psychology, they have taken somewhat different career paths. Now that you have "met" them, let's try to summarize what we have learned from their interviews. Each of them highlight the importance of a solid foundation in the traditional roots of psychology.

Although it may be tempting to try to select all of your undergraduate courses in the specific area you hope to study in graduate school, you may want to remember what they are suggesting about breadth and context. Their suggestions about courses in other disciplines are quite different from each other. These differences may be a reflection of their own history and interests within health psychology or may reflect their current perceptions of the field and where it is going. Regardless of the specific courses you may select as electives outside psychology, they suggest the importance of broad exposure. They also both note the importance of developing good writing skills. This exposure is helpful no matter how certain you may feel about your career direction.

Their responses to the rewards of this career area also illustrate the breadth of this specialty. Dr. Rozensky focuses on his clinical work, while Dr. Tucker is most rewarded by her professional research and writing. Their frustrations illustrate parts of the profession not usually addressed on the undergraduate level—the challenges of paperwork and required meetings that may not really interest you but which you are required to complete. Perhaps these comments are a reminder that regardless of your specialty, you will not be able to spend all of your time in clinical work. Both Drs. Rozensky and Tucker are employed within the university setting. Even if they were in full-time clinical practice, they would have considerable paperwork to complete as part of their business.

Clinical Forensic Psychology

The specialty that connects psychology and the legal system is forensic psychology. According to information on the website of the American Psychology-Law Society, "the field of psychology and law involves the application of scientific and professional aspects of psychology to questions and issues relating to law and the legal system" (http//www. unl.edu/ap-ls/careers.html). Clinical psychology is not the only specialty within psychology that contributes to psychology-law studies. Students who are interested in psychology-law combined careers other than clinical psychology should go to the website for further information. We are limiting this discussion to **clinical forensic psychology.**

Mental health practitioners have worked with the legal system for many years. This is not a new activity. Psychiatrists testified in courts about mental disorders for many years before psychologists were given this right. In 1962, the United States Court of Appeals for the District of Columbia stated in a majority opinion that appropriately trained psychologists qualified as expert witnesses regarding mental disorders (*Jenkins v. United States,* 1962). This was the first time psychologists were given this privilege. Since that time, the role of the psychologist in the courtroom has expanded. Today, psychologists are found as expert witnesses in both criminal and civil courts and serve as consultants to many legal agencies. They may even be named by the court to provide mandated evaluations of litigants to the court rather than being part of the adversarial process. For example, family court judges may name a psychologist to provide an evaluation of the entire family unit before making a decision regarding custody during a divorce proceeding. This process is different from the earlier one in which each parent hired an individual psychologist and these psychologists became part of the adversarial procedures. When the psychologist is named by the judge to do the evaluation, the results are sent directly to the judge as well as to each of the attorneys. Usually the judge will also mandate how much of the psychologist's fees are paid by each of the parents based on their finances.

It was not until the 1970s, however, that this interaction between psychologists and the legal system led to the development of formal training programs and scholarly outlets devoted to the interface of law and psychology. The first university to establish a graduate program leading to a combination of a doctoral degree in psychology and a law degree was the University of Nebraska at Lincoln. This was also the decade when the first scholarly journal devoted to psychology and law, *Law and Human Behavior,* was started. This is an interdisciplinary journal. Another important journal is *Psychology, Public Policy, and Law,* which began publication in 1995. Since the 1970s, this field has continued to grow. Every other March, a national conference is held to discuss current issues and research in the field. There are now a number of predoctoral and postdoctoral training programs in psychology and the law. Books and journals are available to those who want to learn more about the field (e.g., Bartol, 1996; Hess & Weiner, 1999).

Clinical-forensic psychologists are clinical psychologists who specialize in the assessment and/or treatment of persons who, in some way, are involved in the legal process or legal system (http://www.unl.edu/ap-la/careers.html/). Some of them have doctoral degrees in clinical psychology as well as law degrees, while others have doctoral degrees in clinical psychology with a specialty in forensic psychology. The website given here includes a list of programs offering these specialties. Those psychologists with both degrees are licensed as clinical psychologists as well as having passed the bar exam as attorneys. These psychologists work in both the criminal and civil court settings. To do their work appropriately, they use their training in normal and abnormal development plus assessment procedures in combination with their legal knowledge. Forensic psychologists may help provide information about whether or not a defendant has some mental defect that legally prevents that person from assisting in his or her own defense or understanding the legal proceedings. In other words, forensic psychologists help determine whether or not defendants are legally competent to stand trial or competent to plead guilty. In the U.S. legal system, if the prosecution, the defense, or the judge raises the issue of competence of the defendant to stand trial at any point during a criminal proceeding, the judge must order an evaluation. If the defendant is found incompetent, one of several things may happen. The judge may remand the person to a treatment facility until the person is found competent and then the legal process continues. In other cases, a plea bargain may occur such that the person will not be prosecuted if he or she seeks the needed treatment. This latter option is used most often in cases of lesser offenses.

What does it take to be called an "expert witness"? The final decision on this question is made by the trial judge. Possession of a valid license as a psychologist is the first step to be named an expert witness. Over time, the courts have made rulings about this topic because of the importance such testimony has for the trial's outcome. The two rulings most often cited in discussion about expert witness status are the **Frye rule** and **Daubert.** In the case of *Frye v. United States* (1923), the courts ruled that the basis of the testimony must be generally accepted in the scientific community upon which that testimony is based. As you can see, this ruling applies to professions in addition to psychology. A question here is how to determine what is "generally accepted" within the profession of psychology. By now you probably realize that psychologists from different theoretical orientations may disagree with each other about what they find acceptable psychological science. According to "Frye," however, it is really the psychological community rather than the judge who provides the basis for deciding whether or not information should be admitted in court. In 1993, a ruling by the United States Supreme Court in *Daubert v. Merrell Dow Pharmaceuticals* placed more of the responsibility on the judge regarding the decision about expert witness testimony. According to this ruling, the issue is not whether the relevant scientific community accepts the procedures but rather whether the expert used the scientific reasoning process to reach the stated conclusions. During the process of qualification as an expert witness, the psychologist can expect to be asked questions about such factors as the reliability and validity of the assessment measures used as well as the empirical basis for them.

Among juvenile offenders, competence to stand trial is the most frequently requested form of mental health evaluations (Melton, Petrila, Poythress, & Slobogin, 1997), although only recently has attention been paid to consistency of this practice across legal jurisdictions (Nicholson & Norwood, 2000). In other cases, the focus may be on an estimate of the defendant's state of mind at the time a criminal act occurred. There are also cases in which the clinical forensic psychologist is asked to indicate the type of treatment that would be of greatest benefit to a convicted criminal. Criminal cases are the ones for forensic psychologists that seem to get the majority of media attention. Clinical forensic psychologists also work in civil cases. These cases include such issues as whether an adult is capable of making life decisions or perhaps needs a guardian, child custody, or whether a person has been emotionally harmed as a result of another person's negligence. Other clinical forensic psychologists are active researchers. They may develop and evaluate assessment tools designed specifically for a forensic population or treatment procedures used in these settings. The 1992 APA Ethical Principles of Psychologists and Code of Conduct had a separate section on forensic activities; however, the most recent version does not separate this activity from overall activities of psychologists. This change may be a reflection of the fact that many psychologists now find they are required to testify in court even if they do not view themselves as forensic psychologists and thus the ethical principles are broadly applicable.

Clinical forensic psychologists work in a range of settings. They may have an independent private practice on either a full-time or part-time basis. Others are employed by forensic hospitals, prison systems, or mental health centers. A good example of a forensic hospital is St. Elizabeth's hospital in Washington, DC. Among the famous patients at that hospital is John Hinkley, who shot then U.S. President Ronald Reagan in 1981. In late 2003, he remained in St. Elizabeth's and was just granted by the courts permission to have unsupervised visits to his parents' home. Psychologists were part of the team that evaluated John Hinkley for the courts to determine if he should be granted these visits. Those forensic psychologists who are primarily researchers typically work in university settings. Popular films and television programs have given the mistaken impression that many forensic clinical psychologists are criminal profilers, usually described as someone who has strong training in psychology who is able to help law enforcement find a criminal by describing the person based on the criminal act the person committed. The Behavioral Sciences Unit of the Federal Bureau of Investigation (FBI) does engage in some of this activity. It does not, however, employ large numbers of psychologists who do this. Students who have an interest in the work with this FBI unit must first become FBI agents. They must have experience in criminal investigation before they will even be considered for this unit and there are only a limited number of positions within this program. Thus, we do not recommend pursuing a career in clinical psychology if your career goal is to become a criminal profiler. Some psychologists have suggested that the work in criminal profiling continues to lack sufficient empirical support and perhaps should be scrutinized more closely (Homant & Kennedy, 1998).

There are clinical psychologists who do work with law enforcement agencies and who do become involved as "part" of their job in considering characteristics of a potential criminal. Some police departments have a psychologist called whenever their SWAT team is called to a scene. In these cases, the psychologist does not have the advantage of the usual interview information or making a tentative judgment like those we discussed earlier in this book. The police expect their clinical psychologist to advise them about whether the suspect can be talked out of a hostage situation or whether they should attack the building. The clinical psychologist's opinion has life-and-death consequences in these cases. At another time that day these same police psychologists might be working individually with a police officer who needs support following the death of his or her partner in the line of duty. Thus, clinical skills are used in a variety of ways in this law enforcement setting. Police use of psychologists has been increasing over the years. Another role that psychologists play in police work is the psychological evaluation of potential offenders. In this case, the psychologist is probably not employed by the police department but rather has been asked to do this evaluation either by the defendant's attorney or by the courts. As psychologists' roles evolve within police departments, the need for sharing information can be expected to increase. In 1997, a group representing police chiefs in the United States met with leadership from the APA to discuss ways psychologists could assist police departments.

Following the events of September 11, 2001, when dealing with the aftermath of a terrorist attack became part of American life, psychologists were actively involved with police, fire services, and emergency medical personnel. With increased attention to homeland security, there are likely to be additional roles for psychologists within a range of law enforcement agencies. A start on this road of increased collaboration between psychologists and the law enforcement community occurred in February 2002 at a conference cosponsored by APA, the FBI Academy, and the University of Pennsylvania Center for Study of Ethnopolitical Conflict. The purpose of this conference was to discuss ways social scientists and law enforcement could work together on issues related to terrorism. Another example of this type of collaboration is the fact that the Department of Homeland Security (DHS) designates four of its fifty graduate student fellowships to students in psychology who are studying counterterrorism. These psychology graduate students are involved in research, curriculum development, public policy, and clinical work on terrorism. Thus, both researchers and practitioners are needed in this evolving field. Students who want to read more about this specialty may wish to read one or more of the textbooks available in the field (e.g., Melton, Huss, & Tomkins, 1999; Wrightsman, Nietzel, & Fortune, 1998).

LISA R. GROSSMAN received her J.D. and Ph.D. degrees from a joint degree program at Northwestern University called Law and the Social Sciences. Her Ph.D. specialty field is clinical psychology. At the time of this interview, she was in full-time private practice of clinical and forensic psychology.

Lisa R. Grossman
*Photo courtesy of
Lisa R. Grossman.*

If you were talking to an undergraduate student who is considering a career in clinical and forensic psychology, what psychology courses would you recommend as good preparation? "When I was an undergraduate, the psychology department in my university did not have a clinical component. I would like to have taken courses in clinical psychology, including personality theories, assessment, treatment orientations, law and psychology, and ethics. On a graduate level, I would recommend a solid foundation in psychology, including courses in abnormal psychology, developmental psychology, research design and statistics, personality theories, ethics, treatment theories, psychometrics, normal development, and neuropsychology."

What courses in other disciplines would you recommend? "As an undergraduate, I was interested in anything that dealt with human behavior. Because sociology and social psychology so closely overlapped, I took as many courses as I could in sociology. As a result, I was able to earn a second major in it. Because of my double major, I did not have time to take as many courses as I would have liked in such areas as art, history, and literature. On the graduate level, I would recommend courses in law and the legal process, including civil procedure, criminal law, torts, family law, and mental health law."

What courses didn't you have that you wish you had taken? "Because I was in a joint degree program where I earned both my law degree and my doctorate in psychology, I was fortunate to have taken all of the legal courses that have helped me to prepare to be a forensic psychologist. However, I would have liked to have taken a course specifically in forensic psychology, but that was not offered at the time I was in school. I would also have liked a course in ethics, but that was not offered when I was in school, either. I believe that ethics needs to be introduced to students as early in their training as possible."

When you think about the work you do, what do you find most rewarding? "There are many aspects of forensic work that I find rewarding. I am gratified when my forensic report/recommendations are sufficient to settle a case instead of having a long and protracted trial. I also find it very rewarding when I can make recommendations that are in the best interest of the child, despite rancorous and/or alienating parents. I also find it rewarding to detect a malingerer who is trying to deceive the justice system."

What do you find most frustrating? "I am always dismayed when I see divorcing parents who are more concerned about their own needs than those of their children. I also find it frustrating when attorneys create more of an adversarial process than necessary. Further, it is upsetting when ill-qualified psychologists attempt forensic work, write inadequate reports, testify poorly, and have no real understanding of the forensic process."

Were there specific life experiences that influenced you to become a psychologist? "I knew I wanted to be a psychologist since I was in junior high school. I was fascinated with why people acted in the way they did, and gross psychopathology intrigued me. The unconscious mind has always been a powerful concept to me."

Why did you decide to work in forensic psychology? "I went into forensic psychology because I found the interface between the law and psychology to be intriguing. Also, when I was thinking about careers in psychology, there were very few forensic psychologists at that time. I wanted to be somewhat different than all the rest of the clinical psychologists in the country."

Did you have a mentor or role model who influenced you to become a psychologist? If so, please tell us about this person. "When I was an undergraduate at Northwestern University, Dr. Bruce Sales was the instructor for my class in research design. At that time, he was a psychologist who was just taking his bar exam. It was because of him that I first became interested in combining law and psychology, and I have been indebted to him ever since."

Please write one or two paragraphs about each of two days in your professional life that describe a sample of what you do. "As a forensic psychologist, I conduct a variety of forensic evaluations, including custody/visitation, insanity, disability, emotional damage after an injury, malpractice issues, etc. On a typical day, I might see a parent who is fighting for custody of his/her child(ren). I would conduct a structured, in-depth clinical interview that includes an assessment of parenting capacity. I would also begin psychometric testing with only those instruments that have appropriate validity and reliability. This assessment would take the entire morning. In the afternoon I would see several clinical patients in psychotherapy or mediation. I would then return various business calls, contact some collaterals associated with the morning evaluation, and then do a home visit of the other parent. That evening I would prepare for a deposition to be given the next day. The next morning, I would go to an attorney's office where I am deposed for a maximum of three hours. That afternoon, I would supervise a psychologist who was on probation from the Department of Regulation, conduct a parent-child observation, observe and assess the child, and then return phone calls. That evening, as president of Forensic

Forum, a Chicago organization composed of judges, lawyers, and mental health professionals, I might chair a dinner/presentation of a forensic topic delivered by one of our members."

Looking toward the future of forensic psychology, what are your predictions for such factors as growth, new directions, and so on? "As I look toward the future in forensics, I see a greater determination of what constitutes scientific evidence that psychologists bring to the courts, à la Daubert [she is referring to the Daubert v. Merrell Dow case we cited before]. I also see greater use of collaborative law so that the judicial system becomes less adversarial and more interested in settlements with quicker and more humane resolutions."

What changes would you like to see occur in your specialty? "I would like to see all states give immunity to all court-ordered experts so that unhappy litigants can't manipulate the judicial system by filing spurious licensing board, ethics, or legal complaints."

Looking over the time since you received your degree, how has your identity as a professional changed, and to what do you attribute these changes? "My graduate training mainly focused on psychodynamic theory. Over the years, while I still conceptualize using a psychodynamic framework, I have become less rigid in my techniques and far more eclectic. I have come to realize that any particular intervention can be justified by a variety of different orientations that merely use different language and terminology."

If you could have dinner with any person, living or dead, who would you select and why? "I would have dinner with Sigmund Freud for two basic reasons. First, Freud was known to do 'quick' psychoanalyses and to be analyzed by Freud would be mesmerizing. Second, I would like to set Dr. Freud straight about women and sexuality."

It is obvious from her responses to our questions that Dr. Grossman has a very busy schedule. We wondered if she had any hobbies outside her work. She told us her favorite hobby is people. She said, "I love to observe and interact with people and consider myself blessed to have such wonderful friends and family."

Interview Summary

Dr. Grossman has a law degree in addition to her degree in clinical psychology. Although not all forensic psychologists have these dual degrees, she feels it has been essential for her work. She noted the importance of psychological assessment in the forensic arena and thus the importance of taking an assessment course. In terms of rewards and frustrations of this specialty, Dr. Grossman noted rewards on an individual level such as being able to settle a case without a long trial and the frustration of those cases that become adversarial and take more time. She also noted that she would like to be able to have the outcome of her work occur more quickly than it often does. It is also important to note one of Dr. Grossman's comments if you are thinking about forensic psychology as a career. When she talked about changes in her profession she noted one problem with unhappy litigants filing unfounded charges against the psychologist. Doing the type of work she does, such as child custody, tends to lead to at least one party in the case being really upset. That person may try to get revenge by filing a complaint against the professional he or she views as responsible for outcome—the psychologist. Even though you know you did nothing wrong, it can take both time and money to defend yourself against such charges.

Sport Psychology

A form of "coaching" provided by psychologists involves work with athletes. Although psychologists have worked with athletes for many years, the definition of **sport psychology** and the qualifications for practicing this specialty evolved over a period of time. A survey of one thousand members of the APA Division of Clinical Psychology reported that 22 percent of those responding had consulted either with individual athletes or with teams and that 48 percent had provided therapy to athletes (Petrie & Diehl, 1995). Today, sport psychology is seen as an interdisciplinary field including psychology, physical education, and sport and exercise science. Clinical psychologists who wish to work with this population obtain specialized training in sport science in addition to their clinical training. A special section on sport psychology in *Professional Psychology: Research and Practice* addressed the types of training needed, ethical issues to consider, relationship to family systems psychology, eating disorders, and employment as a team psychologist (Hays & Chan, 2001).

Although there are some doctoral programs in sport psychology, most of the training occurs either in specialized postdoctoral fellowships or through various forms of cross-discipline training. "Sport psychology is a science in which the principles of psychology are applied in a sport or exercise setting" (Cox, 1998, p. 4). Some experts trace the history of sport psychology to a study published by psychologist Norman Triplett in the *American Journal of Psychology* in 1897. His research investigated the impact of observers on one's performance. He noted, for example, that cyclists improved more when competing with other cyclists than when they were riding alone. The first sport psychology laboratory, the Athletic Research Laboratory, was opened at the University of Illinois in 1925 under the direction of Coleman Roberts Griffith. During his career, he was an active researcher in sport psychology and wrote one of the early textbooks in the field. He was an integral part of the specialty during the period from 1920 to 1940. Some of you may be wondering why a field that has existed for over one hundred years is not more fully developed by now. Like many other topics, sport psychology did not become sufficiently popular to continue once these original researchers were no longer active. During the 1940s and 1950s, little work was done in this specialty. This does not mean that it would never reappear. It was during the mid-1960s that sport psychology once again appeared in the profession. Research in the field began to appear at that time and textbooks were published. Today, many such books are available (e.g., Anshel, 2003; Cox, 1998; Van Raalte & Brewer, 2002).

Professional associations have added to the growth of sports psychology as well as to keeping it alive as a specialty. These organizations provide both scholars and practitioners of sport psychology with an identity as well as a professional meeting where they can exchange ideas and debate controversial topics in the field. The first meeting of the North American Society for the Psychology of Sport and Physical Activity (NASPSPA) was held in 1967. The primary goal of this organization is advancement of the field through experimental research. The NASPSPA journal, *Journal of Sport and Exercise Psychology,* provides a site for publishing data from these studies. At about the same time, sport psychology in Canada also began to organize. The Canadian Society for Psychomotor Learning and Sports Psychology (CSPLSP) was founded in 1969. Interest in sport psychology is not limited to North America. For example, sport psychology is an integral part of the Australian Psychological Society (APS). In Australia, use of the title and practice of sport psychology is more fully regulated than it is in North America at this time. The International Society for Sport Psychology (ISSP) is an organization that illustrates the global nature of this specialty.

Not all psychologists interested in the application of the field to sports focus on the research perspective. As a result, applied sport psychology developed. Applied sport psychology focuses on the professional and applied side of the field. Interest in applied aspects of sport psychology led to the formation of the Association for the Advancement of Applied Sport Psychology (AAASP) in 1985. Both professionals and students can join AAASP. AAASP began publication of its journal, *Journal of Applied Sport Psychology,* in 1989. Information about this organization can be found on its website (www. aaasponline.org). Applied sport psychology includes "performance enhancement, life skills training, organizational consulting with teams, clinical and counseling interventions with athletes, and rehabilitation" (Meyers, Coleman, Whelan, & Mehlenbeck, 2001, p. 5).

The United States Olympic Committee recognized that applied sport psychology had a range of contributions to make to training elite athletes. They subdivided the areas of sport psychology into clinical/counseling sport psychology, educational sport psychology, and research sport psychology. The clinical/counseling sport psychologists, the type most closely related to clinical psychology, assist athletes in addressing problems that fall within traditional clinical psychology (e.g., anxiety, depression). The educational sport psychologist teaches principles of sport psychology to both athletes and coaches. Much of their emphasis is on performance enhancement. They also work with athletes about how to use sport to improve the quality of their lives. The research of sport psychologists provides the knowledge foundation upon which the others base their work.

Psychologists interested in sport psychology formed Division 47 of APA, the Division of Exercise and Sport Psychology. Information about APA Division 47 can be obtained through the APA website (www.apa.org/divisions).

As the field has grown, some organizations have started to address the issue of qualifications to practice this specialty. The AAASP developed a certification process leading to the title of certified consultant, Association for the Advancement of Applied Sport Psychology (Cox, 1998). The qualifications for this certificate include possession of an earned doctoral degree in an area related to sport psychology. These areas include psychology, sport science, and physical education. In addition to the degree, specific courses are listed. Not all sport psychologists agree with this certification process. Like most professions, however, it is highly probable that in the future some form of certification will be accepted by its practitioners. Only time will tell whether these professionals will be regulated by psychology licensing boards or some other specialty group or will become an independent profession.

Just as certification or licensure is often seen as a major component of a profession, so is an ethical code. In 1982, NASPSPA issued a set of ethical standards for services provided by its members (Staff, 1982). These standards cover nine basic areas: responsibility, competence, moral and legal standards, public statements, confidentiality, welfare of the client, professional relationships, assessment techniques, and research with human participants. These standards do not apply to all practitioners who call themselves "sport psychologists" but only to those individuals who are members of NASPSPA. Of course, sport psychologists who are also licensed psychologists must adhere to the ethical principles required by their state licensing board. If they are members of APA, they are also expected to follow the APA Ethics Code. Moore (2003) noted that there are some areas of sport psychology practice that lead to ethical dilemmas for the practitioner. When sport psychologists are hired by teams and organizations, it is important for them to establish clear limitations for confidentiality and maintenance of boundaries. For example, the sport psychologist may be expected to attend social functions with the team. Such a social relationship with a former or future patient is not generally acceptable. These needs are somewhat similar to those of organizational psychologists but different from those faced by clinical psychologists in traditional employment settings. Athletes may be traded to other teams and thus no longer are considered patients. The traditional period of transition to another psychologist may not be possible in these cases. This does not mean, however, that the psychologist is excused from the need to prepare the athlete for the possibility of abrupt change when first working with him or her.

Psychologists who work with teams need to pay particular attention to Standard 3.11, psychological services delivered to or through organizations, of the APA Ethics Code (APA, 2002). This standard is new in the most recent version of the code and is perhaps a reflection of the increasing number of psychologists who find their work involving organizations rather than individuals. The seven areas covered in this standard provide the psychologist with a framework for evaluating a range of issues that arise in this type of practice. The following interview information illustrates some of the work of a sport psychologist as well as an opportunity for you to compare his responses to those of the other professionals in this chapter.

RICHARD M. SUINN has a Ph.D. in clinical psychology from Stanford University. At the time of this interview he was a professor emeritus at Colorado State University. He is a past president of the American Psychological Association. The specific questions we asked Dr. Suinn are followed by his responses.

If you were talking to an undergraduate student who is considering specializing in sport psychology, what courses in psychology would you recommend as good preparation? Dr. Suinn listed learning theory, behavioral psychology, behavioral intervention, functional analysis of behavior, and cognitive/behavior therapy.

What courses in other disciplines would you recommend? He noted that a course in logic is important. Other courses he felt would be helpful were any course in interviewing/listening skills, introduction to health/physical education, introduction to coaching, and introduction to nutrition.

When you think about the work you do, what do you find most rewarding? Dr. Suinn told us that the most rewarding part of being a sport psychologist is having actual behavioral outcomes confirm the fact that a brief intervention can make a real difference in performance. He noted that this is different from just having the athlete report in subjective terms that his work was helpful.

What do you find most frustrating about your work? In this case, Dr. Suinn noted that he finds it frustrating when a coach turns over the athlete, or even entire team, to him to "work my magic" and then fails to provide the follow-through contributions that are part of the sport psychology program to effect improvements.

Richard M. Suinn
*Photo courtesy of
Richard M. Suinn.*

Were there specific life experiences that influenced you to become a psychologist?
He noted that he took several core courses in other areas and then took his first psychology course. That combination led him to psychology.

Why did you decide to work in clinical and sport psychology? "Clinical psychology
blends my interest in science/logic with my interest in helping people. Sport psychology
was an accident developing from a private clinical case in which I used visualization to
strengthen coping responses (as opposed to eliminating fear responses). The coach of a
ski team was looking for a psychologist to help eliminate anxiety via short-term intervention (other psychologists said they needed months/years to do successful treatment), and
I traded doing stress management for an opportunity to test my visualization-to-reinforce-
adaptive-behavior program. The U.S. Nordic Ski Team then 'discovered' me . . . and I
had a new place to do my 'experiments.'"

Did you have a mentor or role model who influenced you to become a psychologist?
Although Dr. Suinn did not have a mentor, he noted that he had been planning to major in
speech. One of his speech professors told him not to major in speech because it would be
a waste of time.

*Please write one or two paragraphs about each of two days in your professional life
that describe a sample of what you do.* "Since I am retired, my professional life typically involves going to my office about 7:15 A.M., checking and answering emails and
chatting with first-year counseling graduate students as they arrive to their office, which
is directly across from mine. Then I focus on whatever task I have agreed to do, such as

write a preface for a new book, prepare for an invited address in Japan, and coordinate the responses of the APA Task Force on Enhancing Diversity in APA." Dr. Suinn maintains contacts with professional colleagues, mainly through email. After sorting his regular mail and scanning professional journals that have arrived he is able to go home for the remainder of the day.

Looking toward the future of clinical and sport psychology, what are your predictions for such factors as growth, new directions, and so on? "Clinical psychology will continue its success, merging with services and research on health psychology. Prescription authority will become a formal part of some clinicians' orientation. Neuropsychology will continue to be highly respected by other professionals as the strongest aspect of clinical work. New severe disorders will continue to be recognized as challenges for treatment; more joint treatment approaches will evolve that combine psychological interventions with pharmaceutical interventions. Sport psychology will take a long time before reaching common acceptance and use by the public. The transfer of principles from sport psychology work with athletes to 'behavioral coaching' with leaders will continue to expand through the effort of practitioners willing to do the required marketing. Traditional (existing) departments of psychology will continue to bypass sport psychology doctoral training; new programs aiming at such doctoral training will be organized within something like the 'Institutes' model that will integrate sport science and sport psychology from an applied emphasis."

What changes would you like to see occur in clinical and sport psychology? "Clinical doctoral programs need to strengthen the appeal of research activities to their students in the way social psychology does. Early emphasis needs to be placed on teaching careers. Practicum experiences should be truly integrated with theory/principle courses (e.g., a lab section along with a didactic section). Sport psychology needs a clear foundation in behavioral psychology including functional analysis, with an exposure to the cognitive-behavioral therapy model of psychotherapy. Training should emphasize core courses in abnormal psychology, professional ethics, and interviewing and conceptualization of cases and should include personal qualities as a criterion for the degree."

Looking over the time since you received your degree, how has your identity as a professional changed, and to what do you attribute these changes? "I might have had some glimmer of being an applied psychologist at some vague point in time, but somehow I always knew I would be a faculty person . . . as confirmed by my enrolling in a nonrequired course 'How to Teach Psychology.' My primary identity has always been as an educator who happens to have a specialty area."

If you could have dinner with any person, living or dead, who would you select and why? Dr. Suinn would select either his grandfather or his great-grandfather. He said he has always been told that his lineage traces to Sun Yat-Sen, the first president of China. Although this information was passed to Dr. Suinn by his parents, and to his cousins by their parents, they have no documentation of it because the personal history was lost.

We asked Dr. Suinn about his hobbies to give you some idea about his life outside psychology. He said his hobbies are fishing, Alpine skiing, and tennis.

Although Dr. Suinn is retired, and therefore his typical day does not include active work as a sport psychologist, we chose to interview him because he has done so much to establish sport psychology as a specialty. Also, his work is not in the traditional areas most students associate with sport psychology, such as football, but rather in skiing. His work has been with athletes who are among the elite rather than those who are typical professional athletes.

We hope you have found some careers in this chapter that seem worth further exploration. In the next chapter, we will use this same format to introduce you to some additional specialties.

Key Terms

clinical forensic
psychology

clinical health
psychology

clinical neuro-
psychology

commisurotomy

Daubert

Frye rule

sport psychology

CHAPTER 15

Specialties in Clinical Psychology II

Geropsychology, Clinical Child Psychology, and Pediatric Psychology

In chapter 1, we noted that some clinical psychologists specialize in working with specific age groups. This interest in developing age-specific assessment and intervention procedures has led to the development of specialty tracks in clinical training programs, internships, and postdoctoral fellowships for students interested in working with particular age groups. It has also led to a large body of literature specific to each stage of life. In this chapter, we describe three careers in clinical psychology that are age related: clinical geropsychology, child clinical psychology, and pediatric psychology.

Clinical Geropsychology

The number of people who are considered "older" has increased significantly over time. By 2011, the first of the seventy-seven million "Baby Boomers" in the United States will become part of this older (age sixty-five or above) generation. Current developmental psychology textbooks discuss issues related to the three-generational family that comes from increased longevity and use such terms as **sandwich generation** to refer to the adult who has obligations to both parents and children. Researchers are now suggesting that we start to think about four-generational families and the issues they face (Takamura, 1998). For example, in these four-generational families we may now see more than one generation living in retirement.

Psychologists who want to work with older adults are encouraged to consider their own attitudes about this population before beginning their work. Both positive and negative stereotypes may influence clinical interactions. Some of us think only of negative terms when we use the word *stereotype*. With older adults these attitudes may center on them being "cranky" or "set in their ways." Viewing patients in this group as difficult may lead the psychologist to avoid working with them. It may be, however, that regular contact with older adults really makes the psychologist face personal issues of aging that are uncomfortable. These issues may involve the psychologist's aging parents or even his or her own aging. Thus, personal issues arise that are sufficiently uncomfortable that the psychologist is unable to maintain an appropriate therapeutic perspective of the patient. When viewing older patients and their limitations the psychologist also needs to guard against behaving in a paternalistic way that may compromise the therapeutic relationship (Horvath & Bedi, 2002). Positive stereotypes such as viewing older patients as "cute" or "grandparentlike" may also compromise the clinical process. These stereotypes may lead the psychologist to overestimate older patients' abilities and fail to provide needed intervention (Kimerling, Zeiss, & Zeiss, 2000). Although examination of one's prejudices is important when working with *any* patient, the literature suggests that we may not be as effective in doing so with older patients.

Within the APA-archived definitions of specialties and proficiencies, **clinical geropsy-chology** is listed as a proficiency. Its definition includes the statement that "Clinical geropsychology is a proficiency in professional psychology concerned with helping older persons and their families maintain well-being, overcome problems, and achieve maximum potential during later life" (http/www.apa.org/crsppp/gero.html). Clinical psychologists who specialize in this area need to understand both normal and abnormal aging processes. They also must attend to the psychological and social aspects of aging and the role the person's cultural background and ethnicity may play in the aging process. For example, ads for exercise programs are common. Some of these ads are targeted to specific populations, such as women or older adults. Clinical geropsychologists must be aware of the specific exercise and nutritional needs of the elderly population if they are going to practice effectively in this area.

As life expectancy has increased, there has even been the addition of such terms as *younger-old* (ages sixty-five to seventy-five), *older old* (ages seventy-five to eighty-five) and *oldest-old* (over age eight-five+) to our vocabulary (Abeles et al., 1998). Research on

Probability a 65-Year-Old Will Live until Age	
Age	Percentage
70	95.5%
75	83.5%
80	78.0%
85	63.0%
90	43.9%
95	24.2%
100	9.6%

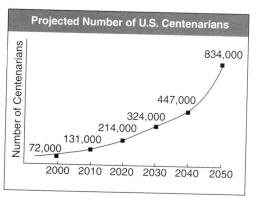

U.S. Census data on life expectancy *Adapted from U.S. Census Bureau,* Centenarians in the United States. *Washington, DC: U.S. Government Printing Office, 1999.*

centenarians (those over one hundred years old) is not uncommon. In fact, centenarians are the fastest growing segment of our population (U.S. Census Bureau, 2001). In the accompanying figures, you can see that the probability of a sixty-five-year-old person living to be a centenarian is almost 10 percent. What factors contribute to long life? Will you live to be one hundred years old? Would you want to be one hundred years old? Consider how life may be different for people in this age range than it is for those who are in the younger categories of "old." Psychologists are in a unique position to help answer these questions.

The issues at each of the three developmental periods we mentioned here are somewhat different. Special forms of intervention used by clinical geropsychologists include teaching the process of life review, work with family caregivers, and grief therapy. If you have not studied developmental psychology or psychology of aging, the term **life review** may be new to you. Some older adults benefit from evaluating their contributions over their lifespan. Actually making a journal or some other form of written summary of the things of which they are proud and considering the impact of some of their life choices may help both the older adult and that person's family. You may wonder if doing a life review would lead a person to become depressed about life choices. Specialists in this area have found, however, that conducting a life review may allow people to resolve lingering issues and have a better understanding of their past (McDougall, Blixen, & Suen, 1997).

When our projected lifespan was shorter than it is today, we tended to think of issues of old age as being similar across people. Today, clinical geropsychologists talk about the continuum of impairment and functional ability among their patients. When working in outpatient settings, the patients are often quite functional, while those patients seen in extended care facilities may have a much more limited range of ability. Clinical geropsychologists must also be aware of the effects of various types of medication, often taken by the elderly, on their daily functioning. For example, certain medication for cardiac conditions may also contribute to an inability for men to obtain or maintain an erection. The importance of sexuality for men needs to be addressed with cardiologists in medication selection. If other medications are not an option, then ways to handle this changed sexual responsivity can be addressed by the psychologist.

The settings where clinical geropsychologists see patients include outpatient settings, medical and psychiatric inpatient settings, extended care facilities, and nursing homes. Regardless of the location of the patient, clinical geropsychologists need to remember that unless the patient has previously been declared incompetent, the same rights apply to these older people as to any other patient. They have the right to refuse treatment or stop treatment at any time. Even if the original appointment with the psychologist was made by an adult child of the patient, that does not mean that this adult child is the patient. The psychologist cannot talk to the adult child without a written authorization from the actual patient. If the patient is a resident of an assisted care facility, the psychologist will also need to obtain a release of information from the patient to discuss issues with the staff of that facility about the patient's mental health care. In this case, the psychologist may want to obtain information from the staff members as well as work with them to provide needed services to the patient.

Societal changes have influenced the range of people with whom clinical geropsychologists work. Traditionally, they worked with other healthcare professionals and people related by blood or marriage to the older adult. Today, however, most clinical geropsychologists use the term *family* to refer to a much larger group. We discussed changing concepts of family in chapter 12. Here we will add some ideas specific to older adults. For financial reasons, many older people who form new romantic relationships do not marry. There are concerns about loss of pensions and healthcare insurance that may be tied to a deceased spouse. They may, therefore, choose to cohabit rather than marry. They are emotionally committed to their new partners, however, and these partners need to be considered part of the treatment process. Another change confronting clinical geropsychologists is the ethnicity of the older adult. The population of the United States is becoming more ethnically diverse. Federal government projections suggest that by 2020, the number of elderly Hispanic Americans will increase by 300 percent, elderly African Americans by 102 percent, and elderly people of Asian and Pacific Island heritage by 358 percent (Takamura, 1998).

Older adults display almost the entire range of emotional problems seen in younger adults. About 20–22 percent of older adults can be expected to meet the criteria for a diagnosable mental disorder (Gatz & Smyer, 2001). Unfortunately, older adults are more likely to experience multiple problems than are younger adults. For example, many physical disorders are more common among older adults than young adults. Thus, the person who may have a psychological disorder as described in DSM-IV may also be experiencing the debilitating cognitive symptoms of Alzheimer's disease or cerebrovascular pathology. Death of peers at this stage of life is also more common than it is for younger adults, and so dealing with depression is often part of the intervention process. Because there are some special depression issues with this population, resources written for professionals are now available (e.g., Karel, Ogland-Hand, & Gatz, 2002). Despite the common factors among older adults, some research has suggested that this population may be more heterogeneous than any other age group. It is important for the geropsychologist to understand the impact of the age cohort as well as more traditional factors such as gender, culture, and ethnicity when making treatment plans (Crowther & Zeiss, 2003). Forensic issues including the ability to live independently or to make major life decisions such as medical directives are often part of the clinical geropsychologist's evaluation activities and intervention requirements. A range of psychological interventions have been found to be helpful to older adults (Abeles et al., 1998; Duffy, 1999; Gatz et al., 1998; Zarit & Knight, 1996; Zarit & Zarit, 1982). The first session of psychotherapy is always important. We discussed many of the requisite skills in chapters 5 and 11. As the geriatric population has increased, specialized resources have been developed to apply these basic skills to the initial session with the older patient (e.g., Scogin, 2000). The research base for the efficacy of various forms of intervention with ethnic minority older adults needs further investigation (Arean, 2003).

Several national conferences have discussed the needed training for clinical psychologists who want to specialize in this emerging area. In 1981, the Conference on Training Psychologists for Work in Aging met in Boulder, Colorado. This conference is sometimes called the **Older Boulder** conference, referring to the original scientist-practitioner conference we discussed in chapter 1, but in this case applying those concepts to work with older adults. Delegates to "Older Boulder" made recommendations about training as well as needed services (Santos & VandenBos, 1982). Eleven years later, a second conference was held in Washington, DC, to further develop recommendations for training, as well as identify needed areas of clinical research (Teri, Storandt, Gatz, Smyer, & Stricker, 1992; reproduced in Knight, Teri, Santos, & Wohlford, 1995). To continue the work of this conference, and to provide more specific information on the topics raised by the delegates, Section II (Clinical Geropsychology) of APA's Division 12 (Clinical Psychology) and APA's Division 20 (Adult Development and Aging) formed a task force to write guidelines for psychological practice with older adults. Those guidelines were approved as APA policy by the Council of Representatives in August 2003 (APA, 2004). Those twenty guidelines address attitudes; general knowledge about adult development, aging, and older adults; clinical issues; assessment; intervention, consultation, and other service provision; and education.

Despite the growing needs for mental health services for older adults, many students are not being exposed to work with this population. For example, a survey of forty-five psychology externs and forty-nine interns at one training site found that only 1 percent of these trainees had completed three courses in adult development or geriatric mental health (Hinrichsen, 2000). Prior to coming to this training site, 63 percent of these trainees had never been supervised in providing psychotherapy to an elderly patient, and 65 percent of them had no previous assessment experience with this population. Even among practicing psychologists, fewer than 30 percent report having had any coursework in geropsychology, although 69 percent of that same sample reported conducting at least some clinical work with older adults (Qualls, Segal, Norman, Niederhe, & Gallagher-Thompson, 2002). For the interested reader, a list of predoctoral and postdoctoral training opportunities can be found on the Division 12, Section II, website (http://bama.ua.edu/~appgero/apa12_2/training/trainmain.html). Relevant publications, some of which can be downloaded, can be found on the APA website (http://www.apa.org/pi/aging).

As one way to begin to address this educational need, the California psychology licensing board in 2002, through a statute taking effect January 1, 2003, made either graduate or continuing education coursework in aging and long-term care a requirement for licensure as a psychologist in California (Board of Psychology, 2003). Candidates for California psychology licensure who began their graduate studies on or after January 1, 2004, must complete at least ten contact hours of coursework in the biological, social, and psychological aspects of aging in order to become licensed. California psychologists who are already practicing must complete either a three-hour continuing education course in this area or demonstrate its equivalent in their teaching or practice experience before they can renew their license. They do not have to take this coursework each time they renew their license. They must have this background, however, the next time they are scheduled to renew their licenses. This statute illustrates how psychologists who wish to learn about this population but who did not have formal coursework on the topic can begin to obtain some basic information. These psychologists, however, are not the ones who will be providing the training and research to increase the knowledge base in clinical geropsychology. Qualls (1998) summarized the knowledge base recommended by the 1996 APA Interdivisional Task Force on Qualifications for Practice in Clinical and Applied Geropsychology. Table 15.1 is an adaptation of that material. It will be the psychologists who obtain specialized degrees plus supervised practical experience in clinical geropsychology who will further our understanding of this domain.

Table 15.1 Clinical Geropsychology Training
Specialized research and theory
Biological aspects
Cognitive aspects
Psychosocial aspects
Sociocultural and socioeconomic aspects
Daily living issues
Psychopathology applied to aging
Specialized psychological assessment
Specialized forms of intervention
Prevention and crisis intervention
Consultation
Work with other disciplines
Ethical issues

Source: Adapted from Qualls, S. H. Training in geropsychology: Preparing to meet the demand. Professional Psychology: Research and Practice, 29(1998): 23–27.

WILLIAM E. HALEY has a Ph.D. in clinical psychology from the University of Massachusetts-Amherst. At the time of this interview, Dr. Haley was professor and chair of the Department of Gerontology at the University of South Florida in Tampa. He held joint appointments in the Department of Psychology and the Division of Geriatric Medicine at the University of South Florida. Among his many professional activities, he was associate editor of *Psychology and Aging,* a former president of the Section on Clinical Geropsychology of the APA Division of Clinical Psychology (Division 12, Section II), and chair-elect of the Behavioral and Social Sciences Section of the Gerontological Society of America. The specific questions we asked Dr. Haley are followed by his responses.

If you were talking to an undergraduate student who is considering specializing in clinical geropsychology, what courses in psychology would you recommend as good preparation? "There are three courses that I think are particularly important for undergraduate students who are interested in clinical geropsychology. First, the cornerstone course for any student interested in clinical psychology is abnormal psychology. Second, a course in health psychology would be very useful since most of the unique problems faced by older adults are related to health difficulties. Finally, a course in psychology of aging would be very useful to provide a background in both normal aging and the clinical problems of older adults."

What courses in other disciplines would you recommend? "Many universities have multidisciplinary gerontology programs. These often include courses such as sociology of aging and biology of aging. If there are courses available in pharmacology or pathophysiology, these would also be very valuable. Many gerontology programs also offer internships or field placements. I strongly advise students to get this type of multidisciplinary coursework, and to get some real world experience that will help them decide whether they enjoy working with certain populations."

William E. Haley
*Photo courtesy of
William E. Haley.*

What courses didn't you have that you wish you had? "I never had a single course
in geropsychology, either as an undergraduate or graduate student. It is the sad truth that
many universities still don't have courses focused on aging, even though older adults
are the fastest growing part of the U.S. population. Actually, the course that I didn't
get that I really wish that I had would be a course in English literature. I went through
undergraduate school in only three years, and designed my own special major, and never
took any courses in this area. As I have gotten out in the world of academia more, and
expanded my horizons, I wished that I knew more about the great works of literature
and how to fully appreciate them. I am trying to make up for this deficit in my education by reading on my own, and listening to books on tape—my latest project, great fun
for me, was listening to an audiobook of Chaucer's *Canterbury Tales.* This was utterly
entertaining for me."

   Dr. Haley's response to this question illustrates an important point about undergraduate education. Once you start graduate school your training becomes highly focused.
While you are an undergraduate student, consider taking some courses just for "fun."

   When you think about the work you do, what do you find most rewarding? "The most
rewarding aspect of my job is the opportunity to make a positive impact on a large number of students, researchers, service providers, and older adults and their families. When
I teach my undergraduate course in psychology of aging, I routinely have students tell
me that what I have taught them has either helped them to understand their own parents

or grandparents or has opened their eyes to geropsychology as a field. When I see that my research has been used and cited by others, and applied by practitioners who are providing services out in the field, that is very gratifying as well. Finally, I do a lot of presentations for professionals who provide services, and for older adults and their families. It is very rewarding to see that what I have to say seems to be meaningful and helpful to these people who are in the trenches every day, trying to help older people live full and active lives."

What do you find most frustrating? "The most frustrating part of my work now is that I am something of a victim of my own success. I have been a specialist in clinical geropsychology for about twenty years now and have gotten busier as the time goes by. I work closely with many graduate students and collaborate with colleagues from several other universities and have too many papers and grants that I am working on at one time. I also increasingly get opportunities to deliver lectures, to attend conferences, or to consult with colleagues, usually traveling to interesting places and meeting fascinating people. So I am busier than I would like to be. However, part of me really enjoys all of this, because I really believe in what I am doing, and I gain so much satisfaction from what I do."

Although his comments sound more positive than frustrating, think about doing *all* of this at the same time. Now try to consider having a personal life. Where does it fit with his schedule? Thinking of it this way, you will be able to understand Dr. Haley's frustration.

Were there specific life experiences that influenced you to become a psychologist? "My father was a police captain. He came home from work every day with amazing stories about the people that he encountered on the job. I was fascinated with their personalities and with the question of whether criminals could be rehabilitated. When I went to college, I thought I wanted to be a prison psychologist! I worked for a semester at Marion Federal Penitentiary and it was not for me; those guys scared me to death, and I didn't think I could do much good for them."

Why did you decide to work in clinical geropsychology? "I went into clinical geropsychology mainly by accident, but also because of the availability of training money from the National Institute of Mental Health. I had finished my clinical internship at the University of Washington-Seattle School of Medicine. I wanted to stay there, and they had postdocs in geriatrics and pediatrics, both funded by NIMH. I could have flipped a coin, but picked geriatric psychology. Once I started it, I was hooked. My first experience was in working with family members who cared for someone with Alzheimer's disease. I found that there were many things I could do to help them and that they were very grateful for any help they got. I also learned that there were very few people going into the field of clinical geropsychology. It was a great choice but also a lucky choice."

Did you have a mentor or role model who influenced you to become a psychologist? "There were three psychologists who were particularly important in mentoring me. One was Dr. Kenneth Wilson. He was a psychologist and criminologist at Southern Illinois University (SIU)-Carbondale. He agreed to supervise directed readings with me, and also got me the opportunity to work at the prison. The second person was Dr. Janet Rafferty, also SIU-Carbondale. She was a very famous psychologist but very kindly agreed to supervise my undergraduate honors thesis, and helped me get into graduate school. The third person was Dr. Bonnie Strickland, who was my mentor in graduate school at the

University of Massachusetts-Amherst. She was a very famous scholar, wonderful mentor, and became president of the American Psychological Association. She gave me many opportunities, provided very good guidance of my work, and was very supportive. I was very lucky to get to work with such outstanding mentors."

Please write one or two paragraphs about each of two days in your professional life that describe a sample of what you do. "On Tuesday, after handling my email, I spent the morning working on two journal articles. One of these involves collaboration with colleagues at three other universities and is a five-year study of effectiveness of counseling family caregivers of patients with Alzheimer's disease. The results show that the intervention decreases depression in these family caregivers, and the effects last for three years. The second paper is coauthored with four colleagues, all at other universities, and it reviews what psychologists' contributions have been and could be in the area of care of terminally ill patients and their families. In the afternoon, I taught my section of undergraduate psychology of aging. It is a three-hour summer course and has about seventy-five students. I lectured about Alzheimer's disease, and depression, in older adults. I used a number of case examples and gave students information about the latest treatments available for these conditions. I then met with several students after class to talk about whether they might want to go into clinical psychology, or geropsychology, after graduating.

"On Wednesday morning, I met with three of my graduate students about their research and writing. Two of them are working with me on coauthoring a book chapter about family care-giving, so we reviewed my comments on their writing. One of the students is getting ready to start a study of bereavement in older adults who have lost a spouse to cancer. Another student is working on an article reviewing how ethnic minority older adults and their families may differ in their preferences for care when they are terminally ill. The third student is managing my research grant that focuses on the psychological experiences of older women who have survived breast cancer. In the afternoon, I worked on writing a grant to fund a five-year study of older breast cancer survivors. This grant will involve collaboration with two oncologists, a nurse, two other psychologists, and a sociologist. If it is funded, I will be able to do some work that will be very interesting and important for improving care for older adults."

Looking toward the future of clinical geropsychology, what are your predictions for such factors as growth, new directions, and so on? Clinical geropsychology is destined for greatness. One recent study estimated there were only seven hundred clinical geropsychologists in the United States but that we should have seven thousand of them based on the number of older adults. America is rapidly aging, and this is a specialty with a lot of opportunity for psychologists."

What changes would you like to see occur in clinical geropsychology? "There are two important changes I would like to see. First, we need to improve Medicare reimbursement for psychological services. Medicare does cover psychological assessment and intervention, but there are gaps in this coverage. Second, I believe that all clinical psychologists should be required to have some training in clinical geropsychology. Older adults are currently 13 percent of the U.S. population, and about 20 percent of the Florida population, but APA does not require training in geropsychology for accreditation of programs. But everyone should know that the national licensure exam now includes items in the area of geropsychology! A group of geropsychologists developed these items last year at a meeting in Tampa. Maybe that will provide some incentive for psychologists to get some training in geropsychology."

Looking over the time since you received your degree, how has your identity as a professional changed, and to what do you attribute these changes? "When I first got my degree, I wanted to do clinical and research work that would benefit patients and their families, and I wanted to have the chance to teach and lead an academic lifestyle. Because I was so successful in my research, and because I had good abilities in working with other people, I have ended up being a department chair and involved in leadership positions in several journals and professional organizations. It is very flattering to have many people contact me and want my advice or assistance with their projects and to be nominated for different awards and offices. I was the first person in my family to finish college, and I never thought that I would be doing so many things that have me traveling and being called on to be a leader of interesting projects."

If you could have dinner with any person, living or dead, who would you select and why? "I would pick a psychologist, Dr. Powell Lawton, who died several years ago. Dr. Lawton was one of the first pioneers in the field of clinical geropsychology and was once president of the Gerontological Society of America. I met him on several occasions, and he was one of the kindest and most helpful and thoughtful people that I have ever met. He was also the ultimate professional when he was editor of the APA journal *Psychology and Aging,* for which I am currently an associate editor. I know that Dr. Lawton was a Quaker and that he was also a role model for other colleagues of mine in psychology and gerontology. I would like to find out a bit more about him as a person. Since he was so humble, he never spoke about himself when I did get to see him."

As a final bit of information about our interviewees, we asked each of them about their hobbies. Dr. Haley noted that his hobbies are reading, working out, travel, and playing the banjo. Dr. Matthews has had the opportunity to hear him play the banjo at a social function following a professional meeting and suggests that if Dr. Haley ever tires of being a psychologist he might consider touring as a musician!

GEORGE NIEDEREHE has a Ph.D. in clinical psychology from the University of Chicago. At the time of this interview, Dr. Niederehe was a psychologist at the National Institute of Mental Health (NIMH) in Rockville, Maryland. Before joining the staff at NIMH, Dr. Niederehe was a member of the faculty in the Department of Psychiatry and Behavioral Sciences at the University of Texas Medical School in Houston, Texas. He served as one of the leaders of the group who developed the guidelines for working with older persons that were passed by the APA Council in August 2003. The specific questions we asked Dr. Niederehe are followed by his responses.

If you were talking to an undergraduate student who is considering specializing in clinical geropsychology, what courses in psychology would you recommend as good preparation? "In my opinion, the strongest basis on which a student can build a special emphasis in the clinical psychology of aging is first to get a rounded background in psychology in general, and in clinical psychology in particular. Assuredly, such a preparation should include coursework in such critical areas as developmental psychology, cognitive psychology, and biological bases of behavior and in general clinical areas

George Niederehe
Photo courtesy of
George Nierderehe.

such as assessment and intervention methods and consultation. From that sort of general grounding, one can move in many directions to pursue particular lines of work with older adults—for which differing sorts of additional coursework may be useful. Special areas of study that I expect will prove useful to almost anyone who is preparing to work with a broad spectrum of older adults include neuropsychology and, perhaps somewhat surprising, organizational psychology."

What courses in other disciplines would you recommend? "I think that may depend on the student's general style and approach to clinical work. Overall, I would think coursework on medical conditions that are commonly encountered in older persons and on pharmacology could be especially valuable. Likewise, the same is apt to be true of courses that provide useful perspectives for understanding older adults as social beings operating in social contexts, e.g., anthropology, law, social work, and family therapy."

What courses didn't you have that you wish you had? "I entered graduate study in psychology without strong undergraduate underpinnings in the field, having majored in philosophy. I never had the benefit of a number of basic courses such as history and systems, biopsychology, motivation, and industrial/organizational psychology and only audited certain others (personality theories, basic social psychology). Although I later had more advanced coursework covering aspects of some of these areas, I believe I would have been better off to have come to these things with a more 'complete' grasp of the field already under my belt."

When you think about the work you do, what do you find most rewarding? "The most rewarding aspects of my current work at NIMH are the times when I get to interact and confer with investigators (including aspiring investigators) regarding the research plans they are developing for prospective grant applications."

What do you find most frustrating? "Most frustrating are the demands of dealing with seemingly endless administrative and bureaucratic details that are far removed from the work of actually planning and conducting research projects, and the lack of opportunity to spend time pursuing my own research directions."

Were there life experiences that influenced you to become a psychologist? "I was attracted to the notion of assisting others via one-on-one counseling well before I narrowed this down to an activity I wanted to pursue specifically through psychology as a profession. I cannot identify any single experience that led to this. To some degree, I may have developed these interests through a variety of interactions during my youth with Catholic priests. As a teenager, I envisioned becoming a priest and for some years studied in seminaries before deciding on which aspects of that overall career concept I preferred to focus, and on those which I did not. At the point when I entered graduate studies, I was still rather diffuse in my appreciation of the differences among psychology, psychiatry, medicine, and so forth. After gaining some experience working in a neurosurgical unit, I reaffirmed my initial inclination to study psychology rather than medicine because of a sense of wanting to try to put my career efforts toward improving people's quality of life and interpersonal relationships rather than toward attending primarily to their general physical health."

Why did you decide to work in clinical geropsychology? "My initial interests in geropsychology arose during graduate school when I began to think seriously about my eventual focus within clinical psychology and about how to develop a dissertation topic. I became interested in exploring the issue of what allowed some people to 'change with the times' as they aged and to stay vital and full of fresh ideas—which I thought stood in contrast to the typical pattern of aging, the general stereotype that most older people were helplessly 'stuck in their ways' and longstanding attitudes. For this inspiration, I credit several TV interviews I had seen with Maggie Kuhn, a social worker who in her retirement had become an even bolder firebrand and social activist than she had been previously. She took up living in a commune, founded the Gray Panthers, and so forth.

"As there were numerous faculty members specializing in gerontology at the University of Chicago, I was able to pursue this incipient interest by enrolling in some aging-related courses with professors who were leading figures in the field (e.g., Robert Kahn, Bernice Neugarten). I found the coursework fascinating, and the professors involved became mentors. As I learned more about what a complex issue it really was, my initial interests in 'mental flexibility' shifted and evolved to emphasize other problems, but this learning process led me to make subsequent career choices that kept aging as a focal point. In part, I chose to follow this path for the very practical reason that my mentors had convinced me that the projected growth of the older population was going to make aging a societally important issue in future years and assure a continuing 'marketability' or livelihood for professionals with expertise in gerontology."

Did you have a mentor or role model who influenced you to become a psychologist? If so, please tell us about this person. "Early in my college experience, I had the opportunity to work for a while for a psychologist who served as a role model, which positively contributed to my growing interests in psychology. At the college I attended, everyone had work assignments on campus. I was lucky as a freshman to get assigned as an office assistant to the one faculty member who was a psychologist, Dr. Eugene Kennedy. His responsibilities included doing a lot of work in recruiting applicants to the college, and he used the MMPI as a screening device. Based on this ongoing work, he was also collecting and analyzing data for studies of young people who aspired to religious life (in seminaries and convents). As part of my office assistant duties, he taught me how to score MMPIs and how to calculate correlations between MMPI data and other variables (a process done by hand in those days). He was also a terrific public speaker and wrote compelling books. He turned me on to the work of Carl Rogers, with which I became very taken and on which I later wound up focusing my philosophy thesis."

Please write one or two paragraphs about each of two days in your professional life that describe a sample of what you do. "Relative to what most clinical geropsychologists do, it is apt to be most informative to differentiate what I do nowadays from how I spent my time earlier in my professional career. Both days that I will describe are rather hypothetical, in the sense that it is atypical to intermingle so many disparate activities in a single day—but such a day conveys a better sense of the whole of the job.

"Fifteen to twenty years ago, when I worked in a clinical service context, I was also engaged in conducting research and leading training programs in that setting. My day begins with several supervisory appointments with some of the trainees who are seeing patients in the Gerontology Center psychiatric clinic to which I am attached as a staff psychologist. These include psychology interns, psychiatric residents, and postdoctoral clinical fellows in geriatric psychiatry or psychology who are conducting intakes, assessments, or treatment sessions as part of their rotations in the clinic. While I have varying degrees of responsibility for direction of these various training programs, today no particular meetings of the program faculty are scheduled. By mid-morning, I transition into seeing a clinical patient whom I have previously assessed as part of a 'Memory Clinic' evaluation, a special assessment program in the clinic for which I am responsible. I go over the test results with the woman, who had complained of memory difficulties. She is relieved to hear that the cognitive changes she displays are within the range of those attributable to normal aging. I suggest that symptoms of depression are perhaps a complicating issue, and have the clinic psychiatrist come in to help discuss treatment options. Before lunch, I conduct a psychotherapy session with an ongoing patient, an elderly gentleman being treated with both medications and psychotherapy for chronic anxiety problems. We include his wife, as our focus is on how these issues are affecting his marriage.

"After lunch, I co-lead a seminar on research methods for our postdoctoral fellows in psychogeriatric research, a program which I direct and administer with the support of an NIMH training grant. Some weeks I make presentations to the group on various topics or lead discussions of assigned readings, but today I have arranged a guest lecture by a statistician from a neighboring university, so I simply have to sit in and oversee the session as the organizer. Following the seminar, I meet briefly with one of the fellows to discuss progress on her fellowship research project. I then move on to a scheduled meeting with the project coordinator and research assistants who are working on my funded research, which has been developing methods and measures for assessing family dynamics surrounding the care of elderly patients with dementia. Currently we are conducting pilot work to assess how well the methods can be extended to family evaluations when the index patients suffer from depression rather than dementia and to determine the sorts of modifications necessary. We go over progress on data collection and discuss yesterday's orientation and training session with student volunteers who will serve as coders for the videotaped interactions that we are recording between patients and their spouses/partners. After the staff meeting, I sit down at the personal computer in my office (still a novelty at this point) to end the day puzzling over the initial data on intercoder reliability, and hopefully drafting out a few more paragraphs in that next research grant proposal that I am preparing."

Dr. Niederehe then goes on to describe his work in 2003. "Many people are surprised to learn that the responsibilities of NIH project officers involve mainly the stimulation and shaping of new project proposals, much more so than exercising oversight over already funded projects. When I first get into the office, I spend an hour going through email and voicemail messages to ascertain what inquiries have come in and field or appropriately refer as many as possible of those I can handle immediately. Some of these people request basic information about what is known about a particular clinical issue; others want to find out how to proceed to discuss a briefly described research idea with an appropriate staff contact at NIMH; other messages come from established investigators about proposals we have previously discussed or about technical issues that have arisen in their funded projects. Following this, I have a phone appointment with a researcher who has sent me a draft of a planned grant application, which I have reviewed. I go over my informal review with him and provide 'technical assistance,' pointing out aspects of the draft that I think can be improved or clarified or where important methodological details need to be filled in. We discuss aspects of the tentative research design or plans that I find questionable, as well as possible alternatives to strengthen the approach. Late in the morning, I sit in on the review of a grant application that is being held in another part of the building. Although such peer review of most applications is usually conducted in large committee meetings, this particular application was judged to be a special case because of certain conflicts of interest involved, so a special review has been arranged by an ad hoc committee which is convening via conference call. Program staff members like me are allowed to sit in as observers during reviews; the investigator will soon be contacting me to learn and discuss the results, well in advance of the time he will receive a written summary.

"After spending part of the lunch hour returning several phone calls, I move on to a meeting of the Aging Research Consortium, a crosscutting internal committee composed of staff from various branches and programs within NIMH which has the task of monitoring and coordinating the institute's overall efforts in support of aging research. At today's meeting, we focus primarily on finalizing a program announcement that will be published in the *NIH Guide for Grants and Contracts,* informing the research community about NIMH's current interests and priorities relative to aging research. We also discuss progress on plans for a workshop the group is organizing. The workshop will aim to define more clearly the key issues in a particular aspect of aging research and to stimulate greater investigator interest in this area, which the consortium has identified as a relatively unattended gap in current scientific knowledge. Following the meeting, I return to my office to review the annual progress report from one of the funded treatment studies for which I am the responsible project officer; my approval of the report and of the study's progress is necessary before the next year's pending grant award will be issued. Next on the agenda is another teleconference call, this time the monthly meeting of the Executive Committee for a large, multisite clinical trial that NIMH has funded. As the government project officer for the contract that supports this particular study (awarded to a centralized coordinating center, which in turn has subcontracted with more than a dozen clinical sites around the country to carry out the treatment and data collection activities), I participate as a member of the Executive Committee in reviewing the various facets of the trial and in discussing any policy decisions that the group needs to make. After the call, I do a final check on my email and fire off a few more messages, as necessary. Then I have to dash off to a local university, where I am teaching an evening class on the psychological aspects of aging."

Looking toward the future of clinical geropsychology, what are your predictions for such factors as growth, new directions, and so on? "Because of the escalating size of the elderly population and increased acceptance of psychological services by the generation now reaching old age, I expect more and more psychologists will be encountering older adults in their clinical work and taking an interest in expanding this aspect of their practice. At the same time, the knowledge base of clinical geropsychology is increasing rapidly. I believe all of this will lead to increases in how much training psychologists are given with respect to the aging process and in how professional psychology tends to be organized relative to work with older adults. About a decade ago, I described the typical practice of clinical geropsychology as a 'cottage industry.' Today, that has begun to change. The American Psychological Association has formally recognized clinical geropsychology as a 'proficiency' or area of professional concentration within psychology, and has adopted guidelines for practice with older adults. In the coming years, I expect the area may be recognized as a full-fledged specialty, and I would anticipate an increasing formalization and professionalization of various aspects of working in this area.

"At the same time, certain lines of work with older adults are apt to grow in prominence. Among these, I expect to see considerably more attention given to the issues of competency evaluation and determining the appropriateness of fit between individual older persons and various potential living/care environments. I anticipate that psychologists with expertise in issues of aging may spend increasing portions of their time consulting with frontline care staff, providing necessary training and supervision, and the like. Also, if work with older adults becomes a greater priority for psychology as a whole, I would anticipate that there will be many more positions for academically and research-oriented geropsychologists in clinical training programs."

What changes would you like to see in your specialty? "I hope that we are evolving toward a situation in which substantial information about aging and relevant clinical experiences will be integrated into the training of all professional psychologists. I expect that eventually having some degree of knowledge in this area will be included among the criteria for general licensure, and imparting such knowledge will figure among the accreditation criteria for training programs. I hope that more continuing education activities will be developed in which practicing psychologists can have ready access to appropriate types of preparation for work with older adults. I also hope that more methods or systems of credentialing will be established whereby psychologists who have acquired considerable expertise in geropsychological work can be recognized for their special degree of expertise."

Looking over the time since you received your degree, how has your identity as a professional changed, and to what do you attribute these changes? "When I came out of graduate school, although I was most intent on assuring that there would be a research component to my work as psychologist, I very much thought of myself as the traditional 'triple threat,' who would stay active in clinical service and training pursuits, as well as research. In the first part of my career, indeed my work was structured along such lines. Today, I think this has shifted somewhat, such that my work has come to concentrate predominantly on the research component. In addition, within that realm, I have had to come to see myself as mainly a facilitator for others' work. Much of my focus is on the growth and directions of the mental health and aging research field as a whole, rather than on the various particulars of what is happening in the subareas in which I used to concentrate.

"These shifts in perspective stem partly from my move to a project officer position at NIMH, and the special vantage point associated with this kind of responsibility. Also, to some degree the identity changes no doubt have reflected my passage into a different stage and set of family circumstances. Furthermore, I assume that some of the change (e.g., increased focus on research) represents a natural evolution over time, as I have gravitated toward emphasizing pursuits and interests that had a greater priority for me and for which I am probably better suited temperamentally."

If you could have dinner with any person, living or dead, who would you select and why? "I have difficulty with questions like this, recognizing their projective nature. In reality, I do not have a single role model or fixed ideal person whom I would consistently name in reply to this question. My answer is likely to change according to my moods, current interests, etc. What I would say in general is that I have strong interests in the history of ideas and tend to be curious about the lives of 'big thinkers'—people who have contributed major ideas or perspectives that led to historical shifts in people's ways of viewing things or organizing their lives. Such people are found in all walks of life—scientists, artists, humanitarians, political and religious leaders. Darwin, Einstein, Freud, Joyce, Gandhi, Wittgenstein are just some of the names from relatively recent history that come to mind in this respect, and there are many others whose influence has been just as noteworthy, even if somewhat less sweeping in scope. I would love to be able to meet with such people and understand in a more personal vein how their ideas developed, what motivated them to live the ways they did, what circumstances may have led to a flourishing and acceptance of their ideas as opposed to alternative ideas and innovations offered by others. A problem with this pipedream is that I would want to have an interchange at a personal and genuine level and I suspect few of these folk would likely be of the sort to suffer fools like me gladly."

As a final bit of information about each of our interviewees, we asked them about their hobbies. Dr. Niederehe told us that his hobbies include family genealogy and do-it-yourself projects. These projects include home/car maintenance, computer repairs, and rough woodworking. His wife is an artist and teacher and they have two daughters.

Integrating the Interviews

Both Dr. Haley and Dr. Niederhe see clinical geropsychology as a growing field. We certainly agree with them on their perception. Another common theme in their work settings is that as each became more well known in the field, he found he had less and less time for personal interests. When they discussed undergraduate preparation for clinical geropsychology, they agreed that a solid background in psychology is important. Because of the importance of health issues for this population, having some background in health psychology or other areas of health is useful preparation. They also point out that psychology is not the only field with interests in issues of aging. It is important for students to seek related courses from diverse disciplines even if they are certain they want to become psychologists. Each of these clinical geropsychologists also illustrates the fact that you do not need to be certain about your direction within the profession when you are an undergraduate. Some career directions are influenced by events that occur in your training cycle, such as Dr. Haley having two choices at the opposite ends of the life spectrum when selecting a postdoctoral fellowship. Once again, first becoming a solid clinical psychologist and then *adding* the specialty area seems to be a focus of our interviewees.

Clinical Child Psychology

As you may have learned in a developmental psychology class, children are not just miniature adults. Their cognitive abilities, problems, and reactions to these problems are very different from those of adults. Within the DSM-IV system, there are separate diagnoses that are reserved for problems of children and adolescents. Our diagnostic classification system has not always viewed children and adolescents that way. In the first two editions of the DSM, psychiatric problems in children were seen as analogous to those in adults. Starting with DSM-III, diagnostic categories specific to children became part of the system. Older epidemiological studies suggest that about 12 percent of children in the United States show significant emotional or behavioral problems (Gould, Wunsch-Hitzig, & Dohenwend, 1980). More recent researchers have found, depending on the particular study, that between 8 percent and 20 percent of children are diagnosed with these problems, suggesting a relatively stable rate of diagnosis over a period of years (Costello et al., 1996; Mash & Dozois, 1996; Roberts, Attkisson, & Rosenblatt, 1998). It is not surprising, therefore, that some psychologists have chosen to work exclusively with this population.

According to the APA archived definition of specialties and proficiencies, **clinical child psychology** is a specialty of professional psychology which integrates basic tenets of clinical psychology, developmental psychology, and principles of child and family development" (http://www.apa.org/crsppp/childclin/html). The term *child* in this definition is used more broadly than we tend to use it in other contexts. Specialists in clinical child psychology work with infants, toddlers, children, and adolescents. In other words, they work with all preadult age groups. To do their work, these psychologists must have a solid understanding of normal child development and normal family processes. When either or both of these systems is not functioning within the expected range, the clinical child psychologist may be in a position to suggest remediation.

As society changes, so do the types of problems likely to lead to the need for intervention. For example, teenage mothers are usually less able to provide the type of environment conducive to psychologically healthy growth that older mothers provide for their children. Thus, as the rate of teenage pregnancy rises, so do the number of children needing psychological services. The same can be said of children adjusting to parental divorce and interactions with stepfamilies. As the divorce and remarriage rates rise, so does the number of children who are impacted by this societal factor. Child clinical psychologists also work on the behavioral problems associated with the use of alcohol and illegal drugs. Clinical child psychologists also assist children who are at risk for developing problems. These psychologists may find they have special ethical issues to consider. For example, what about issues of confidentiality? Who is the patient—the adult bringing the child or the child? There are also separate laws related to the welfare of children. An example is the case of a child telling the psychologist of some form of abuse. As long as the child is credible, the psychologist may be required to report this situation to a state governmental agency. Failure to do so can lead to the psychologist being disciplined by the state licensing board and/or the courts. Clinical child psychologists need to be aware of those special laws and how they relate to the practice of psychology.

As we noted in chapter 3, Witmer started his clinic in Philadelphia to treat children with learning problems. Binet's work in assessment was started because of his concerns about the special needs of children in French schools. Clinical child psychology courses have been offered in U.S. universities for many years. One of the earliest clinical child psychology courses in the United States was offered in 1941 by Charlotte Buhler at Clark University (Routh, 1994). In 1959, Alan Ross published one of the early books on the practice of clinical child psychology. As you can see, this is not a new specialty, although there have been changes in its focus over time.

Research by clinical child psychologists covers many areas. When we talked about interviewing earlier in this book, we noted that it is important to learn not only about the person's problems but also about strengths upon which to build. Related to this concept is the child clinical literature that addresses the development of competence in children. Not all children who live in unfavorable environments develop problems. The question for researchers is to determine what leads to resilience in children and adolescents. Although the early research in clinical child psychology tended to address issues of deficit, as the specialty moved toward the twenty-first century there was a tendency to address strengths as well. The literature on competence and resilience is part of the trend and will be used to illustrate the clinical child specialty. Those students who want to read further in this area might start with Masten and Coatsworth's (1998) review article. We will provide a few of their findings here to illustrate the material.

Although the terms **competence** and **resilience** are not unique to psychology, they do have specific meanings in the psychological literature. Broadly speaking, competence refers to the person's ability to handle expected developmental tasks. Thus, the specific abilities that define competence will change with the person's age, time in history, and culture, to name a few of the relevant variables. Clinical child psychologists study children who are viewed as competent in order to learn about the variables that are related to this ability. They can then use that information to develop interventions for use with those children who do not currently demonstrate competence. Resilience refers to the ability to demonstrate competence when you have been faced with significant adversity. As psychologists have studied children, they have found that children who live in abusive environments or face the death of a parent, for example, do not all exhibit poor competence. On the other hand, such conditions do seem to place the child "at risk" to develop problems. Thus, it is of interest to psychologists to discover the factors that lead one child to be resilient while another child is not.

Research on the developing brain suggests that what happens during the early years may be important in understanding the development of resilience (Nelson & Bloom, 1997). Freud suggested that early childhood is crucial in terms of personality development. As neuroscience research progresses we are finding support for the importance of that developmental period for a different reason. This information is shaping current research in the field. The resilience literature thus far has suggested two major predictors for psychological health: having good cognitive or intellectual abilities and a relationship with a caring prosocial adult. As intervention programs develop, these factors are usually central to the planning. One of the factors about resilience of interest to twenty-first century researchers is the impact of resilience on the psychological well-being of the child or adolescent. Some studies cited in Masten and Coatsworth's (1998) review found that although these children may be demonstrating competence in the traditional areas measured, they may also be experiencing internal distress. Current researchers are investigating the factors that may impact the development of these psychological reactions to repeated challenges to healthy development.

Next we will provide comments by two psychologists who are leaders in clinical child psychology. One works in a hospital setting, and the other directs a specialty doctoral training program.

JESSICA HENDERSON DANIEL received her Ph.D. in educational psychology from the University of Illinois. At the time of this interview, she was employed as a clinical psychologist at Children's Hospital in Boston where she had been working in various positions for thirty-one years. Among her professional roles are Massachusetts representative on the APA Council of Representatives, member of APA's Committee for the Advancement of Professional Practice, member of APA's Board of Directors, and representative of "senior" psychologists to APA's Ad Hoc Committee on Early Career Psychologists. She served as president of APA's Division 35, the Society for the Psychology of Women. She is also working on a pictorial book to document the contributions of ethnic minority psychologists to the discipline. The specific questions we asked Dr. Daniel are followed by her responses to them.

If you were talking to an undergraduate student who is considering specializing in clinical child psychology, what psychology courses would you recommend as good preparation? She noted that many courses are helpful. Among those she recommended are child-adolescent development, clinical child-adolescent development, personality, health psychology, social psychology, history of psychology, racial-ethnic psychology, family psychology, abnormal psychology, statistics and research design, gender and psychology, and prejudice and psychology.

As you can see, she is recommending a blend of the traditional basis of psychology with courses specific to her interest area. Of course, not all of these courses will be offered at any specific university.

What courses in other disciplines would you recommend? Dr. Daniel recommended courses that might be found in such departments as sociology, education, and business, depending on the university. The specific courses she noted are public policy and child

Jessica Henderson Daniel
*Photo courtesy of Jessica
Henderson Daniel.*

welfare, public health and child-adolescent welfare, demography and children/adolescents, history of policy and practices related to children and adolescents in the United States, child-adolescent literature, and economics and children-adolescents.

What courses didn't you have that you wish you had? Many of the courses she listed in response to this question are the ones she recommended from departments other than psychology in response to the previous question. For this question she listed public policy and children-adolescents, demography and children-adolescents, history and children-adolescents, economics and children-adolescents, children's/adolescent literature, race/ethnicity in the lives of children/adolescents, and health policy and children-adolescents.

When you think about the work you do, what do you find most rewarding? Dr. Daniel works in a direct service setting. What she finds most rewarding in this setting is working with children/adolescents and their families to improve the quality of their lives, providing instruction and training to graduate students and pre/postdoctoral fellows, and mentoring persons in training as well as early career psychologists.

What do you find most frustrating? Like many of our other interviewees, Dr. Daniel refers to the paperwork side of her work in response to this question. She noted that she is frustrated by the paperwork associated with billing and justifying additional sessions as well as the fact that insurance companies have so much power in determining who can receive care, when, and from whom.

Were there specific life experiences that influenced you to become a psychologist? Dr. Daniel told us there were no specific experiences that led to her career choice.

Why did you decide to work in clinical child psychology? "I have always enjoyed children. I was the superintendent of the Sunday School at my church when I was a college student. I taught preschoolers while I was in graduate school. I am fascinated by how children learn and develop. I have a particular interest in the role of families in the lives of children and adolescents."

Did you have a mentor or role model who influenced you to become a psychologist? "No."

Please write one or two paragraphs about each of two days in your professional life that describe a sample of what you do. "One day: I began the day (8 A.M.) by attending the Research Rounds in Adolescent Medicine where the fellows present their research ideas to the faculty and other fellows. Then it was on to check and respond to my email. I grab a cup of coffee. The next hour, I attended Grand Rounds in psychiatry. The following hour, I attended the Child Protection team meeting where I have served as the psychologist for thirty-one years. (The team reviews cases involving child abuse/neglect, sexual abuse, and domestic violence). A quick run to check my snail mail in the Department of Psychiatry—this is part of my exercise regimen—I walk up to the eighth floor. That afternoon, I attend a faculty meeting at Boston University, where I am adjunct faculty in the clinical psychology program. It is a twenty-minute walk each way. Then I see a patient. Then I check my email and try to sort and answer the snail mail. That evening, I have a conference call.

"Another day: I begin the day by teaching the postdoc seminar from 8 to 9 A.M. Following the seminar, I meet with one of the postdoctoral fellows who is concerned about finding a job the following year. I have an hour free to run to the eighth floor to check my mail. Then I supervise the postdoc psychology fellow in adolescent medicine. I grab a quick lunch and check my email at the same time. That afternoon, I am meeting with representatives from Children's Museum (I am a past member of the board) who want to consult with me about an installation. I then begin to contact psychology faculty about teaching in the clinical seminar for the time period January through March. Then it is off to run a group for African-American women leaders in Boston. I walk into my house at 8:30 that evening."

Dr. Daniel also told us that she tries to keep Friday as a writing day. So far, this has not worked. Because of days like the two she described to us, she has to do her writing on weekends.

Looking toward the future of clinical child psychology, what are your predictions for such factors as growth, new directions, and so on? Dr. Daniel directed her response to this question to issues at Children's Hospital. She predicts an increased awareness of the skills that psychologists can bring to the various medical specialties: first, in providing support for parents and children through difficult procedures and in decision-making about end-of-life issues; second, in working directly with parents and staff to provide developmentally appropriate care and options for patients; third, in assisting providers who work with developmentally delayed, chronically ill children and those with medical diagnoses that compromise their cognitive development; and fourth, in helping track pain and other symptoms that may have a psychological component.

What changes would you like to see occur in your specialty? Dr. Daniel would like to see modifications of some treatment modalities to ensure that they are effective with a range of cultural groups. She believes more programs will include instruction and training about sexual orientation, race/ethnicity, socioeconomic status, immigration, and religion. All faculty members will have some level of familiarity with these issues.

Looking over the time since you received your degree, how has your identity as a professional changed, and to what do you attribute these changes? "I began as an educational psychologist who was focused on instruction. Then I moved to instruction with children who have psychological challenges and then on to being a therapist. It was a matter of opportunities. I was a very good teacher of children, including those who have received minimal stimulation and nurturance. Also, I was effective in working with teachers and parents as a trainer and demonstration teacher. At one point, I worked with severely compromised children and was very effective as a teacher and trainer. Then I was a postdoc at Judge Baker Guidance Center, where I received formal clinical training. So much of what I was taught I was already doing intuitively. I had already been trained in behavioral techniques. I also learned how to provide family therapy along with psychodynamic therapy."

If you could have dinner with any person, living or dead, who would that be and why? "I would have dinner with Ida B. Wells. She was a woman of color at the turn of the last century. She was a courageous newspaper woman who wrote about injustice. She returned to the South to interview black people about lynching and then wrote about it in her Chicago newspaper. She was a leader who understood the era and was not overwhelmed by challenges. She persuaded blacks to move out of Memphis after the lynching of black businessmen. The latter had been successful and consequently competed with the white-owned businesses. She understood power, communications, and social justice."

As a final bit of information to help us get a more complete picture of Dr. Daniel, we asked her about her hobbies. She told us she enjoys reading novels, walking, and the arts. Within the arts, she enjoys visual arts (art museums and galleries); performance (theater and dance); films, especially foreign films; and music (jazz, classical, and '60s-era soul rock). Perhaps this range of interests grew out of her childhood, when she had the opportunity to live in a variety of places because her father was in the Air Force.

MICHAEL C. ROBERTS received his Ph.D. in clinical psychology from Purdue University. He holds a diplomate in clinical psychology from the American Board of Professional Psychology (ABPP). At the time of this interview, Dr. Roberts chaired the psychology department at the University of Kansas, which has a doctoral program in clinical psychology that is widely known for its training in clinical child psychology. He identifies himself as both a clinical child and a pediatric psychologist. Although we have presented these specialties as somewhat different, Dr. Roberts' combined interest is not unusual.

If you were talking to an undergraduate student who is considering specializing in clinical child/pediatric psychology what psychology courses would you recommend as good preparation? Dr. Roberts suggested either child psychology or developmental psychology, depending on what is offered in the student's program. He also recommended a course in abnormal child psychology or developmental psychopathology. Finally, he noted the importance of basic research methods and basic statistics as preparation.

Michael C. Roberts
*Photo courtesy of
Michael C. Roberts.*

What courses in other disciplines would you recommend? Dr. Roberts suggested human development as well as human biology. Although the latter was not viewed as mandatory, he felt it was good preparation. A course in public health or health promotion is also useful. Because of the changes in the world of clinical practice, he felt a course in business or accounting would be useful to later practice. Finally, he suggested a course in scientific or technical writing. He noted that this course is not necessarily the type of writing taught in English departments.

What courses didn't you have that you wish you had? He only listed one course in response to this question. He would like to have had a course in behavior analysis. For work with children, he finds this methodology is more suitable than the large group designs he was taught.

When you think about the work you do, what do you find most rewarding? "I enjoy on a daily basis: working with students, both undergraduate and graduate, in teaching, supervising research, and guiding professional development. As a program consultant and clinical supervisor, and in earlier years as a more active clinician, I enjoy seeing and being able to document that patients/clients change and improve. It is rewarding to have people function better in a variety of ways." As an example, he said he was once told in the grocery store by excited parents, "Jeffrey pooped in the potty!" (Note that the way parents express their excitement may not be through the use of professional language!) Other things he finds rewarding are testing hypotheses, discovering new things and being a detective of human behavior, being a professional and living up to the standards of a profession, gaining insights on his own behaviors and thoughts as well those of others, and having a scientific approach. Finally, he noted the use of critical thinking that is different from that of many people but serves one well even outside of psychology.

What do you find most frustrating? He started his response by noting the assumption that people know automatically what it is that psychologists do and financial concerns for funding education and healthcare services. He then commented on the lack of coordination between service providers, especially for children and adolescents. "Because children are involved in multiple systems, in the United States (and often elsewhere), these various services are administered by different agencies with different missions, backgrounds, and funding streams (e.g., school systems, mental health systems, family court or juvenile justice, medical system, social welfare system). All too often, there is little reason or mechanisms for these agencies and services to cooperate, resulting in a fragmented array of services. All too frequently these services are inadequate to meet the needs. This is particularly true for the more complex situations posed by children with serious emotional disturbances. It is frustrating when children and adolescents with severe problems cannot get the effective services they need. I am frustrated that the length of time for students to graduate with a doctorate and become recognized as having the credentials to be licensed psychologists is getting too long. Compared to about fifty years of history of clinical psychology, in the last few years licensing laws and expectations have drawn out the sequence for subservient status even more. Currently students who are graduating from strong APA-accredited training programs have much more experience than ever before and, frankly, do not need an additional postdoctoral experience to be qualified as a practitioner."

Were there specific life experiences that influenced you to be come a psychologist? Why did you decide to work in clinical child psychology? "There were a number of events in my childhood that likely led to my interest in psychology. As a young boy, I saw the emotional impact on a family friend who had unintentionally killed a boy on a bicycle on a highway. There was an immense complexity in the situation (e.g., I reminded the man of the boy; but my parents were adept at explaining this; his children were affected by his agony). I was puzzled and intrigued by what could be done to have prevented it, what could be done to have helped this man recover and his family adjust. My parents exhibited a strong sense of professionalism and ethics, altruism and caring, curiosity and inquiry, and a pragmatic orientation of trying to understand how things work in their own lives, so their models were available to me. I had virtually no restrictions on what I read and I sampled a wide variety in fiction and nonfiction and discovered that human beings are interesting animals. These sorts of issues pointed me to clinical psychology. As I focused myself for graduate school applications, I realized that changing children's lives in mental health and in physical health would have a lifelong impact, so I looked for the few programs at the time that provided strong child-oriented clinical psychology. While in graduate school, I discovered pediatric psychology as a subset of clinical child psychology—wherein psychological techniques were applicable to treating several medical issues as well as to resolving psychological problems that arose as a result of the medical condition or treatment. I was hooked—and was fortunate to work with a number of outstanding mentors who opened doors for me. It is because of my various mentors' influence in being 'door openers' to psychology that I am able to be effective as a scientist-practitioner in clinical child/pediatric psychology."

Did you have a mentor or role model who influenced you to become a psychologist? If so, please tell us about this person. "Professor Mark Thelen, now retired from the University of Missouri-Columbia, was my undergraduate mentor. He opened the world of psychology research to me through my work with him and his research team of graduate students. With his supervision, I completed two undergraduate honors projects that were eventually published. He demonstrated to me how to be a good research detective, an effective teacher, and a decent human being as a professional psychologist. In his interactions with people around him, he modeled what it must be like to be in therapy with him, always clarifying, summing up, extending hypotheses, and offering thoughtful insights. Dr. Thelen mentored me as an undergraduate, kept up a long-distance mentoring while I went to graduate school, and nurtured my early career as well. We would meet at conventions and discuss our recent work and design research projects (twenty-five years later, I still have some of the cocktail napkins on which major projects were outlined). He treated me with respect and gave me confidence to search for answers to questions using research methods. Had I not found this mentor who was incredibly knowledgeable, who had standards, who had a huge sense of humor, and who was willing to take the time with a fledgling, I probably would be something else and unhappy (probably a lawyer)."

Please write one or two paragraphs about each of two days in your professional life that describe a sample of what you do. "It does not sound appealing, but I spend lots of time in meetings. A typical day will start with reading and writing in the morning because that time is when I have the clearest mind and motivation. In late mornings, over lunch, and in the afternoon, I hold meetings on a variety of topics and missions. I discuss the therapeutic classrooms that our program runs, in conjunction with the local school district, for children who have serious emotional disturbances. This is a clinical application where we are conducting research evaluations and students receive clinical practicum experience. This is known as the Intensive Mental Health Program, and information is starting to be published on it. I collaborate with other faculty and students on preparing a research grant proposal to continue evaluating the therapeutic classrooms program. I meet with my graduate and undergraduate students' research team and then break for individual meetings with students about their particular projects (e.g., master's thesis on the development of hope as a positive psychology perspective in children and their parents who are Native American; master's thesis on the impact of insulin pumps for children who have diabetes; undergraduate honors thesis evaluating educational outcomes of the therapeutic classrooms program; and a dissertation project on impacting parents' perceptions of vulnerability of their children to unintentional injuries). Late afternoons, I may meet with the dean and other department chairs to discuss issues related to the training program I direct and changes in university policies, or visit schools where our classrooms are, or visit a local mental health center or the medical center in Kansas City where I collaborate with colleagues."

Looking toward the future of clinical child/pediatric psychology, what are your predictions for such factors as growth, new directions, and so on? "I believe that the movement to establish the evidence base for psychological assessments and empirically supported psychotherapy will be enhanced to help the professional decide what works best for what types of clients under what circumstances. I sense there will be more involvement of clinical psychology with biological/physiological aspects of human functioning, including considerations of genetics. The Human Genome Project will likely open up more avenues for clinical psychology applications than can be envisioned. I also think that greater expansion will come with the integration of cognitive neurosciences in applications with clinical psychology. With this integration, I think there will be less mind/body dualism in health care. I think there will be a better understanding over time of the role of human behavior in health care and better methods of shaping behavior change will be discovered. Even without additional focus on the brain–behavior relationship, there are many important areas to investigate and make evaluation of clinical applications. There will always be a role for psychologists who can adapt to changes, learn, and contribute to the bases of the field; provide competent services based on a scientific approach; incorporate critical thinking; and have specialty skills to bring to bear on problems and their resolution. I think these will be important because what is believed now will be improved upon or even debunked and changed in the future. Additionally, the problems may change over the course of a professional career."

What changes would you like to see occur in your specialty? "I hope to see diminished fractionating between scientific psychology and clinical psychology practitioners. I view the 'scientist-practitioner' model as an important one that has staying power over time and I fear some anti-science movements within the field. At the same time, I would like to see more relevance in the science to clinical applications."

Looking over the time since you received your degree, how has your identity as a psychologist changed, and to what do you attribute these changes? "It amazes me to see how much more information there is now than there was when I was in graduate school— the bigger problem now is how to gather information and sort through it. There are many more excellent journals and books, many more valid and reliable assessment and intervention techniques than ever before, and I hope to see the demise of methods that are not empirically supported. I think my identity as a psychologist has changed from one of clinical psychology to being a clinical child psychologist and pediatric psychologist. I think that the specialty field has grown so much in terms of knowledge base and effective assessment and intervention that the generalist model of training just is not sufficient. There is too much material and experience to master in order to be proficient as a clinical child psychologist or a clinical adult psychologist. Inevitably, one specializes anyway, and I believe that it is better for the professional to have a stronger knowledge and experience base in the specialty than to have a little of everything, but nothing of true substance. Specialization does not narrow the professional, it actually broadens the perspective and makes one more competent and effective."

If you could have dinner with any person, living or dead, who would you select and why? "I would select Albert Bandura (still living). His social learning theory influenced me greatly in my early research into imitation and modeling (I never did a Bobo clown study, but I published a range of studies relying on his theories). Although I only met him once at an APA convention many years ago, he was a long-distance mentor of a different type—he influenced me through his writing. He has continued to be an active force in psychology over a long time of contributions to theory." Dr. Roberts suggested that a second person he might also like to meet was Samuel J. Crumbine, MD. He noted that he has become interested in the life and contributions of Dr. Crumbine, who implemented innovative public health interventions in Kansas and later worked with Herbert Hoover in the American Child Health Association.

As a final piece of information to give us an understanding of Dr. Roberts as a person, we asked about his hobbies. He noted they are photography, his children's activities, and travel.

Integrating the Interviews

Both Dr. Daniel and Dr. Roberts do a range of things as part of their professional lives. Although they came from very different academic backgrounds and work in different types of settings, they both seem to enjoy serving as mentors. As with most of our interviewees, they note the importance of a solid background in psychology as a foundation for graduate study. To work with children, however, they note the importance of learning about children from many perspectives, for example, learning about children's literature such as you might find in an education course. Electing a course of this type may not be an idea that comes readily to mind for undergraduates. They both note the importance of advocacy for children as part of the role of psychologists in their specialty. Dr. Daniel noted the importance of learning about gender and culture as you prepare for this specialty. This comment certainly fits with our perspective on the future direction of the entire profession. Dr. Roberts noted the importance of generating clinically relevant research data for the continued growth of clinical child psychology. As you can see, they are both excited about their specialty and predict it will continue to grow, suggesting there is room for those students reading this book who may wish to join them.

Pediatric Psychology

As the name suggests, these psychologists work closely with pediatricians. Pediatric psychologists can be found in pediatrician's offices, clinics, and children's hospitals. Their focus is on the behavioral and emotional aspects of the physical problems of patients who are seen by pediatricians. Thus, they see the same age range as child clinical psychologists but usually focus on very different types of problems. Many of these children suffer from chronic illnesses. About 2 percent of the children in the United States are diagnosed with a severe chronic illness that has the potential to impair their daily functioning, with an additional 20 percent having a less serious chronic illness (Thompson & Gustafson, 2005).

The term **pediatric psychology** was first used by Brennemann in 1933 (Routh, 1994) but did not seem to continue in either the literature or in the development of training models. Modern pediatric psychology traces its roots to the late 1960s. At that time, three psychologists (Dorothea Ross, Lee Salk, and Logan Wright) within the APA Division of Clinical Psychology (Division 12) formed a committee to try to identify the psychologists who were working in departments of pediatrics at medical schools or in hospitals. Ross surveyed chairs of departments of pediatrics in U.S. medical schools and located about three hundred such psychologists. A Division 12 committee conducted a similar study in

1957 but nothing seems to have followed from the data. After the 1968 survey, Lee Salk organized the production of a newsletter, *Pediatric Psychology,* to continue discussion of the activities of these specialists. He also popularized the work pediatric psychologists do with children through writing books intended for the lay public and made TV appearances on programs such as the NBC *Today* show. By 1976, interest in the specialty had grown to the point that the newsletter started by Salk evolved into a scholarly journal, the *Journal of Pediatric Psychology.* Over the years, many definitions have been given for pediatric psychology. The early definitions were fairly narrow and focused exclusively on the role of pediatric psychologists in medical settings. More recent definitions include a broad range of responsibilities and healthcare contexts to reflect the actual practice of pediatric psychology in the twenty-first century.

Pediatric psychology came into existence to meet an unfilled need; pediatricians were confronted with a large number of problems that required both a medical and a psychological treatment approach (Roberts, 1986). According to early data from pediatric practices (Duff, Rowe, & Anderson, 1973) only 12 percent of all patients presented problems that were considered purely physical; 36 percent had problems that were considered psychological, and the remaining 52 percent had problems that were both physical and psychological in nature. Pediatric psychology developed as a result of pediatricians needing psychological services to meet the needs of their practices; pediatric psychologists thus have the goal of providing more accessible, competent services for children and families needing psychological interventions. Pediatric psychologists often practice in healthcare settings rather than in psychiatric or mental health facilities, so they see problems that include behavioral concomitants of physical illness, disability, or medical procedures. It is not uncommon for these psychologists to see children and their families because of sequelae to burns or spina bifida, adjustment to diabetes or hemophilia, or anxiety over surgical procedures or cancer treatment (Roberts, 1986). A review of articles published in the *Journal of Pediatric Psychology* illustrates the range of topics within the specialty (Mullins & Chaney, 2001). Among the articles were social support and adjustment among adolescents with cancer, role of the family support system in HIV risk reduction, and interaction between infants with orofacial clefts and their mothers. Not only do pediatric psychologists work with a range of topics, but they also have a range of professional positions, including educator, clinician, diagnostician, and administrator.

Pediatric psychologists, like their pediatrician colleagues, have been leaders in the area of prevention. Many unhealthy lifestyles have their roots in childhood. Behaviors such as smoking, overeating, and lack of exercise often start in childhood. School-based health promotion and health education programs developed with the assistance of pediatric psychologists are ways to start addressing these problems. Pediatric psychologists can be seen in schools, day care centers, and playgrounds teaching parenting skills, accident prevention, and child management skills to teachers and teachers' aides.

Pediatric psychologists, like child clinical psychologists, deeply appreciate the developmental perspective in their work (Tinsley & Park, 1984). Development refers to orderly changes over time, and understanding the rapidity and extensiveness of these changes is vital to sound pediatric and child clinical psychology practice (Maddux, Roberts, Sledden, & Wright, 1986). Thus, the developmental perspective requires some background in Piaget's cognitive development theory, Freud's psychodynamic theory of personality development, Kohlberg's theory of moral development, and Erickson's theory of social development. If these theories are not familiar to you, some additional reading may be needed. As you can see, pediatric psychologists must be broadly trained in human development and psychopathology and must have an understanding of family dynamic issues. In addition, both pediatric psychologists and child clinical psychologists should understand the jargon of pediatricians so that good communication between different types of providers can be maintained. One of the most positive contributions that pediatric psychologists make is the furtherance of the interdisciplinary team model, in which the focus is on the complex, interactive nature of psychopathology, family dynamics, and physical health.

As you can see, all three of these specialties will rely more and more in future years upon knowledge gained from science. Knowledge about physiology, pharmacology, and diseases such as Alzheimer's in the elderly and ADHD in the young will require increased understanding by psychologists of these areas. Recent research demonstrates that more and more children are being prescribed medication that affects their behavior (Zito et al., 2000). Knowledge gleaned from genetics and a better understanding of the physiological mechanisms of aging will help psychologists better predict the behavior of the elderly and tailor interventions that will make life easier for them and their caregivers.

The following two interviews with pediatric psychologists illustrate hospital practice by a new member of the specialty and a senior member of the specialty. The questions, followed by their responses, are the same as those we have used throughout this chapter and the previous one.

NABIL HASSAN EL-GHOROURY received his Ph.D. in clinical psychology from the State University of New York at Binghamton. At the time of this interview, he was working in Cleveland, Ohio, in the Department of Pediatrics of MetroHealth Medical Center. The specific questions we asked Dr. El-Ghoroury are followed by his responses.

If you were talking to an undergraduate student who is considering a career specializing in pediatric psychology, what courses in psychology would you recommend as good preparation? He responded that he would recommend general courses in abnormal, developmental, social, and health psychology. Specialized coursework would be helpful in behavior modification, child clinical psychology, and psychopharmacology.

What courses in other disciplines would you recommend? He noted that coursework in biology or medicine covering human health and illness would be useful. From sociology, courses in deviance as well as medical organizations would provide a good foundation.

What courses didn't you have that you wish you had? He wished he had taken more advanced coursework in both developmental psychology and sociology. Finally, fluency in a commonly occurring foreign language is tremendously helpful.

When you think about the work you do, what do you find most rewarding? "I find most rewarding that I am contributing to an urban, ethnic minority community. Being the only bilingual psychologist in a department, and being able to service a community that otherwise might have been ignored or underserved in my hospital setting is fulfilling on a personal, professional, and spiritual level. While I recognize that my work is 'only a drop in the bucket' for the needs of the hospital community, I find comfort in the fact that I am

Nabil Hassan El-Ghoroury
Photo courtesy of Nabil Hassan El-Ghoroury.

helping at least one family every day. I feel that my work contributes to my personal mission and is consistent with my values."

What do you find most frustrating? "The most frustrating thing about my work as a pediatric psychologist is logistical. There simply is not enough time in any given day to complete all the paperwork required for the number of patients I generally see. Being able to balance work demands with a fulfilling personal life is particularly difficult."

Were there specific life experiences that influenced you to become a psychologist? Why did you decide to work in pediatric psychology? "I have a younger brother with autism; he has definitely influenced my decision to be a psychologist. I knew very little about autism and my family did not speak about it much, but it was always present in my family. When I entered college, I was curious about autism, so I examined the behavioral treatment of autism for a paper in my abnormal psychology class. I happened to attend UCLA, where Dr. Ivar Lovaas, a well-known expert on autism, worked. I became involved working with children with autism as a behavior therapist and then as a researcher. I started using the behavioral techniques I used with preschoolers with my brother (who at that time was about eighteen years old), and found them to be incredibly successful with him and reinforcing for both of us. The clinical and research experience, including teaching children how to play appropriately with peers, and coleading a study, hooked me into psychology, and I decided to go to graduate school to become a clinical psychologist.

"It's really an accident how I became a pediatric psychologist. This is my first position out of my postdoctoral training. My training has primarily been child clinical, despite having an internship and postdoctoral fellowship in medical schools. I was always interested in working in a university-affiliated hospital because I felt that would allow me to be primarily a clinician, but maintain roles as researcher and teacher, which were both important to me. When this job came up, it seemed like a good match because it required the general clinical skills I had already, and I met the hospital's need for a Spanish-speaking psychologist. Ultimately, it was my Spanish skills that helped me secure this position. My training in child clinical psychology also served as a nice base for my emerging work as a pediatric psychologist."

Did you have a mentor or role model who influenced you to become a psychologist? "My inspiration for my work as a psychologist has to be my brother Omar, who has autism. When I was in high school, I described my heroes as Omar's special education teachers because they worked with kids like my brother when I could never imagine having the patience to do so. My role model for being a caregiver is my mother. I saw her work tirelessly to help my brother. After my mother passed away, a family friend shared with me that she had been training me when I was a child to take care of my brother when I was an adult. As it turns out, she may have done too good a job, because instead of taking care of my brother, I've helped many children with autism as well as other mental health needs."

Please write one or two paragraphs about each of two days in your professional life that describe a sample of what you do. "Wednesday: My day generally starts early, around 8 A.M. I don't schedule patients until 9 A.M., so I have a chance to get some paperwork done, review notes and email, and maybe make a phone call or two. I have one patient in the morning and then supervision with my clinical supervisor (because I am working on accruing postdoctoral hours, I still have to be supervised). Afternoons are very busy with patients, with six scheduled patients per afternoon. On Wednesdays, I stay until 7 P.M. to allow working families to come in. My morning and early afternoon sessions are generally parent training, which focus on teaching parenting skills. This allows me to maximize my afterschool slots for direct work with children. Most evening slots are either more direct work with children or with working parents. Today was a good day, and I had only one family not show up for their session. I stay until 7:30 to write up notes, and then leave for the night.

"Friday I start at 8 A.M. and attend pediatric grand rounds. Even when the topic is not directly related to mental health issues, I attend to learn what behavioral issues are related to the topic and to learn more about general pediatric issues. I have two clients in the morning, both working on parenting skills. I have two patients in the afternoon, including one new patient. When I have a new patient, I invite a medical student rotating through our clinic to observe a diagnostic assessment. My day ends a little early on Friday (because I work ten- to twelve-hour days two to three days/week), so I get to leave a little after 3:30 P.M."

Looking toward the future of pediatric psychology, what are your predictions for such factors as growth, new directions, and so on? "I see integrating health care into primary care as a particular area of growth for pediatric psychology. I also find it exciting to be in a position to teach medical students and residents about behavioral and developmental issues related to children's mental and physical health."

What changes would you like to see occur in your specialty? "I would like to see an increased emphasis on multicultural issues in pediatric psychology. Service delivery to children from non-English speaking households and research on the health needs of children from different ethnic groups would be desirable."

Looking over the time since you received your degree, how has your identity as a professional changed, and to what do you attribute these changes? "It's been about nine months since I got my degree, and my identity had not changed too much. One change is that I am incorporating the title 'Dr.' into my identity and make an effort to use that title. The change that is different for me is thinking of myself as a pediatric psychologist. I am learning how to work as a psychologist in a medical setting, how to communicate with physicians, and how to teach residents about the importance of behavioral and developmental issues. On a different level I have been more appreciative of the spiritual aspects of being a therapist. Working in a hospital is definitely one reason for changes in my professional identity. There is a definite culture that exists, and I am quickly learning about it. Another cause for change is that my career is a slightly different area than my training (from child clinical to pediatric). I think my appreciation of spirituality in my career is a reflection of increasing spirituality in my personal life and a desire to have my career be congruent with my personal values and beliefs."

If you could have dinner with any person, living or dead, who would you select and why? "I would like to have dinner one last time with my mother, who passed away about two years ago. I would like to hear her laugh one last time and hear her stories about her childhood and her experiences as a mother of a son with autism."

As you read about Dr. El-Ghoroury, you can see he is very busy. You can also note some similarities between his background and that of Dr. Roberts, whose identity also blurs the lines between child clinical and pediatric psychology. He noted that it is hard to maintain a balance between his work and his outside life. He does, however, have hobbies. At the time of this interview, his hobbies included volleyball, reading, movies, history, and wine tasting.

GERALD P. KOOCHER received his Ph.D. in clinical psychology with a minor in developmental psychology from the University of Missouri, Columbia. At the time of this interview, he was the Dean of the Graduate School for Health Studies of Simmons College in Boston. Although Dr. Koocher views himself as specializing in pediatric psychology, he also has a secondary specialization in forensic psychology. Thus, some of his responses relate to a career covered in the previous chapter. He works with children and families confronting chronic and life-threatening illness and with families involved in child custody disputes. He also has a long history of service to his profession, including ten years as APA treasurer followed by election as its president in 2004 (the term actually began in 2006 although the election was two years earlier).

If you were talking to an undergraduate student who is considering specializing in pediatric psychology, what psychology courses would you recommend as good preparation? "Strong preparation in adult and child psychopathology, along with courses on

Gerald P. Koocher
*Photo courtesy of
Gerald P. Koocher.*

psychodiagnosis and assessment, are important. In addition, courses focused on fundamentals of health psychology, as applied to children, and basic child psychopathology
would be useful."

What courses in other disciplines would you recommend? "Courses in child health
and development, sociology of deviance or criminology, and developmental disabilities
are good preparation for this career."

What courses didn't you have that you wish you had taken? "I wish I had taken
some courses in legal research and management. I now have a managerial role and
had to acquire practical information in business operations and negotiation long after
graduate school. I have also had to learn legal research techniques and sources on my
own. Scholarly legal courses are quite different from those used to conduct research in
the behavioral sciences."

When you think about the work you do, what do you find most rewarding? "Making
a difference! Whether I am helping a family to cope with serious illness or helping to
resolve a contentious child custody dispute, I take pride and find great reward in making a difference in people's lives. Even with respect to my teaching and research, I enjoy
hearing of my students' career accomplishments or finding that my work is cited and used
by others."

What do you find most frustrating? "The bureaucracy of our current healthcare system
that demands I spend nearly as much time completing paperwork as treating patients."

Were there specific life experiences that influenced you to become a psychologist? "I was the oldest of three sons and often 'babysat.' In addition, I spent many years as a summer camp counselor. I found great rewards and delights in working with children."

Why did you decide to work in pediatric psychology? "I began graduate school with an interest in mentally ill adult offenders, following in the footsteps of an undergraduate professor I admired. I soon became frustrated by recidivism and the difficulty of treating this population, while also having great fun and personal rewards treating child and family cases. I went on internship to a pediatric hospital and fell in love with the work."

Did you have a mentor or role model who influenced you to become a psychologist? "There were really three very influential people in my career as a psychologist. One was Dr. Murray Cohen, who taught me abnormal psychology when I was an undergraduate at Boston University. The second was Dr. Freda Rebelsky, my undergraduate child psychology professor. Both were gifted teachers with the capacity to challenge and reinforce students. Most influential, however, was Dr. Fred McKinney. Fred was my advisor in graduate school at the University of Missouri from my first day through the completion of my Ph.D. Fred completed his doctorate in the 1930s, long before modern clinical psychology was born. Nonetheless, he was up-to-date in his knowledge of the field and provided a fantastic role model as a scientist-practitioner with the warmth of a grandfather. Aside from the content of their teaching, each of these people gave me encouragement and support while communicating a love of the field."

Please write one or two paragraphs about each of two days in your professional life that describe a sample of what you do. "I currently work as an academic dean and professor. A typical week finds me meeting with faculty and other administrators to focus on boosting enrollment, developing new programs, resolving concerns raised by students or faculty, dealing with assorted appeals, developing budgets, and writing materials for fund-raising letters or alumni bulletins. I also spend a day each week continuing working as a psychologist at a pediatric hospital two blocks away. I supervise one intern, one postdoctoral fellow, and typically do two to three hours of psychotherapy with pediatric patients each week. In addition to my primary work, I also consult with attorneys in cases requiring psychological expertise. Such cases typically involve wrongful death (e.g., evaluating the effects of a homicide or accidental death on the surviving children in the family), child custody, and malpractice. In some of these legal cases, I actually perform evaluations and generate reports, while in others I read documentation such as case notes and depositions in order to give advice to attorneys. I spend about six to seven hours each week in that work."

Looking toward the future of pediatric psychology, what are your predictions for such factors as growth, new directions, and so on? "Pediatric psychology will grow although at a somewhat reduced pace as America struggles to contain healthcare costs. As the economy improves, the demand for pediatric psychologists will boom as research documents the efficacious interventions in a range of content areas (e.g., adaptation to illness, enhancing medical adherence, and pain and weight control). Growth in forensic psychology is already booming and will continue to grow as courts increasingly see the benefit of using psychological expertise to resolve disputes."

What changes would you like to see occur in your specialty? "I would like to see the value of pediatric psychology recognized sufficiently so that no pediatrician would think of practicing without one as a partner and treatment team member."

Looking over the time since you received your degree, how has your identity as a professional changed, and to what do you attribute these changes? "I have learned to value my experience in understanding people and social systems, making assessments based on data and formulating interventions to change behavior as applying to work well beyond the role of a pediatric psychologist. I use these same skills as an administrator, classroom teacher, manager, and leader in civic and professional activities. Psychological training is great training for a wide range of activities beyond the traditional office roles most people envision. I have learned to 'change hats' as I move from one setting to another, without putting aside the skills I have learned as a psychologist."

If you could have dinner with any person, living or dead, who would you select and why? Dr. Koocher selected Dr. Martin Luther King, Jr. He told us he regards Dr. King as one of the most effective revolutionary leaders in history based on the power of his ideas, oratory, and effective use of nonviolent protest. He would have liked to know Dr. King as a person and to talk with him about the realities of his life, ideas, and motivation. He would also like to hear Dr. King's view of his successes and failures.

When asked about his hobbies, Dr. Koocher noted that he has served as an elected member of town government. He also told us that for over a decade he has avidly pursued his interests in digital photography and psitticine aviculture. We debated whether to let our readers pursue this latter hobby or give a more common phrase for it. He is referring to the fact that he raises parrots.

Integrating the Interviews

Although Dr. El-Ghoroury and Dr. Koocher are at different points in their careers in pediatric psychology and have quite different job settings, they noted the frustration of the mandatory paperwork of the current healthcare system. Students who enter clinical psychology because of a desire to help others often have this reaction. They are not prepared for the amount of paperwork required in almost any employment setting. Do not think that if you are in independent practice you will avoid this problem. It will be part of *any* clinical practice. Also note that neither of these psychologists started graduate school with a goal of becoming a pediatric psychologist. We point out this fact to remind undergraduates that they do not need to have strong specialty interests at this time. Based on practical experiences in graduate school or even the first job, those interests may become more apparent. Dr. El-Ghoroury noted that a major reason he was hired was his fluency in Spanish. As we noted elsewhere in this book, the segment of the U.S. population that is growing the fastest is Hispanic. Thus, students may wish to consider taking more language courses, especially conversational language, while they are undergraduates. Both of our pediatric psychologists continue the theme of their colleagues who recommend a broad psychology background plus the specialty courses in health and development. The importance of having a career that fits with your value system was also noted here. Finding such a career helps with issues of burnout. Both of our pediatric psychologists noted how important it is to them to feel they "make a difference" in the lives of the people with whom they work.

We hope that reading about the foundation of these age-based specialties combined with the personal information from specialists in these areas has clarified what these careers entail. Of course, if we had unlimited space, we could have interviewed others in these specialties who do quite different things. Overall, however, we believe these interviews illustrate the breadth of the specialties.

Key Terms

clinical child
 psychology
clinical gero-
 psychology

competence
life review

Older Boulder
pediatric psychology

resilience
sandwich generation

CHAPTER 16

The Dynamic Future of Clinical Psychology

It seems to be a tradition in clinical psychology books to have a chapter in which the authors attempt to predict what the future holds for the profession. We are not seers, and therefore we do not really *know* what clinical psychology will be like when undergraduate students who read this book complete their graduate studies and are ready to enter the profession. What we are going to try to do in this chapter is to consider some of the emerging trends in the profession, in health care, and in the country that seem relevant to the future of clinical psychology. Our comments are generally limited to the practice of clinical psychology in the United States, although because of the close relationship between practice groups in Canada and those in the United States, most of our comments are probably also applicable to practice in Canada. For example, the licensing boards of these two countries belong to a joint international organization that meets twice a year to discuss issues of importance to psychologists practicing in the two countries. Among their initiatives is one to increase the ease of movement of licensed psychologists not only among the states of the United States but also among all of the Canadian provinces. You might hear this discussion talked about in terms of "mobility." The APA accredits doctoral programs in both countries, adding to the close ties they maintain. As you think about your future as a clinical psychologist, therefore, consider the fact that you might elect to attend graduate school in either Canada or the United States.

As we noted earlier in this book, a major activity of clinical psychology is psychotherapy. What can we expect in the future for this aspect of the profession? Noted psychotherapy researcher Dr. John Norcross and his colleagues used the Delphi model of data-gathering to attempt to predict the future of psychotherapy on three occasions: 1980,

1990, and 2000 (Norcross, Alford, & DeMichele, 1992; Norcross, Hedges, & Prochaska, 2002; Prochaska & Norcross, 1982). We'll call these researchers "futurists" for easy reference. This research methodology was originally developed in the early 1950s for use by the military to deal with complex problems. A core part of the methodology is the use of a panel of experts to provide ideas about the topic. The most recent panel of experts in 2000 consisted of sixty-two participants. All of these participants were doctoral-level practitioners. These practitioners reported an average of thirty years of postdoctoral clinical experience. They were selected based on either having served on the previous panels or currently serving as editor of a leading mental health journal. Men outnumbered women by about 3 to 1 in this group. This difference is not surprising given the nature of psychology leadership in the past. By the time of their next survey, we predict this degree of gender imbalance should reverse in line with the overwhelming shift toward women entering the profession (APA, 1995). One change we see is a more visible presence of women in leadership positions—serving as editors of leading mental health journals, as department chairs, and as foundation presidents and being selected to participate in "think tank" projects such as the futurist project we just mentioned.

The futurists we mentioned predicted that four psychotherapy formats would increase from 2000 to 2010: short-term psychotherapy, psychoeducational groups for specific disorders, crisis intervention, and group and couples therapy. The increased use of short-term psychotherapy fits with our earlier discussion of the role of managed care in shaping the profession. The psychoeducational groups fit with the community model we discussed in chapter 13. The discussion of psychotherapy with suicidal patients in chapter 11 is one illustration of crisis intervention. In chapter 12, you read about group and couples therapy. The expert panel also suggested that the use of computer technology would characterize psychotherapy in the first decade of the millennium. We discussed some examples of this use of technology in chapter 11.

As we noted there, there are other areas that are just starting to be explored. The panel predicted that one of the theoretical orientations that would increase in importance would be culture-sensitive/multicultural. In chapter 9, we discussed some cultural considerations that are important when doing psychotherapy. Throughout this book, we have tried to illustrate the importance of sensitivity to cultural issues in the overall practice of clinical psychology. We will talk more about this issue in the section of this chapter on the impact of the changing demographic. The only form of psychotherapy the panelists felt would show a decline during this period was long-term therapy. This suggestion is not surprising when we consider the dramatic role that both managed care and economic factors currently play in mental health care.

When Norcross' panel of experts summarized what they thought psychotherapy would be like in 2010, they found that four key themes emerged: efficiency, evidence, evolution, and integration. *Efficiency* means that psychotherapy will be the shortest and least expensive type available. Economic efficiency is currently viewed as a major driver of the American healthcare industry. Thus, it is not surprising that almost all of the theoretical orientations were predicted to support and develop brief versions of their approach to meet the requirements of this industry. The panel predicted this economic trend would also impact the practice of psychology from the perspective that doctoral-level practitioners would begin to lose business to mental health practitioners with less than a doctoral degree (e.g., social workers, licensed counselors). Interventions that can be used in the home (e.g., self-control procedures and self-help materials) were also viewed as being on the rise.

They predicted that psychotherapy with scientific support, often called empirically supported or evidence based treatment, would be the most important form of intervention. This is what the panel meant by *evidence.* The panel did not imply that the therapies with the greatest efficacy would always be the ones reimbursed by insurance companies. Rather, they suggested that in the coming years those forms of therapy with the greatest involvement in controlled research would be those preferred by insurance carriers. Change would continue to be gradual based on theory and research.

This *evolution* of theory and therapy development has been typical of psychotherapy over the years. Very few forms of psychotherapy have actually just disappeared. Instead, one form of psychotherapy frequently provides the basis or foundation for the development of other forms of psychotherapy.

The panel also predicted there would be an *integration,* rather than fragmentation, of the field. Their use of *integration* was to suggest a more intentional process than "evolution" implies. They predicted that those aspects of current types of psychotherapy that have the greatest support will be selected and combined to form newer intervention approaches. Based on this prediction, we should see considerable psychotherapy research in the future as these new forms of psychotherapy are developed. Even if specific aspects of psychotherapy have been found to be useful, data on the combined format will be needed.

Changing Demographics

As the United States entered the twenty-first century, the U.S. Census Bureau analyzed population trends from the previous decade. The U.S. population experienced faster growth, in terms of percentage change of the population, than was found in most of the other major developed countries. In the 1990s, the U.S. population grew by 13.2 percent. Contrast that growth to the 12.6 percent in Canada, 2.4 percent in Japan, and –1.4 percent in Russia. Historically, not all parts of the country or the world have grown at the same rate. Thus, it is important to determine specifically where the population is growing to determine where the services of clinical psychologists may be needed. The 1990s were the only decade of the twentieth century in which every state gained in population, although some counties lost population. Counties losing population tended to be in the Great Plains region of the country. There were also differences in this growth pattern on a regional basis. The South and West grew faster than did other parts of the country. The fastest growing state in the 1990s was Nevada, with a 66 percent increase in its population. One factor that seems to be related to this growth pattern is the increase in the percentage of the population who are age fifty-five or over. Retirement communities in the South and West may be contributing to the population growth in these regions. Future clinical psychologists in these parts of the country may need to have training in geropsychology to meet the needs of those who seek their services.

According to Census Bureau data (U.S. Department of Commerce, 2001), the ethnic composition of the United States had also changed by the end of the twentieth century and would continue to change significantly for the next fifty years. In 1990, the largest number of identified ethnic minorities in the United States was listed as black. In 2000, Hispanics comprised a slightly higher percentage of the U.S. population than did blacks. Those individuals self-identified as Asian had also increased their percentage of the U.S. population over that time period, while American Indians and Pacific Islanders remained fairly constant. For the first time, the U.S. Census Bureau also included a category for "two or more" races in their survey; these individuals comprised over 2 percent of the people responding to the 2000 U.S. census questionnaire.

Just as population growth varied by region of the country, so did the report of the percentage of the population in various parts of the country who indicated they were members of these various ethnic groups. Brewer and Suchan (2001) used the term *high-diversity states* to refer to those states that included counties with populations that were 60 to 70 percent ethnic. High-diversity states were Arizona, California, New Mexico, Texas, and Virginia. Thus, psychologists who practice in these states have an even greater obligation to develop multicultural competence. Census data also found that the percentage of the U.S. population who were foreign born had reached levels not seen in fifty years. About 11 percent of the U.S. population in 2000 was foreign born, with over half of that group coming from Latin American. Coincidental with increases in the Latino population was the finding that about twenty-seven million Americans in 2000 reported speaking Spanish at home. These changes in the U.S. population suggest the importance of cultural diversity training and linguistic training for clinical psychologists.

In the chapter on assessment, we discussed some of the attempts to develop specialty tools for use with culturally diverse groups. A much more recent development in addressing diversity issues has been attention to linguistic factors in therapy with patients for whom English is not the primary language. With the increasing number of Spanish-speaking patients in the United States, this group seems to be receiving early attention by the profession, but the issues and potential solutions may also be applicable to other groups (Santiago-Rivera & Altarriba, 2002). Researchers have reported that the selection of language used with Hispanic patients may place limitations on both the emotions that are expressed in the therapy session as well as the type of information that is presented (Altarriba & Santiago-Rivera, 1994; Marian & Neisser, 2000). Furthermore, individuals from diverse cultures are more likely to be misdiagnosed than are white Americans (Hoernicke, Kallam, & Tablada, 1994), in part due to communication problems related to language differences, cultural nuances, and, at times, clinician bias (Pumariega & Cross, 1997; Singh, 1998).

Until the publication of the DSM-IV (American Psychiatric Association, 1994), therapists did not have the benefit of standard cultural formulation guidelines for psychiatric diagnosis. There is even a "V" code, those other factors that may need clinical attention, for acculturation problems. Prior to DSM-IV, the focus was on treating mental disorders rather than on the people who manifest these disorders within a broad ecological context (Sue, Bingham, Porsche-Burke, & Vasquez, 1999). Focus on the individual, including use of that person's cultural concepts as part of psychotherapy, does not mean that the psychologist ignores the literature about the most effective treatment for the overall problem (Chen & Davenport, 2005; Martinez-Toboas, 2005).

Practice in a Diverse World

Cultural awareness has been defined as the understanding of differences among and between cultures (Casas, Pavelski, Furlong, & Zanglis, 2001). **Cultural sensitivity** is considered to represent a step beyond awareness—not attributing positive or negative values to the differences within and between cultures. These nonjudgmental perspectives set the stage for **cultural competence,** or the possession of skills and knowledge necessary to work with individuals from different cultures in a manner congruent with their values. Future clinical psychologists will be expected to be culturally competent.

The APA developed guidelines to assist psychologists to develop the needed skills to reach cultural competence (APA, 2003). Psychologists are expected to continue to learn after receiving their final academic degrees. The multicultural guidelines provide a framework for learning in this specific area. These guidelines address not only practice issues but also education and research. The need to help students develop cultural competence is now a requirement for APA accreditation for clinical psychology doctoral programs (APA, 2002b). When these programs are evaluated for either their initial accreditation or regular re-accreditation, they must demonstrate to the satisfaction of the evaluators how they have included diversity training in the program. There has also been increased attention to including diversity issues in both undergraduate and graduate textbooks (Jackson, 2004). We expect that these various sources will combine to lead to greater discussion of cultural competence within the educational process, including continuing professional education in the future.

Although many Hispanic patients are bilingual, Spanish is often their primary language. When speaking Spanish, they are more closely tied to their culture and heritage—factors that are important within the therapeutic setting. Merely studying Spanish in the traditional way does not appear to be sufficient to teach the clinical psychologist the cultural factors needed to conduct effective psychotherapy.

Our Lady of the Lake University in San Antonio, Texas developed a model program designed to address the mental health needs of the 56 percent of the population of their greater urban area who self-identify as Latino (Biever et al., 2002). We chose to describe this program to provide an example of the type of training we expect to see develop in more doctoral programs to help graduates better serve the diverse population. This program, Psychological Services for Spanish Speaking Populations (PSSSP), is a subspecialty within an APA-accredited counseling psychology training program. A major goal of PSSSP is to train psychologists who are equally comfortable providing mental health services in English and Spanish. The program developers had previously found that even among their students for whom Spanish was the primary language these therapist-trainees were more comfortable providing clinical services in English than in Spanish. Further exploration of this topic revealed that because their clinical skills had been learned in English and were still quite new for the students, they were not comfortable translating them into their primary language for use in therapy. It would therefore be important for some of these skills to be taught in Spanish rather than in English if they were to be used immediately in the clinic. The requirements of this subspecialty include immersion language training, as well as training about factors such as ethnic self-identification and traditional healing practices and the work of leading Latino psychologists. To accomplish these goals, the subspecialty program includes seven 3-hour courses plus three consecutive semesters of practica at bilingual sites. The program developers note that in order to have such a subspecialty program, the university must have sufficient bilingual faculty members and practicum supervisors to meet student needs. It may be difficult for many programs to meet this requirement, and addressing more than one linguistic group would certainly be both time and cost prohibitive.

We hypothesize that in the future similar specialty programs will be developed to train psychologists for work with other linguistic groups. If the PSSSP model is used for such program development, early programs are likely to be located in geographic settings with large numbers of individuals who speak the desired language. Such a location would ensure local professionals who could serve as adjunct faculty to teach specialized courses as well as the availability of relevant practicum sites. These programs, and their trainees, would also provide needed services to the community.

With African-American patients the primary concern tends to be more cultural than linguistic. Clinical psychologists need to learn which aspects of culture are important to the mental health of their African-American patients (Whaley, 2001a, 2001b). On the other hand, clinical psychologists who have been trained to avoid stereotypes and other generalizations when working with patients from cultural backgrounds different from their own may find that this approach interferes with the provision of adequate psychological services. For these practicing psychologists, their training is to view all people as equal, and this translates as being alike. Thus, they do not attend to those aspects of the patient's background that are quite different from their own. They may actively restrict themselves from asking such questions because they view them as indicating some form of prejudice. This approach may lead the psychologist to avoid asking questions about the strength of an African-American patient's identity with the local African-American community as well as developing an understanding of the worldview of that community. The same issues that may impede the progress of psychotherapy may also interfere with the mentoring experience of African-American graduate students whose mentors come from a different cultural group. When a match for the graduate student's background is not found among the training program faculty, an alternative may be to enlist professionals from the community as mentors to complement the regular faculty (Walker, Wright, & Hanley, 2001). We are not suggesting that the only good mentor comes from the same cultural background as the student. It is important, however, for the mentor to be comfortable discussing a range of personal issues with the student and for the student to be comfortable with these discussions.

Psychologists must be aware of sensitive ethical implications when working with diverse populations. This issue is sometimes called a professional's **multicultural responsibility** (Ridley, Liddle, Hill, & Li, 2001). By multicultural responsibility we mean a fusion of personal and professional commitment to consider culture in their work. Psychologists do this by exploring their own prejudices, including stereotypes they may hold, and considering how these perceptions influence their interactions with patients from different cultures. Practitioners can also strive to understand how culture is always relevant in psychotherapy (Ridley, Li, & Hill, 1998) and be mindful of when cultural issues come into play rather than wondering if cultural factors affect the patient-therapist relationship.

The APA Ethics Code (APA, 2002a) addresses this topic in several sections. The inclusion of this information throughout the code is another illustration of the profession's commitment to addressing diversity issues. When addressing *Competence,* Standard 2, the Ethics Code specifies that psychologists should work only with those populations with whom they have adequate training or make appropriate referrals of such individuals. This standard also acknowledges that for some groups the discipline may not yet have adequate materials available. In those cases of emerging groups, psychologists are obligated to take reasonable steps to ensure that these individuals are not harmed by the psychologist's interventions.

When addressing *Use of Assessments,* Standard 9.02, the code specifies that psychologists must use only those instruments that have established reliability and validity for the population from which that person comes. We talked about this a bit in our earlier discussion of assessment. As U.S. demographics continue to change, these ethical standards will become even more important for clinical psychologists. It is a bit easier to determine whether or not a test is appropriate for a particular patient than it is to determine whether or not you have actually reached a level of cultural competence to work with a specific patient. To assist psychologists in this decision-making process, Hansen and her colleagues developed a model of multicultural practice competencies with case examples that provides a foundation for interested students to read (Hansen, Pepitone-Arreola-Rockwell, & Greene, 2000).

Textbooks discussing intervention with specific ethnic groups are now available (Jackson & Greene, 2000; LaFramboise, 1996; Parham, White, & Ajamu, 1999). There are also textbooks addressing the more general topic of multicultural counseling (Ponterotto, Casas, Suzuki, & Alexander, 2001; Pope-Davis & Coleman, 1997; Sciarra, 1999; Sue & Sue, 1999). All clinical psychology trainees can benefit from training and supervision in this domain. More specialized resources can be expected as the population continues to change and additional specialized graduate programs are developed.

As clinical psychologists work with families, they must also learn expanded definitions of "family" based on the changing demographics of the country. According to the U.S. Census Bureau (2000), people who live alone outnumber those living in "traditional" households of a married couple with children under the age of eighteen. Over two million grandparents were live-in caregivers according to the 2000 U.S. Census. At that time, there were four million multigenerational households. Remember our discussion of the changing definition of *sandwich generation* in chapter 15? These multigenerational households may include varying numbers of generations. Unmarried-partner households increased from 3.2 to 5.5 million from 1990 to 2000. Once again, remember the information from chapter 15. It can be easy to jump to the conclusion that these unmarried partners are young people who are "living together." We know that at least some of these households are senior citizens. Thus, you can see why knowledge of the extended family in family therapy training has become increasingly important.

We noted that one of the specialties emerging from clinical psychology was clinical geropsychology. The changing demographics are also relevant to this specialty. The U.S. Census Bureau tends to group the population in age ranges: under 15, 15–34, 35–54, and 55 and over. In 2000, the ranking of these groups in terms of their percentage of the U.S. population was 35–54, 15–34, under 15, and 55 and over. As you can see, if you are a traditional age college student, your cohort is not among the larger ones in this country. Based on life expectancy data, the projections for 2020 place the order of these age groups as 55 and over, 15–34, 35–54, and under 15. As the baby boomers continue to add to this older age group, the need for specialized psychological services can also be expected to increase. The clinical geropsychologists you met in chapter 15 also suggested this trend. For example, in 1995, there were approximately 3.6 million people in the United States in the 85 years of age and older group. The current prediction is that this age group will contain 8.5 million people in 2030.

Traditionally, older adults have been underrepresented among those individuals seeking outpatient mental health services (Qualls, 1998). As we move into the twenty-first century, however, the use of mental health services by older citizens has come close to their percentage in the population. Why has this change occurred? No one can give a definite answer to this question. It is probably due to a combination of factors. The growth of specialties like health psychology, which we described in chapter 14, has led to increased interaction between primary care physicians and psychologists. Thus, they may be more likely than their predecessors to make referrals to mental health professionals.

The growth of multidisciplinary outpatient practices has also made the availability of mental health services more visible. A factor that may impact future use of mental health services by older persons is the aging of the baby boomers. The baby boomer generation has been reported to have a higher rate of diagnosed mental disorders than other age groups within the population (Klerman & Weissman, 1989). Whether this increased level of diagnosis is due to a true increase in psychopathology or merely an increased use of mental health services is not important. As baby boomers age, they can be expected to continue to seek the services of psychologists. In contrast to outpatient services, older adults have tended to be overrepresented among patients in inpatient psychiatric settings (Qualls, 1998). Furthermore, it is estimated that about a third of the residents of nursing homes have a mental illness other than dementia and about half of these residents suffer from dementia. Thus the need for services of both clinical geropsychologists and clinical neuropsychologists for this age group is very important. Both of these specialties should be growth areas for psychologists in the future.

Residents of other forms of housing for the elderly have not been studied as completely as those individuals who live in nursing homes, but it is estimated that these people also have a high rate of diagnosable psychopathology. We can only hypothesize why these groups have not been studied in more depth. One possible explanation is that ageism biases in the culture have led to symptoms of psychopathology being ignored in many elderly who are not living in nursing homes. Let's consider memory loss to illustrate this issue. If the person experiencing memory loss is elderly, a common assumption is that this condition is just part of "getting old." His or her family or friends may overlook the possibility that this person is clinically depressed. Remember Joyce from our patient group. Even her psychologist did not consider the possibility of PTSD and acquaintance rape based on her presenting symptoms. Her age and personal expression of concern pointed more toward a traditional view such as the early stages of one of the dementias. Because insurance reimbursement rates are often greater for physical problems than for mental health issues, there may also be less motivation for people to train for the clinical geropsychology specialty as well as to seek out those settings where eldercare services are needed. Perhaps the future will include better education of such lobbying groups for the elderly as the AARP who might be successful in obtaining changes in healthcare coverage for their members.

As clinical geropsychologists have begun to develop training materials and programs, they have noted that practice in this specialty will require not only special knowledge but also a break with the traditional view of clinical practice. Clinical geropsychologists are much less likely to be able to see their patients in a traditional office setting than are other clinical psychologists. These elderly patients need to be seen in a variety of settings. Concerns about slower reaction times may lead them to stop driving. In communities where public transportation is poor or expensive, these individuals may be unable to come to the psychologist's office. Medically fragile patients are often excluded from traditional psychiatric inpatient units because of their medical needs. Thus, they must be seen on medical units of the hospital. It is also important to be able to learn about these patients in their daily context.

Work in geropsychology often requires integration of services with a number of other professions. It is not uncommon to coordinate services with medical specialists, housing staff, and social service agencies. This complex level of service provision may require dealing with a network of providers and institutions rather than a single insurance carrier or hospital administration. In a real sense, geropsychologists will have to assume a greater advocacy role when they care for their patients. This advocacy might include lobbying for better transportation services as well as improved access to psychological care. Clinical psychologists of the twenty-first century will need to have a solid foundation in a variety of skills as they provide services to this older group. Students who are interested in learning about training opportunities in this specialty can find information on the website of the Section on Clinical Geropsychology of APA's Division of Clinical Psychology (http://www.bama.ua.edu/~appgero/apa12_2).

Clinical psychologists who are already in practice may also find they are being asked to see elderly patients whose needs may be different from the patients they have traditionally seen. The American Psychological Association published *Guidelines for Psychological Practice with Older Adults* (APA, 2004) as a document that can assist those psychologists in evaluating their background for this area of practice. These guidelines are subdivided into attitudes about the population, general knowledge, clinical issues, assessment, service provision, and education. As we noted earlier, guidelines are not considered standards. They are not mandatory but rather suggestions for psychologists to improve their practice. Use of these guidelines is similar to the information we provided for the multicultural guidelines.

Diversity training in psychology also includes work with lesbian, gay, bisexual, and transgender (LGBT) individuals. Diversity training in graduate school for work with LGBT patients has been somewhat behind that of programs addressing race and ethnicity. Currently this topic is most likely to be addressed as part of a multicultural course rather than as a separate course (Sherry, Whilde, & Patton, 2005). Some models of cultural competence have broadened the earlier definition to include sexual identity, gender identity, race and ethnicity, and religious identity (Sue, 2001). Using this approach has the potential to lead clinicians to an appreciation of many specialty issues. Until we have more training materials, however, it remains difficult for faculty to know what information should be included at the doctoral level and what should be left for later specialty training.

Future training in these areas can be expected to increase as national policies such as defining marriage and family gain prominence and as textbooks become available for student use in such a course (e.g., Perez, Dubord, & Bieschke, 2000; Ritter & Terndrup,

2002). An illustration of integrating this type of training into doctoral programs is the Safe Zone project, a training module designed to increase awareness and knowledge of LGBT issues at the University of Denver. This project involved mandatory training sessions for all students entering the program in a specified year. The first session was held at the start of their graduate school experience and the second session was held at the beginning of the spring term. This training included didactics about terminology and available research as well as experiential exercises on LGBT subjects. Finkel and her colleagues (2003) provided a preliminary evaluation of this program as well as suggestions about how this approach can impact further practice.

Serious Mental Illness

Although many of the newer areas in clinical psychology are quite different from the traditional mental health activities of the profession, recent years have also witnessed a growth of interest in psychological services for the seriously mentally ill. This group includes people with diagnoses such as schizophrenia and bipolar disorder. With the movement to discharge these patients from long-term care facilities into the community, there was also a tendency to rely on medication as the primary form of treatment for them. Unfortunately, medication compliance rates have been found to be poor with older adults as well as those who become easily confused.

Psychologists can assist with compliance improvement. Psychologists also have skills to assist those individuals who have recovered from serious mental illnesses and now work in peer treatment programs. The empirical literature suggests that a combination of medication and newer forms of intervention designed to assist these individuals to live independently provides the best opportunity for recovery (Coursey, Alford, & Safarjan, 1997). Psychologists are trained not only to provide such services but also to develop and evaluate additional forms of intervention. The seriously mentally ill comprise about 5.4 percent, or about ten million people, of the U.S. adult population (Center for Mental Health Services, 1996) but are usually viewed as receiving inadequate care.

Another role for psychologists working with the seriously mentally ill that can be expected to increase in the future is assisting them in obtaining and maintaining employment. Most people who are considered seriously mentally ill need vocational services. Traditionally, however, this group has continued to have a high rate of unemployment despite a stated interest in working (Mueser, Salyers, & Mueser, 2001). Some preliminary data even suggest that return to work may also benefit mental health and life satisfaction (Bond et al., 2001). Psychologists have begun to use their skills to develop specialty programs to assist these individuals with vocational issues. Students interested in this area of work may wish to start by reading about the Hartford Study (Mueser et al., 2004).

The issue of serious mental illness is not limited to adults. Serious emotional disturbance also exists in children. There are estimates that between 4.5 million and 6.3 million children and adolescents in the United States have a diagnosable mental disorder that seriously interferes with their ability to function (Marsh, 2004). On the other hand, at least two-thirds of these children do not receive services for their disorder. Thus, in the future psychologists can be expected not only to provide such services but also to work on public policy that makes such treatment more accessible.

Trauma

Clinical psychologists have a long history of working with victims of traumatic events. They have also used their research skills to evaluate the efficacy of various forms of intervention (Gist & Lubin, 1998). This area of practice, however, was highlighted following the terrorist attacks on the World Trade Center in New York City on September 11, 2001. Following this event, psychologists not only applied their clinical skills to work with victims, their families, and their communities, but also attempted to develop theories to help them understand people's reactions to this type of threat (Pyszczynski, Solomon, & Greenberg, 2002). These theories can then be tested through clinical research as well as applied to the development of specialized interventions. Psychologists also discovered that they needed better assessment tools to measure the acute stress disorder (ASD) found in people who are at greatest risk for later development of post-traumatic stress disorder (PTSD). Psychologists working in this specialty learned that their skills were needed not only for individuals in New York City but also for American citizens who were working at sites around the world where security was heightened following this attack.

The World Trade Center attack was not the first act of terrorism in the United States in which psychologists took an active role to assist victims. On April 19, 1995, Timothy McVeigh bombed the Murrah Federal Building in Oklahoma City. Every employee who worked in the building and survived was automatically given a diagnosis of PTSD by the federal government. This was done so that they would qualify for psychological services. Research with survivors of the Oklahoma City bombing has suggested that just talking about the event is accompanied by physiological changes long after the event had occurred (Foxhall, 2001). The reported physiological changes included increased heart rate and excessive perspiration. These physiological changes are consistent with other anxiety-based problems.

Within the APA, the Practice Directorate maintains a list of volunteer psychologists called the Disaster Response Network (DRN). When there is a large-scale disaster like the September 11, 2001, tragedy, the Red Cross contacts the DRN through the Practice Directorate. For that trauma, psychologists provided their services at Ground Zero, the name given to the site around the World Trade Center in New York City. Psychologists also provided services at a compassion center in New York City; at the Pentagon outside Washington, DC; at a rural area of Pennsylvania where another plane crashed; and at the scheduled arrival and departure airports of the hijacked planes in order to work with families of the victims. These were psychologists not only from the greater New York and Washington, DC, areas, but also from other parts of the country. Psychologists who had specialty training working with trauma victims drove and took trains from many parts of the country to those sites because air travel had been suspended and thus was not an option. In traumatic events like the September 11 terrorist attacks, psychologists also use their skills to counsel the rescuers. Rescuers are trained for specific jobs. Their training does not have any way to include what they will face in a massive trauma like the September 11 attack or the great Indonesian tsunami of December 2004. Thus, rescuers also benefit from the help of psychologists so they may continue to do the jobs for which they are needed. Two days after the September 11 disaster, APA posted on their website guidelines for practitioners who wanted to host youth forums around the country to help young people understand and cope with the aftermath of this tragedy. Psychologists also provided their services to anxious flyers once air travel was resumed. Supervised clinical psychology graduate students in some communities made regular school visits for many weeks after September 11 to help students normalize their world. On college campuses, psychology faculty adapted their courses to help students deal with their reactions.

As clinical psychologists continue to gain experience working with trauma victims, they have also developed books so that others may learn from their experiences (Zubenko & Capozzoli, 2002). In addition to the therapeutic role psychology plays in addressing trauma, the science of psychology can also contribute to our knowledge base as we attempt to learn how to decrease the chances of similar events in the future. Graduate study related to counterterrorism is an emerging area of interdisciplinary study that includes psychology. One illustration of this work is the ten-week course on the psychology of terrorism that is included in the U.S. Naval Postgraduate School's Homeland Security master's degree program. This course includes material related to the psychological consequences of terrorism, psychological treatment of the victims, and fear management.

Terrorism is just one form of **trauma.** There is also an emotional toll from natural disasters. Among the common forms of natural disaster in the United States are severe storms and earthquakes. Anyone who lives along the Gulf Coast of the United States is familiar with concepts such as "hurricane tracking maps" and the "hurricane season." The importance of mental health services for both immediate and long-term problems following the devastation of hurricanes Katrina and Rita in 2005 illustrates this form of trauma. Residents of states such as California and Washington tend to be knowledgeable about the meaning of various points on the Richter scale for measuring earthquake intensity.

Jacobs (1995) referred to **"disaster mental health"** as the specialty for providing services to disaster victims as well as disaster relief personnel. He noted that mental health professionals have a long history of providing such services as well as studying reactions to trauma. We will briefly describe a program Jacobs directs at the University of South Dakota to illustrate the type of training students in clinical psychology who are interested in this area might pursue. This clinical psychology doctoral program offers a specialty track in *clinical/disaster* psychology through the Disaster Mental Health Institute. Students in this specialty receive training in the management of mental health responses to both large- and small-scale disasters. In addition to their work following disasters, they also provide consultation to organizations and communities about the development of prevention programs. As a foundation for their work, they conduct research in disaster psychology. Information about this program can be found on their website (http://www.usd.edu/dmhi).

An early description of survivor reactions to trauma was based on a description of a nightclub fire in which 491 people died (Lindemann, 1944). A later description of trauma reaction discussed a program of stress management for public safety personnel (Linton, 1995). This author proposed that psychologists provide **pro bono** (free of charge) counseling as a service to their communities. Public safety workers face chronic stress as a result of their occupation. They may also be faced with acute stress reactions following unusually intense experiences. Because every community has the potential to face emergencies, this type of program is not geographically limited.

More recently, several authors have described how to develop community educational programs designed to prevent psychological trauma in communities often facing the consequences of hurricanes and how living in such communities impacts the psychologists who practice there (Barnard & Rothgeb, 2000; Dudley-Grant, Mendez, & Zinn, 2000). Hurricanes are different from other natural disasters in that they often move quite slowly. Hurricane preparation, once a storm path is projected to hit a given community, can be emotionally and physically draining. Purchasing needed emergency supplies may involve waiting in long lines and the inability to obtain all the items that the person wants. Covering windows, possibly moving furniture to block windows, or perhaps moving to higher levels of the residence in case of flooding on the ground floor may be needed prior to the arrival of a hurricane. Decisions may also need to be made about whether to leave home, travel to another community, and spend money on a hotel room or perhaps go to an evacuation center. These decisions are often required at a time when the person is already under stress. The actual duration of the storm may be six hours or more without abating. Depending on the storm, recovery after it has ended may also require an extended period of time. Thus, it is not unusual for a range of psychological reactions to develop following this type of trauma. Because this is something that impacts many people, future work by psychologists is likely to include the development of public education programs and material for the lay public as well as clinical services.

When psychologists write about trauma, we tend to focus on how we can help others. That was our intent when we started this section of the book. As we reviewed some of the literature on this topic, however, we were reminded that clinical psychologists often deal with unstable people and therefore have the potential to become the victims of violence from them. Thus, our ability to apply our skills to our own lives is also important. An article in the *APA Monitor* (Daw, 2001) illustrates this point. This article describes the shooting of a clinical psychologist by a man who was angry about the outcome of his fitness-for-duty evaluation. This former patient came to the psychologist's home and shot him. The psychologist describes how his practice and his life changed as a result of this incident. We are not suggesting that such an event is common; fortunately it is not. It does provide an example, however, of dealing with trauma from an individual perspective.

Other psychologists have also found the need to make personal changes as a result of the patients with whom they practice even when the patient behavior is not as extreme as the previous example. A survey of a random sample of practicing psychologists who are APA members revealed that about 10 percent of the respondents had been stalked by a patient (Gentile, Asamen, Harmell, & Weathers, 2002). Although we tend to associate "stalking" with celebrities, patients may also stalk. The sample for this study was limited and so it is important not to generalize too much. The study did find, however, that the majority of patients who were reported as stalking their psychologist were single women. The most likely diagnoses of these patients were mood disorders on Axis I and borderline personality disorder on Axis II. A higher percentage of male psychologists than female psychologists responding to this survey reported having been stalked. This is different from what has been found in the general population, in which over 75 percent of stalking victims are female (Tjaden & Thoennes, 1997). The most frequent life change these psychologists made after being stalked was to have an unlisted home address in the telephone book. These psychologists noted a range of other precautions they used to protect themselves and their families from intrusive patient behavior. As this literature grows, students of psychology may be instructed about safety issues as part of their practical training. Using the term *trauma* in the diverse ways we have described suggests that this will be a growing area of both training and practice in clinical psychology in the coming years. For example, in 2005 a proposal to create a Division of Trauma Psychology within the APA structure showed psychologists' interest in this topic.

Public Policy Activities

In chapter 13, we described some of psychologists' activities in public policy. We believe this area will continue to grow in multiple ways. More psychologists will be trained about how to shape public policy through short-term training programs designed for practitioners, educators, and researchers. In addition, the growth of the number of psychologists who run for public office can also be expected to continue. Other psychologists will attempt to impact public policy through community programs. As more psychologists demonstrate the potential contributions the profession of psychology can make in this arena, it has the potential to grow.

Executive Coaching

Another growth area related to clinical psychology is called **executive coaching.** Probably the original "executive coaches" were senior leaders in a company who were expected to mentor and develop junior executives. As executive life has become more hectic and downsizing has led to executives assuming more roles, less time has been available for this activity. These changes have led to the development of specialists who serve this function.

In this case, clinical skills are applied to making top business leaders more effective in their roles. This is different from other forms of coaching done by psychologists, such as coaching for sports performance. These executives are not necessarily experiencing personal problems. Some of the most common goals of executive coaching are skill-building, performance improvement, development for future assignments, and definition and implementation of the executive's leadership and the organization's business objectives (Krall, 2001). Clinical psychologists interested in executive coaching need additional training in organizational behavior. Many psychologists in this field recommend supervision or apprenticing in the field with someone who is already successful in the field. Psychologists can use available journal articles and books to gain a better understanding of this emerging specialty and to determine whether this area fits their interests and background (e.g., Brotman, Liberi, & Wasylyshyn, 1998; Goldsmith, Lyons, & Freas, 2000; Kilburg, 2000; Laske, 1999; Witherspoon & White, 1998).

Executive coaches serve as sounding boards for strategic decision-making, coach newly promoted employees in supervising other employees, teach stress management, help a team "fight fair" as its members divide up resources in product development, teach how to manage uncertainty when there are multiple correct strategies that could be pursued, and mediate conflicts between executives. Notice how many of these skills are the ones clinical psychologists use with their patients.

The term *coach* is used, rather than psychologist, partially because of concern on the part of the executive recipients of this service that they might be viewed as mentally ill. According to Rodney Lowman, Ph.D., executive coaching is "about positive things like growth and maximizing potential" (Foxhall, 2002). His comment highlights the stigma that often accompanies mental health delivery. It is also important to note that many of these applications of clinical skills are not the ones traditionally associated with DSM-type disorders. Because the term *psychologist* is not used, there are questions about who provides services in this area and what entity regulates this profession. Many people now seem to refer to themselves as *executive coaches,* whether they come from a business background or from a psychology background, and they bring a variety of skills to this broad, yet-to-be-defined profession. Psychologists have made attempts to integrate the work of their profession, however, as it is applied to work with executives (Kilburg, 2000). Although executive coaching appears to be a growth area among clinical psychologists, experts in this specialty have often stated that only those clinical psychologists who have a background in business, in addition to their psychology background, should enter this area of practice. It is important to understand the climate of the business setting in addition to having an understanding of adjustment issues. Even those psychologists who have a business background need to advise executives about the areas of executive coaching in which they have expertise and those in which they do not. This specialty is likely to continue to define itself and its boundaries but seems to be an area of practice with much to offer in the future.

Emerging Topics in Clinical Practice

We started this chapter with a description of the approach Norcross and his colleagues used to predict changes in psychotherapy. In February 2002, the American Psychological Association's Board of Professional Affairs (BPA) members asked eleven psychology leaders what they viewed as cutting-edge areas for psychological practice in 2020 (Callan, Jerome, & Grossman, personal communication, March 15, 2002). This is similar to the Delphi model used by Norcross and his colleagues. Although the term *psychological practice* is certainly not synonymous with *clinical psychology,* most of the areas identified by the participants could be viewed as potential components of the future profession of clinical psychology. When BPA integrated and summarized the responses to this inquiry, seven areas emerged: prescriptive authority, behavioral health, assessment, positive psychology, diversity, technology, and lifespan psychology. We have addressed some of these topics in this book; others were not covered. We will briefly discuss each of these areas here from the perspective of their relationship to the future of clinical psychology.

Prescriptive Authority

These respondents believed that prescribing psychologists would become more commonplace than at the onset of the century. Advances in pharmacology and more sophisticated drug treatments would impact this growth. By 2020, psychotherapy plus concomitant drug therapy may become the "best practice" for many patients.

The suggestion that **prescriptive authority** will become of greater interest to psychologists in the twenty-first century is supported by the growth of postdoctoral training programs in psychopharmacology for psychologists. At the time of this writing, there are at least eleven such programs in existence (Holloway, 2004). About nine hundred psychologists have either enrolled in, or completed, these programs. To provide a standardized form of evaluating psychologists' academic understanding of psychopharmacology, the College of Professional Psychology within the APA developed an examination in psychopharmacology. This test development occurred over an extended period of time using content experts, experts in test development, and pilot testing. Reliability and validity studies were conducted so that the test would be psychometrically sound. In chapter 1, we discussed some of the legislative processes related to this practice area. As of 2006, at least eighteen U.S. jurisdictions had introduced such legislation and three had passed laws granting psychologists prescribing authority—Guam in 1998, New Mexico in 2002, and Louisiana in 2004.

Not all psychologists who complete these training programs either plan to actually prescribe or expect that laws allowing them to do so will pass during their professional careers. Some psychologists who seek this type of training find that it helps them communicate more effectively in the growing world of multidisciplinary health care. These psychologists act as collaborators and consultants, often to primary-care physicians rather than as actual prescribers. Others who complete these courses do so in the expectation that their state will pass a law similar to the three already enacted and want to be ready to qualify for prescribing status. Because the required education in these statutes takes considerable time to obtain, they need to start in advance of actual passage.

As the option for prescriptive authority becomes a reality for the practice of psychology, questions will arise about how this change may impact the identity of the profession. Some authors have already suggested that it is important for psychologists to develop "a uniquely psychological model of prescribing" (McGrath et al., 2004, p. 159). One of the challenges for clinical psychology in the twenty-first century is to determine just what that model may be.

Because some psychologists have been prescribing within the military system for a number of years, we asked one of them to answer the same questions we asked the psychologists covered in chapters 13, 14, and 15. The following section provides his responses.

MORGAN T. SAMMONS received his Ph.D. in counseling psychology from Arizona State University. At the time of this interview, he was a captain in the United States Navy serving as director, Clinical Operations, U.S. Navy Bureau of Medicine and Surgery.

If you were talking to an undergraduate student who is considering a career in clinical psychology with prescribing authority, what psychology courses would you recommend as good preparation? "First, a good two-semester sequence in general psychology should serve to pique the student's interest in what lies ahead in the graduate curriculum. Second, I'd strongly recommend a senior-level course in biological bases of behavior, principles of neuroscience, or something similar to that. These courses significantly add to the core knowledge base necessary for success in the graduate curriculum. The student will find herself or himself well ahead of peers if this is accomplished. A course in drugs and human behavior, frequently offered at the undergraduate level, when well taught can enrich the understanding of biological bases of behavior courses."

Morgan T. Sammons *Photo by Katharina Pellegrin.*

What courses in other disciplines would you recommend? "General chemistry and biology would be helpful. Otherwise, a solid liberal arts undergraduate track will serve the student well. I would recommend to any student a solid two-semester sequence in philosophy, epistemology, or logic. A structured approach to problem-solving is the hallmark of good researchers and clinicians. These courses, once a cornerstone of the liberal arts curriculum, will assist the student in acquiring the proper intellectual skills to enter the profession. Perhaps most importantly, the student should seek traditional or nontraditional coursework that refers directly to the human experience. Whether these be courses in art that explore our enduring need to create, or theological examinations of the universality of humans' spirituality, these are essential to our understanding of the needs and motivations of those with whom we work or study. I found an undergraduate sequence of philosophy and theology to be quite useful in expanding my worldview and strongly recommend this to others."

What courses didn't you have that you wish you had taken? Dr. Sammons told us that he would like to have taken an advanced course in psychophysiology as well as some courses in statistics for the social sciences. He also noted that since the PC was quite new when he was in school, he would recommend some computer science courses.

When you think about the work you do, what do you find the most rewarding? "This is hard to differentiate. Working with patients and their families, either in individual, couples or group work, is always intrinsically rewarding. On the other hand, developing and implementing mental health policy that has the capability of affecting mental health service provision on a large scale also is highly gratifying."

What do you find most frustrating? "The lack of recognition of the potency of psychological interventions and the persistent difficulties in getting reimbursement for various forms of psychological services by private or governmental payers. The absence of good outcomes data regarding evidence-based interventions and the relative lack of data on cost offsets of providing behavioral health interventions is also a frustration."

Were there any specific life experiences that influenced you to become a psychologist? "Yes. My undergraduate training was in a separate field [he got a BS degree in foreign service]. I did not entertain the notion of becoming a psychologist until I took a temporary job working with Cuban refugees who came to this country in the Mariel boatlift of 1980. As a result of my experiences working with these refugees, many of whom had demonstrable mental illness and all of whom were suffering the effects of forced separation from their homeland and their families, in addition to a history of oppression by the Castro regime, I returned to graduate school and sought a degree in psychology."

Why did you decide to work in psychopharmacology? "The courses I enjoyed most in graduate school were those in psychopharmacology and psychophysiology. I had the benefit of a great professor, Dennis Glanzman, who, though not a psychologist, brought a very applied understanding to both these fields. He made some rather difficult concepts quite understandable and piqued an enduring interest in these areas. At the same time, his acknowledgment of how tentative our understanding of neural processes is also helped shape my enduring skepticism of purely biological explanations of behavior. With rare exceptions, there aren't direct links between neuronal dysfunction and the expression of psychopathology. For example, we can point to all sorts of neuronal variability among patients with depression, but we can't establish true causality between this and the expression of depression itself, which is unique to every person who suffers from the condition. The human response is too complex and variable to be broken down to universally identifiable aberrations in neuronal function."

Did you have a mentor or role model who influenced you to become a psychologist? If so, please tell us about this person. "Where to begin? I think my first role models were friends who were working in the field, whose efforts I admired tremendously. Janis Herman Steenberg was one. She worked with Native Americans and sparked my interest in those cultures. Once in graduate school, Sharon Robinson-Kurpius became my role model. Sharon is still on faculty at Arizona State University and she's had an enduring influence on my career. Of course, for many years I've had tremendous admiration for Dr. Pat DeLeon, who is without doubt one of the foremost American psychologists of any generation [remember his interview from chapter 13]. Pat understands the vital importance of mentorship and is extremely generous in providing mentorship to more junior psychologists. I've benefited tremendously from his example, vision, and incessant work on behalf of psychologists.

Please write one or two paragraphs about each of two days in your professional life that describe a sample of what you do. "Well, interestingly enough, I don't do very much work these days that could be considered directly psychological in nature. I'm currently director for Clinical Support at the Navy's Bureau of Medicine and Surgery, and this job involves developing policy and programs not just in behavioral health, but in all aspects of medical service delivery in the Navy's treatment facilities. We look at a multitude of programs—from behavioral health to our blood bank programs, from risk management and quality assurance to the delivery of surgical services, and try to identify best practices, look at evidence-based standards for healthcare delivery, and improve efficiencies in the delivery of medical services. I work closely with professionals from all medical disciplines to ensure quality, economical health service delivery.

"I get to spend an afternoon a week in the clinic, and this is always a welcome break from administrative work and allows me to keep up my clinical skills. Right now, because of the demands of my job, I tend to provide most of my services via teleconsultations. Telehealth is an important area of emerging practice for psychologists, and we need to continue to refine the ability of psychologists to provide such services. Of course, because I'm a prescribing psychologist, I often work with patients referred from other psychologists or primary care managers to find the appropriate pharmacological intervention for those patients."

Looking forward to the future of psychopharmacology, what are your predictions for such factors as growth, new directions, and so on? "As I said, I think that telehealth is an important emerging aspect of practice. I also think that direct involvement of psychologists in the primary care environment is vital, not only to the health of our patients but to the health of the profession. I think it's important that we examine the prevailing specialty model of mental health service delivery. We know that most patients in need of psychological services don't seek them from a specialist—including psychologists—but ask for care in the primary care setting. As a result, we don't reach the majority of patients who could truly benefit from our services. This needs to change. I also think that prescriptive authority is the way of the future. Psychologists will use medications in a fundamentally different way than do practitioners who've been trained in the medical model. My bias, of course, is that the psychological model provides for far more effective use of medications and that psychologists are the best trained professionals to assess when medications might be the best intervention or when other treatments, like psychotherapy, should be offered instead."

What changes would you like to see occur in your specialty? "More training in psychopharmacology and in the ability of psychologists to work in the primary care environment. Our models of education haven't kept up with the changing face of psychological practice; it's time we examined these closely."

Looking over the time since you received your degree, how has your identity as a professional changed, and to what do you attribute these changes? "Well, I never thought that I would be a prescribing psychologist, and that's been a very rewarding change. Of course, my friend and mentor Dr. Pat DeLeon is the father of the prescriptive authority movement for psychologists, so I would attribute all of my involvement to him. I also never thought that I'd be so deeply involved in the nonpsychological aspects of medical service delivery. I think that many psychologists should consider nontraditional career paths. As vital as our services are to individual patients, our ability to affect entire systems of healthcare service delivery is, I think, ultimately of more value to the profession."

If you could have dinner with any person, living or dead, who would you select and why? "If you want the best answers, you go to the experts, so the best dinner would be one planned and prepared by gourmands. So, if I were to have *dinner* with any person, it would clearly be Jean Anthelme Brillat-Savarin, the French gastronome and author of *Psychology of Taste,* since he was arguably the most accomplished expert on food in recorded Western history. Brillat-Savarin also understood the importance of conversation and a good selection of guests at dinner—that food, if it is to have a balanced role in our lives, is about much more than the consumption of calories. If I were to have a conversation—that's harder, because there are so many interesting things to talk about. Marcus Aurelius, whom many consider to be the founder of the philosophical school of stoicism, which in turn has influenced some modern psychological treatments like cognitive behavior therapy, would be, I think a rather dull conversationalist but one worth listening to. Perhaps with Galileo Galilei, because he challenged the orthodox view and had the courage to persist in his convictions. In this category would fall many who carefully question current orthodoxy. But in the end, I think we have to recognize that philosophy and science really don't persist. New assumptions and speculations replace what we once accepted as scientific truth, new religions arise to take the place of older faiths. What remains as a constant is the urge to satisfy our senses and tell stories that describe our motives, emotions, and reactions in our everyday dealing with people around us and our environment, as well as an exploration of our connectedness to the mystical and divine. So ultimately, it is the voice of the poet that persists. Because of this, I'd begin at the beginning, and choose Homer as the ultimate dinner companion."

Dr. Sammons leads a busy life. He does, however, have hobbies. He told us he enjoys backpacking, skiing, and conservation. He is involved in professional activities outside his position in the military as well. At the time of this interview, he was serving as chairperson of the National Register of Health Service Providers in Psychology and as a member of both APA's Council of Representatives and its Policy and Planning Board.

Dr. Sammons' career includes not only the prescriptive authority component but also some of the public policy issues we discussed in chapter 13. His career illustrates the point that where you start may be quite different from where you go later in your career. Life events can have an impact you did not expect. His responses also support the importance of a broad undergraduate background for the future practice of psychology. Although he made frequent reference to the importance of evidence-based practice, which students may think implies taking nothing but statistics and research courses, he noted the importance of philosophy for background preparation.

Behavioral Health

Behavioral health psychology, health psychology, and behavioral prevention were also seen by BPA as becoming much more prominent by 2020. The growing recognition and quantification of mind–body interactivity will allow psychologists to become more seamlessly integrated into both healthcare and wellness activities. As a result of these changes, psychology is likely to find expanded services in a range of areas. For example, psychological counseling for patients diagnosed with breast, prostate, and other cancers may become standard practice rather than used only in specialized centers or individual cases.

The U.S. Department of Health and Human Services has pointed out that the seven top health risk factors—tobacco use, diet, alcohol, unintentional injuries, suicide, violence, and unsafe sex—are behavioral (Levant et al., 2001; VandenBos et al., 1991). Moreover, there is a significant psychological component in seven of the nine actual leading causes of death (McGinnis & Foege, 1993). Psychological interventions have been found to be useful in treating a broad range of physical health problems across the life span in a cost-effective manner (Friedman, Sobel, Myers, Caudill, & Benson, 1995).

An emerging area for psychologists trained in behavioral health is community health center practice (DeLeon, Giesting, & Kenkel, 2003). Community health centers are federally funded comprehensive primary healthcare facilities designed to provide services to communities and populations that are medically underserved. Among the services provided in these centers are mental health and substance abuse treatment. Psychologists may find themselves expanding their roles in these facilities because of their behavioral health training as well as their background in integrating cultural issues with treatment planning.

As psychologists continue to search for behavioral factors that have a positive impact on both physical and mental health, a growing area of investigation involves religion and religious involvement (George, Ellison, & Larson, 2002; Koenig, McCullough, & Larson, 2001). For example, researchers have reported that religious beliefs and spirituality have a positive impact on healthy behavior and survival among people with HIV/AIDS (Ironson et al., 2002) and improved psychological well-being among a small sample of Latinos with arthritis (Abraido-Lanza, Vasquez, & Echeverria, 2004). Further research will continue to evaluate the role of religion and spirituality not only on an individual level but also from the perspective of the family and the role of beliefs in that system. This family perspective on the impact of spirituality and disease progression with hemodialysis patients has already provided preliminary data from a sample of forty-eight African-American families who are being studied longitudinally (Holder et al., 1998). This study, dealing with people with a common physical problem and ethnic heritage combined with spirituality, illustrates the breadth of this research area. Although we introduced you to this area in chapter 14 when you read about the careers of Drs. Rozensky and Tucker, this specialty is predicted to expand considerably in the near future.

Assessment

Advances in diagnostic tools, functional imaging technology, simulations, and global databases will provide more reliable assessments for all aspects of health care. Assessments by psychologists are likely to be more authentic, integrated, and specialized with greater focus on intervention and remediation than on the diagnosis itself. Also, valid and reliable tools will become more available for people of color. As we noted earlier in this book, the changing demographics of the United States make this latter change of even greater importance than in the past.

Another growth area for assessment is the Internet. Use of the Internet is extremely common. More than half of all U.S. citizens have access to the Internet from their homes (U.S. Department of Commerce, 2002). Of course, many others have such access from their places of employment, libraries, and other public sites. A popular topic among Internet users is mental health. One recent report indicated that 23 percent of all U.S. Internet users have searched for information about mental health issues on the Internet (Naglieri et al., 2004). The Internet has also grown as a site for psychological testing, test development, and test research. Because of this growth, the APA Committee on Psychological Tests and Assessment (CPTA) recommended to its parent boards that they establish a task force to investigate issues that need to be addressed related to Internet testing. This task force was composed of psychologists who are active users of psychological tests, test developers, and researchers about tests. Among the issues this task force raised about Internet testing are test reliability and validity, test administration, security of test items, and confidentiality of test-takers' responses. From the perspective of state licensing boards, there is also a question of how this assessment process relates to state laws about who can administer which types of psychological test. To whom are complaints made when Internet assessment occurs—the regulatory body in the state where the tester resides or the state where the patient resides if these are different? These topics are among the assessment issues that will need to be addressed in the future.

Positive Psychology

A shift is slowly taking place in which measures of optimism, well-being, resilience, happiness, excellence, and optimal human functioning will become as meaningful and in demand as measures of distress and pathology. One definition of **positive psychology** is "the study of the conditions and processes that contribute to the flourishing or optimal functioning of people, groups, and institutions" (Gable & Haidt, 2005, p. 103). The field of positive psychology is about valued subjective experiences: well-being, contentment, and satisfaction related to the past; hope and optimism for the future; and flow and happiness in the present (Seligman & Csikszentmihalyi, 2000). At the personal level, positive psychology is about the capacity for love and vocation, courage, interpersonal skill, aesthetic sensibility, and other positive traits. At the group level, positive psychology centers around better citizenship, responsibility, tolerance, and other virtues. These measures will be used in health care to encourage healthy lifestyles and preclude disease states; in education, to help children focus on their strengths and achieve their individual potential; and in occupational settings, toward greater productivity, more desirable working environments, enhanced job satisfaction, and the resolution of conflicts.

According to Martin Seligman, one of the leaders of the positive psychology movement (Seligman & Csikszentmihalyi, 2000), psychology can show what actions lead to well-being, to positive individuals, and to thriving communities. Psychology should be able to document what kinds of families result in children who flourish, what work settings support the greatest satisfaction among workers, what policies result in the strongest civic engagement, and how people's lives can be most worth living. Early well-known endeavors in the positive psychology movement included Watson's work on effective parenting (Watson, 1928), Jung's work on the search for and discovery of meaning in life (Jung, 1933) and Terman's studies of giftedness (Terman, 1939).

As psychology has evolved, positive, proactive movements within the profession have emphasized areas such as prevention. Instead of focusing on how to relieve suffering and mental illness, research has begun to explore proactive areas such as prevention and physical health. How psychologists can prevent problems such as substance abuse and bullying and increase resilience are subjects coming to the forefront of our research. Notice the range of types of topics we are considering in this movement. Although psychology has a long history of work on the treatment of substance abuse, with some of it considered prevention research, our work on dealing with bullies and increasing our understanding of resilience is not as extensive.

In fact, research links positive emotional states to physical health (Salovey, Rothman, Detweiler, & Steward, 2000). Thus, we have an integration of two of our growth areas—positive psychology and behavioral health. This is really no surprise. As far back as Hippocrates, the father of clinical medicine, four bodily fluids (humors— blood, phlegm, yellow bile, and black bile) were proposed to affect health. According to Hippocrates, when these fluids became unbalanced, illness ensued. Similarly, ancient Chinese medical lore posits that when the energy that flows along the bodily meridians becomes blocked, illness is likely. The restoration of bodily energy using techniques like acupuncture and massage is vital for health according to this belief system.

Behaviorally, depressed individuals report somatic ailments in greater numbers than do nondepressed individuals (Katon, 1984). When health plans offer psychological services at parity with physical illnesses, the utilization of medical services is reduced (Cummings & Follette, 1976; Jones & Vischi, 1979).

Even Sigmund Freud recognized the importance of the healthcare provider's role in inspiring hope in others. Freud (1953) described the patient's expectancies, which, when "colored by hope and faith," are "an effective force . . . in all our attempts at treatment and cure" (p. 289).

The link between hopeful expectations and health outcomes becomes emphasized when we study the placebo effect. Placebos are pharmacologically inert substances given to patients in lieu of an active medication. The word *placebo* comes from the Latin, meaning "I will please"; by the nineteenth century, it was a medicine given "more to please than to benefit the patient," according to Shapiro (1997). A controversial meta-analysis found that the correlation between placebo effect and drug effect in antidepressants was 90 percent (Kirsch & Sapirstein, 1998).

Laughter is a positive emotion that is also currently being studied. For example, bereaved individuals who are able to laugh and smile when discussing their loss recover more completely over time than individuals who were unable to show these positive emotions (Bonnano & Keltner, 1997). Bonner and Keltner hypothesized that this positive emotional response helps to undo the effects of a negative emotion. Positive emotional responses have also been found to predict better mental health among young adult survivors of childhood sexual trauma (Bonanno, 2004). These studies, however, have only started to explore a very large area. As psychologists take greater roles in bereavement counseling and end-of-life decision-making, the role of positive emotional factors is likely to be a growing area of interest. Students who want to learn more about positive psychology can start with one of the books available on this subject (e.g., Aspinwall & Staudinger, 2003; Keyes & Haidt, 2003; Snyder & Lopez, 2002). A journal developed to further both research and good practice from this perspective, *The Journal of Positive Psychology,* published its first issue in 2006. This journal was designed to be multidisciplinary and encouraged authors from such specialties outside psychology as anthropology, medicine, neuroscience, and organizational sciences to submit their articles for review.

Diversity

The continuing evolution of societies into a global community and the subsequent change in demographics and geographical composition will make issues of diversity of fundamental importance. All aspects of psychology will be impacted, from concrete necessities such as the renorming of standard assessment tools to the basics in understanding health, pathology, and human development from multifaceted perspectives. We have already addressed this topic in several chapters of the book. We believe, however, that issues of diversity will continue to be central to the profession in the near future. Also, the topic of diversity will be viewed in a broader way. For many people, this term seems reserved for cultural and ethnic factors. As psychologists use this term, it refers not only to those factors but also to age, lifestyle choices, and physical condition, to name just a few. Thus, future psychologists will think more broadly about these topics and perhaps even be trained in a different way than they have been in the past.

Technology

Varied, global options for wireless and multimedia telecommunications will vastly increase opportunities for distributed learning and remote health care (Jerome et al., 2000; Koocher & Morray, 2000; Newman, 1998; Nickelson, 1996, 1998). Ubiquitous computing and portability such as voice recognition and embedded technologies will facilitate these changes, allowing psychologists to expand services in health care and education. Three-dimensional, virtual reality simulation environments will make possible new opportunities for training, entertainment, and interventions. We described some of these techniques related to psychotherapy in chapter 11. We believe this is a major growth area and propose additional uses for the future.

Psychologists will need to develop new ways of conceptualizing their role as well as to evaluate these new approaches. For example, Strom and his colleagues developed and evaluated an Internet-based treatment program for patients with insomnia (Strom, Pettersson, & Andersson, 2004). This study provides a model for the type of research that is likely to increase as a result of improved access to technology as well as an indication of some of the problems than can arise in this area of investigation. Students who are interested in Internet service provision might start with this study as a way to consider other potential applications. Along with these advances in telecommunications and technological enhancements will come a bewildering array of ethical challenges and practical safeguards for both patients and clinicians (Reed, McLaughlin, & Milholland, 2000).

Lifespan Psychology

Advances in gene therapy, nanotechnology, robotics, imaging, and biosensors will allow people to live longer and healthier lives. As the lifespan lengthens, our understanding of lifespan development must accommodate the changes. How we perceive our families, friendships, education, work, and play will be impacted by these changes. These changes will also impact how we practice clinical psychology and with whom. This topic is broader than the geropsychology specialty we described in chapter 15. Students of clinical psychology will need to have a solid foundation in developmental psychology theory to apply to these changes in their world.

Sample Resources

As we look toward the future, clinical psychologists will continue to develop materials to assist those practitioners who are already in the field. These tools provide information about emerging practice areas as well as information about training needed to enter these areas of practice. Many of the professional groups we described in chapter 2 provide these materials. Because this is an ongoing process that often changes, we will not discuss this topic in great detail here. One example of this type of assistance is APA Division 42, the Division of Psychologists in Independent Practice. Division 42 has developed a series of niche guides, such as *Psychologist-Dentist Collaboration* (Barnett & Rodino, 2000), *Psycho-oncology* (Haber, 1999), *Infertility* (Kolt, 1999), *Consulting with Business on Workplace Behavior* (Gindes, 1999), *Assisting Clients with End-of-Life Decisions* (Werth, 2002), and *Sport Psychology* (Hays, 1995), to name a few. The Division 42 website (www.division42.org) is a valuable resource for aspiring and established clinicians.

Closing Comments

We hope you have enjoyed your trip through our view of clinical psychology. Because this is such a large topic, we were selective about what we presented. If you have now decided to seek more information about any of the topics we have raised, we have reached our goal.

Key Terms

behavioral health psychology	cultural sensitivity	multicultural responsibility	prescriptive authority
cultural awareness	disaster mental health	positive psychology	pro bono
cultural competence	executive coaching		trauma

Glossary

A-B-A-B: a research design in which the patient serves as his or her own control; progresses from baseline to intervention to removal of intervention and then return to it

accommodation: alteration of testing procedure or apparatus because of a patient's specific disability

Achenbach System of Empirically Based Assessment (ASEBA): behavioral assessment checklist with separate forms for children and adolescents

achievement tests: tests designed to measure amount of learning of specific content domains, especially those associated with formal education

Ackerman, Nathan: child psychiatrist who was one of the early leaders in the development of a specialty of family diagnosis and treatment

Activating Event: in Rational-Emotive Therapy: what most people associate with what causes their distress

active listening: clinical skill that includes a combination of hearing what the patient says and communicating that the patient is not being judged for anything said

adjunctive marital therapy: couples therapy designed to improve the relationship by treating only one of the partners

advocacy: speaking for another person or group in an attempt to try to change someone's opinion or gain support, often used in the context of politics and obtaining funds for particular services

affect: the conscious experience of an emotion experienced by a person and viewed by others

allegiance effect: a researcher's therapeutic preference

alternate-form (parallel form) reliability: the form of determining the consistency of test results by administering alternate forms of a test to a heterogeneous representative sample and then correlating the scores

anal stage of psychosexual development: Freud's second developmental period in which the focus of pleasure and potential for conflict is centered on the anus

analog study: a study conducted in a laboratory or controlled setting that is believed to be "analogous to" the clinical situation of interest

anima/animus: Jungian archetypes indicating bisexual nature of humanity; anima is the feminine archetype for men and animus is the masculine archetype for women

apperception: perceiving something in the present based on past perceptions

aptitude tests: tests designed to measure the person's ability to learn rather than current knowledge about a particular subject

archetypes: Jungian term for universal thought types resulting from the common evolutionary history of humanity; a hereditary predisposition to respond to the world in a certain way

art therapy: therapeutic technique using a combination of verbalization and various forms of art media as a means to help patients express emotional issues

assessment: term sometimes used as a synonym for psychological testing

association techniques: projective personality tests for which the task is to say what the stimulus suggests to the person

automatic thoughts: in Beck's cognitive therapy, habitual dysfunctional thoughts that occur rapidly, and automatically, often without much awareness

bariatric medicine: that branch of medicine that deals with issues related to obesity

base rates: the extent to which a particular variable, such as a personality trait, occurs in the population from which the patient comes

BASIC-ID: Arnold Lazarus' term describing the seven modalities comprising the human personality: behavior, affect, sensation, imagery, cognition, interpersonal processes, and drugs/biology

Bayley Scales of Infant Development: developmental scale, used with children from one month to three and one-half years of age; includes Motor Scale, Mental Scale, and Behavior Rating Scale

Beck Depression Inventory II (BDI-II): self-report twenty-one-item inventory of symptoms of depression utilizing a list of four statements arranged in increasing order of severity to evaluate each symptom

behavioral health psychology: use of psychological data and interventions to address health risk behaviors across the lifespan

behavioral observation: method of behavioral assessment in which a clearly defined problem is evaluated in the setting/s in which it occurs

Bender Visual-Motor Gestalt Test: test of complex visual processing often used as part of a neuropsychological screening; nine geometric designs presented on individual cards usually as a copying task

bibliotherapy: a form of psychotherapy in which selected reading materials are used to assist a person in solving personal problems or for other therapeutic purposes

biophysical theories: definitions of personality that focus on internal factors as being the most important ones for understanding people

Boston Process Approach: flexible neuropsychological battery with the number of tests varying depending on patient response

Boulder model: also known as scientist-practitioner model; training model for practicing psychologists that strives to integrate the role of scientist and practitioner

boundary permeability: term from family therapy; refers to the kind of contact various family members have with each other; some have rigid boundaries, while others who are enmeshed have highly permeable ones

Bowen, Murray: early family therapist; tended to work with the parents so they could then interact more appropriately with their families

brief psychotherapy: intervention using a planned approach intended to be completed in a specified period of time; often problem focused

burnout: a reaction to job stress in which the professional is no longer as productive and may elect to leave the profession

California Verbal Learning Test (CVLT-2): list learning test that measures such factors as immediate memory span, learning curve, and the effects of retroactive and proactive interference

catharsis: the release of pent-up psychic energy; the release of emotion following expression of an unconscious conflict; one of the goals of Freudian psychoanalysis

clinical child psychology: applied specialty centered on the assessment and treatment of children and adolescents with symptoms of psychopathology

clinical forensic psychology: the assessment and/or treatment of people who are involved in the legal process or legal system in some way

clinical geropsychology: applied specialty focusing on the needs of individuals in later life and their families

clinical health psychology: psychological specialty addressing the promotion and maintenance of health, components of disease, and rehabilitation

clinical neuropsychology: psychological specialty focused on the application of assessment and intervention principles to normal and abnormal functioning of the central nervous system

clinical psychology: specialty within psychology that integrates science, theory, and practice and applies results to a range of human areas of distress

clinical significance: the "real-life" impact of an intervention; often contrasted to statistical significance, meaning a mathematical difference between groups

closed panel: health maintenance organization (HMO) model in which patients were assigned to providers rather than choosing one

closed therapy group: type of group therapy in which no new members are added after the group is formed regardless of attrition

collaborative family therapy: each member of the family sees a different therapist and therapists coordinate with each other

collective unconscious: Jung's term for the part of the psyche containing instincts and archetypes resulting from evolutionary history of the species that lead to predispositions to interpret our world selectively

commisurotomy: surgical procedure in which the left and right hemispheres of the brain are separated by cutting a thick bundle of fibers that form a bridge between the left and right hemispheres

comorbidity: the occurrence of more than one disorder at the same time in a given person

competence: a person's ability to handle expected developmental tasks that change with age, historical time, and culture

completion techniques: psychological tests in which the task is for the person to complete a process started by the test stimuli

component analysis: use of specific parts of a test for understanding specific subsets of the construct measured by that test

concurrent family therapy: each member of the family sees the same therapist but in individual rather than group sessions

concurrent validity: a form of criterion-related validity that is obtained at the same time as the test scores with which it is compared

congruence: psychotherapist characteristic generally synonymous with "genuineness"; one of Rogers' three basic therapist characteristics

congruent communicators: term used by family therapists to refer to people who are open and genuine in their interpersonal interactions

conjoint family therapy: form of family therapy in which one therapist (or cotherapists) meet with whole family at same time

construct validity: the measure of test validity referring to the extent to which test results correlate with the quality or trait the test is supposed to measure

construction techniques: psychological tests, often personality measures, in which the test stimuli are used by the person to produce material

content validity: the measure of test validity referring to the degree to which the test or its items are found to be representative of the characteristics of the quality or trait the test is supposed to measure

Corrective Emotional Experience: a reenactment in therapy of emotional situations from a child's life, but with different consequences to the child's responses

cost-effectiveness: economical in terms of goods or services received for the money spent

counseling: term used interchangeably with "psychotherapy" by some authors; others suggest that counseling implies a developmental process rather than remediation

counseling psychology: psychology specialty often associated with less severe forms of psychopathology than those seen by those practicing clinical psychology, often including such areas as career issues and marital problems

countertransference: the emotional reactions of a therapist toward a patient; interpreted by Freud as representing feelings the therapist had for significant others earlier in the patient's life

couples therapy: psychotherapy provided simultaneously to two individuals who are in a committed relationship

criterion-related validity: the measure of test validity referring to the degree to which a test is successful in predicting performance on an outcome measure

crystallized intelligence: that part of our intelligence that is believed to be the result of accumulated knowledge; term associated with Cattell's two-factor theory of intelligence

cultural awareness: the understanding of differences among and between cultures

cultural competence: the possession of skills and knowledge necessary to work with individuals from different cultures in a manner congruent with their values

cultural sensitivity: this is considered to be a step further than cultural awareness; the ability to refrain from attributing either positive or negative values to the differences that may exist between or among cultures

culture: a way of life that is transmitted from one generation to another within an identified segment of the population

culture-fair: in psychological assessment this term refers to a procedure or instrument designed to minimize the influence of culture on the evaluation process

culture-free: term used to describe tests developed with special sensitivity to issues of cultural bias

curative factors in group therapy: term associated with the work of psychiatrist Irving Yalom to refer to the primary ways this form of therapy works

Daubert: 1993 United States Supreme Court ruling in the case of *Daubert v. Merrell Dow Pharmaceuticals* giving judges the responsibility to determine whether an expert witness has used scientific reasoning in reaching conclusions

Dementia Rating Scale (DRS-2): screening test used to measure the mental status of adults with cognitive impairment

determinants: the qualities of a blot used by the patient in making a response to the Rorschach considered to be representative of the cognitive processes used in formulating that response

diagnosis: clinical activity involving the classification of behavior based on an accepted system, such as the DSM-IV, as part of the treatment process

Diagnostic and Statistical Manual of Mental Disorders, fourth edition (DSM-IV): published by the American Psychiatric Association, a classification system for emotional problems; most commonly used system in the United States

Differential Ability Scales (DAS): three separate batteries for children and adolescents used to measure intelligence

differentiation of self: a person's ability to understand which processes are intellectual and which ones are emotional

disaster mental health: specialty designed to provide mental health services to both victims of disaster and the first responders who may be affected by what they experience helping those victims

doctor of philosophy (Ph.D.): one potential degree possessed by a clinical psychologist; this degree typically requires at least five years of postbaccalaureate study including the production of a research dissertation and the completion of a twelve-month internship in an applied setting; traditional research degree

doctor of psychology (Psy.D.): one potential degree possessed by a clinical psychologist; this degree typically requires at least five years of postbaccalaureate study including the production of a publishable-quality clinical paper and the completion of a twelve-month internship in an applied setting; newer than Ph.D.

double-blind experiment: experiment in which neither the experimenter nor the subject is aware of the condition in which the subject is participating

dream analysis: a Freudian technique used for diagnosing a patient's mental state by studying his or her dreams to unmask the unconscious; also called oneiroscopy

eclectic (integrative) psychotherapy: approach to psychological intervention involving a combination of theory and techniques from a variety of approaches

ectomorph: Sheldon's basic body type referring to a thin person with fine hair and sensitive nervous system correlated with personality characteristics of inhibition and predominance of intellect over activity

effectiveness research: field research using actual patients to investigate the outcome of clinical intervention

efficacy research: random assignment of patients to treatment groups, including control groups, to evaluate intervention methods

ego: term used by many personality theorists usually to refer to that aspect of the personality that helps the person deal with the real world

ego ideal: Freudian term for the part of the superego that is learned from being rewarded for certain behaviors and later allows us to be pleased about our own behavior

emotional cutoff: term used by some family therapists to refer to children who emotionally distance themselves from their families as a way to deal with overinvolvement in family problems

empathy: understanding on an affective level the thoughts, feelings, and emotions of another person from that person's point of view; the ability to enter another person's psychological world without being influenced by that world

empirically supported treatments (EST): those methods of intervention that have been evaluated using controlled research conducted with a specific patient group

endomorph: Sheldon's body type referring to a person who is predominantly soft and round and correlated with personality characteristics of sociability and easy communication of feelings

epidemiological studies: research about the rate and distribution of specified forms of psychopathology in a named population or sample of a population

e-therapy: Internet-based psychotherapy

ethnicity: a group of shared characteristics such as country of origin of one's family, language, and culture

executive coaching: growth area of psychology in which clinical skills are applied to the needs of individuals in leadership positions to facilitate their work efficiency

expressive therapies: general term encompassing those forms of psychotherapy that make use of the creative arts as a central point of their procedures

face validity: how well the surface content matches with the stated purpose of the test

faking good/faking bad: an underreporting (good) or overreporting (bad) of symptoms in an attempt to look different than one actually feels

false negative: occurs when the outcome of testing suggests the person does not have a characteristic the person actually has

false positive: occurs when the outcome of testing suggests the person has a characteristic the person does not have

familismo: tradition central in many Hispanic/Latino cultures of emphasizing the needs of the family above individual needs

family life chronology: term used by Virginia Satir to describe process of having each family member describe self-views, view of each other, and view of family activities

family mapping: procedure used by structural family therapists to diagram the ways a family is currently interacting

Family Problem-Solving Task (FPST): behavioral procedure to assess family interaction patterns when one member of the family meets the DSM criteria for a diagnosis of schizophrenia, schizoaffective disorder, or schizophreniform disorder

family projection process: Murray Bowen's term for parents projecting their stress onto their children

family systems theorist: general term used to describe a therapist who conceptualizes the family as a system rather than as component parts

family therapy: intervention with multiple members of a family group with one often viewed as the "identified" patient; communication is often viewed as a core problem

feminist therapy: emphasizing giving the patient more power by reducing the power differential between therapist and client and empowering the client

fixation: term often associated with psychodynamic theories of personality referring to a person who continues to grow physically and intellectually but is emotionally stuck at a prior developmental period

fixed batteries: use of a standardized group of tests administered in a standardized manner to evaluate specific types of problems; often associated with neuropsychological evaluations

flexible batteries: selection of specific tests for an individual patient to best answer questions being asked with results of one test suggesting the next one to use

fluid intelligence: the genetically based part of our intelligence in Cattell's two-factor theory, said to include speed, flexibility, skill in acquiring new information and the ability to understand relationships and abstractions

form quality: Rorschach scoring term referring to the degree to which the percept provided by the patient actually fits the space on the inkblot

free association: a Freudian psychotherapeutic technique where the patient lies on a couch and says anything that comes to mind making no effort to censor or inhibit their speech; assumed to give insight into the unconscious

Frye rule: resulted from case of *Frye v. United States* in 1932; used to qualify expert witnesses; places more emphasis on the professional community than on the judge in determining whether or not testimony will be admitted in court

fully functioning person: Rogers' term for people who are growing in a healthy way; demonstrate the basic characteristics in common of openness to experience, existential living, organismic trust, and creativity; and lead rich lives

functional analysis of behavior: foundation of behavioral assessment process often credited to Skinner; refers to determining the antecedents and consequences of an identified behavior

game: in Berne's Transactional Analysis: a complex series of ulterior transactions that progress to a psychological payoff—a feeling such as guilt, depression, or anger

gatekeeper: term associated with HMOs referring to the use of a general physician to determine whether or not a patient needs a referral to a specialist

genital stage of psychosexual development: Freud's final stage of development starting with the onset of puberty when people learn to put the needs of others ahead of their own needs, develop sexual identity, and start to form relationships leading to pairing and procreation

genogram: a diagram depicting interrelationships within a family system; used as part of some forms of family therapy as part of understanding family dynamics

Global Assessment of Function (GAF): Axis V of the DSM-IV classification system; a single summary score on a 100-point scale indicating the psychologist's evaluation of the patient's current overall level of functioning in occupational, psychological, and social areas

Graduate Record Examination (GRE): test frequently required for admission to doctoral programs in clinical psychology; developed by Educational Testing Service (www.gre.org); includes both general aptitude section and an advanced test in psychology

group therapy: term referring to a broad range of techniques for the simultaneous provision of psychotherapy to a number of people

guidelines: description of aspirational behaviors in clinical practice; often contrasted to standards

Halstead-Reitan Neuropsychological Battery (HRNB): fixed battery for neuropsychological assessment used with people age fifteen or older; originally developed by Ward Halstead and expanded by Ralph Reitan

Health Insurance Portability and Accountability Act (HIPAA): promulgated by the U.S. Department of Health and Human Services; provides rules about patient record-keeping

health maintenance organization (HMO): approach to health insurance initiated by 1973 Health Maintenance Organization Act to help control cost of insurance

heterogeneous therapy group: therapy group that includes members with diverse characteristics such as age, diagnosis, or educational level

homogeneous therapy group: therapy group composed of individuals who are similar on relevant characteristics such as age, diagnosis, or educational level

humors: Hippocrates' basic body fluids of blood, phlegm, black bile, and yellow bile; imbalance among humors was correlated with various temperaments

id: in Freudian theory that part of the personality that is present at birth and reacts based on the pleasure principle

idiographic approach: research method utilizing an in-depth case study of one person to understand some specific subject, such as personality

incongruent emotions: an emotion that doesn't fit with the message that is being sent: a significant difference between the emotions the patient feels and the patient's self-view of what emotions should be felt in that situation

indicated prevention: term used in the prevention literature to describe programs designed to alleviate a current problem but also including a strong relapse prevention component

inquiry: phase 2 of many systems of Rorschach administration in which the patient explains where the percept was seen and what blot characteristics were used

intake: clinical interview designed to determine why the individual has contacted the particular provider, whether or not the provider can meet the person's needs, and to explain relevant provider policies and procedures

intelligence: no commonly accepted definition; usually refers to the ability to do certain tasks rather than to knowledge of specific information

insight: in Freudian theory: bringing unconscious, troubling material to consciousness; self-understanding

International Classification of Functionality (ICF): diagnostic system developed by the World Health Organization (WHO) focused on what is needed to allow person to fully function

interpretation: Freud: The therapists referring to something the patient has said or done in such a way as to identify features of the behavior of which the patient had not been fully aware

intervention: term used to refer to the broad range of methods used by clinical psychologists to attempt to alter problematic behavior

invasive procedures: term associated with medical procedures involving the introduction of an outside element, such as a dye prior to a scanning procedure into the body as part of the assessment process; often used to contrast neurological and neuropsychological assessment procedures

Jacobson, Neil: a pioneer in the behavioral approach to couples therapy who developed Integrative Couple Therapy

Kaufman Brief Intelligence Scale (K-BIT): developed by Alan and Nadeen Kaufman as a brief measure of both crystallized and fluid intelligence

latency stage of psychosexual development: in Freudian theory the developmental period between the phallic and genital stages of psychosexual development when the child learns social and cognitive skills needed to function in society

latent content: dream representation of the unconscious motives of a person

Leiter International Performance Scale-Revised: a nonlanguage test of intelligence designed for children and adolescents whose English language speaking skills are weak

libido: term used in many personality theories; according to Freud it is the energy that drives the personality

life review: the process of evaluating one's contributions over a lifespan; may include a written summary of things of which the person is proud and their impact of their life choices

Luria-Nebraska Neuropsychological Battery (LNNB): fixed battery for neuropsychological assessment used with people age fifteen and older; developed by Charles Golden and his colleagues; separate children's version for ages eight to twelve

making the rounds: in Perl's Gestalt therapy: when one member of a group becomes the focus of the activity

malingering: refers to faking one's psychological state when taking a psychological test or participating in psychotherapy, usually for personal gain

managed care organization (MCO): grew out of HMO movement to help insurance companies to carve out benefits

manifest content: what the patient actually reports in a dream

Masters, William, and Johnson, Virginia: pioneers in modern sex therapy for sexual dysfunctions whose work focused on education about sexual functioning and improved couple communication

mesomorph: Sheldon's body type of well-developed muscles and upright posture correlated with personality characteristics of high activity and assertiveness

meta-analysis: a statistical technique that combines data from many studies as a way to increase sample size and better evaluate statistical significance

metacognition: thinking about thinking

Millon Multiaxial Clinical Inventory (MCMI): 175-item true-false personality inventory based on Theodore Millon's biopsychosocial theory of personality

Mini-Mental State Examination (MMSE): brief quantitative measure of cognitive status in adults

Minnesota Multiphasic Personality Inventory (MMPI): second edition released in 1989; 567-item true-false personality test used with adults

Minuchin, Salvador: developer of structural family therapy

mood: an enduring period of a specified emotion

multicultural responsibility: a fusion of personal and professional commitment to consider culture as part of one's clinical work

multigenerational transmission process: Bowen's term in family therapy referring to the concept that family problems are transmitted through more than one generation and therefore learning about previous generations is necessary to understand family pathology

music therapy: the combination of a range of music modalities with psychological and/or biological forms of intervention to attain therapeutic goals with patients of all ages

need: according to Murray this refers to the internal factors that motivate a person

NEO Personality Inventory-Revised (NEO PI-R): personality inventory based on Costa and McCrae's five-factor model of personality

network: an informal link between/among psychologists with similar interests

neuropsychological assessment: specialized form of psychological assessment designed to evaluate brain functioning across the lifespan; most often used if there are questions of neurological insult

nomothetic approach: research approach designed to develop general laws or principles of behavior by studying large samples

normalizing: the process of helping the patient realize that the situation is not hopeless and that you can help

nuclear family emotional systems: Murray Bowen's concept that people tend to seek partners whose level of differentiation is similar to their own

objective personality tests: personality tests in which the person selects from among provided responses rather than generating unique responses

Oedipus complex: Freudian term for the feeling experienced by boys during the phallic stage of psychosexual development when they develop possessive love toward their mother and resentment of their father

Older Boulder: term used to refer to the 1981 Conference on Training Psychologists for Work in Aging held in Boulder, Colorado, the site of the original scientist-practitioner training conference

open panels: approach to managed health care in which providers are not employees of the HMOs

open therapy group: therapy group that maintains its size by adding new members as members leave the group

oral stage of psychosexual development: Freud's first stage, starting at birth, in which the focus of pleasure and potential for distress is the mouth

organic dysfunction: general term used to refer to abnormal behavior that is assumed to have a biological, or organic, basis

paraphrasing: skill used clinical psychologists whereby they restate what they have heard the patient say using different words and then check to determine the accuracy of their perceptions

parapraxis: a Freudian slip, using one word while actually meaning to use a word with a very different meaning

pathognomic signs: specific deficits on psychological test performance that are rarely seen in people who are not impaired

pattern of responding: method of analyzing certain test performance utilizing the relationship among test or subtest scores to understand patient behavior and problems

Peabody Picture Vocabulary Test (PPVT): test of receptive vocabulary used with people from two and one-half through ninety years old

pediatric psychology: psychological specialty in which psychologists work with children and adolescents who have psychological problems associated with their medical problems; treatments are often short-term and integrated with the work of a pediatrician

penis envy: Freudian term for females' realization that they do not have a penis, leading to resentment of the mother for this lack, masturbation, and a desire to share their father's penis; occurs during phallic stage of psychosexual development

percept: term associated with projective tests of personality, especially the Rorschach; refers to each individual response by the patient to the test stimuli

person-centered psychotherapy: a name for Carl Roger's therapy, also called nondirective therapy and client-centered therapy: goals of therapy are set by the patient rather than the therapist

persona: Jungian term for archetype of mask or façade worn in public, or public personality

personal unconscious: Jungian term for the part of the personality composed of thoughts and feelings of which we are not currently aware but can be brought to consciousness under the right circumstances

personality: derived from Greek *persona*, referring to masks worn by early Roman actors in Greek dramas that were intended to indicate major characteristics of the individual; general term referring to those characteristics unique to an individual

Personality Inventory for Children (PIC): objective measure of children's personality based on parent/guardian responses to true-false items

personality tests: assessment tools designed to measure a range of characteristics such as traits or qualities that illustrate an individual's distinctiveness; often subdivided into objective and projective types

phallic stage of psychosexual development: Freud's third stage in which the focus of both pleasure and potential conflict is the genitals; stage in which the child develops attachment to opposite-sex parent

phenomenal field: also known as field of experience; term used by Rogers and others to refer to our internal definition of reality based on the uniqueness of one's history

phrenology: technique developed by Gall and Spurzheim to study personality based on the "bumps" and "dents" on a person's head as indications of excess or lack of certain characteristics

placater: term used by family therapists to refer to those family members who respond to others in a weak and tentative way

play therapy: a psychotherapeutic technique that uses play as a modality to help a child deal with problems or conflicts

pleasure principle: Freudian term for governing process of the id in which fantasy is not distinguished from reality and the object is to satisfy needs and wishes immediately

point of service (POS): an HMO option allowing patients to select their own provider, regardless of whether or not that provider was part of the organization

policy research: studies designed to generate empirical data about social issues of interest to the profession of psychology

positive psychology: movement within psychology emphasizing measures of optimism, well-being, resilience, and health in contrast to a focus on distress and illness

practica: supervised clinical field experiences occurring prior to the required yearlong predoctoral internship in clinical psychology

precertification: term associated with health insurance when the insurance company decides in advance of service provision how much it will cover, such as number of days of hospitalization allowed

predictive validity: the form of criterion-related validity using scores obtained in the future and comparing them to scores on the test being evaluated

pregenital stages of psychosexual development: collective term for Freud's first three stages of psychosexual development in which the person's sexual needs are gratified from stimulation of one's own body

prescriptive authority: the right of members of a specified profession to provide medication for individuals in their care

press: term used by Henry A. Murray to refer to relevant environmental influences on behavior

primary listening skills: general term for skills used by the psychologist to become more aware of the patient's true self; sometimes called a phenomenological understanding of the patient

primary prevention: attempting to change conditions that have the potential to lead to problems before those problems actually arise; often associated with community psychology

pro bono: free of charge; term used in clinical practice to refer to the provision of clinical services without charge to those who cannot afford to pay for them as a form of service to the community

process notes: therapy notes from the perspective of the psychologist's impression of what happened in the session rather than the actual content

progress notes: therapy notes from the perspective of describing how the patient is changing on factors relevant to the reason for treatment

projective hypothesis: basis of projective personality tests; people place structure on unstructured stimuli consistent with their personal pattern of conscious and unconscious processes

projective tests: tests of personality often contrasted with "objective tests"; ambiguous test stimuli are presented to the patient, who is hypothesized to interpret them based on his or her pathology, thus "projecting" personal issues onto these stimuli

protection: community intervention term for personal and environmental factors that help a person cope with stress and function successfully in the environment

protocol validity: validity of an individual's scores; can be influenced by both non-content-based invalid responding and content-based invalid responding

Psychoanalysis: Freudian Insight oriented psychotherapy

psychodrama: specialized form of group therapy developed by Jacob L. Moreno combining concepts of psychotherapy and acting

psychopharmacology: the development and use of psychoactive or psychotropic drugs that ameliorate the symptoms of psychological or psychiatric disorders

psychophysiology: term used to indicate that some of our physical changes are the result of our behavioral or emotional responses to our environment

psychosexual development: term associated with Freud and other psychodynamic theorists emphasizing the central role of sexuality in the developmental process

psychotherapy: trained professionals systematically applying principles derived from psychological theory and research to help troubled people become more functional

psychotherapy integration: the combination of aspects of both theory and techniques from various approaches to psychotherapy in order to better meet the needs of a specific patient

public policy: policy at the community or governmental levels that provides the foundation for making decisions about what resources are allocated and where they are used within the community

QUOID: abbreviation for the undesirable psychotherapy patient who is quiet, ugly, old, institutionalized, and different culturally

race: selected physical characteristics, such as skin color or eye shape, used to group members of various ethnic or cultural groups under a single title

rapport: the comfortable working relationship between the psychologist and the patient

reality principle: guiding rule of Freud's ego utilizing the limitations of the real world when seeking to gratify personal needs

reconstructive psychotherapy: in Wolberg's description of psychotherapy forms this type refers to psychotherapy in which a major goal is for the patient to develop insight into unconscious conflicts that are viewed as underlying the distress

reeducative psychotherapy: in Wolberg's description of psychotherapy forms this type refers to psychotherapy in which the emphasis is on basically observable behavior

reflection: an attempt by the therapist to acknowledge an important feeling expressed by the patient

reliability: term used in psychological assessment to refer to the consistency of test scores across time, across forms, and within a given test

resilience: characteristics of the person associated with the patient's ability to overcome stresses and obtain a positive outcome from psychotherapy; the ability to demonstrate competence when one has been faced with significant adversity

Rey Complex Figures Test: neuropsychological test designed to assess visuospatial memory ability

risk: psychological term for those features of individuals and environments that decrease a person's biological, psychological, and/or social ability to function adaptively in his or her world

Rorschach: a projective test of personality developed by Dr. Hermann Rorschach using ten bilaterally symmetrical standard blots

sandwich generation: people who are expected to meet the needs of both their parents and their children; although originally used to refer to middle-age individuals, currently this term also refers to older adults who have older parents, adult children, and grandchildren depending on them

Satir, Virginia: pioneer in the development of conjoint family therapy

schedule of reinforcement: term associated with learning theories; denotes when a person is to be rewarded and may be based on passage of time or number of responses

screening batteries: the use of shortened versions of standard tests or preliminary tests to determine whether more extensive assessment procedures are needed; term often associated with neuropsychological assessment in which a combination of short evaluation measures has been normed for the purpose of determining whether a full battery is needed

secondary listening skills: those techniques that facilitate communication but are not directly intended to obtain information

secondary prevention: treatment focus in which attempts are made to alter maladaptive behaviors or conditions when they are in their early stages rather than waiting until a full-blown problem has developed

selective prevention: programs that are designed for groups of people who appear to be at greater risk of developing a target problem than are members of the general population

self-esteem: the way people feel about themselves

self-monitoring: behavioral assessment procedure; especially useful when the patient is functional and the behavior of interest is internal and/or infrequent; the patient keeps a record of his or her own behavior of interest

shadow: Jungian archetype representing our animal instincts, the shameful desires we have but do not like to admit exist

short form: an abbreviated version of a test, separately evaluated for reliability and validity that is often used as a screening assessment

sibling position: birth order

social work: mental health profession traditionally associated with provision of community services but currently includes full range of services; entry level at master's-degree level, although doctoral programs now exist

societal regression: term used by Murray Bowen to indicate situation where societal leaders make decisions based on emotion rather than on intellectual comprehension of the issues

Socratic questioning: a Cognitive therapy technique which refers to asking leading questions that guide a patient to a conclusion the therapist wishes them to make

SORC model: behavioral assessment model developed by Kanfer and Phillips; "S" refers to stimulus conditions preceding behavior of interest, "O" refers to relevant organismic variables, "R" refers to the person's response to both "S" and "O", and "C" refers to the consequences of the response

split-half reliability: the form of test reliability in which scores on two equal parts of the test are correlated to determine test consistency

sport psychology: a science in which the principles of psychology are applied in a sport or exercise setting

standard of care: the usual and customary practice

standard error of the measurement: refers to the variability of a person's scores on comparable forms of a test

standards: term used by psychologists to refer to behaviors that are considered mandatory and for which failure to behave in that way can result in malpractice actions

Stanford-Binet: Lewis Terman's translation/adaptation of Binet's original measures of cognitive ability

structural family therapy: family therapy developed by Salvador Minuchin focusing on boundaries among family members

structuring: the process by which the psychologist explains to the patient what to expect from therapy

superego: that part of the personality structure that incorporates the norms and standards of society; in Freudian theory it is subdivided into the conscience and ego ideal and operates based on the morality principle

supportive psychotherapy: term associated with Wolberg's model based on goals of psychotherapy; the major goal is preventing the patient's symptoms from getting worse

synchrony: the correlation of two variables that do not seem to be related, such as increasing therapist speaking time leading to increased speaking time by patients and decreasing speaking time leading to decreased patient speech

systematic desensitization: the therapeutic approach to treating fears and phobias that emphasizes the incompatibility of anxiety and relaxation at the same time. Includes developing a fear hierarchy and systematic exposure to imagined, feared events while maintaining a relaxed state

telepsychotherapy: psychotherapy provided via the Internet; can be synchronous (real time) or asynchronous (delayed time)

Tell-Me-A-Story-Test (TEMAS): projective personality test designed for use with urban Hispanic children

termination: the agreement between patient and therapist that treatment will end at some agreed upon point

tertiary prevention: traditional intervention approach in which attempts are made to reduce or eliminate the impairment that occurs as a result of some illness or problem

test anxiety: general term describing any combination of behavioral, physiological, and phenomenological reactions a person may experience related to concerns about possible failure in a testing situation

test bias: refers to differential validity of test scores for various subgroups with whom it is used; often associated with differential test scores for women and people of color on certain psychological tests

test fairness: term used in psychological assessment to refer to the degree to which the outcome of using scores on a particular test leads to equal social consequences for all subgroups

test-retest reliability: evaluation of consistency of test scores by administering the same test twice to a heterogeneous representative sample and then correlating the two scores

thema: term in Murray's system of personality referring to the interaction of needs and presses

Thematic Apperception Test (TAT): projective test of personality using a storytelling process; test stimuli are thirty-one standard black-and-white pictures

therapeutic alliance: a general term referring to both the quality and the strength of the collaborative relationship that exists between a therapist and a patient

thriving: term used to describe people who continue to grow and develop when faced with negative life situations

token economy: the rewarding of specific behaviors, usually in institutionalized patients, by way of tokens or other rewards in response to an acceptable behavior

top dog-underdog: in Gestalt therapy: when parts of the personality have conversations with each other and the patient plays both parts; similar to Superego in Freudian psychotherapy

Trails A & B: the two parts of the Trail Making Test, a neuropsychological test that is considered a measure of visual-conceptual ability and visual-motor tracking

transactional analysis: a variant of Freudian therapy, introduced by Eric Berne, which describes personality theory in terms of child, parent, and adult; and considers neurosis as maladaptive games

transference: a major component of psychoanalysis; description of the process of a patient reacting to the therapist "as if" the therapist were an important person from the patient's past

trauma: exposure to an extreme stressor; usually involves a threat to one's life or the life of a significant person in the individual's life, such as natural disasters, war, and rape

treatment goals: the desired outcome of therapy

treatment manual: term associated with empirically supported treatments; refers to a precise description of the procedure to be used for intervention so that each therapist approaches the process in the same way

treatment plans: an overview of what the therapist hopes to accomplish with the patient

triangulation: term used by family therapists to refer to a technique for dealing with tension in which a third person is brought into a stressful interpersonal interaction to level the tension

trichotillomania: hair-pulling to the point of baldness

unconditional positive regard: term associated with Carl Rogers' person-centered psychotherapy; therapist characteristic involving the ability to refrain from judging the positive or negative characteristics of the patient while also communicating that this does not mean the therapist agrees with all of the patient's behaviors

universal prevention: similar to primary prevention; refers to programs designed to decrease the rate of new cases of a problem within a specified population

validity: the degree to which a test measures what it says it measures; see also *face validity, construct validity, construct validity, criterion-related validity*

Vineland Adaptive Behavior Scales (VBAS): measure of child's social competence assessing daily living, socialization, motor function, and communication skills

unconditional positive regard: according to Carl Rogers: an environment in which a person is accepted without having to meet the conditions of others; the experience of caring for and accepting a person regardless of what the person says or does

Wechsler Abbreviated Scale of Intelligence (WASI): developed for use when screening rather than full testing is sufficient; raw scores are converted to T scores rather than scaled scores when computing IQ

Wechsler Individual Achievement Test (WIAT): measures academic skills in eight areas with both children and adults; covers all areas specified in Individuals with Disabilities Act

Wechsler Memory Scale, third edition (WMS-III): extensive test of memory including seventeen subtests yielding eight primary indices of memory

Wechsler tests: term used to refer to a series of three tests of intelligence developed by David Wechsler; used with people from preschool through late adulthood

Wide Range Achievement Test, third edition (WRAT-III): released in 1993; measure of academic skills in reading, spelling, and mathematics

working through: emotionally reexperiencing an event and learning different emotional responses to it

YAVIS: abbreviation for the "ideal" psychotherapy patient, who is young, attractive, verbal, intelligent, and successful

References

Chapter 1 Foundations of Clinical Psychology

American Psychological Association (APA). (2002). Ethical principles of psychologists and code of conduct. *American Psychologist, 57,* 1060–1073.

Ayad, F. M. (2004). Psychological factors contributing to the development of obesity and the conditions that must be treated preoperatively. In L. F. Martin (Ed.), *Obesity surgery* (pp. 67–93). New York: McGraw-Hill.

Belar, C. (1992). Conferences on internship and postdoctoral training. In A. E. Puente, J. R. Matthews, & C. L. Brewer (Eds.), *Teaching psychology in America: A history* (pp. 301–310). Washington, DC: American Psychological Association.

Belar, C. D., Bieliauskas, L. A., Larsen, K. G., Mensh, I. N., Poey, K., & Roehlke, H. J. (Eds.). (1989). *Proceedings: National Conference on Internship Training in Psychology.* Washington, DC: American Psychological Association.

Belar, C. D., & Perry, N. W. (1992). The National Conference on Scientist-Practitioner Education and Training for the Professional Practice of Psychology. *American Psychologist, 47,* 71–75.

Callan, J. E., Peterson, D. R., & Stricker, G. (1986). *Quality in professional psychology training: A national conference and self-study.* National Council of Schools of Professional Psychology.

Daw, J. (2002). Making a life-or-death difference. *Monitor on Psychology, 33*(3), 60–62. Farberman, R. K. (2000). When is a new psychologist ready for independent practice? *Monitor on Psychology, 31*(8), 44–47.

Farrenkopf, T., & Bryan, J. (1999). Psychological consultation under Oregon's 1994 Death With Dignity Act: Ethics and procedures. *Professional Psychology: Research and Practice, 30,* 245–249.

Fenn, D. S., & Ganzini, L. (1999). Attitudes of Oregon psychologists toward physician-assisted suicide and the Oregon Death With Dignity Act. *Professional Psychology: Research and Practice, 30,* 235–244.

Hoch, E. L., Ross, A. O., & Winder, C. L. (1966). Conference on the professional preparation of clinical psychologists: A summary. *American Psychologist, 21,* 42–51.

Ilardi, S. S., Rodriguez-Hanley, A., Roberts, M. C., & Seigel, J. (2000). On the origins of clinical psychology faculty: Who is training the trainers? *Clinical Psychology: Science and Practice, 7,* 346–354.

Keith-Spiegel, P., & Wiederman, M. W. (2000). *The complete guide to graduate school admission.* Mahwah, NJ: Lawrence Erlbaum Associates, Inc.

Korman, M. (1974). National Conference on Levels and Patterns of Professional Training in Psychology: The major themes. *American Psychologist, 29,* 441–449.

Magreb, P. R., & Wohlford, P. (Eds.). (1990). *Improving psychological services for children and adolescents with severe mental disorders: Clinical training in psychology.* Washington, DC: American Psychological Association.

Matarazzo, J. D. (1983). Education and training in health psychology: Boulder or bolder. *Health Psychology, 2,* 73–113.

Mayne, T. J., Norcross, J. C., & Sayette, M. A. (2000). *Insider's guide to graduate programs in clinical and counseling psychology 2000/2001 edition.* New York: Guilford Publications.

Pederson, S. L., DePiano, F., Kaslow, N., Klepac, R. K., Hargrove, D. S., & Vasquez, M. (1997). *Proceedings from the National Working Conference on Supply and Demand: Training and Employment Opprtunities in Professional Psychology.* Washington, DC: American Psychological Association.

Rogers, P. (1993). Research in music therapy with sexually abused clients. In H. Payne (Ed.), *Handbook of inquiry in the arts therapies: One river many currents* (pp. 197–217). London: Kingsley.

Smith, D. (2003). 10 ways practitioners can avoid frequent ethical pitfalls. *Monitor on Psychology, 23*(1), 50–56.

Tarnowski, K. J., & Simonian, S. J. (1999). *Directory of graduate programs in clinical child and pediatric psychology* (3rd ed). Mahwah, NJ: Lawrence Erlbaum Associates.

Von Staden, H. (1996). In a pure and holy way: Personal and professional conduct in the Hippocratic Oath. *Journal of the History of Medicine and Allied Health Sciences, 51,* 406–408.

Wadeson, H., Durkin, J., & Perach, D. (Eds). (1989). *Advances in art therapy.* New York: Wiley.

Walfish, S., & Hess, A. K. (2001). *Succeeding in graduate school: The career guide for the psychology student.* Mahwah, NJ: Lawrence Erlbaum Associates.

Chapter 2 Professional Activities and Introduction to Managed Care

Beers, C. (1908). *A mind that found itself.* Garden City, NY: Doubleday.

Hilgard, E. R. (1987). *Psychology in America: A historical survey.* San Diego: Harcourt Brace Jovanovich.

Holloway, J. D. (2003). A thriving practice built on a rare specialty. *Monitor on Psychology, 34*(4), 26–27.

Kubiszyn, T. W., Meyer, G. J., Finn, S. E., Eyde, L. D., Kay, G. G., Moreland, K. L., et al. (2000). Empirical support for psychological assessment in clinical health settings. *Professional Psychology: Research and Practice, 31,* 119–130.

Nicol, A. A. M., & Pexman, P. M. (2003). *Displaying your findings: A practical guide for creating figures, posters, and presentations.* Washington, DC: American Psychological Association.

Rothbaum, P. A., Bernstein, D. M., Haller, O., Phelps, R., & Kohout, J. (1998). New Jersey psychologist's report on managed mental health care. *Professional Psychology: Research and Practice, 29,* 37–42.

Rupert, P. A., & Baird, K. A. (2004). Managed care and the independent practice of psychology. *Professional Psychology: Research and Practice, 35,* 185–193.

Sharkin, B. S., & Knox, D. (2004). Pet loss: Issues and implications for the psychologist. *Professional Psychology: Research and Practice, 34,* 414–421.

Starr, P. (1982). *The societal transformation of American medicine.* New York: Basic Books.

Williams, C. (2001a). What is APAGS, anyway? *Monitor on Psychology, 32*(8), 54–55.

Williams C. (2001b). This year's APAGS priorities. *Monitor on Psychology, 32*(8), 56–58.

Chapter 3 History and Research

Ackerman, N. W. (1958). *The psychodynamics of family life.* New York: Basic Books.

Adler, A. (1927). *Practice and theory of individual psychology.* New York: Harcourt, Brace, & World.

Adler, A. (1935). The fundamental views of individual psychology. *International Journal of Individual Psychology, 1,* 5–8.

Albee, G. W. (2005). A contrary view about prescription authority. *The ABPP Specialist, 24,* 2, 11, 23.

American Psychological Association (APA). (2002). Ethical principles of psychologists and code of conduct. *American Psychologist, 57,* 1060–1073.

Anastasi, A., & Urbina, S. (1997). *Psychological testing* (7th ed). Upper Saddle River, NJ: Macmillan.

Appignanesi, L., & Forrester, J. (1992). *Freud's women.* New York: Basic Books.

Barlow, D. H., & Durand, V. M. (2002). *Abnormal psychology: An integrative approach* (3rd ed). Belmont, CA: Wadsworth.

Beck, S. J. (1937). *Introduction to the Rorschach method.* New York: American Orthopsychiatric Association.

Boring, E. G. (1950). *A history of experimental psychology.* New York: Appleton-Century-Crofts.

Brown, D. C. (1994). Subgroup norming: Legitimate testing practice or reverse discrimination? *American Psychologist, 49,* 927–928.

Chambless, D. L., Baker, M. J., Baucom, D. H., Beutler, L. E., Calhoun, K. S., Crits-Christoph, P., et al. (1998). Update on empirically validated therapies II. *The Clinical Psychologist, 51*(1), 3–16.

Chambless, D. L., & Hollon, S. D. (1998). Defining empirically supported therapies. *Journal of Consulting and Clinical Psychology, 66,* 7–18.

Christensen, A-L. (1975). *Luria's neuropsychological investigation.* New York: Spectrum Publications.

Cohen, R. J., & Swerdlik, M. E. (2002). *Psychological testing and assessment: An introduction to testing and assessment.* Boston: McGraw-Hill.

Comer, R. J. (2001). *Abnormal psychology* (4th ed.). New York: Worth Publishers.

Cranston, A. (1986). Psychology in the Veteran's Administration: A storied history, a vital future. *American Psychologist, 41,* 990–995.

Cuellar, I., Arnold, B., & Maldonado, R. (1995). Acculturation Rating Scale for Mexican-Americans-II: A revision of the original ARSMA scale. *Hispanic Journal of Behavioral Sciences, 17,* 275–304.

DeNelsky, G. Y. (1991). Prescription privileges for psychologists: The case against. *Professional Psychology: Research and Practice, 22,* 188–193.

Diana v. California State Board of Education (1970). No. C-70-37, United States District Court of Northern California.

Follette, W. C., & Callaghan, G. M. (2001). The evolution of clinical significance. *Clinical Psychology: Science and Practice, 8,* 431–435.

Francher, R. E. (1998). Alfred Binet, general psychologist. In G. A. Kimble & M. Wertheimer (Eds.), *Portraits of pioneers in psychology* (Vol. III, pp. 66–83). Mahwah, NJ: Lawrence Earlbaum.

Frank, L. K. (1939). Projective methods for the study of personality. *Journal of Psychology, 8,* 389–413.

Freud, S. (1910). The origin and development of psychoanalysis. *American Journal of Psychology, 21,* 181–218.

Freud, S. (1914). *Leonardo da Vinci: A study in psychosexuality.* New York: Vintage Books.

Freud, S. (1938). *The basic writings of Sigmund Freud.* New York: Modern Library.

Freud, S. (1953–1964). *The standard edition of the complete psychological works of Sigmund Freud* (24 vols.). London: Hogarth Press.

Garfield, S. L. (1981). Psychotherapy: A 40-year appraisal. *American Psychologist, 36,* 174–183.

Garfield, S. L. (1998). The Division of Clinical Psychology: A 50 year appraisal. *The Clinical Psychologist, 51*(2), 3–9.

Gilgen, A. R. (1982). *American psychology since World War II: A profile of the discipline.* Westport, CT: Greenwood Press.

Goldfried, M. R., & Wolfe, B. E. (1996). Psychotherapy practice and research: Repairing a strained alliance. *American Psychologist, 51,* 1007–1016.

Gregory, R. J. (2004). *Psychological testing: History, principles, and applications* (4th ed). Boston, MA: Pearson/Allyn & Bacon.

Gutierrez, P. M., & Silk, K. R. (1998). Prescription privileges for psychologists: A review of the psychological literature. *Professional Psychology: Research and Practice, 29,* 213–222.

Halstead, W. C. (1947). *Brain and intelligence.* Chicago: University of Chicago Press.

Hayes, S. C., Walser, R. D., & Follette, V. M. (1995). Psychology and the temptation of prescription privileges. *Canadian Psychology, 36,* 313–320.

Heiby, E. (1998). The case against prescription privileges: An overview. In S. C. Hayes & E. M. Heiby (Eds.), *Prescription privileges for psychologists: A critical appraisal* (pp. 51–73). Reno, NV: Context Press.

Herman, E. (1995). *The romance of American psychology.* Berkeley: University of California Press.

Herrnstein, R. J., & Murray, C. (1994). *The bell curve: Intelligence and class structure in American life.* New York: Free Press.

Hilgard, E. R. (1987). *Psychology in America: A historical survey.* San Diego: Harcourt Brace Jovanovich.

Hilgard, E. R., & Hilgard, J. R. (1983). *Hypnosis in the relief of pain* (rev. ed.). Los Altos, CA: William Kaufmann.

Holmes, D. S. (2001). *Abnormal psychology* (4th ed.). Boston: Allyn & Bacon.

Holmes, T. H., & Rahe, R. H. (1967). Holmes-Rahe life changes scale. *Journal of Psychosomatic Research, 11,* 213–218.

Humphreys, K. (1996). Clinical psychologists as psychotherapists: History, future, and alternatives. *American Psychologist, 51,* 190–197.

Hutt, M. L., & Milton, E. O. (1947). An analysis of duties performed by clinical psychologists in the Army. *American Psychologist, 2,* 52–56.

James, W. (1890). *The principles of psychology* (2 vols.). New York: Henry Holt.

Jones, E. (1953, 1955, 1957). *The life and works of Sigmund Freud* (Vols. 1–3). New York: Basic Books.

Jones, M. C. (1924). The elimination of children's fears. *Journal of Experimental Psychology, 7,* 383–390.

Jung, C. G. (1959). The concept of the collective unconscious. In *Collected works* (Vol. 9, Part 1). Princeton, NJ: Princeton University Press.

Kazdin, A. E. (1998). *Research design in clinical psychology* (3rd ed). Boston: Allyn & Bacon.

Kazdin, A. E. (1999). The meanings and measurement of clinical significance. *Journal of Consulting and Clinical Psychology, 67,* 332–339.

Klopfer, B., & Kelley, D. M. (1937). The techniques of Rorschach performance. *Rorschach Research Exchange, 2,* 1–14.

Larry P. v. Riles, 343 F. Supp. 1306 (N.D. Cal. 1972) (preliminary injunction), aff'd, 502 F. 2d 963 (9th Cir. 1974), opinion issued No. C-71-2270 RFP (N.D. Cal. October 16, 1979).

Lopez, S. R. (2000). Teaching culturally informed psychological assessment. In R. H. Dana (Ed.), *Handbook of crosscultural and multicultural personality assessment* (pp. 669–687). Mahwah, NJ: Erlbaum.

Louttit, C. M. (1939). The nature of clinical psychology. *Psychological Bulletin, 36,* 361–389.

Lubin, B. (1976). Group therapy. In I. B. Weiner (Ed.), *Clinical methods in psychology.* New York: Wiley-Interscience.

Luria, A. R. (1980). *Higher cortical functions in man* (2nd ed.). New York: Basic Books.

Mason, E. E. (1998). Quality of Life. *IBSR Newsletter, 13,* 13–14.

Matarazzo, J. D. (1990). Psychological assessment versus psychological testing: Validation from Binet to the school, clinic, and courtroom. *American Psychologist, 45,* 999–1016.

Miller, J. G. (1946). Clinical psychology in the Veterans Administration. *American Psychologist, 1,* 181–189.

Moyer, D. M. (1995). An opposing view on prescription privileges for psychologists. *Professional Psychology: Research and Practice, 26,* 586–590.

Newman, R., Phelps, R., Sammons, M. T., Dunivin, D. L., & Cullen, E. A. (2000). Evaluation of the Psychopharmacology Demonstration Project: A retrospective analysis. *Professional Psychology: Research and Practice, 31,* 598–603.

Norcross, J. C., Karg, R. S., & Prochaska, J. O. (1997). Clinical psychologists in the 1990s: II. *The Clinical Psychologist, 50*(3), 4–11.

PASE v. Hannon, 506 F. Supp. 831 (N.D. ILL. 1980).

Pavlov, I. P. (1906). The scientific investigation of the psychical faculties of processes in higher animals. *Science, 24,* 613–619.

Prochaska, J. O., & Norcross, J. C. (2002). *Systems of psychotherapy: A transtheoretical analysis* (5th ed.). Belmont, CA: Brooks/Cole.

Reisman, J. M. (1991). *A history of clinical psychology* (2nd ed). New York: Hemisphere.

Rogers, C. R. (1942). *Counseling and psychotherapy.* Boston: Houghton Mifflin.

Rogers, C. R. (1951). *Client-centered therapy.* Boston: Houghton Mifflin.

Rogers, C. R. (1957). The necessary and sufficient conditions of therapeutic personality change. *Journal of Consulting Psychology, 21,* 95–103.

Rogers, C. R. (1967). Autobiography. In E. G. Boring & G. Lindzey (Eds.), *A history of psychology in autobiography* (Vol. 5, pp. 341–384). New York: Appleton-Century-Crofts.

Rogers, C. R. (1970). *Carl Rogers on encounter groups.* New York: Harper & Row.

Rogers, C. R. (1972). *Becoming partners: Marriage and its alternatives.* New York: Delacorte.

Rogers, C. R., & Dymond, R. F. (Eds). (1954). *Psychotherapy and personality change: Co-ordinated studies in the client-centered approach.* Chicago: University of Chicago Press.

Rorschach, H. (1921). *Psychodiagnostik.* Bern and Leipzig: Ernst Bircher Verlag.

Sammons, M. T., & Brown, A. (1997). The Department of Defense Psychopharmacology Demonstration Project: An evolving program for postdoctoral education in psychology. *Professional Psychology: Research and Practice, 28,* 107–112.

Sammons, M. T., Gorny, S. W., Zinner, E. S., & Allen, R. P. (2000). Prescriptive authority for psychologists: A consensus of support. *Professional Psychology: Research and Practice, 31,* 604–609.

Seligman, M. E. P. (1995). The effectiveness of psychotherapy: The Consumer Reports study. *American Psychologist, 50,* 965–974.

Seligman, M. E. P., Walker, E. F., & Rosenhan, D. L. (2001). *Abnormal psychology* (4th ed.). New York: W. W. Norton & Company.

Shakow, D. (1969). *Clinical psychology as a science and as a profession: A forty-year odyssey.* Chicago: Aldine.

Sharf, R. S. (2000). *Theories of psychotherapy and counseling: Concepts and cases* (2nd ed.). Belmont, CA: Brooks/Cole.

Skinner, B. F. (1938). *The behavior of organisms.* New York: Appleton-Century-Crofts.

Skinner, B. F. (1953). *Science and human behavior.* New York: Macmillan.

Temkin, O. (1947). Gall and the phrenological movement. *Bulletin of the History of Medicine, 21,* 275–321.

Terman, L. M. (1961). Trails to psychology. In C. Murchinson (Ed.), *A history of psychology in autobiography* (Vol II., pp. 297–331). New York: Russell & Russell.

Vandiver, B. J., Cross, W. E., Jr., Worrell, F. C., & Fhagen-Smith, P. E. (2002). Validating the Cross Racial Identity Scale. *Journal of Counseling Psychology, 49,* 71–85.

Watson, J. B., & Rayner, R. (1920). Conditioned emotional reactions. *Journal of Experimental Psychology, 3,* 114.

Witmer, L (1907). Clinical psychology. *Psychological Clinic, 1,* 1–9.

Wolf, T. (1973). *Alfred Binet.* Chicago: University of Chicago Press.

Woodworth, R. S. (1920). *Personal data sheet.* Chicago: Stoelting.

Yalom, I. D. (1975). *The theory and practice of group psychotherapy.* New York: Basic Books.

Yalom, I. D. (1995). *The theory and practice of group psychotherapy* (4th ed). New York: Basic Books.

Chapter 4 Personality Theory

Allen, B. P. (2003). *Personality theories: Development, growth, and diversity* (4th ed.). Boston, MA: Allyn & Bacon.

Allport, G. W. (1937). *Personality: A psychological interpretation.* New York: Holt.

Allport, G. W., & Odbert, H. S. (1936). Trait names: A psychological study. *Psychological Monographs, 47* (Whole No. 211).

Ayllon, T., & Azrin, N. H. (1965). The measurement and reinforcement of behavior of psychotics. *Journal of Experimental Analysis of Behavior, 8,* 357–383.

Cattell, R. B. (1943). The description of personality: Basic traits resolved into clusters. *Journal of Abnormal and Social Psychology, 38,* 476–506.

Costa, P. T., Jr., & McCrae, R. R. (1992). *Revised NEO Personality Inventory (NEO-PI-R) and NEO Five-Factor Inventory (NEO-FFI) professional manual.* Odessa, FL: Psychological Assessment Resources.

Engler, B. (2006). *Personality theories* (7th ed.). Boston: Houghton Mifflin.

Ellis, A. (1958). Rational psychotherapy. *Journal of General Psychology, 59,* 35–49.

Ellis, A. (1978). Toward a theory of personality. In R. J. Corsini (Ed.), *Readings in current personality theories.* Itasca, IL: Peacock.

Ellis, A. (1996). Responses to criticisms of Rational Emotive Behavior Therapy. *Journal of Rational-Emotive and Cognitive Behavior Therapy, 14,* 17–22.

Ellis, A., & Dryden, W. (1997). *The practice of rational emotive therapy.* New York: Springer.

Engler, B. (2006). *Personality theories: An introduction* (7th ed.). Boston: Houghton Mifflin.

Eysenck, H. J. (1970). *The structure of human personality* (3rd ed). London: Metheun.

Frager, R., & Fadiman J. (2005). *Personality and personal growth.* Upper Saddle River, NJ: Pearson/Prentice Hall.

Freud, A. (1936). *The ego and the mechanisms of defense.* New York: International Universities Press.

Hall, C. S., Lindzey, G., & Campbell, J. B. (1998). *Theories of personality* (4th ed.). New York: John Wiley & Sons.

Jung, C. G. (1954). The practice of psychotherapy. In *The collected works of C. G. Jung* (Vol. 16). London: Routledge & Kegan Paul.

Jung, C. G. (1959). The archetypes and the collective unconscious (R. C. F. Hull, Trans.). In *Collected works* (Vol. IX, Part 2). Princeton, NJ: Princeton University Press.

Kazdin, A. E. (1989). *Behavior modification in applied settings* (4th ed.). Pacific Grove, CA: Brooks/Cole.

Kirschenbaum, H., & Jourdan, A. (2005). Current status of Carl Rogers and the person-centered approach. *Psychotherapy: Theory, Research, Practice, Training, 42,* 37–51.

Lakin, M. (1998). Carl Rogers and the culture of psychotherapy. In G. A. Kimble & M. Wertheimer (Eds.), *Portraits of pioneers in psychology* (Vol. III). Washington, DC: American Psychological Association.

Lazarus, A. A. (1973). Multi-modal behavior therapy: Treating the BASIC-ID. *Journal of Nervous and Mental Disorders, 156,* 404–412.

Lazarus, A. A. (1997). *Brief but comprehensive psychotherapy: The multimodal way.* New York: Springer.

Lazarus, A. A. (2000). Multimodal replenishment. *Professional Psychology: Research and Practice, 31,* 93–94.

Loevinger, J. (1976). *Ego development: Conceptions and theories.* San Francisco, CA: Jossey-Bass.

McCrae, R. R. (1992). The Five-Factor Model: Issues and applications. *Journal of Personality, 60,* 175–215.

McCrae, R. R., & Costa, P. T., Jr. (1997). Personality trait structure as a human universal. *American Psychologist, 52,* 509–516.

Rogers, C. R. (1959). A theory of therapy, personality, and interpersonal relationships, as developed in the client-centered framework. In S. Koch (Ed.)., *Psychology: A study of a science* (Vol. 3, pp. 184–256). New York: McGraw-Hill.

Rogers, C. R. (1961). *On becoming a person.* Boston: Houghton-Mifflin.

Rogers, C. R. (1977). *Carl Rogers on personal power.* New York: Delacorte Press.

Rogers, C. R., & Stevens, B. (1967). *Person to person: The problem of being human.* New York: Simon & Schuster.

Sanchez, L. M., & Turner, S. M. (2003). Practicing psychology in the era of managed care. *American Psychologist, 58,* 116–129.

Schultz, D., & Schultz, S. E. (2004). *Theories of personality* (8th ed.). Belmont, CA: Wadsworth/ Thompson Learning.

Sheldon, W. H. (1942). *Varieties of temperament.* New York: Harper.

Skinner, B. F. (1953). *Science and human behavior.* New York: Macmillan.

Skinner, B. F. (1990). Can psychology be a science of mind? *American Psychologist, 45,* 1206–1210.

Triandis, H. C., & Suh, E. M. (2002). Cultural influences on personality. *Annual Review of Psychology, 53,* 133–160.

Westen, D. (1998). The scientific legacy of Sigmund Freud: Toward a psychodynamically informed psychological science. *Psychological Bulletin, 124,* 333–371.

Chapter 5 Diagnosis and Interviewing

Ablow, J. C., Measelle, J. R., Kraemer, H. C., Harrington, R., Luby, J., Smider, N., Dierker, L., Clark, V., Dubicka, B., Heffelfinger, A., Essex, M., & Kupfer, D. J. (1999). The MacArthus Three-City Outcome Study: Evaluating multi-informant measures of young children's symptomatology. *Journal of the American Academy of Child and Adolescent Psychiatry, 38,* 1580–1590.

American Psychiatric Association. (1994). *Diagnostic and statistical manual of mental disorders* (4th ed). [DSM-IV]. Washington, DC: Author.

American Psychological Association (1993). *Record keeping guidelines.* Washington, DC: Author.

American Psychological Association (APA). (2002). Ethical principles of psychologists and code of conduct. *American Psychologist, 57,* 1060–1073.

Berg, R. A., Franzen, M., & Wedding, D. (1987). *Screening for brain impairment: A manual for mental health practice.* New York: Springer Publishing.

Beutler, L. E. (1996). The clinical interview. In L. E. Beutler & M. R. Berren (Eds.), *Integrative assessment of adult personality* (pp. 94–120). New York: Guilford Press.

Beutler, L. E., Machado, P. P., Neufeldt, S. A. (1994). Therapist variables. In A. E. Bergin & S. L. Garfield (Eds.), *Handbook of psychotherapy and behavior change* (4th ed, pp. 229–269), New York: Wiley.

Birren, J. E., & Sloane, R. B. (1977). *Manpower and training needs in mental health and illness of the aging.* Los Angeles: Ethel Percy Andrus Gerontology Center, University of Southern California.

Brammer, R. (2002). Effects of experience and training on diagnostic accuracy. *Psychological Assessment, 14,* 110–113.

Chambers, W. J., Puig-Antich, J., Hirsch, M., Paez, P., Ambrosini, P. J., Tabrizi, M. A., & Davies, M. (1985). The assessment of affective disorders in children and adolescents by semistructured interview: Test-retest reliability of the Schedule for Affective Disorders and Schizophrenia for School-Age Children, Present Episode version. *Archives of General Psychiatry, 42,* 696–702.

Endicott, J., & Spitzer, R. L. (1978). A diagnostic interview: The Schedule for Affective Disorders and Schizophrenia. *Archives of General Psychiatry, 35,* 837–844.

Endicott, J., Spitzer, R. L., Fleiss, J. L., & Cohen, J. (1976). The Global Assessment Scale: A procedure for measuring overall severity of psychiatric disturbance. *Archives of General Psychiatry, 33,* 766–771.

Evans, D. R., Hearn, M. T., Uhlemann, M. R., & Ivey, A. E. (1998). *Essential interviewing: A programmed approach to effective communication* (5th ed.). Pacific Grove, CA: Brooks/Cole.

Fallon, T., & Schwab-Stone, M. (1994). Determinants of reliability in psychiatric surveys of children aged 6–12. *Journal of Child Psychology and Psychiatry and Allied Disciplines, 35,* 1391–1408.

Gatz, M. (Ed.). (1995). *Emerging issues in mental health and aging.* Washington, DC: American Psychological Association.

Goldfried, M., Greenberg, L., & Marmar, C. (1990). Individual psychotherapy: Process and outcome. In M. Rosenzweig & L. Porter (Eds.), *Annual review of psychology* (pp. 659–688). Palo Alto, CA: Annual Reviews.

Groth-Marnat, G. (1997). *Handbook of psychological assessment* (3rd ed.). New York: John Wiley.

Hall, H. V., & Pritchard, D. A. (1996). *Detecting malingering and deception.* Delray Beach, FL: St. Lucie Press.

International Classification of Functionality. (2001). http://www.who.int/inf-pr-2001/en/pr2001-48.html.

Kane, E. W., & Macauley, L. J. (1993). Interviewer gender and gender attitudes. *Public Opinion Quarterly, 57,* 1–28.

Kanfer, F. H., & McBrearty, J. F. (1962). Minimal social reinforcement and interview content. *Journal of Clinical Psychology, 18,* 210–215.

La Rue, A., Dessonville, E., & Jarvik, L. F. (1985). Aging and mental disorders. In J. E. Birren & K. W. Schaie (Eds.), *Handbook of the psychology of aging* (2nd ed., pp. 664–702). New York: Van Nostrand Reinhold.

Luborsky, L. (1962). Clinicians' judgments of mental health. *Archives of General Psychiatry, 7,* 407–417.

Matarazzo, J. D. (1965). The interview. In B. B. Wolman (Ed.), *Handbook of clinical psychology* (pp. 403–450). New York: McGraw-Hill.

Morrison, J. (1995). *DSM-IV made easy: The clinician's guide to diagnosis.* New York: Guilford Press.

Morton, A. (1995). The enigma of non-attendance: A study of clients who do not turn up for their first appointment. *Therapeutic Communities: International Journal for Therapeutic and Supportive Organizations, 16,* 117–133.

Nietzel, M. T., Bernstein, D. A., & Milich, R. (1998). *Introduction to clinical psychology* (5th ed). Upper Saddle River, NJ: Prentice-Hall.

Othmer, E., & Othmer, S. C. (1994). *The clinical interviewing DSM-IV.* Washington, DC: American Psychiatric Press.

Nystul, M. S. (1999). *Introduction to counseling: An art and science perspective.* Boston: Allyn & Bacon.

Piacentini, J., Roper, M., Jensen, P., Lucas, C., Fisher, P., Bird, H., Bourdon, K., Schwab-Stone, M., Rubio-Stipec, M., Davies, M., & Dulcan, M. (1999). Informant-based determinants of symptom attenuation in structured child psychiatric interviews. *Journal of Abnormal Child Psychology, 27,* 417–428.

Pope, B., Nudler, S., Vonkorff, M. R., & McGhee, J. P. (1974). The experienced professional interviewer versus the complete novice. *Journal of Consulting and Clinical Psychology, 42,* 680–690.

Pope, K. S., & Vasquez, M. T. (1998). *Ethics in psychotherapy and counseling* (2nd ed.). San Francisco: Jossey-Bass.

Reynolds, C. R., & Bigler, E. D. (2001). *Clinical Assessment Scales for the Elderly.* Odessa, FL: Psychological Assessment Resources.

Robinson, R. C., & Chapman, B. (1997). *Brain calipers: A guide to a successful mental status exam.* Gratito, MI: Rapid Psychler Press.

Rogers, R. (1995). *Diagnostic and structured interviewing: A handbook for psychologists.* Odessa, FL: Psychological Assessment Press.

Shaffer, D., Fisher, P., Lucas, C. P., Dulcan, M. K., & Schwab-Stone, M. E. (2000). NIMH Diagnostic Interview Schedule for Children Version IV (NIMH DISC-IV): Description, differences from previous versions, and reliability of some common diagnoses. *Journal of the American Academy of Child and Adolescent Psychiatry, 39,* 28–38.

Shea, S. C. (1988). *Psychiatric interviewing: The art of understanding.* Philadelphia: W. B. Saunders.

Siegman, A., & Feldstein, S. (Eds.) (1987). *Nonverbal behavior and communication.* Hillsdale, NJ: Erlbaum.

Somers-Flanagan, J., & Somers-Flanagan, R. (1995). Intake interviewing with suicidal patients: A systematic approach. *Professional Psychology: Research and Practice, 26,* 41–47.

Spiegel, A. (2005). The dictionary of disorder: How one man revolutionized psychiatry. *The New Yorker,* January 3, 2005.

Spitzer, R. L., Fleiss, J. L., Burdock, E. I., & Hardesty, A. S. (1964). The mental status schedule: Rationale, reliability, and validity. *Comprehensive Psychiatry, 5,* 384–395.

Spitzer, R. L., Fleiss, J. L., Endicott, J., & Cohen, J. (1967). Mental status schedule: Properties of factor-analytically derived scales. *Archives of General Psychiatry, 16,* 479–493.

Spitzer, R. L., Williams, J. B., Gibbon, M., & First, M. B. (1992). The Structured Clinical Interview for DSM-III-R (SCID): I. History, rationale, and description. *Archives of General Psychiatry, 49,* 624–629.

Szasz, T. S. (1960). The myth of mental illness. *American Psychologist, 15,* 113–118.

Trzepacz, P. T., & Baker, R. W. (1993). *The psychiatric mental status examination.* New York: Oxford University Press.

Tuokko, H., & Hadjistavropoulos, T. (1998*). An assessment guide to geriatric neuropsychology.* Mahway, NJ: Lawrence Erlbaum Associates.

Valla, J., Bergeron, L., & Smolla, N. (2000). The Dominic-R: A pictorial interview for 6 to 11-year-old children. *Journal of the American Academy of Child and Adolescent Psychiatry, 39,* 85–93.

VandeCreek, L., & Knapp, S. (1997). Record keeping. In J. R. Matthews & C. E. Walker (Eds.), *Basic skills and professional issues in clinical psychology* (pp. 155–172). Boston: Allyn and Bacon.

Chapter 6 Intellectual Assessment

Alessandri, S. M., Bendersky, M., & Lewis, M. (1998). Cognitive functioning in 8- to 18-month-old drug-exposed infants. *Developmental Psychology, 34,* 565–573.

American Psychological Association (APA). (2002). Ethical principles of psychologists and code of conduct. *American Psychologist, 57,* 1060–1073.

Anastasi, A., & Urbina, S. (1997). *Psychological testing* (7th ed). Upper Saddle River, NJ: Prentice-Hall, Inc.

Bayley, N. (1969). *Manual for Bayley Scales of Infant Development.* New York: Psychological Corporation.

Bayley, N. (1993). *Bayley Scales of Infant Development (2nd edition) manual.* San Antonio, TX: Psychological Corporation.

Bayley, N. (2005). *Bayley Scales of Infant and Toddler Development (3rd edition) manual.* San Antonio, TX: Psychological Corporation.

Brazelton, T. B., & Nugent, J. (1995). *Neonatal Behavioral Assessment Scale* (3rd ed.). London: Cambridge University Press.

Brown, L., Sherbenou, R., & Johnsen, S. (1998). *Test of Nonverbal Intelligence-3.* Austin, TX: Pro-Ed.

Burns, E. (1998). *Test accommodations for students with disabilities.* Springfield, IL: Charles C. Thomas.

Campbell, J., Bell, S., & Keith, L. (2001). Concurrent validity of the Peabody Picture Vocabulary Test-Third Edition as an intellectual and achievement screener for low SES African American children. *Assessment, 8,* 85–94.

Caruso, J. C. (2001). Reliable component analysis of the Stanford-Binet: Fourth Edition for 2- to 6-year olds. *Psychological Assessment, 13,* 261–266.

Caruso, J. C., & Cliff, N. (2000). Increasing the reliability of Wechsler Intelligence Scale for Children-Third Edition difference scores with reliable component analysis. *Psychological Assessment, 12,* 89–96.

Cassel, R. N. (1995). Accountability for early childhood education (assessing global functioning). *Reading Improvement, 32* (1) 32–37.

Cattell, R. B. (1971). *Abilities: Their structure, growth, and action.* Boston: Houghton Mifflin.

Chin, C., Ledesma, H., Cirino, P., et al. (2001). Relation between Kaufman Brief Intelligence Test and WISC-III scores of children with RD. *Journal of Learning Disabilities, 34,* 2–8.

Cohen, R. J., & Swerdlik, M. E. (2002). *Psychological testing and assessment: An introduction to test and measurement* (5th ed). Boston: McGraw-Hill.

Corcoran, K., & Fischer, J. (1994). *Measures for clinical practice: A sourcebook, Vols. 1, 2* (2nd ed.) New York: Free Press.

Dana, R. H. (1993). *Multicultural assessment perspectives for professional psychology.* Boston: Allyn & Bacon.

Dana, R. H. (1996). Culturally competent assessment practice in the United States. *Journal of Personality Assessment, 66,* 472–487.

DiCerbo, K., & Barona, A. (2000). A convergent validity study of the Differential Ability Scales and the Wechsler Intelligence Scale for Children-Third Edition with Hispanic children. *Journal of Psychoeducational Assessment, 18,* 344–352.

Doll, E. A. (1953). Measurement of social competence: A manual for the Vineland *Social Maturity Scale.* Circle Pines, MN: American Guidance Service.

Donders, J. (1995). Validity of the Kaufman Brief Intelligence Test (K-BIT) in children with traumatic brain injury. *Assessment, 2,* 219–224.

Donders, J. (1997). A short form of the WISC-III for clinical use. *Psychological Assessment, 9,* 15–20.

Dumont, R., Cruse, C., Price, L., & Whelley, P. (1996). The relationship between the Differential Ability Scales (DAS) and the Wechsler Intelligence Scale for Children-Third Edition (WISC-III). *Psychology in the Schools, 33,* 203–209.

Dunn, L. M., & Dunn, E. S. (1997). *Peabody Picture Vocabulary Test-III*. Circle Pines, MN: American Guidance Service.

Elliott, C. D. (1990). *The Differential Ability Scales: Introductory and technical handbook*. San Antonio, TX: The Psychological Corporation.

Elliott, C. D. (1997). The Differential Ability Scales. In D. P. Flanagan, J. Genshaft, & P. Harrison (Eds.), *Contemporary intellectual assessment: Theories, tests and issues*. New York: Guilford.

Ertl, J. P., & Schafer, E. W. P. (1969). Brain response correlates of psychometric intelligence. *Nature, 223*, 421–422.

Farrell, M., & Phelps, L. (2000). A comparison of the Leiter-R and the Universal Nonverbal Intelligence Test (UNIT) with children classified as language impaired. *Journal of Psychoeducational Assessment, 18*, 268–274.

Frankenberg, W., Dodds, J., Archer, P., Bresnick, B., Mashka, P., Edelman, N., & Shapiro, H. (1990). *Denver Developmental Screening Test (Denver III)*. Denver, CO: Denver Developmental Materials, Inc.

Gardner, H. (1983). *Frames of mind: The theory of multiple intelligence*. New York: Basic Books.

Gardner, H. (1999). Are there additional intelligences? The case for naturalistic, spiritual, and existential intelligences. In J. Kane (Eds.), *Education, information, and transformation: Essays on learning and thinking* (pp. 111–131). Englewood Cliffs, NJ: Prentice-Hall.

Goldman, B. A., & Mitchell, D. F. (1995). *Directory of unpublished experimental measures* (Vol. 6). Washington, DC: American Psychological Association.

Gregory, R. J. (2004). *Psychological testing: History, principles, and applications* (4th ed.) Boston: Allyn & Bacon.

Gridley, B. E., & McIntosh, D. E. (1991). Confirmatory factor analysis of the Stanford-Binet: Fourth Edition for a normal sample. *Journal of School Psychology, 29*, 237–248.

Groenveld, M., & Jan, J. E. (1992). Intelligence profiles of low vision and blind children. *Journal of Visual Impairment and Blindness, 86*, 68–71.

Guilford, J. P. (1967). *The nature of human intelligence*. New York: McGraw-Hill.

Haier, R. J. (1993). Cerebral glucose metabolism and intelligence. In P. A. Vernon (Ed.), *Biological approaches to the study of human intelligence* (pp. 317–332). Norwood, NJ: Ablex.

Hooper, S., Hatton, D., Beranek, G., Roberts, J., & Bailey, D. (2000). Nonverbal assessment of IQ, attention, and memory abilities in children with fragile-X syndrome using the Leiter-R. *Journal of Psychoeducational Assessment, 18*, 255–267.

Horn, J. L. (1994). Theory of fluid and crystallized intelligence. In R. J. Sternberg (Ed.), *Encyclopedia of human intelligence* (pp. 443–451).

Hoza, B., Pelham, W. E., Waschbush, D. A., Kipp, H., & Owens, J. S. (2001). Academic task persistence of normally achieving ADHD and control boys: Performance, self-evaluations, and attributions. *Journal of Consulting and Clinical Psychology, 69*, 271–284.

Jensen, P. S., Martin, B. A., & Cantwell, D. P. (1997). Comorbidity in ADHD: Implications for research, and the DSM-V. *Journal of the American Academy of Child and Adolescent Psychiatry, 36*, 1065–1079.

Kaplan, S. L., & Alfonso, V. C. (1997). Confirmatory factor analysis of the Stanford-Binet: Fourth Edition with preschoolers with developmental delays. *Journal of Psychoeducational Assessment, 15*, 226–237.

Kaufman, A. S., & Kaufman, N. L. (1990). *Kaufman Brief Intelligence Test: Manual*. Circle Pines, MN: American Guidance Service.

Levy, P. (1968). Short-form tests: A methodological review. *Psychological Bulletin, 69*, 410–416.

Maddox, T. (2003). *Tests: A comprehensive reference for assessments in psychology, education, and business* (5th ed.). Austin, TX: Pro-Ed.

Maltby, J., Lewis, C., & Hill, A. (2001). *Commissioned review of 250 psychological tests* (Vols. 1–2). Lewiston, NY: Edwin Mellen Press.

McCallum, R. S., Bracken, B., & Wasserman, J. (2001). *Essentials of nonverbal assessment.* New York: Wiley.

Miller, L. T., & Lee, C. J. (1993). Construct validation of the Peabody Picture Vocabulary Test-Revised: A structural equation model of the acquisition order of words. *Psychological Assessment, 5,* 438–441.

Murphy, L. L., Plake, B. S., Impara, J. C., & Spies, R. A. (Eds.). (2002). *Tests in print VI.* Lincoln: University of Nebraska Press.

Naugle, R. I., Chelune, G., & Tucker, G. (1993). Validity of the Kaufman Brief Intelligence Test. *Psychological Assessment, 5,* 182–186.

Niccols, A., & Latchman, A. (2002). Stability of the Bayley Mental Scale of Infant Development with high risk infants. *British Journal of Developmental Disabilities, 48,* 3–13.

Plake, B. S., Impara, J. C., & Spies, R. A. (Eds.). (2003). *The fifteenth mental measurements yearbook.* Lincoln, NE: Buros Institute of Mental Measurements.

Raz, S., Glogowski-Kawamoto, B., Yu, A. W., Kronenberg, M. E., Hopkins, T. L., Lauterbach, M. D., Stevens, C. P, & Sander, C. J. (1998). *Neuropsychology, 12,* 459–467.

Roid, G. H., & Miller, L. J. (1997). *Examiner's manual for the Leiter International Performance Scale-Revised.* Wood Dale, IL: Stolting.

Sattler, J. M. (2001). *Assessment of children: Cognitive applications.* San Diego, CA: Jerome M. Sattler, Publisher.

Siegman, A. W. (1956). The effect of manifest anxiety on a concept formation task, a nondirected learning task, and on timed and untimed intelligence tests. *Journal of Consulting Psychology, 20,* 176–178.

Silverstein, A. B. (1990). Short forms of individual intelligence tests. *Psychological Assessment, 2,* 3–11.

Smith, G. T., McCarthy, D. M., & Anderson, K. G. (2000). On the sins of short-form development. *Psychological Assessment, 12,* 102–111.

Sparrow, S. S., Balla, D. A., & Cicchetti, D. V. (1984). *Vineland Adaptive Behavior Scales, Interview Edition: Expanded form manual.* Circle Pines, MN: American Guidance Service.

Sternberg, R. J., Conway, B. E., Ketron, J. L., & Bernstein, M. (1981). People's conceptions of intelligence. *Journal of Personality and Social Psychology, 41,* 37–55.

Sternberg, R. J., & Kaufman, J. C. (1998). Human abilities. *Annual Review of Psychology, 49,* 479–502.

Suzuki, L. A., & Valencia, R. R. (1997). Race-ethnicity and measured intelligence: Educational implications. *American Psychologist, 52* (10) 1103–1114.

Uzgiris, I. C., & Hunt, J. M. (1989). *Assessment in infancy: Ordinal scales of psychological development.* Urbana: University of Illinois Press.

Wang, M. C., Haertel, G. D., & Walberg, H. J. (1990). What influences learning? A content analysis of review literature. *Journal of Educational Research, 84,* 30–43.

Washington, J., & Craig, H. (1999). Performance of at-risk, African American preschoolers on the Peabody Picture Vocabulary Test-III. *Language, Speech, & Hearing Services in Schools, 30,* 75–82.

Wechsler, D. (1958). The measurement and appraisal of adult intelligence (4th ed.). Baltimore: Williams & Wilkins.

Wechsler, D. (1975). Intelligence defined and undefined: A relativistic appraisal. *American Psychologist, 30,* 135–139.

Wechsler, D. (1999). *WASI manual.* San Antonio, TX: The Psychological Corporation/Harcourt Brace & Company.

Wechsler, D. (2001). *Wechsler Individual Achievement Test manual.* San Antonio, TX: The Psychological Corporation.

Wilkinson, G. S. (1993). *Wide Range Achievement Test-3.* Wilmington, DE: Wide Range.

Williams, K. T., & Wang, J. (1997). *Technical references to the Peabody Picture Vocabulary Test-Third Edition (PPVT-III).* Circle Pines, MN: American Guidance Service.

Chapter 7 Personality Assessment

Ames, L. B., & August, J. (1966). Rorschach responses of Negro and white 5-to-10-year-olds. *Journal of Genetic Psychology, 10,* 297–309.

Anastasi, A., & Urbina, S. (1997). *Psychological testing* (7th ed). Upper Saddle River, NJ: Prentice Hall.

Baer, R. A., & Miller, J. (2002). Underreporting of psychopathology on the MMPI-2: A meta-analytic review. *Psychological Assessment, 14,* 16–26.

Baer, R. A., Wetter, M. W., & Berry, D. T. R. (1995). Effects of information about validity scales on underreporting symptoms on the MMPI-2: An analogue investigation. *Assessment, 2,* 189–200.

Beck, S. J. (1944). *Rorschach's test. I: Basic Processes.* New York: Grune and Stratton.

Beck, S. J. (1945). *Rorschach's test. II: A variety of personality pictures.* New York: Grune and Stratton.

Beck, S. J. (1952). *Rorschach's test. III: Advances in interpretation.* New York: Grune and Stratton.

Bellak, L. (1993). *The TAT, CAT, and SAT in clinical use* (5th ed.). New York: Grune and Stratton.

Buck, J. N. (1948). The H-T-P technique: A qualitative and quantitative scoring manual. *Journal of Clinical Psychology, 4,* 319–396.

Buck, J. N. (1981). *The House-Tree-Person technique: A revised manual.* Los Angeles: Western Psychological Services.

Burns, R. C., & Kaufman, S. H. (1970). *Kinetic Family Drawings (K-F-D): An introduction to understanding through kinetic drawings.* New York: Bruner/Mazel.

Butcher, J. N., Dahlstrom, W. G., Graham, J. R., Tellegen, A., & Kaemmer, B. (1989). *Minnesota Multiphasic Personality Inventory-2 (MMPI-2): Manual for administration and scoring.* Minneapolis: University of Minnesota Press.

Butcher, J. N., Williams, C. L., Graham, J. R., Archer, R. P., Tellegen, A., Ben-Porath, Y. S., & Kaemmer, B. (1992). *MMPI-A (Minnesota Multiphasic Personality Inventory-Adolescent) manual for administration, scoring, and interpretation.* Minneapolis: University of Minnesota Press.

Camara, W. J., Nathan, J. S., & Puente, A. E. (2000). Psychological test usage: Implications in professional psychology. *Professional Psychology: Research and Practice, 31,* 141–154.

Cohen, R. J., & Swerdlik, M. E. (2002). *Psychological testing: An introduction to tests and measurement.* Boston: McGraw-Hill.

Costa, P. T., Jr., & McCrae, R. R. (1992). *Revised NEO Personality Inventory (NEO-PI-R) and NEO Five-Factor Inventory (NEO-FFI) professional manual.* Odessa, FL: Psychological Assessment Resources.

Costantino, G., & Malgady, R. G. (1983). Verbal fluency of Hispanic, black, and white children on TAT and TEMAS. *Hispanic Journal of Behavioral Sciences, 5,* 199–206.

Costantino, G., Malgady, R. G., Casullo, M. M., & Castillo, A. (1991). Cross-cultural standardization of TEMAS in three Hispanic cultures. *Hispanic Journal of Behavioral Sciences, 13,* 48–62.

Costantino, G., Malgady, R. G., & Rogler, L. H. (1988). *Tell-Me-A-Story TEMAS-manual.* Los Angeles: Western Psychological Services.

Costantino, G., Malgady, R. G., & Vazquez, C. (1981). A comparison of the Murray-TAT and a new thematic apperception test for urban Hispanic children. *Hispanic Journal of Behavioral Sciences, 3,* 291–300.

Douglas, C. (1993). *Translate this darkness: The life of Christiana Morgan.* New York: Simon & Schuster.

Exner, J. E. (1974). *The Rorschach: A comprehensive system.* New York: Wiley.

Exner, J. E. (1990). *A Rorschach workbook for the comprehensive system* (3rd ed.). Asheville, NC: Rorschach Workshops.

Flanagan, R., & di Guiseppe, R. (1999). Critical review of the TEMAS: A step within the development of thematic apperception instruments. *Psychology in the Schools, 36,* 21–30.

Friedman, A. F., Lewak, R., Nichols, D. S., & Webb, J. T. (2001). *Psychological assessment with the MMPI-2.* Mahwah, NJ: Lawrence Erlbaum Associates.

Garb, H. N. (1999). Call for a moratorium on the use of the Rorschach Inkblot Test in clinical and forensic settings. *Assessment, 6,* 311–318.

Garb, H. N., Florio, C., & Grove, W. (1998). The validity of the Rorschach and the MMPI: Results from meta-analyses. *Psychological Science, 9,* 402–404.

Gregory, R. J. (2004). *Psychological testing: History, principles, and applications* (4th ed.). Boston: Pearson/Allyn & Bacon.

Harkness, A. R. (1992). Fundamental topics in personality disorders: Candidate trait dimensions from lower regions of the hierarchy. *Psychological Assessment, 4,* 251–259.

Harkness, A. R., McNulty, J. L., & Ben-Porath, Y. S. (1995). The personality psychopathology five (PSY-5): Constructs and MMPI-2 scales. *Psychological Assessment, 7,* 104–114.

Harkness, A. R., McNulty, J. L., Ben-Porath, Y. S., & Graham, J. R. (2002). *MMPI-2 Personality-Psychopathology Five (PSY-5) scales: Gaining an overview for case conceptualization and treatment planning.* Minneapolis: University of Minnesota Press.

Hathaway, S. R., & McKinley, J. C. (1943). *The Minnesota Multiphasic Personality Inventory manual.* Minneapolis: University of Minnesota Press.

Hertz, M. R. (1992). *Frequency Tables for Scoring Rorschach Responses* (5th ed.). Los Angeles: Western Psychological Services.

Hiller, J. B., Rosenthal, R., Bornstein, R. F., Berry, D. T. R., & Brunell-Neulieb, S. (1999). A comparative meta-analysis of Rorschach and MMPI validity. *Psychological Assessment, 11,* 278–296.

Hulse, W. G. (1951). The emotionally disturbed child draws his family. *Quarterly Journal of Child Behavior, 3,* 151–174.

Hunsley, J., & Bailey, J. M. (1999). The clinical utility of the Rorschach: Unfulfilled promises and an uncertain future. *Psychological Assessment, 11,* 266–277.

Jankowski, D. (2002). *A beginner's guide to the MCMI-III.* Washington, DC: American Psychological Association.

Joiner, T. E., Jr., & Schmidt, K. L. (1997). Drawing conclusions—or not—from drawings. *Journal of Personality Assessment, 69,* 476–481.

Keiser, R. E., & Prather, E. N. (1990). What is the TAT? A review of ten years of research. *Journal of Personality Assessment, 55,* 800–803.

Klopfer, B., & Kelley, D. (1942). *The Rorschach technique.* Yonkers: World Book.

Lachar, D., & Gruber, C. (2001). *Manual: Personality Inventory for Children-2.* Los Angeles: Western Psychological Services.

Lah, M. I. (1989). New validity, normative, and scoring data for the Rotter Incomplete Sentences Blank. *Journal of Personality Assessment, 53,* 607–620.

Lamb, D. G., Berry, D. T. R., Wetter, M. W., & Baer, R. A. (1994). Effects of two types of information on closed head injury on the MMPI-2: An analogue investigation. *Psychological Assessment, 6,* 8–13.

Lerner, P. M. (1998*). Psychoanalytic perspectives on the Rorschach.* Hillsdale, NJ: The Analytic Press.

Lilienfeld, S. O., Fowler, K. A., & Lohr, J. M. (2003). And the band played on: Science, pseudoscience, and the Rorschach inkblot method. *The Clinical Psychologist, 56* (1), 6–7.

Lindzey, G. (1961). *Projective techniques and cross-cultural research.* New York: Appleton-Century-Crofts.

Machover, K. (1949). *Personality projection in the drawing of the human figure.* Springfield, IL: Charles C. Thomas.

Malgady, R. G., Costantino, G., & Rogler, L. H. (1984). Development of a Thematic Apperception Test (TEMAS) for urban Hispanic children. *Journal of Consulting and Clinical Psychology, 52,* 986–996.

McRae, R. R., & Costa, P. T., Jr. (2004). A contemplated revision of the NEO Five-Factor Inventory. *Personality and Individual Differences, 36,* 587–596.

McRae, R. R., Costa, P. T., Jr., & Martin, T. A. (2005). The NEO-PI-3: A more readable revised NEO Personality Inventory. *Journal of Personality Assessment, 84,* 261–270.

McRae, R. R., Costa, P. T., Jr., Terracciano, A., Parker, W. D., Mills, C. J., De Fruyt, F., et al. (2002). Personality trait development from 12 to 18: Longitudinal, cross-sectional, and cross-cultural analyses. *Journal of Personality and Social Psychology, 83,* 1456–1468.

Meyer, G. J. (Ed.). (1999). Special section: I. The utility of the Rorschach in clinical assessment. *Psychological Assessment, 11,* 235–303.

Meyer, G. J. (Ed.). (2001). Special section: II. The utility of the Rorschach in clinical assessment. *Psychological Assessment, 13,* 419–503.

Meyer, G. J., & Handler, L. (1997). The ability of the Rorschach to predict subsequent outcome: Meta-analysis of the Rorschach Prognostic Rating Scale. *Journal of Personality Assessment, 69,* 1–38.

Millon, T. (1969). *Modern psychological pathology: A biosocial approach to maladaptive learning and functioning.* Philadelphia: Saunders.

Millon, T. (1997). *MCMI-III manual* (2nd ed). Minneapolis, MN: National Computer Systems.

Millon, T., Millon, C., & Davis, R. (1993). *Millon Adolescent Personality Inventory: manual.* Minneapolis, MN: National Computer Systems.

Millon, T., Millon, C., & Davis, R. (1994). *MCMI-III manual: Millon Clinical Multiaxial Inventory-III.* Minneapolis, MN: National Computer Systems.

Morgan, C. D., & Murray, H. A. (1935). A method for investigating fantasies: The Thematic Apperception Test. *Archives of Neurology and Psychiatry, 34,* 289–306.

Osberg, T. M., & Poland, D. L. (2002). Comparative accuracy of the MMPI-2 and the MMPI-A in the diagnosis of psychopathology in 18-year-olds. *Psychological Assessment, 14,* 164–169.

Piotrowski, Z. (1947). *A Rorschach compendium.* Utica, NY: State Hospital Press.

Rapaport, D., Gill, M. M., & Schafer, R. (1968). *Diagnostic psychological testing* (rev. ed.). New York: International Universities Press.

Ranseen, J. D., Campbell, D. A., & Baer, R. A. (1998). NEO-PI-R profiles in adults with Attention Deficit Disorder. *Assessment, 5,* 19–24.

Retzlaff, P. (1995). *Tactical psychotherapy of the personality disorder: An MCMI-III-based approach.* Boston: Allyn & Bacon.

Rogers, R., Salekin, R. T., & Sewell, K. W. (1999). Validation of the Millon Clinical Multiaxial Inventory for Axis II disorders: Does it meet the Daubert standard? *Law and Human Behavior, 23,* 425–443.

Rotter, J. R., Lah, M., & Rafferty, J. (1992). *Manual-Rotter Incomplete Sentences Blank* (2nd ed.). Orlando, FL: The Psychological Corporation.

Rouse, S. V., Finger, M. S., & Butcher, J. N. (1999). Advances in clinical personality measurement: An item response theory analysis of the MMPI-2 PSY-5 scales. *Journal of Personality Assessment, 72,* 282–307.

Rubenzer, S. J., Faschingbauer, T. R., & Ones, D. S. (2000). Assessing the U.S. presidents using the revised NEO Personality Inventory. *Assessment, 7,* 403–420.

Schoenberg, M. R., Dorr, D., Morgan, C. D., & Burke, M. (2004). A comparison of the MCMI-III personality disorder and modifier indices with the MMPI-2 clinical and validity scales. *Journal of Personality Assessment, 83,* 273–280.

Sivek, T. M., & Hosterey, U. (1992). The Thematic Apperception Test as an aid in understanding the psychodynamics of development of chronic idiopathic pain syndrome. *Psychotherapy and Psychosomatics, 57,* 57–60.

Strack, S., & Craig, R. J. (2004). The Millon Clinical Multiaxial Inventory-III (MCMI-III). *SPA Exchange, 16*(1), 6–7.

Stricker, G., & Gold, J. R. (1999). The Rorschach: Toward a nomothetically based, Idiographically applicable configurational model. *Psychological Assessment, 11,* 240–250.

Tellegen, A., Ben-Porath, Y. S., McNulty, J. L., Arbisi, P. A., Graham, J. R., & Kaemmer, B. (2003). *The MMPI-2 Restructured Clinical (RC) Scales: Development, validation, and interpretation.* Minneapolis: University of Minnesota Press.

Tharinger, D. J., & Stark, K. (1990). A qualitative versus quantitative approach to evaluating the Draw-A-Person and Kinetic Family Drawing: A study of mood- and anxiety-disorder children. *Psychological Assessment, 2,* 365–375.

Thomas, A., & Chess, S. (1977). *Temperament and development.* New York: Brunner/Mazel.

Thomas, A., Chess, S., & Birch, H. B. (1968). *Temperament and behavior disorders in children.* New York: New York University Press.

Thomas, A. D., & Dudek, S. Z. (1985). Interpersonal affect in Thematic Apperception Test responses: A scoring system. *Journal of Personality Assessment, 49,* 30–36.

Thompson, C. E. (1949). The Thompson modification of the Thematic Apperception Test. *Rorschach Research Exchange, 13,* 469–478.

Waehler, C. A. (1997). Drawing bridges between science and practice. *Journal of Personality Assessment, 69,* 482–487.

Weiner, I. B. (2000). Using the Rorschach properly in practice and research. *Journal of Clinical Psychology, 56,* 435–438.

Weiner, I. B., Spielberger, C. D., & Abeles, N. (2003). Once more around the park: Correcting misinformation about Rorschach assessment. *The Clinical Psychologist, 56*(1), 8–9.

Wetter, M. W., & Corrigan, S. K. (1995). Providing information to clients about psychological tests: A survey of attorneys' and law students' attitudes. *Professional Psychology: Research and Practice, 26,* 474–477.

Wood, J. M., Nezworski, M. T., & Stejskal, W. J. (1996). The Comprehensive System for the Rorschach: A critical examination. *Psychological Science, 7,* 3–10.

Chapter 8 Neuropsychological Assessment and Behavioral Assessment

Abeles, N. (2001, December). Challenges of test coaching for assessment. *Testing International, 11*(2), 4–6.

Achenbach, T. M. (1991). Integrative guide for the 1991 CBCL/4–18, YSR, and TRF *Profiles.* Burlington: University of Vermont, Department of Psychiatry.

Achenbach, T. M. (2000). Assessment of psychopathology. In A. Sameroff & M. Lewis (Eds.), *Handbook of developmental psychopathology* (2nd ed., pp. 41–56). New York: Kluwer/Plenum Academic Press.

Anderson, R. M. (1994). *Practitioner's guide to clinical neuropsychology.* New York: Plenum Press.

Arnold, B. R., Montgomery, G. T., Casteneda, I., & Longoria, R. (1994). Acculturation and performance of Hispanics on selected Halstead-Reitan neuropsychological tests. *Assessment, 1,* 239–248.

Aucone, E. J., Wagner, E. E., Raphael, A. J., Golden, C. J., Espe-Pfeifer, P., Dornheim, L., et al. (2001). Test-retest reliability of the Advanced Psychodiagnostic Interpretation

(API) scoring system for the Bender Gestalt in chronic schizophrenics. *Assessment, 8,* 351–353.

Baron, I. S. (2003). *Neuropsychological evaluation of the child.* New York: Oxford University Press.

Batchelor, E., Jr., Sowles, G., Dean, R. S., & Fischer, W. (1991). Construct validity of the Halstead-Reitan Neuropsychological Battery for children with learning disorders. *Journal of Psychoeducational Assessment, 9,* 16–31.

Beck, A. T., Steer, R. A., & Brown, G. K. (1996). *Manual for the Beck Depression Inventory-II (BDI-II).* San Antonio, TX: Psychological Corporation.

Bellack, A. S., Haas, G. L., & Tierney, A. M. (1996). A strategy for assessing family interaction patterns in schizophrenia. *Psychological Assessment, 8,* 190–199.

Bellack, A. S., & Hersen, M. (Eds.). (1998). *Behavioral assessment: A practical handbook.* Boston: Allyn & Bacon.

Bender, L. A. (1938). A visual motor gestalt test and its clinical use. *American Orthopsychiatric Association Research Monographs,* No. 3.

Berg, R., Franzen, M., & Wedding, D. (1987). *Screening for brain impairment: A manual for mental health practice.* New York: Springer Publishing Company.

Christensen, A. (1983). Reactive effects during naturalistic observation of families. *Behavioral Assessment, 5,* 349–362.

Compas, B. E., & Gotlib, I. H. (2002). *Introduction to clinical psychology: Science and practice.* Boston: McGraw-Hill.

Delis, D. C., Kramer, J. H., Kaplan, E., & Ober, B. A. (2000). *California Verbal Learning Test* (2nd ed). San Antonio, TX: The Psychological Corporation.

Di Sclafani, V., Mackay, R. D. S., Meyerhoff, D. J., Norman, D., Weiner, M. W., & Fein, G. (1997). Brain atrophy in HIV infection is more strongly associated with CDC clinical stages than with cognitive impairment. *Journal of the International Neuropsychological Society, 3,* 276–287.

Doze, S., Simpson, J., Hailey, D., & Jacobs, P. (1999). Evaluation of a telepsychiatry pilot project. *Journal of Telemedicine and Telecare, 5,* 38–46.

Essig, S., Mittenberg, W., Petersen, R., Strauman, S., & Cooper, J. (2001). Practices in forensic neuropsychology: Perspectives of neuropsychologists and trial attorneys. *Archives of Clinical Neuropsychology, 16,* 271–291.

Faibish, G. M., Auerbach, V. S., & Thornby, J. I. (1986). Modifications of the Halstead-Reitan in geriatrics. *British Journal of Psychiatry, 149,* 698–709.

Fletcher-Janzen, E., Strickland, T. L., & Reynolds, C. R. (Eds.). (2000). *Handbook of cross-cultural neuropsychology.* New York: Kluwer Academic/Plenum Publishers.

Folstein, M. F., Folstein, S. E., & McHugh, P. R. (2001). *Mini-Mental State Examination.* Lutz, FL: Psychological Assessment Resources.

Franzen, M., & Berg, R. (1989). *Screening children for brain impairment.* New York: Springer Publishing Company.

Freund, K., & Blanchard, R. (1989). Phallometric diagnosis of pedophilia. *Journal of Consulting and Clinical Psychology, 57,* 1–6.

Freund, K., & Watson, R. J. (1991). Assessment of the sensitivity and specificity of a phallometric test: An update of phallometric diagnosis of pedophilia. *Psychological Assessment, 3,* 254–260.

Gavett, B. E., Lynch, J. K., & McCaffrey, R. J. (2003). Third party observers: The effect size is larger than you might think. *Archives of Clinical Neuropsychology, 18,* 789–790.

Getka, E. J., & Glass, C. R. (1992). Behavioral and cognitive-behavioral approaches to the reduction of dental anxiety. *Behavior Therapy, 23,* 433–448.

Golden, C. J. (1987). *Luria-Nebraska Neuropsychological Battery: Children's revision manual.* Los Angeles: Western Psychological Services.

Golden, C. J., Hammeke, T. A., & Purisch, A. D. (1980). *A manual for the administration and interpretation of the Luria-Nebraska Neuropsychological Battery.* Los Angeles: Western Psychological Services.

Golden, C. J., Kane, R., Sweet, J., Moses, J. A., Cardellino, J. P., Templeton, R., Vicente, P., & Graber, B. (1981). Relationship of the Halstead-Reitan Neuropsychological Battery to the Luria-Nebraska Neuropsychological Battery. *Journal of Consulting and Clinical Psychology, 49,* 410–417.

Golden, C. J., & Kuperman, S. K. (1980). Graduate training in clinical neuropsychology. *Professional Psychology, 11,* 55–63.

Golden, C. J., Purisch, A. D., & Hammeke, T. A. (1985). *Luria-Nebraska Neuropsychological Battery: Forms I and II.* Los Angeles: Western Psychological Services.

Goodglass, H. (1986). The flexible battery in neuropsychological assessment. In T. Incagnoli, G. Goldstein, & C. J. Golden (Eds.), *Clinical applications of neuropsychological test batteries* (pp. 121–134). New York: Plenum Press.

Gottman, J. M., & Levenson, R. W. (1992). Marital processes predictive of later dissolution: Behavior, physiology, and health. *Journal of Personality and Social Psychology, 63,* 221–233.

Halstead, W. C. (1947). *Brain and intelligence.* Chicago: University of Chicago Press.

Halstead, W. C., & Wepman, J. M. (1959). The Halstead-Wepman Aphasia Screening Test. *Journal of Speech and Hearing Disorders, 14,* 9–15.

Haynes, S. N., & O'Brien, W. H. (2000). *Principles and practice of behavioral assessment.* New York: Kluwer Academic/Plenum Press.

Heaton, R. K., Grant, I., Butters, N., White, D. A., Kirson, D., Atkinson, J. H., McCutchan, J. A., Taylor, M. J., Kelly, M. D., Ellis, R. J., Wolfson, T., Velin, R., Marcotte, T. D., Hesselink, J. R., Jernigan, T. L., Chandler, J., Wallace, M., Abramson, I., & the HNRC Group. (1995). The HNRC 500-Neuropsychology of HIV Infection at different disease stages. *Journal of the International Neuropsychological Society, 1,* 231–251.

Heaton, R. K., Nelson, L. K., Thompson, D. S., Burks, J. S., & Franklin, G. M. (1985). Neuropsychological findings in relapsing-remitting and chronic-progressive multiple sclerosis. *Journal of Consulting and Clinical Psychology, 53,* 103–110.

Hollister, J. M., Mednick, S. A., Brennan, P., & Cannon, T. D. (1994). Impaired autonomic nervous system habituation in those at risk for schizophrenia. *Archives of General Psychiatry, 51,* 552–557.

Hutt, M. L. (1985). The Hutt adaptation of the Bender-Gestalt Test (4th ed.). Orlando, FL: Grune & Stratton.

Jacobsen, S. E., Sprenger, T., Andersson, S., & Krogstad, J-M. (2003). *Journal of the International Neuropsychological Society, 9,* 472–478.

Johnson-Greene, D. (2004). Dementia Rating Scale-2 (DRS-2): By P. J. Jurica, C. L. Leitten, and S. Mattis: Psychological Assessment Resources: 2001. *Archives of Clinical Neuropsychology, 19,* 145–147.

Jurica, S. J., Leitten, C. L., & Mattis, S. (2001). *Dementia Rating Scale: Professional manual.* Odessa, FL: Psychological Assessment Resources.

Kamphaus, R. W., DiStefano, C., & Lease, A. M. (2003). A self-report typology of behavioral adjustment for young children. *Psychological Assessment, 15,* 17–28.

Kane, R. L., Sweet, J. J., Golden, C. J., Parsons, O. A., & Moses, J. A. (1981). Comparative diagnostic accuracy of the Halstead-Reitan and standardized Luria-Nebraska Neuropsychological batteries in a mixed psychiatric and brain-damaged population. *Journal of Consulting and Clinical Psychology, 49,* 484–485.

Kanfer, F. H., & Phillips, J. S. (1970). *Learning foundations of behavior therapy.* New York: Wiley.

Kaplan, E. (1990). The process approach to neuropsychological assessment of psychiatric patients. *Journal of Neuropsychiatry and Clinical Neurosciences, 2,* 72–87.

Kennepohl, S., Shore, D., Nabors, N., & Hanks, R. (2004). African American acculturation and neuropsychological test performance following traumatic brain injury. *Journal of the International Neuropsychological Society, 10,* 566–577.

Kiernan, R. J., Mueller, J., & Langston, J. W. (1995). *Cognistat: Neurobehavioral Cognitive Status Examination.* Fairfax: The Northern California Neurobehavioral Group, Inc.

Koppitz, E. M. (1975). *The Bender-Gestalt Test for young children* (Vol. 2). New York: Grune & Stratton.

Lees-Haley, P. R., Smith, H. H., Williams, C., & Dunn, J. T. (1996). Forensic neuropsychological test usage: An empirical survey. *Archives of Clinical Neuropsychology, 11,* 45–51.

Lezak, M. D. (1995). *Neuropsychological assessment* (3rd ed.). New York: Oxford University Press.

McGlynn, F. D., & Rose, M. P. (1998). Assessment of anxiety and fear. In A. S. Bellack & M. Hersen (Eds.), *Behavioral assessment: A practical handbook* (pp. 179–209). Elmsford, NY: Pergamon Press.

Meyers, J. E., & Meyers, K. R. (1995). *The Meyers Scoring system for the Rey Complex Figure and the Recognition Trial: Professional Manual.* Odessa, FL: Psychological Assessment Resources.

O'Donnell, J. P. (1983). Neuropsychological test findings for normal, learning disabled, and brain damaged young adults. *Journal of Counseling and Clinical Psychology, 51,* 726–729.

Pascal, G. R., & Suttell, B. J. (1951). *The Bender-Gestalt Test: Quantification and validity for adults.* New York: Grune & Stratton.

Patterson, G. R. (1977). Naturalistic observation in clinical assessment. *Journal of Abnormal Child Psychology, 5,* 307–322.

Patterson, G. R., & Forgatch, M. S. (1995). Predicting future clinical adjustment from treatment outcome and process variables. *Psychological Assessment, 7,* 275–285.

Peterson, L., & Sobell, L. C. (1994). Introduction to the state-of-the-art review series: Research contributions to clinical assessment. *Behavior Therapy, 25,* 523–531.

Piotrowski, C., & Keller, J. W. (1992). Psychological testing in applied settings: A literature review from 1982–1992. *Journal of Training & Practice in Professional Psychology, 6,* 74–82.

Raphael, A. J., & Golden, C. J. (1998). *Objective scoring form and booklet for the API Bender Gestalt.* Miami, FL: International Assessment Systems.

Raphael, A. J., & Golden, C. J. (2002). Relationships of objectively scored Bender variables with MMPI scores in an outpatient psychiatric population. *Perceptual and Motor Skills, 95,* 1217–1232.

Reichenberg, N., & Raphael, A. J. (1992). *Advanced Psychodiagnostic Interpretation of the Bender Gestalt Test: Adults and children.* New York: Praeger.

Reitan, R. M. (1955). Investigation of the validity of Halstead's measure of biological intelligence. *Archives of Neurology and Psychiatry, 73,* 28–35.

Reitan, R. M. (1986). Theoretical and methodological bases of the Halstead-Reitan Neuropsychological Battery. In I. Grant & K. M. Adams (Eds.), *Neuropsychological assessment of neuropsychiatric disorders* (pp. 3–30). New York: Oxford University Press.

Reitan, R. M., & Wolfson, D. (1993). *The Halstead-Reitan Neuropsychological Test Battery: Theory and clinical interpretation.* Tucson, AZ: Neuropsychology Press.

Rey, A. (1941). L'examen psychologique dan les cas d'encephalopathie traumatique. *Archives de Psychologie, 28,* 286–340.

Reynolds, C. R., & Kamphaus, R. W. (1992). *Behavior Assessment System for Children.* Circle Pines, MN: American Guidance Service.

Rosiers, G. des, & Kavanaugh, D. (1987). Cognitive assessment in closed head injury: Stability, validity, and parallel forms for two neuropsychological measures of recovery. *International Journal of Clinical Neuropsychology, 9,* 162–173.

Schaefer, C. E., Gitlin, K., & Sandgrund, A. (Eds.). (1991). *Play diagnosis and assessment.* New York: Wiley.

Schopler, E., Reichler, R. J., & Renner, B. R. (1988). *The childhood autism rating scale.* Los Angeles: Western Psychological Services.

Schopp, L., Johnstone, B., & Merrell, D. (2000). Telehealth and neuropsychological assessment: New opportunities for psychologists. *Professional Psychology: Research and Practice, 31,* 179–183.

Skinner, B. F. (1953). *Science and human behavior.* New York: Macmillan.

Spreen, O., & Strauss, E. (1998). *A compendium of neuropsychological tests* (2nd ed). New York: Oxford University Press.

Street, L. L., & Barlow, D. H. (1994). Anxiety disorders. In L. W. Craighead, W. E. Craighead, A. E. Kazdin, & M. J. Mahoney (Eds.), *Cognitive and behavioral interventions: An empirical approach to mental health problems* (pp. 71–87). Boston: Allyn & Bacon.

Taussig, I. M., Mack, W. J., & Henderson, V. W. (1996). Concurrent validity of Spanish-language versions of the Mini-Mental State Examination, Mental Status Questionnaire, Information Concentration Test, and Orientation-Memory-Concentration Test: Alzheimer's disease patients and non-demented elderly comparison subjects. *Journal of the International Neuropsychological Society, 2,* 286–298.

Taylor, C. B., Agras, W. S., Losch, M., Plante, T. G., & Burnett, K. (1991). Improving the effectiveness of computer-assisted weight loss. *Behavior Therapy, 22,* 229–236.

Taylor, J. S., Harp, J. A., & Elliott, T. (1992). Preparing the plaintiff in the mild brain injury case. *Trial Diplomacy Journal, 15,* 65–72.

Tomarken, A. J. (1995). What is the critical evidence favoring expectancy bias theory and where is it? *Behavioral and Brain Sciences, 18,* 313–314.

Tombaugh, T. N. (1996). *Test of Memory Malingering (TOMM).* New York: Multi-Health Systems.

Tombaugh, T. N. (1997). The Test of Memory Malingering (TOMM): Normative data from cognitively impaired individuals. *Psychological Assessment, 9,* 260–268.

Tombaugh, T. N., & McIntyre, N. J. (1992). The Mini-Mental State Examination: A comprehensive review. *Journal of American Geriatric Society, 40,* 922–935.

Victor, T. L., & Abeles, N. (2004). Coaching clients to take psychological and neuropsychological tests: A clash of ethical obligations. *Professional Psychology: Research and Practice, 35,* 373–379.

Wadsworth, M. E., Hudziak, J. J., Heath, A. C., & Achenbach, T. M. (2001). Latent class analysis of Child Behavior Checklist anxiety/depression in children and adolescents. *Journal of the American Academy of Child and Adolescent Psychiatry, 40,* 106–114.

Waters, A. M., Lipp, O. V., & Cobham, V. E. (2000). Investigation of threat-related attentional bias in anxious children using the startle eyeblink modification paradigm. *Journal of Psychophysiology, 14,* 142–150.

Wechsler, D. (1945). A standardized memory scale for clinical use. *Journal of Psychology, 19,* 87–95.

Wechsler, D. (1997). *Wechsler Memory Scale-Third Edition.* San Antonio, TX: Psychological Corporation.

Williams, A. D. (2000). Fixed versus flexible batteries. In R. J. McCaffrey, A. D. Williams, J. M. Fisher, & L. C. Laing (Eds.), *The practice of forensic neuropsychology: Meeting challenges in the courtroom* (pp. 57–70). New York: Plenum.

Wysocki, J. J., & Sweet, J. J. (1985). Identification of brain-damaged, schizophrenic, and normal medical patients using a brief neuropsychological screening battery. *International Journal of Clinical Neuropsychology, 7,* 40–44.

Chapter 9 Introduction to Psychotherapy

Allen, B. P. (2003). *Personality theories: Development, growth, and diversity* (4th ed). Boston: Allyn & Bacon.

Axline, V. M. (1979). *Play therapy.* New York: Ballentine Books.

Berry, J. W., & Kim, U. (1988). Acculturation and mental health. In P. R. Dansen, J. W. Berry, & N. Sartorius (Eds.), *Health and cross-cultural psychology.* Newbury Park, CA: Sage.

Beutler, L. E., Crago, M., & Arezmendi, T. G. (1986). Research on therapist variables in psychotherapy. In S. L. Garfield (Ed.), *Handbook of psychotherapy and behavior change* (3rd ed., pp. 257–310). New York: Wiley.

Borkovec, T. D., & Castonguay, L. G. (1998). What is the scientific meaning of empirically supported therapy? *Journal of Consulting and Clinical Psychology, 66,* 136–142.

Burlingame, G. M., Fuhriman, A., & Johnson, J. E. (2001). Cohesion in group psychotherapy. *Psychotherapy: Theory/Research/Practice/Training, 38,* 373–379.

Butz, M. R., Bowling, J. B., & Bliss, C. A. (2000). Psychotherapy with the mentally retarded: A review of the literature and the implications. *Professional Psychology: Research and Practice, 31,* 42–47.

Cantor, D. W. (2005). Patient's rights in psychotherapy. In G. P. Koocher, J. C. Norcross, & S. S. Hill (Eds.), *Psychologists' desk reference* (2nd ed., pp. 181–183). New York: Oxford University Press.

Capuzzi, D., & Gross, D. R. (Eds.). (2003). *Counseling and psychotherapy: Theories and interventions* (3rd ed.). Columbus, OH: Merrill Prentice-Hall.

Cardemil, E. V. (2003). Guess who's coming to therapy? Getting comfortable with conversations about race and ethnicity in psychotherapy. *Professional Psychology: Research and Practice, 34,* 278–286.

Cardemil, E. V., & Battle, C. L. (2003). Guess who's coming to therapy? Getting comfortable with conversations about race and ethnicity in psychotherapy. *Professional Psychology: Research and Practice, 34* (3) 278–286.

Chambless, D. L., & Hollon, S. D. (1998). Defining empirically supported therapies. *Journal of Consulting and Clinical Psychology, 66,* 7–18.

Christensen, A., & Jacobson, N. S. (1994). Who (or what) can do psychotherapy: The status and challenge of nonprofessional therapies. *Psychological Science, 5,* 8–14.

Crits-Christoph, P. (1992). The efficacy of brief dynamic psychotherapy: A meta-analysis. *The American Journal of Psychiatry, 149,* 151–158.

Cullari, S. (Ed.). (1998). *Foundations of clinical psychology.* Boston: Allyn & Bacon.

Egan, G. (1998). *The skilled helper: A problem-management approach to helping* (6th ed.). Pacific Grove, CA: Brooks/Cole.

Elkin, I. E., Shea, T., Watkins, J. T., Imber, S. D., Stotsky, S. M., Collins, J. F., Glass, D. R., Pilkonis, P. A., Leber, W. R., Docherty, J. P., Fiester, S. J., & Parloff, M. B. (1989). National Institute of Mental Health Treatment of Depression Collaborative Research Program: General effectiveness of treatment. *Archives of General Psychiatry, 46,* 974–982.

Ellis, A., & Dryden, W. (1997). *The practice of rational-emotive therapy.* New York: Springer.

Eysenck, H. J. (1952). The effects of psychotherapy: An evaluation. *Journal of Consulting Psychology, 16,* 319–324.

Eysenck, H. J. (1965). The effects of psychotherapy. *International Journal of Psychiatry, 1,* 99–143.

Eysenck, H. J. (1966). *The effects of psychotherapy.* New York: International Science Press.

Farber, B. A., & Lane, J. S. (2001). Positive regard. *Psychotherapy: Theory/Research/Practice/Training, 38,* 390–395.

Gold, J. R. (1996). *Key concepts in psychotherapy integration.* New York: Plenum Press.

Greenberg, L., Elliott, R., & Lietaer, G. (1994). Research on experiential psychotherapies. In A. E. Bergin & S. L. Garfield (Eds.), *Handbook of psychotherapy and behavior change* (4th ed., pp. 509–539). New York: Wiley.

Hall, C. S., Lindzey, G., & Campbell, J. B. (1998). *Theories of personality* (4th ed). New York: John Wiley & Sons.

Hellman, I. D., & Morrison, T. L. (1987). Practice setting and type of caseload as factors in psychotherapist stress. *Psychotherapy, 24*(3), 427–432.

Horner, A. J. (1991). *Psychoanalytic object relations therapy*. Northvale, NJ: Aronson.

Horvath, A. O. (2001). The alliance. *Psychotherapy: Theory/Research/Practice/Training, 38*, 365–372.

Hurley, A. D., Pfadt, A., Tomasulo, D., & Gardner, W. I. (1996). Counseling and psychotherapy. In J. W. Jacobson & J. A. Mulick, *Manual of diagnosis and professional practice in mental retardation* (pp. 371–380). Washington, DC: American Psychological Association.

Hutchinson, G. T., Patock-Peckham, J. A., Cheong, J., & Nagoshi, C. T. (1998). Irrational beliefs and behavioral misregulation in the role of alcohol abuse among college students. *Journal of Rational Emotive and Cognitive Behavior Therapy, 16*, 61–74.

Kaslow, F. W. (1986). Therapy with distressed psychotherapists: Special problems and challenges. In R. R. Kilburg, P. E. Nathan, & R. W. Thoreson (Eds.), *Professionals in distress: Issues, syndromes, and solutions in psychology* (pp. 187–210). Washington, DC: American Psychological Association.

Kazdin, A. E. (1994). Methodology, design, and evaluation in psychotherapy research. In A. E. Bergin & S. L. Garfield (Eds.), *Handbook of psychotherapy and behavior change* (4th ed., pp. 19–72). New York: Wiley.

Kendall, P. C., & Chambless, D. L. (Eds.). (1998). Empirically supported psychological therapies (Special section). *Journal of Consulting and Clinical Psychology, 66*, 3–150.

Lafferty, P., Beutler, L. E., & Crago, M. (1989). Differences between more and less effective psychotherapists: A study of select therapist variables. *Journal of Consulting and Clinical Psychology, 57*, 76–80.

Lambert, M. J., & Bergin, A. E. (1994). The effectiveness of psychotherapy. In A. E Bergin & S. L. Garfield (Eds.), *Handbook of psychotherapy and behavior change* (4th ed., pp. 143–189). New York: Wiley.

Lambert, M. J., Bybee, T., Houston, R., Bishop, M., Sanders, A. D., Wilkinson, R., et al. (2005). Compendium of psychotherapy treatment manuals. In G. P. Koocher, J. C. Norcross, & S. S. Hill (Eds.), *Psychologists' desk reference* (2nd ed., pp. 192–202).

La Roche, M. J., & Maxie, A. (2003). Ten considerations in addressing cultural differences in psychotherapy. *Professional Psychology: Research and Practice, 34*, 180–186.

Luborsky, L., & Barber, J. P. (1993). Benefits of adherence to psychotherapy manuals and where to get them. In N. E. Miller, L. Luborsky, J. P. Barber, & J. P. Docherty (Eds.), *Psychodynamic treatment research* (pp. 211–226). New York: Basic Books.

Lyons, L. C., & Woods, P. J. (1991). The efficacy of rational-emotive therapy: A quantitative review of the outcome research. *Clinical Psychology Review, 11*, 357–369.

Mental Health Bill of Rights Project. (1997). Principles for the provision of mental health and substance abuse treatment services. *Independent Practitioner, 17*(2), 57–58.

Murdock, N. L. (2004). *Theories of counseling and psychotherapy: A case approach*. Upper Saddle River, NJ: Pearson/Merrill Prentice Hall.

Norcross, J. C. (2001). Purposes, processes, and products of the task force on empirically supported therapy relationships. *Psychotherapy: Theory/Research/Practice/Training, 38*, 345–356.

Nystul, M. S. (1999). *Introduction to counseling: An art and science perspective*. Boston: Allyn & Bacon.

Prochaska, J. O., & Norcross, J. C. (1999). *Systems of psychotherapy: A transtheoretical analysis* (4th ed.). Pacific Grove, CA: Brooks/Cole.

Rogers, C. R. (1951). *Client-centered therapy*. Boston: Houghton Mifflin.

Rogers, C. R. (1957). The necessary and sufficient conditions of therapeutic change. *Journal of Consulting Psychology, 21*, 95–103.

Schofield, W. (1964). *Psychotherapy: The purchase of friendship*. Englewood Cliffs, NJ: Prentice-Hall.

Schultz, D. P., & Schultz, S. E. (2005). *Theories of personality* (8th ed.). Belmont, CA: Wadsworth.

Seligman, M. E. P. (1995). The effectiveness of psychotherapy: The Consumer Reports Study. *American Psychologist, 50,* 965–974.

Sharf, R. S. (2000). *Theories of psychotherapy and counseling: Concepts and cases.* Belmont, CA: Brooks/Cole.

Skovholt, T. M. (2001). *The resilient practitioner: Burnout prevention and self-care strategies for counselors, therapists, teachers, and health professionals.* Needham Heights, MA: Allyn & Bacon.

Smith, M. L., & Glass, G. V. (1977). Meta-analysis of psychotherapy outcome studies. *American Psychologist, 32,* 752–760.

Sue, D. W., & Sue, D. (1999). *Counseling the culturally different: Theory and practice* (3rd ed.). New York: John Wiley & Sons.

Sundberg, N. D., Taplin, J. R., & Tyler, L. E. (1983). *Introduction to clinical psychology: Perspectives, issues, and contributions to human services.* Englewood Cliffs, NJ: Prentice-Hall.

Truax, C. B., & Mitchell, K. M. (1971). Research on certain therapist interpersonal skills in relation to process and outcome. In A. E. Bergin & S. L Garfield (Eds.), *Handbook of psychotherapy and behavior change: An empirical analysis* (pp. 299–344). New York: Wiley.

U.S. Bureau of the Census. (2001). *The Hispanic population.* Washington, DC: Government Printing Office.

VandenBos, G. R. (1996). Outcome assessment of psychotherapy. *American Psychologist, 51,* 1005–1006.

Weston, D. (1998). The scientific legacy of Sigmund Freud: Toward a psychodynamically informed science. *Psychological Bulletin, 124,* 333–371.

Wolberg, L. R. (1967). *The technique of psychotherapy* (2nd ed.). New York: Grune and Stratton.

Woodside, M. R., & Legg, B. H. (1990). Patient advocacy: A mental health perspective. *Journal of Mental Health Counseling, 12,* 38–50.

Worell, J., & Remer, P. (1992). *Feminist perspectives in therapy: An empowerment model for women.* New York: Wiley.

Wyatt v. Stickney, 344F Supp. 373 (M.D. Ala. 1972).

Young, M. E. (2001). *Learning the art of healing: Building blocks and techniques* (2nd ed.). Upper Saddle River, NJ: Merrill Prentice-Hall.

Chapter 10 Schools of Psychotherapy

Alford, B. A., & Beck, A. T. (1997). *The integrative power of cognitive therapy.* New York: Guilford.

Anderson, E. M., & Lambert, M. J. (1995). Short-term dynamically oriented psychotherapy: A review and meta-analysis. *Clinical Psychology Review, 15,* 503–514.

Ayllon, T., & Azrin, N. H. (1965). The measurement and reinforcement of behavior of psychotics. *Journal of Experimental Analysis of Behavior, 8,* 357–383.

Beck, A. T. (1976). *Cognitive therapy and the emotional disorders.* Madison, WI: International Universities Press.

Beck, A. T. (2005). The current state of cognitive therapy: A 40-year retrospective. *Archives of General Psychiatry, 62,* 953–959.

Beck, J. S. (1995). *Cognitive therapy: Basics and beyond.* New York: Guilford.

Brown, G. K., Have, T. T., Henriques, G. R., Xie, S. X., Hollander, J. E., & Beck, A. T. (2005). Cognitive therapy for the prevention of suicide attempts. *Journal of the American Medical Association, 294,* 563–570.

Comas-Diaz, L. (2005). Becoming a multicultural psychotherapist: The confluence of culture, ethnicity, and gender. *Journal of Clinical Psychology: In Session, 61,* 973–982.

Davanloo, H. (1979). Techniques of short-term psychotherapy. *Psychiatric Clinics of North America, 2,* 11–22.

Demos, V. C., & Prout, M. F. (1993). A comparison of seven approaches to brief psychotherapy. *International Journal of Short-Term Psychotherapy, 8,* 3–22.

Dobson, K. S. (1989). A meta-analysis of the efficacy of cognitive therapy for depression. *Journal of Consulting and Clinical Psychology, 57,* 414–419.

Elliott, R., Watson, J., Goldman, R., & Greenberg, L. (2004). *Learning emotion-focused therapy: The process-experiential approach to change.* Washington, DC: American Psychological Association.

Ellis, A. (1962). *Reason and emotion in psychotherapy.* New York: Lyle Stuart.

Ellis, A. (1991). The philosophical basis of rational-emotive therapy (RET). *Psychotherapy in Private Practice, 8,* 97–106.

Ellis, A. (2000). Rational-emotive behavior therapy as an internal control psychology. *Journal of Rational-Emotive and Cognitive Behavior Therapy, 18,* 19–38.

Ellis, A., & Dryden, W. (1997). *The practice of rational-emotive therapy.* New York: Springer.

Ellis, A., & Greiger, R. (Eds.). (1977). *Handbook of rational-emotive therapy: Vol 1.* New York: Springer.

Engles, G. I., Garnefski, N., & Diekstra, R. F. (1993). Efficacy of rational-emotive therapy: A quantitative analysis. *Journal of Consulting and Clinical Psychology, 61,* 1083–1090.

Fishman, D. B., & Franks, C. M. (1997). The conceptual evolution of behavior therapy. In P. L. Wachtel & S. B. Messer (Eds.), *Theories of psychotherapy: Origins and evolution* (pp. 131–180). Washington, DC: American Psychological Association.

Frankl, V. (1967). *Psychotherapy and existentialism: Selected papers on logotherapy.* New York: Washington Square Press.

Freud, S. (1953). The interpretation of dreams. In J. Strachey (Ed. and Trans.), *The standard edition of the complete psychological works of Sigmund Freud* (Vol. 5, pp. 339–627). London: Hogarth. (Original work published in 1900.)

Freud, S. (1964). An outline of psycho-analysis. In J. Strachey (Ed. and Trans.), *The standard edition of the complete psychological works of Sigmund Freud* (Vol. 23, pp. 144–207). London: Hogarth. (Original work published in 1940.)

Glasser, W. (1965). *Reality therapy: A new approach to psychiatry.* New York: Harper & Row.

Glasser, W. (1969). *Schools without failure.* New York: Harper & Row.

Glasser, W. (1992). Reality therapy. In J. K. Zeig (Ed.), *The evolution of psychotherapy: The second conference* (pp. 270–278). New York: Brunner/Mazel.

Glasser, W. (2003). *Warning: Psychiatry can be hazardous to your mental health.* New York: HarperCollins.

Gloaguen, V., Cottraux, J., Cucherat, M., & Blackburn, I. (1998). A meta-analysis of the effects of cognitive therapy in depressed patients. *Journal of Affective Disorders, 49,* 59–72.

Grawe, K., Donati, R., & Bernauer, F. (1998). *Psychotherapy in transition.* Seattle: Hogrefe & Huber.

Howatt, W. A. (2001). The evolution of reality therapy to choice theory. *International Journal of Reality Therapy, 21,* 7–11.

Jacobson, E. (1938). *Progressive relaxation.* Chicago: University of Chicago Press.

Jones, M. C. (1924). The elimination of children's fears. *Journal of Experimental Psychology, 7,* 383–390.

Kovacs, M., & Beck, A. T. (1978). Maladaptive cognitive structures in depression. *The American Journal of Psychiatry, 135,* 525–533.

Leichsenring, F., Rabung, S., & Leibing, E. (2004). The efficacy of short-term psychodynamic psychotherapy in specific psychiatric disorders: A meta-analysis. *Archives of General Psychiatry, 61,* 1208–1216.

Luborsky, L. (1984). *Principles of psychoanalytic psychotherapy: A manual for supportive-expressive treatment.* New York: Basic Books.

McGovern, T. E., & Silverman, M. (1986). A review of outcome studies of rational-emotive therapy from 1977 to 1982. In A. Ellis & R. M. Grieger (Eds.), *Handbook of rational-emotive therapy* (pp. 81–102). New York: Springer.

Meador, R. D., & Rogers, C. R. (1984). Client-centered therapy. In R. J. Corsini (Ed.), *Current psychotherapies* (2nd ed.). Itasca, IL: Peacock.

Miller, C. A., & Capuzzi, D. (1984). A review of transactional analysis outcome studies. *American Mental Health Counselors Association Journal, 6*(1), 30–41.

Norcross, J. C., Beutler, L. L. E., & Levant R. F. (Eds.). (2005). *Evidence-based practice in mental health: Debate and dialogue on the fundamental questions.* Washington, DC: American Psychological Association.

Norcross, J. C., & Goldfried, M. R. (2005). *Handbook of psychotherapy integration* (2nd ed.). New York: Oxford University Press.

Paul, G. L., Redfield, J. P., & Lentz, R. J. (1976). The Inpatient Scale of Minimal Functioning: A revision of the Social Breakdown Syndrome Gradient Index. *Journal of Consulting and Clinical Psychology, 44,* 1021–1022.

Perls, F. S. (1969). *Gestalt therapy verbatim.* Lafayette, CA: Real People Press.

Perls, F. S., Hefferline, R. F., & Goodman, P. (1951). *Gestalt therapy.* New York: Julian Press.

Prochaska, J. O., & Norcross, J. C. (2007). *Systems of psychotherapy: A transtheoretical analysis* (6th ed.). Belmont, CA: Thomson Brooks/Cole.

Radtke, L., Sapp, M., & Farrell, W. C. (1997). Reality therapy: A meta analysis. *Journal of Reality Therapy, 17,* 4–9.

Rogers, C. R. (1957). The necessary and sufficient conditions of therapeutic personality change. *Journal of Consulting Psychology, 21,* 95–103.

Rogers, C. R., & Dymond, R. F. (Eds.). (1954). *Psychotherapy and behavior change: Coordinated studies in the client-centered approach.* Chicago: University of Illinois Press.

Seligman, L. (2001). *Systems, strategies, and skills of counseling and psychotherapy.* Upper Saddle River, NJ: Prentice-Hall.

Smith, M. L., & Glass, G. V. (1977). Meta-analysis of psychotherapy outcome studies. *American Psychologist, 32,* 752–760.

Smith, M. L., Glass, G. V., & Miller, T. I. (1980). *The benefits of psychotherapy.* Baltimore, MD: Johns Hopkins University Press.

Strupp, H. H. (1992). The future of psychodynamic psychotherapy. *Psychotherapy, 29* (1), 21–27.

Sue, S. (2003). In defense of cultural competency in psychotherapy and treatment. *American Psychologist, 53,* 964–970.

Walen, S., DiGiuseppe, R., & Wessler, R. L. (1980). *A practitioner's guide to rational-emotive therapy.* New York: Oxford University Press.

Wallerstein, R. S. (1986). *Forty-two lives in treatment.* New York: Guilford.

Watson, J. B., & Rayner, R. (1920). Conditioned emotional reactions. *Journal of Experimental Psychology, 3,* 114.

Wolpe, J. (1958). *Psychotherapy by reciprocal inhibition.* Stanford, CA: Stanford University Press.

Wubbolding, R. E. (2000). *Reality therapy for the 21st century.* Philadelphia: Brunner-Routledge.

Chapter 11 Individual Psychotherapy

American Psychological Association (APA). (2002). Ethical principles of psychologists and code of conduct. *American Psychologist, 57,* 1060–1073.

Anastopoulos, A. D., DuPaul, G. J., & Barkley, R. A. (1992). Stimulant medication and parent training therapies for attention deficit-hyperactivity disorder. *Journal of Learning Disabilities, 24,* 210–218.

Anastopoulos, A. D., & Shaffer, S. D. (2001). Attention-deficit hyperactivity disorder. In C. E. Walker & M. C. Roberts (Eds.), *Handbook of clinical child psychology* (3rd ed., pp. 470–494). New York: Wiley.

Axline, V. M. (1979). *Play therapy.* New York: Ballantine Books.

Barkley, R. A. (1998). *Attention-deficit/hyperactivity disorder: A handbook for diagnosis and treatment* (2nd ed.). New York: Guilford Press.

Bongar, B. (2002). *The suicidal patient: Clinical and legal standards of care* (2nd ed.). Washington, DC: American Psychological Association.

Bongar, B., & Sullivan, G. R. (2005). Treatment and the management of the suicidal patient. In G. P. Koocher, J. C. Norcross, & S. S. Hill (Eds.), *Psychologists' desk reference* (pp. 240–245). New York: Oxford.

Broverman, I. K., Broverman, D., Clarkson, F. E., Rosenkrantz, P., & Vogle, S. (1970). Sex role stereotypes and clinical judgments of mental health. *Journal of Consulting and Clinical Psychology, 34,* 1–7.

Brown, L. S. (1994). *Subversive dialogues: Theory in feminist therapy.* New York: Basic Books.

Brown, L. S. (2000). Feminist therapy. In C. R. Snyder & R. E. Ingram (Eds.), *Handbook of psychological change: Psychotherapy processes and practices for the 21st century* (pp. 358–380). New York: Wiley.

Brown, L. S., & Mueller, F. A. (2005). Guidelines for treating women in psychotherapy. In G. P. Koocher, J. C. Norcross, & S. S. Hill (Eds.), *Psychologists' desk reference* (pp. 295–298). New York: Oxford.

Castelnuovo, G., Gaggioli, A., Mantovani, F., & Riva, G. (2003). New and old tools in psychotherapy: The use of technology for the integration of traditional clinical treatments. *Psychotherapy: Theory, Research, Practice, Training, 40,* 33–44.

Comas-Diaz, L., & Greene, B. (Eds.). (1994). *Women of color: Integrating ethnic and gender identities in psychotherapy.* New York: Guilford.

Deutsch, C. (1984). Self-report sources of stress among psychotherapists. *Professional Psychology: Research and Practice, 15,* 833–845.

Enns, C. Z. (1997). *Feminist theories and feminist psychotherapies: Origins, theses, and variations.* New York: Haworth.

Falco, K. (1991). *Psychotherapy with lesbian clients: Theory into practice.* New York: Brunner/ Mazel.

Gilbert, L. A., & Scher, M. (1999). *Gender and sex in counseling and psychotherapy.* Boston: Allyn & Bacon.

Hall, R. C. W., Platt, D. E., & Hall, R. C. W. (1999). Suicide risk assessment: A review of risk factors for suicide in 100 patients who made severe suicide attempts: Evaluation of suicide risk in a time of managed care. *Psychosomatics, 40,* 18–27.

Jongsma, A. E. (2005). Psychotherapy treatment plan writing. In G. P. Koocher, J. C. Norcross, & S. S. Hill (Eds.), *Psychologists' desk reference* (2nd ed.). New York: Oxford.

Kaduson, H. G., & Schaefer, C. (1997). *101 favorite play therapy techniques.* Northvale, NJ: Jason Aronson.

Kortte, K. B., Hill-Briggs, F., & Wegener, S. T. (2005). Psychotherapy with cognitively impaired adults. In G. P. Koocher, J. C. Norcross, & S. S. Hill (Eds.), *Psychologists' desk reference* (2nd ed). New York: Oxford.

Krijn, M., Emmelkamp, P. M. G., Olaffson, R. P., & Biemond, R. (2004). Virtual reality exposure therapy for anxiety disorders: A review. *Clinical Psychology Review, 24,* 259–281.

Landreath, G. L. (Ed.). (1982). *Play therapy: Dynamics of the process of counseling with children.* Springfield, IL: Charles C. Thomas.

Marshall, R. D., & Pierce, D. (2000). Implications of recent findings in posttraumattic stress disorder and the role of pharmacotherapy. *Harvard Review of Psychiatry, 7,* 247–256.

MTA Cooperative Group. (1999). A 14-month randomized clinical trial of treatment strategies for attention deficit/hyperactivity disorder. *Archives of General Psychiatry, 56,* 1073–1086.

National Institutes of Health (NIH). (2000). National Institutes of Health consensus development conference statement: Diagnosis and treatment of attention-deficit/hyperactivity disorder (ADHD). *Journal of the American Academy of Child and Adolescent Psychiatry, 39,* 182–193.

Oordt, M. S., Jobes, D. A., Rudd, M. D., Fonseca, V. P., Runyan, C. N., Stea, J. B. et al. (2005). Development of a clinical guide to enhance care for suicidal patients. *Professional Psychology: Research and Practice, 36,* 208–218.

Pelham, W., Wheeler, T., & Chronis, A. (1998). Empirically supported psychosocial treatments for attention deficit hyperactivity disorder. *Journal of Clinical Child Psychology, 27,* 190–225.

Philpott, L. L., Brooks, G. R., Lusterman, D. D., & Nutt, R. L. (1997). *Bridging separate gender worlds: Why men and women clash and how therapists can bring them together.* Washington, DC: American Psychological Association.

Rothbaum, B. O., Hodges, L., Smith, S., & Lee, J. H. (2000). *Journal of Consulting and Clinical Psychology, 68,* 1020–1026.

Russ, S. W., & Freedheim, D. K. (2001). Psychotherapy with children. In C. E. Walker & M. C. Roberts (Eds.), *Handbook of clinical child psychology* (3rd ed, pp. 840–859.). New York: Wiley.

Schaefer, C. (Ed.). (1979). *Therapeutic use of child's play.* New York: Aronson.

Singer, D. (1993). *Playing for their lives.* New York: Free Press.

Wolf, A. W. (Ed.). (2003). The technology of psychotherapy [Special issue], *Psychotherapy: Theory, Research, Practice, Training, 40*(1/2).

Worrell, J., & Remer, P. (2003). *Feminist perspectives in therapy: Empowering diverse women* (2nd ed.). New York: Wiley.

Chapter 12 Couples, Family, and Group Psychotherapy

Ackerman, N. W. (1958). *The psychodynamics of family life: Diagnosis and treatment of family relationships.* New York: Basic Books.

Alexander, J. F., Holtzworth-Monroe, A., & Jameson, P. B. (1994). The process and outcome of marital and family therapy: Research review and evaluation. In A. E. Bergin & S. L. Garfield (Eds.), *Handbook of psychotherapy and behavior change* (pp. 595–630). New York: John Wiley & Sons.

American Psychological Association (APA). (2002). Ethical principles of psychologists and code of conduct. *American Psychologist, 57,* 1060–1073.

Beckvar, D. S., & Beckvar, R. J. (2003). *Family therapy* (5th ed.). Boston: Allyn & Bacon.

Blatner, A. (1997). Psychodrama: The state of the art. *Arts in Psychotherapy, 24,* 23–30.

Blatner, A. (2000). *Foundtions of psychodrama* (4th ed.). New York: Springer.

Bowen, M. (1960). A family concept of schizophrenia. In D. D. Jackson (Ed.), *The etiology of schizophrenia* (pp. 346–372). New York: Basic Books.

Bowen, M. (1966). The use of family theory in clinical practice. *Comprehensive Psychiatry, 7,* 345–374.

Bowlby, J. (1969). *Attachment and loss, Vol. 1: Attachment.* New York: Basic Books. Christensen, A., & Heavey, C. L. (1999). Interventions for couples. *Annual Review of Psychology, 50,* 165–190.

Butler, T., & Fhuriman, A. (1986). Professional psychologists as group treatment providers: utilization, training, and trends. *Professional Psychology, Research and Practice, 17* (3) 273–275.

Corey, M. S., & Corey, G. (1997). *Groups: Process and practice* (5th ed.). Pacific Grove, CA: Brooks/Cole.

DeGenova, M. K., & Rice, F. P. (2002). *Intimate relationships, marriages, & families* (5th ed). Boston: McGraw-Hill.

Ezriel, H. (1973). Psychoanalytic group therapy. In L. R. Wolberg & E. K. Schwartz (Eds.), *Group psychotherapy 1973* (pp. 183–210). New York: International Medical Book Corp.

Frank, J. D. (1979). Thirty years of group therapy: A personal perspective. *International Journal of Group Psychotherapy, 29,* 439–452.

Glass, T. A. (1998). Ethical issues in group therapy. In R. M. Anderson, Jr., & T. L. Needels (Eds.), *Avoiding ethical misconduct in psychology specialty areas* (pp. 95–126). Springfield, IL: Charles C. Thomas.

Guerney, B. G. (1984). Relationship enhancement therapy and training. In D. Larson (Ed.), *Teaching psychological skills: Models for giving psychology away* (pp. 171–206). Monterey, CA: Broooks/Cole.

Gurman, A. S., & Jacobson, N. S. (Eds.). (2002). *Clinical handbook of couple therapy* (3rd ed.). New York: Guilford Press.

Haynes, S. N., Jensen, B. J., Wise, E., & Sherman D. (1981). The marital intake interview: A multi-method criterion validity assessment. *Consulting and Clinical Psychology, 49* (3) 379–387.

Heiman, J. R., & LoPiccolo, J. (1983). Clinical outcome of sex therapy: Effects of daily versus weekly treatment. *Archives of General Psychiatry, 40,* 443–449.

Hersen, M., Kazdin, A. E., & Bellack, A. S. (Eds.). (1983). *The clinical psychology handbook.* New York: Pergamon Press.

Heyman, R. E., Eddy, J. M., Weiss, R. L., & Vivian, D. (1995). Factor analysis of the Marital Interaction Coding System (MICS). *Journal of Family Psychology, 9,* 209–215.

Imber-Black, E. (1990). Multiple embedded systems. In M. P. Mirkin (Ed.), *The social and political contexts of family therapy* (pp. 3–18). Boston: Allyn & Bacon.

Jacobson, N. S., & Christensen, A. (1996). *Integrative couple therapy: Promoting acceptance and change.* New York: W. W. Norton.

Jacobson, N. S., & Margolin, C. (1979). *Marital therapy: Strategies based on social learning and behavior exchange principles.* New York: Brunner/Mazel.

Johnson, S. M., & Greenberg, L. S. (1995). The emotionally focused approach to problems in adult attachment. In N. S. Jacobson & A. S. Gurman (Eds.), *Clinical handbook of couple therapy* (pp. 121–141). New York: Guilford Press.

Johnson, T. W., & Colucci, P. (1999). Lesbians, gay men, and the family cycle. In B. Carter & M. McGoldrick (Eds.), *The expanded family life cycle* (3rd ed., pp. 346–361). Boston: Allyn & Bacon.

Kaslow, F. W. (1987). Trends in family psychology. *Journal of Family Psychology, 1,* 77–90.

Kaslow, N. J., & Aronson, S. G. (2004). Recommendations for family interventions following a suicide. *Professional Psychology: Research and Practice, 35,* 240–247.

Kerr, M. E. (1981). Family systems theory and therapy. In A. S. Gurman & D. P. Kniskern (Eds.), *Handbook of family therapy* (pp. 226–264). New York: Brunner/Mazel.

Kipper, D. A., & Ritchie, T. D. (2003). The effectiveness of psychodramatic techniques: A meta-analysis. *Group Dynamics: Theory, Research, and Practice, 7,* 13–25.

Klontz, B. T. (2004). Ethical practice of group experiential psychotherapy. *Psychotherapy: Theory, Research, Practice, Training, 41,* 172–179.

Leiblum, S. R., & Rosen, R. C. (Eds.). (2000). *Principles and practice of sex therapy* (3rd ed.). New York: Guilford Press.

Lieberman, M. A. (1977). Problems in integrating traditional group therapies with new forms. *International Journal of Group Psychotherapy, 27,* 19–32.

LoPiccolo, J., Heiman, J. R., Hogan, D. R., & Roberts, C. W. (1985). Effectiveness of single therapists versus cotherapy teams in sex therapy. *Journal of Consulting and Clinical Psychology, 53,* 287–294.

Markus, H. E., & King, D. A. (2003). A survey of group psychotherapy training during predoctoral psychology internship. *Professional Psychology: Research and Practice, 34,* 203–209.

Mash, E. J., & Wolfe, D. A. (2005). *Abnormal child psychology* (3rd ed). Belmont, CA: Thompson.

Masters, W., & Johnson, V. (1970). *Human sexual inadequacy.* Boston: Little, Brown.

Minuchin, S. (1974). *Families and family therapy.* Cambridge, MA: Harvard University Press.

Minuchin, S., & Fishman, H. C. (1981). *Family therapy techniques.* Cambridge, MA: Harvard University Press.

Minuchin, S., Montalvo, B., Gurney, B., Rosman, B., & Schumer, F. (1967). *Families of the slums.* New York: Basic Books.

Moline, M. E., Williams, G. T., & Austin, K. M. (1998). *Documenting psychotherapy: Essentials for mental health practitioners.* Thousand Oaks, CA: Sage.

Moreno, J. L. (1946). *Psychodrama* (2nd ed.). (Vol. 1). New York: Beacon House.

Moreno, J. L. (1959). Psychodrama. In S. Arieti (Ed.), *American handbook of psychiatry* (Vol. 2) (pp. 1375–1396). New York: Basic Books.

Nichols, M. P. (2002). *The essentials of family therapy.* Boston: Allyn & Bacon.

Nichols, M. P., & Schwartz, R. C. (2001). *Family therapy: Concepts and methods.* Boston: Allyn & Bacon.

Nystul, M. S. (1999). *Introduction to counseling: An art and science perspective.* Boston: Allyn & Bacon.

O'Leary, K. D., Vivian, D., & Malone, J. (1992). Assessment of physical aggression against women in marriage: The need for multimodal assessment. *Behavioral Assessment, 12,* 5–14.

Ormont, L. (2003). *Group psychotherapy.* New York: Jason Aronson.

Patterson, C. J., & Redding, R. (1996). Lesbian and gay families with children: Implications of social science research for policy. *Journal of Social Issues, 52*(3), 29–50.

Petry, S. S., & McGoldrick, M. (2005). Genograms in assessment and therapy. In G. P. Koocher, J. C. Norcross, & S. S. Hill (Eds.), *Psychologists' desk reference* (2nd ed., pp. 366–373). New York: Oxford.

Rivas-Vazquez, R. A., Blais, M. A., Rey, G. J., & Rivas-Vazquez, A. A. (2001). A brief reminder about documenting the psychological consultation. *Professional Psychology: Research and Practice, 32,* 194–199.

Sacks, J. M., Bilaniuk, M. T., & Gendron, J. M. (Eds.). (1995). *Bibliography of psychodrama: Inception to date.* New York: Psychodrama Center of New York.

Sadock, H., & Kaplan, B. (Eds.). (1993). *Comprehensive group psychotherapy* (3rd ed.). Baltimore: Williams and Wilkins.

Satir, V. M. (1972). *Peoplemaking.* Palo Alto, CA: Science and Behavior Books.

Satir, V. M. (1983). *Conjoint family therapy* (3rd ed.) Palo Alto, CA: Science and Behavior Books.

Satir, V. M., & Baldwin, M. (1983). *Satir step by step.* Palo Alto, CA: Science and Behavior Books.

Snyder, D. K., Wills, R. M., & Grady-Fletcher, A. (1991). Long-term effectiveness of behavioral versus insight-oriented marital therapy: A 4-year follow-up study. *Journal of Consulting and Clinical Psychology, 59,* 138–141.

Sue, D. W., & Sue, D. (2003). *Counseling the culturally diverse: Theory and practice* (4th ed.). New York: Wiley.

U.S. Bureau of the Census. (1999). *Statistical abstract of the United States, 1999.* Washington, DC: U.S. Government Printing Office.

Waschbusch, D. A., Kipp, H. L., & Pelham, W. E., Jr. (1998). Generalization of behavioral and psychostimulant treatment of attention-deficit/hyperactivity disorder (ADHD): Discussion and examples. *Behaviour, Research and Therapy, 36,* 675–694.

Weinstein, M., & Rossini, E. D. (1998). Academic training in group psychotherapy in clinical psychology doctoral programs. *Psychological Reports, 82,* 955–959.

Weiss, R. L., & Halford, W. K. (1996). Managing marital therapy: Helping partners change. In V. B. Van Hasselt & M. Hersen (Eds.), *Sourcebook of psychological treatment manuals for adult disorders* (pp. 489–537). New York: Plenum Press.

Wetchler, J. L., & Piercy, F. P. (1996). Transgenerational family therapies. In F. P. Piercy, D. H. Sprenkle, J. L. Wetchler, et al. (Eds.), *Family therapy sourcebook* (2nd ed., pp. 25–49). New York: Guilford.

Wile, D. B. (1981). *Couples therapy.* New York: Wiley.

Wincze, J. P., & Carey, M. P. (2001). *Sexual dysfunction: A guide for assessment and treatment.* New York: Guilford Press.

Wolcott, I., & Glazer, H. (1989). *Marriage counseling in Australia: An evaluation.* Melbourne: Australian Institute of Family Studies.

Yalom, I. D. (1970). *Theory and practice of group psychotherapy.* New York: Basic Books.

Yalom, I. D. (1995). *The theory and practice of group psychotherapy* (4th ed.). New York: Basic Books.

Yalom, I. D., Houts, P. S., Newell, G., & Rand, H. K. (1967). Preparation of patients for group therapy. *Archives of General Psychiatry, 17,* 416–427.

Zilbergeld, B. (1992). *The new male sexuality.* New York: Bantam Books.

Zohn, J., & Carmody, T. P. (1978). Training opportunities in group treatment methods in APA-approved clinical psychology programs. *Professional Psychology: Research and Practice, 9,* 50–62.

Chapter 13 Community Intervention and Public Policy

Beers, C. (1908). *A mind that found itself.* Garden City, NY: Doubleday.

Brendtro, L., Brokenleg, M., & Van Brockern, S. (1990). *Reclaiming youth at risk: Our hope for the future.* Bloomington, IN: National Educational Service.

Buffmire, J. A. (1995). Are politics for you? *Professional Psychology: Research and Practice, 26,* 453–455.

Cicchetti, D., & Toth, S. L. (1998). The development of depression in children and adolescents. *American Psychologist, 53,* 221–241.

Commission on Chronic Illness. (1957). *Chronic illness in the United States, Vol. 1.* Cambridge, MA: Harvard University Press.

Cullari, S. (Ed.). (1998). *Foundations of clinical psychology.* Boston: Allyn and Bacon.

Dalton, J. H., Elias, M. J., & Wandersman, A. (2001). *Community psychology: Linking individuals and communities.* Belmont, CA: Wadsworth.

Dingfelder, S. F. (2004, July/August). Behavioral health—a primary concern. *Monitor on Psychology, 35*(7), 32–33.

Duffy, K. G. (1998). Community psychology. In S. Cullari (Ed.), *Foundations of clinical psychology* (pp. 348–374). Boston: Allyn & Bacon.

Forsythe, S. L. (2004, May). Grassroots . . . what's the big deal? *Monitor on Psychology, 35,* 80–82.

Gordon, R. (1987). An operational classification of disease prevention. In J. A. Steinberg & M. M. Silverman (Eds.), *Preventing mental illness* (pp. 20–26). Rockville, MD: Department of Health and Human Services.

Haggerty, R., Sherrod, L., Garmezy, N., & Rutter, M. (Eds.). (1994). *Stress, risk, and resilience in children and adolescents.* New York: Cambridge University Press.

Karakashian, M. (1998). Armenia: A country's history of challenges. *Journal of Social Issues, 54,* 381–392.

Kennemer, W. N. (1995). Psychology and the political process. *Professional Psychology: Research and Practice, 26,* 456–458.

Maddi, S. R. (1987). Hardiness training at Illinois Bell Telephone. In J. P. Opatz (Ed.), *Health promotion evaluation* (pp. 101–115). Stevens Point, WI: National Wellness Institute.

Maddi, S. R. (2002). The story of hardiness: Twenty years of theorizing, research, and practice. *Consulting Psychology Journal, 54,* 173–185.

Mrazek, P., & Haggerty, R. (1994). *Reducing risks for mental disorders: Frontiers for preventive intervention research.* Washington, DC: National Academy Press.

O'Leary, V. (1998). Strengths in the face of adversity: Individual and social thriving. *Journal of Social Issues, 54,* 425–446.

Rodgers, A. Y. (1993). The assessment of variables related to the parenting behavior of mothers with young children. *Child and Youth Services Review, 15,* 385–402.

Smith, M. B., & Hobbs, N. (1966). The community and the community mental health center. *American Psychologist, 21,* 499–509.

Sullivan, M. J., & Reedy, S. D. (2005). Psychologists as legislators: Results of the 2004 elections. *Professional Psychology: Research and Practice, 36,* 32–36.

Sundberg, N. D., Winebarger, A. A., & Taplin, J. R. (2002). *Clinical psychology: Evolving theory, practice, and research.* Upper Saddle River, NJ: Prentice-Hall.

Veroff, J., Douvan, E., & Kulka, R. A. (1981). *Mental health in America: Patterns of help-seeking from 1957 to 1976.* New York: Basic Books.

Chapter 14 Specialties in Clinical Psychology I: Neuropsychology, Health Psychology, Forensic Psychology, and Sport Psychology

American Psychological Association (APA). (1992). *Ethical principles of psychologists and code of conduct.* Washington, DC: Author.

American Psychological Association (APA). (2002). Ethical principles of psychologists and code of conduct. *American Psychologist, 57,* 1060–1073.

Anshel, M. H. (2003). *Sport psychology: From theory and practice* (4th ed.). San Francisco, CA: Benjamin Cummings.

Antoni, M. (2003). *Stress management intervention for women with breast cancer.* Washington, DC: American Psychological Association.

Bartol, C. (1996). Police psychology: Then, now, and beyond. *Criminal Justice and Behavior, 23,* 70–89.

Baum, A., & Andersen, B. L. (Eds.). (2001). *Psychosocial interventions for cancer.* Washington, DC: American Psychological Association.

Brannon, L., & Feist, J. (2000). *Health psychology: An introduction to behavior and health* (4th ed.). Belmont, CA: Wadsworth/Thompson Learning.

Broca, P. (1960). Remarks on the seat of the faculty of articulate language, followed by an observation of aphaesia. In G. von Bonin (Trans.), *Some papers on the cerebral cortex.* Springfield, IL: C. C. Thomas. (Original work published in 1865.)

Brown, R. T., Freeman, W. A., Brown, R. A., Belar, C., Hersch, L., Hornyak, L. M., et al. (2002). The role of psychology in health care delivery. *Professional Psychology: Research and Practice, 33,* 536–545.

Browne, R. J. (1983). Sex differences in neuropsychological functioning. In C. J. Golden & P. J. Vicente (Eds.), *Foundations of clinical neuropsychology* (pp. 429–458). New York: Plenum Press.

Carter, C. L., & Hailey, B. (1999). Psychological issues in genetic testing for breast cancer. *Women and Health, 28,* 73–91.

Cox, R. H. (1998). *Sport psychology: Concepts and applications* (4th ed.). Boston: WCB McGraw Hill.

Daubert v. Merrell Dow Pharmaceuticals, 509 U.S. 579 (1993).

Filskov, S. B., & Catanese, R. A. (1986). Effects of sex and handedness on neuropsychological testing. In S. B. Filskov & T. J. Boll (Eds.), *Handbook of clinical neuropsychology* (Vol. 2), (pp. 198–212). New York: John Wiley.

Fletcher-Janzen, E., Strickland, T. L., & Reynolds, C. R. (Eds.). (2000). *Handbook of cross-cultural neuropsychology.* Hingham, MA: Kluwer Academic Plenum.

Frank, R. G., McDaniel, S. H., Bray, J. H., & Heldring, M. (2003). *Primary care psychology.* Washington, DC: American Psychological Association.

Frye v. United States, 392 F, 1013 (DC Cir 1923).

Golden, C. J., Hammeke, T., & Purisch, A. (1980). *A Manual for the Luria-Nebraska Neuro-psychological Battery* (rev. ed). Los Angeles: Western Psychological Services.

Hays, K., & Chan, C. (Eds.). (2001). Sport psychology [Special section]. *Professional Psychology: Research and Practice, 32,* 5–40.

Hess, A. L., & Hart, R. (1990). The specialty of neuropsychology. *Neuropsychology, 4,* 49–52.

Hess, A., & Weiner, I. (Eds.). (1999). *The handbook of forensic psychology* (2nd ed.). New York: John Wiley.

Hoffman, H. G., Doctor, J. N., Patterson, D. R., Carrougher, G. J., & Furness, T. A. (2000). Virtual reality as an adjunctive pain control during burn wound care in adolescent patients. *Pain, 85,* 305–309.

Homant, R., & Kennedy, D. (1998). Psychological aspects of crime scene profiling: Validity research. *Criminal Justice and Behavior, 23,* 319–343.

Incagnoli, T. (1986). Current directions and future trends in clinical neuropsychology. In T. Incagnoli, G. Goldstein, & C. J. Golden (Eds.), *Clinical application of neuropsychologi-cal test batteries* (pp. 1–45). New York: Plenum Press. *Jenkins v. United States,* 307 F.2d 637 (D.C. cir. 1962).

Johnson, S. B., Perry, N., & Rozensky, R. R. (2002). (Eds.) *Handbook of clinical health psychol-ogy: Volume I.* Washington, DC: American Psychological Association.

Keefe, F. J., Buffington, A. L. H., Studts, J. L., & Rumble, M. E. (2002). Behavioral medicine: 2002 and beyond. *Journal of Consulting and Clinical Psychology, 70,* 852–856.

Kirkwood, K. T., Peck, D. F., & Bennie, L. (2000). The consistency of neuropsychological assess-ments performed via telecommunication and face-to-face. *Journal of Telemedicine and Telecare, 6,* 147–151.

Kolb, B., & Whishaw, I. O. (2003). *Fundamentals of human neuropsychology* (6th ed.). New York: Worth Publishers.

Kral, M. C., Brown, R. T., & Hynd, G. W. (2001). Neuropsychological aspects of pediatric sickle cell disease. *Neuropsychological Review, 11,* 179–196.

Kuther, T. L., & Morgan, R. D. (2003). *Careers in psychology: Opportunities in a changing world.* Belmont, CA: Wadsworth/Thompson Learning.

Lamminen, H., Lamminen, J., Ruohonen, K., & Uusitalo, H. (2003). A cost study of teleconsul-tation for primary-care ophthalmology and dermatology. *Journal of Telemedicine and Telecare, 7,* 167–173.

Matthews, J. R. (1992). Sex and gender. In A. E. Puente & R. J. McCaffrey (Eds.), *Handbook of neuropsychological assessment: A biopsychosocial perspective* (pp.121–139). New York: Plenum Press.

McCaffrey, R. J., Duff, K., & Westervelt, H. J. (2000). *Practitioner's guide to evaluating change with neuropsychological assessment instruments.* Norwell, MA: Kluwer Academic/Plenum.

McDaniel, S. H., Belar, C. D., Schroeder, C., Hargrove, D. S., & Freeman, E. L. (2002). A training curriculum for professional psychologists in primary care. *Professional Psychology: Research and Practice, 33,* 65–72.

McKay, G. H., Glasgow, R. E., Feil, E. G., Boles, S. M., & Barrera, M. (2002). Internet-based diabetes self-management and support: Initial outcomes from the Diabetes Network Project. *Rehabilitation Psychology, 47,* 31–48.

Melton, G. B., Huss, M. T., & Tomkins, A. J. (1999). Training in forensic psychology and the law. In K. Hess & I. B. Weiner (Eds.), *The handbook of forensic psychology* (2nd ed., pp. 700–720). Danvers, MA: Wiley.

Melton, G. B., Petrila, J., Poythress, N., & Slobogin, C. (1997). *Psychological evaluation for the courts* (2nd ed.). New York: Guilford Press.

Meyers, A. W., Coleman, J. K., Whelan, J. P., & Mehlenbeck, R. S. (2001). Examining careers in sport psychology: Who is working and who is making money? *Professional Psychology: Research and Practice, 35,* 5–11.

Moore, Z. E. (2003). Ethical dilemmas in sport psychology: Discussion and recommendations for practice. *Professional Psychology: Research and Practice, 34,* 601–610.

Nicholson, R. A., & Norwood, S. (2000). The quality of forensic psychological assessments, reports, and testimony: Acknowledging the gap between promise and practice. *Law and Human Behavior, 24,* 9–44.

Parsons, O. A., & Prigatano, G. P. (1978). Methodological considerations in clinical neuropsychological research. *Journal of Consulting and Clinical Psychology, 46,* 608–619.

Petrie, T. A., & Diehl, N. S. (1995). Sport psychology in the profession of psychology. *Professional Psychology: Research and Practice, 26,* 288–291.

Prigatano, G. P., Parsons, O. A., & Bortz, J. J. (1995). Methodological considerations in clinical neuropsychological research: 17 years later. *Psychological Assessment, 7,* 396–403.

Quick, J. C. (1999). Occupational health psychology: The convergence of health and clinical psychology with public health and preventive medicine in an organizational context. *Professional Psychology, 30,* 123–128.

Raymond, J. S., Wood, D. W., & Patrick, W. D. (1990). Psychology training in work and health. *American Psychologist, 45,* 1159–1161.

Rice, P. L. (1998). *Health psychology.* Pacific Grove, CA: Wadsworth/Thompson Learning.

Ritterband, L. M., Cox, D.C., Walker, L., Kovatchev, B., McKnight, L., Patel, K., et al. (2003). A Web-based treatment intervention as adjunctive therapy for pediatric encopresis. *Journal of Consulting and Clinical Psychology, 71,* 910–917.

Rodrigue, J. R. (1996). Promoting healthier behaviors, attitudes, and beliefs toward sun exposure in parents of young children. *Journal of Consulting and Clinical Psychology, 64,* 1431–1436.

Sheridan, E. P., Matarazzo, J. D., Boll, T. J., Perry, N. W., Weiss, S. M., & Belar, C. D. (1988). Postdoctoral education and training for clinical service providers in health psychology. *Health Psychology, 7*(1), 1–17.

Sperry, R. W. (1982). Some effects of disconnecting the cerebral hemispheres (Nobel Lecture). *Science, 217,* 1223–1226.

Spira, J. L., & Reed, G. M. (2003). *Group psychotherapy for women with breast cancer.* Washington, DC: American Psychological Association.

Staff. (1982, Fall). *Ethical standards for the provision of services by NASPSPA members.* NASPSPA Newsletter, addendum.

Stirling, J. (2001). *Introducing neuropsychology.* Philadelphia: Psychology Press.

Streisand, R. M., Rodrigue, J. R., Sears, S. F., Jr., Perri, M. G., Davis, G. L., & Banko, C. G. (1999). A psychometric normative data base for pre-liver transplantation evaluation: The Florida cohort 1991–1996. *Psychosomatics, 40,* 479–485.

Tate, D. F., Wing, R. R., & Winett, R. A. (2001). Using Internet technology to deliver a behavioral weight loss program. *Journal of the American Medical Association, 285,* 1172–1177.

Tjemsland, L., Soreide, J. A., & Malt, U. F. (1996). Traumatic distress symptoms in early breast cancer. I: Acute response to diagnosis. *Psycho-Oncology, 5,* 1–8.

Van Raalte, J. L., & Brewer, B. W. (2002). *Exploring sport and exercise psychology* (2nd ed.). Washington, DC: American Psychological Association.

Weineke, M. H., & Dienst, E. R. (1995). Neuropsychological assessment of cognitive functioning following chemotherapy for breast cancer. *Psycho-Oncology, 4,* 61–66.

Whitfield, K. E., Weidner, G., Clark, R., & Anderson, N. B. (2002). Sociodemographic diversity and behavioral medicine. *Journal of Consulting and Clinical Psychology, 70,* 463–481.

Wilson, J. F. (2003). *Biological foundations of human behavior.* Belmont, CA: Wadsworth/ Thompson Learning.

Wrightsman, L. S., Nietzel, M. T., & Fortune, W. H. (1998). *Psychology and the legal system* (4th ed). Pacific Grove, CA: Brooks/Cole.

Chapter 15 Specialties in Clinical Psychology II: Geropsychology, Clinical Child Psychology, and Pediatric Psychology

Abeles, N., Cooley, S., Deitch, I. M., Harper, M. S., Hinrichsen, G., Lopez, M. A., & Molinari, V. A. (1998). What practitioners should know about working with older adults. *Professional Psychology: Research and Practice, 29,* 413–427.

American Psychological Association (APA). (2004). Guidelines for psychological practice with older adults. *American Psychologist, 59,* 236–260.

Arean, P. A. (2003). Advances in psychotherapy for mental illness in late life. *American Journal of Geriatric Psychiatry, 11,* 4–6.

Board of Psychology. (March, 2003). New law specifies aging, long-term care coursework. *Update,* 3.

Costello, E. J., Angold, A., Burns, B. J., Erkanli, A., Stangl, D. K., & Tweed, D. L. (1996). The Great Smokey Mountains Study of youth: Functional impairment and serious emotional disturbance. *Archives of General Psychiatry, 53*(12), 1137–1143.

Crowther, M. R., & Zeiss, A. M. (2003). Aging and mental health. In J. S. Mio & G. Y. Iwamasa (Eds.), *Culturally diverse mental health: The challenge of research and resistance* (pp. 309–322). New York: Brunner-Routledge.

Duff, R. S., Rowe, D. S., & Anderson, F. P. (1973). Patient care and student learning in a pediatric clinic. *Pediatrics, 50,* 839–846.

Duffy, M. (Ed.). (1999). *Handbook of counseling and psychotherapy with older adults.* New York: John Wiley & Sons.

Gatz, M., Fiske, A., Fox, L. S., Kaskie, B., Kasl-Godley, J. E., McCallum, T. J., & Wetherell, J. L. (1998). Empirically validated treatments for older adults. *Journal of Mental Health and Aging, 4,* 9–46.

Gatz, M., & Smyer, M. A. (2001). Mental health and aging at the outset of the twenty-first century. In J. E. Birren & K. W. Schaie (Eds.), *Handbook of the psychology of aging* (5th ed., pp. 532–544). San Diego: Academic Press.

Gould, M. S., Wunsch-Hitzig, R., & Dohrenwend, B. P. (1980). Formulation of hypotheses about the prevalence, treatment, and prognostic significance of psychiatric disorders in children in the United States. In B. P. Dohrenwend, B. S. Dohrenwend, M. S. Gould, B. Link, P. R. Neugebaur, & R. Wunsch-Hitzig (Eds.), *Mental illness in the United States: Epidemiological estimates* (pp. 9–44). New York: Praeger.

Hinrichsen, G. A. (2000). Knowledge of and interest in geropsychology among psychology trainees. *Professional Psychology: Research and Practice, 31,* 442–445.

Horvath, A. O., & Bedi, R. P. (2002). The alliance. In J. C. Norcross (Ed.), *Psychotherapy relationships that work* (pp. 37–70). New York: Oxford University Press.

Karel, M. J., Ogland-Hand, S., & Gatz, M. (2002). *Assessing and treating late-life depression: A casebook and resource guide.* New York: Basic Books.

Kimerling, R. E., Zeiss, A. M., & Zeiss, R. A. (2000). Therapist emotional responses to patients: Building a learning based language. *Cognitive and Behavioral Practice, 7,* 312–321.

Knight, B. G., Teri, L., Santos, J., & Wohlford, P. (Eds.). (1995). *Mental health services for older adults: Implications for training and practice in geropsychology.* Washington, DC: American Psychological Association.

Maddux, J. E., Roberts, M. C., Sledden, E. A., & Wright, L. (1986). Developmental issues in child health psychology. *American Psychologist, 41,* 25–34.

Mash, E. J., & Dozois, D. J. A. (1996). Child psychopathology: A developmental systems perspective. In E. J. Mash & R. A. Barkley (Eds.), *Child psychopathology* (pp. 3–60). New York: Guilford Press.

Masten, A. S., & Coatsworth, J. D. (1998). The development of competence in favorable and unfavorable environments. *American Psychologist, 53,* 205–220.

McDougall, G. J., Blixen, C. E., & Suen, L. (1997). The process and outcome of life review psychotherapy with depressed homebound older adults. *Nursing Research, 46,* 277–283.

Mullins, L. L., & Chaney, J. M. (2001). Pediatric psychology: Contemporary issues. In C. E. Walker & M. C. Roberts (Eds.) *Handbook of clinical child psychology* (3rd ed., pp. 910–928). New York: John Wiley & Sons.

Nelson, C. A., & Bloom, F. E. (1997). Child development and neuroscience. *Child Development, 68,* 970–987.

Qualls, S. H. (1998). Training in geropsychology: Preparing to meet the demand. *Professional Psychology: Research and Practice, 29,* 23–27.

Qualls, S. H., Segal, D., Norman, S., Niederhe, G., & Gallagher-Thompson, D. (2002). Psychologists in practice with older adults: Current patterns, sources of training, and need for continuing education. *Professional Psychology: Research and Practice, 33,* 435–442.

Roberts, M. C. (1986). *Pediatric psychology: Psychological interventions and strategies for pediatric problems.* Elmsford, NY: Pergamon Press.

Roberts, R. E., Attkisson, C. C., & Rosenblatt, A. (1998). Prevalence of psychopathology among children and adolescents. *American Journal of Psychiatry, 155*(6), 715–725.

Ross, A. O. (1959). *The practice of clinical child psychology.* New York: Grune & Stratton.

Routh, D. K. (1994). *Clinical psychology since 1917: Science, practice, and organization.* New York: Plenum.

Santos, J. F., & VandenBos, G. R. (Eds.). (1982). *Psychology and the older adult: Challenges for training in the 1980s.* Washington, DC: American Psychological Association.

Scogin, F. (2000). *The first session with seniors: A step by step guide.* San Francisco: Jossey-Bass.

Takamura, J. C. (1998). An aging agenda for the 21st century: The opportunities and challenges of population longevity. *Professional Psychology: Research and Practice, 29,* 411–412.

Teri, L., Storandt, M., Gatz, M., Smyer, M., & Stricker, G. (1992). *Recommendations from a national conference on clinical training in psychology: Improving psychological services for older adults.* Unpublished manuscript. Washington, DC: American Psychological Association.

Thompson, R. J., & Gustafson, K. E. (2005). Psychological interventions in childhood chronic illness. In G. P. Koocher, J. C. Norcross, & S. S. Hill (Eds.), *Psychologists' desk reference* (2nd ed., pp. 406–409). New York: Oxford.

Tinsley, B. R., & Parke, R. D. (1984). The historical and contemporary relationship between developmental psychology and pediatrics; A review and an empirical survey. In H. E. Fitzgerald, B. M. Lester, & M. W. Yogman (Eds.), *Theory and research in behavioral pediatrics* (Vol. 2, pp. 1–30). New York: Plenum.

Zarit, S. H., & Knight, B. G. (Eds.). (1996). *A guide to psychotherapy and aging: Effective clinical interventions in a life-stage context.* Washington, DC: American Psychological Association.

Zarit, S. H., & Zarit, J. M. (1982). Families under stress: Interventions for caregivers of senile dementia patients. *Psychotherapy: Theory, Research, and Practice, 19,* 461–471.

Zito, J. M., Safer, D. J., dosReis, S., Gardner, J. F., Boles, M., & Lynch, F. (2000). Trends in the prescribing of psychotropic medications to preschoolers. *Journal of the American Medical Association, 283*(8), 1025–1030.

Chapter 16 The Dynamic Future of Clinical Psychology

Abraido-Lanza, A. F., Vasquez, E., & Echeverria, S. E. (2004). En las manos de Dios [in God's hands]: Religious and other forms of coping among Latinos with arthritis. *Journal of Consulting and Clinical Psychology, 72,* 91–102.

Altarriba, J., & Santiago-Rivera, A. L. (1994). Current perspectives on using linguistic and cultural factors in counseling the Hispanic client. *Professional Psychology: Research and Practice, 25,* 388–397.

American Psychiatric Association. (1994). *Diagnostic and statistical manual for mental disorders* (4th ed.). Washington, DC: Author.

American Psychological Association (APA). (1995). *Report of the task force on the changing gender composition of psychology.* Washington, DC: Author.

American Psychological Association (APA). (2002a). Ethical principles of psychologists and code of conduct. *American Psychologist, 57,* 1060–1073.

American Psychological Association (APA). (2002b). *Guidelines and principles for accreditation.* Washington, DC: Author.

American Psychological Association (APA). (2003). Guidelines on multicultural education, training, research, practice, and organizational change for psychologists. *American Psychologist, 58,* 377–402.

American Psychological Association (APA). (2004). Guidelines for psychological practice with older adults. *American Psychologist, 59,* 236–260.

Aspinwall, L. G., & Staudinger, U. M. (Eds.). (2003). *A psychology of human strengths: Fundamental questions and future directions for a positive psychology.* Washington, DC: American Psychological Association.

Barnard, A. G., & Rothgeb, I. V. (2000). Rebuilding a private practice in psychology following a hurricane: The experience of two psychologists. *Professional Psychology: Research and Practice, 31,* 393–397.

Barnett, J. E., & Rodino, E. (2000). *Psychologist-dentist collaboration. A guide for niche practice in Practice Information Clearinghouse of Knowledge.* Phoenix, AZ: Psychologists in Independent Practice.

Biever, J. L., Castano, M. T., de las Fuentes, C., Gonzalez, C., Servin-Lopez, S., Sprowls, C., & Tripp, C. G. (2002). The role of language in training psychologists to work with Hispanic clients. *Professional Psychology: Research and Practice, 33,* 330–336.

Bonanno, G. A. (2004). Loss, trauma, and human resilience: Have we underestimated the human capacity to thrive after extremely aversive events? *American Psychologist, 59,* 20–28.

Bonanno, G. A., & Keltner, D. (1997). Facial expressions of emotion and the course of conjugal bereavement. *Journal of Abnormal Psychology, 106,* 126–137.

Bond, G. R., Resnick, S. G., Drake, R. E., Xie, H., McHugo, G. J., & Bebout, R. R. (2001). Does competitive employment improve nonvocational outcomes for people with severe mental illness? *Journal of Consulting and Clinical Psychology, 69,* 489–501.

Brewer, C. A., & Suchan, T. A. (2001). *Mapping Census 2000: The geography of U.S. diversity.* Washington, DC: U.S. Government Printing Office.

Brotman, L. E., Liberi, W. P., & Wasylyshyn, K. M. (1998). Executive coaching: The need for standards of competence. *Consulting Psychology Journal, Practice & Research, 50*(1), 40–46.

Casas, J. M., Pavelski, R., Furlong, M. J., & Zanglis, I. (2001) Advent of systems of care: Practice and research perspectives and policy implications. In J. G. Ponterotto, J. M. Casas, L. Suzuki, & C. Alexander (Eds.), *Handbook of multicultural counseling* (2nd ed., pp. 189–221). Thousand Oaks, CA: Sage.

Center for Mental Health Services. (1996). *Mental health, United States 1996* (R. Manderscheid & M. Sonnenschein, Eds.). DHHS Publication No. SMA 96–3098. Washington, DC: U.S. Government Printing Office.

Chen, S. W., & Davenport, D. S. (2005). Cognitive-behavior therapy with Chinese American clients: Cautions and modifications. *Psychotherapy: Theory, Research, Practice, Training, 42,* 101–110.

Coursey, R. D., Alford, J., & Safarjan, W. (1997). Significant advances in understanding and treating serious mental illness. *Professional Psychology: Research & Practice, 28,* 205–216.

Cummings, N. A., & Follette, W. T. (1976). Brief psychotherapy and medical utilization. In H. Darken (Ed.), *The professional psychologist today* (pp. 165–174). San Francisco: Jossey-Bass.

Daw, J. (2001, October). A wounded psychologist goes back to work. *Monitor on Psychology, 32,* 29.

DeLeon, P. H., Giesting, B., & Kenkel, M. B. (2003). Community health centers: Exciting opportunities for the 21st century. *Professional Psychology: Research and Practice, 34,* 579–585.

Dudley-Grant, G. R., Mendez, G. I., & Zinn, J. (2000). Strategies for anticipating and preventing psychological trauma of hurricanes through community education. *Professional Psychology: Research and Practice, 31,* 387–392.

Finkel, M. J., Storaasli, R. D., Bandele, A., & Schaefer, V. (2003). Diversity training in graduate school: An exploratory evaluation of the Safe Zone project. *Professional Psychology: Research and Practice, 34,* 555–561.

Foxhall, K. (2001, October). Learning to live past 9:02 a.m., April 19, 1995. *Monitor on Psychology, 32,* 26–28.

Foxhall, K. (2002, April). More psychologists are attracted to the executive coaching field. *Monitor on Psychology, 33*(4), 52–53.

Friedman, R., Sobel, D., Myers, P., Caudill, M., & Benson, H. (1995). Behavioral medicine, clinical health psychology, and cost offset. *Health Psychology, 14,* 509–518.

Freud, S. (1953). *The complete psychological works of Sigmund Freud.* Vol. 7. (J. Strachey, Ed. and Trans.). London: Hogarth Press & Institute of Psychoanalysis.

Gable, S. L., & Haidt, J. (2005). What (and why) is positive psychology? *Review of General Psychology, 9,* 103–110.

Gentile, S. R., Asamen, J. K., Harmell, P. H., & Weathers, R. (2002). The stalking of psychologists by their clients. *Professional Psychology: Research and Practice, 33,* 490–494.

George, L. K., Ellison, C. G., & Larson, D. B. (2002). Explaining the relationships between religious involvement and health. *Psychological Inquiry, 13,* 190–200.

Gindes, M. (1999). *Consulting with business on workplace behavior. A guide for niche practice in Practice Information Clearinghouse of Knowledge.* Phoenix, AZ: Psychologists in Independent Practice.

Gist, R., & Lubin, B. (Eds.). (1998). *Response to disaster: Psychosocial, community, and ecological approaches.* Bristol, PA: Taylor and Francis.

Goldsmith, M., Lyons, L., & Freas, A. (Eds.). (2000). Foundations of coaching. In *Coaching for leadership: How the world's greatest coaches help leaders learn.* San Francisco: Jossey-Bass/Pfeiffer.

Haber, S. (1999). *Psycho-oncology. A guide for niche practice in Practice Information Clearinghouse of Knowledge.* Phoenix, AZ: Psychologists in Independent Practice.

Hansen, N. D., Pepitone-Arreola-Rockwell, F., & Greene, A. F. (2000). Multicultural competence: Criteria and case examples. *Professional Psychology: Research and Practice, 31,* 652–660.

Hays, K. F. (1995). Putting sport into (your) practice. *Professional Psychology: Research and Practice, 26,* 33–40.

Hoernicke, P. A., Kallam, M., & Tablada, T. (1994). Behavioral disorders in Hispanic American culture. In R. L. Peterson & S. Ishii-Jordon (Eds.), *Multicultural issues in the education of students with behavioral disorders* (pp. 115–125). Cambridge, MA: Brookline.

Holder, B., Turner-Musa, J., Kimmel, P., Alleyne, S., Kobrin, S., Simmens, S., Cruz, I., & Reiss, D. (1998). Engagement of African-American families in research of chronic illness: A multi-system approach. *Family Process, 37*(2), 127–151.

Holloway, J. D. (2004, June). Gaining prescriptive authority. *Monitor on Psychology, 35,* 22–24.

Ironson, G., Solomon, G., Balbin, E., O'Cleirigh, C., George, A., Kumar, M., Larson, D., & Woods, T. (2002). The Ironson-Woods Spirituality/Religiousness Index is associated with long survival, health behaviors, less distress, and low cortisol in people with HIV/AIDS. *Annals of Behavioral Medicine, 24*(1), 34–48.

Jackson, L. C. (2004). Putting on blinders or bifocals: Using the new multicultural guidelines for education and training. *The Clinical Psychologist, 57*(1–2), 11–16.

Jackson, L. C., & Greene, B. (2000). (Eds.). *Psychotherapy with African American women.* New York: Guilford.

Jacobs, G. A. (1995). The development of a national plan for disaster mental health. *Professional Psychology: Research and Practice, 26,* 543–549.

Jerome, L. W., DeLeon, P. H., James, L. C., Folen, R., Earles, J., & Gedney, J. J. (2000). The coming of age of telecommunications in psychological research and practice. *American Psychologist, 51,* 407–421.

Jones, K., & Vischi, T. (1979). Impact of alcohol, drug abuse, and mental health treatment on medical care utilization: Review of the research literature. *Medical Care, 17* (Suppl. 12), 1–82.

Jung, C. G. (1933). *Modern man in search of a soul.* New York: Harcourt.

Katon, W. (1984). Depression: Relationship to somatization and chronic medical illness. *Journal of Clinical Psychiatry, 45,* 4–11.

Keyes, C. L. M., & Haidt, J. (Eds.). (2003). *Flourishing: Positive psychology and the life well lived.* Washington, DC: American Psychological Association.

Kilburg, R. R. (2000). *Executive coaching: Developing managerial wisdom in a world of chaos.* Washington, DC: American Psychological Association.

Kirsch, I., & Sapirstein, G. (1998). Listening to Prozac but hearing placebo: A meta-analysis of antidepressant medication. *Prevention & Treatment, 1,* Article 0002a, posted June 26, 1998. http://www.journals.apa.org/pt/prevention/volume1/pre001002a.html

Klerman, G. L., & Weissman, M. M. (1989). Increasing rates of depression. *Journal of the American Medical Association, 261,* 2229–2235.

Koenig, H. G., McCullough, M. E., & Larson, D. B. (2001). *Handbook of religion and health.* New York: Oxford University Press.

Kolt, L. (1999). *Infertility. A guide for niche practice in Practice Information Clearinghouse of Knowledge.* Phoenix, AZ: Psychologists in Independent Practice.

Koocher, G., & Morray, E. (2000). Regulation of telepsychology: A survey of state attorneys general. *Professional Psychology: Research & Practice, 31,* 503–508.

Krall, M. (2001, Fall). An introduction to executive coaching. *The Register Report, 27,* 13–15.

LaFramboise, T. (1996). *American Indian life skills curriculum.* Madison: University of Wisconsin Press.

Laske, O. E. (1999). An integrated model of developmental coaching. *Consulting Psychology Journal: Practice & Research, 51*(3), 139–159.

Levant, R. F., Reed, G. M., Ragusea, S., Stout, C., DiCowden, M., Murphy, M., Sullivan, F., & Craig, P. (2001). Envisioning and accessing new roles for professional psychology. *Professional Psychology: Research and Practice, 32,* 79–87.

Lindemann, E. (1944). Symptomatology and management of acute grief. *American Journal of Psychiatry, 101,* 141–148.

Linton, J. C. (1995). Acute stress management with public safety personnel: Opportunities for clinical training and pro bono community service. *Professional Psychology: Research and Practice, 26,* 566–573.

Marian, V., & Neisser, U. (2000). Language-dependent recall of autobiographical memories. *Journal of Experimental Psychology: General, 129,* 361–368.

Marsh, D. T. (2004). Serious emotional disturbance in children and adolescents: Opportunities and challenges for psychologists. *Professional Psychology: Research and Practice, 35,* 443–448.

Martinez-Toboas, A. (2005). Psychogenic seizures in an *Espiritismo context:* The role of culturally sensitive psychotherapy. *Psychotherapy: Theory, Research, Practice, Training, 42,* 6–13.

McGinnis, J. M., & Foege, W. H. (1993). Actual causes of death in the United States. *JAMA, 270,* 2207–2212.

McGrath, R. E., Wiggins, J. G., Sammons, M. T., Levant, R. F., Brown, A., & Stock, W. (2004). Professional issues in pharmacotherapy for psychologists. *Professional Psychology: Research and Practice, 35,* 158–163.

Mueser, K. T., Clark, R. E., Haines, M., Drake, R. E., McHugo, G. J., Bond, G. R., et al. (2004). The Hartford study of supported employment for persons with severe mental illness. *Journal of Consulting and Clinical Psychology, 72,* 479–490.

Mueser, K. T., Salyers, M. P., & Meuser, P. R. (2001). A prospective analysis of work in schizophrenia. *Schizophrenia Bulletin, 27,* 281–296.

Naglieri, J. A., Drasgow, F., Schmit, M., Handler, L., Prifitera, A., Margolis, A., & Velasquez, R. (2004). Psychological testing on the Internet: New problems, old issues. *American Psychologist, 59,* 150–162.

Newman, R. (1998, May). How are managed care and telehealth alike? *APA Monitor, 29.*

Nickelson, D. W. (1996). Behavioral telehealth: Emerging practice, research and policy opportunities. *Behavioral Sciences and the Law, 14,* 443–457.

Nickelson, D. W. (1998). Telehealth and the evolving health care system: Strategic opportunities for professional psychology. *Professional Psychology: Research and Practice, 29,* 527–535.

Norcross, J. C., Alford, B. A., & DeMichele, J. T. (1992). The future of psychotherapy: A Delphi poll. *Psychotherapy, 29,* 150–158.

Norcross, J. C., Hedges, M., & Prochaska, J. O. (2002). The face of 2010: A Delphi poll on the future of psychotherapy. *Professional Psychology: Research and Practice, 33,* 316–322.

Parham, T. A., White, J. L., & Ajamu, A. (1999). *The psychology of blacks: An African centered perspective* (rev. ed.). Upper Saddle River, NJ: Prentice-Hall.

Perez, R. M., Dubord, K. A., & Bieschke, K. J. (2000). *Handbook of counseling and psychotherapy with lesbian, gay, and bisexual clients.* Washington, DC: American Psychological Association.

Ponterotto, J. G., Casas, J. M., Suzuki, L. A., & Alexander, C. M. (2001). *Handbook of multicultural counseling* (2nd ed.). Thousand Oaks, CA: Sage.

Pope-Davis, D. B., & Coleman, H. K. (Eds.). (1997). *Multicultural counseling competencies: Assessment, education, and training.* Thousand Oaks, CA: Sage.

Prochaska, J. O., & Norcross, J. C. (1982). The future of psychotherapy: A Delphi poll. *Professional Psychology, 13,* 620–627.

Pumariega, A., & Cross, T. (1997). Cultural competence in child psychiatry. In J. Noshpitz & N. Alessi (Eds.), *Basic handbook of child and adolescent psychiatry* (Vol. 4, pp. 473–484). New York: John Wiley.

Pyszczynski, T., Solomon, S., & Greenberg, J. (2002). *In the wake of 9/11: The psychology of terror.* Washington, DC: American Psychological Association.

Qualls, S. H. (1998). Training in geropsychology: Preparing to meet the demand. *Professional Psychology: Research and Practice, 29,* 23–28.

Reed, G. M., McLaughlin, C. J., & Milholland, D. K. (2000). Ten interdisciplinary principles for professional practice in telehealth: Implications for psychology. *Professional Psychology: Research and Practice, 31,* 170–178.

Ridley, C. R., Li, L. C., & Hill, C. L. (1998). Multicultural assessment: Reexamination, reconceptualization, and practical application. *The Counseling Psychologist, 26,* 827–910.

Ridley, C. R., Liddle, M. C., Hill, C. L., & Li, L. C. (2001). Ethical decision making in multicultural counseling. In J. G. Ponterotto, J. M. Casas, L. Suzuki, & C. Alexander (Eds.), *Handbook of multicultural counseling* (2nd ed., pp. 165–188). Thousand Oaks, CA: Sage.

Ritter, K. Y., & Terndrup, A. I. (2002). *Handbook of affirmative psychotherapy with lesbians and gay men.* New York: Guilford Press.

Salovey, P., Rothman, A. J., Detweiler, J. B., & Steward, W. T. (2000). Emotional states and physical health. *American Psychologist, 55*(1), 110–121.

Santiago-Rivera, A. L., & Altarriba, J. (2002). The role of language in therapy with the Spanish-English bilingual client. *Professional Psychology: Research and Practice, 33,* 30–38.

Sciarra, D. T. (1999). *Multiculturalism in counseling.* Itasca, IL: F. E. Peacock.

Seligman, M. E. P., & Csikszentmihalyi, M. (2000). Positive psychology: An introduction. *American Psychologist, 55,* 5–15.

Shapiro, A. K. (1997). *The powerful placebo: From ancient priest to modern physician.* Baltimore, MD: Johns Hopkins Press.

Sherry, A., Whilde, M. R., & Patton, J. (2005). Gay, lesbian, and bisexual training competencies in American Psychological Association accredited graduate programs. *Psychotherapy: Theory, Research, Practice, Training, 42,* 116–120.

Singh, N. N. (1998). Cultural diversity: A challenge for evaluating systems of care. In M. H. Epstein, K. Kutash, & A. Duchnowski (Eds.), *Outcomes for children and youths with emotional and behavioral disorders and their families* (pp. 425–455). Austin, TX: Pro-Ed.

Snyder, C. R., & Lopez, S. J. (Eds.). (2002). *Handbook of positive psychology.* New York: Oxford University Press.

Strom, L., Pettersson, R., & Andersson, G. (2004). Internet-based treatment for insomnia: A controlled evaluation. *Journal of Consulting and Clinical Psychology, 72,* 113–120.

Sue, D. W. (2001). Multidimensional facets of cultural competence. *The Counseling Psychologist, 29,* 790–821.

Sue, D. W., Bingham, R. P., Porsche-Burke, L., & Vasquez, M. (1999). The diversification of psychology: A multicultural revolution. *American Psychologist, 54,* 1061–1069.

Sue, D. W., & Sue, D. (1999). *Counseling the culturally different: Theory and practice* (3rd ed). New York: John Wiley & Sons.

Terman, L. M. (1939). The gifted student and his academic environment. *School and Society, 49,* 65–73.

Tjaden, P., & Thoennes, N. (1997). *Stalking in America: Findings from the National Violence Against Women Survey.* Denver, CO: Center for Policy Research.

U.S. Department of Commerce. (2001). *Current population survey, 1998, 1999, and 2000.* Washington, DC: U.S. Government Printing Office.

U.S. Department of Commerce. (2002). *A nation online: How Americans are expanding their use of the Internet.* Washington, DC: Author.

VandenBos, G., DeLeon, P., & Belar, C. (1991). How many psychological practitioners are needed? It's too early to know! *Professional Psychology: Research and Practice, 22,* 441–448.

Walker, K. L., Wright, G., & Hanley, J. H. (2001). The professional preparation of African American graduate students: A student perspective. *Professional Psychology: Research and Practice, 32,* 581–584.

Watson, J. B. (1928). *Psychological care of infant and child.* New York: Norton.

Werth, J. W. (2002). *Assisting clients with End-of-Life decision making. A guide for niche practice.* Practice Information Clearinghouse of Knowledge. Phoenix, AZ: Psychologists in Independent Practice.

Whaley, A. L. (2001a). Cultural mistrust and mental health services for African Americans: A review and meta-analysis. *The Counseling Psychologist, 29,* 513–531.

Whaley, A. L. (2001b). Cultural mistrust: An important psychological construct for diagnosis and treatment of African Americans. *Professional Psychology: Research and Practice, 32,* 555–562.

Witherspoon, R., & White, P. R. (1998). *Four essential ways that coaching can help executives.* Greensboro, NC: Center for Creative Leadership.

Zubenko, W. N., & Capozzoli, J. (Eds.). (2002). *Children and disasters: A practical guide to healing and recovery.* New York: Oxford University Press.

Index

A-B-A-B design, 63–64
Abbreviated Battery IQ, 167–68
ABC model, 230, 231
A-B-C model, 282–84
A-B-C theory of personality, 112–13
accommodation, 159
Achenbach System of Empirically Based
    Assessment (ASEBA), 235–36
achievement tests, 67, 174
Ackerman, Nathan, 325
activating event, 283
activity record, 281–82
addictions, positive and negative, 289
Adler, Alfred, 81
advocacy, 35, 37, 42, 358–59
affect, 113, 141. *See also* feelings;
    psychotherapy, schools of,
    emphasizing emotions and sensations
aid-in-dying laws, 26
Alcoholics Anonymous (AA), 339
alignments (family dynamics), 335
"all but dissertation" (ABD), 12, 13
allegiance effect, 274
Allport, Gordon W., 93
alter egos (psychodrama), 346
alternate-form reliability, 155
alternative problem-solving strategies, 302
altruism, 342
American Association for Marriage
    and Family Therapy (AAMFT),
    40, 41
American Association for the
    Advancement of Behavior Therapy
    (AABT), 40, 41
American Group Psychotherapy Association
    (AGPA), 40–41

American Psychological Association (APA),
    15, 31–32, 88
    boards and committees, 38–39
    Ethics Code, 2, 3, 344, 365, 391, 398
    governance, 32
    publications, 33, 35
        journals, 35, 36
    standards and guidelines, 3, 145, 446
    structure, 33, 35, 37–38
        Central Office, 35, 38
        divisions, 30–31, 33–35
        Education Directorate, 37
        Practice Directorate, 35
        Public Interest Directorate, 38
        Science Directorate, 37
American Psychological Association
    of Graduate Students (APAGS), 32
American Psychological Association
    Practice Organization (APAPO),
    35, 37
American Psychological Foundation
    (APF), 364
anal-expulsive personality, 97
analog studies, 87
anal-retentive personality, 97
anal stage of psychosexual development, 97
anima/animus, 103
antecedent conditions, 230
Anton, Barry, 2
anxiety, 98, 159, 286
anxiety hierarchy, 286, 287
Aphasia Screening Test, 214
apperception, 188
aptitude tests, 67
archetypes, 102–3
Arithmetic (WAIS-III subtest), 161